HADITH, PIETY, AND LAW

Selected Studies

RESOURCES IN ARABIC AND ISLAMIC STUDIES

series editors

Joseph E. Lowry
Devin J. Stewart
Shawkat M. Toorawa

Number 3
Hadith, Piety, and Law: Selected Studies

HADITH, PIETY, AND LAW
Selected Studies

Christopher Melchert

LOCKWOOD PRESS

Atlanta, Georgia
2015

HADITH, PIETY, AND LAW
Selected Studies

ISBN: 978-1-937040-49-9

Library of Congress Control Number: 2015954883

Cover image: Page from *Ṣaḥīḥ al-Bukhārī*, Egypt or Syria, 14th–15th century AD. Ink and gold on paper. The The Nasli M. Heeramaneck Collection, gift of Joan Palevsky (M.73.5.600), Los Angeles County Museum of Art. (Image in the public domain.)

Printed in the United States of America on acid-free paper.

CONTENTS

Law

Series Editors' Preface

Professor Christopher Melchert has spent his career illuminating the early history of Islamic religious sentiment, thought, and institutions. His first book, *The Formation of the Sunni Schools of Law* (1997), provided a convincing framework for dating the emergence of the Sunni schools of legal thought (*madhhabs*). Subsequent articles investigated regional and ideological alignments among 8th- and 9th-century religious scholars, trends in piety among religious figures committed to the study and transmission of traditions—hadiths—from the Prophet Muḥammad, the distinction between asceticism and mysticism in early Islamic religious practice, and scholarship of the Qur'an by early Muslim savants.

Professor Melchert's evident sympathy for the historical figures whose lives and thought he has studied, most of whom belong to pietistic currents of various kinds that were often skeptical of the intellectualizing adventures of their co-religionists, has lent a unique scholarly depth and empathy to his work. It must be said that non-mystical piety, especially when associated with the transmission of Prophetic hadiths, has not received the attention it might have in the field of Islamic studies. This lack of attention stems partly from the field's enduring interest in and perhaps overemphasis of rationalism and Hellenism in early Islam, and partly from a suspicion of traditionalist Islam, especially among many modern scholars who choose to see in Sufism a potential for ecumenism. Melchert recognized more than two decades ago that this major blind spot in modern scholarship required urgent redress, and the fifty or so articles he has published are eloquent testimony to his perseverance and success.

All of Professor Melchert's scholarship is characterized by the methodological rigor of the historian, the judicious deployment of traditional categories of analysis from the discipline of religious studies, and the philological tools of Arabic and Islamic studies. The essays collected here, on the themes of hadith, piety, and law, bear witness to all of these.

We feel bound to disclose that we have known Christoph Melchert since all of us were in graduate school together at the University of Pennsylvania in the late 1980s and early 1990s. It was a heady time at Penn, due in no small part to the enormous inspiration provided to all of us by the late George Makdisi, whose footsteps we continue to try to follow in our various ways. We hope Melchert will agree that this fine collection of studies is also in a way a tribute to that time and to our teacher and mentor, *raḥimahu 'llāh.*

Joseph E. Lowry
Devin J. Stewart
Shawkat M. Toorawa

Author's Preface

I am often asked how I came to take up Arabic or Islamic History or whatever my subject seems to be. That is fairly easy to answer: at UC Santa Cruz, I was pretty sure I wanted to major in History; I thought I should prefer to study the history of some part of the world besides the United States and Europe (they had been studied enough, I thought); and I wandered by accident (distributing class-evaluation forms) into Terry Burke's introductory survey of Middle Eastern history. Finding that I enjoyed all four parts of that (the late Ottoman Empire, then twentieth-century Egypt and Iran, finally the Arab-Israeli conflict), I thought the Middle East should be as good a place as any. A bit over a year later, I took my first Arabic class, a ten-week intensive summer course at Cal. I made the Middle East my major area of concentration for the History degree and enjoyed further classes with Burke and with Alan Richards in Economics. At Burke's suggestion, I applied to spend a year at the American University in Cairo. I prepared for that with a second ten-week summer course at Cal. I thought I should come back able at least to read a newspaper, which was a good estimate of what nine more months would do, also to make sure I didn't hate Arabs or something—better to find out before I embarked on a Ph.D.

This collection is dedicated to my teachers. The unsuspected influence a teacher can have hit me when I wrote a two-page review of Marshall Hodgson, *The Venture of Islam*, for a graduate-student forum at Princeton. A little later, I read Terry Burke's own review and was astonished to see that we had made pretty much the same points, although I had read only the second half of volume 3 with him at Santa Cruz (Edmund Burke III , "Islamic History as World History: Marshall Hodgson, 'The Venture of Islam,'" *IJMES* 10 [1979]: 241–64). It was thanks to a fellow student at Santa Cruz, though, that I first read Max Weber. I have often recalled an observation in his late lecture "Science as a Vocation" on scholarship as a career: "Certainly, chance does not rule alone, but it rules to an unusually high degree. I know of hardly any career on earth where chance plays such a role" (*From Max Weber*, trans. Hans H. Gerth & C. Wright Mills [London: Routledge & Kegan Paul, 1948], 132). I remain a believer in what he says of the professor and politics, that the professor has no business trying to convert students to his own point of view. Rather, he says, for every political position there are inconvenient facts, and the professor's job is to habituate his students to facing those facts, whatever they may be. More generally,

I also keep to an interpretation of history as dominated by the struggle of groups. Weber thought the most important groups of his time were the nation states and committed himself to the German, a position I find appalling; however, he presumably did it more self-consciously and responsibly than most.

Weber's idea of groups was more flexible than the Marxist idea of classes, more applicable to pre-modern history. But my college years were also the high tide of academic Marxism in the United States and I was affected. I continue to organize history into stages, expect to find conflict, look for explanations of historical change (why things went one way rather than another, resisting Mark Twain's characterization of history as "one damned thing after another"), and to explain in terms of the conflict of groups. I suppose Marxism inoculated me against the linguistic turn, feminism, postmodernism, and other academic fads, although they have anyway had less influence on Islamic history than other fields. It also made me permanently suspicious of nationalism, which tends to deny conflict within the nation, blaming all ills on outsiders. Weber said that materialism was not a street car one boards and gets off at will, and I suppose I should concede that, if Louis XVI and Nicolas II were bound to be incompetent monarchs when revolution was imminent, so the Left was bound to fritter away its energies on side issues in a time when capital was increasing its share of income. Besides, I myself have drifted into apolitical Mennonitism at the same time.

I initially planned to devote myself to problems of development—how it came to be that we are rich and they poor. However, I found that modern Middle East studies is a highly politicized field. People who pursue it have to spend a lot of time arguing about Arabs and Israelis, and there seemed to be an oversupply of people who were there first for the sake of promoting some political line, only secondly for the sake of scholarship. Therefore, I pushed my studies back in time. Study of the medieval Middle East also turns out to be regrettably politicized, but at least the linguistic demands reduce the number of dilettantes. In graduate school, first at Princeton, then U. Penn., I found my way to the study of Islamic movements and institutions, especially in the ninth century C.E. (A qualifying exam written by Roy Mottahedeh and Bernard Lewis at Princeton probably disposed me to look at the ninth century a few years later, but I was more conscious at the time that it fell within the scope of Fuat Sezgin, *GAS*, without, I then thought, all the difficulties of attribution that plague the study of earlier centuries.) At different points, I proposed various topics for my dissertation: Ibn Khaldūn, Syrian cities in the twelfth century, judges, the Jarīri school, the formation of Sunnism—as it turned out, I had enough material for the law chapter of the last to constitute a whole dissertation by itself. (Besides, I could stand on the shoulders of a giant, mainly George Makdisi, whose attention to the school of law as a teaching institution was crucial to my identifying the teachers with whom they reached their classic forms.) My later articles on Ibn Mujāhid and the transition from asceticism to mysticism are roughly the Qur'an and piety chapters I planned for the dissertation on Sunnism. Maybe I'll write such a book in the future.

My first published article was something I actually prepared as a graduate student:

"Sectaries in the Six Books: Evidence for Their Exclusion from the Sunni Community," *Muslim World* 82 (1992): 287–95. I was using Ibn Ḥajar, *Taqrīb* al-Tahdhīb, to look up men in my dissertation research and noticed what seemed like a lot of heretics amongst traditionists in the Six Books. I thought to rearrange them chronologically and thought I saw a pattern of increasing numbers of Murjiʾa, Qadariyya, and Shiʿa into the early ninth century, then drastically declining from about the time of the Inquisition. I began something more substantial in the summer of '92 before taking up my first job out of graduate school, teaching History at Wake Forest University, what became "Religious Policies of the Caliphs From al-Mutawakkil to al-Muqtadir," *Islamic Law and Society* 3 (1996): 316–42. I think it turned out to be my most-cited article. I had taken to heart J. H. Hexter's advice, referring to an article of his that provoked a massive historiographical debate in the 1950s and '60s after it had been rejected by the *AHR*: "A letter of rejection is not a divine decree ..., but the decision of one or two fallible men, subject to reversal by other men equally fallible" (*Reappraisals in History* [London: Longmans, 1961], xxi). "Religious Policies" was rejected by two journals before being accepted by a third. "Revise and resubmit" was the usual response to my submissions in the 1990s, before my particular point of view had become part of common wisdom, or at least well-enough known not to seem aberrant.

My first invitational article was "The Imāmīs between Rationalism and Traditionalism," for Lynda Clarke. It eventually appeared in *Shīʿite Heritage: Essays on Classical and Modern Traditions*, ed. L. Clarke (Binghamton, N.Y.: Global Publications, 2001), 273–83. I wrote it mainly over the summer of '93 between my first job, at Wake Forest, and my second, at Southwest Missouri State University. It was my first experience of Shiʿi biographical dictionaries. They seem recalcitrant after Sunni biographical dictionaries, but I was pleased to discover that some of the categories I and others had made out among the Sunnis also appeared among the Shiʿis. The conference, in a suburb of Philadelphia, brought together four groups of scholars: North American academics, Muslim and non-Muslim, Middle Eastern academics, and Middle Eastern Shiʿi religious authorities. The North Americans spoke the same language and easily communicated with one another, the Middle Eastern religious authorities spoke their own language with confidence—it was the Middle Eastern academics who looked demoralized, having some idea of the scholarly game that the North Americans were playing, always driving to overturn preconceptions, but feeling pressured at the same time to uphold the tradition more easily represented at the meeting by the men in gowns and turbans.

While I was at SMSU, I finished and submitted the articles that eventually appeared as "The Transition from Asceticism to Mysticism at the Middle of the Ninth Century C.E." [*HPL 6] and "The Adversaries of Aḥmad Ibn Ḥanbal" [*HPL 1]. "Transition" is the one I expected to make my name but for years it was actually very little cited. The polarity of asceticism and mysticism had been pushed to my attention especially by one of my teachers at U. Penn., Lowell Clucas, who made much of the contrast between the Latin and Greek outlooks in the Middle Ages. I have found it very helpful, myself, at giving me things to notice (in different churches' hymnals, for example), and some such transition was an ill-defined part of the Islamic scholarly tradition, besides. However, scholarly fashion had turned strongly against Weber in the mid-'90s, and the concept of mysticism has come under attack, too. I would still defend it. Pointing to marginal cases proves nothing—every scheme of classification breaks down at the margins. (The weather normally changes little from December 20th to 21st, for example, but "fall" and "winter" remain useful categories.) Some hold to the idea that Islamic mysticism (or at least something like Sufism) was there from the time of the Prophet—usually scholars with private commitments to Sufism they would do better to keep away from their scholarship. "Mysticism" has often been used too loosely to be illuminating, but the solution is to define it carefully.

I presented one more convention paper while I was teaching at SMSU, the one that eventually became "The Ḥanābila and the Early Sufis," *Arabica* 48 (2001): 352–67. I did not submit any more articles from SMSU, though, because I lost my job, mostly for being an insufficiently popular teacher. I did present a paper on Sufi movements in Khurasan to MESA in December 1995, which eventually became "Sufis and Competing Movements in Nishapur, 9th–10th Centuries C.E.," *Iran* 39 (2001): 237–47. It was based heavily on excerpts from al-Ḥākim al-Naysābūrī, *Tārikh Naysābūr*, preserved in al Dhahabī, *Tārīkh al-islām*, of which I had purchased a dozen volumes from a dealer in Damascus by money transfer to Switzerland. Getting books from the Middle East was to become much easier with the Internet in years to come. I also travelled by bus to Philadelphia to present a paper to AOS in March 1996, which eventually became "Ibn Mujāhid and the Establishment of Seven Qurʾanic Readings," *SI*, no. 91 (2000), 5–22. It was based mainly on three weeks of note-taking at the U. Penn. library in Philadelphia the previous November, before the MESA meeting in Washington. I was interested by differences between the study of variant readings and of hadith, surprised to discover that there was apparently no connection between Ibn Mujāhid's seven and hadith reports by which the Qurʾan was revealed in seven *aḥruf* (contrary to a great deal of secondary literature), also that there was no clear traditionalist impulse behind the establishment of seven (contrary to what Makdisi had assumed) and that it was not accomplished by Ibn Mujāhid himself or even in his time but by later generations of scholars (actually confirming what Bergsträsser and Pretzl had said in the '30s). I travelled to Providence, Rhode Island, to present what would eventually become "The Piety of the Hadith Folk" [*HPL 8], my tribute to Marshall Hodgson. That was for a pre-arranged panel, so attendance was better than the previous year, and my paper was well received. In some ways, on the other hand, it seemed a low point in my exile from academe, as, having no friends in Providence as I had in Philadelphia, I arranged to arrive there by bus around noon, then left again for the bus station that same evening to begin the trip back to Missouri around 24 hours later. Submission of a draft for publication was held up for another year and a half, till Matthew Gordon invited me to another gathering (this time finding money to pay for it, so I flew instead) and Michael Bates got me into the Columbia library to look at a relevant German book.

The warmer parts of 1996 and most of 1997 I supported myself by painting houses, but in September '97 we moved to South Carolina for me to teach in a Mennonite secondary school. I learnt a lot more about conservative Mennonitism from interacting so closely with children and parents, some of it disappointing, some encouraging. I got away in November to attend another pre-arranged MESA panel in San Francisco to present an early version of a paper on hadith that is now slated to appear as "The transmission of hadith: changes in the ninth and tenth centuries C.E.' among selected papers of the Union Européenne des Arabisants et Islamisants, 2012. I was invited to appear in yet another pre-arranged panel in 1998, where someone kindly read aloud what would become "Early Renunciants as *Ḥadīth* Transmitters," *The Muslim World* 92 (2002): 407–18, but by this time I was in Damascus on a Social Science Research Council grant. Having had such difficult access to primary sources for so long, I threw myself onto the riches of the Asad Library and l'Institut français des études arabes de Damas with great energy. I framed, researched, wrote, and submitted three articles from there: "How Ḥanafism Came to Originate in Kufa and Traditionalism in Medina" [*HPL 12], "Bukhārī and Early Hadith Criticism" [*HPL 2], and "The Concluding Salutation in Islamic Ritual Prayer," *Le Muséon* 114 (2001): 389–406. I also framed and researched what became "Qurʾanic Abrogation Across the Ninth Century," *Studies in Islamic Legal Theory*, ed. Bernard Weiss, Islamic Law and Society 15 (Leiden: Brill, 2002), 75–98, my laptop succumbing to a virus two months before my grant expired. I will say that my experience of writing articles as an "independent scholar" has made me pretty stony-hearted about "publish or perish." Getting a job is such a dice game, it would be absurd to blame anyone for rolling the dice as often as possible or for accepting any job offered. However, we who have jobs should also, I believe, work to deserve our luck. Anyone with a good job means two or three holders of doctorates without. I feel scant sympathy for people who hold down good jobs but don't publish.

My research in the 1990s was overwhelmingly based on biographical dictionaries. My time in Damascus was something of a turning point. "How Ḥanafism Came to Originate in Kufa" certainly came from digging in biographical dictionaries, and some biographical dictionaries were at the center of "Bukhārī and Early Hadith Criticism," but with the latter my technique shifted from what biographical dictionaries could tell us about networks and parties of the men of religion to the dictionaries themselves. Bukhārī, *al-Tārīkh al-kabīr*, had struck me as the most boring biographical dictionary ever, but trying to work out its relation to Bukhārī's *Ṣaḥīḥ* and how it might have been used in the ninth century, I was led to a theory of how hadith criticism worked (largely confirming the way Eerik Dickinson had described it in his dissertation, contra other secondary literature on hadith based on later theoretical syntheses; subsequent reading has not confirmed my idea of a distinct Khurasani approach). But "The Concluding Salutation" and "Abrogation" came of comparing what different law books said of a given problem. It's the obvious way to study the history of Islamic law and probably where the most progress is to be made.

My luck continued to improve when I was awarded a fellowship at the Institute for Advanced Study in Princeton for the year 1999–2000. I had proposed to write (in effect) the book on Sunnism of which a chapter had become my actual dissertation. What I mostly did was to catch up on my secondary reading and to tidy up various earlier works for publication. The only publication that I framed, researched, and mostly wrote from the Institute was the AOS convention paper that became "Traditionist-Jurisprudents and the Framing of Islamic Law" [*HPL 13]. It also has turned out to be much-cited. Perhaps it does make a difference what journal an article appears in. A European historian at Pembroke College, Oxford, once suggested that scholars be restricted to four articles across their careers. I can easily see advantages to such a restriction, but I doubt whether authors would choose the same four as their readers.

I cannot find a copy of my presentation to the Islamic Legal Studies conference at Harvard two months later, it must have seemed so little worth preserving, but it probably formed part of my retrospective for Wael Hallaq two years later, "The Formation of the Sunnī Schools of Law," *The Formation of Islamic Law*, ed. Wael B. Hallaq, The Formation of the Classical Islamic World 27 (Aldershot: Ashgate, 2004), 351–66. I did get a much better idea there at the Institute of how my work fit into the larger field: tending to the skeptical end of the spectrum as to the reliability of ninth-century and later sources for the history of the seventh and eighth, insisting on the importance of the traditionalists as well as writers more congenial to most educated American sensibilities, and insisting on the importance of theology and piety to the jurisprudents and the way they developed the law. It seems it normally takes a while to see where one fits in, as I have now observed from being on hiring committees. Perhaps uncertainty is one reason graduate students so often make exaggerated claims for the originality of their own approaches and the foolishness of earlier students. This said, I have also found that graduate students seem to be my best readers. A peculiar point of view is the most valuable thing a new entrant brings to a scholarly field, but we evidently risk becoming inflexibly attached to our own, resisting other points of view, as we begin to publish.

In February 2000, then, I was offered my present job at Oxford. That was the ultimate turn of the wheel. Now I especially recalled Hamlet's conversation with Rosencrantz and Guildenstern, concluding, "In the secret parts of Fortune? O, most true! She is a strumpet." I had applied for dozens of jobs, as usual, but I was on just two other short lists, at the University of Sunderland (for a department that would be abolished a year later) and Northwest Georgia State—another indication of how much luck determines who goes where and how little in demand I was still, never mind I presume to say a pretty strong publication record. Teaching at all levels has its special rewards, but I do get to work with an unusually high average level of undergraduates, here. Because British higher education is more specialized than American, they soon go to a higher skill level, so I don't have to rely on translations for the third- and fourth-year students, rather ask them to read anything I like in Arabic. We have almost no money for graduate students, so the best undergraduates usually go on to the United States; however, we get a few good ones who wish to be in the UK for family reasons, so I have had several outstanding doctoral students, as well. If the Arabic collection here were moved to the United States, I doubt it would figure in the top half-dozen, but it might in the next half-dozen. Interlibrary Loan is a good deal less vigorous than in the US. So much is now available electronically, though, and shipping costs from the Middle East are lower for what I purchase than they would be in the US, that altogether it is an excellent place from which to conduct research.

The first piece of research I remember conducting in Oxford is my contribution to what became the George Makdisi memorial volume, "The Etiquette of Learning in the Early Islamic Study Circle," *Law and Education in Medieval Islam*, ed. Joseph E. Lowry, Devin J. Stewart, and Shawkat M. Toorawa (n.p.: E. J. W. Gibb Memorial Trust, 2004), 33–44. This seems as good an illustration as any of the importance of technical skill in reading Arabic. It's like differential equations to a chemist—not what he studies, not what he teaches, but totally necessary for what he does study and teach. Graduate students for whom reading Arabic remains painful may write publishable dissertations and get good jobs (one is seldom hired by fellow Arabists, almost never by fellow specialists), but if all they read is what's directly relevant to the research question at hand, they will not notice interesting things on the periphery and they will not accumulate material for future projects. "Religious Policies," "Adversaries," "The Ḥanābila and the Early Sufis," "Piety of the Hadith Folk," "Etiquette," and other articles all developed out of notes I had accumulated while working on something else. People who don't accumulate notes on the periphery tend to become scholars of single books, little heard from after they get tenure.

The first convention paper I prepared at Oxford was "The Holy Man in Early Islam" for the AOS in Toronto. This was inspired by a collection of essays from some of my new colleagues in Oxford, *The Cult of Saints in Late Antiquity and the Middle Ages: Essays on the Contribution of Peter Brown*, ed. James Howard-Johnston and Paul Antony Hayward (Oxford: University Press, 1999). No version of this has been published. It has been rejected twice by journals, partly for good reasons (unclear focus, unevenness of citations, &c.), partly for bad, mainly that it didn't talk about what the Europeanists talk about. I am reminded of inter-religious dialogue. The naïve approach is to say, "The important questions are A, B, C; our answers are 1, 2, 3; now what are your answers?" It always turns out that the questions are part of the tradition as well as the answers; for example, the problem of sin seems great to Christians, minor to Muslims, as problems of law seem crucial to Muslims, peripheral to Christians. In the same way, the Arabic sources for Islamic history are very different from the Latin and Greek for European history, so naturally the problems that Arabists address are different from what Europeanists do. There is also a sort of scholarly imperialism: European topics seem intrinsically interesting, whereas extra-European demand special justification, so an article on monastic ritual in late-medieval France, say, is welcome, whereas an article on Sufi ritual in late-medieval Syria is obviously for specialists only and unwelcome in a journal for historians, not just Islamicists. (The *Journal of the American Academy of Religion* expressly rejected "Transition" in 1995 for not including inter-religious comparisons and therefore interesting too few readers. They have somewhat mended their ways since the World Trade Center attack.) I suppose the material of "The Holy Man" will show up as part of my projected book on Islamic piety before Sufism.

My 2002 presentation to the AOS became "Baṣran Origins of Classical Sufism" [*HPL 9]. Based mainly on biographical dictionaries, still, this one proposed three stages in the development of early piety: pervasive respect for renunciation in the early eighth century, increasing doubt in the later eighth century and into the ninth, then the emergence of Sufism as a safely Sunni approach at the end of the ninth century. Later that year, I presented a paper to the revived School of Abbasid Studies at Cambridge that became "The Meaning of *qāla 'l Shāfiʿī* in Ninth Century Sources" [*HPL 14]. This was based mainly on reading books of law, largely inspired by Norman Calder, *Studies in Early Muslim Jurisprudence* (New York: Clarendon Press, 1993). It makes out that apparent quotations are often paraphrastic, sometimes speculative, although probably more as Wael Hallaq had described in his contribution to the Weiss volume than as Calder had in Studies. I got quite a kicking a few years later by Ahmed El Shamsy in *JAOS*. I was wrong to overlook Siyar al-Wāqidī buried within the *Umm* ("it seems that no copy of *Siyar al-Wāqidī* is extant," 278)—it is preserved in the *Umm* at 4:176–94, presumably placed there in the revision of al-Bulqīnī (d. 805/1403). I was also wrong to overlook the survival in manuscript of Buwayṭī's *Mukhtaṣar* ("presumably quoting al-Buwayṭī's *Mukhtaṣar*, still extant in the late Mamluk period," 300). But I did say that Muḥammad ibn Naṣr al-Marwazī, over whom El Shamsy takes me to task, evidently had access to the *Umm* pretty much as we know it, whereas I do not see that El Shamsy has new evidence that the *Umm* as we know it was published before mid-century.

It must have been already in 2002 that Patricia Crone invited me to contribute to her series of short biographies. She was a great editor, so I was happy to offer something. She suggested Ibn Qutayba, but I said I didn't respect him sufficiently, offering to treat Aḥmad b. Ḥanbal if Cook had turned her down. Indeed, it transpired that she had asked him and Aḥmad was free, so my next several conference papers were bound to be about him. To the AOS in Nashville I presented what would become "The *Musnad* of Aḥmad ibn Ḥanbal" [*HPL 3], to a local gathering organized by Ron Nettler what would become "The Ḥanbali Law of *Ǧihâd*," *The Maghreb Review* 29 (2004): 22-32, and to the 2003 SOAS Qurʾan conference what would become "Aḥmad ibn Ḥanbal and the Qurʾan," *Journal of Qurʾanic Studies* 6/2 (2004): 22–34. I reproduced very little prose from these in the book that eventually came out in Crone's series, *Ahmad ibn Hanbal*, Makers of the Muslim World (Oxford: Oneworld, 2006), but they all involved important background reading. I had a terrible time with the publisher of that book, who set an overactive proofreader to rewrite my text, among other things continually making it read better at the cost of saying more than my sources would support. The resultant book is at least 90 percent mine, though. Had it been a Brill book, there would have been an additional chapter on the secondary literature, which it is as well I never wrote (it would have sounded ill-tempered), and another on the works ascribed to Aḥmad ibn Ḥanbal, which, not done by me, left the way open to Saud Al-Sarhan, whose 2011 dissertation at Exeter covered that ground at least as capably as I should have.

I regret I could not show my second book to George Makdisi. His idea for a dissertation was to pick a man, read his works, and make him one's window into his century. He had picked Ibn ʿAqīl, his teachers had picked Ḥallāj (Massignon) and Ibn Taymiyya (Laoust), others had picked Jāḥiẓ (Pellat), Ibn Qutayba (Lecomte), and so on. At my penultimate meeting with him, he still asked me, "When are you going to pick a man?" I had instead written about a problem for my dissertation, but I did come to see the advantages of beginning with a person or a text, especially when I began to supervise graduate students. If one starts with a problem, there is always the danger that one will read and read and never find the needed data; alternatively, that one will force the given data to provide a solution they really cannot. I have regularly set master's students an exam comprising four or five photocopies of pages from original sources with instructions to come back in a week having characterized the place of any one of them in the larger work, compared it with similar pages in other works, identified persons and technical terms, finally having sketched one or more research problems that the page suggested. A few historical incidents have been exhaustively written up (the fall of Jerusalem in 1099, perhaps), a few persons (I doubt anyone will add much to Rosenthal's biography of al-Ṭabarī, for example, although no doubt reading his works will add much about law, qur'anic interpretation, and history), but I think a graduate student could hardly fail to come up with a workable topic for a seminar paper by reading a page from some relevant source in the first week, then lining up parallel pages from other works. It might not be publishable, but it will certainly leave the student with a much firmer knowledge of what different sources will yield.

In 2004, I began to attend the biennial meetings of l'Union européenne des arabisants et islamisants. My first contribution was published as "Whether to Keep Women Out of the Mosque: A Survey of Medieval Islamic Law," *Authority, Privacy and Public Order in Islam*, ed. B. Michalak-Pikulska and A. Pikulski, Orientalia Lovaniensia analecta 148 (Leuven: Peeters, 2006), 59–69. This was based on comparing law books from the different schools. To my surprise, I discovered that the Ḥanbali school seemed the friendliest to women's participation in group prayer, to the point of calling for women to lead some group prayers, the *tarāwīḥ* prayers in Ramadan if a woman should know the Qurʾan but none of the men present (the whole school's position) or any prayer if a woman should be the one who best knows the Qurʾan (a minority position in the school). I go to UEAI meetings to keep up with Continental scholarship, to represent the UK in a European-wide organization (actually, French scholarship seems the least well-represented there, although French remains the second language of meetings after English), and, admittedly, because they meet in picturesque places with good food and drink. I continued to be a regular at AOS until they took to scheduling meetings early enough in March to intersect with Hilary Term in Oxford, when it is difficult for me to get away. The attractions of AOS are seeing old pals and a fairly high average level of papers presented, but I admit they also weigh ever less against the ordeals of intercontinental air travel.

I have accepted over many invitations to conferences since coming to Oxford. When I was starting out, I was eager to publish my ideas, of course, and jumped at every chance. Now, conferences can too easily distract from my chosen research program. But they tend to be organized by friends, who are hard to turn down, or I am drawn to present something from loyalty to the subject. But this paper on women in the mosque and a series of presentations to future SOAS Qurʾan conferences are examples of distraction. (At least the most substantial of the Qur'an articles, "The Relation of the Ten Readings to One Another," *Journal of Qurʾanic Studies* 10/2 [2008]: 73–87, addresses a problem I had wondered about for a long time, how many discrepant readings could have been generated by oral transmission, also whether readings from the same metropolis are notably more similar—it transpires not.)

Reading Wael B. Hallaq, *The Origins and Evolution of Islamic Law*, Themes in Islamic Law 1 (Cambridge: University Press, 2005), it seemed as though my ideas were well represented, from which I concluded that I had had my say about Islamic law and that it was time to move to another field. I do not wish to be another who, on finding that he has not converted everyone to his opinion, repeats it over and over in hopes of attracting notice that way. The field I chose was renunciant piety (*zuhd*) before Sufism. "Baṣran Origins" was a sketch of my historical scheme, the piety chapter of *Ahmad ibn Hanbal* was a sketch of renunciant activities and attitudes (as exemplified in the earliest Ḥanbali works). I came up with "The History of the Judicial Oath in Islamic Law," *Oralité et lien social au Moyen Âge (Occident, Byzance, Islam)*, ed. Marie-France Auzépy and Guillaume Saint-Guillain, Centre de recherche d'histoire et civilization de Byzance Monographies 29 (Paris: ACHCByz, 2008), 309–26, because I had accepted an invitation from Denise Aigle to a conference in Paris on a topic too far from what I thought to talk about. It was great to sit in the Sorbonne where Makdisi had studied, but I really should have declined. What became "Māwardī, Abū Yaʿlá, and the Sunni Revival" [*HPL 15], was my contribution to a small conference in Cracow. The problem I addressed, whether Māwardī's famous treatise *al-Aḥkām al-sulṭāniyya* depended on Abū Yaʿlā's treatise by the same name or the other way around, had been on my mind since it came up in a seminar under Makdisi, and I am pleased to have come up with an answer, but it was a distraction. The same goes for "The Relation of Ibn Taymiyya and Ibn Qayyim al-Jawziyya to the Ḥanbali School of Law," *Islamic Theology, Philosophy and Law: Debating Ibn Taymiyya and Ibn Qayyim al-Jawziyya*, ed. Birgit Krawietz and Georges Tamer with Alina Kokoschka, Studien zur Geschichte des islamischen Orients, n.F. 27 (Berlin: de Gruyter, 2013), 146–61, which afforded a pleasant trip to Berlin and I hope usefully extends Henri Laoust's history of the Ḥanbali school.

Encyclopaedia articles were the provocation for two articles on hadith: "The Life and Works of Abū Dāwūd al-Sijistānī," *Al Qanṭara* 29 (2008): 9–44, and "Bukhārī and His *Ṣaḥīḥ*" [*HPL 4]. I had had a bad experience with al-Ḥasan al-Baṣrī, having agreed to write a thousand-word article on him for *The Encyclopaedia Iranica* and devoted a week to researching it, which seemed sufficient for a piece of that size. Some time later, Michael

Cooperson and Shawkat Toorawa prevailed on me to write a 5,000-word article on him (*Dictionary of Literary Biography* 311: *Arabic Literary Culture, 500–925*, ed. Cooperson and Toorawa [Detroit: Thomson Gale, 2005], 121–27). I spent over a month on that and discovered many things I wished I had said differently in the earlier article. When asked to write about Abū Dāwūd and Bukhārī for *EI3*, I resolved to submit précis of longer studies. They were fun to write, too. A third hadith article, "The Life and Works of Al Nasā'ī" [*HPL 5], was provoked by reading a good book in Arabic, which I happened to pick up in Damascus where I was looking for books in Arabic on Aḥmad b. Ḥanbal and Abū Dāwūd. My latest hadith article, "The Early Controversy over Whether the Prophet Saw God," *Arabica* 62 (2015): 459–76, was provoked mainly by my noticing some odd reports in a Ḥanbali creed I was translating.

I got to take off all of calendar 2008 from teaching. I had two terms of normal sabbatical leave coming and was able to secure a third thanks to a sabbatical-leave-extension grant from the Arts and Humanities Research Council. For a time, it was fairly easy to get such grants if one's sabbatical leave was not quite adequate to finish some worthy project, but word spread and the year I applied the success rate fell from half to a third. It fell again the next year, then the category was abolished. Funding bodies increasingly prefer a few large projects over many small ones. Perhaps they are easier to administer. I doubt that one "principal investigator" and several others working on a topic of his choice will come up with better work than the same number of scholars working on projects of their own choosing. Moreover, I strongly doubt whether funding bodies have the capacity to decide which topics will be most fruitful. They are too vulnerable to following fads (e.g., interdisciplinarity, an import from the natural sciences) and politics (e.g., encouraging scholarship to make Muslims happy citizens). But in 2007 I pleaded with success that my studies of the holy man and Ahmad's book *al-Zuhd* (what became "Aḥmad ibn Ḥanbal's Book of Renunciation," *Der Islam* 85 [2008]: 345–59) constituted a coherent project, which my study of exaggerated fear (what became "Exaggerated Fear in the Early Islamic Renunciant Tradition" [*HPL 10]) would complete. I was able to submit all three as promised, along with another article analysing an early Sufi work I happened to take along on a trip to Japan, "Khargūshī, *Tahdhīb al-asrār*," *BSOAS* 73 (2010): 29–44. Still, I noticed some discomfort with having a deadline; with having to work on just these three articles I had told a funding body I would produce. I don't think it made them better, and it reinforces my feeling that the best course is to let scholars follow their noses wherever their reading leads them. It also illustrates how important it is to have time off. People with short contracts may well envy me my permanent teaching position, but they need not think that I have an easier time than they doing research during term time. On the contrary, I can wrest away no more than one or two hours a day, which is all right for mechanical data collection but not original thinking. I do research between terms, the same as if I were an adjunct.

I managed to adapt some invitations to my project of historicizing the renunciant period. "Abū Nuʿaym's Sources for *Ḥilyat al-awliyāʾ*, Sufi and Traditionist," *Les maîtres soufis et* *leurs disciples*, ed. Geneviève Gobillot and Jean-Jacques Thibon, Études arabes, médiévales et modernes (PIFD 273) (Beirut: Presses de l'IFPO, 2012), 145–60, was ostensibly about the tenth century and Sufi literature but provided me with valuable background on our largest single source for renunciant sayings. "Renunciation (*zuhd*) in the Early Shiʿi tradition" [*HPL 11] started as a presentation to a conference at the Institute of Ismaili Studies. It attracted an unusual editorial introduction when it was published. Editors of collected articles usually purport to identify common themes and convergent results, never mind that the actual articles go off in many different directions. Here, Mohyddin Yahia objected to my making out mysticism as something that arrived in time and was not there from the beginning, likewise overlooking that the modest austerities endorsed by the Sufis' ninth-century critics were exactly what the Qurʾan itself had called for two centuries before. "The Islamic Literature on Encounters between Muslim Renunciants and Christian Monks," *Medieval Arabic Thought: Essays in Honour of Fritz Zimmermann*, ed. Rotraud Hansberger, M. Afifi al-Akiti, and Charles Burnett, Warburg Institute Studies and Texts 4 (London: Warburg Institute, 2012), started as a conference presentation on a panel organized by my colleague Afifi al-Akiti. "Three Qur'anic Terms (*Siyāḥa*, *Ḥikma* and *Ṣiddīq*) of Special Interest to the Early Renunciants," *The Meaning of the Word: Lexicography and Qur'anic Exegesis*, ed. S. R. Burge (London: Oxford University Press, 2015), started as another presentation to the Institute of Ismaili Studies. "Ibn al-Mubārak's *Kitāb al-Jihād* and Early Renunciant Literature," *Violence in Islamic Thought from the Qur'ān to the Mongols*, ed. Robert Gleave and István Kristó-Nagy, Legitimate and Illegitimate Violence in Islamic Thought 1 (Edinburgh: University Press, 2015), 49–69, managed to combine Rob Gleave's catchy theme of violence with mine of renunciant piety.

On the other hand, "The Destruction of Books by Traditionists," *Al Qanṭara* 35 (2014): 213–31, represented my thanks to Maribel Fierro for bringing me to Barcelona for a conference. "Public Baths in Islamic Law," *25 siècles de bain collectif en Orient*, ed. Marie-Françoise Boussec, &al., Études urbaines 9 and PIFD 282 (Cairo: Institut français d'archéologie orientale, 2014), 1001–10, was prepared for a conference in Damascus I ended up being unable to attend because of visa difficulties and credit-card fraud. "Abū Isḥāq al-Šīrāzī and Ibn al-Ṣabbāġ and the Advantages of Teaching at a madrasa," *Annales Islamologiques*, no 45 (2011): 141–66, was a favor to Mathieu Tillier. "Whether to Keep Unbelievers out of Sacred Zones: A Survey of Medieval Islamic Law," *JSAI*, no 40 (2013): 177–94, was a follow-up to my article on women and mosques but also a tribute to Yohanan Friedmann, who solicited it.

And then there have been yet more articles on Islamic law. "Basra and Kufa as the Earliest Centers of Islamic Legal Controversy," *Islamic Cultures, Islamic Contexts: Essays in Honor of Professor Patricia Crone*, ed. Behnam Sadeghi, &al., Islamic History and Civilization, Studies and Texts, 114 (Leiden: Brill, 2015), 173–94, was more on my continuing quest to identify regional traditions, although less conclusive than I hoped. "The Early Ḥanafiyya and Kufa," *Journal of Abbasid Studies* 1 (2014): 23–45, was a follow-up to "How Ḥanafism Came to Originate in Kufa," again finding no evidence in the biographical and legal literature of a flourishing Ḥanafi school in Kufa after Abū Ḥanīfa himself transferred to Baghdad but, surprisingly, finding much transmission of hadith in Kufa purportedly going back to Abū Ḥanīfa. "The Spread of Ḥanafism to Khurasan and Transoxania," *Medieval Central Asia and the Persianate World*, ed. A. C. S. Peacock & D. G. Tor, I. B. Tauris & BIPS Persian Studies Series (London: I. B. Tauris, 2015), 13–30, was for a pleasant trip to St Andrews, Scotland, and built on notes I had accumulated over a long period. Roy Mottahedeh once told me and some other graduate students to be sure we liked our dissertation topics, since that is what people would ask us to talk about for the next ten years. "Twenty years" is my experience.

I used to say that younger scholars should work close to the sources when they have lots of energy, leaving the grand syntheses till they reach their sixties. I find myself still preferring to write articles, where it's easy to stick to what I know. It sometimes seemed regrettable that George Makdisi did not spend more time reading secondary literature, so that his articles would address current debates. On the other hand, work close to the sources seems likely to survive longer than the synthetic overview. Makdisi took pleasure in contrasting Joseph Schacht, whose work continues to provoke debate, whose methods continue to be fruitful, with H. A. R. Gibb, a pleasure to read when one does go back to him but seldom any longer the subject of debate. It is the fate of scholars for their work to be superseded, but I hope mine continues to find readers for at least another generation.

Editorial Note

As the articles in this volume were originally published in a variety of journals and edited collections, the transliteration systems vary. We have made no attempt to standardize transliteration across this volume. This should not pose a problem for specialists (especially now that they have been warned), and we suspect it will not matter much to readers who do not know Arabic.

The transliteration of names in the index follows the system employed by Brill in *Encyclopaedia of Islam Three*.

The abbreviation *HPL appearing in square brackets after the title of a Melchert article indicates that it appears also in this volume. Thus [*HPL 9] means it appears as chapter 9 here.

Rather than append a corrigendum, we have corrected typographical, dating and other errors, and also incorporated some light emendations supplied by Melchert.

We are grateful to the original copyright holders for allowing us to reproduce the articles.

Abbreviations

BSOAS	*Bulletin of the School of Oriental and African Studies*
EI1	*Encyclopaedia of Islam*, 1st ed. (Leiden, 1913–38)
EI2	*Encyclopaedia of Islam*, new ed. [= 2nd edn] (Leiden, 1954–2009)
EI3	*Encyclopedia of Islam Three* (Leiden, 2007–)
GAS	Fuat Sezgin, *Geschichte des arabischen Schrifttums* (Leiden, 1967–)
IBLA	*L'Institut des belles lettres arabes*
IJMES	*International Journal of Middle East Studies*
JAOS	*Journal of the American Oriental Society*
JSAI	*Jerusalem Studies in Arabic and Islam*
JRAS	*Journal of the Royal Asiatic Society*
NASB	*New American Standard Bible*
REI	*Revue des études islamiques*
SI	*Studia Islamica*
ZDMG	*Zeitschrift der Deutschen Morgenländischen Gesellschaft*

HADITH

1
THE ADVERSARIES OF AḤMAD IBN ḤANBAL

Thanks mainly to the researches of Josef van Ess, our understanding of the *Muʿtazila* during the ninth century C.E. has undergone a revolution.[1] We can now say that the Inquisition of al-Maʾmūn was not mainly about *Muʿtazilī* ideas.[2] Although some Muʿtazila later became involved with the Inquisition, we can now say that the *Muʿtazila* of the early ninth century were only loosely connected with the classical *Muʿtazilī* movement we know from the later ninth century and onwards. I should like to extend this revolution by arguing for a new identification of all the major opposing theological parties of the ninth century C.E.

In the main, we should cease to classify the opposing parties as *Ahl al-Sunna*, the *Šīʿa*, and the *Muʿtazila*. "*Ahl al-sunna*" was certainly one of the traditionalists' names for themselves; however, it was later claimed by too many to be useful in discussing the ninth century. In Baghdad, the *Šīʿa* were not a major force until the tenth century. We might even then classify them variously as traditionalists, rationalists, and semi-rationalists.[3]

---

1. For a convenient summary, *v.* now *The Encyclopaedia of Islam*, new ed. (Leiden: E. J. Brill, 1960), *s.v.* "*Muʿtazila*," by D. Gimaret, with references.

2. For the Inquisition, *v. The Encyclopaedia of Islam*, new edn., *s.v.* "Miḥna," by Martin Hinds, with fairly full references to sources and previous studies. V. in particular Josef van Ess, "Ḍirār b. ʿAmr und die 'Cahmiya': Biographie einer vergessenen Schule," *Der Islam* 44 (1968): 34, where he points out particular differences between Muʿtazili thought concerning the create *Qurʾān* and Bišr al-Marīsī's; also, now, *Theologie und Gesellschaft im 2. und 3. Jahrhundert Hidschra*, 3 vols. to date (New York: Walter de Gruyter, 1992), 3:175–188.

3. Two convenient summaries are Heinz Halm, *Shīʿism*, trans. Janet Watson and Marian Hill, Islamic Studies (Edinburgh: Edinburgh Univ. Press, 1991), and Moojan Momen, *An Introduction to Shīʿi Islam: The History and Doctrines of Twelver Shīʿism* (New Haven: Yale Univ. Press, 1985). On the Imāmīya in particular between traditionalism and rationalism, *v.* Wilferd Madelung, "Imāmism and Muʿtazilite Theology," pp.

Originally published in *Arabica* 44 (1997): 234–53.

As for the *Muʿtazila*, to identify all rationalists with them [235] is to exaggerate their importance and correspondingly to depreciate other groups of rationalists, such as a wing of the nascent Ḥanafi school of law. Instead, we had better conceive of the main opposing parties as traditionalists (respecting only scriptuary sources of law and theology) and rationalists (including the *Muʿtazila* but not limited to them), with a third party of semi-rationalists in the middle.

What I present here is mainly a short survey of the polemics of Aḥmad Ibn Ḥanbal against various other Muslims. It confirms that the *Muʿtazila* were no more important than other rationalists. The party that most alarmed Aḥmad was not the *Muʿtazila*, the *Šīʿa*, or the rationalist *Ḥanafīya*, but rather the semi-rationalist middle party.

Aḥmad against the Rationalists

The popular, traditionalist party in Baghdad collected in the first half of the ninth century C.E. around Aḥmad Ibn Ḥanbal (d. 241/855). Aḥmad, already an extremely knowledgeable traditionist and jurisprudent, made himself especially notable by refusing to confess the *Qurʾān* create at the Inquisition of al-Maʾmūn and his successors (began 218/833, abolished by stages 232–237/847–852).[4] The chief consequence of the Inquisition, or rather of its failure, was to discredit the caliph as arbiter of orthodoxy. Henceforward, Islamic orthodoxy might be defined only by consensus of the community, or its spokesmen the men of religion; no longer, certainly, by the caliph.[5]

In the field of jurisprudence, Aḥmad Ibn Ḥanbal himself upheld a style very different from that of the later handbooks of jurisprudence. He staunchly opposed the teaching of law apart from the transmission of *ḥadīṯ* reports, staunchly opposed the collection and transmission of juridical opinions from anyone later than the Companions and Successors, staunchly opposed, that is, both the practice of his rationalistic contemporaries, the nascent Ḥanafi school (also the nascent Māliki [236] and Šāfiʿi schools), and the basis of *Sunnī* jurisprudence from the tenth century onwards.[6]

132–9 in T. Fahd, ed., *Le Shîʿisme imâmite* (Paris: Presses Universitaires de France, 1979); Hossein Modaressi, "Rationalism and Traditionalism in Shîʿî Jurisprudence: A Preliminary Survey," *Studia Islamica*, no. 59 (1984), 141–158; and Christopher Melchert, "The Imāmīs between Rationalism and Traditionalism," in Linda Clarke, ed., *Shīʿite heritage* (Binghamton: Global Publications), 273–283.

4. Note my distinction between "traditionist," one who collected hadith reports (*muḥaddiṯ*), and "traditionalist," one who required a strictly textual basis for all law and theology (one of the party that called itself *ahl al-sunna* in the 9th century C.E., now more often called *ahl al-ḥadīṯ*). This distinction goes back to George Makdisi, "Ashʿarī and the Ashʿarites in Islamic Religious History 1: The Ashʿarite Movement and Muslim Orthodoxy," *Studia Islamica* 17 (1962): 49.

5. V. George Makdisi, *The Rise of Colleges* (Edinburgh: Edinburgh Univ. Press, 1981), ch. 1.

6. For a brief, accurate survey of Aḥmad's juridical practice, *v.* Susan A. Spectorsky, "Aḥmad Ibn Ḥanbal's *Fiqh*," *Journal of the American Oriental Society* 102 (1982): 461–465.

Aḥmad was most hostile towards *aṣḥāb al-raʾy*, jurisprudents who relied heavily on *raʾy* (common sense or reason) and the opinions of previous jurisprudents in preference to hadith reports. This is what one expects to find on the plane of jurisprudence: that Aḥmad should recommend burying books of *raʾy*,[7] that he should direct traditionists to deduce the law from what they know without asking *aṣḥāb al-raʾy*,[8] that he should forbid someone to study *raʾy* even for the sake of arguing against *aṣḥāb al-raʾy*,[9] and so on.

Aḥmad's hostility towards *raʾy* went beyond disagreement over points of jurisprudence. He was willing to attribute unbelief (*kufr*) to someone who gave juridical opinions on the basis of *Kitāb al-Ḥiyal*.[10] According to Aḥmad, Abū Ḥanīfa rejected *ḥadīṯ* reports in favor of his *raʾy*.[11] At the conclusion of one creed, Aḥmad imprecates *aṣḥāb al-raʾy* together with the rejected theological parties the *Murǧiʾa*, the *Qadarīya*, the *Rāfiḍa*, the *Ḥarūrīya*, and the *Ǧahmīya*.[12]

In the creeds and elsewhere, Aḥmad defines the *Rāfiḍa* as those who prefer ʿAlī to Abū Bakr,[13] who reject Abū Bakr and ʿUmar,[14] or who insult any of the Companions.[15] In addition to their hostility toward [237] certain Companions, Aḥmad holds against the *Rāfiḍa* their avoiding ritual prayer in the mosque[16] and rejecting *ḥadīṯ*.[17] Most of the great *riǧāl* critics distinguished between *tašayyuʿ*, a sort of mild *Šīʿism* including Zaydism, and *rafḍ*, an extreme position foreshadowing later *Imāmism*; however, Aḥmad explicitly includes the *Zaydīya* among the *Rāfiḍa*.[18]

7. Aḥmad Ibn Ḥanbal, *K. al-Waraʿ*, ed. Zaynab Ibrāhīm al-Qārūt (Cairo: n.p., 1340; repr. Beirut: Dār al-Kutub al-ʿIlmīya, 1983), 81; Ibn Abī Yaʿlā, *Ṭabaqāt al-ḥanābila*, ed. Muḥammad Ḥāmid al-Fiqī, 2 vols. (Cairo: Maṭbaʿat al-Sunna al-Muḥammadīya, 1952), 1:347.

8. Ibn Abī Yaʿlā, 1:238.

9. Ibn Abī Yaʿlā, 1:327.

10. Ibn Abī Yaʿlā, 1:218, with possible reference to books by Abū Ḥanīfa, Abū Yūsuf, and Muḥammad al-Šaybānī. Cf. al-Ḫaṭīb al-Baġdādī, *Tārīḫ Baġdād aw Madīnat al-Salām*, 14 vols. (Cairo: Maktabat al-Ḫānǧī, 1931), 13:403f, where Ibn al-Mubārak is quoted (improbably) as calling it an act of unbelief to give opinions according to the *K. al-Ḥiyal* of Abū Ḥanīfa.

11. ʿAbd Allāh ibn Aḥmad, *Ǧāmiʿ al-ʿilal wa-maʿrifat al-riǧāl lil-imām Aḥmad ibn Muḥammad ibn Ḥanbal*, ed. Muḥammad Ḥusām Bayḍūn, 2 vols. (Beirut: Muʾassasat al-Kitāb, 1990), 2:51.

12. Creed I, *apud* Ibn Abī Yaʿlā, 1:36. Henri Laoust has identified and numbered six creeds: *La Profession de foi d'Ibn Batta* (Damascus: Institut Français de Damas, 1958), xv, xvi. They are to be found *apud* Ibn Abī Yaʿlā, 1:2436 (Creed I); 130f (II); 241246 (III); 294f, repeated 329f (IV); 311–313 (V); 341–345 (VI).

13. Creed VI, *apud* Ibn Abū Yaʿlā, 1:343. Al-Ḫallāl, *Musnad min masaʾil Abī ʿAbd Allāh Aḥmad ibn Muḥammad ibn Ḥanbal*, ed. Ziyauddin Ahmed, Asiatic Society of Bangladesh Publication 29 (Dacca: Asiatic Society of Bangladesh, 1975), 219.

14. Ibn Abī Yaʿlā, 1:182.

15. Creed I, *apud* Ibn Abī Yaʿlā, 1:30. Al-Ḫallāl, 219.

16. Aḥmad Ibn Ḥanbal, *Kitāb fī al-ṣalāh*, *apud* Ibn Abī Yaʿlā, 1:371.

17. Ibn Abī Yaʿlā, *Ṭabaqāt al-ḥanābila* 1:172.

18. Creed I, *apud* Ibn Abī Yaʿlā, 1:33.

Indeed, Aḥmad did not recognize these rejected theological parties as Muslims at all. One should not pray behind one who drinks intoxicants (including *nabīḏ*), nor even one who sits with one who drinks;[19] yet, says Aḥmad, one who drinks may still be counted a Muslim, whereas the *Qadarīya*, *Murǧiʾa*, *Rāfiḍa*, and *Ǧahmīya* are not to be counted Muslims.[20] Of these four groups, the *Qadarīya* and *Murǧiʾa* come up for condemnation the least often, the *Ǧahmīya* most often.

Aḥmad's practice as a traditionist was sometimes more lenient than his pronouncements would suggest. One does find instances of his rejecting traditionists for their aspersing Companions (a standard charge against various brands of *Šīʿa*). For example, he related *ḥadīṯ* reports for a time from the Kufan al-Ḥusayn ibn al-Ḥasan al-Ašqar (d. 208/823–824), then ceased on being informed of his having written about the faults of Abū Bakr and ʿUmar.[21] Likewise, he forbade his son ʿAbd Allāh to relate from ʿAlī ibn al-Ǧaʿd (d. 230/845) on hearing that he had aspersed some of the Companions.[22] To the contrary, however, he was willing to relate hadith reports of the Kufan ʿAbd Allāh ibn Šarīk al-ʿĀmirī (fl. early second/eighth century), although he was a Muḫtārī; indeed, he counted him trustworthy (*ṯiqa*).[23] He reportedly justified his relating hadith reports of the great Yemeni traditionist ʿAbd al-Razzāq (d. 211/827), well known for his Šīʿism, on the ground of his having been no propagandist,[24] or (more dubiously) having repented.[25] Aḥmad refused to return the salute of ʿAlī ibn al-Madīnī (d. 234/849) and forbade his son ʿAbd Allāh to relate hadith reports of him, so great was [238] his disgust at ʿAlī's behaviour during the Inquisition; yet, observes al-Ḏahabī, *ḥadīṯ* reports from ʿAlī do appear in the *Musnad*, as well as many in the *Ṣaḥīḥ* of al-Buḫārī.[26]

Western scholars have usually identified the doctrine of a create *Qurʾān* with the *Muʿtazila*, but it was actually associated with other parties, as well. Abū l-Ḥasan al-Ašʿarī states that those who held the *Qurʾān* to be create were "the *Muʿtazila*, the *Ḫawāriǧ*, most of the *Zaydīya*, the *Murǧiʾa*, and many of the *Rawāfiḍ*."[27] Josef van Ess and Martin Hinds have pointed out that the theologian chiefly associated with the doctrine of al-Maʾmūn

---

19. Ibn Abī Yaʿlā, 1:230f, 311f.

20. Ibn Abī Yaʿlā, 1:326.

21. Ibn Ḥaǧar, *Tahḏīb "al-Tahḏīb,"* 12 vols. (Hyderabad: Maṭbaʿat Maǧlis Dāʾirat al-Maʿārif al-Niẓāmīya, 1325–1327), 2:336.

22. Ibn Ḥaǧar, 7:291.

23. Ibn Abī Ḥātim, *K. al-Ǧarḥ wa-al-taʿdīl*, 9 vols. (Hyderabad: Maṭbaʿat Ǧamʿīyat Dāʾirat al-Maʿārif, 1360), 5:80f.

24. Ibn Abī Yaʿlā, 1:182.

25. Ibn Ḥaǧar, 7:53.

26. Al-Ḏahabī, *Siyar aʿlām al-nubalāʾ*, 25 vols. (Beirut: Muʾassasat al-Risāla, 1981–1988), 11 (ed. Ṣāliḥ al-Samr, 1982): 59.

27. Abū l-Ḥasan al-Ašʿarī, *Die dogmatischen Lehren der Anhänger des Islam*, ed. Hellmut Ritter, 2nd edn., Bibliotheca Islamica 1 (Wiesbaden: Franz Steiner, 1963), 582.

was Bišr al-Marīsī (d. 218/833–834), certainly identified a *Ḥanafī* jurisprudent but not as a *Muʿtazilī*.[28] Abū l-Ḥasan al-Ašʿarī discusses the views of Bišr al-Marīsī in his chapter concerning the *Murǧiʾa*, among whom he includes Abū Ḥanīfa, not in his chapter concerning the *Muʿtazila*.[29] There is no entry for Bišr in the chief extant biographical dictionaries of the *Muʿtazila*.[30]

The man chiefly associated with the prosecution of the Inquisition after the death of al-Maʾmūn, chief qadi Ibn Abī Duwād (d. 240/854), was probably a *Ḥanafī* and *Muʿtazilī*. With one dubious exception, early biographers say nothing of Ibn Abī Duwād's formation or affiliation in the field of jurisprudence. The classical schools of law were yet forming in his time, and he may have been closest to the abortive Basran school. The dubious exception is Abū l-Qāsim al-Balḫī (d. 319/931?). The printed edition of his *Maqālāt al-islāmīyīn* includes two entries for Ibn Abī Duwād. The first entry states that he championed Ḥanafi jurisprudence and strengthened it with *ḥadīṯ* reports, the second says nothing whatever after the name.[31] Ibn al-Nadīm uses the exact words of the first entry concerning not Ibn Abī Duwād but rather [239] Ibn al-Ṯalǧī (d. 266/880).[32] I strongly suspect that Abū l-Qāsim's first entry for Ibn Abī Duwād originally referred to Ibn al-Ṯalǧī, and that Ibn al-Nadīm quotes it correctly; that Abū l-Qāsim's originally single entry for Ibn Abī Duwād provided no information beyond the name, and that this is the basis of Ibn al-Murtaḍā's similarly uninformative entry.[33] Ibn al-Nadīm does state that Ibn Abī Duwād's son, at least, was a follower of Abū Ḥanīfa.[34] Ibn Abī Duwād is acknowledged as a Ḥanafi by the later biographer Ibn Abī l-Wafāʾ (d. 775/1373).[35] As for Ibn Abī Duwād's affiliation in *kalām*, Abū l-Qāsim's inclusion of his name among the *Muʿtazila* is probably to be trusted (insofar as the *Muʿtazila* were, in his time, a coherent theological party). Ibn al-Nadīm identifies him

28. V. *supra*, note 2.

29. V. Abū l-Ḥasan al-Ašʿarī, index.

30. Abū l-Qāsim al-Balḫī, *Maqālāt al-islāmīyīn*, *apud* Fuʾād Sayyid, ed. and comp., *Faḍl al-iʿtizāl wa-ṭabaqāt al-muʿtazila* (Tunis: al-Dār al-Tūnisīya lil-Našr, 1974), 57119; al-Qāḍī ʿAbd al-Ǧabbār, *Faḍl al-iʿtizāl wa-ṭabaqāt al-muʿtazila*, *apud* Sayyid, 129350; Ibn al-Murtaḍā, *Die Klassen der Muʿtaziliten*, ed. Susanna DiwaldWilzer, Bibliotheca Islamica 2 (Beirut: Imprimerie Catholique, 1961). On the Ḥanafīya and the Inquisition, *v.* also W. Montgomery Watt, *The Formative Period of Islamic Thought* (Edinburgh: Univ. Press, 1973), 285f, and Hinds, "Miḥna."

31. Sayyid, 105.

32. Ibn al-Nadīm, *Kitâb al-Fihrist*, ed. Gustav Flügel, with Johannes Roediger and August Mueller (Leipzig: F. C. W. Vogel, 1872), 206.

33. Ibn al-Murtaḍā, *Klassen*, 62.

34. Apud Ibn Ḥaǧar, *Lisān "al-Mīzān,"* 7 vols. (Hyderabad: Maǧlis Dāʾirat al-Maʿārif, 13291331), 1:171.

35. Ibn Abī l-Wafāʾ, *al-Ǧawāhir al-muḍīya*, ed. ʿAbd al-Fattāḥ Muḥammad al-Ḥulw, 2 vols. published (Cairo: ʿĪsā al-Ḥalabī, 1978), 1:134f; also idem, 2 vols. (Hyderabad: Dāʾirat al-Maʿārif al-Niẓāmīya, 1914), 2:390.

as a leading *Muʿtazilī*, while Ibn al-Murtaḍā suggests that he learnt his doctrine from Abū l-Huḏayl al-ʿAllāf (d. 235/849–850?).[36]

Altogether, then, the Inquisition is to be identified less with the *Muʿtazila* than with the nascent Ḥanafi school of law. Traditionalists widely accused Abū Ḥanīfa of professing the *Qurʾān* create.[37] Aḥmad, too, repeated such accusations.[38] Confirming the slight significance of the *Muʿtazila* in the Inquisition, one finds very little from Aḥmad Ibn Ḥanbal against them. Twice, in Ibn Abī Yaʿlā's biographical dictionary, Aḥmad is quoted as rejecting *Muʿtazilī* doctrine concerning responsibility for actions;[39] once, in what Laoust calls Creed VI, he rejects [240] their alleged equation of sin and unbelief.[40] He never blames them for advocating a create *Qurʾān*. "*Ǧahmīya*" is the name he reserves for the advocates of a create *Qurʾān*.

The *Muʿtazila* evidently did become a more pressing concern to *Ḥanābila* in the last quarter of the ninth century, for creeds from this period have more to say about the Muʿtazila's errors than creeds from Aḥmad. ʿAbd Allāh ibn Aḥmad (d. 290/903) devotes a long section of his *Kitāb al-Sunna* to aspersions against ʿAmr ibn ʿUbayd, only the first from Aḥmad himself.[41] The short presentation of Aḥmad's creed by the Ḥanbali jurisprudent Abū Bakr al-Ḫallāl (d. 311/923) includes statements on the *Muʿtazilī* questions of *istiṭāʿa* and *ʿadl* without direct quotations.[42] In his Šarḥ *"Kitāb al-Sunna,"* al-Barbahārī (d. 329/941) denounces by name the ninth-century *Muʿtazila* Hišām al-Fūṭī (or Fuwaṭī—different sources support each) (twice), Ṯumāma ibn Ašras, and Abū l-Huḏayl.[43] This new prominence of the *Muʿtazila* in later *Ḥanbalī* creeds confirms the recent finding that the classical period of *Muʿtazilism* began only in the last quarter of the century.[44]

36. Ibn al-Nadīm, *apud* Ibn Ḥaǧar, *Lisān* 1:171; Ibn al-Murtaḍā, 125.

37. Al-Buḫārī, K. *al-Ḍuʿafāʾ wa-al-matrūkīn*, ed. Būrān al-Ḍinnāwī (Beirut: ʿĀlam al-Kutub, 1984), 149; al-Sāǧī, *K. al-ʿIlal, apud* Ibn ʿAbd al-Barr, *al-Intiqāʾ fī faḍāʾil al-ṯalāṯa al-aʾimma al-fuqahāʾ Mālik wa-l-Šāfiʿī wa-Abī Ḥanīfa* (Cairo: Maktabat al-Qudsī, 1350), 150; al-Ḫaṭīb al-Baġdādī, *Tārīḫ Baġdād* 12:349, 13:375, 378, 379, 382, 386; Wilferd Madelung, "The Origins of the Controversy Concerning the Creation of the Koran," *Orientalia Hispanica: sive studia F. M. Pareja octogenaria dicata* (Leiden: E. J. Brill, 1974), 509, citing Abū l-Ḥasan al-Ašʿarī, *al-Ibāna* (Hyderabad, 1948), 29.

38. Aḥmad Ibn Ḥanbal, *K. al-ʿIlal*, ed. Waṣī Allāh ibn Muḥammad ʿAbbās, 2:545, 546, 3:276; ʿAbd Allāh ibn Aḥmad, *Ǧāmiʿ al-ʿilal* 2:51, 52, 190. Wilferd Madelung has stated that Aḥmad Ibn Ḥanbal himself would not accuse Abū Ḥanīfa of advocating a create *Qurʾān* (Madelung, "Origins," 509f), but this was before the publication of the Ḥanbali works just named.

39. Ibn Abū Yaʿlā, *Ṭabaqāt al-ḥanābila* 1:145, 184.

40. Apud Ibn Abī Yaʿlā, 1:343.

41. ʿAbd Allāh ibn Aḥmad, *K. al-Sunna*, ed. Muḥammad ibn Saʿīd ibn Sālim al-Qaḥṭānī, 2 vols. (Dammam: Dār Ibn al-Qayyim, 1986), 2:434422.

42. Aḥmad Ibn Ḥanbal (i.e., al-Ḫallāl), *al-ʿAqīda lil-imām Aḥmad ibn Ḥanbal*, ed. ʿAbd al-ʿAzīz ʿIzz al-Dīn al-Sayrawān (Damascus: Dār Qutayba, 1988), 114.

43. Apud Ibn Abī Yaʿlā, 2:27, 38.

44. On the early and classical periods of Muʿtazilism, *v.* Gimaret, "*Muʿtazila*," esp. 784.

More than of any other group, one finds from Aḥmad condemnations of the *Ǧahmīya*; that is, of those who held the *Qurʾān* create, denied that God spoke audibly, and so on.[45] Not only is Aḥmad quoted against them more often, but his language concerning them goes further than concerning any other group, including the *Rāfiḍa* and *Muʿtazila*. For example, he recommends that someone who has declared the *Qurʾān* create be asked to repent, then killed if he refuse.[46] Alternatively, he is quoted as calling for the death at least of their propagandists (*duʿā, ḫuṭabāʾ*).[47] [241]

Aḥmad against the Semi-Rationalists

Aḥmad includes among the *Ǧahmīya* both the *Wāqifa*, those who would not say whether the Qurʾān was create or increate, and the *Lafẓīya*, those who said that the *Qurʾān* itself was increate but that their pronunciation of it (*lafẓ*) was create; indeed, he states that they are worse than the (original) *Ǧahmīya*.[48] In later times, traditionalist Muslims would accept such a distinction between an increate *Qurʾān* and its create pronunciation.[49] However, Aḥmad Ibn Ḥanbal emphatically rejected it, expressly identifying it with the Ǧahmi doctrine of the create *Qurʾān*.[50]

Several members of the *Lafẓīya* are actually named. Denounced by name the most often is al-Ḥusayn al-Karābīsī (d. 248/862–863?), a onetime student of al-Šāfiʿī's and the most important transmitter of his Baghdadi teaching ("*al-qadīm*").[51] He seems to have been the first and most prominent to assert that one's pronunciation of the *Qurʾān* was create.[52] Aḥmad identified al-Karābīsī himself as a successor to Bišr al-Marīsī.[53] Al-Karābīsī expressed exasperation: "What shall we do with this boy? If we say 'create,' he

45. On the supposed party of the Ǧahmīya, *v.* esp. Watt, *Formative*, 143147. For a contrary treatment that takes *Ǧahm* ibn Ṣafwān seriously as an earlier Muslim thinker, *v.* Ḫālid al-ʿAṣalī, Ǧahm *ibn Ṣafwān wa-makānatuhu fī al-fikr al-islāmī* (Baghdad: al-Maktaba al-Ahlīya, 1965). Al-ʿAṣalī argues that Ǧahm was not dependent on the *Muʿtazila* but rather they on him (161–167); however, relying on Ibn Taymīya, he also distinguishes between the positions of Ǧahm and the Muʿtazila concerning the way God speaks (168f).

46. Ibn Abī Yaʿlā, 1:156; Abū Saʿīd al-Dārimī, *Kitāb ar-Radd ʿalā l-*Ǧahmīya, ed. Gösta Vitestam (Lund: C. W. K. Gleerup, 1960), 101.

47. Ibn Abī Yaʿlā, 1:95; al-Dārimī, *Radd al-imām al-Dārimī ʿUtmān ibn Saʿīd ʿalā l-Marīsī al-ʿanīd*, ed. Muḥammad Ḥāmid al-Fiqī (Cairo: Maṭbaʿat Anṣār al-Sunna al-Muḥammadīya, 1358), 118 = (n.p.: Dār al-Furqān, 1985?), 120.

48. Ibn Abī Yaʿlā, 1:21, 29, 165, 172, 414.

49. E.g., al-Ḏahabī: *v. Siyar* 12 (ed. Ṣāliḥ al-Samr, 1983): 82.

50. Al-Ḫaṭīb al-Baġdādī, *Tārīḫ Baġdād* 8:65f; Ibn Abī Yaʿlā, *Ṭabaqāt al-ḥanābila* 1:41, 62, 75, 94, 111, 120, 121, 288.

51. V. al-Nawawī, *Tahḏīb al-asmāʾ wal-luġāt*, 4 vols. in 3 (Cairo: Idārat al-Ṭibāʿa al-Munīrīya, 1927), 2:284.

52. Abū l-Ḥasan al-Ašʿarī, *Dogmatischen Lehren*, 602; Ibn al-Nadīm, *Fihrist*, 181.

53. Al-Ḫaṭīb al-Baġdādī, 8:66; Ibn Abī Yaʿlā, 1:62.

says 'innovation'; if we say 'increate,' he says 'innovation.'"[54] Al-Karābīsī's doctrine of the pronunciation was taken up after him by Aḥmad al-Šarrāk (fl. ca. 240/854–855), Abū Ṯawr (d. 240/854), Ibn Kullāb (d. ca. 240/854–855), al-Ḥāriṯ al-Muḥāsibī (d. 243/857–858), Dāwūd al-Ẓāhirī (d. 270/884), and possibly al-Buḫārī (d. 256/870).[55]

According to Ḥanbali tradition, Aḥmad was most bothered, after al-Karābīsī, by Abū Ṯawr. Abū Ṯawr was another of al-Šāfiʿī's students [242] in Baghdad, and another important transmitter of his Baghdadi teaching.[56] He aligned himself with the traditionalists, calling *raʾy* a form of innovation (*bidʿa*).[57] Abū Ṯawr was sometimes denounced by himself, sometimes alongside al-Karābīsī.[58] As for Abū Ṯawr's particular error, Aḥmad once disparaged him for insufficient severity in condemning someone who said, with al-Karābīsī, that the *Qurʾān* was increate but his pronunciation of it create.[59] More often, Abū Ṯawr's error seems to have concerned the hadith report, "God created Adam in his image": Abū Ṯawr interpreted it, *contra* Aḥmad, to mean "in Adam's image," not "in God's image."[60]

Al-Ḫaṭīb al-Baġdādī does quote contrary reports of Aḥmad's praising Abū Ṯawr; for example, comparing his stature to that of Sufyān al-Ṯawrī.[61] The *Ḥanbalī* jurisprudent Abū Bakr al-Ḫallāl would explain that Aḥmad had praised Abū Ṯawr until he heard of his heretical doctrines, then condemned him;[62] however, this explanation is impossible to reconcile with the particular report that Aḥmad praised Abū Ṯawr when his son ʿAbd Allāh had just returned from his funeral.[63] Al-Ḫaṭīb al-Baġdādī was a Šāfiʿī in jurisprudence, an Ašʿarī in theology, on poor terms with the *Ḥanābila*;[64] perhaps, therefore, the pro-Ṯawri tradition he indicates is to be classified with the pro-*Šāfiʿī* tradition we have previously noticed.

---

54. Al-Ḫaṭīb al-Baġdādī, 7:65.

55. For Aḥmad al-Šarrāk, *v.* al-Ḫallāl, *Musnad*, 541–547, esp. 547. For Ibn Kullāb and Abū Ṯawr, *v.* Ibn ʿAbd al-Barr, *Intiqāʾ*, 156. For Ibn Kullāb, Dāwūd al-Ẓāhirī, and al-Buḫārī, *v.* Ibn Ḥaǧar, *Tahḏīb* 2:361f. For al-Muḥāsibī, *v. infra*. Aḥmad denounced the Damascene traditionist Hišām ibn ʿAmmār (d. 244/858–859?) for the same heresy, but without connecting him with al-Karābīsī: al-Ḫallāl, *Musnad min masāʾil*, 556. He also heard it alleged that Nuʿaym ibn Ḥammād, who actually died in prison for refusing to confess the *Qurʾān* create (228/843), had said his pronunciation of the *Qurʾān* was create, again without any connection with al-Karābīsī: *ibid.*, 549.

56. V. *supra*, note 51.

57. Al-Ḫaṭīb al-Baġdādī, 6:67f.

58. Ibn Abī Yaʿlā, 1:211, 212, 255, 414.

59. Al-Ḫallāl, *Musnad min masāʾil*, 544.

60. Ibn Abī Yaʿlā, 1:93, 212, 309.

61. Al-Ḫaṭīb al-Baġdādī, 6:66–69.

62. Apud Ibn Abī Yaʿlā, 1:328.

63. Al-Ḫaṭīb al-Baġdādī, 6:68f.

64. V. Ibn al-Ǧawzī, *al-Muntaẓam*, 6 vols. published (Hyderabad: Maṭbaʿat Dāʾirat al-Maʿārif al-ʿUṯmānīya, 1357–1360), 8:267f.

Aḥmad Ibn Ḥanbal's hostility seems to have inspired violence against two of the *Lafẓīya*: the ascetics Aḥmad al-Šarrāk and al-Ḥāriṯ al-Muḥāsibī. Aḥmad received letters from Tarsus denouncing Aḥmad al-Šarrāk for saying his pronunciation of the *Qurʾān* was create. When al-Šarrāk returned to Baghdad, he denied having said such a thing, but Aḥmad would not believe him, and commanded that no one sit with him. He fled to ʿAbbādān, but an associate of Aḥmad's prevailed on the ruler to have a crier announce at all the inns that no one was to sit with him, and he was expelled from that city as well.[65]

[243] Al-Muḥāsibī first fled to Kufa, where he announced his repentance of all that Aḥmad held against him. When Aḥmad refused to accept his repentance, perhaps on the ground of its vagueness, al-Muḥāsibī returned to Baghdad but hid. When he died and was buried there, two years after Aḥmad's death, only four persons prayed over him.[66]

No early *Ḥanbalī* source explicitly states Aḥmad's complaint with al-Muḥāsibī; however, it seems most likely to have been, again, his position concerning the pronunciation of the *Qurʾān*. The early *Ṣūfī* biographer, Abū Saʿīd Ibn al-Aʿrābī (d. 341/952?), states that al-Muḥāsibī talked (theologized) about the pronunciation (*lafẓ*) and faith (*īmān*).[67] Aḥmad himself associated al-Muḥāsibī with Ǧahmism, probably for saying that a man's pronunciation of the *Qurʾān* was create, possibly also for arguing that faith must be create.[68] (On the nature of faith, Aḥmad is quoted inconsistently: usually, that one should say of faith neither "create" nor "increate," a position of *waqf*; alternatively, that the faith that is heard is increate, the faith that comprises human actions create.[69]) Aḥmad angrily complained that al-Muḥāsibī had impelled the prominent ascetic Badr al-Maġāzilī (d. Baghdad, 282/895) as well to take up the opinion of Ǧahm.[70] Additionally, Aḥmad heard of al-Muḥāsibī's casting doubt on the audibility of God's voice.[71]

There is one report that Aḥmad shunned al-Muḥāsibī simply for engaging in *kalām*, dialectical theological reasoning.[72] Although vague, this agrees with Aḥmad's distrust of all *kalām*, even apologetic: with his excluding the practitioner of *kalām* from *Ahl al-Sunna*, and forbidding a follower to sit with practitioners, even though they defend the *Sunna*.[73]

65. Al-Ḫallāl, *Musnad min masāʾil*, 547.

66. Al-Ḏahabī, *Tārīḫ al-islām*, ed. ʿUmar ʿAbd al-Salām Tadmurī, 40 vols. to date (Beirut: Dār al-Kitāb al-ʿArabī), 18 (A.H. 241–250; 1991): 209 (Kufa, repentance); al-Ḫaṭīb al-Baġdādī, 8:216 (hiding, death). On the contrary, the early Šāfiʿī biographer al-ʿAbbādī states that al-Muḥāsibī died in Basra: *Kitāb Ṭabaqāt al-fuqahāʾ al-šāfiʿīya*, ed. Gösta Vitestam, Veröffentlichungen der "De Goeje Stiftung" 21 (Leiden: E. J. Brill, 1964), 27.

67. Ibn al-Aʿrābī, *Ṭabaqāt al-nussāk*, *apud* al-Ḏahabī, *Tārīḫ al-islām* 18:209.

68. Ibn Abī Yaʿlā, *Ṭabaqāt al-Ḥanābila* 1:62f, 233f.

69. Ibn Abī Yaʿlā, 1:93f, 2:176; al-Ḫallāl, *Musnad min masāʾil*, 560; cf. Aḥmad Ibn Ḥanbal (i.e., al-Ḫallāl), *ʿAqīda*, 117f.

70. Ibn Abī Yaʿlā, 1:233. Cf. al-Ḫallāl, *Musnad min masāʾil*, 352f.

71. Al-Ḏahabī, *Tārīḫ al-islām* 18:209f.

72. Apud al-Sulamī, probably *Miḥan al-ṣūfīya*, *apud* al-Ḫaṭīb al-Baġdādī, *Tārīḫ Baġdād* 8:215f.

73. Ibn Abī Yaʿlā, 1:242, 334.

It also agrees with al-Muḥāsibī's own denial that he upheld any special doctrine of the pronunciation.[74] Abū l-Ḥasan al-Ašʿarī may have [244] preserved one of al-Muḥāsibī's positions in *kalām* in his report that one Ḥāriṯ held that God is not other than his characters (*ṣifāt*), although they are different from one another.[75] By contrast, Bišr al-Marīsī evidently proposed that God's hearing is not different from his sight, his face from his hand, and so on—an example of what al-Muḥāsibī opposed, if indeed this Ḥāriṯ was al-Muḥāsibī.[76]

Additionally, there is a story from al-Ḥākim al-Naysābūrī that Aḥmad went with a follower to eavesdrop on a session of al-Muḥāsibī's, was moved to tears by al-Muḥāsibī's wisdom, then forbade his follower to sit with al-Muḥāsibī for fear that this was too advanced for him.[77] Some later writers preferred this explanation for Aḥmad's hostility to al-Muḥāsibī to an explanation involving *kalām*, but probably because they were less hostile to *kalām*, themselves, and more respectful of al-Muḥāsibī.[78] I am more inclined to agree with al-Ḏahabī, that the story simply does not sound right.[79]

Aḥmad spurned Dāwūd al-Ẓāhirī as well for accepting the position of al-Karābīsī, that the pronunciation of the *Qurʾān* was create.[80] Additionally, Dāwūd distinguished between an increate heavenly prototype and a create *Qurʾān* among the people.[81] He was known especially for asserting that the *Qurʾān* was *muḥdaṯ*, not *qadīm*; that is, for holding that although it might be increate, there had been a time when the *Qurʾān* was not.[82] In later times, traditionalist Muslims would accept this distinction, too, between an increate *Qurʾān* and a *Qurʾān* that had always been;[83] however, it was heartily rejected by Aḥmad and contemporary traditionalists. Muḥammad ibn Yaḥyā al-Ḏuhlī (d. 258/872?), chief (*raʾīs*) of Nishapur, wrote Aḥmad and others to warn against Dāwūd, and [245] when Dāwūd came to Baghdad, Aḥmad refused to see him.[84]

74. Josef van Ess, *Die Gedankenwelt des Ḥāriṯ al-Muḥāsibī*, Bonner orientalische Studien, n.s., 12 (Bonn: Selbstverlag des orientalischen Seminars der Univërsität Bonn, 1961), 205f.

75. Abū l-Ḥasan al-Ašʿarī, *Dogmatischen Lehren*, 546.

76. Abū Saʿīd al-Dārimī, *Radd al-imām al-Dārimī*, ed. Fiqī, 22 = Dār al-Furqān, 24f.

77. Apud al-Ḫaṭīb al-Baġdādī, 8:214f.

78. E.g., al-Subkī, *Ṭabaqāt al-šāfiʿīya al-kubrā*, ed. Maḥmūd Muḥammad al-Ṭināḥī & ʿAbd al-Fattāḥ al-Ḥulw, 10 vols. (Cairo: ʿĪsā al-Bābī al-Ḥalabī, 19641976), 2:279; Ibn Kaṯīr, *al-Bidāya wal-nihāya fī l-tārīḫ*, 14 vols. (Cairo: Maṭbaʿat al-Saʿāda, 19321939), 10:330; Ibn Ḥağar, *Tahḏīb* 2:136.

79. Al-Ḏahabī, *Mīzān al-iʿtidāl*, ed. ʿAlī Muḥammad al-Biğāwī, 4 vols. (Cairo: ʿĪsā al-Bābī al-Ḥalabī wa-Šurakāh, 1963), 1:430.

80. Al-Ḫallāl (*K. al-Sunna?*), *apud* al-Ḏahabī, *Siyar* 13 (ed. ʿAlī Abū Zayd, 1983): 103; al-Ḫaṭīb al-Baġdādī, 8:374.

81. Al-Ḫaṭīb al-Baġdādī, 8:374.

82. Abū l-Ḥasan al-Ašʿarī, 583.

83. V. Ibn Kaṯīr, 10:272.

84. Al-Ḫaṭīb al-Baġdādī, 8:373f; Ibn Abī Yaʿlā, 1:58.

Finally, Aḥmad is said to have associated al-Karābīsī's doctrine of the create pronunciation of the *Qur'ān* with the Ḥanafi jurisprudent Ibn al-Ṯalǧī (d. 266/880?).[85] We have only hostile accounts of Ibn al-Ṯalǧī's position concerning the *Qur'ān*, and they are contradictory. At an extreme, he is said to have made an exception in his will, "No one is to be given (any part of) my third save who says the *Qur'ān* is create."[86] He is repeatedly attacked by Abū Saʿīd al-Dārimī (d. 280/894?), traditionalist chief of Herat.[87] Sometimes, his position is identified as *waqf*; that is, refusal to declare the *Qur'ān* either create or increate.[88] Aḥmad himself, though, is said to have denounced him for talking, with al-Karābīsī, about the pronunciation of the *Qur'ān*.[89]

Less fiercely, Aḥmad is said to have denounced two Basran *Mālikīya* for agnosticism concerning the *Qur'ān*, namely Aḥmad ibn (al-)Muʿaḏḏal (d. ca. 240/855–854) and his disciple Yaʿqūb ibn Šayba (d. 262/875–876). Ibn Muʿaḏḏal had reportedly introduced *Mālikī* jurisprudence to Iraq.[90] The very enterprise of teaching jurisprudence apart from hadith was scorned by contemporary traditionalists. He discouraged Abū Dāwūd from seeking hadith,[91] and appears in no encyclopedia of *riǧāl* criticism, himself. Altogether, then, he appears to have been a semi-rationalist in both theology and jurisprudence. Aḥmad disparaged him for refusing to declare whether the *Qur'ān* was create or increate.[92] He disparaged Yaʿqūb ibn Šayba for the same offense.[93]

The Semi-Rationalists

We can identify additional figures as semi-rationalists on the basis of conflicts with the *Ḥanābila* after Aḥmad. Al-Buḫārī, the famous traditionist (d. 256/870), was expelled from Nishapur near the end of his [246] life for suggesting one's pronunciation of the *Qur'ān* was create. The man responsible was Muḥammad ibn Yaḥyā al-Ḏuhlī, the traditionalist

85. More usually called "Ibn Šuǧāʿ" in Ḥanafi tradition.

86. Ibn Ḥaǧar, *Tahḏīb* 9:221.

87. V. works cited above, notes 46, 47; also van Ess, *Theologie* 1:181f.

88. Abū l-Ḥasan al-Ašʿarī, *Dogmatischen Lehren*, 583; al-Ḫaṭīb al-Baġdādī, 5:351.

89. Ibn Abī Yaʿlā, 1:94, 120.

90. Ibn Ḥazm, *al-Iḥkām fī uṣūl al-aḥkām*, ed. Aḥmad Muḥammad Šākir, 8 vols. in 1 (Cairo: Maktabat al-Ḫānǧī, 1345), 5:98. On the form of his name, *v.* Ibn Ḥaǧar, *Tabṣīr al-muntabih bi-taḥrīr "al-Muštabih,"* ed. Muḥammad ʿAlī al-Naǧǧār, with ʿAlī Muḥammad al-Biǧāwī, Turāthunā, 4 vols. (Cairo: al-Dār al-Miṣrīya lil-Ta'līf wal-Tarǧama, 1964?–1967), 4:1299.

91. Al-Ḏahabī, *Siyar* 11:520.

92. Al-Ḏahabī, *Tārīḫ al-islām* 17 (A.H. 231–240), 54.

93. Al-Ḫaṭīb al-Baġdādī, 14:282.

leader who had earlier warned Aḥmad not to receive Dāwūd al-Ẓāhirī.[94] This time, some Baghdadis, doubtless *Ḥanābila*, had warned Muḥammad ibn Yaḥyā.[95]

It is well established that al-Muzanī (d. 264/878?), influential Egyptian Šāfiʿī, was engaged in *kalām*. One famous traditionalist, Abū Zurʿa al-Rāzī (d. 264/878), avoided studying under him, for he was interested only in *ḥadīṯ* whereas al-Muzanī taught only *kalām* and disputation (*munāẓara*).[96] One of al-Muzanī's positions in *kalām* is known, and it clearly identifies him with the semi-rationalists of Baghdad: that the name is other than the named.[97] Ibn Kullāb took up the same position.[98] Al-Muzanī was also accused of holding that the pronunciation of the *Qurʾān* was create.[99] According to another story, his Egyptian students abandoned him for a time because he had said the *Qurʾān* itself was create.[100] The accusation may have been related to the arrest of another student of al-Šāfiʿī's, al-Buwayṭī (d. 231/846?), who was hauled away to Iraq and there died in prison for affirming the *Qurʾān* increate. Al-Muzanī was said to have been among those who denounced him.[101] The connection with Aḥmad is that al-Muzanī is also said to have responded to an accusation concerning the *Qurʾān* by producing a summary of the creed of Aḥmad Ibn Ḥanbal with his endorsement.[102]

We can also identify the historian and *Qurʾān* commentator al-Ṭabarī (d. 310/923) with the semi-rationalists. Near the end of his life, the *Ḥanābila* blockaded him in his house, preventing him from receiving visitors.[103] Our medieval sources give various accounts of the accusation [247] against him, but most have to do with semi-rationalist

94. Al-Ḫaṭīb al-Baġdādī, 2:31, 8:373f; Ibn Abī Yaʿlā, 1:58; al-Ḏahabī, *Siyar* 13:99, 103.

95. Al-Ḫaṭīb al-Baġdādī, *Tārīḫ Baġdād* 2:31.

96. Ibn Abī Ḥātim, Ǧarḥ 2:204.

97. Al-Ḫušanī, *Ṭabaqāt ʿulamāʾ Ifrīqiya*, *apud* Abū l-ʿArab, *Classes des savants de l'Ifriqiya*, ed. Mohammed ben Cheneb, Publications de la Facultée des lettres d'Alger, Bulletin de Correspondance africaine 51 (Paris: Leroux, 1915), 213 = *apud* Abū l-ʿArab, *Quḍāt Qurṭuba wa-ʿUlamāʾ Ifrīqīya*, ed. ʿIzzat al-ʿAṭṭār al-Ḥusaynī, Min turāṯ al-Andalus 2 (Cairo: Maktabat al-Ḫānǧī, 1953), 179.

98. Al-ʿAbbādī, *Ṭabaqāt*, 27 (ʿAbd Allāh ibn Saʿīd = Ibn Kullāb).

99. Al-Ḫalīlī, *al-Iršād fī maʿrifat ʿulamāʾ al-ḥadīṯ*, abr. al-Silafī, Aya Sofya (Istanbul) 2951, 56a.

100. Ibn ʿAbd al-Barr, *Intiqāʾ*, 110, 111.

101. Al-Ḏahabī, *Tārīḫ al-islām* 17 (A.H. 231–240): 423f; *Siyar* 12:61f.

102. Şehit Ali Paşa (Istanbul) 2763/3. V. *GAS* 1:493, #II; 508, #22a.

103. Al-Ḥākim al-Naysābūrī, *Tārīḫ Naysābūr*, *apud* al-Ḏahabī, *Siyar* 14:272; al-Ḫaṭīb al-Baġdādī, *Tārīḫ Baġdād* 2:164.

positions in either theology or jurisprudence.[104] His association with Dāwūd al-Ẓāhirī and the students of al-Šāfiʿī is further evidence of al-Ṭabarī's semi-rationalism.[105]

Indeed, most of the known semi-rationalists were loosely associated with al-Šāfiʿī. The only members of the supposed ninth-century Kullābi school not associated with al-Šāfiʿī were Ibn Kullāb himself and, in the next generation, al-Qalānisī.[106] So very little is known of Ibn Kullāb, it seems possible that later generations made him a scapegoat, exaggerating his importance and blaming him for the worst of semi-rationalist doctrine in order to exonerate the *Šāfiʿīya*. For example, it is easy to see how it might have been more convenient for Ibn Ḫuzayma to have condemned the Kullābīya than the *Šāfiʿīya*.[107] A possible parallel would be the *Ǧahmīya*, blamed for the doctrine of the create *Qurʾān* to exonerate the *Ḥanafīya*. [248]

Several of these *Šāfiʿī* semi-rationalists are also known to have elaborated *uṣūl al-fiqh*, the application of *kalām* to jurisprudence. Two eleventh-century biographers report that al-Karābīsī wrote on both the theory of jurisprudence (*uṣūl al-fiqh*) and the ramifica-

104. Explanations include that al-Ṭabarī was accused of *rafḍ*, extreme Šīʿism (so Ibn Miskawayh, *The Concluding Portion of the Experiences of the Nations* 1: *Reigns of Muqtadir, Qahir and Radi*, ed. H. F. Amedroz [Oxford: Basil Blackwell, 1920], 84; Ibn al-Ǧawzī, *Muntaẓam* 6:172); that al-Ṭabarī offered a different interpretation of certain Qurʾanic verses (so Yāqūt, *The Irshád al-aríb ilá maʿrifat al-adíb*, ed. D. S. Margoliouth, E. J. W. Gibb Mem. ser. 6, 7 vols. [Leiden: E. J. Brill, 1907–1927], 6:436, concerning Q.17.79; Ibn al-Ǧawzī, 6:172, concerning Q.5.64); that al-Ṭabarī had refused to consider Aḥmad Ibn Ḥanbal a jurisprudent (so Ibn al-Aṯīr, *al-Kāmil fī al-tārīḫ*, s.a. 310; ed. C. J. Tornberg, 13 vols. [repr. Beirut: Dār Ṣādir, 1965–1967], 8:134); finally, that al-Ṭabarī took a heretical position concerning the pronunciation of the *Qurʾān* (*lafẓ*; so Ibn Ḥağar, *Lisān* 3:295). I would contest some aspects of Rosenthal's biography (Franz Rosenthal, "The Life and Works of al-Ṭabarī," *The History of al-Ṭabarī* 1: *General Introduction and From the Creation to the Flood*, Bibliotheca Persica and SUNY Series in Near Eastern Studies [Albany: State Univ. of New York Press, 1989], 1–154); for example, his neglect of information from Ibn al-Ǧawzī, like this controversy over Q.5.64, and his identification *tout court* of rationalism with Muʿtazilism. On the whole, though, Rosenthal's biography seems a splendid piece of work for which we must all be grateful whose studies involve al-Ṭabarī.

105. Ibn al-Nadīm, *Fihrist*, 234. Al-Ṭabarī and Ibn Surayǧ recommended that someone ignore Ibn Qutayba and Abū ʿUbayd in favor of al-Šāfiʿī and Dāwūd: al-Ḏahabī, *Siyar* 13:102, 301. Al-Ṭabarī is included in the earliest extant biographical dictionary of the Šāfiʿi school: al-ʿAbbādī, *Ṭabaqāt*, 52.

106. At that, Ibn Kullāb is claimed for the Šāfiʿi school by al-Subkī; however, without evidence of his activity as a jurisprudent: *Ṭabaqāt al-šāfiʿīya* 2:299f. The extant material on Abū l-ʿAbbās al-Qalānisī has been gathered by Daniel Gimaret, "Cet autre théologien sunnite: Abū l-ʿAbbās al-Qalānisī," *Journal asiatique* 277 (1989): 227–261. Gimaret cites no evidence of his affiliation in jurisprudence, and cites Ibn Ṭāhir al-Baġdādī to the effect that all his works concerned *kalām* (234). He doubts whether we should consider al-Qalānisī a follower of Ibn Kullāb (234f), which agrees with my contention that we should refer to a loose semi-rationalist grouping rather than, with misleading precision, a Kullābi school.

107. In 309/921, Ibn Ḫuzayma (d. 311 or 312/ca. 924) repudiated some of his students for being *Kullābīya*. He asserted that Aḥmad had been denounced that party with exceptional severity. V. al-Ḥākim al-Naysābūrī (*Tārīḫ Naysābūr*), *apud* al-Ḏahabī, *Siyar* 14 (ed. Akram al-Būšayyī, 1983): 379f; cf. Josef van Ess, "Ibn Kullāb et la miḥna," *Arabica* 37 (1990): 187fn (résumé by Gilliot).

tions (*al-furūʿ*).[108] One relates al-Karābīsī's position concerning a classic question of *uṣūl al-fiqh*, whether a report necessarily produces certain knowledge.[109] Al-ʿAbbādī preserves a position of al-Muḥāsibī's concerning another classic question, whether the consensus of the scholars in one age was not a source of law if the scholars of a previous age had disagreed over the same question.[110] Dāwūd al-Ẓāhirī is famous for his rejection of *qiyās*. More positively, the list of his works includes a number that must have dealt with other classic questions of *uṣūl al-fiqh*.[111] Finally, there is extant from al-Muzanī a short work on some questions of *uṣūl*.[112]

If the semi-rationalists were largely *Šāfiʿīya*, we should find that Aḥmad and his followers were peculiarly hostile to that school. Indeed, the latest researches confirm that al-Šāfiʿī himself was no traditionalist, but rather a figure in the middle, what I have called a "semi-rationalist."[113]

Accordingly, Ḥanbali assessments of al-Šāfiʿī from the generation after Aḥmad tend to be negative. Aḥmad is described as helping al-Šāfiʿī to assess *ḥadīṯ* reports[114]; as saying "He did not benefit from us more than we benefitted from him," as though his followers had assumed that most of the benefit had gone to al-Šāfiʿī[115]; and as recommending [249] students to avoid the books of al-Šāfiʿī.[116] A Mālikī tradition even quotes Aḥmad as saying of al-Šāfiʿī, "He was trustworthy (as a traditionist), a partisan of *raʾy* and *kalām*, without knowledge of *ḥadīṯ*, and a Shiite."[117]

108. Al-ʿAbbādī, *Ṭabaqāt*, 24f; Abū Isḥāq al-Šīrāzī, *Ṭabaqāt al-fuqahāʾ*, ed. Iḥsān ʿAbbās (Beirut: Dār al-Rāʾid al-ʿArabī, 1970), 102.

109. Al-ʿAbbādī, 24. Cf. Bernard Weiss, *The Search for God's Law* (Salt Lake City: Univ. of Utah Press, 1992), 294f; *contra* Wael B. Hallaq, who disputes al-Karābīsī's contribution in either field on the ground that we have no particular information about it, "Was al-Shafiʿi the Master Architect of Islamic Jurisprudence?" *International Journal of Middle East Studies* 25 (1993): 602, n. 23.

110. Al-ʿAbbādī, 27. For later Šāfiʿi discussions, *v.* Weiss, 247f.

111. V. Ibn al-Nadīm, *Fihrist*, 216f, esp. *K. al-Iǧmāʿ*, *K. al-Ḫabar al-wāḥid*, *K. al-Ḫabar al-mūǧib lil-ʿilm*, *K. al-Ḥuǧǧa*, *K. al-Ḫuṣūṣ wal-ʿumūm*, and *K. al-Mufassar wal-muǧmal*.

112. *K. al-Amr wal-nahy*, ed. and trans. R. Brunschvig, "'Le livre de l'ordre et de la défense' d'al-Muzani," *Bulletin de l'études orientales* 11 (1945–1946): 145–194. There is also attributed to him a *K. al-Qiyās*: v. George Makdisi, "The Juridical Theology of Shâfiʿî," *Studia Islamica*, no. 59 (1984), 31.

113. Hallaq, 587–605, esp. 593f.

114. ʿAbd Allāh ibn Aḥmad, *apud* Abū Nuʿaym, 9:170; Ibn Abī Yaʿlā, *Ṭabaqāt al-ḥanābila* 1:6.

115. Aḥmad Ibn Ḥanbal, *K. al-ʿIlal wa-maʿrifat al-riǧāl*, ed. Waṣī Allāh ibn Muḥammad ʿAbbās, 4 vols. (Beirut: al-Maktab al-Islāmī, 1988), 1:469 = ed. Talât Koçyiğit & Ismail Cerrahoğlu, Ankara Üniversitesi Ilâhiyat Fakültesi Yayínlarín 49, only first vol. published (Ankara: Doğuş Matbaacílík ve Ticaret Matbaasí, 1963), 1:158; Abū Nuʿaym, 9:170.

116. Ibn Abī Yaʿlā, 1:38; al-Ḏahabī, *Siyar* 13:550.

117. Al-Qāḍī ʿIyāḍ, *Tartīb al-madārik wa-taqrīb al-masālik li-maʿrifat aʿlām madhab Mālik*, ed. Aḥmad Bakīr Maḥmūd, 5 vols. (Beirut: Maktabat al-Ḥayāt, 1967–1968?), 1:389, l. 11; 390, l. 9.

Only with the second generation after Aḥmad did traditionalists begin to praise al-Šāfiᶜī. Al-Ḫallāl quotes Aḥmad as saying, "Al-Šāfiᶜī is among the beloved of my heart."[118] The first writer to devote a *manāqib* work to al-Šāfiᶜī was a semi-rationalist, Dāwūd al-Ẓāhirī,[119] but the second was a traditionalist, the *riğāl* critic Ibn Abī Ḥātim al-Rāzī (d. 327/938).[120] Perhaps the change was effected in part by publication of the *Risāla* of (it was said) al-Šāfiᶜī, recently redated to around 300/912–913.[121] The rehabilitation of al-Šāfiᶜī did not make semi-rationalist *Šāfiᶜīya* acceptable to the *Ḥanābila*. The blockade of al-Ṭabarī's house has been mentioned already. In 323/935, the *Ḥanābila* incited blind men to attack the *Šāfiᶜīya* from mosques.[122]

It is an admitted difficulty that the semi-rationalists had scant conception of themselves as a distinct group. Some were on poor terms with one another; for example, Abū Ṯawr joined Aḥmad in questioning whether al-Karābīsī had really studied under al-Šāfiᶜī.[123] Following Abū l-Ḥasan al-Ašᶜarī, Josef van Ess has called them *ahl al-iṯbāt*[124]; however, this has the double disadvantage that they did not use it of themselves in the ninth century C.E. and that it was later used to designate all [250] traditionalists, whether involved in *kalām* or not.[125] "The *mutakallimīn* of *ahl al-sunna*" is a term they themselves might have recognized and accepted; however, it not only seems long, it assumes that *ahl al-sunna* did include *mutakallimīn*, which Aḥmad and other traditionalists of the ninth century strenuously denied.

For all the vagueness of its boundaries, the semi-rationalist party was extremely important. Semirationalism, neither outright traditionalism nor rationalism, was the matrix of the classical schools of law.[126] Ibn Surayğ, virtual founder of the classical Šāfiᶜi

118. Aḥmad Ibn Ḥanbal (i.e., al-Ḫallāl), *ᶜAqīda*, 127.

119. Kātib Çelebī, *Kašf al-ẓunūn*, ed. Şerefeddin Yaltkaya & Rifat Bilge, 2nd ed., 2 vols. (Istanbul: Maarif Matbaasí, 1941–1943), 2:1839.

120. Ibn Abī Ḥātim, *Ādāb al-Šāfiᶜī wa-manāqibuh*, ed. ᶜAbd al-Ġanī ᶜAbd al-Ḫāliq (Aleppo: Maktabat al-Turāṯ al-Islāmī, 1954).

121. Norman Calder, *Studies in Early Muslim Jurisprudence* (Oxford: Clarendon Press, 1993), 242. George Makdisi has found the *Risāla* thoroughly traditionalist in establishing a criterion of orthodoxy that has nothing to do with *kalām* or reason: "Juridical Theology" 5–47, esp. 43–47. There is a separate, Šāfiᶜi tradition by which Aḥmad highly admired al-Šāfiᶜī, for which *v.*, e.g., al-Bayhaqī, *Manāqib al-Šāfiᶜī*, ed. Aḥmad Ṣaqr, 2 vols. (Cairo: al-Mağlis al-Aᶜlā lil-Šuʾūn al-Islāmīya, 1969).

122. Ibn al-Aṯīr, s.a. 323; 8:308. Of course, al-Ḫallāl was active mainly as a jurisprudent, developing a Ḥanbali school of law very like the contemporary Šāfiᶜi school of Ibn Surayğ, whereas the assaults on al-Ṭabarī and the Šāfiᶜīya were led by others (Ibn Abī Dāwūd and al-Barbahārī, respectively). On the division of the *Ḥanābila* in the fourth/tenth century among jurisprudents, ascetics, and activists, *v.* Ibn Abī Yaᶜlā, 2:43.

123. Ibn Ḥağar, *Tahḏīb* 2:361.

124. Van Ess, "Ibn Kullāb und die Miḥna," 126–131 = "Ibn Kullāb et la *miḥna*," 219–225.

125. Ibn ᶜAsākir, *Tabyīn kaḏib al-muftarī* (Damascus: Maṭbaᶜat al-Tawfīq, 1347), 163.

126. What I call the "classical" schools are precisely equivalent to what George Makdisi calls the

school, was almost certainly of this party.[127] Abū Bakr al-Ḫallāl, virtual founder of the classical Ḥanbali school, was close to it, with his untraditionalist devotion to the sayings of Aḥmad as a source of law, in addition to hadith; also, as we have seen, with his praise of al-Šāfiʿī.[128] The Māliki school of Baghdad, led by the students of Aḥmad ibn Muʿaḏḏal, most importantly Ismāʿīl ibn Isḥāq (d. 282/896), was associated with semi-rationalism. Three other schools of the time were also semi-rationalist: those named for Abū Ṯawr, Dāwūd al-Ẓāhirī, and al-Ṭabarī. These schools gave formal priority to *Qurʾān* and *ḥadīṯ*, as did the traditionalists, but they also allowed a great deal of play to rational methods like analogy.

Semirationalism was the matrix of classical Sufism, as well, for al-Ǧunayd, its virtual founder, was disciple to Abū Ṯawr and al-Muḥāsibī, [251] and may have met Ibn Kullāb.[129] Abū ʿAlī al-Rūḏabārī (d. 322/933–934) adhered to the Šāfiʿi school, Ruwaym (d. 303/915–916) and Ibn al-Aʿrābī to the Ẓāhiri school, al-Šiblī (d. 334/946) to the Mālikī.[130] None of the known early *Ṣūfis* of Baghdad adhered to either the more traditionalist Ḥanbali school or the more rationalist Ḥanafi. (Partial exceptions are a few figures from the generation before al-Ǧunayd, who at some time at least sat with Aḥmad.[131]) Classical Sufism

guild schools: *v.* "*Ṭabaqāt*-Biography: Law and Orthodoxy in Classical Islam," *Islamic Studies* (Islamabad) 32 (1993): 371–196, esp. 389–392. That is, they are the schools as we know them from the fifth/eleventh century onwards, the schools with a regular procedure of forming jurisprudents.

127. On the importance of Ibn Surayǧ, *v.* Hallaq, "Was al-Shafiʿi the Master Architect?," 595f. For a discussion of his theological position, *v.* Louis Massignon, *The Passion of al-Hallāj*, trans. Herbert Mason, Bollingen ser. 98, 4 vols. (Princeton: Princeton Univ. Press, 1982), 1:374–376. No *kalām* work of his survives, but among the dozen titles that are mentioned (compared with over 400 works he is said to have written: Abū Isḥāq al-Šīrāzī, *Ṭabaqāt al-fuqahāʾ*, 109), only one seems to deal with a problem of *uṣūl al-fiqh*: *Naqd kitāb al-Ǧārūf ʿalā al-qāʾilīn bi-takāfuʾ al-adilla*, cited by Ibn Ṭāhir al-Baġdādī, *al-Farq bayna l-firaq*, ed. Muḥyī l-Dīn ʿAbd al-Ḥamīd (Cairo: Maktabat Muḥammad ʿAlī Ṣabāḥ, n.d.), 363. His writing about *uṣūl al-fiqh* at all establishes that he was no traditionalist. So does the prominence in *kalām* alleged by al-Ḍiyāʾ al-Ḫaṭīb, *Ġāyat al-marām*, *apud* al-Subkī, *Ṭabaqāt al-šāfiʿīya* 3:22. Ibn al-Murtaḍā asserts that he was a Muʿtazili, having studied under Abū l-Ḥusayn al-Ḫayyāṭ: Ibn al-Murtaḍā, *Klassen*, 129. Unfortunately, the theological work in the Süleymaniye library attributed to him (*v.* *GAS* 1:495, #1) must date from a century later.

128. Al-Ḏahabī states that there was no independent Ḥanbali school (*maḏhab mustaqill*) before about 300/912–913, when al-Ḫallāl collected Aḥmad's sayings and justified them: *Siyar* 14:298.

129. For al-Ǧunayd and Abū Ṯawr, *v.* Ibn ʿAṭāʾ, *apud* Ibn al-Ǧawzī, *Naqd al-ʿilm wal-ʿulamāʾ* (n.p.: Idārat al-Ṭibāʿa al-Munīrīya, 1966), 167 = *Talbīs Iblīs*, ed. Ḫayr al-Dīn ʿAlī (Beirut: Dār al-Waʿy al-ʿArabī, 1970?), 193. For al-Ǧunayd and Ibn Kullāb, *v.* Josef van Ess, "Ibn Kullāb und die Miḥna," *Oriens* 18–19 (1965–1966): 101 = "Ibn Kullāb et la *miḥna*," 186f.

130. On Ruwaym, *v.* al-Sulamī, *Kitāb Ṭabaqāt al-Ṣūfiyya*, ed. Johannes Pedersen (Leiden: E. J. Brill, 1960), 170; al-Ḫaṭīb al-Baġdādī, *Tārīḫ Baġdād* 8:430. On Ibn al-Aʿrābī, *v.* al-Sulamī (presumably *Tārīḫ al-ṣūfiya*), *apud* Ibn Ḥaǧar, *Lisān* 1:309. On al-Šiblī, *v.* al-Ḏahabī, *Tārīḫ al-islām* 25 (331–350): 117f.

131. Notably Muḥammad Ibn Abī l-Ward (d. 263/877?), for whom *v.* Ibn Abī Yaʿlā, 1:317f, and Abū Ḥamza (d. 269/882–883?), for whom ʿ Ibn Abī Yaʿlā, 1:268f. In Basra, Ibn Sālim (d. 350's/960's?) was said to have learnt the jurisprudence of Abū Ḥanīfa, while those of the *Sālimīya* who had learnt jurisprudence

was a compromise mysticism designed to mollify the traditionalists. Al-Ǧunayd wanted no repeat of Ġulām Ḫalīl's Inquisition of 264/877–878, in which 70–odd *Ṣūfīs* had been arrested.[132] Perhaps it was natural that the *Ṣūfīs* should choose a compromise theology and jurisprudence.[133]

Possibly, through Ibn Muǧāhid (d. 324/936), the semi-rationalist party was furthermore the matrix of the classical organization of *Qur'ān* recitation.[134] Further research will surely demonstrate connections in grammar [252] and *belles-lettres* (*adab*). The *Ṣūfī* al Rūḏabārī boasted that his teacher (*ustaḏ*) in Ṣūfism had been al-Ǧunayd, in jurisprudence Ibn Surayǧ, in *adab* Ṯaʿlab, and in *ḥadīṯ* Ibrāhīm al-Ḥarbī.[135] Al-Rūḏabārī is also said to have studied *Qur'ān* recitation under Ibn Muǧāhid.[136]

Conclusion

This examination of Aḥmad's remembered polemics against heretics suggests some amendments to the usual view of theological politics in the ninth century. First, the traditionalists' main struggle was not against the *Muʿtazila*. Had they been the main adversaries, we should have many more statements against them from Aḥmad, his contemporaries, and his followers. Doubtless Aḥmad and other traditionalists disagreed with the *Muʿtazila* and would use strong language about them; however, they saw their main adversaries elsewhere. The great theological struggle of the ninth century was between traditionalists and rationalists, among whom the *Muʿtazila* (perhaps, in Aḥmad's time, the proto-*Muʿtazila*) were merely one group. Only near the end of the century did the *Muʿtazila* emerge as the main group among the rationalists.

---

were *Mālikīya*, according to al-Muqaddasī (i.e., al-Maqdisī), *Aḥsan al-taqāsīm*, 126. However, this school was a rival movement to Baghdadi Sufism. Al-Barbahārī, the Ḥanbali leader, was associated with it as a disciple to Sahl al-Tustarī, for which *v.* Ibn Abī Yaʿlā, *Ṭabaqāt al-ḥanābila* 2:18.

132. For a brief account of the Inquisition, *v.* Carl Ernst, *Words of Ecstasy in Sufism*, SUNY Series in Islam (Albany: State Univ. of New York Press, 1985), 97–101. As for its association with traditionalism, Ibn al-Aʿrābī makes clear that it began among traditionalists in Basra: *Ṭabaqāt al-nussāk*, *apud* al-Ḏahabī, *Siyar* 13 (ed. ʿAlī Abū Zayd, 1983): 284. Ibn Abī Yaʿlā does not own Ġulām Ḫalīl as a Ḥanbali; however, the *K. al-Sunna* attributed to him is extremely close to that of the later Ḥanbali al-Barbahārī: *v.* Louis Massignon, ed., *Recueil de textes inédits*, Collection de textes inédits relatifs à la mystique musulmane 1 (Paris: Paul Geuthner, 1929), 213f; cf. al-Barbahārī, Šarḥ *"K. al-Sunna," apud* Ibn Abī Yaʿlā, *Ṭabaqāt al-ḥanābila* 2:18–43, esp. 19, 26, 34.

133. For connections between Sufism and Ašʿarism in the next century, *v.* Tilman Nagel, *Die Festung des Glaubens* (Munich: C. H. Beck, 1988); cf. Claude Gilliot, "Quand la théologie s'allie á l'histoire," *Arabica* 39 (1992): 241–260.

134. V. *Encyclopaedia of Islam*, new ed., s.v. "Ibn Mudjāhid," by J. Robson, with references, to which add al-Subkī, 3:57f.

135. Al-Sulamī, *Ṭabaqāt*, 369. Cf. al-Ḫaṭīb al-Baġdādī, 1:331, missing Ibn Surayǧ.

136. Ibn al-Ṣalāḥ al-Šahrazūrī, *Ṭabaqāt al-šāfiʿīya*, ed. al-Nawawī, Hamidiye (Istanbul) 537, 74a.

Second, the struggle between hadith and *ra*ʾ*y* was very sharp (at least in Baghdad), and extended well beyond disagreements over juridical problems. It included the Inquisition of al-Maʾmūn and his successors, when they tried to establish a doctrine not of the *Muʿtazila* but of the traditional juridical allies of their dynasty, the *Ḥanafiya*. The situation was complicated by there having developed a more traditionalist party among the *Ḥanafiya*, who did not, for example, affirm a create *Qur*ʾ*ān*. Until late in the ninth century, however, the *Ḥanafiya* are mainly to be placed on the rationalist side of the great struggle.

Third, where Aḥmad directed his sharpest polemics was not against either *Muʿtazila* or rationalist *Ḥanafiya*, but rather against a semi-rationalist middle party: self-proclaimed traditionalists who threatened to insinuate the tools of the rationalists into traditionalist practice. In theology, they used sophisticated arguments in defense of traditionalist doctrine. Their jurisprudence was formally based on scriptuary sources, *Qur*ʾ*ān* and [253] *ḥadīṯ*, but they actually relied heavily on analogy and other methods originally developed by the rationalists. It was the *Ašāʿira* who took up the semi-rationalist theological position of Aḥmad's chief enemies in the next century and upheld it the longest. But virtually all Muslims became semi-rationalists in jurisprudence.

2
BUKHĀRĪ AND EARLY HADITH CRITICISM

A few years ago, Norman Calder questioned the attribution of *al-Taʾrīkh al-kabīr* to Muḥammad ibn Ismāʿīl al-Bukhārī (d. 256/870), the great Transoxanian traditionist.

> Apparently the product of the devoted and orderly activity of a single person, works like the *Ṣaḥīḥ*s of Bukhārī and Muslim should probably be recognized as emerging into final form at least one generation later than the dates recorded for the deaths of the putative authors....
>
> A fortiori the *rijāl* works associated with these collections. Bukhārī's *Al-Taʾrīkh al-kabīr* is probably a post facto description of the *Ṣaḥīḥ*, not a set of criteria governing the collection of its materials.[1]

The first goal of this study is to determine whether *al-Taʾrīkh al-kabīr* is a post facto description of the *Ṣaḥīḥ* (usually referred to in the sources as *al-Jāmiʿ al-ṣaḥīḥ*, *al-Jāmiʿ*, or *Ṣaḥīḥ* al-Bukhārī; however, its full title is reportedly *al-Jāmiʿ al-musnad al-ṣaḥīḥ al-mukhtaṣar min umūr rasūl Allāh . . . wa-sunanihi wa-ayyāmih*).[2]

Calder redated various early juridical texts—the *Mudawwanah* of Saḥnūn, the *Muwaṭṭaʾ* of Mālik (recension of Yaḥyá ibn Yaḥyá al-Laythī), and others—according to how much they adduced Prophetic hadith or how much the evidently older sources of Companion hadith and especially the opinions of eighth-century jurisprudents. It was Calder's essential argument that it makes better sense to suppose a gradually increasing deference

Much of the research behind this paper was made possible by a grant from the Social Science Research Council with funds mainly from the United States Information Agency.

1. Norman Calder, *Studies in Early Muslim Jurisprudence* (Oxford: Clarendon Press, 1993), 194.
2. Al-Nawawī, *Tahdhīb al-asmāʾ wa-al-lughāt*, 2 vols. in 3 (Cairo: Idārat al-Ṭibāʿah al-Munīrīyah, 1927; rpr. Beirut: Dār al-Kutub al-ʿIlmīyah, n.d.), 1: 73.

Originally published in *Journal of the American Oriental Society* 121 (2001): 7–19.

to Prophetic hadith than to suppose early recognition of its priority (in the *Muwaṭṭa*ʾ of Mālik, some Ḥanafi works, and virtually all the works of al-Shāfiʿī), succeeded by deference instead to reason and the opinions of early jurisprudents (the *Mudawwanah*), succeeded by a rediscovery of the priority of Prophetic hadith. Accordingly, he assigned the *Mudawwanah* of Saḥnūn and the works of al-Shaybānī that constitute *Kitāb al-Aṣl* to about 250/864–65; the *Mukhtaṣar* of al-Muzanī to around 270/883–84; and the *Umm* and *Risālah* of Shāfiʿī to around 300/912–13.

The attribution of *al-Taʾrīkh al-kabīr*, as of the collections of sound hadith that go by the names of Bukhārī, Muslim (d. 261/875), Abū Dāwūd (275/889), al-Tirmidhī (279/892), and Ibn Mājah (273/887), calls into question Calder's redating of various eighth- and ninth-century legal texts partly inasmuch as such texts presuppose an exclusive interest in Prophetic hadith as opposed to Companion hadith and the opinions of later jurisprudents. Prophetic hadith reports make up only about twenty-two percent of all items in the *Muṣannaf* of ʿAbd al-Razzāq (d. 211/827), as one might expect in so early a collection (although they make up almost half the material of the last [8] volume alone, where we presumably meet the most later additions).[3] Prophetic hadith reports constitute twenty-five percent of the material in the *Muṣannaf* of Abū Bakr Ibn Abī Shaybah (d. 235/849), and I have the impression of fewer opinions there from eighth-century jurisprudents.[4] The *Musnad* of Aḥmad ibn Ḥanbal (d. 241/855) stresses Prophetic hadith, but it seems to have been compiled after his lifetime, and Aḥmad's surviving juridical works (or rather collections by others of his opinions) show heavy reliance on hadith from Companions.[5] But the Six Books are organized by juridical category, plainly for the benefit of jurisprudents and presumably for jurisprudents who had accepted that Prophetic hadith (with the Qurʾan) constituted the principal basis of the law—this at least a generation before, by Calder's reckoning, Shāfiʿī's *Risālah* had told them so.

Actually, the *Ṣaḥīḥ* of Bukhārī seems not to have been widely published until well into the tenth century, for virtually all known transmissions were through a single man, Muḥammad ibn Yūsuf ibn Maṭar al-Firabrī (d. 320/932).[6] Somehow, no one else of the

---

3. ʿAbd al-Razzāq, *al-Muṣannaf*, ed. Ḥabīb al-Raḥmān al-Aʿẓamī, Min Manshūrāt al-Majlis al-ʿIlmī 39, 11 vols. (Johannesburg: Majlis Ilmi, 1390–92/1970–72). Based on samples of over 400 (all 11 volumes) and 50 (last volume alone).

4. Abū Bakr Ibn Abī Shaybah, *al-Muṣannaf*, ed. Muḥammad Salīm Ibrāhīm Samārah, et al., 4 vols. (Beirut: ʿĀlam al-Kutub, 1989). Based on a sample of 200.

5. See Susan A. Spectorsky, "Aḥmad Ibn Ḥanbal's *Fiqh*," *JAOS* 102 (1982): 461–65.

6. J. W. Fück, "Zur Überlieferungsgeschichte von Buḫārī's Traditionssammlung," *Zeitschrift der Deutsche Morgenländischen Gesellschaft* 92 (N.F. 17, 1938): 60–87. Fuat Sezgin names five important transmitters of the *Ṣaḥīḥ* directly from Bukhārī but admits that its first commentator, al-Khaṭṭābī (d. 386/996), already knew only the recensions of Firabrī and Ibrāhīm ibn Maʿqil al-Nasafī (d. 295/907–908). Kātib Çelebī describes Nasafī as relating merely a part near the end by *ijāzah*. (I suppose that the date he gives for Nasafī's death, 240, is an unrelated mistake.) V. Fuat Sezgin, *Geschichte des arabischen Schrifttums*, 9 vols.

many illustrious traditionists who related hadith of Bukhārī (al-Mizzī lists over eighty) recognized the value of his collection of sound hadith and transmitted it. Its organization, in particular its chapter headings, seem not to have stabilized until the mid-tenth century.[7] It first attracted commentaries in the later tenth century.[8] The earliest hadith collection based on the *Ṣaḥīḥ* of Muslim is said to have been that of Abū Bakr ibn Rajāʾ al-Sindī al-Isfarāyinī (d. 286/899–900)[9]; however, the earliest that might have been based on the *Ṣaḥīḥ* of Bukhārī is that of Abū ʿAlī Saʿīd ibn ʿUthmān ibn al-Sakan (d. 353/964).[10] Inasmuch as the *Ṣaḥīḥ* of Bukhārī (as we know it) was apparently not widely published until well after Calder's date for the *Risālah* of Shāfiʿī, its organizing principle, the sufficiency of Prophetic hadith for the derivation of the law, cannot decisively refute Calder's chronology.

al-Taʾrīkh al-Kabīr: Not What Calder Guessed

Al-Taʾrīkh al-kabīr (henceforward *TK*) describes over 12,300 traditionists.[11] A typical entry reads so:

to date (Leiden: E. J. Brill, 1967–84), 1: 117f; Kātib Çelebī, *Keşf-el-zunun*, ed. Şerefettin Yaltkaya and Rifat Bilge, 2 vols. (Istanbul: Maarif Matbaası, 1941, 1943), 1: 545. See also Rosemarie Quiring-Zoche, "How al-Buḫārī's *Ṣaḥīḥ* was Edited in the Middle Ages: ʿAlī al-Yūnīnī and His *rumūz*," *Bulletin d'études orientales* 50 (1998): 191–222. Yūnīnī (d. 701/1302), whose edition of the *Ṣaḥīḥ* is apparently the most common text in use today, collated recensions going back to different disciples to Firabrī but found no alternative to Firabrī himself. For more on Firabrī (alternatively, Farabrī), see al-Dhahabī, *Taʾrīkh al-islām*, ed. ʿUmar ʿAbd al-Salām Tadmurī, 46 vols. to date (Beirut: Dār al-Kitāb al-ʿArabī, 1987–), 23 (A.H. 301–20): 613–15.

7. Kātib Çelebī, *Keşf* 1: 542.

8. See Sezgin, *GAS*, 1: 118 (*Iʿlām al-sunan* by al-Khaṭṭābī), 126 (selections by Ayyūb al-Firabrī [*fl.* later 4th/10th century] and al-Marwazī al-Kushmayhānī [d. 389/998–999]), 130f. (*Asāmī man rawá ʿanhum al-Bukhārī* by Ibn ʿAdī al-Qaṭṭān [d. 365/976] and various treatments of Bukhārī's authorities by al-Dāraquṭnī [d. 385/995]).

9. He composed his *Ṣaḥīḥ* "according to the criterion of Muslim": al-Dhahabī, *Taʾrīkh al-islām* 21 (A.H. 281–90): 288. Of course, "the criterion of Muslim" might have been formulated retrospectively.

10. *Al-Muntaqá al-ṣaḥīḥ* or *Muntaqá "al-Ṣaḥīḥ"*: see al-Dhahabī, *Taʾrīkh* 26 (A.H. 351–80): 89; Kātib Çelebī, *Keşf* 1: 1070.

11. Not subject to extensive discussion hitherto except in the work of various editors. See F. Krenkow, "The Tarikh of the Imam al-Bukhari," *Islamic Culture* 8 (1934): 643–48, which notified the world that most of *TK* was extant in manuscript and described two copies in Istanbul; also the introduction to Umm ʿAbd Allāh bt. Maḥrūs al-ʿAsalī, *Fihris Muṣannafāt al-imām . . . al-Bukhārī . . . al-manshūrah fīmā ʿadā "al-Ṣaḥīḥ,"* arr. Muḥammad ibn Ḥamzah ibn Saʿd, supv. Abū ʿAbd Allāh Maḥmūd ibn Muḥammad al-Ḥaddād (Riyadh: Dār al-ʿĀṣimah, 1408), 9–61.

> Ad'ham al-Sadūsī, Abū Bishr. Ḥajjāj al-Aʿwar quoted Shuʿbah, "He was client to Shaqīq ibn Thawr." He heard [9] ʿAbd Allāh ibn Buraydah. There related (hadith) from him Shuʿbah and Hushaym. His hadith is among the Basrans.[12]

According to a story from Firabrī, transmitter of the *Ṣaḥīḥ* of Bukhārī, and from an Abū Jaʿfar Muḥammad ibn Abī Ḥātim, described as a copyist (*warrāq*) and sometimes as Bukhārī's own copyist, Bukhārī wrote *TK* on moonlit nights in Mecca, when he was a youth fairly new to the collection of hadith.[13] Through the same source comes the story that Isḥāq ibn Rāhawayh (d. 238/853?) showed a copy to the governor of Khurasan, ʿAbd Allāh ibn Ṭāhir (d. 230/844), who could scarcely believe it.[14] Its composition is thus placed well before the *Ṣaḥīḥ*, supposedly assembled at the instigation of someone in Isḥāq's circle.[15]

The textual history of *TK* is complex, and what I offer is provisional (perhaps waiting for someone to make Bukhārī's histories the center of a doctoral dissertation). It raises considerably less doubt than the transmission of the *Ṣaḥīḥ*, as we have several witnesses from the ninth century. Admittedly like the *Ṣaḥīḥ*, *TK* survived through the transmission of a single man, Abū al-Ḥasan Muḥammad ibn Sahl ibn ʿAbd Allāh (alternatively al-Kurdī), a Basran Qurʾan reciter and grammarian.[16] Almost nothing seems to be known of the man apart from his transmitting *TK*.[17] One colophon states that he heard *TK* from Bukhārī in Basra, 246/860–61 (*TK* 1: 3). However, other recensions evidently circulated in the Middle Ages. Abū Zurʿah al-Rāzī worked from a copy provided him by al-Faḍl ibn al-ʿAbbās (Faḍlak al-Rāzī, d. 270/883).[18] Al-Khaṭīb al-Baghdādī quotes *TK* with a chain ending < Abū Aḥmad ibn Fāris < al-Bukhārī.[19] The association with Bukhārī of a professional copyist

---

12. Bukhārī, *K. al-Taʾrīkh al-kabīr*, 4 vols. in 8 (Hyderabad: Maṭbaʿat Jamʿīyat Dāʾirat al-Maʿārif al-ʿUthmānīyah, 1358–62; 2nd edn., 1377/1958; rpr. 8 vols. + index, Beirut: Dār al-Kutub al-ʿIlmīyah, 1986), 2: 65f.

13. Al-Khaṭīb al-Baghdādī, *Taʾrīkh Baghdād*, 14 vols. (Cairo: Maktabat al-Khānjī, 1349/1931; rpr. Cairo: Maktabat al-Khānjī and Beirut: Dār al-Fikr, n.d.), 2: 7, ll. 10f.

14. Al-Khaṭīb al-Baghdādī, *Taʾrīkh Baghdād* 2: 7, ll. 16–22.

15. Al-Khaṭīb al-Baghdādī, *Taʾrīkh Baghdād* 2: 8, ll. 13–17.

16. See the colophon of the Köprülü ms apud Bukhārī, *TK* (rpr. Beirut, 1986) 1: 10, identical to the chain of transmission described in Asad (Damascus) 3802/15.

17. E.g., see Ibn Ḥajar, *Lisān "al-Mīzān,"* 7 vols. (Hyderabad: Majlis Dāʾirat al-Maʿārif, 1329–31), 5: 194, which quotes an early commentator on the *Ṣaḥīḥ* as calling him an unknown, and Ibn al-Jazarī, *Ghāyat al-nihāyah fī ṭabaqāt al-qurrāʾ*, ed. Gotthelf Bergsträßer, 3 vols. in 2 (Cairo: Maktabat al-Khānjī, 1351–52/1932–33; rpr. Beirut: Dār al-Kutub al-ʿIlmīyah, 1400/1980), 2: 151, which scarcely says more than what might be deduced from his name and his transmitting *TK*.

18. Ibn Abī Ḥātim, *Bayān khaṭaʾ Muḥammad ibn Ismāʿīl al-Bukhārī fī taʾrīkhih* (Hyderabad: Maṭbaʿat Dāʾirat al-Maʿārif al-ʿUthmānīyah, 1961), 2.

19. In one hundred sixty-five places, according to Akram Ḍiyāʾ al-ʿUmarī, *Mawārid al-Khaṭīb al-Baghdādī fī "Taʾrīkh Baghdād"* (n.p.: Maktabat Muḥammad Hāshim al-Kutubī, 1395/1975), 347, 558. ʿUmarī cites nine examples, 348fn., which I have checked. They are all unquestionably from *TK*, not *al-Taʾrīkh al-awsaṭ*.

(Abū Jaʿfar Muḥammad ibn Abī Ḥātim) suggests, following Calder, deliberate authorship and multiple identical copies. It also means that someone besides Bukhārī himself stood to profit by the publication of works attributed to him, so one might suspect the copyist of organizing material in Bukhārī's name; yet our text of *TK* seems to have by-passed this copyist.

The earliest extant commentary on *TK* appeared a generation earlier than any treatment of the *Ṣaḥīḥ*, namely Ibn Abī Ḥātim al-Rāzī (d. 327/938), *Bayān khaṭaʾ Muḥammad ibn Ismāʿīl al-Bukhārī fī taʾrīkhih*, based on the criticism of Abū Zurʿah al-Rāzī (d. 264/878) and Abū Ḥātim al-Rāzī (d. 277/890). It presupposes an alphabetical collection like our *TK*, with a section on *kuná* an integral part at the end. It also presupposes a somewhat different text from ours. In a sample of seventy-two items (from seven hundred seventy-one proposed corrections), fifty-one have to do with changing the names of main entries in *TK*. (Most of the rest deal with chains of transmitters in *TK*.) In five cases (ten percent), Ibn Abī Ḥātim proposes to change a name altogether missing from our present text of *TK*. In twenty-one cases (forty-one percent), the change proposed by Ibn Abī Ḥātim is what is already in our present text of *TK*. The editor of *Bayān*, anxious to defend Bukhārī, suggests that either Faḍlak al-Rāzī had taken his copy of *TK* from an early, unfinished draft by Bukhārī or Abū Zurʿah actually used another, bad copy from some unnamed source.[20] The first of these proposals better squares with Abū Zurʿah's own reported description of the copy he used, and as Bukhārī is said to have spent sixteen years compiling the *Ṣaḥīḥ*, he must also have spent a great deal of time reworking *TK*.[21] [10] Contrary to the story from Firabrī and Abū Jaʿfar Muḥammad ibn Abī Ḥātim of composition in a few years in Mecca, another traditionist is quoted as explaining Bukhārī's many mistakes in this wise:

> He is a man who looked into the books of every Bukharan who came to him from Iraq. When he saw a name he did not know and hadn't his books with him (they did not write carefully and their books are without points), he would add to his own book by mistake. Otherwise, I never saw a Khurasani who understood more than he except for his stammering (*law lā ʿī fī lisānih*).[22]

As Bukhārī continually made additions, so also he must have continually made corrections.

Still, at least some corrections in *TK* must have been posthumous. Either Bukhārī or someone else might have accommodated many of Abū Zurʿah's criticisms, but only

20. ʿAbd al-Raḥmān ibn Yaḥyá al-Muʿallimī al-Yamānī, introduction to Ibn Abī Ḥātim, *Bayān*, d.

21. For sixteen years, see al-Khaṭīb al-Baghdādī, *Taʾrīkh Baghdād* 2: 14, ll. 13–17. Whatever Isḥāq ibn Rāhawayh showed ʿAbd Allāh ibn Ṭāhir obviously could not have been the present text of *TK*.

22. Abū ʿAlī Ṣāliḥ ibn Muḥammad, apud al-Khaṭīb al-Baghdādī, *Mūḍiḥ awhām al-jamʿ wa-al-tafrīq*, al-Silsilah al-Jadīdah min Maṭbūʿāt Dāʾirat al-Maʿārif al-ʿUthmānīyah 14/1, 2 vols. (Hyderabad: Maṭbaʿat Majlis Dāʾirat al-Maʿārif al-ʿUthmānīyah, 1378/1959), 1: 7.

someone else might have commented on the notice for ʿUbayd ibn Ismāʿīl al-Habbārī (d. 250/864–865), "His name in the original (*aṣl*) is "ʿAbd Allāh"" (*TK* 5:442f).[23] According to the colophon, of course, every date after 246 should indicate an addition by someone else than Bukhārī. Both our text of *TK* and the one quoted by al-Khaṭīb al-Baghdādī through Ibn Fāris include a note of Kawsaj's death in 251.[24] Presumably, the recensions of Muḥammad ibn Sahl and Ibn Fāris were combined at some point.

As for dating *TK*, the latest express date I have come across in it is A.H. 252, for Ziyād ibn Ayyūb Dallawayh, said to have died then (*TK* 3:345), and Muḥammad ibn Bashshār Bundār, said to have died in Rajab 252 (*TK* 1:49). A substantial number of transmitters in the *Ṣaḥīḥ* postdeceased Bukhārī, but I have not found any of their names in *TK*. Altogether, the evidence seems to be consistent with Bukhārī's having assembled *TK* in about the size and form in which we have it; however, the present text shows some rearrangement and probably extensive correction by later transmitters.

Since the *Ṣaḥīḥ* is said to name altogether 1,525 persons in its various chains of transmitters, it is hard to see how the huge *TK* might be merely "a post facto description of the *Ṣaḥīḥ*."[25] To further test Calder's suggestion, I selected 200 names from *TK* at random, then looked up each man in the sample in al-Mizzī, *Tahdhīb "al-Kamāl,"* an exhaustive treatment of all the transmitters mentioned in the Six Books.[26] It turns out that Calder's suggestion is indeed impossible. Only twenty-nine men (fourteen percent) in the sample from *TK* are included in the *Ṣaḥīḥ* of Bukhārī. An additional five (two percent) are not in the *Ṣaḥīḥ* but do appear in one or more of Bukhārī's other collections of hadith (*al-Adab al-mufrad*, *Khalq afʿāl al-ʿibād*, or *al-Qirāʾah khalfa al-imām*). The remaining one hundred sixty-three (eighty-two percent) appear in none of Bukhārī's collections of hadith. There is not enough material in the *Ṣaḥīḥ* of Bukhārī or in all the collections of Bukhārī together for anyone to have abstracted from them *TK*.

Likewise, I collected from Mizzī a sample of 200 names that appear in one of Bukhārī's hadith collections. Not all of them can be found in *TK*—twenty-five (twelve percent) seem to be missing, including nineteen (fourteen percent) of those whose names appear in the *Ṣaḥīḥ* itself. (Only about half as large a proportion from *Adab* is missing from *TK*.) Again, it seems impossible that *TK* should have been deduced from the *Ṣaḥīḥ* or even from all of Bukhārī's hadith collections together.

23. Additionally, he appears as ʿUbayd in the *Ṣaḥīḥ*: see Mizzī, *Tahdhīb "al-Kamāl" fī asmāʾ al-rijāl*, ed. Bashshār ʿAwwād Maʿrūf, 35 vols. (Beirut: Muʾassasat al-Risālah, 1413/1992), 19: 186f.

24. Bukhārī, *TK* 1: 404; al-Khaṭīb al-Baghdādī, *Tārīkh Baghdād* 6: 364, ll. 14–17.

25. Calder, *Studies*, 194fn. Transmitters in the *Ṣaḥīḥ* are numbered in al-Kalābādhī, *Rijāl "Ṣaḥīḥ" al-Bukhārī al-musammá al-Hidāyah wa-al-irshād*, ed. ʿAbd Allāh al-Laythī, 2 vols. (Beirut: Dār al-Maʿrifah, 1407/1987).

26. See n. 23 above; also *The Encyclopaedia of Islam*, new ed., *s.v.* "Mizzī," by G. H. A. Juynboll.

What, then, of Calder's alternative description (which he evidently assumed to be traditional), that *TK* offers "a set of criteria governing the collection" of Bukhārī's *Ṣaḥīḥ*? Medieval scholars often refer to "Bukhārī's criterion (*sharṭ al-Bukhārī*)" as a means to sort sound from unsound hadith reports. Calder's "criteria" may allude to it. However, it was deduced in retrospect from the *Ṣaḥīḥ*, never expounded directly by Bukhārī.[27] Ibn Ḥibbān al-Bustī (d. 354/965) was the first traditionist to define his [11] own criterion, so far as I know.[28] Al-Ḥākim al-Naysābūrī (d. 405/1014) was the earliest to define Bukhārī's criterion, asserting that a hadith report met Bukhārī's criterion if it had at least two reliable transmitters (*ʿadlayn*) at every generation; yet the *Ṣaḥīḥ* includes significant examples that do not meet such a criterion.[29] In the *Mustadrak*, al-Ḥākim appears to consider a link to meet Bukhārī's criterion simply if it appears in Bukhārī's *Ṣaḥīḥ*, without reference to *TK* or other biographical literature. Such is expressly Bukhārī's criterion as defined by al-Nawawī in the introduction to his commentary on the *Ṣaḥīḥ* of Muslim.[30] Al-Suyūṭī reviews a number of other definitions for Bukhārī's criterion but finds none satisfactory except that Bukhārī trusted only uninterrupted chains of reliable transmitters.[31]

The most persistent alternative definition of Bukhārī's criterion seems to be that every transmitter be proven to have met and heard directly from the person from whom he is represented as transmitting.[32] It is hard to see on what other basis than links in accepted chains of transmitters any traditionist might have been certain of two men's having met. (Nevertheless, some traditionists evidently thought they could know; e.g., Abū Bakr al-Marrūdhī reported asking Aḥmad whether Ibn ʿAwn had heard anything

---

27. "It has not been transmitted of any of them (the Six) that he said, 'I have made it a condition of putting (a hadith report) in my book that it meet such and such a criterion'": so expressly Ibn al-Qaysarānī (d. 507/1113), *Shurūṭ al-aʾimmah al-sittah*, pp. 83–105 in *Thalāth rasāʾil fī ʿilm muṣṭalaḥ al-ḥadīth*, ed. ʿAbd al-Fattāḥ Abū Ghuddah (Aleppo: Maktab al-Maṭbūʿāt al-Islāmīyah, 1417/1997), 85.

28. Ibn Ḥibbān, *Ṣaḥīḥ Ibn Ḥibbān bi-tartīb Ibn Balbān*, ed. Shuʿayb al-Arnaʾūṭ, 18 vols., 3rd printing (Beirut: Muʾassasat al-Risālah, 1414/1993), 1: 151.

29. Al-Ḥāzimī (d. 584/1188), *Shurūṭ al-aʾimmah al-khamsah*, pp. 107–189 in *Thalāth rasāʾil*, ed. Abū Ghuddah, 129–137, 140.

30. "If the transmitters of a hadith report are all trustworthy save that among them are, for example, Abū al-Zubayr al-Makkī, Suhayl ibn Abī Ṣāliḥ, al-ʿAlāʾ ibn ʿAbd al-Raḥmān, or Ḥammād ibn Salamah, they say of it, 'This hadith report is sound by the criterion of Muslim but not by the criterion of Bukhārī . . . .' Such is likewise the case of Bukhārī concerning what he included of the hadith of ʿIkrimah, client to ibn ʿAbbās, Isḥāq ibn Muḥammad al-Farawī, ʿAmr ibn Marzūq, et al., by whom Bukhārī argued but Muslim did not": Nawawī, *Sharḥ Ṣaḥīḥ Muslim*, ed. ʿIṣām al-Ṣabābaṭī, Ḥāzim Muḥammad, & ʿImād ʿĀmir, 11 vols. (Cairo: Dār al-Ḥadīth, 1415/1994), 1: 32.

31. Suyūṭī, *Tadrīb al-Rāwī fī sharḥ "Taqrīb" al-Nawawī*, ed. ʿIzzat ʿAlī ʿAṭīyah and Mūsá Muḥammad ʿAlī, 2 vols. (Cairo: Dār al-Kutub al-Islāmīyah, 1980, 1985), 1: 81–85, 155–62 = ed. Ṣalāḥ Muḥammad ʿUwayḍah, 2 vols. in 1 (Beirut: Dār al-Kutub al-ʿIlmīyah, 1996), 1: 30–32, 61–64.

32. E.g., Kātib Çelebī, *Keşf* 1: 541; similarly, Suyūṭī, *Tadrīb* (Cairo) 1: 83 = (Beirut) 1: 31. See also Eerik Nael Dickinson, "The Development of Early Muslim *ḥadīth* Criticism," Ph.D. diss., Yale Univ., 1992, 169.

from Anas. Aḥmad said, "He saw him, but as for hearing, I do not know. Ayyūb saw him but did not hear."[33]) Certainly, *TK* is no exposition of such a criterion. In the sample, not one date of birth is mentioned and only eleven dates of death (six percent).[34] (Why it should be called a *taʾrīkh* when it has so few dates is a minor puzzle. Perhaps it comes of the literature's basis in traditionists' personal diaries.[35]) Thus, *TK* hardly establishes even contemporaneity.

TK does regularly state that someone "heard" (*samiʿa*) one list of transmitters, that another list "heard from him" (*samiʿa minh*), whereas a biographical dictionary of the tenth century, *Kitāb al-Jarḥ wa-al-taʿdīl*, normally records the same respective lists as those from whom he "related" hadith (*rawá ʿan*) and who "related (hadith) from him" (*rawá ʿanh*). However, it seems doubtful whether we see in *al-Jarḥ wa-al-taʿdīl* the blurring of a distinction carefully maintained in *TK*, for Bukhārī's alternation among *samiʿa*, *rawá ʿan*, and simply *ʿan* does not appear to be systematic. Typically, for example, Bukhārī states that ʿAwn ibn Abī Juḥayfah "heard" his father, then mentions that there "said" (*qāla*) Muḥammad ibn Sayf "from (*ʿan*)" Sufyān ibn Ḥurayth "from" ʿAwn "from" (not *samiʿa* again or even *ḥaddathanī*) his father that Bilāl used to put his fingers in his ears (*TK* 7:15). I have never noticed that Bukhārī provides separate lists for shaykhs anyone respectively "heard" and merely "related from." Finally, "heard" in *TK* commonly corresponds to "related from" in *al-Taʾrīkh al-awsaṭ* and less often to "related from" or simply "from" in *Kitāb al-Ḍuʿafāʾ al-ṣaghīr*. They are further early evidence that Bukhārī did not (or at least was not known to) attach precise meanings to the various terms for transmission of hadith. It was Aḥmad and other Iraqi traditionists who continually worried over the implications of *ḥaddathanī*, *akhbaranī*, and so on. [12]

TK also offers few evaluations of personal reliability. In the sample, some evaluation or other is mentioned of only eleven men at most (six percent). Almost as often, evaluations are of particular hadith reports rather than men (most often *munqaṭiʿ*). Seldom, then, does it tell us who was a reliable transmitter, who not. Altogether, it seems unlikely that anyone could use *TK* directly to tell which transmitters to include in a collection of reliable hadith, which not. There is not enough there to go by.

---

33. Aḥmad ibn Ḥanbal, *al-Jāmiʿ fī al-ʿilal wa-maʿrifat al-rijāl*, ed. Muḥammad Ḥusām Bayḍūn, 2 vols. (Beirut: Muʾassasat al-Kutub al-Thaqāfīyah, 1410/1990), 1: 18. Anas ibn Mālik was a Companion usually said to have died in 91 or 92/*ca.* 710.

34. Cf. Franz Rosenthal, *A History of Muslim Historiography* (Leiden: E. J. Brill, 1952), 13: "less than 7 percent of the biographies are provided with dates of death and less than one-half of one percent of the biographies has an indication of date of birth." I should expect a slightly higher percentage of dates in the first two volumes, from which Rosenthal's figures come, because these include the Muḥammads and Aḥmads, hence a smaller proportion of Companions and Followers, a higher proportion of men who lived into the ninth century.

35. See George Makdisi, "The Diary in Islamic Historiography: Some Notes," *History & Theory* 25 (1986): 173–85.

Indeed, Bukhārī's *Ṣaḥīḥ* seems strikingly independent of *TK*. The high proportion of men in the *Ṣaḥīḥ* not found in *TK* (fourteen percent) has been mentioned already. Many of the hadith reports quoted *in extenso* in *TK* do not appear in the *Ṣaḥīḥ* (in my sample of two hundred, nine out of eleven from men who figure in the *Ṣaḥīḥ*). Hadith reports and transmitters that appear in the *Ṣaḥīḥ* are frequently ignored in the appropriate entries in *TK*; that is, the links X < A, < B, and < C may all appear in the *Ṣaḥīḥ* yet only X < A in *TK*, or the links X < A, < B, and < C in the *Ṣaḥīḥ* yet X < A, < D, and < E in *TK*. Of the chains of transmission quoted in full in the sample from *TK*, forty-five (eighty percent) go back to the Prophet, eleven to a Companion or some later figure. Thus, *TK* conforms imperfectly but better than the *Ṣaḥīḥ* to the chronology of interest in Prophetic hadith that Calder posits for the ninth century.

TK may reflect complete reliance on *isnād* analysis to separate the sound from the weak hadith reports. Its compiler was deeply interested in chains of transmission: of two hundred traditionists, we are informed of whom one hundred fifty-one (seventy-six percent) related hadith. Eerik Dickinson has recently proposed that *isnād* analysis was virtually the entire basis of ninth- and tenth-century hadith criticism: that dates of death were speculatively deduced from chains of transmission; that explanations for unacceptable hadith (that a man had become senile at a certain point, lost his books, etc.) were likewise speculative; that, by and large, men were considered trustworthy inasmuch as their names were associated with acceptable hadith reports (*contra* the traditional account that acceptable hadith reports were indicated by trustworthy transmitters).[36]

Yet even on the basis of *isnād* analysis, one could only indirectly use *TK* to distinguish acceptable from unacceptable transmission. Barely a quarter of its subjects are expressly associated with particular hadith reports. To be sure, experienced ninth-century traditionists must have made many associations simply on reading the names. Al-Khalīlī (d. 446/1055) complains that the *rijāl* works of Bukhārī, Ibn Abī Khaythamah, and Ibn Abī Ḥātim are useful only to those who already know prodigious amounts.[37] But even to an expert, *TK* would have been useful primarily to identify men by their names, all its subjects being at least named. Indeed, al-Khaṭīb al-Baghdādī quotes Abū Zurʿah al-Rāzī as expressly referring to "this book of Muḥammad ibn Ismāʿīl's (concerning) the names of men (*asmāʾ al-rijāl*)."[38]

Identification of names is a headache for anyone working with hadith. It is often difficult to identify persons even in *TK*. In the sample from *TK*, ʿAbbās ibn Jāriyah appears in *Kitāb al-Jarḥ wa-al-taʿdīl* as ʿAbbād, ʿAbd Allāh ibn Suhayl appears as ibn Sahl, ʿAbd al-ʿAzīz ibn Abī Saʿd as ibn Abī Saʿīd, and Muḥriz ibn Ḥārithah as ibn Jāriyah. How much more

---

36. Dickinson, "Development," chap. 6.

37. Al-Khalīlī, *al-Irshād fī maʿrifat ʿulamāʾ al-ḥadīth*, abr. al-Silafī, ed. ʿĀmir Aḥmad Ḥaydar (Beirut: Dār al-Fikr, 1993/1414), 5.

38. Al-Khaṭīb al-Baghdādī, *Mūḍiḥ* 1: 7.

do obscure identifications abound in actual collections of hadith. In the literature about hadith and its transmission, one continually meets with comments such as this:

> Bukhārī related hadith from him (Isḥāq ibn Manṣūr Kawsaj [d. 251/865]), saying, "There related to us Isḥāq" without further identification, so that one might think he meant Isḥāq ibn Rāhawayh. In our own time, there is disagreement over which is more probable.[39]

Obscure identifications were sometimes deliberate (*tadlīs*) but more often, surely, just careless. As it could not be used directly to sort sound from unsound hadith reports, the first use of *TK* must have been to clarify ambiguous references that traditionists found in their notebooks. I have used it so myself; for example, to identify Ad'ham al-Sadūsī in *TK* with Ad'ham ibn Ṭarīf al-Sadūsī in *Kitāb al-Jarḥ wa-taʿdīl*, both men being said to have related hadith from ʿAbd Allāh ibn Buraydah. Thus, the closest analogues to *TK* are not such later works as Mizzī, *Tahdhīb "al-Kamāl,"* and al-Dhahabī, *Mīzān al-iʿtidāl*, but rather such as Ibn Mākūlā, *al-Ikmāl*.

Comparison with *al-Taʾrīkh al-Awsaṭ* and *al-Ḍuʿafāʾ*

Bukhārī is said to have compiled his *taʾrīkh* three times.[40] The small version, *al-Taʾrīkh al-ṣaghīr*, evidently dealt only with Companions and is no longer extant. The middle-sized version, *al-Taʾrīkh al-awsaṭ* (henceforward [13] *TA*), is extant and has been published, although at least twice under the mistaken title of *al-Taʾrīkh al-ṣaghīr*.[41] The miscellaneous character of the text makes it difficult to count how many traditionists it covers, but their number seems to be somewhat more than two thousand. *TA* shows some important similarities to *TK*. Its entries are often identical to those in *TK*. In a sample of eighty-five men from *TA*, seventy-seven (ninety-one percent) appear also in *TK*. Like *TK* (and by contrast with contemporary Iraqi works, on which more below), *TA* offers few biographical details about its subjects not immediately relevant to evaluating hadith reports.

TA is also, in ways, quite different from *TK*. First, it arranges its subjects not alphabetically but by decade of death. Second, it expressly names death dates much more often than *TK*—in a sample of eighty-five men, the precise year in which someone died is

39. Al-Dhahabī, *Siyar aʿlām al-nubalāʾ*, 25 vols. (Beirut: Muʾassasat al-Risālah), 12 (ed. Shuʿayb al-Arnaʾūṭ & Ṣāliḥ al-Samr, 1983): 260.

40. Al-Khaṭīb al-Baghdādī, *Taʾrīkh Baghdād* 2: 7, ll. 13–16.

41. Al-Bukhārī, *al-Taʾrīkh al-sʾaghīr* (Hyderabad: Matʾbaʿat Dāʾirat al-Maʿārif al-ʿUthmānīyah, n.d.) = *al-Tārīkh al-sʾaghīr*, ed. Mahʾmūd Ibrāhīm Zāyid, 2 vols. (Beirut: Dār al-Maʿrifah, 1406/1986) = *al-Taʾrīkh al-awsaṭ*, ed. Muḥammad Ibrāhīm al-Luḥaydān, Silsilat Kutub al-Tawārīkh wa-al-Tarājim 2, 2 vols. (Riyadh: Dār al-Ṣumayʿī, 1418/1998). For the misidentification of *al-Taʾrīkh al-awsaṭ* as *al-Ṣaghīr*, see the introduction referred to in note 11, esp. 28f.

given for thirty-three (forty-two percent), compared with six percent of the names in *TK*. Third, it includes somewhat more personal evaluations than *TK*: in the sample, fourteen (sixteen percent), compared again with six percent of the names in *TK*. Fourth, *TA* seems less concerned with chains of transmission. Of eighty-five traditionists in the sample, we are informed of whom only twenty-four (twenty-eight percent) related hadith, by contrast with seventy-six percent of those in *TK*.

Finally, *TA* is far less tightly organized than *TK*. The information in *TK* is fairly stereotyped, one entry presenting more or less the same information about its subject as another. *TA* is much more varied. As an example of its tendency to digress, consider this sequence of data:

1) < ʿAbd Allāh ibn Abī al-Aswad < Saʿīd ibn ʿĀmir: “Ibn ʿAwn died in the year 151.”
2) < Muḥammad ibn Muqātil < Aḥmad < Yaḥyá: “Ḥanẓalah was still alive in the year 151.”
3) Muḥammad ibn Isḥāq, Abū Bakr ibn Yasār, client to Qays ibn Mukharrimah al-Qurashī, al-Madanī, died in Baghdad in the year 151.
4) < al-Muqri’: “Ibn ʿAwn and Ibn Jurayj died in the year 150.”
5) Yaḥyá ibn Bukayr: There died in 151 Ibn ʿAwn, he being ʿAbd Allāh ibn ʿAwn ibn Arṭabān, Abū ʿAwn, client to Muzaynah, al-Baṣrī.
6) < al-Muqriʾ < Ibn al-Mubārak: “I have not seen anyone better than ʿIbn Awn.”[42]

The lack of a named authority for item 3 (and in one manuscript for item 5) does not seem significant, inasmuch as items without authorities are frequent throughout *TA*. Items 2 and 3 were presumably set down at a different time from items 4–6. It seems more likely that 1–3 originally made up a unit concerning the year 151 while 4–6 were a later addition than that 2 and 3 were clumsily inserted into an originally coherent notice concerning Ibn ʿAwn. Furthermore, the terse style of items 1–3 looks earlier than the more elaborate 4–6. Now, why would Bukhārī or anyone else insert 4–6 after item 3 and not immediately after item 1? Most likely, I should guess, we are looking at marginal notes that have moved into the text in the course of transmission. If we had only *TA* to go by, I should probably guess with some confidence that the additions were not by Bukhārī; however, almost the same words appear in *TK*, s.n. ʿAbd Allāh ibn ʿAwn (*TK* 5: 163)—behold the limits of form criticism. From Firabrī comes the story that Bukhārī would get up, light the lamp, and add something (*yuʿalliqu*) eighteen times in a night.[43] (I recall examining an autograph volume of *Taʾrīkh al-islām* by al-Dhahabī with notes in his hand both in the margins and on extra slips attached between leaves. This sort of authorial addition

42. Bukhārī, *al-Taʾrīkh al-ṣaghīr*, ed. Zāyid, 2: 104 = *TA*, ed. Luḥaydān, 2: 86f.
43. Al-Khaṭīb al-Baghdādī, *Taʾrīkh Baghdād* 2: 14, ll. 10–13.

must be as old as codices.[44]) It seems unlikely that *TA* was extracted directly from *TK*, else surely it would be as systematic.

At other points, it seems almost certain that someone else than Bukhārī added material to *TA*. The published editions are based on three manuscripts: one of them quits at men who died in 250, the other two go on to the mid-250s, including at the end a notice for Bukhārī himself. None of the ten men in the extension after 250 appears in *TK*. In the common section for the year 250 alone appear nine men, only two of whom appear also in *TK*. Two out of nine is only twenty-two percent, compared with an intersection of ninety-two percent for *TA* as a whole. Furthermore, the second of them must have been inserted into *TA* by someone other than Bukhārī, for he is ʿUbayd ibn Ismāʿīl al-Habbārī, not ʿAbd Allāh [14] ibn Ismāʿīl as Bukhārī identified him in *TK*; moreover, *TA* states that he died just one day after ʿUbayd ibn Asbāṭ ibn Muḥammad al-Hamdānī, a fact not noted in *TK* (*TK* 5: 442f.). My guess is that Bukhārī had nothing to do with our present text of *TA* from about 238/852–53 onward. From that point noticeably increases the number of men who appear in *TA* but not in *TK*. The extra men are not all Baghdadi, nor even Iraqi, but a predominance of Baghdadis suggests that additions were made there.

Bukhārī is also credited with two books devoted entirely to weak transmitters. The small version, *Kitāb al-Ḍuʿafāʾ al-ṣaghīr*, is extant and has been published several times.[45] It comprises notices for 418 traditionists. I have studied a sample of 42. Every one appears also in *TK*. Like *TK*, *Ḍuʿafāʾ* usually mentions from whom someone related hadith (sixty-four percent of the sample). Also like *TK*, it seldom mentions dates (seven percent of the sample). Unlike *TK*, but naturally for its theme, it usually offers express evaluations of its subjects.

Ḍuʿafāʾ sheds some light on the composition of *TK*. Like the *Bayān* of Ibn Abī Ḥātim, *Ḍuʿafāʾ* suggests that *Kitāb al-Kuná* is an integral part of *TK* at the end. About half the time, *TK* has fuller information: a fuller form of the name, additional evaluations, or additional names of transmitters to or from the subject of the evaluation. Often, though, *TK* and *Ḍuʿafáʾ* present exactly the same information. Occasionally (two cases of the 42), *Ḍuʿafāʾ* has additional information. A little more often, there is additional information in both *TK* and *Ḍuʿafāʾ*. On the general principle that detail is normally added rather than subtracted, *TK* looks like the later work. There are other signs of additions to *TK* as well. For example, Bukhārī says of Kathīr ibn ʿAbd Allāh in *Ḍuʿafāʾ*, "I think him al-Ubullī." By con-

44. From the ninth century, Aḥmad ibn Ḥanbal states that some traditionists repudiated a Muḥammad ibn Jābir when they observed *laḥq* (later additions) in his notebooks: Aḥmad ibn Ḥanbal, *K. al-ʿIlal wa-maʿrifat al-rijāl*, ed. Waṣī Allāh ibn Muḥammad ʿAbbās, 4 vols. (Beirut: al-Maktab al-Islāmī, 1988), 3: 61f. = *Jāmiʿ* 2: 102.

45. My citations here are to Bukhārī, *K. al-Ḍuʿafāʾ al-ṣaghīr*, ed. Maḥmūd Ibrāhīm Zāyid (Aleppo: Dār al-Waʿy, 1396). Sezgin mentions Agra, 1323, and Allahabad, 1325, *GAS* 1: 133. I have also looked at *K. al-Ḍuʿafāʾ al-ṣaghīr*, pp. 405–503 in *al-Majmūʿ fī al-ḍuʿafāʾ wa-al-matrūkīn*, ed. ʿAbd al-ʿAzīz ʿIzz al-Dīn al-Sayrawān (Beirut: Dār al-Qalam, 1405/1985).

trast, *TK* omits "I think him" and adds at the end that Ibrāhīm al-Harawī was his source for the man's *nisbah*. Ibrāhīm's information must have come along between the writing of *Ḍuʿafāʾ* and of *TK* as we know it.[46]

Quotations in *Taʾrīkh Baghdād* tend to confirm that *Ḍuʿafāʾ* is earlier than *TK*. Akram Ḍiyāʾ al-ʿUmarī says al-Khaṭīb al-Baghdādī quotes from *Ḍuʿafāʾ* 44 times altogether and cites eleven examples.[47] Usually, Khaṭīb's quotations do agree more closely with our text of *Ḍuʿafāʾ* than with the corresponding entries in *TK*; however, they occasionally agree more closely with *TK*, suggesting that Khaṭīb's source was a different text, perhaps the lost *Kitāb al-Ḍuʿafāʾ al-kabīr*.[48] Probably, then, the small version of *Ḍuʿafāʾ* was written first and the long version on the basis of it and *TK*.

Comparison with Aḥmad ibn Ḥanbal, *al-ʿIlal wa-Maʿrifat al-Rijāl*

Another ninth-century work expressly intended to help identify traditionists is Aḥmad ibn Ḥanbal (d. 241/855), *al-ʿIlal wa-maʿrifat al-rijāl* (henceforward *ʿMR*).[49] *ʿIlal* in the title indicates subtle defects in chains of transmitters but *maʿrifat al-rijāl*, "the knowledge of the men," intersects with what seems to be the main subject of *TK*. To be precise, a quarter of the entries in *ʿMR* seem to have the main purpose of establishing someone's identity, in the same fashion as nearly all the entries in *TK*; for example, "My father said, 'I more than once heard Ismāʿīl ibn ʿUlayyah say, "There related to me Yaḥyá, Abū Humām," meaning Abū Humām ibn Yaḥyá'" (ʿAbbās 2: 542, Bayḍūn 2: 50), thus identifying a man in chains of transmission from Ibn ʿUlayyah. A mere two percent of all entries mention dates. [15]

46. Cf. *TK* 3: 278f., *Ḍuʿafāʾ*, 44, s.n. Rabīʿ ibn Ṣabīḥ (addition of clientship at end of entry in *TK*—it would normally appear right after the name); *TK* 6: 165, *Ḍuʿafāʾ*, 80, s.n. ʿUmar ibn Ṣuhbān (addition of full name and place at end of entry in *TK*); *TK* 6: 401f., *Ḍuʿafāʾ*, 86, s.n. ʿĪsá ibn Maymūn (addition of clientship at end of entry in *TK*); *TK* 7: 429, *Ḍuʿafāʾ*, 111, s.n. Mihrān ibn Abī ʿUmar (addition of *kunyah* at end of entry in *TK*).

47. ʿUmarī, *Mawārid*, 319f.

48. Cf. *Taʾrīkh Baghdād* 12: 326, ll. 14–16, *Ḍuʿafāʾ*, 93, *TK* 7: 109 (*Ḍuʿafāʾ* missing *nisbah* and Kufan connection); *Taʾrīkh Baghdād* 13: 431, *Ḍuʿafāʾ*, 115, *TK* 8: 114 (*Ḍuʿafāʾ* missing *nisbah*); *Taʾrīkh Baghdād* 11: 23, ll. 8–11, *Ḍuʿafāʾ*, 77, *TK* 6: 98 (evaluation agrees with *Ḍuʿafāʾ* but *kunyah* and *nisbah* with *TK*).

49. Three editions have appeared: Aḥmad ibn Ḥanbal, *K. al-ʿIlal wa-maʿrifat al-rijāl*, ed. Talât Koçyiğit and Ismail Cerrahoğlu, Ankara Üniversitesi Ilâhiyat Fakültesi Yayinlarin 49 (Ankara: Doğuş Matbaacilik ve Ticaret Matbaasi, 1963), which includes half the extant material from ʿAbd Allāh ibn Aḥmad; *K. al-ʿIlal wa-maʿrifat al-rijāl*, ed. ʿAbbās (see n. 44 above), which includes the other half of the material from ʿAbd Allāh and has the most extensive notes; and *al-Jāmiʿ fī al-ʿilal wa-maʿrifat al-rijāl*, ed. Bayḍūn (see n. 33 above), which adds to ʿAbbās' material answers by Aḥmad (and others) to al-Marrūdhī, Maymūnī, and Ṣāliḥ ibn Aḥmad collected by Abū Aḥmad Ḥusaynak al-Tamīmī (d. 375/985), 1: 15–68. References that follow are to the editions of ʿAbbās and Bayḍūn.

A difference is that ʿ*MR* also presents many more of the evaluations of personal reliability that one expects in hadith criticism. Where six percent of the entries in *TK* include a personal evaluation, a quarter of the entries in ʿ*MR* report Aḥmad's evaluation of some traditionist. For example, Aḥmad states that Ad'ham ibn Ṭarīf was highly trustworthy (ʿAbbās 2:206, Bayḍūn 1:269). Evaluations of personal reliability also comprise about a third of the entries in ʿ*MR* not from Aḥmad.

A particularly glaring difference between *TK* and ʿ*MR* is the systematic ordering of information in *TK* and the almost random ordering of information in ʿ*MR*. *TK* is not fully alphabetical (e.g., the sons of ʿUmars, ʿUthmāns, and ʿAlīs normally appear in that order), but once one has found the right section, one expects to find any given name without having to read more than eight or ten pages. In ʿ*MR*, such information as Aḥmad's identification of ʿUqbah ibn ʿAbd al-Ghāfir (ʿAbbās 2: 87f., Bayḍūn 1: 233) can hardly be found except by skimming from the very start. Sometimes there is repetition; for example, Aḥmad pronounces Muḥammad ibn Qays al-Asadī trustworthy four times in three widely scattered places (ʿAbbās 2: 189, 505, 3: 86, Bayḍūn 1: 263, 2: 37f., 114).

How could the collectors of ʿ*MR* hold up their heads without troubling to order their material more systematically? Unlike *TK*, I would say, ʿ*MR* is only partly a reference work to be consulted as written. The form of every entry stresses its oral character: whereas only occasionally does an entry in *TK* include "Abū ʿAbd Allāh said," "Muḥammad said," or "al-Bukhārī said," almost every entry in ʿ*MR* reaffirms its orality, beginning "My father related to me," "I asked Abū ʿAbd Allāh," "I asked my father," and so forth. ʿ*MR* continually refers to notebooks (and Aḥmad was a strong advocate of relating hadith from notebooks as an aid to accuracy), but its disorganization suggests a book to be memorized, not kept on the shelf for periodic reference.

In contrast to *TK* and Bukhārī, no one would assign ʿ*MR* directly to Aḥmad as his deliberate composition: what we have is several collections of his answers to various traditionists of the next generation. Some entries, perhaps one in seven, are not from Aḥmad at all but rather from contemporaries, most often Yaḥyá ibn Maʿīn (d. 233/848). The additions are closely related to the work's oral character: the recorder of data from one traditionist felt free to add data from elsewhere, just as his conversation at the mosque would not consist solely of transmission from one shaykh.

About a quarter of the entries in ʿ*MR* consist of neither identifications nor evaluations of reliability but rather stories about the transmission of hadith; for example, so many people gathered to hear ʿIkrimah that he got onto the roof of a house to dictate (Bayḍūn 1: 45). Stories about hadith are completely missing from *TK*. (They were missed from at least the tenth century. Bukhārī is quoted as explaining, "There is scarcely a name in the *Taʾrīkh* for which I haven't a story; however, I disliked to make the book longer."[50]) Firabrī's story of Isḥāq ibn Rāhawayh's taking *TK* to the governor of Khurasan suggests

50. Al-Khaṭīb al-Baghdādī, *Taʾrīkh Baghdād* 2: 7, ll. 11f.

a very different social setting for *TK*, mainly the world of *adab*, polite letters. Above all, though, *TK*'s systematic character calls to mind a working professional, not, as *ʿMR* calls to mind, a pious Muslim with a stock of miscellaneous observations and anecdotes.

I have sampled three other ninth-century Iraqi collections as well, two from Yaḥyá ibn Maʿīn, one from Abū Dāwūd.[51] Similarly to *ʿMR*, they were not deliberately composed by their principal authorities but collected by disciples. Similarly to *ʿMR*, they are not systematically arranged by date or alphabetical order; however, the collection from Abū Dāwūd and the *Taʾrīkh* of Yaḥyá ibn Maʿīn are ordered geographically. They vary somewhat in the proportions they offer of personal evaluations, identifications, and anecdotes about traditionists of the past, also in the amount of material they present from other experts. The proportion of personal evaluations ranges from fifty-nine percent of the sample from Yaḥyá ibn Maʿīn, *Maʿrifat al-rijāl*, fifty-eight percent of the sample from Abū Dāwūd, to twenty-nine percent of the sample from Yaḥyá ibn Maʿīn, *al-Taʾrīkh*. Identifications range from forty percent of the sample in Yaḥyá ibn Maʿīn, *al-Taʾrīkh*, to sixteen percent of the sample from Yaḥyá ibn Maʿīn, *Maʿrifat al-rijāl*, sixteen percent of the sample from Abū Dāwūd. Anecdotes and biographical material concerning traditionists comprise sixteen percent of the sample from Abū Dāwūd but only six or seven percent of the two samples from Yaḥyá ibn Maʿīn. Compared with *ʿMR*, then, they confirm a distinct Iraqi interest in personal evaluations but not in stories about traditionists. As usual, Aḥmad and his followers appear to be the extreme conservatives of the traditionalist movement, here most strongly resisting professionalization. [16]

Comparison with *al-Jarḥ wa-al-Taʿdīl*

Kitāb al-Jarḥ wa-al-taʿdīl of Ibn Abī Ḥātim al-Rāzī is said to have been based on *TK*, so it should make another useful comparison.[52] Information on names and those to and from whom they related hadith are usually attributed to the author's father, the famous traditionist Abū Ḥātim al-Rāzī.[53] A typical entry runs so:

51. Yaḥyá ibn Maʿīn, *al-Taʾrīkh*, ed. ʿAbd Allāh Aḥmad Ḥasan, 2 vols. (Beirut: Dār al-Qalam, n.d.); *idem*, *Maʿrifat al-rijāl* 1, ed. Muḥammad Kāmil al-Qaṣṣār (Damascus: Majmaʿ al-Lughah al-ʿArabīyah, 1405/1985); *idem*, *Maʿrifat al-rijāl* 2, ed. Muḥammad Muṭīʿ al-Ḥāfiẓ and Ghazwah Budayr (Damascus: Majmaʿ al-Lughah al-ʿArabīyah, n.d.); Abū Dāwūd, *Suʾālāt Abī ʿUbayd al-Ājurrī Abā Dāwūd*, ed. Muḥammad ʿAlī Qāsim al-ʿUmarī, Iḥyāʾ al-Turāth al-Islāmī 7 (Medina: al-Jāmiʿah al-Islāmīyah, al-Majlis al-ʿIlmī, 1399/1979).

52. Al-Khaṭīb al-Baghdādī, *Mūḍiḥ* 1: 8f.

53. Ibn Abī Ḥātim, *Kitāb al-Jarḥ wa-al-taʿdīl*, introduction + 4 vols. in 8 (Hyderabad: Jamʿīyat Dāʾirat al-Maʿārif al-ʿUthmānīyah, 1360; rpr. 9 vols., Beirut: Dār Iḥyāʾ al-Turāth al-ʿArabī, n.d.). A large proportion of the entries in volume 2, the first volume of regular biographies, are attributed jointly to Abū Ḥātim and Abū Zurʿah al-Rāzī (d. 264/878). It is easy to imagine, although unlikely to be proven, that Ibn Abī Ḥātim simply tired of writing Abū Zurʿah's name and that most of the information in *Jarḥ* should

> Ad'ham ibn Ṭarīf al-Sadūsī, Abū Bishr, client to Shaqīq ibn Thawr. He related (hadith) from Muṭarrif ibn ʿAbd Allāh ibn Shikhkhīr, Salmān Abū ʿAbd Allāh, and ʿAbd Allāh ibn Buraydah. There related from him Shuʿbah, Hushaym, and Bishr ibn al-Mufaḍḍal. I heard my father say that. Abū Muḥammad said there related from him Ismāʿīl ibn ʿUlayyah. ʿAbd al-Raḥmān < ʿAbd Allāh ibn Aḥmad ibn Ḥanbal, in writing, < his father, "Ad'ham ibn Ṭarīf is thoroughly trustworthy."[54]

Ibn Abī Ḥātim states that his intention was to include everyone from whom *ʿilm* had been transmitted, even if this required including many whom no critic had expressly evaluated.[55] *Jarḥ* comprises entries for over 18,000 traditionists.

Ibn Abī Ḥātim owns no debt to Bukhārī and *TK*, but his cursory entry for Bukhārī himself might indicate a reason for reticence:

> He came to them in Ray in 250. He related (hadith) of ʿAbdān al-Marwazī, Abū Humām al-Ṣalt ibn Muḥammad, al-Firyābī, and Ibn Abī Uways. My father and Abū Zurʿah heard from him. Then they left his hadith when Muḥammad ibn Yaḥyá al-Naysābūrī wrote to them that he had declared among them that one's pronunciation of the Qur'an was created.[56]

Muḥammad ibn Yaḥyá al-Dhuhlī (d. 258/872) also had Bukhārī expelled from Nishapur.[57]

There are some important similarities between *TK* and *Jarḥ*. Above all is their authors' overriding concern with chains of transmission. *Jarḥ* is even less concerned than *TK* with dates of death: in a sample of one hundred eighty entries, only one includes a date of death. None, of course, includes a date of birth. But of one hundred fifty-six (eighty-seven percent), substantially more than the seventy-five percent of those in *TK*, we are told from whom they transmitted hadith; of one hundred sixty-two (ninety percent), who transmitted hadith from them. Indeed, *Jarḥ* often reads like an improved version of *TK*, providing the same information about transmitters with additions.

Still, it does not appear possible to demonstrate direct textual dependence of *Jarḥ* on *TK*. About eighty-four percent of the men in my sample from *TK* appear in *Jarḥ*, a high proportion but it would surely be close to one hundred if *Jarḥ* were simply an expansion of *TK*. The order of names is only superficially similar, so *TK* could not have provided Ibn Abī Ḥātim even with a list of names to start from.[58]

---

be attributed to them jointly. Sometimes, information in *Bayān* is attributed to Abū Zurʿah but in *Jarḥ* to Abū Ḥātim; e.g., s.n. Muḥammad ibn ʿAbd al-Raḥmān ibn Yuḥannas, *TK* 1: 477, *Bayān*, 15, *Jarḥ* 7: 322.

54. Ibn Abī Ḥātim, *Jarḥ* 2: 348. "Salmān Abū ʿAbd Allāh" is not a corruption of "ibn ʿAbd Allāh": cf. Ibn Abī Ḥātim, *Jarḥ* 4: 298. "Abū Muḥammad" and "ʿAbd al-Raḥmān" both refer to Ibn Abī Ḥātim.

55. Ibn Abī Ḥātim, *Jarḥ* 2: 38.

56. Ibn Abī Ḥātim, *Jarḥ* 7: 191.

57. For more on Bukhārī's difficulties in Nishapur, see al-Khaṭīb al-Baghdādī, *Taʾrīkh Baghdād* 2: 30–33.

58. Cf. Dickinson, "Development," 50f.

The outstanding difference between *TK* and *Jarḥ* is in the interest they show in evaluations of traditionists (*thiqah*, *ṣadūq*, etc.). Where *TK* expressly rates only six percent of its subjects, *Jarḥ* does forty-nine percent. Concerning seventy-three percent of the men rated, Abū Ḥātim is quoted; concerning thirty-eight percent, usually but not always alongside Abū Ḥātim, Yaḥyá ibn Maʿīn; concerning twenty-two percent, Aḥmad ibn Ḥanbal; and concerning nineteen percent, Abū Zurʿah. ʿAlī ibn al-Madīnī and other critics are also quoted, but much less often. Although Yaḥyá ibn Maʿīn is quoted more often than Aḥmad, Aḥmad seems to be more highly respected, as his opinion is nearly always quoted before Yaḥyá's. Ibn Abī Ḥātim tells stories to point up the ideal character of the traditionist only in the introductory volume (*al-Taqdimah*).

Placing *al-Taʾrīkh al-Kabīr*

Roy Mottahedeh has recently proposed that hadith science was especially vigorous in the Islamic Northeast [17] (Transoxania, Khurasan, and the Jibal) and that the Six Books are a representative expression.[59] Perhaps Mottahedeh exaggerates Northeastern self-reliance. The two common features he makes out in the Six Books are arrangement of hadith reports by topic, not by transmitter, and a lively concern with "the discipline of *rijāl*, the examination of the aspects of the lives of transmitters considered relevant to their acceptability as transmitters."[60] Neither is exclusively Northeastern. There have already come up the earlier collections of hadith arranged by topic of ʿAbd al-Razzāq and Abū Bakr Ibn Abī Shaybah, respectively Yemeni and Kufan. Also, the knowledge of *rijāl* that Mottahedeh indicates is clearly the sort of anecdotes and evaluations one finds in Aḥmad's *ʿMR* rather than Bukhārī's *TK*.[61] Furthermore, although the reputed authors of the Six Books all have *nisbahs* indicating Northeastern origins, Abū Dāwūd settled in Basra while Nasāʾī (d. 303/915?) worked mainly in Old Cairo. Abū Dāwūd's extant *rijāl* criticism resembles Aḥmad's *ʿMR* rather than Bukhārī's *TK*, while a comment from Bukhārī's early commentator Khaṭṭābī indicates that Abū Dāwūd's *Sunan* found its audience in Iraq, Egypt, and the Maghrib.[62]

It seems more reasonable to identify a distinctive Northeastern approach within the larger field of hadith criticism. *TK* might constitute its defining example, almost single-

59. Roy Mottahedeh, "The Transmission of Learning: The Role of the Islamic Northeast," 63–72 in *Madrasa: La transmission du savoir dans le monde musulman*, dir. Nicole Grandin and Marc Gaborieau (Paris: AP Éditions Arguments, 1997), esp. 66–72.

60. Mottahedeh, "Transmission," 70.

61. G. H. A. Juynboll offers a list of 47 outstanding *rijāl* critics, *Muslim Tradition*, Cambridge Studies in Islamic Civilization (Cambridge: Univ. Press, 1983), appendix IV. Although there are some odd omissions (e.g., Aḥmad ibn Ḥanbal and Abū Ḥātim al-Rāzī) and many figures were active in more than one region, the Iraqis seem to outnumber the Northeasterners by two to one.

62. Khaṭṭābī apud al-Nawawī, *Tahdhīb al-asmāʾ* 2: 227.

mindedly concerned with the names of men and the links in which they figure, not with evaluations of their personal reliability. Keith Lewinstein has observed identifiable Eastern (Khurasani and Transoxanian) and Western (Iraqi) traditions of heresiography.[63] The Eastern tradition was distinguished by stress on refutation rather than description and by lack of interest in history or anecdote. The Eastern tradition seldom associates individual persons with the heresies under discussion. "For anyone accustomed to the standard heresiographical accounts," says Lewinstein, "the Eastern sources look confused and superficial."[64] Analogously, *TK* might appear to be the most boring piece of hadith literature in print. *Jarḥ* seems slightly more interesting, as Ibn Abī Ḥātim occasionally explains an evaluation by reference to someone's theological views.[65] But *Jarḥ* shows the Northeastern tradition in process of absorption by the Iraqi, as it takes up Iraqi enthusiasm for personal evaluations.

It fits the distinct emphasis of Northeastern hadith science that the extant *rijāl* works of Muslim, *al-Ṭabaqāt* and *Kitāb al-Kuná wa-al-asmāʾ*, are about the names of men rather than their reliability.[66] It does not fit the proposed pattern of Northeastern hadith science so well that Bukhārī also wrote *TA* and *Ḍuʿafāʾ*, respectively full of dates and evaluations of personal reliability (although, unlike contemporary Iraqi works, neither presents many anecdotes suggesting the ideal character of the Muslim traditionist). As they appear to be earlier compilations than *TK*, we might set them down to the early influence on Bukhārī of the Iraqi tradition: after all, he collected hadith in the Hijaz, Syria, and Iraq as well as Khurasan, repeatedly visited Baghdad in particular, quotes ʿAlī ibn al-Madīnī, Yaḥyá ibn Maʿīn, Aḥmad ibn Ḥanbal, and other Iraqi hadith critics, and is said to have dictated *TK* in Basra.[67] Additionally, though, the *ʿIlal* and *Ṣaḥīḥ* of Tirmidhī are full of Bukhārī's evaluations of individual traditionists, so it was not only as an impressionable young man that Bukhārī took an interest in such evaluations. These works show that the respective Iraqi and Northeastern versions of hadith science cannot have been more than general tendencies. Likewise, examples of Northeastern-style concern with names and chains of transmitters are not hard to find in as thoroughly Iraqi works as *ʿMR*.

Further research is needed to test Norman Calder's suggestion that *isnād* analysis was restricted not geographically but temporally: "The common-link phenomenon as a feature [18] of hadith literature relates to a method of *isnād* criticism current amongst

63. Keith Lewinstein, "Notes on Eastern Ḥanafite Heresiography," *JAOS* 114 (1994): 583–98.

64. Lewinstein, "Notes," 592.

65. The entry for Dāwūd ibn ʿAlī (al-Ẓāhirī) was a notable eye-opener for me: Ibn Abī Ḥātim, *Jarḥ* 3: 410f.; Christopher Melchert, *The Formation of the Sunni Schools of Law*, Studies in Islamic Law and Society 4 (Leiden: Brill, 1997), 180.

66. Muslim, *al-Ṭabaqāt*, ed. Abū ʿUbaydah Mashhūr ibn Ḥasan ibn Maḥmūd ibn Salmān, 2 vols. (Riyadh: Dār al-Hijrah, 1411/1991); *al-Kuná wa-al-asmāʾ*, ed. ʿAbd al-Raḥīm Muḥammad Aḥmad al-Qashqarī, Iḥyāʾ al-Turāth al-Islāmī 8, 2 vols. (Medina: al-Jāmiʿah al-Islāmīyah, 1404/1984).

67. Al-Khaṭīb al-Baghdādī, *Taʾrīkh Baghdād* 2: 22, ll. 19–22, 2: 6f. on his early travels more generally.

jurists and others in the second half of the third century."[68] It is weakly confirmed inasmuch as *TA* and *Ḍuʿafāʾ* are from early in Bukhārī's career, *TK* from late; also inasmuch as the various material considered from Aḥmad and Yaḥyá ibn Maʿīn is from early in the century. It seems to be contradicted by the stress on personal evaluations in the answers of Abū Dāwūd.

A sharper contrast between *TK* and *ʿMR* is not geographical but social: the apparent professionalism of *TK*'s context, the informality and amateurism of *ʿMR*'s. *TA* and *Ḍuʿafāʾ* fit better with this typology, inasmuch as the first methodically includes dates and the second evaluations, similar entries grouped together and ordered chronologically or alphabetically for easy reference rather than scattered about as in *ʿMR*.

Mottahedeh speaks of the superior *rigor* of Northeastern hadith science, "motivated in large part by the attempts of its scholars to base Islamic law on *ḥadīth* rather than *raʾy*."[69] But one can hardly maintain that the struggle of *ḥadīth* against *raʾy* was fiercer in the ninth-century Northeast than in ninth-century Iraq. Moreover, Bukhārī and Muslim do not represent Northeastern traditionalism. The local traditionalist leader expelled Bukhārī from Nishapur, as noted above, and became estranged from Muslim.[70] In law and theology alike, Bukhārī and Muslim represent rather the semi-rationalist party, upholding the central tenets of the traditionalists but borrowing the methods of their rationalist adversaries.[71] If anything, Northeastern traditionists should have been more willing than the Iraqi to accommodate jurisprudents (as by arranging their hadith reports topically) just because the struggle of *ḥadīth* against *raʾy* (which overlapped with *fiqh*) was less bitter outside Iraq.

The professionalism evident in the style of *TK*, the amateurism in that of *ʿMR*, may also have had something to do with the higher degree of patronage for the men of religion from Northeastern rulers, an issue Mottahedeh himself helpfully raises.[72] The story of Isḥāq ibn Rāhawayh's showing *TK* to the governor of Khurasan has already come up. The governor of Bukhara is supposed to have asked Bukhārī himself, near the end of his life, to come dictate his *Ṣaḥīḥ* and *Taʾrīkh* to him or his sons. (Bukhārī refused this request and so, it is said, died in exile; however, one version further involves theological opposition from the ulema of Bukhara.)[73] The Iraqi entry among the Six Books is from Abū Dāwūd, who was taken near the end of his life under the wing of the shadow ca-

68. Calder, *Studies*, 240.

69. Mottahedeh, "Transmission," 72.

70. Al-Khaṭīb al-Baghdādī, *Taʾrīkh Baghdād* 2: 30–33, 13: 103, ll. 4–15.

71. On the semi-rationalists, see Christopher Melchert, "The Adversaries of Aḥmad Ibn Ḥanbal," *Arabica* 44 (1997): 234–53 [*HPL 1]. On traditionalist discontent with collections consisting solely of sound Prophetic hadith, see Melchert, *Formation*, 26–28.

72. Mottahedeh, "Transmission," 66, 71.

73. Al-Khaṭīb al-Baghdādī, *Taʾrīkh Baghdād* 2: 33f.

liph Muwaffaq.[74] He may have been in close communication with Aḥmad ibn Ḥanbal at one time[75]; however, his own description of *al-Sunan*, his collection of Prophetic hadith reports ordered by topic, stresses the use of these particular hadith reports by jurisprudents and so sounds far closer to semi-rationalist Shāfiʿi theorizing than contemporary Ḥanbali works.[76]

Rulers naturally wanted a predictable jurisprudence. For example, when a dispute over *waqf* properties arose in Egypt, none other than Mutawakkil, the caliph who had ended the Inquisition and bidden Aḥmad to come instruct his son, called on a panel of Ḥanafi jurisprudents to adjudicate, not Ḥanbali traditionists.[77] The hadith science promoted by Aḥmad and his followers in Iraq was designed for amateurs, men who spent all their spare [19] time at the mosque because they liked to (because it was their religious duty), not because it was their livelihood; who spent their time at the mosque exchanging stories about exemplary Muslims of the past equally with sorting out which hadith reports to trust for the purpose of establishing the law. As an alternative form of hadith science emerged—especially, it seems, in Khurasan—, the amateurism represented by *ʿMR* was progressively pushed back to the margins.[78]

To return to the question of authorship with which this study began, *al-Taʾrīkh al-awsaṭ* and *Kitāb al-Ḍuʿafāʾ al-ṣaghīr* appear to be earlier works than *al-Taʾrīkh al-kabīr*, although *TA* shows signs of extensive interpolation and extension by Bukhārī and others. Compared with *Kitāb al-Jarḥ wa-al-taʿdīl*, on the other hand, *TK* looks early. Entries in *Jarḥ* commonly name more transmitters and offer fuller versions of men's names (compare

74. Khaṭṭābī, apud Ibn ʿAsākir, *Taʾrīkh Madīnat Dimashq*, ed. Muḥibb al-Dīn Abū Saʿīd ʿUmar ibn Gharāmah al-ʿAmrawī, 65 vols. (Beirut: Dār al-Fikr, 1415/1995), 22: 199 (s.n. Sulaymān ibn al-Ashʿath). For the tendency of Muwaffaq's patronage (Māliki, semi-rationalist), see Christopher Melchert, "Religious Policies of the Caliphs from al-Mutawakkil to al-Muqtadir," *Islamic Law and Society* 3 (1996): 316–42.

75. Al-Khaṭīb al-Baghdādī reports its being said that Abū Dāwūd made his hadith collection early and showed it to Aḥmad for approval in a doubtful tone without quoting his source: *Taʾrīkh Baghdād* 9: 56, ll. 3f.

76. Abū Dāwūd, *Risālat Abī Dāwūd al-Sijistānī Sulaymān ibn al-Ashʿath fī waṣf sunanih*, pp. 27–54 in *Thalāth rasāʾil fī ʿilm muṣṭalaḥ al-ḥadīth*, ed. ʿAbd al-Fattāḥ Abū Ghuddah (Aleppo: Maktab al-Maṭbūʿāt al-Islāmīyah, 1417/1997). Express references to Shāfiʿī and his rejection of *marāsīl* (followed by Aḥmad) sound as though they belong more properly to a later generation. On the other hand, the assertion that no one else had made such extensive researches as he (*lā aʿrifu aḥadan ajmaʿa ʿalá al-istiqṣāʾ ghayrī*) sounds as though it must have come before the books of Bukhārī and Muslim had become known, at least in Iraq and the Hijaz. Whether directly from Abū Dāwūd or not, the letter does serve as an early commentary on the *Sunan*'s chief concerns, not notably traditionalist.

77. Al-Kindī, *Governors and Judges of Egypt*, ed. Rhuvon Guest, E. J. W. Gibb Memorial Ser. 19 (Leiden: E. J. Brill, 1912), 474f.

78. On the marginalization but not disappearance of the old amateurism, see Jacqueline Chabbi, "La figure du *maître* dans l'Islam médiéval," *Maître et disciples dans les traditions religieuses*, ed. Michel Meslin (Paris: Cerf, 1990), 79–96, esp. 92–94, and Calder, *Studies*, chap. 7, esp. 183.

the two entries quoted above). Also compared with *Jarḥ*, *TK* has less in common with Iraqi *rijāl* criticism of the ninth century, which stresses personal evaluations and the language of personal encounter equally with chains of transmission. *Jarḥ* evidently combines Northeastern concern with *isnād* analysis and Iraqi concern with personal evaluations. *TK*'s omission of about one man in seven mentioned in the *Ṣaḥīḥ* strongly suggests to me that *TK* was finished earlier. (Similarly, the *ʿIlal* of al-Tirmidhī seems to be earlier than his *Ṣaḥīḥ*.[79]) Reversing Norman Calder's suggestion, the attribution of our present *Ṣaḥīḥ* to Bukhārī remains questionable; however, *TK* we may well assign to Bukhārī's lifetime or at least, considering the advanced specialization to which it appeals, not later than the end of the ninth century.

79. Ḥamzah Dīb Muṣṭafá, "Introduction," *ʿIlal al-Tirmidhī al-kabīr, tartīb Abū* [*sic*] *Ṭālib al-Qāḍī*, ed. Muṣṭafá, 2 vols. (Amman: Maktabat al-Aqṣá, 1406/1986), 1: 52.

3
THE *MUSNAD* OF AḤMAD IBN ḤANBAL: HOW IT WAS COMPOSED AND WHAT DISTINGUISHES IT FROM THE SIX BOOKS

The *Musnad* dictated by Aḥmad ibn Ḥanbal (d. Baghdad, 241/855) to his son ᶜAbd Allāh (d. Baghdad, 290/903) is the largest of the great ninth-century collections of *ḥadīṯ* to survive. It did not gain a place among "the Six Books" that became more or less the Sunni canon of *ḥadīṯ* from the tenth to the twelfth century C.E. But it was included in most lists that went beyond the Six Books; for example, al-Ḥusaynī's directory of men in the ten books.[1] What follows is an attempt to determine above all how it was collected and what makes it so much longer than other collections.

Earlier Studies of the *Musnad*

The most important medieval discussions of the *Musnad* were published by Aḥmad Muḥammad Šākir in the first volume of his edition: Abū Muṣᶜab al-Madīnī (d. Isfahan, 581/1184), *Ḫaṣāʾiṣ al-Musnad*, and Ibn al-Ǧazarī (d. Shiraz, 833/1429), *al-Maṣᶜad al-aḥmad fī Musnad al-imām Aḥmad*.[2] Both describe the *Musnad* and quote stories of how it was composed. Ibn al-Ǧazarī, most notable for his work on the Qur'ānic readings, also pays

1. Al-Ḥusaynī, *al-Taḏkira bi-maᶜrifat riǧāl al-kutub al-ᶜašara*, ed. Rifᶜat Fawzī ᶜAbd al-Muṭṭalib (Cairo 1418/1997), covering the six plus a collection from each eponym, mainly Abū Ḥanīfa, Mālik, al-Šāfiᶜī, and Aḥmad ibn Ḥanbal.

2. Aḥmad ibn Ḥanbal, *al-Musnad*, ed. Aḥmad Muḥammad Šākir (Cairo 1368–75/1948–56), I, 19–27 (al-Madīnī), 28–56 (Ibn al-Ǧazarī).

Originally published in *Der Islam* 82 (2005): 32–51.

a good deal of attention to the transmission of the *Musnad* across the centuries. Additionally, there is a famous debate over certain *ḥadīṯ* reports in the *Musnad*. Ibn al-Ğawzī (d. Baghdad, 597/1201) selected and assembled weak *ḥadīṯ* reports in *Kitāb al-mawḍūʿāt*.[3] Some [33] of his aspersions on *ḥadīṯ* in the *Musnad* were refuted by Abū l-Faḍl al-ʿIrāqī (d. Cairo, 806/1404), Ibn Ḥağar al-ʿAsqalānī (d. Cairo, 852/1449), and al-Saḫāwī (d. Medina, 902/1497).[4] Al-Suyūṭī (d. Cairo, 911/1505) also wrote a treatment of *ġarīb* locutions in an abridgement of the *Musnad* that is in print.[5] However, he was long preceded by a Ḥanbalī grammarian, Ġulām Ṯaʿlab (d. Baghdad, 345/957).[6] A commentary on the *Musnad* was written by Muḥammad ibn ʿAbd al-Hādī (d. Medina, 1138/1726).[7]

As for transmitters who appear in the *Musnad*, Ibn ʿAsākir (d. Damascus, 571/1176) treated the Companions among them.[8] The *Kamāl* of al-Ğammāʿīlī (d. Cairo, 600/1203) and its famous reworking by al-Mizzī (d. Damascus, 742/1341), *Tahḏīb al-Kamāl*, discuss the *ḥadīṯ* transmitters who appear in the Six Books. Two books by Mizzī's younger contemporary al-Ḥusaynī (d. Damascus, 765/1364) treat transmitters who appear in Aḥmad's *Musnad*: *al-Ikmāl*, devoted exclusively to transmitters who appear in the *Musnad* but not the Six Books, and *al-Taḏkira*, which covers transmitters of *ḥadīṯ* mentioned in the Six Books and in collections of *ḥadīṯ* attributed to the eponyms of the four main schools of law.[9] Ibn [34] al-Ğazarī wrote an improvement on Ḥusaynī's *Ikmāl* called *al-Maqṣid al-aḥmad fī riğāl*

3. Ibn al-Ğawzī, *K. al-Mawḍūʿāt min al-aḥādīṯ al-marfūʿa*, ed. Nūr al-Dīn ibn Šukrī ibn ʿAlī Bawyāğīlāz (Riyadh 1418/1997), is plainly the best edition.

4. Abū l-Faḍl is mentioned by al-Kattānī (d. Fez, 1345/1927), *al-Risāla al-mustaṭrafa li-bayān mašhūr kutub al-sunna al-mušarrafa*, ed. Abū ʿAbd al-Raḥmān Ṣalāḥ Muḥammad ʿUwayḍa (Beirut 1416/1995), 23. The work in question by Ibn Ḥağar is *al-Qawl al-musaddad fī l-ḏabb ʿan al-Musnad li-l-imām Aḥmad* (Hyderabad A.H. 1319), reprinted numerous times. The supplement to Ibn Ḥağar's work is al-Saḫāwī, *al-Ḏayl al-mumahhad*, mentioned in al-Suyūṭī, *Tadrīb al-rāwī*, *nawʿ* 2: *al-ḥasan* = ed. Abū ʿAbd al-Raḥmān Ṣalāḥ Muḥammad ʿUwayḍa (Beirut 1417/1996), I, 88.

5. Al-Suyūṭī, *ʿUqūd al-zabarğad fī iʿrāb al-ḥadīṯ al-nabawī*, ed. Salmān al-Quḍāh (Beirut 1414/1994). The abridgement, by the Šāfiʿī Ibn al-Mulaqqin (d. Cairo, 804/1401), is not extant so far as I know.

6. According to al-Ḫaṭīb al-Baġdādī, *Tārīḫ Baġdād* (Cairo 1349/1931, repr. Cairo and Beirut n.d.), II, 358f.

7. According to ʿAbd al-Qādir Ibn Badrān, *al-Madḫal ilā maḏhab al-imām Aḥmad ibn Ḥanbal* (Cairo n.d.), 246 = ed. ʿAbd Allāh ibn ʿAbd al-Muḥsin al-Turkī (Beirut 1401/1981), 473.

8. Ibn ʿAsākir, *Tartīb asmāʾ al-ṣaḥāba allaḏīna ahrağa ḥadīṯahum Aḥmad ibn Ḥanbal fī l-Musnad*, ed. ʿĀmir Ḥasan Ṣabrī (Beirut 1989).

9. Ḥusaynī, *al-Ikmāl fī ḏikr man lahu riwāya fī Musnad al-imām Aḥmad min al-riğāl siwā man ḏukira fī Tahḏīb al-Kamāl*, ed. ʿAbd al-Muʿṭī Amīn Qalʿağī (al-Manṣūra, Egypt 1409/1989); for *al-Taḏkira*, v. n. 1. The *Musnad* of Aḥmad was assembled by his son ʿAbd Allāh. *Al-Taḏkira* treats the *Musnad* of Abū Ḥanīfa assembled by al-Ustāḏ al-Subaḏmūnī (d. Buḫara? 340/951), the *Muwaṭṭaʾ* of Mālik assembled by the Andalusian Yaḥyā ibn Yaḥyā (d. 234/849), and the *Musnad* of al-Šāfiʿī assembled by a disciple to Abū l-ʿAbbās al-Aṣamm (d. Nishapur, 346/957).

Aḥmad.[10] Ibn Ḥağar al-ʿAsqalānī corrected and extended Ḥusaynī's work concerning men quoted by all the eponyms of the schools of law in *Taʿǧīl al-manfaʿa*.[11]

The *Musnad* was first printed, in six volumes, in Egypt in the earlier 1890s, under the direction of Aḥmad al-Bābī al-Ḥalabī.[12] Wensinck's concordances refer to this edition by volume number and page.[13] In the 1940s and '50s, Aḥmad Muḥammad Šākir re-edited the *Musnad*, completing a little more than a third of it before his death.[14] Since then several other reworkings of the old Egyptian edition have appeared. These have featured easier-to-read type but only some have been supplied with the marginal cross-references to the Egyptian edition that alone make it possible to use them with Wensinck's concordances, while the marginal cross-references in these have sometimes been off by a page—*caveat emptor*. What deserves to be the standard edition is now anyway that of Šuʿayb al-Arnaʾūṭ and many assistants in 50 volumes, as fully annotated as Šākir's.[15] It has been indispensable to this study. (References to the *Musnad* in what follows are to the Cairo edition in Roman, then Arnaʾūṭ in italic; e.g. I, 131 *II, 331*.) [35]

Aḥmad's *Musnad* is arranged according to Companion: first come *ḥadīṯ* reports transmitted from the Prophet by Abū Bakr, next by ʿUmar, and so on until the end, where one finds *ḥadīṯ* reports transmitted by women. Al-Ḏahabī lamented that no one had re-arranged the *Musnad* either alphabetically or topically.[16] Ibn Ḥağar mentions that a certain Isfahani had re-arranged the *Musnad* alphabetically but that he himself has never seen it; however, he does point out a recent re-arrangement by topic from Nāṣir al-Dīn Ibn Zurayq (d. 803/1401).[17] Ibn al-Muḥibb al-Ṣāmit (d. Damascus, 789/1387) rearranged at

10. Ibn al-Ğazarī, *Maṣʿad*, in *Musnad*, ed. Šākir, I, 40.

11. Ibn Ḥağar, *Taʿǧīl al-manfaʿa bi-zawāʾid riǧāl al-aʾimma al-arbaʿa*, of which the principal editions are these: (Hyderabad A.H. 1324); ed. Ikrām Allāh Imdād al-Ḥaqq (Beirut 1416/1996); and ed. Ayman Ṣāliḥ Šaʿbān (Beirut 1996). The rest of Ḥusaynī, *Ikmāl*, on men in the Six Books, is part of the basis of Ibn Ḥağar, *Tahḏīb al-Tahḏīb*.

12. Aḥmad, *Musnad imām al-muḥaddiṯīn wa-l-qudwa fī l-zuhd wa-l-waraʿ* (Cairo n.d). The only date provided is at the end of the sixth volume, Ğumādā II 1313 (November-December 1895): presumably, the other volumes were issued over the previous several years.

13. A.J. Wensinck, et al., *Concordance et indices de la tradition Musulmane* (Leiden 1936–69); idem, *A Handbook of Early Muhammadan Tradition* (Leiden 1927). Also referring to volume and page number of the old Egyptian edition is *Fahāris Musnad al-imām Aḥmad ibn Ḥanbal (164–241)* (Mecca 1420/1999), less useful than Wensinck for finding particular *ḥadīṯ* reports but including an index of shaykhs; superfluous, however, if one has the new edition of Arnaʾūṭ, for which *v.* n. 15.

14. *V.* n. 2.

15. Aḥmad, *Musnad al-imam Aḥmad ibn Ḥanbal*, ed. Šuʿayb al-Arnaʾūṭ, et al. (Beirut 1413–21/1993–2001).

16. Al-Ḏahabī, *Siyar aʿlām al-nubalāʾ* (Beirut 1401–9/1981–88), XIII (ed. ʿAlī Abū Zayd), 525.

17. Ibn Ḥağar, *al-Muʿǧam al-mufahras*, ed. Muḥammad Šākir Maḥmūd al-Ḥāǧǧī Umrayr al-Mayādīnī (Beirut 1418/1998), 129.

least the shorter sections in alphabetical order.[18] Sezgin mentions one re-arrangement: Ibn Zuknūn (d. Damascus, 837/1434), *al-Kawākib al-darārī fī tartīb Musnad Aḥmad ʿalā abwāb al-Buḫārī*.[19] Saḫāwī describes it as including long quotations from later books of law, *tafsīr*, and so forth, and so coming altogether to 120 volumes.[20] I have used before a twentieth-century re-arrangement by ʿAbd al-Raḥmān al-Bannā al-Sāʿātī, father of the famous leader of the Muslim Brethren, published in the later 1930s.[21]

Selections of the *Musnad* have also been assembled. Ibn al-Ǧawzī composed a *Ǧāmiʿ al-masānīd* that included most of the individual texts of the *Musnad* (*mutūn*, meaning alternative *asānīd* were omitted), along with *ḥadīṯ* from al-Buḫārī, Muslim, and al-Tirmiḏī.[22] Ibn Kaṯīr (d. Damascus, 774/1373) likewise composed a *Ǧāmiʿ al-masānīd*, combining *ḥadīṯ* from Aḥmad's *Musnad* (omitting what he considered weak) with other *ḥadīṯ* from the Six Books and three other collections, arranging [36] it all alphabetically by Companion.[23] Ibn Ḥaǧar al-Hayṯamī (d. Cairo, 807/1405), *Ġāyat al-maqṣid fī zawāʾid al-Musnad*, arranges by topic such *ḥadīṯ* reports as he found in the *Musnad* but not in the Six Books. Nearly all the same material also appears in the same author's *Maǧmaʿ al-zawāʾid*.[24]

Another sort of re-arrangement is now in print, *Iṭrāf al-musnid al-muʿtalī bi-aṭrāf al-musnad al-ḥanbalī* by Ibn Ḥaǧar, that isolates *ḥadīṯ* in the *Musnad* by Companion and Successor (*ṣaḥābī*, *tābiʿ*), just as Mizzī had done a century earlier for *ḥadīṯ* in the Six Books with *Tuḥfat al-ašrāf*.[25] This arrangement makes it easier to compare different transmis-

---

18. Ibn al-Ǧazarī, *Maṣʿad*, in *Musnad*, ed. Šākir, I, 39; Ibn Ḥaǧar, *Muʿǧam*, 129, restricting it to *al-muqillīn* (i.e. I take it, those Companions who are credited with relatively few *ḥadīṯ* reports, where the *Musnad* as ʿAbd Allāh left it shows the most confusion). On Abū Bakr Ibn al-Muḥibb al-Ṣāmit, *v.* ʿUmar Riḍā Kaḥḥāla, *Muʿǧam al-muʾallifīn* (Damascus 1957–61), X, 196.

19. Sezgin, *Geschichte des arabischen Schrifttums* (Leiden 1967–2000), I, 506.

20. Al-Saḫāwī, *al-Ḍawʾ al-lāmiʿ li-ahl al-qarn al-tāsiʿ* (Cairo A.H. 1353–55), V, 214, s.n. ʿAlī ibn Ḥusayn ibn ʿUrwa.

21. ʿAbd al-Raḥmān al-Bannāʾ al-Sāʿātī, *al-Fatḥ al-rabbānī li-tartīb Musnad al-imām Aḥmad ibn Ḥanbal al-Šaybānī* (Cairo n.d.).

22. Ḏahabī, *Siyar* XIII, 525; Carl Brockelmann, *Geschichte der arabischen Litteratur* (Leiden 1943–49), I, 662 (503); Supplementband, I, 917.

23. Ibn Kaṯīr, *Ǧāmiʿ al-masānīd wa-l-sunan*, ed. ʿAbd al-Muʿṭī al-Qalʿaǧī (Beirut 1994). The others are the *Musnad* of al-Bazzār (d. Ramla, 291/904?), the *Musnad* of Abū Yaʿlā al-Mawṣilī (d. 307/919–20?), and *al-Muʿǧam al-kabīr* of al-Ṭabarānī (d. Isfahan, 360/971).

24. Ibn Ḥaǧar al-Haytamī, *Ġāyat al-maqṣid fī zawāʾid al-Musnad*, ed. Ḫallāf Maḥmūd ʿAbd al-Samīʿ (Beirut 1421/2001); *idem*, *Maǧmaʿ al-zawāʾid wa-manbaʿ al-fawāʾid* (Cairo A.H. 1352–53) = ed. Muḥammad ʿAbd al-Qādir Aḥmad ʿAṭā (Beirut 1422/2001).

25. Ibn Ḥaǧar, *Aṭrāf Musnad al-imām Aḥmad ibn Ḥanbal al-musammā Iṭrāf al-musnid al-muʿtalī bi-aṭrāf al-musnad al-ḥanbalī*, ed. Zuhayr ibn Nāṣir al-Nāṣir (Damascus 1414/1993). G.H.A. Juynboll has publicized al-Mizzī, *Tuḥfat al-ašrāf*. For a brief guide, *v. EI2*, s.v. "al-Mizzī," by G.H.A. Juynboll; for a more extended, idem, "Some *isnād*-Analytical Methods Illustrated on the Basis of Several Woman-Demeaning Sayings from the *ḥadīth* Literature," in *al-Qanṭara* 10 (1989): 343–83, at 345–50.

sions of effectively the same *ḥadīṯ* report. Another work of Ibn Ḥaǧar's, *Itḥāf al-mahara*, follows the same plan but concerning eleven books, including the *Musnad*.[26]

As for modern studies of the *Musnad*, Ignaz Goldziher published a brilliant survey of it very soon after its appearance in printed form, stressing its testimony to the wider state of *ḥadīṯ* criticism and collection in the ninth century.[27] A decade later, Martin Hartmann published a supplementary survey with a close description of its main organizing [37] principle, mainly the Companions who transmitted from the Prophet.[28] G.H.A. Juynboll's account of Šākir's edition has much to say about the *Musnad* itself, as well.[29] Still more recently, ʿĀmir Ḥasan Ṣabrī has published several studies in Arabic: an annotated list of additions to the *Musnad* from ʿAbd Allāh; a very useful annotated list of Aḥmad's immediate authorities; and an annotated list of *ḥadīṯ* reports in the *Musnad* and elsewhere taken from Aḥmad's written notes, not oral dictation.[30]

The Number of *Ḥadīṯ* Reports in the *Musnad*

Widely varying estimates are available of how many *ḥadīṯ* reports the *Musnad* comprises. Medieval estimates of its extent range from 30,000 to 50,000.[31] One modern estimate counts 30,000 *ḥadīṯ* reports from Aḥmad himself, another 10,000 added by his son ʿAbd Allāh.[32] Another counts 30,000 *ḥadīṯ* reports without repetition, another 10,000 repeated.[33] Modern editions vary less widely. By counting *ḥadīṯ* reports differently, particularly where variant *asānīd* are presented one after another, different reworkings of the 1890s Cairo edition come up with slightly different numbers: one edition counts 27,634, while

26. Ibn Ḥaǧar, *Itḥāf al-mahara bi-l-fawāʾid al-mubtakira min aṭrāf al-ʿašara*, ed. Zuhayr ibn Nāṣir al-Nāṣir (Medina 1415/1994). The title refers to ten books, but Ibn Ḥaǧar used the *Sunan* of al-Dāraquṭnī as number 11 to supply missing parts of Ibn Ḫuzayma's *Ṣaḥīḥ*.

27. Ignaz Goldziher, "Neue Materialien zur Litteratur des Ueberlieferungswesens bei den Muhammedanern," *ZDMG* 50 (1896), 465–506; also *Gesammelte Schriften*, ed. Joseph Desomogyi (Hildesheim 1967–73), IV, 69–110.

28. Martin Hartmann, "Die Tradenten erster Schicht im Musnad des Aḥmad Ibn Ḥanbal," *Mitteilungen des Seminars für orientalische Sprachen* 9 (1906), 148–76.

29. Gualtherus H.A. Juynboll, "Aḥmad Muḥammad Shākir (1892–1958) and His Edition of Ibn Ḥanbal's Musnad," *Der Islam* 49 (1972), 221–47.

30. ʿĀmir Ḥasan Ṣabrī, *Zawāʾid ʿAbd Allāh ibn Aḥmad ibn Ḥanbal fī l-Musnad* (Beirut 1410/1990); idem, *Muʿǧam šuyūḫ al-imām Aḥmad ibn Ḥanbal fī l-Musnad* (Beirut, 1413/1993); idem, *al-Wiǧādāt fī musnad al-imām Aḥmad ibn Ḥanbal* (Beirut 1416/1996).

31. E.g. different manuscripts of Ibn Ḫaldūn, *al-Muqaddima*, for which *v. The Muqaddima*, trans. Franz Rosenthal (New York 1958), II, 461. One tenth-century Ḥanbali estimate is 30,000: al-Ḫaṭīb, *Tārīḫ Baġdād*, IX, 375. Another is 40,000, less thirty or forty: Ibn al-Ǧazarī, *Maṣʿad*, in *Musnad*, ed. Šākir, I, 33. Ḥusaynī reports 40,000, including repeats and additions from ʿAbd Allāh: *Taḏkira*, I, 3.

32. Ibn Badrān, *Madḫal*, 245 = ed. Turkī, 471.

33. ʿAbd al-Ḥalīm al-Ǧundī, *Aḥmad ibn Ḥanbal imām ahl al-sunna* (Cairo, 1977), 190.

the recent edition of Šuʿayb al-Arnaʾūṭ, et al., counts 27,647.[34] (Because different editions count *ḥadīṯ* differently, citations by number are not more satisfactory than volume [38] and page in the 1890s edition.[35]) Different estimates also reflect different manuscripts. The editor of Ibn Ḥaǧar's *Iṭrāf* identifies some *ḥadīṯ* reports and many *asānīd* mentioned by Ibn Ḥaǧar but not found in the 1890s edition.[36] I have also noticed *ḥadīṯ* reports in the 1890s edition not covered in the *Iṭrāf* (unfortunately, the same goes for Wensinck's *Concordance*). Presumably Ibn Ḥaǧar's manuscript of the *Musnad* differed substantially from what is extant today (however, analysis of a sample of 1 percent suggests that Ibn Ḥaǧar's manuscript comprised very nearly the same number of *ḥadīṯ* reports as our published versions). Arnaʾūṭ, et al., include 92 supernumerary *ḥadīṯ* reports missing from the section on *anṣār* that they gathered from Ibn Kaṯīr, *Ǧāmiʿ al-masānīd*, Ibn Ḥaǧar, *Iṭrāf al-musnid* and *Itḥāf al-mahara*, Ibn Ḥaǧar al-Hayṯamī, *Ġāyat al-maqṣid*, and Ibn ʿAsākir, *Tartīb asmāʾ al-ṣaḥāba*.[37]

The main reason for the greater bulk of the *Musnad* by comparison with the Six Books is that it includes many more repeats; that is, effectively identical texts (*mutūn*) with (usually) different *asānīd*. This must have been evident to anyone accustomed to Wensinck's concordances, where a given text will be located at one or two points in some number of the Six Books, then half a dozen times or more in Aḥmad's *Musnad*. Here is an example: Buḫārī quotes one *ḥadīṯ* report by which the Prophet states, "God created Adam in his image (*ʿalā ṣūratih*)," Muslim two, then the *Musnad* six, not including one exact repeat.

Ibn Ḥaǧar's *Iṭrāf* comes up with 12,787 separate reports, counting as an individual *ḥadīṯ* report what one Successor related from one Companion from the Prophet. For example, Ibn Ḥaǧar counts the following as three different *ḥadīṯ* reports, not variants of one.

> < Sufyān < Abū l-Zinād < al-Aʿraǧ < Abū Hurayra < the Prophet: "If one of you strikes (someone), let him avoid the face, for God created Adam in his image."[38]
>
> < Yaḥyā ibn Saʿīd < Ibn ʿAǧlān < Saʿīd < Abū Hurayra < the Messenger of God: "If one of you strikes (someone), let him avoid the face. Let him not say "May God make your face far away and likewise whatever face resembles yours," for God created Adam in his image."[39] [39]

34. Aḥmad ibn Ḥanbal, *al-Musnad*, ed. Samīr Ṭāhā al-Maǧdūb, et al. (Beirut 1413/1993). *Fahāris Musnad al-imām* apparently comes up with yet another count.

35. Cf. R. Marston Speight, "A Look at Variant Readings in the *ḥadīth*," *Der Islam* 77 (2000), 169–79.

36. E.g. Ibn Ḥaǧar, *Iṭrāf* I, 445.

37. Aḥmad, *Musnad*, XXXIX, 434–535.

38. Aḥmad, *Musnad*, II, 244 *XII*, *275*f; Ibn Ḥaǧar, *Iṭrāf*, VII, 347.

39. Aḥmad, *Musnad*, II, 251, 434 XII, 382–85, *XV*, *371*; Ibn Ḥaǧar, *Iṭrāf*, VII, 239.

> < Sulaymān ibn Dāwūd < al-Muṯannā < Qatāda < Abū Ayyūb < Abū Hurayra < Prophet: "When one of you fights (another), let him avoid the face, for God (mighty and glorious is he) created Adam in his image."[40]

By contrast, Ibn Ḥağar counts it the same *ḥadīṯ* report if almost the same *isnād* is attached to a version that ends at "let him avoid the face" without explanation (i.e. without saying that God created Adam in his image), as do half a dozen further variants in the *Musnad* of the first and third, above. Ibn Ḥağar's figure suggests that repeats constitute a little over half the *Musnad*, but his definition of "repeat" seems unnecessarily restrictive.

Judging from my own sample selected at random, 274 items represent 1,460 *ḥadīṯ* reports in the whole *Musnad*. My count includes repeats whether transmitted by the same Successor or no; that is, it considers such variants as the above three *ḥadīṯ* reports on Adam and the image of God as examples of repetition. This gives us a ratio of more than four to one. It suggests that, among some 27,700 in the whole *Musnad*, there should be around 5,200 individual reports, with the rest repeats. This compares with the *Ṣaḥīḥ* of Buḫārī, said to comprise 2,762 individual reports, 7,397 including repeats (normally parallel versions), a ratio of about two to one.[41] The *Ṣaḥīḥ* of Muslim presents many more multiple, parallel *asānīd* in succession (i.e. for easy comparison), although its repeat ratio is probably somewhat lower.[42] Thus, the *Musnad* appears to offer many more repeats (normally parallel versions) than any of the Six Books, which more than anything else is responsible for its greater bulk. (By Ḏahabī's estimate, the total number of known, distinct prophetic *ḥadīṯ* reports is scarcely ten thousand.[43])

The *Musnad* does not contain all the *ḥadīṯ* ascribed to Aḥmad. Ibn al-Ğawzī names 414 men and one woman from whom Aḥmad learnt *ḥadīṯ*, [40] whereas the *Musnad* comprises *ḥadīṯ* from only 292 shaykhs, 70 percent of Ibn al-Ğawzī's total.[44] I have looked up eighteen prophetic *ḥadīṯ* reports in the *Kitāb al-ašriba* collected by Abū l-Qāsim al-Bağawī

40. Aḥmad, *Musnad*, II, 519 *XVI, 427*; Ibn Ḥağar, *Iṭrāf* VIII, 96.

41. *EI2*, s.v. "Bukhārī," by J. Robson. But estimates vary; e.g. al-Nawawī counts 7,275 *ḥadīṯ* reports altogether, about 4,000 without repeats: *Tahḏīb al-asmāʾ wa-l-luġāt* (Cairo 1927, repr. Beirut n.d.), I, 75. Suyūṭī mentions someone who counted 6,397 without *muʿallaqāt* and *mutābiʿāt*, 2,513 without repeats: *Tadrīb al-rāwī, nawʿ* 1: *al-ṣaḥīḥ* = ed. Abū ʿAbū al-Raḥmān, I, 48.

42. Cf. Juynboll, "Some *isnād*-Analytical," 361: "The only observation which it seems safe to make at this point is that, *on the whole*, in the majority of bundles, Muslim's strands are slightly more elaborate than Bukhārī's." Nawawī estimates about 4,000 *ḥadīṯ* reports in Muslim's collection, not counting repeats: Suyūṭī, *Tadrīb al-rāwī* I, 49.

43. Al-Ḏahabī, *Siyar*, XI (ed. Ṣāliḥ al-Samr), 187.

44. Ibn al-Ğawzī, *Manāqib al-imām Aḥmad ibn Ḥanbal*, ed. Muḥammad Amīn al-Ḫānğī al-Kutubī (Cairo A.H. 1349), 33–54; Ṣabrī, *Muʿğam*, 9. According to Ibn al-Ğazarī, Aḥmad cites 283 different shaykhs in the *Musnad*, ʿAbd Allāh another 173: *Maṣʿad*, in *Musnad*, ed. Šākir, I, 34. Ibn al-Ğawzī's list is not quite complete; e.g. *v*. Ziyād Muḥammad Manṣūr, Introduction, *Suʾālāt Abī Dāwūd . . . li-l-imām Aḥmad ibn Ḥanbal* (Medina 1414/1994), 137.

(d. 317/929), all related by Aḥmad to al-Baġawī, and found only fourteen in the *Musnad*.[45] The missing four are also not in Ibn Ḥağar, *al-Iṭrāf*, which provides some assurance that they were not simply in parts of the *Musnad* lost between the fifteenth and nineteenth centuries.

The Ḥanbali tradition sometimes maintains that all of what Aḥmad put in the *Musnad* he regarded as sound. For example, Ḥanbal ibn Isḥāq (d. 273/886) quotes him as saying, "I have collected and selected this book from 750,000. Whatever the Muslims disagree about by way of the *ḥadīṯ* of the Messenger of God . . . , consult it. If you find it there . . . ; otherwise, it is not probative."[46] In other words, one should resort to the *Musnad* in case of doubt. If a disputed *ḥadīṯ* report was found there, one might safely act on it, whereas if it was not found there, one should disregard it. But comparison with the *masāʾil* collections presenting his juridical opinions shows that Aḥmad did not respect so highly everything in the *Musnad* nor, it seems, include in the *Musnad* everything he did respect. For example, I have looked up 34 prophetic *ḥadīṯ* reports quoted in the first volume of the *Masāʾil* of Ibn Hāniʾ and found only 30 in the *Musnad*. Some of those not found in the *Musnad* are dismissed by Aḥmad in the *Masāʾil* as unsound, hence we might not expect them. For example, there is a *ḥadīṯ* report about the Prophet's not saluting someone because he was not in a state of ritual purity that Aḥmad describes as *munkar* on account of not being *marfūʿ*; that is, it is missing a link in its *isnād* (not, as normally in later usage, the Companion who quotes the Prophet but rather the link between that Companion and al-Ḥasan al-Baṣrī, a Successor).[47] But [41] one also finds Aḥmad endorsing a *ḥadīṯ* report that is not in the *Musnad*, as well as disparaging one that is. Aḥmad is once asked about a *ḥadīṯ* report from Ḥamna over menstruation and the ritual prayer. He answers: "In my opinion, it is nothing. The *ḥadīṯ* report of Fāṭima is stronger, in my opinion, and has a sounder *isnād*." Yet the *Musnad* apparently includes Ḥamna's *ḥadīṯ* report and not Fāṭima's.[48] Numbers of *ḥadīṯ* reports from the Prophet are found in Aḥmad's collection *al-Zuhd* but not in the *Musnad*. One does not suppose that Aḥmad regarded them either as weak.

45. Aḥmad (attrib.; actually, Abū l-Qāsim al-Baġawī), *al-Ašriba*, ed. Ṣubḥī al-Sāmarrāʾī (Beirut 1405/1985).

46. Ibn Abī Yaʿlā, *Ṭabaqāt al-ḥanābila*, ed. Muḥammad Ḥāmid al-Fiqī (Cairo 1371/1952), I, 143; al-Madīnī, *Ḫaṣāʾiṣ*, in *Musnad*, ed. Šākir, I, 21.

47. Ibn Hāniʾ al-Naysābūrī, *Masāʾil al-imām Aḥmad ibn Ḥanbal*, ed. Zuhayr al-Šāwīš (Beirut 1400), I, 22; cf. *Musnad* IV, 345 *XXXI, 381f*, V, 80 *XXIV, 361f*, where it is presented with al-Ḥuṣayn Abū Sāsān between al-Ḥasan and Companion al-Muhāğir ibn Qunfuḏ. Elsewhere in the *Musnad*, there are a few *ḥadīṯ* reports in which al-Ḥasan al-Baṣrī quotes the Prophet directly; e.g. *Musnad*, II, 290 *XIII, 273*.

48. Ibn Hāniʾ, I, 30, 33; *Musnad*, VI, 381f, 439 XLV, 121–23, 467–69, 469. Ibn Ḥağar, *Iṭrāf*, indicates that there was no such *ḥadīṯ* report from Fāṭima in the version of the *Musnad* available to him, either.

When the *Musnad* Was Assembled

One source quotes ʿAbd Allāh as stating: "My father composed the *Musnad* after coming from ʿAbd al-Razzāq"; that is, from about 204/819–20.[49] He seems to have experimented with arrangement by topic. Abū Ḥātim al-Rāzī (d. 277/890) recalled:[50]

> I first met Aḥmad in the year 213 (828–29). He had brought out with him to the prayer the book of drinks and the book of faith. He then prayed. Nobody asked him anything, so he returned his books to his house. I came to him another day. Lo and behold, he had brought out the same two books. I thought he was doing so to fulfill his duty of upholding public morals, for the book of faith is the root of the faith, while the book of drinks means turning people away from evil, all evil coming from drunkenness.

In other words, he had brought out to the mosque, probably at the dawn prayer, these two topical collections of *ḥadīṯ*, and stubbornly kept on bringing them out even though no one seemed to be interested.

Aḥmad ceased to relate *ḥadīṯ* well before he died. Presumably, his work on the *Musnad* ceased at the same time. Exactly when and why is uncertain. This is not the place to treat the problem in full, which would require listing many contradictory accounts. Al-Maʾmūn's second letter concerning the Inquisition certainly includes a threat to forbid narration [42] (*ḥikāya*), presumably of *ḥadīṯ* in mosques, which were the caliph's preserve.[51] Al-Muʿtaṣim is said to have imposed house arrest on Bišr ibn al-Walīd al-Kindī (d. 238/853), the Ḥanafī *qāḍī*, and forbidden him to relate *ḥadīṯ*. The sentence was renewed by al-Wāṯiq and rescinded only by al-Mutawakkil.[52] It seems credible, then, that Aḥmad, too, was prevented from relating *ḥadīṯ* in public from the start of the Inquisition in 218/833. This agrees with accounts by which Aḥmad related the *Musnad* at home to his sons Ṣāliḥ and ʿAbd Allāh and his cousin Ḥanbal ibn Isḥāq (that is, not to a great audience in public), also that he joyfully resumed relating *ḥadīṯ* in public at the death of al-Muʿtas.im in 227/842.[53] But then came a letter from al-Wāṯiq warning him to make himself scarce,

49. Al-Madīnī, *Ḫaṣāʾiṣ*, in *Musnad*, ed. Šākir, I, 25. For 204, *v.* also Ibn al-Ǧawzī, *Manāqib*, 188.

50. Ibn Abī Ḥātim, *K. al-Ǧarḥ wa-l-taʿdīl* (Hyderabad A.H. 1360–71, repr. Beirut n.d.), I, 303.

51. Al-Ṭabarī, *Annales*, ed. M. J. de Goeje (Leiden 1879–1901), III, 1120 = *Tārīḫ al-Ṭabarī*, ed. Muḥammad Abū l-Faḍl Ibrāhīm (Cairo 1960–69), VIII, 636.

52. Ibn Abī l-Wafāʾ, *al-Ǧawāhir al-muḍīya fī ṭabaqāt al-ḥanafīya*, ed. ʿAbd al-Fattāḥ Muḥammad al-Ḥulw (Cairo 1398–1408/1978–88, repr. Giza, 1413/1993), I, 454. *V.* now Holger Winkelmann-Liebert, "Die *miḥna* im Kalifat des al-Muʿtaṣim," *Der Islam* 80 (2003), 224–83. He does not mention Bišr ibn al-Walīd, an account of whose confinement would weaken his case for Muʿtaṣim's general neglect of the Inquisition (cf. *op. cit.*, 275, where the energetic prosecution of the Inquisition in Egypt is relegated to a footnote).

53. Al-Ḫalīlī, *al-Iršād fī maʿrifat ʿulamāʾ al-ḥadīṯ*, abr. al-Silafī, ed. ʿĀmir Aḥmad Ḥaydar (Mecca 1993/1414), 188; Ibn al-Ǧawzī, *Manāqib*, 191f (chap. 27), 328 (chap. 71).

causing Aḥmad at first to go into hiding, then to stick to his house for the remainder of that caliph's reign, not venturing out even for Friday prayers.[54] By most accounts, this is about the point at which he swore to relate no more *ḥadīṯ*.

Even if fear of the caliph was the principal motive for Aḥmad's oath, he did adhere to it even after al-Mutawakkil had suspended the Inquisition. This is in line with the policy expressed in the *masāʾil* collections, that persons are to be held to their words.[55] But it is also said expressly that he quit relating *ḥadīṯ* of his own volition a little before being forbidden by al-Wāṯiq.[56]

Whether Aḥmad foreswore not to relate *ḥadīṯ* before or after being forbidden by the caliph, a leading motivation was probably to avoid the public attention that came with relating *ḥadīṯ*, hence the temptation to pride, a notable theme of early renunciant literature. Aḥmad's renunciant contemporary Bišr al-Ḥāfī (d. Baghdad, 227/841), much quoted by the next [43] generation of Ḥanābila, prayed God to forgive every step he had taken in quest of *ḥadīṯ*.[57] Bišr is directly quoted as explaining that he did not relate *ḥadīṯ* because he desired to do so, "and whenever I desire something, I renounce it."[58] Aḥmad's leading disciple al-Marrūḏī quoted Aḥmad himself as saying, on being told that somebody wanted to meet him, "I have taken rest. I have had no repose (*farağ*) except since I swore not to relate *ḥadīṯ*. Would that they left us (alone). The way (*al-ṭarīq*) is what Bišr ibn al-Ḥāriṯ followed."[59] Aḥmad also cited the precedents of the Yemeni Rabāḥ ibn Zayd (d. 187/802–3) and the Baṣran Abū Ḥabīb Ḥayyān (d. 216/831–32), who had likewise ceased to relate *ḥadīṯ* well before their deaths.[60]

Authorities in the *Musnad* but Not in the Six Books

As concerns transmitters cited, the intersection between the *Musnad* and other early collections of *ḥadīṯ* can be summarized in a table. Column A shows the average number of transmitters shared with the rest of the Six Books (for Aḥmad's *Musnad*, with all of the Six Books) from a randomly selected sample of 1,012 (10 percent) from Ḥusaynī, *al-Taḏkira*. Column B shows the number in common with Aḥmad's *Musnad*. Column C is then simply the ratio between A and B.

54. Ibn al-Ğawzī, *Manāqib*, 328 (chap. 71).

55. Susan Spectorsky, *Chapters on Marriage and Divorce: Responses of Ibn Ḥanbal and Ibn Rāhwayh* (Austin 1993), 7.

56. Ibn al-Ğawzī, *Manāqib*, 328 (chap. 71).

57. Al-Ḫaṭīb, *Tārīḫ Baġdād*, IV, 344f.

58. *Ibid.*, VII, 70, ll. 2–6; similarly, Abū Nuʿaym, *Ḥilyat al-awliyāʾ* (Cairo 1352–57/1932–38), VIII, 355.

59. Apud Ḏahabī, *Siyar*, XI, 216. At least part of Marrūdī's *masāʾil* collection is said to have been published by al-Dār al-Salafīya, but I have not seen it, myself.

60. Ibn Abī Yaʿlā, *Ṭabaqāt*, I, 324.

A) book	B) Average number of transmitters shared with the rest of the Six Books	C) Number in common with Aḥmad's Musnad	D) Ratio of B to C
Aḥmad, Musnad	43	—	—
Buḫārī	27	22	81%
Muslim	32	33	103%
Abū Dāwūd	43	52	123%
Tirmiḏī	40	46	115%
Nasāʾī	42	51	121%
Ibn Māǧa	40	52	130%

[44] The smallest intersection of transmitters is between Aḥmad and Buḫārī, greatest between Aḥmad and Abū Dāwūd. Abū Dāwūd was the one of the Six personally closest to Aḥmad, so it is not surprising that he quoted so many of the same transmitters; however, Buḫārī and Muslim also transmitted *ḥadīṯ* from Aḥmad, so it is a little puzzling that the four *sunan* should all agree markedly more with the *Musnad* than the *ṣaḥīḥayn*. In general, Aḥmad cites many more different Companions, fewer later Ḥiǧāzīs, and more Syrians by comparison with Buḫārī and Muslim. The *Musnad* and the *ṣaḥīḥayn* are roughly equal as to Baṣrans and Kūfans.

As for Aḥmad's immediate authorities, 34 percent of the *ḥadīṯ* reports in my sample from the *Musnad* (omitting additions from ʿAbd Allāh) came from Baghdadi shaykhs, 28 percent from Baṣran, 15 percent from Kūfan. Altogether, the *Musnad* is about 86 percent Iraqi. Significant numbers of *ḥadīṯ* reports in the *Musnad* also came from Syrian, Meccan, and Yemeni shaykhs. (Compare the *Ṣaḥīḥ* of Muslim: about 62 percent of its *ḥadīṯ* reports came from Iraqi shaykhs, 20 percent Khurasani and Transoxanian, 10 percent Egyptian, 5 percent Meccan.) However, there are scarcely two dozen *ḥadīṯ* reports in the whole *Musnad* from Medinese shaykhs (not one in a thousand).[61] It seems a good guess that Aḥmad heard them in Mecca or Baṣra, not Medina, in spite of reports in the biographical literature that his travels in search of *ḥadīṯ* included time in Medina.[62] Judging by entries in biographical dictionaries, Scott Cameron Lucas has found that the significance

61. They are Anas ibn ʿIyāḍ (eleven *ḥadīṯ* reports), on whom *v.* Ibn Ḥaǧar, *Tahḏīb*, I, 375f; Muḥammad ibn Ismāʿīl ibn Muslim (ten), *Tahḏīb*, IX, 61; and Yūsuf ibn Yaʿqūb ibn Abī Salama (two), *Tahḏīb*, XI, 430f. One shaykh, Abū l-Qāsim ibn Abī l-Zinād (six *ḥadīṯ* reports), is identified in standard sources as Medinese but evidently lived in Baghdad: Ibn Ḥaǧar, *Tahḏīb*, XII, 203; al-Ḫaṭīb, *Tārīḫ Baġdād*, XIV, 398.

62. E.g. Ibn al-Ǧawzī, *Manāqib*, 22.

of Medina in *ḥadīṯ* dwindled rapidly from the death of al-Zuhrī (125/742–43 or earlier).[63] The incidence of Medinese shaykhs in Aḥmad's *Musnad* (and the Six Books) confirms the insignificance of Medina. Meccan prominence was also somewhat artificial: of the four Meccans from whom Aḥmad related the most *ḥadīṯ* in the *Musnad*, three had moved there from Baṣra, one from Kūfa.[64] [45]

Al-Tarġīb wa-l-tarhīb in the *Musnad*

G.H.A. Juynboll once distinguished between the standard of authentification demanded for *ḥadīṯ* having to do with legal duties and a lower standard for *ḥadīṯ* having to do with *al-tarġīb wa-l-tarhīb*, making to aspire and making to fear (i.e. encouraging piety and discouraging impiety). He then asserted that the *Musnad* was swollen with *ḥadīṯ* of the latter category.[65] There is some evidence for a double standard, on which more below. However, it does not appear that the *Musnad* has a great deal more of *al-tarġīb wa-l-tarhīb* than other collections. In his introduction to *al-Ǧāmiʿ al-ṣaḥīḥ*, Muslim summarizes its contents as God's "*sunan al-dīn* (beliefs), *aḥkām* (ordinances), reward and punishment, *al-tarġīb wa-l-tarhīb*, and so forth."[66] I estimate that *aḥkām* comprise 52 percent of the *Musnad* (cf. 43 percent of Muslim); *al-tarġīb wa-l-tarhīb* 17 percent (cf. 11 percent of Muslim); history, including prophetic biography, 13 percent (cf. 20 percent of Muslim); *sunan al-dīn* 13 percent (cf. 4 percent of Muslim); devotions (e.g. prayers to repeat) 6 percent (cf. Muslim, 7 percent); reward and punishment 5 percent (cf. 6 percent of Muslim); eschatology 3 percent (cf. 2 percent of Muslim); and Qurʾānic glosses 1 percent (cf. 2 percent of Muslim). It appears, then, that there is somewhat more of *al-tarġīb wa-l-tarhīb* in the *Musnad* than elsewhere, but hardly by enough to put the *Musnad* in a separate category.

It appears that there is more substance to the allegation that the *Musnad* is swollen by formally weak *ḥadīṯ* reports. By the estimate of Arnaʾūṭ, et al., mainly based on evaluations in *riǧāl* encyclopaedias, about 57 percent of *ḥadīṯ* reports in the *Musnad* are sound (*ṣaḥīḥ*, *ṣaḥīḥ ʿalā šarṭ al-šayḫayn*, etc.), 19 percent are passable (*ḥasan*, *qawī*, etc.), but 24

63. Scott Cameron Lucas, "The Arts of *ḥadīth* Compilation and Criticism: A Study of the Emergence of Sunnism in the Third/Ninth Century," Ph. D. dissertation, Univ. of Chicago 2002, 435–39.

64. Sufyān ibn ʿUyayna (d. 198/814), Kūfan, 759 *ḥadīṯ* reports in the *Musnad*; Abū Saʿīd ʿAbd al-Raḥmān ibn ʿAbd Allāh (d. 197/812–13), Baṣran, 252 *ḥadīṯ* reports; ʿAbd Allāh ibn Yazīd al-Muqriʾ (d. 213/828?), Baṣran, 195 *ḥadīṯ* reports; Muʾammal ibn Ismāʿīl (d. 205/822?), Baṣran, 134 *ḥadīṯ* reports. Based on Ṣabrī, *Muʿǧam*, 76f, and the appropriate entries in Ibn Ḥaǧar, *Tahḏīb al-Tahḏīb*.

65. G.H.A. Juynboll, *Muslim Tradition* (Cambridge 1983), 189.

66. Cf. G.H.A. Juynboll, "Muslim's Introduction to his *Ṣaḥīḥ*," *Jerusalem Studies in Arabic and Islam*, no. 5 (1984), 263–311, at 265, interpreting *sunan al-dīn* as "usages" rather than precisely "beliefs," meaning those theological propositions that constitute orthodoxy.

percent are weak (*ḍaʿīf, mursal, ġayr ṣaḥīḥ*). Aḥmad Muḥammad Šākir found that about 11 percent of the *ḥadīṯ* reports in the *Musnad* were weak.[67]

Aḥmad and other traditionists are sometimes quoted in favour of rigour when it comes to assessing *ḥadīṯ* reports concerning the ordinances [46] and dogma, lenience when it comes to *ḥadīṯ* in other categories. For example, "When we relate (*ḥadīṯ*) from the Messenger of God . . . concerning the licit and illicit, the precedents and ordinances, we are strict about *asānīd*; but when we relate (*ḥadīṯ*) from the Prophet concerning the virtues of works and what neither lays down nor suspends any ordinance, then we are easygoing about *asānīd*."[68] Nevertheless, it does not appear that *ḥadīṯ* reports in the *Musnad* pertaining to *al-tarġīb wa-l-tarhīb* are particularly liable to be weak: by the evaluations of Arnaʾūṭ, et al., 63 percent of the *Musnad*'s *ḥadīṯ* concerning *aḥkām* are sound, 63 percent of those concerning *al-tarġīb wa-l-tarhīb* (respective figures for the outright weak are 22 percent and 20).

Moreover, this is not to say that Aḥmad himself regarded these *ḥadīṯ* as weak, whether concerning *aḥkām* or *al-tarġīb wa-l-tarhīb*. On the contrary, he presumably saw fit to include most of them because they had parallels elsewhere. Aḥmad's actual policy (whatever his professed theory) is best shown by an example. He is once quoted as saying of Muḥammad ibn Isḥāq (d. 151/768–69?), the famous biographer of the Prophet, "Such *ḥadīṯ* reports as these, meaning *maġāzī* (stories of raids) and the like, are to be written down. As for the licit and forbidden, we require strength like this" and clenched his fist.[69] Ḥanbal ibn Isḥāq recalled that Aḥmad said Ibn Isḥāq was not a *ḥuǧǧa*; that is, one did not argue by *ḥadīṯ* he related.[70] (But Ibn Hāniʾ recalled the opposite.[71]) ʿAbd Allāh ibn Aḥmad said Aḥmad would not argue by Ibn Isḥāq's *ḥadīṯ* concerning the *sunan* (i.e. ordinances as opposed to history).[72] One might then expect the *Musnad* to include from Ibn Isḥāq only historical reports. Actually, Ibn Isḥāq appears in almost 600 *asānīd*, of which the first dozen (for example) are divided seven-to-five between *aḥkām* (mostly ritual law) and history, roughly the same proportion of *aḥkām* as in the whole *Musnad*. What makes Ibn Isḥāq worth quoting in the *Musnad* is that his transmission corroborates and is corroborated by parallel *asānīd*. To conclude, Aḥmad's method of *ḥadīṯ* criticism was not to classify transmitters, then mechanically apply those classifications to all the *ḥadīṯ* they transmit, as do his modern editors. Rather, the normal case was for someone to relate *ḥadīṯ* sometimes correctly, sometimes not, so Aḥmad accepted as sound [47] what was

67. Juynboll, "Aḥmad Muḥammad Shākir," 226.

68. Al-Ḫaṭīb al-Baġdādī, *al-Kifāya fī ʿilm al-riwāya, bāb al-tašdīd fī aḥādīṯ al-aḥkām* = ed. Aḥmad ʿUmar Hāšim (Beirut 1406/1986), 163.

69. Ibn Abī Ḥātim, *Ǧarḥ*, VII, 193.

70. Al-Ḫaṭīb, *Tārīḫ Baġdād*, I, 230.

71. *Aḥtaǧǧu bih*: Ibn Hāniʾ, *Masāʾil*, II, 242.

72. *Loc. cit.*

corroborated, rejected as dubious what was not.[73] Also, it appears that Aḥmad only occasionally, not systematically, applied a stricter criterion to *ḥadīṯ* concerning *aḥkām* than concerning *al-tarġīb wa-l-tarhīb*.

Additions from ʿAbd Allāh ibn Aḥmad

We also have widely different estimates of the number of additional *ḥadīṯ* reports (*zawāʾid*) from ʿAbd Allāh ibn Aḥmad as opposed to Aḥmad himself. ʿĀmir Ḥasan Ṣabrī found only 1,300 in the Bulaq edition (under 5 percent). About 900 of them are variants on Aḥmad's; that is, basically the same texts with different, corroboratory *asānīd*.[74] I should guess that medieval estimates of additions from ʿAbd Allāh, ranging as high as 10,000, are likewise based on different manuscripts, fuller versions no longer extant. (Ibn Ḥağar identified five additions from al-Qaṭīʿī [d. Baghdad, 368/979], who transmitted the *Musnad* from ʿAbd Allāh, but his modern editor found only two of them in the Cairo edition.[75]) There are certainly parallels in other works. For example, Ibn Ḥağar worked from a *K. al-Zuhd* that comprised about a third as many *ḥadīṯ* reports as Aḥmad's *Musnad*;[76] that is, at around 9,000, over three times as many as the standard published version of the *Zuhd*.[77] About a third of the items in the extant *Zuhd* are from ʿAbd Allāh, not from his father, and quotations in *Ḥilyat al-awliyāʾ* indicate that ʿAbd Allāh's learning in this area was great.

It is also a question to what extent the *Musnad* is Aḥmad's assemblage, to what extent ʿAbd Allāh's. ʿAbd Allāh asserts that he heard almost everything in the *Musnad* two or three times, which suggests that Aḥmad selected the *ḥadīṯ* therein but that its final arrangement was up to ʿAbd Allāh.[78] Ḏahabī describes Aḥmad as having only somewhat more to do with the actual arrangement of our *Musnad*:[79] [48]

> The imam Aḥmad disbelieved in composing books. This book of his, the *Musnad*, he did not compose or set in order; neither did he take care with its *ḥadīṯ*. Rather, he would relate it to his son from his copies and fascicles, telling him: "Put this in so-and-so's *musnad*, this in so-and-so's *musnad*."

73. On Aḥmad's transmission from weak and heretical shaykhs, *v.* further Ṣabrī, *Muʿǧam*, 15–64.

74. Ṣabrī, *Zawāʾid*, 118, 131.

75. Al-Nāṣir, *muqaddima*, Ibn Ḥağar, *Iṭrāf*, I, 61f. Cf. Ṣabrī, *Zawāʾid*, 118.

76. Ibn Ḥağar, *Taʿǧīl*, ed. Imdād al-Ḥaqq, I, 243.

77. Aḥmad ibn Ḥanbal, *K. al-Zuhd* (Mecca A.H. 1357, repr. Beirut 1403/1983).

78. Aḥmad ibn Ḥanbal, *K. al-ʿIlal wa-maʿrifat al-riǧāl*, ed. Waṣī Allāh ibn Muḥammad ʿAbbās (Beirut 1988), III, 157 = *K. al-Ǧāmiʿ fī l-ʿilal wa-maʿrifat al-riǧāl*, ed. Muḥammad Ḥusām Bayḍūn (Beirut 1410/1990), II, 141.

79. Ḏahabī, *Siyar*, XIII, 522.

Occasional comments from ʿAbd Allāh in the *Musnad* do confirm that Aḥmad meant to put together a particular collection of sound *ḥadīṯ*, although not exactly the collection we have. For example, we read < Aḥmad < ʿAlī ibn Ṯābit al-Ǧazarī < Nāṣiḥ, Abū ʿAbd Allāh, < Simāk ibn Ḥarb < Ǧābir ibn Samura < Prophet: "That a man should educate his child or that one of you educate his child is better than giving daily alms of half a *ṣāʿ*." Then comes this surprising comment: "My father did not bring out this *ḥadīṯ* report in his *Musnad* on account of Nāṣiḥ, since he was weak in *ḥadīṯ*. He dictated it to me in *al-Nawādir*."[80] Some *ḥadīṯ* reports were up to the standard of the *Musnad*, according to Aḥmad's plan, others were not; but the final selection was patently ʿAbd Allāh's.

Ibn al-Ǧazarī explained occasional confusion in the *Musnad* and omission of sound *ḥadīṯ* by its unfinished state at Aḥmad's death:[81]

> When the imam Aḥmad began to collect the *Musnad*, he wrote on individual sheets and distributed them among individual fascicles . . . . He started to dictate it to his sons and the people of his house. He died before purifying and amending it, so it remained as it was. Then his son ʿAbd Allāh took over what seemed to make it up and joined to that what he had heard that was similar to it to fill it out . . . . Many *ḥadīṯ* reports remained in leaves and fascicles he never came across.

Ibn al-Ǧazarī's account is presumably his inference from ʿAbd Allāh's occasional comments on his work that he wrote into the *Musnad* itself. For example, there appears a *ḥadīṯ* report < ʿAbd al-Malik ibn ʿAmr < Hišām < Yaḥyā ibn Abī Kaṯīr < Abū Sallām < Abū Umāma < the Messenger of God: "Learn the Qurʾān, for it will be an intercessor on the Day of the Resurrection . . . ."[82] There follows this comment: "I found this *ḥadīṯ* report in my father's notebook in his hand. He had struck it out. I thought he had struck it out because it was a mistake. It is actually < Zayd < Abū Sallām < Abū Umāma." Then comes the *ḥadīṯ* report Aḥmad had struck out, < ʿAbd al-Razzāq < Maʿmar < Yaḥyā ibn Abī Kaṯīr < Abū Salama < Abū Umāma < the Messenger of God: "Learn the Qurʾān, for it will be an intercessor on the Day of the Resurrection . . . ."[83] [49] We easily imagine ʿAbd Allāh going through his father's notes as Ibn al-Ǧazarī describes. Ṣabrī, who has studied ʿAbd Allāh's additions more closely than anyone else, takes it that the arrangement of the *Musnad* was ʿAbd Allāh's doing.[84]

This is not to say that ʿAbd Allāh departed widely from his father's plan. He apparently retained items of which he disapproved. For example, we read < Aḥmad < Aswad ibn

---

80. Aḥmad, *Musnad*, V, 96 *XXXIV, 459*; Ṣabrī, *Zawāʾid*, 119f.
81. Ibn al-Ǧazarī, *Maṣʿad*, in *Musnad*, ed. Šākir, I, 30.
82. Aḥmad, *Musnad*, V, 249 *XXXVI, 462f.*
83. Aḥmad, *Musnad*, V, 250f *XXXVI, 481*.
84. Ṣabrī, *Zawāʾid*, 112.

ʿĀmir < Abū Isrāʾīl < Hilāl al-Hağarī < ʿAbd Allāh ibn ʿAmr < the Messenger of God: "The Muslim is the one from whose tongue the Muslims are safe . . . ." There follows this comment from Abū ʿAbd al-Raḥmān (i.e. ʿAbd Allāh): "This is a mistake. It was (transmitted) only < al-Ḥakam < Sayf < Rušayd al-Hağarī."[85] Hartmann is of the opinion that ʿAbd Allāh's work was quite mechanical, since the text itself looks so little like the product of active, intelligent re-arrangement.[86]

In conclusion, Fuat Sezgin seems typically overeager when he argues against Goldziher from Abū Mūsā l-Madīnī's account that Aḥmad himself assembled the *Musnad*.[87] However, it does appear that as ʿAbd Allāh assembled the *Musnad*, he earnestly strove to represent his father's teaching accurately. He lived just when the culture of writing had definitely prevailed over that of purely oral transmission, when exact transmission was coming to prevail over loose paraphrase and extrapolation. His departures from his father's plan apparently comprise mainly accidental omission and clearly labelled addition.

Further on What Distinguishes the *Musnad* from the Six Books

The advantage of arrangement by topic is making it much easier to look up a given *ḥadīṯ* report. Surely, this is one reason the Six Books, the most popular Sunni collections of *ḥadīṯ*, are all arranged by topic. Aḥmad's *Musnad* did not make the grade in part because it was inconveniently arranged. (No doubt, easily-searchable CD-ROM versions are even now raising its popularity.) Arrangement by Companion reflects the habit of traditionists, thinking first of *isnād*, also used to the memory [50] contest (*muḏākara*) in which traditionists would sit about competing with one another to recall alternative *asānīd*. Arrangement by Companion was introduced in the generation before Aḥmad, subsequently to arrangement by category.[88] Perhaps, half-consciously, Aḥmad and ʿAbd Allāh preferred a difficult arrangement just to make the point that anyone who proposed to offer opinions about Islamic law had to be a competent traditionist. Topical arrangement would let in too many dilettantes unable to resist facile reasoning because they did not know which *ḥadīṯ* reports were well attested, which not.

---

85. Aḥmad, *Musnad*, II, 209 *XI, 545f*. Further examples collected by Ṣabrī, *Zawāʾid*, 77–85.

86. Hartmann, "Tradenten," 153.

87. Sezgin, *GAS*, I, 504.

88. The first to arrange *ḥadīṯ* by Companion were Abū Dāwūd al-Ṭayālisī (d. 204/819?) in Baṣra and ʿUbayd Allāh ibn Mūsā (d. 213/829?) in Kūfa, according to Ḫalīlī, *Iršād*, 149, s.n. Abū Dāwūd Sulaymān ibn Dāwūd al-Ṭayālisī. Whatever arranging al-Ṭayālisī undertook, however, the *Musnad* of his now extant and published was assembled only in the late ninth century, for which *v*. Robert Marston Speight, "The *Musnad* of al-Ṭayālisī: A study of Islamic Ḥadīth as Oral Literature," Ph. D. dissertation, Hartford Seminary 1971, 11. *V*. also ibid., 18f, for the observation that arrangement by *isnād* was not the earliest pattern.

The main difference between the *Musnad* and the Six Books, besides its arrangement by *isnād*, appears to be what Goldziher stressed: its sheer length, which made it unhandy to work with as well as expensive to copy. Longer collections did not survive. Abū Bakr Ibn Abi ʿĀṣim, the Baṣran Sufi, later *qāḍī* for Isfahan (d. 287/900?), compiled a *Musnad* comprising 50,000 *ḥadīṯ* reports, now lost.[89] The longest *Musnad* ever assembled is said to have been that of the Nishapuran al-Māsirǧisī (d. 365/976), which took up 3,000 fascicles or some 150 volumes.[90] Aḥmad's *Musnad* also came close to disappearing. It took Ibn al-Ǧazarī himself seven years to get the whole *Musnad* by *qirāʾa* (reading aloud from his copy for his shaykh's approval), partly because the *Musnad* is so long, partly because one shaykh was unwilling to share the part he had.[91] Some of Ibn Badrān's shaykhs, presumably in late-nineteenth-century Damascus, asserted that the *Musnad* had been entirely lost. Ibn Badrān asserted against them that he had seen most of it in Damascene libraries — only "most of it," note, and this in probably the main centre of Ḥanbalism from the Mongol destruction of Baghdad to the establishment of Saudi Arabia in the twentieth century.[92]

The outsize length of Aḥmad's *Musnad* was due mainly to the inclusion of parallel *asānīd*, not to its including material substantially different [51] from what was in the Six Books. The purpose of providing parallel *asānīd* was doubtless corroboration. Comparison of *asānīd* was the essential method of ninth-century *ḥadīṯ* criticism.[93] Collectors such as Abū Dāwūd and Tirmiḏī effectively ask us to trust them that the *ḥadīṯ* reports in their collections are sound; that is, that they themselves have made the necessary comparisons to be sure that the transmitters in their *asānīd* are reliable. Muslim to some extent and Aḥmad to a greater do not ask us to take their word for it: they show us the evidence for us to compare *asānīd* ourselves, should we wish. (Buḫārī apparently provides almost as many alternative *asānīd* as Muslim but dispersed under different headings, making comparisons difficult.)

Although the content of the *Musnad* is similar to that of the Six Books, the absence of Medinese shaykhs among Aḥmad's immediate authorities is striking. Patricia Crone has identified Ḥanbalī law, along with Mālikī and Šāfiʿī, with a Medinese bloc, as opposed to a Kūfan bloc comprising Ḥanafī and Šāfiʿī law.[94] But it seems fairly clear that the idea of Kūfa as the centre of jurisprudence by *raʾy* as opposed to Medina the centre of jurisprudence by *ḥadīṯ* was invented in the mid-ninth century.[95] There is no sign that Aḥmad

89. Ḏahabī, *Siyar*, XIII, 436.

90. Ḏahabī, *Siyar*, XVI (ed. Šuʿayb al-Arnaʾūṭ and Akram al-Būšaiyī), 289.

91. Ibn al-Ǧazarī, *Maṣʿad*, in *Musnad*, ed. Šākir, I, 51.

92. Ibn Badrān, *Madḫal*, 245 = ed. al-Turkī, 471.

93. *V.* Eerik Dickinson, *The Development of Early Sunnite* Ḥadīth *Criticism* (Leiden 2001), esp. chap. 6.

94. Patricia Crone, *Roman, Provincial, and Islamic Law* (Cambridge 1987), 23.

95. *V.* Christopher Melchert, "How Ḥanafism Came to Originate in Kufa and Traditionalism in Medina," *Islamic Law and Society* 6 (1999), 318–47 [*HPL 12]. Cf. Harald Motzki, *The Origins of Islamic Jurispru-*

thought himself indebted to any particularly Medinese tradition. The prominence of Baṣran shaykhs among Aḥmad's authorities suggests that we may be dealing rather with a Baṣran bloc identified only from the later ninth century — after Aḥmad's time — as essentially Medinese.

dence: Meccan Fiqh before the Classical Schools, trans. Marion H. Katz (Leiden 2002), asserting that prophetic *ḥadīṯ* was more important in Medina than elsewhere already in the early eighth century.

4
BUKHĀRĪ AND HIS *ṢAḤĪḤ*

Abū ʿAbd Allāh Muḥammad ibn Ismāʿīl ibn Ibrāhīm ibn al-Mughīrah ibn Bardizbah (Badhdizbah? Yazdhibah?) al-Juʿfī was the most highly regarded of all Sunni hadith collectors. He was born in Bukhara, 13 Shawwāl 194/20 July 810, died in Khartank, near Samarqand, 1 Shawwāl 256/1 September 870. What follows is a survey of his life and works, with special emphasis on the *Ṣaḥīḥ*, to which his fame is principally due. A short version of it will appear in *The Encyclopædia of Islam*, and it is the first purpose of this article simply to show more fully the evidentiary basis of what is said there.

Given Bukhārī's importance to the Islamic tradition, it is unsurprising that we have more information about him and his main work than about any other of the Six Books and their collectors. What surprises is how thin the modern literature is, in both Arabic and European languages. A dismissive statement from his recent biographer Ghassan Abdul-Jabbar suggests some probable reasons:[1]

> In Western academia, hadiths are seen as a source to be interpreted in order to identify the interests of the later generations that 'fabricated' them. There is only passing interest in the tradition and technique of hadith study that Muslim scholars developed. Perhaps this is why, despite widespread acknowledgement of Bukhari's importance, there is little more than a few passages here and there about him.

Certainly, the authenticity issue has dominated modern hadith studies; for example, Herald Motzki's recent collection of scholarship on hadith covers nothing else.[2] However, Ab-

1. Gh. Abdul-Jabbar, *Bukhari* (*Makers of Islamic Civilization*), London, 2007, p. 128 (= Abdul-Jabbar, *Bukhari*).

2. H. Motzki, *Ḥadīth: origins and developments* (*Formation of the classical Islamic world*, 28), Aldershot,

Originally published in *Le Muséon* 123 (2010): 425–54.

dul-Jabbar overlooks a brilliant little section of Goldziher's *Muslim Studies* on 'The Ḥadīth Literature,' which includes over ten pages on Bukhārī's *Ṣaḥīḥ* in particular.[3] One guesses that he found Goldziher's doubts about the authenticity of hadith so distasteful that he could not bring himself to read his actual works. It might be added that Muslim writers in European languages, hoping to refute Goldziher and Schacht, have strongly contributed to keeping the authenticity [426] issue prominent. Reluctance to cast doubt on Bukhārī's authority has probably also inhibited Bukhārī scholarship by Muslims, which tends to reproduce material in the commentaries, especially that of Ibn Ḥajar (d. 852/1449), without contributing new research. I was surprised to find it considerably more difficult to get my hands on a useful index of men in Bukhārī's *Ṣaḥīḥ* than I had earlier of men in Abū Dāwūd's *Sunan* and even Aḥmad's massive *Musnad*. However, significant new studies from Scott Lucas and Jonathan Brown show that the situation is changing.[4] The study that follows goes beyond previous accounts especially as to Bukhārī's travels; in offering a more careful description of Bukhārī's works than has hitherto appeared in English, at least; in testing assertions in the biobibliographical literature against the works themselves, with preference for the evidence of the works when (as often) they are in contradiction; and in locating Bukhārī more accurately on the juridico-theological spectrum of his time.

Life

Bukhārī's *nisbah Juʿfī* refers generally to an Arabian tribe, particularly to a one-time governor of Bukhara Yamāni al-Juʿfī, patron to al-Mughīrah, the first Muslim in Bukhārī's line. I have not discovered any trace of this Yamāni independently of his being the reason for Bukhārī's other *nisbah* and his being great-grandfather to one of Bukhārī's leading shaykhs (197 hadith reports in the *Ṣaḥīḥ*, according to Sezgin), Muḥammad ibn ʿAbd Allāh al-Juʿfī (d. 229/844).[5] For example, Yāqūt offers a sketch of how Bukhara was subdued and resubdued in the later seventh century and who was appointed to supervise the region, with admitted gaps in the chronology, then mentions this Yamāni only in connection with Bukhārī and Muḥammad ibn ʿAbd Allāh.[6] Yamāni was presumably part of some family tradition.

2004.

3. I. Goldziher, *Muslim Studies*, ed. S.M. Stern, trans. C. R. Barber - S.M. Stern, Chicago, 1968–71, vol. 2, p. 189–251, esp. p. 216–229 (= Goldziher, *Muslim Studies*).

4. S.C. Lucas, *The Legal Principles of Muḥammad b. Ismāʿīl al-Bukhārī and their Relationship to Classical Salafi Islam*, in *Islamic Law and Society*, 13 (2006), p. 289–324 (= Lucas, *Legal Principles*); J. Brown, *The Canonization of al-Bukhārī and Muslim* (*Islam history and civilization, Studies and texts*, 69), Leiden, 2007 (= Brown, *Canonization*).

5. F. Sezgin, *Buhârî'nin kaynakları*, Istanbul, 1956, p. 210 (= Sezgin, *Buhârî'nin Kaynakları*).

6. Yāqūt, *Geographisches Wörterbuch*, Leipzig, 1866, 1:519–521.

Bukhārī's father was a traditionist before him, hearing hadith from Mālik ibn Anas, among others.[7] He died while Bukhārī was still very [427] young, so that he was reared by his mother alone. He studied law and collected hadith in Transoxania and Khurasan from the age of 11, when he left the *kuttāb*, to 16. In 210/825–826, he made the pilgrimage to Mecca with his brother Aḥmad and travelled widely in quest of hadith over the next decade and a half.[8]

I should like to determine more precisely and certainly than other biographers where and when he travelled. The biographical literature regularly lists places to which he travelled and shaykhs from whom he heard hadith, but some details seem doubtful when tested against the evidence of Bukhārī's own works and the earliest biographical notices. For example, al-Khaṭīb al-Baghdādī states near the beginning of his biography that Bukhārī 'wrote in Khurasan, the Jibal, all the cities of Iraq, the Hijaz, Syria, and Egypt.'[9] This list is only partly confirmed by the *Ṣaḥīḥ*. Here are the percentages of hadith mentioned there from each of these regions: Khurasan (and Transoxania) 20 percent, the Jibal 1 percent, all the cities of Iraq (excluding Mesopotamia) 54 percent, the Hijaz (i.e. Mecca and Medina) 7 percent, Syria 8 percent, and Egypt 10 percent.[10] Bukhārī relates 79 hadith reports in the *Ṣaḥīḥ* from shaykhs of the Jibal, 78 of them from Ibrāhīm ibn Mūsá al-Ṣaghīr (d. 220s/835–845) of Rayy, the other from Marrār ibn Ḥammūyah (d. 254/868) of Hamadhan, who at that is ambiguously identified.[11] There are also a few hadith reports from additional Jibalis in the *Adab* and other smaller works. But this does not look like the record of a significant trip to collect hadith in [428] the region. We also have the

7. Bukhārī, *al-Tārīkh al-kabīr*, Hyderabad, 1358–1362, 2nd edn. 1377/1958, vol. 1, p. 342–343 (= Bukhārī, *TK*).

8. The earliest extant major biographies are two by Ibn ʿAdī al-Qaṭṭān (d. 360/970–971?) in the introductions to *al-Kāmil fī ḍuʿafāʾ al-rijāl*, ed. ʿĀ.A. ʿAbd al-Mawjūd, *et al.*, Beirut, 1418/1997 (= Ibn ʿAdī al-Qaṭṭān, *Kāmil*), and *Asāmī man rawá ʿanhum Muḥammad ibn Ismāʿīl al-Bukhārī* (*Silsilat al-ajzāʾ al-ḥadīthīyah*, 2), ed. ʿĀ.Ḥ. Ṣabrī, Beirut, 1414/1994. Al-Khaṭīb al-Baghdādī (d. 463/1071) provides us with by far the most important early biography, on which virtually all later biographers depend: *Tārīkh Baghdād*, Cairo, 1349/1931, vol. 2, p. 4–34 (= al-Khaṭīb al-Baghdādī, *TB*), alternatively *Tārīkh Madīnat al-Salām*, ed. B.ʿA. Maʿrūf, Beirut, 1422/2001, vol. 2, p. 322–359 (= *TMS*). There was also a substantial biography in a volume by Abū Jaʿfar Muḥammad ibn Abī Ḥātim, Bukhārī's copyist (*warrāq*), called *Shamāʾil al-Bukhārī*, some of which survives in quotation; likewise a substantial biography in al-Ḥākim al-Naysābūrī (d. 405/1014), *Tārīkh Naysābūr*. For other biographies, *v.* F. Sezgin, *Geschichte des arabischen Schrifttums*, Leiden, 1967, vol. 1, p. 115–134 (= *GAS*), to which add al-Dhahabī, *Tārīkh al-islām*, ed. ʿU.ʿA.S. Tadmurī, Beirut, 1407–1421/1987–2000, 18 (251–260 h.), p. 238–274 (= Dhahabī, *Tārīkh*), with further references.

9. Al-Khaṭīb al-Baghdādī, *TB*, vol. 2, p. 4, and *TMS*, vol. 2, p. 322.

10. Working from the list of shaykhs in Sezgin, *Buhârî'nin Kaynakları*, p. 205–303. Sezgin's lists need to be redone, for his numbers add up to only 6,855 hadith reports in all the *Ṣaḥīḥ*. However, I assume his numbers are not systematically distorted.

11. Ibn Ḥajar, *Tahdhīb al-Tahdhīb*, Hyderabad, 1325–1327, repr. Beirut, n.d., vol. 10, p. 80–81 (= Ibn Ḥajar, *Tahdhīb*).

negative evidence of Ibn Abī Ḥātim's report that Bukhārī came to Rayy in 250/864–865.[12] Had he visited earlier as well, Ibn Abī Ḥātim ought to have mentioned it. I am inclined to guess, then, that Bukhārī caught Ibrāhīm ibn Mūsá al-Ṣaghīr in Baghdad or Mecca and never actually visited the Jibal until much later (as I guessed earlier of Abū Dāwūd al-Sijistānī[13]). Regrettably, Bukhārī seldom mentions in *al-Tārīkh al-kabīr* when or where he met someone. Of Ibrāhīm ibn Mūsá al-Ṣaghīr, for example, Bukhārī mentions only that Ibrāhīm heard from Ibn Abī Zāʾidah and ʿĪsá ibn Yūnus, not that he himself ever met him, let alone when and where.[14] By the way, Bukhārī relates two hadith reports in the *Ṣaḥīḥ* of Ibrāhīm ibn Mūsá < Ibn Abī Zāʾidah and six of Ibrāhīm < ʿĪsá ibn Yūnus. By contrast, Bukhārī relates 62 hadith reports of Ibrāhīm < Hishām ibn Yūsuf. His not mentioning this last relationship is a typical example of how the *Tārīkh* is independent of the *Ṣaḥīḥ*.[15]

Bukhārī is quoted from near the end of his life as recalling that he had collected hadith in Syria and Egypt, entered Mesopotamia twice and Basra four times, stayed in the Hijaz six years, and entered Kufa and Baghdad innumerable times.[16] Mesopotamia (*al-Jazīrah*) is the odd name on this list: if he went there twice in the course of collecting hadith, why does the *Ṣaḥīḥ* report hadith from just one Mesopotamian shaykh, Aḥmad ibn ʿAbd al-Malik of Harran (d. 221/835–836)? It is possible that he wrote down hadith from many other shaykhs in Mesopotamia, visitors like himself from the other places with which they are associated in the biographical literature. At least as likely, it seems to me, is that he visited Mesopotamia for the pious purpose of *jihād*, manning an outpost on the frontier, possibly helping raiders in their staging area. A story is quoted of his copyist of Bukhārī's helping to build a *ribāṭ* in Firabr, carrying bricks himself.[17] Another story of the same is that he indulged himself one day by lying down as they worked on his book of qurʾanic commentary in Firabr. Asked to explain himself, he said that they were in a [429] frontier city and so needed to be ready in case of enemy attack.[18] Both stories indicate, at least, his interest in defending the frontier. Of course, it is also possible, and to my mind the most likely, that this is another example of contradiction between the biographical

12. Ibn Abī Ḥātim, *Kitāb al-Jarḥ wa-al-taʿdīl*, Hyderabad, 1360–71, repr. Beirut, n.d., vol. 7, p. 191 (= Ibn Abī Ḥātim, *Jarḥ*).

13. Ch. Melchert, *The Life and Works of Abū Dāwūd al-Sijistānī*, in *Al-Qanṭara*, 29 (2008), p. 9–44, at p. 12.

14. Bukhārī, *TK*, vol. 1, p. 327.

15. Ch. Melchert, *Bukhārī and early hadith criticism*, in *Journal of the American Oriental Society*, 121 (2001), p. 7–19, at p. 12 (= Melchert, *Bukhārī*) [*HPL 2].

16. Ibn ʿAsākir, *Tārīkh Madīnat Dimashq*, ed. M.D.A.S. al-ʿAmrawī, Beirut, 1415/1995, vol. 52, p. 58 (= Ibn ʿAsākir, *TMD*).

17. Dhahabī, *Siyar aʿlām al-nubalāʾ*, ed. Sh. al-Arnaʾūṭ, &al., Beirut, 1401–1409/1981–1988, vol. 12, p. 450 (= Dhahabī, *Siyar*), apparently drawing on M. Ibn Abī Ḥātim, *Shamāʾil al-Bukhārī*.

18. Al-Khaṭīb al-Baghdādī, *TB*, vol. 2, p. 14, and *TMS*, vol. 2, p. 332–3.

record and Bukhārī's own works, the latter forcing us to discard the former. This seems to be the position of al-Dhahabī, who says simply, 'He did not enter Mesopotamia.'[19]

The evidence of death dates gives us *termini ante quem* for his visiting various cities; for example, he states that ᶜAbbās ibn Abī Ṭālib said Saᶜīd ibn al-Rabīᶜ al-ᶜĀmirī died in 211/826–827, which suggests Bukhārī was collecting hadith in Basra before then.[20] In 217/832–833, Bukhārī took his leave of ᶜAlī ibn Ḥafṣ al-Marwazī in Ashkelon, as Bukhārī himself directly states.[21] We have a few other dates in early sources. A story from Bukhārī's copyist places him back in Nishapur in the early 220s/mid-830s, as he related the news of the Inquisition in Baghdad and what Aḥmad ibn Ḥanbal and others had done.[22] In 246/860–861, he was in Basra, for one colophon states that its transmitter heard *al-Tārīkh al-kabīr* from Bukhārī in Basra that year.[23] Al-Khalīlī (d. 446/1055) states that he related hadith in Baghdad for the last time in 248/862–863.[24] But al-Kalābādhī (d. 398/1007) states that Firabrī heard Bukhārī dictate the *Ṣaḥīḥ* in Firabr, Transoxania, in that year.[25] In 250/864–865, as we have seen, he related hadith in Rayy.[26] Al-Ḥākim al-Naysābūrī is quoted, presumably from the lost *Tārīkh Naysābūr*, as saying that Bukhārī first entered Nishapur in 209/824–825 (the year before his pilgrimage), the last time in 250, after which he stayed for five years.[27] According to Kalābādhī, however, he was in Bukhara in 252/866–867, where Firabrī heard the *Ṣaḥīḥ* from him a second time.[28] Al-Dāraquṭnī is quoted as saying that Firabrī heard it from Bukhārī over three years' time, 253–255/867–869.[29] Such [430] dubiously harmonizable dates are more evidence of the unreliability of the biographical literature. I am inclined to trust Ibn Abī Ḥātim and Dāraquṭnī before the other sources just mentioned, since their reports are not only earlier but make it easier to account for the meagre circulation of the *Ṣaḥīḥ* before the mid-tenth century C.E., whereas the other reports make it more difficult to account for that. Jaᶜfar ibn Muḥammad al-Mustaghfirī is quoted from the lost *Tārīkh Nasaf* as saying that Bukhārī came to Nasaf in 256 (the last year of his life), then left for Samarqand in Ramaḍān of that year/August 870.[30]

19. Dhahabī, *Siyar*, vol. 12, p. 396.
20. Bukhārī, *TK*, vol. 3, p. 471.
21. Ibid., *TK*, vol. 6, p. 270.
22. Dhahabī, *Siyar*, vol. 12, p. 417–418.
23. Bukhārī, *TK*, vol. 1, p. 3.
24. Al-Khalīlī, *al-Irshād*, abr. al-Silafī, ed. ᶜĀ.Ḥ. Ḥaydar, Beirut, 1993/1414, p. 378.
25. Kalābādhī, *Rijāl* Ṣaḥīḥ *al-Bukhārī*, ed. ᶜA.A. al-Laythī, Beirut, 1407/1987, vol. 1, p. 24 (= Kalābādhī, *Rijāl*).
26. Ibn Abī Ḥātim, *Jarḥ*, vol. 7, p. 191.
27. Dhahabī, *Tārīkh*, 18 (251–260 h.), p. 250; *Siyar*, vol. 12, p. 404.
28. Kalābādhī, *Rijāl*, vol. 1, p. 24
29. Samᶜānī, *al-Ansāb*, s.n. 'Farabrī' = ed. M.A. Ḥallāq, Beirut, 1419/1999, vol. 3, p. 440 (= Samᶜānī, *Ansāb*).
30. Dhahabī, *Tārīkh*, 18 (251–260 h.), p. 250.

Personally, Bukhārī is described as having been thin and of average height.[31] He spoke little, a sign of piety recommended in hadith.[32] A number of stories indicate Bukhārī's devotion to ritual observances. Stinging hornets could not make him curtail his prayer. He recited the Qurʾan daily during Ramaḍān. He renewed his ritual ablutions and prayed two sets of bowings before entering any hadith report into his *Ṣaḥīḥ*. He said that he never touched money, having someone else buy ink and paper for him.[33]

He must have inherited great wealth. There are stories of his penury as a youth, collecting hadith in Basra. But another story, of his taking 5,000 dirhams' profit from reselling goods from a caravan to the first persons who approached him instead of 10,000 from selling them to a second group that appeared the next day, suggests that he was a rich trader.[34] Landed wealth is indicated by the story of his renting a plot to someone for 700 dirhams a year and paying him back 100 a year for supplying him with cucumbers.[35] There is also a story from his copyist that he refused to involve the ruler in hounding a debtor of his. When the ruler acted on his own without any request from Bukhārī, he arranged for the wretch to pay him just ten dirhams a year, even though the debt was for 520,000.[36] The story is told, of course, to establish Bukhārī's clemency, also, once again, his indifference to worldly gain; however, we may notice the implicit size of his personal fortune, allowing him to deal in sums of such magnitude. [431]

The biographical literature does not tell us of any children of Bukhārī's. There is a story from his copyist, though, of his buying a Khazari concubine in Firabr for 500 dirhams more than she was worth. He later took her along to Nishapur.[37] The point of the story is his unwillingness to haggle, also his pious scruple that by touching this one's chin he had committed himself to buying her, even though there were prettier ones available from the same dealer. Again, however, we may notice his casual expenditure of a considerable sum, also the hint that indeed he never married.

---

31. Ibn ʿAdī al-Qaṭṭān, *Kāmil*, vol. 1, p. 227.

32. Abū ʿAlī Ṣāliḥ ibn Muḥammad, apud al-Khaṭīb al-Baghdādī, *Mūḍiḥ awhām al-jamʿ wa-al-tafrīq* (*al-Silsilah al-jadīdah min maṭbūʿāt Dāʾirat al-Maʿārif al-ʿUthmānīyah 14/1*), Hyderabad, 1378/1959, vol. 1, p. 7; cf. Melchert, *Bukhārī*, p. 10.

33. Al-Khaṭīb al-Baghdādī, *TB*, vol. 2, p. 9, 11–13, and *TMS*, vol. 2, p. 327, 330–331.

34. Al-Khaṭīb al-Baghdādī, *TB*, vol. 2, p. 11–12, and *TMS*, vol. 2, p. 330.

35. Dhahabī, *Tārīkh*, 18 (251–260 h.), p. 263, presumably drawing on *Tārīkh Naysābūr*.

36. Dhahabī, *Tārīkh*, 18 (251–260 h.), p. 261, and *Siyar*, vol. 12, p. 446, apparently drawing on M. Ibn Abī Ḥātim, *Shamāʾil al-Bukhārī*.

37. Dhahabī, *Tārīkh*, 18 (251–260 h.), p. 262, and *Siyar*, vol. 12, p. 447, apparently drawing on M. Ibn Abī Ḥātim, *Shamāʾil al-Bukhārī*.

Works of Bukhārī

Our earliest list of the works of Bukhārī is from Ibn al-Nadīm (*fl.* 377/987):[38]

(1) *Kitāb al-Tārīkh al-kabīr*;
(2) *K. al-Tārīkh al-ṣaghīr*;
(3) *K. al-Asmāʾ wa-al-kuná*;
(4) *K. al-Ḍuʿafāʾ*;
(5) *K. al-Ṣaḥīḥ*;
(6) *K. al-Sunan fī al-fiqh*;
(7) *K. al-Adab*;
(8) *K. al-Tārīkh al-awsaṭ*;
(9) *K. Khalq afʿāl al-ʿibād*;
(10) *K. al-Qirāʾah khalfa al-imām*.

With two or three exceptions, these are extant and have been published. No. 1 is first of all an alphabetical list of traditionists, over 12,300 (al-Ḥākim al-Naysābūrī relates an estimate of 40,000, but this appears to be a mistake[39]). Brown suggests that al-Ḥākim's quoted reference to men and women indicates that a section concerning women has been lost in transmission, which is conceivable but so far lacks confirmation from quotations of such a section in other works.[40] One manuscript includes a statement of having been taken down from Bukhārī in Basra, 246/860–861, but the text itself reports persons as dying in the year 252, indicating [432] that someone, possibly Bukhārī himself, later updated it.[41] Many corrigenda proposed by Ibn Abī Ḥātim al-Rāzī (d. 327/938) are accommodated in the extant text, which suggests that it was edited posthumously.[42] No. 2, which apparently treated only Companions, was still available to Ibn Ḥajar in the recension of ʿAbd Allāh ibn Muḥammad ibn ʿAbd al-Raḥmān al-Ashqar.[43] It is no longer extant. No. 8, a chronological collection of notices concerning over 2,000 traditionists, has sometimes

38. Ibn al-Nadīm, *al-Fihrist*, *fann* 6, *maqālah* 6 (= Ibn al-Nadīm, *Fihrist*).

39. Al-Ḥākim al-Naysābūrī, *al-Madkhal ilá al-ṣaḥīḥ*, ed. R.H.ʿU. al-Madkhalī, Beirut, 1404/1984, p. 111. Incautiously repeated by many modern biographers, e.g. Ḥ.ʿA.M. Hāshim, *al-Imām al-Bukhārī*, Cairo, n.d., p. 271 (= Hāshim, *Imām*). The context is a polemic about how Bukhārī distinguished weak from strong traditionists, so that the more persons mentioned in *al-Tārīkh al-kabīr*, the more stringent Bukhārī seems to have been; hence, I suppose, an inclination to exaggerate.

40. Brown, *Canonization*, p. 68fn.

41. Bukhārī, *TK*, 1:3.

42. Melchert, *Bukhārī*, p. 9–10.

43. Ibn Ḥajar, *Hady al-sārī*, ed. ʿA.ʿA.ʿA.A. Bin Bāz, Beirut, 1428–1429/2008, p. 577 (= Ibn Ḥajar, *Hady*). The *Hady* is Ibn Ḥajar's introduction to his commentary on the *Ṣaḥīḥ*, *Fatḥ al-bārī*, of which it is normally published as the first volume. To my knowledge, this particular edition is as textually adequate as others and easily available commercially; however, I do not propose it as a standard edition to be preferred.

been mistaken for it.[44] Different manuscripts go on to different dates—one includes a notice of Bukhārī's own death in 256—, and I have guessed that it left Bukhārī's hands in about 238/852–853.[45]

A short version of no. 4, *al-Ḍuʿafāʾ al-ṣaghīr*, is extant in the recension of Ādam ibn Mūsá al-Khuwārī and has been published. It lists 418 weak traditionists in alphabetical order. A long version, *al-Ḍuʿafāʾ al-kabīr*, is apparently lost except in quotation, as in al-Khaṭīb al-Baghdādī, *Tārīkh Baghdād* from the recension of a Muḥammad ibn Ibrāhīm ibn Shuʿayb al-Ghāzī.[46] Ibn Ḥajar mentions having a *K. al-Ḍuʿafāʾ* as transmitted from Bukhārī by Abū Bishr Muḥammad ibn Aḥmad ibn Ḥammād al-Dawlābī, an Abū Jaʿfar Shaykh ibn Saʿīd, and Ādam ibn Mūsá al-Khuwārī, the last of whom presumably indicates that what he knew was actually *al-Ḍuʿafāʾ al-ṣaghīr*.[47] A statement in the text and quotations in other works suggest that no. 3 is an integral part at the end of no. 1.[48] However, it comes to us in the recension of another than no. 1, from which some have inferred that it deserves to be considered a separate work, an inference strengthened by Ibn al-Nadīm's listing it separately.[49]

Finally, no. 6 is neither extant today nor even identifiable in quotation. However, Bukhārī is quoted as saying, 'When I got to be eighteen, I took to assembling the cases of the Companions and Followers and their opinions.'[50] [433] Bukhārī periodically mentions the legal opinions of various Companions and Followers in the *Ṣaḥīḥ*—most often, al-Ḥasan al-Baṣrī (d. 110/728), then Ibrāhīm al-Nakhaʿī of Kufa (d. 96/714?), then a number of others: the caliph ʿUmar (d. 23/644), Shurayḥ (d. 78/697–698?) and al-Shaʿbī (d. 103/721–722?) of Kufa, Muḥammad ibn Sīrīn of Basra (d. 110/729), Ṭāwūs of Yemen (d. 106/725?), ʿAṭāʾ of Mecca (d. 114/732?), ʿIkrimah (d. 107/725–726?) and al-Zuhrī (d. 125/743?) of Medina, & al. Presumably, no. 6 was made up of such opinions as these.

Just one work is extant that Ibn al-Nadīm does not name:

(11) *Rafʿ al-yadayn fī al-ṣalāh*.

44. V. M.A. ʿUtūw, *Ithbāt anna tārīkh al-imām al-Bukhārī al-maṭbūʿ bi-ism* al-Tārīkh al-ṣaghīr *huwa* al-Tārīkh al-awsaṭ, in *ʿĀlam al-kutub*, 16 (1415–1416/1995), p. 546–551.

45. Melchert, *Bukhārī*, p. 14.

46. V. A.Ḍ. al-ʿUmarī, *Mawārid al-Khaṭīb al-Baghdādī fī* Tārīkh Baghdād, n.p., 1395/1975, p. 319–320.

47. Ibn Ḥajar, *Hady*, p. 577.

48. Bukhārī, *TK*, vol. 8/2, p. 93, and Melchert, *Bukhārī*, p. 9.

49. Umm ʿAbd Allāh, *Fihris muṣannafāt al-imām . . . al-Bukhārī . . . al-manshūrah fīmā ʿadā* al-Ṣaḥīḥ, arr. M.Ḥ. Ibn Saʿd, supv. A.ʿA.A.M.M. al-Ḥaddād, Riyadh, 1408, p. 31.

50. Al-Khaṭīb al-Baghdādī, *TB*, vol. 2, p. 7, and *TMS*, vol. 2, p. 325.

This was known to Ibn Ḥajar as related from Bukhārī by Maḥmūd ibn Isḥāq al-Khuzāʿī.[51] Besides prophetic hadith, a great deal of this, also, is made up of opinions and precedents reported of Companions and Followers, all in favour of raising the hands throughout the course of the ritual prayer and not only at the initial *takbīr*.

In addition to the above works, Ibn Ḥajar ascribes the following to Bukhārī near the end of the introduction to his commentary on the *Ṣaḥīḥ*:

(12) *Birr al-wālidayn*, recension of Muḥammad ibn Dallawayh al-Warrāq;
(13) *al-Jāmiʿ al-kabīr*, named by Ibn Ṭāhir;
(14) *al-Musnad al-kabīr*;
(15) *al-Tafsīr al-kabīr*, mentioned by al-Firabrī;
(16) *K. al-Ashribah*, mentioned by al-Dāraquṭnī, *al-Muʾtalif wa-al-mukhtalif*, s.n. 'Kīsah';
(17) *K. al-Hibah*;
(18) *Asāmī al-ṣaḥābah*, mentioned by Abū al-Qāsim Ibn Mandah, recension of Ibn Fāris, also quoted by al-Bayhaqī in his directory of Companions;
(19) *K. al-Wuḥdān*, on Companions of whom only one hadith report is related;
(20) *K. al-Mabsūṭ*, mentioned by al-Khalīlī, *al-Irshād*, recension of Muhīb ibn Sulaym;
(21) *K. al-ʿIlal*, mentioned by Ibn Mandah, recension of Abū Muḥammad ʿAbd Allāh ibn al-Sharqī;
(22) *K. al-Fawāʾid*, mentioned by al-Tirmidhī in his *Jāmiʿ*, *k. al-manāqib*.

Firabrī's story of no. 15, *al-Tafsīr al-kabīr*, seems likely to refer to the large chapter of the *Ṣaḥīḥ* devoted to qurʾanic commentary. *Asāmī al-ṣaḥābah*, no. 18, seems likely to be another name for *al-Tārīkh al-ṣaghīr*. In vain have I searched Tirmidhī, *al-manāqib* for some mention of no. 22. In any case, it seems likely to have been another name for no. 6. [434] Some of these unpublished titles are mentioned in modern manuscript catalogues, but they too are probably excerpts or alternative names of extant works, especially of the *Ṣaḥīḥ*.[52] The ones that seem to me most likely to have existed as independent works, not merely extant works or parts thereof under different names, are nos. 12, presumably a collection of hadith on filial piety, 16, presumably a collection of hadith on alcoholic drinks, 17, presumably a collection of hadith on the law of gifts, 19, and 21, presumably a collection of hadith with subtle defects.

---

51. Ibn Ḥajar, *Hady*, p. 577. The only edition I have been able to consult is based on a Cairene MS copied from Ibn Ḥajar's own copy: *K. Rafʿ al-yadayn*, Beirut, 1416/1996.

52. For MSS and unpublished works, *v. GAS*, vol. 1, p. 115–134 and N.ʿA.R. Khalaf, *Istidrākāt ʿalá tārīkh al-turāth al-ʿarabī li-Fuʾād Sizkīn fī ʿilm al-ḥadīth* (*Maktabat Niẓām Yaʿqūbī al-khāṣṣah-Baḥrayn, Dirāsāt wa-buḥūth*, 1), Beirut, 1421/2000, p. 135–264.

The Ṣaḥīḥ

Bukhārī's fame rests chiefly on the *Ṣaḥīḥ*, a collection of hadith, mostly (over 90 percent) going back to the Prophet. Its proper title is *al-Jāmiᶜ al-musnad al-ṣaḥīḥ al-mukhtaṣar*, meaning roughly 'the comprehensive, fully supported, sound epitome.'[53] It is *comprehensive* in comprising hadith on all topics, *fully supported* in providing *asānīd* for nearly all its hadith, *sound* inasmuch as hadith criticism vouches that every item goes back to the putative speaker, and an *epitome* perhaps inasmuch as it presents only a selection of sound hadith; alternatively, inasmuch as its contents are arranged topically (putting it in competition, to some extent, with contemporary *mukhtaṣars* from the nascent schools of law[54]). It is commonly referred to as '*al-Ṣaḥīḥ*' for short, and it is significant that Ibn al-Nadīm so refers to it, when it was just becoming recognized as the pre-eminent collection of hadith.

Different students have counted its hadith reports differently. The chief difficulty is how to count alternative *asānīd*. Sometimes, for example, Bukhārī presents the beginning of an *isnād*, then the letter *ḥāᵓ* (presumably an abbreviation, but whether for *ḥadīth*, *taḥwīl*, or *isnād ākhar* is uncertain), then an alternative *isnād* to the same point (e.g. 1912, with alternative *isnād* from the Follower level down). Less often, he presents an alternative *isnād* without any *ḥāᵓ* (e.g. 1919). Occasionally, he presents alternative *asānīd* in full (e.g. four in a row at 2051). Very often, he presents alternative *asānīd* under different topic headings. [435] Twenty-two hadith reports are said to be repeated under different topic headings with exactly the same *isnād* and wording.[55] Ibn Ḥajar's estimates in the introduction to his commentary may be cited to indicate orders of magnitude: 7,275 hadith reports with full *isnād*, 2,602 excluding repeats, with a further 1,341 mentioned with incomplete *asānīd* for the purpose of corroboration (*taᶜālīq*).[56] This makes it the second longest of the Six Books, after Muslim's, with 11–12,000 hadith reports. Excluding repeats, on the other hand, makes it one of the shortest, about half as long as the book of Abū Dāwūd, roughly two-thirds as long as those of Tirmidhī, Ibn Mājah, and Muslim, and only a little longer than Nasāᵓī's (and then only if we suppose that Nasāᵓī's entrant among the Six is *al-Mujtabá*, not, as al-Mizzī and other traditionists of the Mamluk period supposed, *al-Sunan al-kubrá*).

Since Ibn Ḥajar's is the most important commentary on the *Ṣaḥīḥ* and Muḥammad Fuᵓād ᶜAbd al-Bāqī strove to make his editions compatible with Wensinck's *Concordance*, his numbering of hadith in the *Fatḥ* (followed also now in many editions of the *Ṣaḥīḥ* by

53. ᶜA.F. Abū Ghuddah, *Taḥqīq ismay al-ṣaḥīḥayn wa-ism* Jāmiᶜ *al-Tirmidhī*, Aleppo, 1414/1993.

54. On which v. J.E. Brockopp, *Early Islamic Jurisprudence in Egypt: Two Scholars and Their* Mukhtaṣars, in *International Journal of Middle East Studies*, 30 (1998), p. 167–182.

55. ᶜA.Ḥ.ᶜA.W. al-Hāshimī, *ᶜĀdāt al-imām al-Bukhārī fī ṣaḥīḥih*, ed. M.N. al-ᶜAjamī, Beirut, 1428/2007, p. 56–61.

56. Ibn Ḥajar, *Hady*, p. 562.

itself) is preferable for scholarly citation;[57] however, so many commercial editions of the *Ṣaḥīḥ* are available, it is best also to name the *kitāb* and *bāb*, or at least the *kitāb* and the number of the *bāb* according to Wensinck's usage (indicated in Arabic as the numbering of *al-Muʿjam*). As electronic searching becomes usual, it may become best to quote the beginning of a cited hadith report (its *ṭaraf*) in Arabic.

Bukhārī's usual style of repetition under different headings differs from, for example, Muslim's usual style in his *Ṣaḥīḥ*, which is to report variants one after another, not widely separated. Take the Prophet's command, 'Whoever believes in God and the Last Day, let him not injure his neighbour. Whoever believes in God and the Last Day, let him honour his guest. Whoever believes in God and the Last Day, let him say good or be silent.' This appears in *k. al-adab*, 'the book of etiquette,' *bāb man kāna yuʾminu bi-Allāh wa-al-yawm al-ākhir fa-lā yuʾdhi jārah*, 'section: whoever believes in God and the Last Day, let him not injure his neighbour' (no. 6018), with the *isnād* < Qutaybah ibn Saʿīd < Abū al-Aḥwaṣ < Abū Ḥuṣayn < Abū Ṣāliḥ < Abū Hurayrah. It is immediately followed by a variant with a completely different *isnād*: < ʿAbd Allāh ibn Yūsuf < al-Layth < Saʿīd al-Maqburī < Abū Shurayḥ al-ʿAdawī: 'My ears [436] heard and my eyes saw when the Prophet spoke, saying, "Whoever believes in God and the Last Day, let him honour his neighbour. Whoever believes in God and the Last Day, let him honour his guest and his *jāʾizah*." He was asked, "What is his *jāʾizah*, O Messenger of God?" He said, "A day and a night. Hospitality is for three days. What is beyond that is alms for him. Whoever believes in God and the Last Day, let him say good or be silent"' (no. 6019). Later in *k. al-adab*, in *bāb ikrām al-ḍayf*, 'section: honouring one's guest,' the second reappears with a slightly different *isnād* and more different wording: < ʿAbd Allāh ibn Yūsuf < Mālik < Abū Saʿīd al-Maqburī < Abū Shurayḥ al-Kaʿbī < the Messenger of God: 'Whoever believes in God and the Last Day, let him honour his guest and his *jāʾizah*, a day and a night. Hospitality is for three days. What is beyond that is alms. It is not permitted to him to stay with him until he puts him out' (no. 6135). Bukhārī then mentions a second variant: 'Ismāʿīl related to us that Mālik related to him the like of this, then added, "Whoever believes in God and the Last Day, let him say what is good or be silent."' Then come the very first words here mentioned with a variant *isnād*: < ʿAbd Allāh ibn Muḥammad < Ibn Mahdī < Sufyān < Abū Ḥuṣayn < Abū Ṣāliḥ < Abū Hurayrah < the Prophet (no. 6136). Abū Hurayrah's report appropriately goes first in the section stressing the neighbour, Abū Shurayḥ's in the section stressing the guest. The other versions are there mainly to show that we have corroborative testimony that the Prophet said something to this effect, even if we cannot be sure of his exact words. Still other versions of Abū Hurayrah's and Abū Shurayḥ's reports, slightly different in both *isnād* and wording, appear together a third time in *k. al-riqāq*, roughly 'sayings to soften the heart,' *bāb ḥifẓ al-lisān*, 'section: minding one's tongue' (nos. 6475–6476).

57. Ibn Ḥajar, *Fatḥ al-bārī*, ed. M.D. al-Khaṭīb, Cairo, 1380/1960.

We lack any theoretical statement from Bukhārī, but the *Ṣaḥīḥ* and *al-Tārīkh al-kabīr* indicate fairly strongly that he relied mainly on comparison of different versions to identify sound hadith. Comparison is the main reason for repeating so many hadith reports with variant *asānīd* under different topic headings. The anomaly, the version that disagreed with the rest as to either *isnād* or *matn*, would be discarded. Contrary to numerous modern descriptions of hadith criticism, biographical data were fairly unimportant.[58] *Al-Tārīkh al-kabīr* is primarily useful for [437] identifying men by their names. About three-quarters of the names are provided with lists of those to and from whom they transmitted hadith, also useful in identifying names in *asānīd*. But it seldom offers express evaluations of sample hadith, very seldom of transmitters' overall trustworthiness. Likewise, it seldom mentions when someone was born and died. In short, it bespeaks a reliance on hadith criticism by means of comparing *asānīd*, not by means of character assessment or chronological overlap.

As early as the first extant commentary on the *Ṣaḥīḥ*, from al-Khaṭṭābī (d. 388/998?), students of hadith referred to 'Bukhārī's criterion' (*sharṭ al-Bukhārī*), but repeated attempts to define it have been inconclusive.[59] One early attempt to define it was noticeably unsuccessful: that, as two witnesses establish a fact in law, a hadith report meets Bukhārī's criterion if it is transmitted by two at every level.[60] A very common description in the modern secondary literature has been that Bukhārī would accept a link only if the later transmitter was known to have directly heard from the earlier, not merely that the later transmitter was active in a time and place such that he may have heard directly from the earlier.[61] The usual evidence for someone's having directly heard from someone else was the use of express terms such as *ḥaddathanī* ('he related to me') and *akhbaranī* ('he informed me') as opposed to ambiguous terms such as *qāla* ('he said') and *ʿan* ('from'). It is going too far to say that 'Bukhārī did not . . . attach precise meanings to the various terms for transmission of hadith.'[62] It is widely acknowledged that Bukhārī did not distinguish between *ḥaddathanī* and *akhbaranī*, as many contemporaries did.[63] Occasionally, however, it is plain that Bukhārī was interested in the terminology of transmission. For example, no. 2440 in the *Ṣaḥīḥ* (*k. al-maẓālim* 1, *bāb qiṣāṣ al-maẓālim*) includes the link Qatādah *ʿan* Abū al-Mutawakkil, followed by Yūnus ibn Muḥammad *ḥaddathanā* Shaʿbān *ʿan* Qatādah

58. *V.* E. Dickinson, *The Development of Early Sunnite* Ḥadīth *Criticism* (*Islamic History and Civilization, Studies and Texts*, 38), Leiden, 2001, chap. 6 (= Dickinson, *Development*), for a general description. Abdul-Jabbar, *Bukhari*, chap. 5, is superior to most other modern treatments of Bukhārī's particular practice; *v.* also A.B. al-Kāfī, *Manhaj al-imām al-Bukhārī*, Beirut, 1421/2000 (= Kāfī, *Manhaj*).

59. *V.* Brown, *Canonization*, Hāshim, *Imām*, chap. 3, and Kāfī, *Manhaj*.

60. So apparently al-Ḥākim al-Naysābūrī, on which *v.* Melchert, *Bukhārī*, p. 11, and Brown, *Canonization*, p. 166–168.

61. So even Goldziher, *Muslim Studies*, 2:228–229.

62. Melchert, *Bukhārī*, p. 11.

63. e.g. Hāshim, *Imām*, p. 122–123.

ḥaddathanā Abū al-Mutawakkil. The point of mentioning the second *isnād* is evidently to show that Qatādah did transmit directly from Abū al-Mutawakkil. Similarly, after no. 2481 (*k. al-maẓālim* 34, *bāb idhā kasara qaṣʿah*), we are told, 'Ibn Abī Maryam said (*qāla*) that Yaḥyá ibn Ayyūb informed us (*akhbaranī*) that Ḥumayd related to us (*ḥaddathanā*) that Anas related to us (*ḥaddathanā*) [438] on the authority of (*ʿan*) the Prophet,' all parallel to the previous hadith report with *ʿan* instead of these terms denoting direct audition. This is actually one of seven instances of this *isnād*, with slight variants, all apparently corroborative of the hadith report just mentioned.[64] We have his express statement after no. 3141 (*k. farḍ al-khums* 18, *bāb man lam yukhammis al-aslāb*): 'Muḥammad (i.e. Bukhārī himself) said, "Yūsuf heard from Ṣāliḥ and Ibrāhīm heard from Abū ʿAbd al-Raḥmān ibn ʿAwf",' assuring us about two links in the previous hadith report covered by *ʿan*.

Still, it can easily be shown that Bukhārī does not always confirm somewhere that one of his transmitters heard directly from another. Mohammad Fadel, for example, is demonstrably right when he says, 'Another reason leading to the repetition of *ḥadīth* texts is that al-Bukhārī wished to establish that a meeting had taken place between two transmitters who had appeared in an earlier text cited with *ʿanʿana*' (*ʿanʿana* meaning an *isnād*'s having only *ʿan* between one or more names and another). But he is not demonstrably right to add in a note, 'Al-Bukhārī would not accept transmissions of the *ʿanʿana* variety until he had established that the two transmitters had met and were not just contemporaries.'[65] For example, here is a summary of transmitters from al-Ḥasan al-Baṣrī in *asānīd* of any length in the *Ṣaḥīḥ*:

Ibrāhīm ibn Nāfiʿ 1 hadith report (= h.r.), *ʿan* al-Ḥasan. *Al-Tārīkh al-kabīr* (vol. 1: p. 332–323) does not mention his transmission from al-Ḥasan.

Ashʿath (ibn ʿAbd al-Malik) 1 h.r., *ʿan*. *Al-Tārīkh al-kabīr* (vol. 1: p. 431) *samiʿa*.

Abū al-Ashhab (Jaʿfar ibn Ḥayyān) 1 h.r., *ʿan*. *Al-Tārīkh al-kabīr* (vol. 2: p. 189) does not mention al-Ḥasan.

Al-Aʿlam Ziyād (ibn Ḥayyān) 1 h.r., *ʿan*. *Al-Tārīkh al-kabīr* (vol. 2: p. 189) does not mention al-Ḥasan.

Ayyūb (ibn Abī Tamīmah al-Sakhtiyānī) 1 h.r., *ʿan*. *Al-Tārīkh al-kabīr* (vol. 1: p. 409–410) does not mention al-Ḥasan.

Jarīr ibn Ḥāzim, 8 h.r's, 3 *samiʿtu*, 3 *ʿan*, 2 *ḥaddathanī*. *Al-Tārīkh al-kabīr* (vol. 2: p. 213) does not mention al-Ḥasan.

64. *K. al-wuḍūʾ* 70, *bāb al-buzāq wa-al-mukhāṭ*, no. 241; *k. al-ṣalāh* 32, *bāb mā jāʾa fī al-qiblah*, no. 402; *k. mawāqīt al-ṣalāh* 25, *bāb waqt al-ʿishāʾ ilá niṣf al-layl*, no. 572; *k. al-adhān* 33, *bāb iḥtisāb al-āthār*, no. 656; *k. al-maẓālim* 34, *bāb idhā kasara qaṣʿah*, no. 2481; *k. al-tafsīr* 9, *bāb wa-ittakhadhū min maqām Ibrāhīm*, no. 4483; *k. al-libās* 48, *bāb faṣṣ al-khātam*, no. 5869.

65. M. Fadel, *Ibn Ḥajar's* Hady al-sārī, in *Journal of Near Eastern Studies*, 54 (1995), p. 161–197, at p. 165 (= Fadel, *Ibn Ḥajar's* Hady).

Ḥabīb ibn al-Shahīd one story implying direct audition. *Al-Tārīkh al-kabīr* (vol. 2: p. 320) *samiʿa*.

Ḥazm (ibn Abī Ḥazm) 1 h.r., *ʿan*. *Al-Tārīkh al-kabīr* (vol. 3, p. 111) *samiʿa*. [439]

Ibn Shubrumah (ʿAbd Allāh) 1 h.r., *ḥaddathanā*. *Al-Tārīkh al-kabīr* (vol. 5: p. 117) does not mention al-Ḥasan.

ʿAbbād ibn Rāshid 1 h.r., *ḥaddathanī*. *Al-Tārīkh al-kabīr* (vol. 6: p. 36) *ʿan*.

ʿAbd al-Wāḥid (ibn Ziyād) 1 h.r., *ḥaddathanī*. *Al-Tārīkh al-kabīr* (vol. 6: p. 59) does not mention al-Ḥasan.

ʿAwf (ibn Abī Jamīlah) 7 h.r's, all *ʿan*. *Al-Tārīkh al-kabīr* (vol. 7: p. 58) does not mention al-Ḥasan.

Ibn ʿAwn (ʿAbd Allāh) 1 h.r., *ʿan*. *Al-Tārīkh al-kabīr* (vol. 5: p. 163) *samiʿa*.

Qatādah (ibn Diʿāmah) 3 h.r's, *ʿan*, *akhbaranā*, and *ḥaddathanā*. *Al-Tārīkh al-kabīr* (vol. 7: p. 186) tells a story of direct audition.

Qurrah ibn Khālid story implying direct audition. *Al-Tārīkh al-kabīr* (vol. 7: p. 183) *samiʿa*.

Mubārak (ibn Faḍālah) 1 h.r., *ʿan*. *Al-Tārīkh al-kabīr* (vol. 7: p. 426) *samiʿa*.

Maʿbad ibn Hilāl al-ʿAnazī story implying direct audition. *Al-Tārīkh al-kabīr* (vol. 7: p. 400) does not mention al-Ḥasan.

Muʿallá ibn Ziyād 1 h.r., *ʿan*. *Al-Tārīkh al-kabīr* (vol. 7: p. 394) *ʿan*.

Abū Mūsá (Isrāʾīl ibn Mūsá) 2 h.r's, *ʿan*. *Al-Tārīkh al-kabīr* (vol. 2: p. 56) mentions al-Ḥasan without specifying whether Abū Mūsá heard from him directly.

Hishām (ibn Ḥassān) 1 h.r., *ʿan*. No entry in *al-Tārīkh al-kabīr*.

Yaḥyá ibn ʿAtīq 1 h.r., *ʿan*. *Al-Tārīkh al-kabīr* (vol. 8: p. 295) does not mention al-Ḥasan.

Yūnus (ibn ʿUbayd) 11 h.r's, all *ʿan*. *Al-Tārīkh al-kabīr* (vol. 8: p. 402) *samiʿa*.

Anonymous 1 h.r., *ʿan*.

The total number of hadith reports is 49 (somewhat smaller than the number of his reported legal opinions), including parallel *asānīd*. The total number of different transmitters from al-Ḥasan is 23, for only seven of whom is direct audition documented in the *Ṣaḥīḥ*, with direct audition reported of four others in *al-Tārīkh al-kabīr*. Bukhārī may have known other hadith with *ḥaddathanī* between the twelve remaining men's names and al-Ḥasan's among the hundred thousand sound hadith reports he did not include in the *Ṣaḥīḥ*. That would presumably be the basis for his stating directly in *al-Tārīkh al-kabīr* that someone heard from (*samiʿa*) al-Ḥasan, even though he has only versions with *ʿan* in the *Ṣaḥīḥ*.

Altogether, though, when direct audition is reported in neither the *Ṣaḥīḥ* nor *al-Tārīkh al-kabīr* for a majority of those who related hadith of al-Ḥasan, it seems impossible for this version of Bukhārī's criterion to be inferrable either from the *Ṣaḥīḥ* or the *Ṣaḥīḥ* together with *al-Tārīkh al-kabīr*. (And if both the *Ṣaḥīḥ* and *al-Tārīkh al-kabīr* maintain a careful distinction between *samiʿa* and *ʿan*, how to account for *ʿan* in [440] *al-Tārīkh al-kabīr* for ʿAbbād ibn Rāshid < al-Ḥasan where the *Ṣaḥīḥ* has *ḥaddathanī*?) Invocation of this supposed criterion depends on the uncompelling assumption that, if a dozen versions of how some traditionist transmitted from another have *ʿan* between them, one of them *ḥaddathanī*, it would have been accurate to have said *ḥaddathanī* in the first dozen cases instead of *ʿan*, never that the one discrepant version represents *ḥaddathanī* carelessly substituted for *ʿan*.[66] This is not to argue that *ʿan* is a reliable sign of inaccurate transmission. Rather, I propose that evidence of direct audition is a condition too stringent for the evidence that collectors like Bukhārī had at hand. Expecting evidence of direct audition is like the Muʿtazili demand for twenty or more transmitters at every level before any hadith report should be considered acceptable.[67] Bukhārī evidently preferred reports based on direct audition and pointed out evidence of it when he could but did not exclude reports not demonstrably based on direct audition. He durst not exclude them if the law was to be based primarily on hadith.

Often, Bukhārī himself can be shown to have been fairly careless. For example, a leading authority in the *Ṣaḥīḥ* is Abū al-Yamānī of Homs (d. 222/837?), of whom Bukhārī relates 257 hadith reports, all in turn from Shuʿayb ibn Abī Ḥamzah, also of Homs (d. 162/778–779?). Abū al-Yamānī is widely reported to have heard very little of Shuʿayb (Abū Dāwūd said 'one word'), rather made posthumous use of his notebooks.[68] In *al-Tārīkh al-kabīr*, Bukhārī reports complacently that Abū al-Yamānī heard from (*samiʿa*) Shuʿayb.[69] Another sort of carelessness is evident to anyone who sets out to list Bukhārī's shaykhs, whom he often names ambiguously. For example, no. 4243 (*k. al-maghāzī* 39, *bāb ghazwat Khaybar*) starts with 'there related to me al-Ḥasan.' Kalābādhī thought this was al-Ḥasan al-Zaʿfarānī, al-Ḥākim al-Naysābūrī that this was al-Ḥasan ibn Shujāʿ, with a third possibility proposed by other commentators.[70] No. 2809 (*k. al-jihād wa-al-siyar* 14, *bāb man atāhu sahm*) is related from Muḥammad ibn ʿAbd Allāh. Kalābādhī says this certainly means Muḥammad ibn Yaḥyá ibn ʿAbd Allāh al-Dhuhlī. Altogether, some thirty hadith reports in the *Ṣaḥīḥ* have been identified as coming [441] from Dhuhlī, although Bukhārī never expressly names Dhuhlī, presumably because his persecution of Bukhārī made acknowledgement distasteful to him. This particular identification seems to be confirmed by Ibn Khuzaymah, *al-Tawḥīd*, where the same hadith report is expressly related from Dhuhlī. However, the recension of Abū ʿAlī ibn al-Sakan expressly identifies this as Muḥammad ibn ʿAbd Allāh ibn al-Mubārak al-Mukharramī.[71] It seems likely that Ibn al-Sakan's fuller

66. As one recent commentator has said, 'If hearing is expressly asserted in one *isnād*, *ʿan* is taken to indicate the same in all': Hāshim, *Imām*, p. 91.

67. Muʿtazili criteria are often reviewed in the literature of *uṣūl al-fiqh*; e.g. Abū Isḥāq al-Shīrāzī, *Kitāb al-Lumaʿ* (*Studies in Comparative Legal History*), trans. E. Chaumont, Berkeley, 1999, p. 192–193.

68. V. Ibn Ḥajar, *Tahdhīb*, vol. 2, p. 441–443 for a summary.

69. Bukhārī, *TK*, vol. 2, p. 344.

70. Ibn Ḥajar, *Fatḥ al-bārī*, ed. ʿA.ʿA.ʿA.A. Bin Bāz, Beirut, 1428–1429/2008, vol. 8, p. 214–215 (= Ibn Ḥajar, *Fatḥ*).

71. Ibn Ḥajar, *Fatḥ*, vol. 6, p. 82.

form of the name is his own gloss, which (with many parallels) raises the question of how many other clear identifications have come not from Bukhārī himself but from later redactors' speculative expansion.

Ibn Ḥajar advances as one reason for preferring Bukhārī's *Ṣaḥīḥ* to Muslim's that eighty men in the former, 160 in the latter were ever disparaged as weak traditionists. He goes on to say that Bukhārī never relied heavily on any of these eighty, besides.[72] But one of the shaykhs he relied on most heavily, Ismāᶜīl ibn Abī Uways of Medina (d. 227/842?), source of 207 hadith reports by Sezgin's count, is roundly disparaged: 'weak-minded,' 'stole hadith,' 'a great liar,' and so on.[73] Ibn Ḥajar concludes his biography by saying 'It is not to be thought that the two shaykhs (i.e. Bukhārī and Muslim) brought out from him anything but what was sound of his hadith, which he shared with the trustworthy.'[74] Having pronounced Bukhārī's book the next soundest after the Qurᵓan, Ibn Ḥajar could hardly have said otherwise of Bukhārī's dependence on Ibn Abī Uways; however, it seems plain here that Bukhārī's impeccability had become dogma, impossible to falsify.

Although it appears that Bukhārī's assessments of traditionists were the product of his criticism, not its starting point, his assessments were highly respected by some others. The earliest to quote him frequently is al-Tirmidhī (d. 279/892). Over three-quarters of all items in his *K. al-ᶜIlal al-kabīr* involve quotations of Bukhārī. He also quotes him frequently in his *Jāmiᶜ*, usually commenting on particular hadith reports. Ibn Abī Ḥātim (d. 327/938) does not quote him in his massive *K. al-Jarḥ wa-al-taᶜdīl*, preferring the testimony of his father Abū Ḥātim, Abū Zurᶜah al-Rāzī, Aḥmad ibn Ḥanbal, and Yaḥyá ibn Maᶜīn. However, Bukhārī and Yaḥyá ibn Maᶜīn are the critics most often quoted by Ibn ᶜAdī al-Qaṭṭān in his fairly massive *al-Kāmil fī ḍuᶜafāᵓ al-rijāl*, followed by Nasāᵓī, Aḥmad, and al-Saᶜdī, the last one otherwise obscure.[75] [442]

In *al-Tārīkh al-kabīr*, Bukhārī quotes other critics from time to time. Most often, he offers his own evaluation of the trustworthiness of some traditionist or some hadith report he transmitted. Next most often, Bukhārī quotes Aḥmad ibn Ḥanbal, then Yaḥyá ibn Saᶜīd al-Qaṭṭān (d. 198/813). But he does not quote such evaluations often; for example, none of the 21 biographies cited above of transmitters from al-Ḥasan includes an earlier critic's evaluation.

Bukhārī is quoted as saying that he made up his *Ṣaḥīḥ* over a period of sixteen years out of more than 600,000 hadith reports.[76] He would not have thought that the other

72. Ibn Ḥajar, *Hady*, p. 11.

73. Summary in Ibn Ḥajar, *Tahdhīb*, vol. 1, p. 310–312.

74. Ibn Ḥajar, *Tahdhīb*, vol. 1, p. 312.

75. Most likely Abū ᶜAbd Allāh Muḥammad ibn Isḥāq ibn Saᶜīd ibn Ismāᶜīl al-Saᶜdī al-Harawī, whose book *al-Ṣanāᶜ min al-fuqahāᵓ wa-al-muḥaddithīn* was seen by Samᶜānī in Bukhara. Samᶜānī gives no date, but the list of his shaykhs suggests that Saᶜdī was born in the earlier 240s/later 850s: Samᶜānī, *Ansāb*, vol. 3, p. 35.

76. Al-Khaṭīb al-Baghdādī, *TB*, vol. 2, p. 8–9, 14, and *TMS*, vol. 2, p. 327, 333.

593,000 were unsound; rather, he omitted many sound hadith reports to keep the work to a reasonable length (so he is quoted by Ibn ʿAdī), and most of the 600,000 would have been non-prophetic reports, besides.[77] At that, *600,000* appears to be a conventional number for 'the whole of a large number.'[78] He is also quoted as saying that he knew by heart 100,000 sound hadith reports and 200,000 unsound, which presumably gives a better idea of the expected ratio of sound to unsound that a careful collector would pick up.[79] (Compare the reported estimate of the major Basran traditionist Shuʿbah [d. 160/776]: 'I have looked into it and found that not a third of it is sound.'[80]) The biographical literature offers many such quotations regarding his scholarship, often contradictory. Many harmonizations have been attempted; for example, al-Nawawī reconciles stories that Bukhārī composed his *Ṣaḥīḥ* in each of Bukhara, Mecca, and Basra by proposing that he worked on it in all three.[81] On the whole, contradictions seem to indicate that it is safer to rely on inferences from the works themselves. Among other reports in the biographical literature that I would disbelieve are that he composed the *Ṣaḥīḥ* in Medina, that he composed it at the instigation of someone in Isḥāq ibn Rāhawayh's circle, and that he secured approving reviews of it from Yaḥyá ibn Maʿīn, ʿAlī ibn al-Madīnī, and Aḥmad ibn Ḥanbal.[82] Also dubious, although less plainly contradicted by literature of the [443] ninth and earlier tenth centuries, are reports that he drew crowds of thousands in Basra, tens of thousands in Baghdad.[83] These fit his fame in the late tenth century, not earlier.

To be honest, the presumptive unreliability of the biographical literature must extend to the stated numbers of hadith reports that Bukhārī knew. G.H.A. Juynboll has referred to such figures as 'grotesque exaggerations if not downright fictitious.'[84] Juynboll thinks that later collections of false hadith (*mawḍūʿāt*) must have been much larger had Bukhārī and other collectors actually known so many more hadith reports than they entered into their collections. It is hard to believe that a *Ṣaḥīḥ* of (at the widest possible estimate) 9,000 hadith reports was actually distilled from 600,000 or even 100,000. Juynboll has proposed that 'Tradition collectors in early Islam may be visualized as always presenting virtually everything they had amassed on a certain legal or moral issue, provided, these . . . met their personal standards.'[85] Otherwise, he thinks, they ought to have

77. Ibn ʿAdī al-Qaṭṭān, *Kāmil*, vol. 1, p. 226.

78. A. Silverstein, *Islamic History* (*Very Short Introductions*), Oxford, 2010, p. 88.

79. Ibn ʿAdī al-Qaṭṭān, *Kāmil*, 1:226; al-Khaṭīb al-Baghdādī, *TB*, vol. 2, p. 25, and *TMS*, vol. 2, p. 346.

80. Apud Abū al-Qāsim al-Balkhī, *Qabūl al-akhbār wa-maʿrifat al-rijāl*, ed. A.ʿA.Ḥ.ʿU. ʿAbd al-Raḥīm, Beirut, 1421/2000, vol. 1, p. 21.

81. Al-Nawawī, *Tahdhīb al-asmāʾ wa-al-lughāt*, Cairo, 1927, repr. Beirut, n.d., vol. 1, p. 74.

82. Al-Khaṭīb al-Baghdādī, *TB*, vol. 2, p. 8–9, and *TMS*, vol. 2, p. 326–237; Ibn Ḥajar, *Hady*, p. 575.

83. Al-Khaṭīb al-Baghdādī, *TB*, vol. 2, p. 15, 20, and *TMS*, vol. 2, p. 334–335, 340.

84. G.H.A. Juynboll, *Some* isnād-*Analytical Methods*, in *al-Qanṭara*, 10 (1989), p. 343–383, at p. 375 (= Juynboll, *Some* isnād-*Analytical Methods*).

85. Ibid., p. 374.

been more successful at eliminating contradictory hadith. As so often in hadith studies, a great deal depends on the individual scholar's feel for what is going on. (Regarding the longstanding, unresolved debate over the authenticity of prophetic hadith, Herbert Berg has notably stressed the importance of initial assumptions, a point largely conceded also by Harald Motzki.[86] I would say the same of, for example, more and less stringent *rijāl* criticism in the Middle Ages. If one critic says *ṣadūq* and another *thiqah*, that is a more likely a matter of how they separately felt about the evidence than of their looking at substantially different bodies of evidence.)

If it is conceded that estimates in the biographies of Bukhārī's knowledge are unreliable, can anything better be substituted for them? Kalābādhī counts altogether 1,525 persons who appear in *asānīd* in the *Ṣaḥīḥ*. This means at most about six hadith reports per person in that collection. If we assume the same number of hadith reports per person, *al-Tārīkh al-kabīr* with some 12,300 names suggests knowledge of 73,800 hadith reports. Of course, this is likely to be an overly generous assumption: many more of the persons named in *al-Tārīkh al-kabīr* than those named in the *Ṣaḥīḥ* are likely to have been unknowns who appeared in only one [444] or two hadith reports known to Bukhārī. Moreover, some of the 12,300 probably appeared only in *asānīd* for non-Prophetic hadith. Still, this should be a considerably more plausible high estimate of how many prophetic hadith reports Bukhārī knew than the 600,000 reported in *Tārīkh Baghdād*. My best guess would be that (1) Aḥmad's *Musnad*, comprising somewhat fewer than 26,500 prophetic hadith reports from him (the extant text also includes about 1,300 hadith reports from his son ʿAbd Allāh, actual compiler of the *Musnad*), includes most of what he knew and (2) the extent of Bukhārī's knowledge was similar to Aḥmad's. Aḥmad presumably knew somewhat more non-Prophetic hadith reports going back only to Companions, Followers, and other early Muslims, perhaps likewise Bukhārī.

Besides quoting his comments here and there in his *Jāmiʿ*, Tirmidhī quotes 39 hadith reports with full *isnād* from Bukhārī. Not a single one of them is in the *Ṣaḥīḥ*, although there are five in *al-Tārīkh al-kabīr*, three in *al-Adab*, and one in *Khalq afʿāl al-ʿibād*. Once, he says, 'I asked Muḥammad about this, but he offered no judgement. It was as if he thought that the hadith report of Zuhayr < Abū Isḥāq < ʿAbd al-Raḥmān ibn al-Aswad < his father < ʿAbd Allāh was more likely. He put it in his *Jāmiʿ*.'[87] A related hadith report with this *isnād* is indeed found in Bukhārī's *Ṣaḥīḥ* (*k. al-wuḍūʾ* 21, *bāb lā yustanjá bi-rawth*, no. 156). There can be little doubt that Tirmidhī actually heard Bukhārī, but one may doubt strongly that the *Ṣaḥīḥ* had yet been assembled and made available at that time. On the other hand, it has been observed that Muslim's *Ṣaḥīḥ* avoids duplication of Bukhārī's to an uncanny degree. The tradition makes out that Muslim worked on the basis of Bukhārī's *Ṣaḥīḥ*, which

86. H. Berg, *The Development of Exegesis in Early Islam* (*Curzon Studies in the Qurʾān*), Richmond, Surrey, 2000, chap. 2; H. Motzki, *Dating Muslim Traditions*, in *Arabica*, 52 (2005), p. 204–253.

87. Tirmidhī, *al-Jāmiʿ al-ṣaḥīḥ*, *al-ṭahārah* 13, *bāb al-istinjāʾ bi-al-ḥajarayn*, no. 17.

seems possible. Al-Dāraquṭnī even characterizes Muslim's *Ṣaḥīḥ* as a *mustakhraj*—a collection of Bukhārī's texts with alternative *asānīd*—with additions.[88] Muslim and Bukhārī were together in Nishapur near the end of Bukharī's life.

Quotations and internal evidence together suggest that *al-Tārīkh al-kabīr* and *al-Awsaṭ* are securely attributed to Bukhārī but underwent amendment both by him and others, mostly over the middle third of the ninth century.[89] The *Ṣaḥīḥ* is a little less securely attributed. First, there is the evidence that it did not begin to circulate significantly until well into the tenth century. Tirmidhī's evidently limited access to it has been mentioned already. No commentary appeared until the mid-tenth [445] century, although commentaries on Muslim's *Ṣaḥīḥ* began to appear in the first generation after him.[90] Five men are named as transmitting it from Bukhārī, only two of whose recensions are preserved at all in the extant commentaries, mainly those of Ibrāhīm ibn Maʿqil al-Nasafī (d. 295/908?) and Muḥammad ibn Yūsuf ibn Maṭar al-Firabrī or Farabrī (d. 320/932).[91] Firabrī's reported boast that 'Ninety-thousand men heard *Kitāb al-Ṣaḥīḥ* of Muḥammad ibn Ismāʿīl, but I am the only one left to relate it' is not credible.[92] Presumably, Bukhārī's difficulties with persecuting traditionalists interfered with wider publication in his lifetime and for the half-century afterwards.

Secondly, there is evidence of textual instability into the tenth century. As for literary evidence, one transmitter from Firabrī, Abū Isḥāq Ibrāhīm ibn Aḥmad al-Mustamlī (d. 376/986–987), who heard the *Ṣaḥīḥ* from Firabrī in 314/926–927, is quoted as saying, 'I copied Bukhārī's book from the original copy of it in the possession of Muḥammad ibn Yūsuf al-Firabrī. I saw in it things that were incomplete and things with blank spaces. Among them were topic headings with nothing after them and hadith without topic headings. We therefore joined one thing to another.' Al-Bājī, having related this, continues,[93]

> What confirms this statement is that the recensions of Abū Isḥāq al-Mustamlī, Abū Muḥammad al-Sarakhsī, Abū al-Haytham al-Kushmayhanī, and Abū Zayd al-Marwazī differ as to sequence even though they were all copied from one original. That happened inasmuch as each one estimated where to place something from the margin (*ṭurrah*) or a scrap of paper (*ruqʿah*). This will become clear to you when you see two or more topic headings next to one another with no intervening hadith.

88. Abū Aḥmad al-Naysābūrī and al-Dāraquṭnī apud Ibn Ḥajar, *Hady*, p. 11, 575.

89. Melchert, *Bukhārī*, p. 9–10, 13–14.

90. On the commentary literature, *v.* now ʿA.A.M. al-Ḥabashī, *Jāmiʿ al-shurūḥ wa-al-ḥawāshī*, Abu Dhabi, 1425/2004, 1:396–438, 3:1672–1695, also M.D. ʿAṭīyah, *et al.*, *Dalīl muʾallafāt al-ḥadīth*, Beirut, 1416/1995, esp. vol. 1, p. 259–277.

91. *GAS*, vol. 1, p. 117; J. Fück, *Beiträge zur Überlieferungsgeschichte von Buḫārī's Traditionssammlung*, in *Zeitschrift der Deutschen Morgenländischen Gesellschaft*, 92 (n.F. 17, 1938), p. 60–87.

92. Al-Khaṭīb al-Baghdādī, *TB*, 2:9 *TMS*, 2:328.

93. Ibn Ḥajar, *Hady*, p. 8; Brown, *Canonization*, p. 385.

Copious descriptions of discrepancies among the different recensions from Firabrī may be found in the commentaries, especially Ibn Ḥajar, *Fatḥ al-bārī* and al-Qasṭallānī, *Irshād al-sārī*. These often mention shorter and longer versions of the names of transmitters (as noted above with regard to 'Muḥammad ibn ʿAbd Allāh'), variation among *ḥaddathanī*, *ḥaddathanā*, *akhbaranā* and so forth between names, substitution of words in reports (usually such as would likely have come of misreading [446] someone's handwriting in the course of dictation), omission of pronouns, and so on. The first extant commentary, from Khaṭṭābī, professes to be based mainly on the recension of Nasafī.[94] It often presents hadith considerably out of order by comparison with the text familiar to us today. Regrettably, it usually ignores Bukhārī's topic headings, which means that it cannot be used to assess the state of those headings in the mid-tenth century.

As for manuscript evidence, the earliest extant fragment of the *Ṣaḥīḥ* was found by Alphonse Mingana to present hadith in a different order from that of the familiar text, with occasional variations of spelling, addition or omission of pronouns, and the other sorts of variations that the commentaries preserve.[95] Jonathan Brown is dismissive: 'Mingana's partial manuscript of the *Ṣaḥīḥ* consisted of only three chapters. We have no evidence that the ordering of the remaining ninety-four chapters was irregular.'[96] To the contrary, I would say, it seems highly unlikely that the three chapters preserved in Mingana's Manchester manuscript were exactly the three characterized by such irregularities, the others being identical to the familiar text. Moreover, we actually do have a great deal of evidence, mainly in the commentaries, that such irregularities did characterize the whole of the *Ṣaḥīḥ*. Mingana's manuscript should be welcomed as confirmation of the commentary tradition. However, this is not to say that either Mingana's manuscript or the textual variations pointed out in the commentaries suggests that the *Ṣaḥīḥ* was effectively created posthumously and projected back onto Bukhārī. None of its redactors had an independent reputation as a notable jurisprudent, likely to have written numerous topic headings himself. I propose only that discrepancies among different recensions confirm that Bukhārī composed the *Ṣaḥīḥ* near the end of his life and left it in a somewhat unfinished state.

Only versions of Firabrī's recension, not even the recension of Nasafī as well, were available to al-Yūnīnī (d. 701/1302), whose work formed the textual basis of the so-called Sulṭāni edition of 1311–1313 (mid-1890s), the main basis in turn of subsequent editions

94. Al-Khaṭṭābī, *Aʿlām al-ḥadīth (Min al-turāth al-islāmī)*, ed. M.S.ʿA.R. Āl Saʿūd, Mecca, 1988, vol. 1, p. 106 but cf. A.ʿA.A. al-Bātilī, *al-Imām al-Khaṭṭābī (Silsilat al-rasāʾil al-jāmiʿīyah 45)*, Riyadh, 1426/2005, 2:805, finding that Khaṭṭābī uses the recensions of Nasafī and Firabrī equally.

95. A. Mingana, *An Important MS. of Bukhārī's* Ṣaḥīḥ, in *Journal of the Royal Asiatic Society*, 1936, p. 287–292; Idem, *An Important Manuscript of the Traditions of Bukhāri (sic)*, Cambridge, 1936.

96. Brown, *Canonization*, p. 385.

and the closest we have to a standard text today.[97] (It is said that the standard text in the [447] Maghrib is that of Abū ʿImrān Mūsá ibn Saʿādah [d. 522/1128], going back to Firabrī through Abū Dharr.[98]) The *Ṣaḥīḥ* seems to have been generally recognized as the soundest collection of prophetic hadith from around the beginning of the eleventh century. Scholarly interest peaked in the fifteenth century but has continued to the present.[99] Its earliest champions tended to be Shāfiʿi in law, but jurisprudents of all schools came to cite it with pride when it included a hadith report that supported their school's position. Respect for it as the next soundest book after the Qurʾan grew over time to the point that rituals were devised around it in some parts of the Islamic world.[100]

Law

Bukhārī's *Ṣaḥīḥ* is exalted above other collections partly for the acuity of its legal reasoning, said to be found especially in his topic headings. Bukhārī has been retrospectively claimed by all the four Sunni schools of law, but they actually crystallized after his lifetime and he can be shown to advocate rules peculiar to each of them, rules that none of them would endorse, and rules that go against each one of them.[101] He was accurately classified by Ibn al-Nadīm amongst the traditionist-jurisprudents (*fuqahāʾ aṣḥāb al-ḥadīth*), who stood for basing the law as much as possible on hadith and as little as possible on local custom and reason or convenience.[102] This put him at odds especially with the nascent Ḥanafi school. His books *Rafʿ al-yadayn* and *al-Qirāʾah khalfa al-imām* are directed against well-known Ḥanafi positions, while *al-Ṣaḥīḥ* periodically argues in headings against *baʿḍ al-nās*, 'a certain person,' whose positions are usually identified in the Ḥanafi tradition as those of Abū Ḥanīfah, sometimes of his disciple al-Shaybānī.[103]

The most important study of Bukhārī's particular legal position has recently appeared from Scott C. Lucas. Working mainly from Bukhārī's *kitāb akhbār al-āḥād*, for reliance on solitary reports, and *kitāb* [448] *al-iʿtiṣām bi-al-kitāb wa-al-sunnah*, for reliance on the Qurʾan and hadith (i.e. not reason or *raʾy*), Lucas identifies the major themes of

97. *V.* R. Quiring-Zoche, *How al-Buḫārī's* Ṣaḥīḥ *Was Edited in the Middle Ages: ʿAlī al-Yūnīnī and His* rumūz, in *Bulletin d'études orientales*, 50 (1998), p. 191–222.

98. Y. al-Kattānī, *al-Imām al-Bukhārī* (*Kitāb Jamʿīyat al-Imām al-Bukhārī*, 1), Rabat, n.d., p. 100.

99. *V.* M.ʿI. ʿArār al-Ḥasanī, *Itḥāf al-qāriʾ bi-maʿrifat juhūd wa-aʿmāl al-ʿulamāʾ ʿalá* Ṣaḥīḥ *al-Bukhārī*, Damascus, 1407/1987 (= ʿArār al-Ḥasanī, *Itḥāf*), and Brown, *Canonization*.

100. For a survey, *v.* Brown, *Canonization*, p. 338–349.

101. N.ʿA.K.S. al-Ḥamdānī, *al-Imām al-Bukhārī* (*Silsilat buḥūth al-dirāsāt al-islāmīyah*, 16), Mecca, 1412, p. 155.

102. Ibn al-Nadīm, *Fihrist*, *fann* 6, *maqālah* 6.

103. *V.* Brown, *Canonization*, p. 73–74; Hāshim, *Imām*, p. 192–198; ʿArār al-Ḥasanī, *Itḥāf*, chap. 3; exploited to introduce a polemic against Bukhārī by Ḥ.Gh.Gh. al-Harsāwī, *al-Imām al-Bukhārī wa-fiqh ahl al-ʿIrāq*, Beirut, 1420/2000.

Bukhārī's legal thought as the authority of the Prophet, the secondary authority of the Companions, the authority of consensus, and the necessity of *ijtihād*, meaning personal exertion to discover the rule called for by the Qurʾan and the *sunnah* (i.e. not to practise *taqlīd*, taking someone else's word for it). Bukhārī's doctrine of consensus is slippery, a section heading referring first to the agreement of the scholars (*ahl al-ʿilm*), then to what Mecca and Medina agree upon. Along the way, Lucas observes that the Qurʾan is prominent in Bukhārī's topic headings and that he seems highly mistrustful of *qiyās*, although apparently advocating a form of it under the name of *tashbīh*. Although seldom noted in the secondary literature, Bukhārī does often quote the Qurʾan, as in a little more than a quarter of all section titles—a remarkable proportion, given that there are almost 3,500 sections in the *Ṣaḥīḥ* but only about 500 verses of the Qurʾan traditionally recognized as having legal import.[104] Compare, for example, qurʾanic citations in al-Shāfiʿī, *al-Umm*, where they constitute 8 percent of all items, and in some *masāʾil* collections of Aḥmad ibn Ḥanbal, where they constitute about 1 percent of all items.[105] Bukhārī's quotations frequently come with glosses of words, some Bukhārī's own, some attributed to earlier experts, above all Ibn ʿAbbās the Companion (d. 68/687–688) and Mujāhid the Meccan Follower (d. 103/721–722?).[106]

So far so good. Surprisingly, Lucas thinks that Bukhārī's legal position 'is radically different from that found in al-Shāfiʿī's *Risāla* . . . . There is a notable absence of tension in al-Bukhārī's work between the Qurʾān and Sunna or even between seemingly contradictory *ḥadīths*, topics that preoccupy al-Shāfiʿī in the *Risāla*.' As for contradiction between Qurʾan and *sunnah*, 'al-Bukhārī suggests that if one focuses on ascertaining what the Prophet commanded, prohibited, and did, and then acts upon this information, one will not encounter any contradictions or tensions with the Qurʾan.'[107] Lucas' larger project is to develop the similarity between Bukhārī's outlook and that of modern Salafi Muslims. What interests me more is to locate Bukhārī on the spectrum of opinion in his own [449] century, for which comparison with al-Shāfiʿī is important but insufficient.

Considering the whole range of opinion at the mid-ninth century, I would say that Bukhārī's position is actually much more similar to that of al-Shāfiʿī, or more precisely the first generation of al-Shāfiʿī's followers, than Lucas proposes. During Bukhārī's lifetime, the spectrum of opinion concerning the place of hadith in Islamic law and theology ran from the Muʿtazilah at one extreme, who favoured main reliance on the Qurʾān

104. On 500 verses, *v.* for example al-Māwardī, *Adab al-qāḍī* (*Iḥyāʾ al-turāth al-islāmī*, 4), ed. M.H. al-Sirḥān, Baghdad, 1391–1392/1971–1972, 1:514 = al-Māwardī, *al-Ḥāwī al-kabīr*, ed. M. Maṭrajī, et al., Beirut, 1414/1994, vol. 20, p. 186.

105. *V.* Ch. Melchert, *Aḥmad ibn Ḥanbal and the Qurʾan*, in *Journal of Qurʾanic Studies*, 6/2 (2004), p. 22–34, at p. 28.

106. Bukhārī's literary expertise is remarked by ʿA.Gh. ʿAbd al-Khāliq, *al-Imām al-Bukhārī*, Jedda, 1405/1985, p. 134.

107. Lucas, *Legal Principles*, p. 309–310.

and reason, to the Sunni traditionalists at the other, who favoured maximal reliance on hadith and minimal on reason. In principle, the Muʿtazilah accepted sound hadith as a supplementary source of law but proposed impossibly stringent criteria to identify what was sound. In principle, everyone put the Qurʾan first, but the traditionalists tended to put the Qurʾan near the centre of their devotional lives while finding so much legal material in hadith that they tended to elaborate the law on that basis alone. Near the middle stood those who accepted *kalām* insofar as it was used to defend traditionalist theological tenets, accepted hadith but thought it superfluous to know twenty versions of one prophetic dictum, and devoted their ingenuity to combining texts rather than piling them up.[108]

Bukhārī was devoted to *isnād* comparison, all right, which aligned him with the traditionalists. In Eerik Dickinson's terms, he was with the *hadith critics*, such as Aḥmad ibn Ḥanbal and Abū Zurʿah al-Rāzī, who expected the culling of sound from unsound hadith reports to provide certain answers to legal questions, as opposed to the *hadith commentators*, who dealt with contradictory hadith by relentless harmonization; e.g. al-Shāfiʿī and al-Muzanī.[109] However, this is not the whole story. No one would dispute Goldziher's contrast between Mālik's *Muwaṭṭāʾ* and Bukhārī's *Ṣaḥīḥ* as principally a book of law on the one hand, a collection of hadith on the other. But Goldziher is also correct to contrast Bukhārī's evident concern with the application of the hadith in his *Ṣaḥīḥ* with Muslim's evident unconcern in his.[110] Both Bukhārī and Muslim (and all the other compilers of the Six Books, to varying degrees, Nasāʾī probably the most often, Abū Dāwūd the least) repeat hadith reports with the [450] evident purpose of displaying some of the corroborating evidence that makes them think theirs are sound. A major difference, already observed here, is that Muslim tends to place variant *asānīd* one after the other for easy comparison, whereas Bukhārī usually scatters them under multiple topic headings. This is why Mohammad Fadel is justified in saying of Bukhārī's *Ṣaḥīḥ*, 'technical *ḥadīth* information is made *secondary* to considerations of the text's legal implications.'[111] What Bukhārī foregrounds, in other words, is his ingenuity in finding the right hadith report from which to infer any given point of law, not the means for an expert *isnād* critic to distinguish more likely hadith reports from less. That is, his place on the spectrum is somewhere between Aḥmad and al-Shāfiʿī.

108. V. Ch. Melchert, *The Adversaries of Aḥmad Ibn Ḥanbal*, in *Arabica*, 44 (1997), p. 234–253 [*HPL 1], with stress on theology, and Idem, *Traditionist-Jurisprudents and the Framing of Islamic Law*, in *Islamic Law and Society*, 8 (2001), p. 383–406, with stress on law. On theology, *v.* also J. van Ess, *Ibn Kullāb und die Mihna*, in *Oriens*, 18–19 (1965–1966), p. 92–141, trans. with additional notes by Cl. Gilliot, *Ibn Kullāb et la Mihna*, in *Arabica*, 37 (1990), p. 173–233.

109. Dickinson, *Development*, chap. 1.

110. Goldziher, *Muslim Studies*, vol. 2, p. 198, 226–227.

111. Fadel, *Ibn Ḥajar's* Hady, p. 165.

In nearly every other way, Bukhārī clearly falls in with the moderate Sunni party, the semi-rationalists, not the extreme traditionalists. Lucas is impressed that al-Shāfiʿī's *Risālah* understands hadith to be in tension with the Qurʾan, but the *Risālah* is an argument against rationalists who would dismiss hadith that seem to contradict the Qurʾan, whereas al-Shāfiʿī thinks they are, properly understood, complementary, hadith explaining the Qurʾan. Surely Bukhārī's continual quotation of the Qurʾan is likewise about the complementarity of Qurʾan and hadith, again with hadith normally explaining the Qurʾan. Al-Shāfiʿī's *Risālah* carefully defines and restricts the operation of *qiyās* rather than rejecting it, as Bukhārī seems to do, but Dāwūd al-Ẓāhirī (d. 270/884), who was close enough to al-Shāfiʿī to write the first *manāqib* works about him and the first biographical dictionary of his followers, went on to expressly reject *qiyās* altogether. (Let it be stressed, too, that *qiyās* had a wider range of meaning in Bukhārī's day than later.) As for the authority of the Companions, al-Shāfiʿī has a hard time justifying it in the *Risālah* but cites Companion opinion fairly often in practice. Hadith reports quoted in *K. al-Umm* go back respectively to the Prophet and Companions in a ratio of about three to two. As for consensus, al-Shāfiʿī's exposition in the *Risālah* is still fairly sketchy, while that in *K. Jimāʿ al-ʿilm* comes close to identifying it as the consensus of the Companions.[112] Dāwūd al-Ẓāhirī argued expressly that only the consensus of the Companions is authoritative. The classical Shāfiʿi school held that the consensus of the scholars in any age is authoritative, the early Māliki school of course that the consensual practice of Medina is authoritative. Bukhārī may be read [451] as supporting any of the primitive Shāfiʿi position, the classical Shāfiʿi position, and the early Māliki position on Medina extended to include also Mecca, whence al-Shāfiʿī himself took so much of his doctrine. In sum, although it is regrettable that we have so few points of comparison in the ninth-century literature of *uṣūl al-fiqh* (mainly because so little of it has survived), Bukhārī seems to belong more securely in the Shāfiʿi camp of his day than any other, whether the adherents of *raʾy* or the strict traditionalists loyal to Aḥmad.

This said, it must be admitted that whereas juridical handbooks of the High Middle Ages often mention Bukhārī's including one or another hadith report in his *Ṣaḥīḥ*, they do not mention his advocating one or another opinion as they do of his contemporaries Isḥāq ibn Rāhawayh and Dāwūd al-Ẓāhirī. Bukhārī's self-effacing manner of making his points about the law probably made it easier for later medieval jurisprudents to accept him as a Sunni ecumenist with whom they seldom had to admit disagreement. Both the appearance of transcending the schools and the appearance of devotedly following the Qurʾan have probably kept his prestige high in the modern period, as Muslims have increasingly rejected the schools's claim to a monopoly on legal interpretation.

112. V. J.E. Lowry, *Early Islamic Legal Theory: The* Risāla *of Muḥammad ibn Idrīs al-Shāfiʿī* (*Studies in Islamic law and society*, 30), Leiden, 2007, chap. 7, also A.Y. Musa, *Ḥadīth as scripture*, New York, 2008, chaps. 2, 6.

Theology

Near the end of his life, Bukhārī suffered persecution on account of his theological views, particularly for holding his pronunciation of the Qurʾan to be create, although not the Qurʾan itself (*lafẓī bi-al-Qurʾān makhlūq*). This put him in the company of various others denounced by Aḥmad: al-Ḥusayn al-Karābīsī (d. 248/862–863?), Aḥmad al-Sharrāk (*fl. ca.* 240/854–855), Abū Thawr (d. 240/854), Ibn Kullāb (d. *ca.* 240/854–855), al-Ḥārith al-Muḥāsibī (d. 243/857–858), and Dāwūd al-Ẓāhirī, most of whom were associated with Shāfiʿī in law.[113] Bukhārī's book *Khalq afʿāl al-ʿibād* piles up hadith indicating that actions are create, although not expressly including the pronunciation of the Qurʾan. He was denounced for it in Nishapur in Ramaḍān 252/September 866 by the local traditionalist leader Muḥammad ibn Yaḥyā al-Dhuhlī (d. 258/872?). By one account this was on Dhuhlī's receipt of a letter from unnamed Baghdadis who said he had refused to stop asserting among them that one's pronunciation of the Qurʾan was create.[114] By another, this was after Bukhārī's telling a questioner who had asked about the pronunciation [452], 'Our actions are create and our pronunciations are among our actions.'[115]

Sooner or later (our sources differ), he left for Bukhara. But the governor there wanted him to provide a private session at the palace to teach his sons, which Bukhārī piously refused to do. The governor thereupon incited some scholars to accuse Bukhārī of unbelief, so he left, ultimately for some relatives in the village of Khartank, three miles out of Samarqand, where he died.[116] Alternatively, however, the governor is said to have acted on receipt of a letter from Dhuhlī denouncing Bukhārī.[117] One suspects that the story of the governor's demanding private lessons was based on the caliph al-Mutawakkil's demanding the same from Aḥmad ibn Ḥanbal a few years earlier.[118] A similar story was told of the shadow caliph al-Muwaffaq's demanding private lessons from Abū Dāwūd al-Sijistānī a few years later.[119] There is also a story in *Tārīkh Nasaf*, doubted by al-Dhahabī, that between Bukhara and Samarqand, he stopped at Baykand, which was divided into

113. Melchert, *Adversaries*, pp. 241–242.

114. Al-Khaṭīb al-Baghdādī, *TB*, vol. 2, p. 30–33, and *TMS*, vol. 2, pp. 352–355.

115. Ibn ʿAsākir, *TMD*, vol. 52, p. 92, also by which this took place on Bukhārī's second or third day in Nishapur, which according to al-Ḥākim al-Naysābūrī should have been in 250/864–865.

116. Al-Khaṭīb al-Baghdādī, *TB*, vol. 2, p. 33–34, and *TMS* vol. 2, pp. 355–357; Dhahabī, *Siyar*, vol. 12, p. 464–465, drawing on al-Ḥākim, *Tārīkh Naysābūr*.

117. Ibn ʿAsākir, *TMD*, vol. 52, p. 97; Dhahabī, *Tārīkh*, 18 (251–260 h.), p. 270; Idem, *Siyar*, 12:463.

118. For which *v.* Ṣāliḥ ibn Aḥmad, *Sīrat al-imām Aḥmad ibn Ḥanbal*, ed. F.ʿA.M. Aḥmad, Alexandria, 1984, p. 100–106; Ḥanbal ibn Isḥāq, *Dhikr miḥnat al-imām Aḥmad ibn Ḥanbal*, ed. M. Naghsh, Cairo, 1397/1977, p. 106–109.

119. Al-Khaṭṭābī, *Maʿālim al-sunan*, ed.ʿA.S.ʿA.Sh. Muḥammad, Beirut, 1416/1996, vol. 1, p. 7 = ed. M.R. al-Ṭabbākh, Aleppo, 1351–1352/1932–1934, 1:7–8. On stories patterned on a historical incident, *v.* M. Cooperson, *Classical Arabic Biography* (*Cambridge Studies in Islamic Civilization*), Cambridge, 2000, p. 44–45, 50–51, 60, *et passim*.

parties for and against him, which impelled him to move on to Samarqand, where the same thing happened, hence his withdrawing to a village on the outskirts.[120]

Dhuhlī was alleged to have been actuated by envy, which is possible but does not contradict the charge against Bukhārī (nor explain why so many others turned against Bukhārī). Bukhārī himself is quoted as saying that all the people of Nishapur, Qumis, Rayy, Hamadhan, Hulwan, Baghdad, Kufa, Medina, Mecca, and Basra who quoted him as saying 'My pronunciation of the Qurʾan is created' were liars but also, as we have seen, conceding that actions are create, then expressly that one's pronunciation of something is an action. Ibn Mandah (d. 395/1005), who asserts that Bukhārī had learnt the doctrine of the pronunciation of the [453] Qurʾan from Karābīsī, is perhaps a hostile witness.[121] But friendly witnesses also accepted it, such as Ibn Abī Zayd al-Qayrawānī (d. 386/996).[122] The most likely harmonization seems to be that Bukhārī never did say in so many words that his pronunciation was create, presumably on having seen the hostility of Aḥmad ibn Ḥanbal and his followers to those who had openly said so (Aḥmad's own position was that one should not discuss the question to begin with); that, however, he wrote *Khalq afʿāl al-ʿibād* to support the semi-rationalist Sunni tendency; and that the natural inference (Dhahabī calls it *lāzim qawlih*[123]) was widely made that he did hold the pronunciation of the Qurʾan to be create.

According to Ḥanbali tradition, Aḥmad was most bothered, after al-Karābīsī, by Abū Thawr. Like Bukhārī, he aligned himself with the traditionalists, calling *raʾy* a form of innovation (*bidʿah*).[124] Aḥmad once disparaged Abū Thawr for not condemning someone who said, with al-Karābīsī, that his pronunciation of the Qurʾan was increate.[125] More often, Abū Thawr's error seems to have concerned the hadith report, 'God created Adam in his image': Abū Thawr interpreted it, *contra* Aḥmad, to mean 'in Adam's image,' not 'in God's image.'[126] Bukhārī includes this hadith report in the *Ṣaḥīḥ* but in such a way as to hint that he preferred Abū Thawr's anti-anthropomorphic interpretation. Bukhārī once relates of Yaḥyá ibn Jaʿfar of ʿAbd al-Razzāq by an *isnād* going back to the Prophet, 'God . . . created Adam after his image. His height was 60 cubits. When he had created him, he said to him, "Go and salute that group," meaning a group of angels sitting, "and listen to how they answer you, for it will be your salutation and the salutation of your seed . . . "' (*istiʾdhān* 1, *bāb badʾ al-salām*, no. 6227). Aḥmad ibn Ḥanbal relates the same text directly

---

120. Dhahabī, *Siyar*, vol. 12, p. 463–464; Muḥammad ibn Abī Ḥātim confirms that Bukhārī was forcibly put out of Samarqand, apud Dhahabī, *Siyar*, vol. 12, p. 466.

121. Ibn Mandah, *Masʾalat al-īmān*, apud Ibn Ḥajar, *Tahdhīb*, vol. 2, p. 362–363.

122. Apud Ibn ʿAsākir, *Tabyīn kadhib al-muftarī*, Damascus, 1347, p. 407.

123. Dhahabī, *Siyar*, vol. 12, p. 457.

124. Al-Khaṭīb al-Baghdādī, *TB*, vol. 6, p. 67–68, and *TMS*, vol. 6, p. 580.

125. Al-Khallāl, *al-Musnad min masāʾil Abī ʿAbd Allāh* (*Asiatic Society of Bangladesh public'n*, 29), ed. Ḍ.D. Aḥmad, Dacca, n.d., p. 544.

126. Ibn Abī Yaʿlá, *Ṭabaqāt al-ḥanābilah*, ed. M.Ḥ. al-Fiqī, Cairo, 1371/1952, vol. 1, p. 93, 212, 309.

of ʿAbd al-Razzāq.[127] Elsewhere, however, Bukhārī relates of ʿAbd Allāh ibn Muḥammad of ʿAbd al-Razzāq the same text but beginning rather, 'God created Adam with a height of 60 cubits. When he had created him, he said . . . ' (*aḥādīth al-anbiyā*ʾ 1, *khalq Ādam wa-dhurrīyatih*, no. 3326). Bukhārī thus suggests that God's creating [454] Adam in his image is a dispensible part of the report (all the more strongly by placing the shortened version in the section on Adam's creation), probably another example of Bukhārī's aligning himself with the semi-rationalist party rather than the traditionalists around Aḥmad.

Conclusion

As Jonathan Brown has shown, Bukhārī's *Ṣaḥīḥ* was extolled across the tenth century by a series of moderate Sunnis, mostly Shāfiʿi in law and roughly Ashʿari in theology. The most important of them was al-Ḥākim al-Naysābūrī (d. Nishapur, 405/1014), eminent traditionist, also Shāfiʿi in law and Ashʿari in theology. By the early eleventh century, they had succeeded in elevating Bukhārī's *Ṣaḥīḥ* above all other collections of hadith. (Adherents of the Ḥanafi school were notably slow to recognize its preeminence.) In law, theology, and even *adab*, Bukhārī adhered to precisely the moderate Sunni tendency of his own day that would prevail over competing versions of Islam in the long term. His juridical-theological position was thus not incidental to his future renown but essential to it. That renown was based above all on the consensus of the community, as Ibn Ḥajar said. Although it had to be justified by extolling the authenticity of the hadith in the *Ṣaḥīḥ*, that book's renown did not entail complete faith in the impeccability of every last detail, as Goldziher said, at least until recently.

127. Aḥmad, *al-Musnad*, Cairo, 1313/1895, vol. 2, p. 315 = ed. Sh. al-Arnaʾūṭ, *et al.*, Beirut, 1413–1421/1993–2001, vol. 13, 504–506. It also appears in ʿAbd al-Razzāq, *al-Muṣannaf* (*Min manshūrāt al-Majlis al-ʿilmī*, 39), ed. Ḥ.R. al-Aʿẓamī, Johannesburg, 1390–1392/1970–1972, no. 19435.

5
THE LIFE AND WORKS OF AL-NASĀʾĪ

Abū ʿAbd al-Raḥmān Aḥmad ibn Shuʿayb ibn ʿAlī al-Nasāʾī was a Sunni traditionist, one of whose collections, *al-Mujtabā*, is traditionally counted among the Six Books.[1] He was born in the city of Nasā [378] or Nisā in Western Khurasan (north of Tus, west of Marw) in about 215/830–1. He spent the early 230s/late 840s collecting *ḥadīth* in Khurasan. He travelled to Iraq by the end of the 230s/early 850s, doubtfully ever returning to the East. He collected some *ḥadīth* in Mecca, doubtfully any in Medina or the Jibal, more in Mesopotamia, Syria, and Egypt, but the greatest quantity in Iraq, about 42 per cent of

A version of this study was presented to a conference in Leiden, 15–16 December 2011, organized by Petra Sijpesteijn and Léon Buskens. Like that conference, it is dedicated to the memory of Gautier H.A. Juynboll (1935–2010).

1. The principal modern studies (to my knowledge) are James Robson, 'The transmission of Nasaʾi's "Sunan,"' *JSS* 1 (1956), 38–59, and ʿUmar Īmān Abū Bakr, *al-Imām al-Nasāʾī wa-kitābuhu* al-Mujtabā (Riyadh 1424/2003). Kāmil Muḥammad Muḥammad ʿUwayḍah, *Abū ʿAbd al-Raḥmān Aḥmad ibn ʿAlī ibn Shuʿayb al-Nasāʾī*, Aʿlām al-fuqahāʾ wa-al-muḥaddithīn (Beirut 1416/1996), is insignificant, comprising mostly commonplaces about ḥadīth in general. On the other hand, several introductions are substantial: I have found the most in those to al-Nasāʾī, *ʿAmal al-yawm wa-al-laylah*, ed. Fārūq Ḥamādah (n.p.: Dār al-Salām, 1428/2007), 21–112, and idem, *al-Sunan al-kubrā*, ed. Ḥasan ʿAbd al-Munʿim Shalabī, sup'd by Shuʿayb al-Arnaʾūṭ, 12 vols (Beirut 1421/2001), 1, 11–52. Al-Nasāʾī's *rijāl* criticism in particular is scrutinized by Qāsim ʿAlī Saʿd, *Manhaj al-imām Abī ʿAbd al-Raḥmān al-Nasāʾī fī al-jarḥ wa-al-taʿdīl wa-jamʿ aqwālihī fī al-rijāl*, Silsilat dirāsāt ḥadīthīyah 4, 5 vols (Dubai 1422/2002). There is a 15th-century monograph: al-Sakhāwī, *Bughyat al-rāghib al-mutamannī fī khatm al-Nasāʾī riwāyat Ibn al-Sunnī*, ed. Abū al-Faḍl Ibrāhīm ibn Zakarīyāʾ (Cairo and Beirut 1411/1991). The earliest major extant biography appears to be the entry in Ibn Manẓūr, *Mukhtaṣar* Tārīkh Dimashq, ed. Rawḥīyah al-Naḥḥās, et al., 29 vols (Damascus 1404–9/1984–9), 3, 100–3. This section is evidently missing from the extant manuscripts of Ibn ʿAsākir, *Tarīkh madīnat Dimashq* itself. For other medieval biographies, *v.* al-Dhahabī. *Tārīkh al-islām*, ed. ʿUmar ʿAbd al-Salām Tadmurī, 52 vols (Beirut 1407–21/1987–2000), 23 (301–20 H.), 105–9, with further references.

Originally published in *Journal of Semitic Studies* 59 (2014): 377–407.

al-Mujtabā. He probably settled in Egypt in about 260/873–4, in Zuqāq al-Qanādīl in Old Cairo. In Dhū al-Qaʿdah 302/May-June 915, he left Old Cairo for the last time for Tarsus, where he participated in the ransoming of prisoners. Al-Nasāʾī was severely beaten in Damascus not long afterwards for relating a collection of *ḥadīth* on the virtues of ʿAlī, who was still unpopular there, and failing to produce a similar collection of *ḥadīth* on the virtues of Muʿāwiyah. Alternative early reports place his death in al-Ramlah on 13 Ṣafar 303/28 August 915 and in Mecca in the month of Shaʿbān 303/February-March 916.[2] The present study offers nothing new on al-Nasāʾī's personal life, what little is known having been adequately covered elsewhere. It does review the attributed works in greater detail than has been done before (especially in European languages), identifies where and when al-Nasāʾī collected *ḥadīth* in greater detail and more precisely than previous studies have done, and considers at length his method of *ḥadīth* criticism, along with some other points such as his juridical position. [379]

al-Nasāʾī's Works

The reputed works of al-Nasāʾī are here listed after Shalabī's introduction to *al-Sunan al-kubrā* (no. 14 below).

(1) *Al-Tafsīr*. Quranic commentary. Published.[3] *Ḥadīth* reports (734), about 70 per cent from the Prophet, the rest from Companions, with some repetition under multiple headings or alternative *isnāds* (chains of transmitters). The concluding book (no. 82) of *al-Sunan al-kubrā*, but said to be known only in the recension of Ḥamzah al-Kinānī.[4] (More on the transmitters of *al-Sunan al-kubrā* below.)

(2) *Al-Jumʿah*. On the Friday noon prayer.[5] Book 17 of *al-Sunan al-kubrā*.

2. Both dates are reported by Ibn Manẓūr without attribution. The earlier date is quoted of Ibn Yūnus (d. 347/958; i.e. his lost *Tārīkh Miṣr*), the later of al-Ḥākim al-Naysābūrī (d. 405/1014; i.e. his lost *Tārīkh Naysābūr*), quoting in turn al-Dāraquṭnī (d. 385/995), by Ibn al-Jawzī, *al-Muntaẓam*, 6 vols (Hyderabad 1357–60), 6, 132 = ed. Muḥammad ʿAbd al-Qādir ʿAṭā and Muṣṭafā ʿAbd al-Qādir ʿAṭā, with Nuʿaym Zurzūr, 18 vols (Beirut 1412/1992), 13, 156, and other later biographers. The earlier date is also quoted of al-Ṭaḥāwī (d. 321/933; i.e. his lost *al-Tārīkh*) by al-Mizzī, *Tahdhīb al-Kamāl fī asmāʾ al-rijāl*, ed. Bashshār ʿAwwād Maʿrūf, 35 vols (Beirut 1400–13/1980–92), 1, 340.

3. I have examined *Tafsīr al-Nasāʾī*, ed. Ṣabrī ibn ʿAbd al-Khāliq al-Shāfiʿī and Sayyid ibn ʿAbbās al-Jalīmī, 2 vols (Beirut 1410/1990). Two MSS named by Sezgin, *GAS* 1, 169, no. 6.

4. Ibn Ḥajar, *K. Tahdhīb al-Tahdhīb*, 12 vols (Hyderabad, 1325–7, repr. Beirut: Dār Ṣādir, n.d.), 1, 6. Overlooked by Robson, who makes out that Ibn Ḥajar considered Ibn Aḥmar's recension to be complete: 'Transmission,' 47.

5. For MSS, *v. GAS* 1, 169, no. 9, and Najm ʿAbd al-Raḥmān Khalaf, *Istidrākāt ʿalā tārīkh al-turāth al-ʿarabī li-Fuʾād Sizkīn fī ʿilm al-ḥadīth*, Maktabat Niẓām Yaʿqūbī al-Khāṣṣah-Baḥrayn, Dirāsāt wa-buḥūth 1 (Beirut 1421/2000), 418.

(3) *Khaṣāʾiṣ ʿAlī*. *Ḥadīth* about ʿAlī's special distinctions. Published.[6] Book 77 of *al-Sunan al-kubrā* in the recension of Ibn Sayyār.[7]

(4) *ʿAmal yawm wa-laylah*. On supererogatory devotions. Published.[8] Book 81 of *al-Sunan al-kubrā* in the recensions of Ibn al-Aḥmar and Ibn al-Sayyār.[9]

(5) *Faḍāʾil al-Qurʾān*. On the pious use of the Qurʾān; e.g. encouragements to recite it, discouragements to argue over it. Published.[10] Book 75 of *al-Sunan al-kubrā*.

(6) *Manāsik al-ḥajj*. Ibn al-Athīr alleges that al-Nasāʾī's collection of *manāsik* (rituals, especially at the pilgrimage) follows Shāfiʿi doctrine.[11] This has been taken by some to indicate a separate work, but I see no [380] reason it should not refer to *kitāb manāsik al-ḥajj*, book 24 of *al-Mujtabā* (on which more below).[12]

(7) *Juzʾ min ḥadīth ʿan al-Nabī*. Unpublished Damascus MS.[13] Probably excerpts from *al-Sunan al-kubrā*.

(8) *Al-Ighrāb*. *Ḥadīth* and comments on traditionists from Shuʿbah the Basran client (d. 160/777?) not related by Sufyan al-Thawrī, his Kufan contemporary (d. 161/777?), and the other way around. A quarter or less is extant and has been published.[14] This part comprises 224 *ḥadīth* reports, of which a little over a fourth are in both *al-Sunan al-kubrā* and *al-Mujtabā*, about half in neither. Both Ibn Khayr and al-Sakhāwī report that it was transmitted from al-Nasāʾī by Ibn Ḥayyawayh, Ibn Khayr also that it was transmitted from him by Saʿīd ibn Jābir (d. 327/938–9?).[15]

---

6. Al-Nasāʾī, *Khaṣāʾiṣ al-imām amīr al-muʾminīn ʿAlī ibn Abī Ṭālib*, ed. Muḥammad al-Kāẓim (n.p.: Majmaʿ Iḥyāʾ al-Thaqāfah al-Islāmīyah, 1419), is a relatively careful edition. The editor lists twelve earlier editions at 22–3. For MSS, *v. GAS* 1, 168, no. 2.

7. Ibn Ḥajar, *Tahdhīb* 1, 6. Also overlooked by Robson, who states that *K. Faḍāʾil ʿAlī ibn Abī Ṭālib wa-khaṣāʾiṣuh* 'is not part of the *Sunan*': 'Transmission,' 47.

8. *V.* n. 1 for the fifth edition by this editor. One MS mentioned by *GAS* 1, 169, no. 7.

9. Ibn Ḥajar, *Tahdhīb* 1, 6.

10. Al-Nasāʾī, *Faḍāʾil al-Qurʾān*, ed. Fārūq Ḥamādah (Casablanca 1400/1980).

11. Ibn al-Athīr, *Jāmiʿ al-uṣūl fī aḥādīth al-rasūl*, ed. ʿAbd al-Qādir al-Arnāʾūṭ and Muḥammad Adīb al-Jādir, 15 vols (Beirut 1403–12/1983–91), 1, 196 = ed. Ayman Ṣāliḥ Shaʿbān, 15 vols (Beirut 1418/1998), 1, 131.

12. Cf. Bağdatlı İsmail Paşa, *Hadiyyat al-ʿārifīn*, 2 vols (Istanbul 1951, and Maarif Basımevi, 1955), 1, 56.

13. *GAS* 1, 169, no. 10.

14. Al-Nasāʾī, *Kitāb al-Ighrāb: al-juzʾ al-rābiʿ min ḥadīth Shuʿbah ibn al-Ḥajjāj wa-Sufyān ibn Saʿīd al-Thawrī mimmā aghraba baʿḍuhum ʿalā baʿḍ*, ed. Abū ʿAbd al-Raḥmān Muḥammad al-Thānī ibn ʿUmar ibn Mūsā (Medina 1421/2000).

15. Ibn Khayr al-Ishbīlī, *Index librorum de diversis scientiarum ordinibus quos a magistris didicit Abu Bequer Ben Khair*, ed. Franciscus Codera & J. Ribera Tarrago, Bibliotheca arabico-hispana 9–10, 2 vols (Caesaraugustae 1894–5), no. 197 = *al-Fahrasah*, nn. by Muḥammad Fuʾād Manṣūr (Beirut 1419/1998), 123; Sakhāwī, *Bughyah*, 68. On Saʿīd, *v.* Dhahabī, *Tārīkh al-islām* 24 (321–30 H.), 171–2, with further references.

(9) *Imlāʾāt ḥadīthīyah*. Unpublished Damascus MS.[16] Some miscellaneous comments on traditionists (e.g. listing the reliable and unreliable disciples of Abū Ḥanīfah) transmitted from al-Nasāʾī by Ibn Rashīq al-ʿAskarī have been published and may constitute what is covered by this title.[17] Al-Sakhāwī mentions two sessions of dictation transmitted from al-Nasāʾī by Abyaḍ ibn Muḥammad ibn Abyaḍ (d. 377/987–8).[18]

(10) *Tasmiyat fuqahāʾ al-amṣār min aṣḥāb Rasūl Allāh wa-man baʿdahum*. Lists of leading figures from various regions with occasional comments. Published.[19] Transmitted from al-Nasāʾī by Ibn Rashīq al-ʿAskarī. [381]

(11) *Tasmiyat man lam yarwi ʿanhu ghayr rajul wāḥid*. Those from whom only a single person is known to have related *ḥadīth*. Published.[20]

(12) *Al-Tamyīz*. Identifications of traditionists liable to be confused. For example, al-Nasāʾī comments at one point in *al-Mujtabā*, 'There are three (named) Ismāʿīl ibn Muslim. This is one of them (in the previous *ḥadīth* report), who is not bad (*lā baʾs bih*). (Another) Ismāʿīl ibn Muslim is a shaykh who relates (*ḥadīth*) from Abū Ṭufayl, who (also) is not bad. The Ismāʿīl ibn Muslim who relates (*ḥadīth*) from al-Zuhrī and al-Ḥasan is left as to *ḥadīth*.'[21] Ibn Ḥajar mentions seven traditionists named Ismāʿīl ibn Muslim in *Tahdhīb al-Tahdhīb* and quotes al-Nasāʾī, *al-Tamyīz*, apropos of one of them: 'trustworthy.'[22] This is evidently not one of the three mentioned in *al-Mujtabā*, although Ibn Ḥajar does mention of the one who transmitted from al-Zuhrī and al-Ḥasan that al-Nasāʾī said 'left as to *ḥadīth*.'[23] But the existence of multiple traditionists by this name shows why a book like *al-Tamyīz*

16. Not mentioned by Sezgin, *GAS*. Shalabī identifies it as Ẓāhirīyah 163: *Muqaddimat al-taḥqīq* (v. n. 1), 1, 19.

17. Appended to al-Bukhārī, *K. al-Ḍuʿafāʾ al-ṣaghīr*, ed. Maḥmūd Ibrāhīm Zāyid (Aleppo 1396), 123–5.

18. Sakhāwī, *Bughyah*, 68. On Abyaḍ, v. Dhahabī, *Tārīkh al-islām* 26 (351–80 H.), 606, with further references

19. I have inspected *Majmūʿat rasāʾil fī ʿulūm al-ḥadīth*, ed. Ṣubḥī al-Badrī al-Samarrāʾī (Medina 1389/1969), 7–10, and *Majmūʿat rasāʾil fī ʿulūm al-ḥadīth*, ed. Naṣr Abū ʿAṭāyā and Muṣṭafā Abū Sulaymān al-Nadwī (Beirut 1413/1993), 19–44. References to latter edn henceforth in *italics*. Also appended to Bukhārī, *Ḍuʿafāʾ*, ed. Zāyid, 126–30.

20. I have inspected *Majmūʿat rasāʾil*, 21–2 *65–75*. Also appended to Bukhārī, *Ḍuʿafāʾ*, ed. Zāyid, 118–22. Sezgin mentions a MS copy of 14 ff.: *GAS* 1, 169, no. 5. The published version is very unlikely to have occupied so many folios, but I am more inclined to doubt Sezgin's listing than the completeness of the published version.

21. Nasāʾī, *Mujtabā*, *manāsik al-ḥajj* 49, *al-Qurʾān*, no. 2729.

22. Ibn Ḥajar, *Tahdhīb* 1, 333.

23. Ibn Ḥajar, *Tahdhīb* 1, 332, apparently quoting no. 16. Cf. Nasāʾī, *al-Ḍuʿafāʾ*, appended to Bukhārī, *Ḍuʿafāʾ*, ed. Zāyid, 17.

should have been needed. Al-Sakhāwī mentions *Asmāʾ al-ruwāh wa-al-tamyīz baynahum.*[24]

(13) *Al-Jarḥ wa-al-taʿdīl.* Evaluations of traditionists. Occasionally quoted by Ibn Ḥajar.[25]

(14) *Al-Sunan al-kubrā.* Until recently thought lost but now published.[26] See below for transmitters from al-Nasāʾī.

(15) *Shuyūkh al-Zuhrī.* The shaykhs of the Medinese Muḥammad ibn Muslim ibn Shihāb (d. 124/741–2?). Ibn Ḥajar refers to a *ḥadīth* report [382] that al-Nasāʾī related here, but this work may be the same as no. 22 under a different title.[27]

(16) *Al-Ḍuʿafāʾ wa-al-matrūkīn.* Lists unreliable traditionists. Published.[28] Mentioned by Ibn Khayr and al-Sakhāwī, who both say it was transmitted from him by Ibn Rashīq al-ʿAskarī.[29]

(17) *Al-Ṭabaqāt.* On men who related *ḥadīth* of Nāfiʿ (Medinese, d. 119/737?) and al-Aʿmash (Kufan, d. 148/765?). Published, perhaps defectively.[30] Transmitted from al-Nasāʾī by Ibn Rashīq al-ʿAskarī.

(18) *Al-Asmāʾ wa-al-kunā.* Cross-referencing names and teknonyms. Ibn Khayr mentions a version arranged (*mubawwab*) by Abū ʿAbd Allāh Muḥammad ibn Aḥmad ibn Mufarraj, an Andalusian qadi (d. 380/990).[31] Related from al-Nasāʾī by his son ʿAbd al-Karīm, according to al-Sakhāwī.[32] Muḥammad ibn Aḥmad ibn Mufarraj's source for it may have been either Abū Hurayrah ibn Abī al-ʿIṣām or Ḥamzah al-Kinānī, both of whom transmitted some or all of *al-Sunan al-kubrā* from

24. Sakhāwī, *Bughyah*, 67.

25. Ibn Ḥajar, *Tahdhīb* 1, 97, 419, 4, 91; idem, *Lisān* 2, 300.

26. This began to be published as *Kitāb al-sunan al-kubrā*, recension of Abū Bakr Muḥammad ibn Muʿāwiyah ibn al-Aḥmar al-Andalusī and Abū ʿAbd Allāh Muḥammad ibn Qāsim ibn Sayyār al-Andalusī, ed. Muḥammad Ḥabīb Allāh Amīr al-Dīn al-Atharī, sup'd by ʿAbd al-Ṣamad Sharaf al-Dīn, 3 vols (Bombay 1391–). The first complete and apparently most widely disseminated edition is that edited by ʿAbd al-Ghaffār al-Bundārī and Sayyid Kisrawī Ḥasan, 7 vols (Beirut 1411/1991), with 11,770 numbered *ḥadīth* reports. Distinctly superior is the Shalabī edn, for which *v.* n. 1. It includes 11,949 numbered *ḥadīth* reports. For MSS, *v.* Khalaf, *Istidrākāt*, 412. None reported by Sezgin, *GAS* 1, 167–9.

27. Ibn Ḥajar, *Talkhīṣ al-ḥabīr*, ed. ʿAbd Allāh Hāshim al-Yamānī al-Madanī, 4 vols in 2 (Cairo n.d.), 1, 110 = ed. Abū ʿĀṣim Ḥasan ibn ʿAbbās ibn Quṭb, 4 vols (n.p.: Muʾassasat Qurṭubah and Dār al-Mishkāh, 1416/1995), 1, 195.

28. I have inspected the version in *al-Majmūʿ fī al-ḍuʿafāʾ wa-al-matrūkīn*, ed. ʿAbd al-ʿAzīz ʿIzz al-Dīn al-Sayrawān (Beirut 1405/1985), 39–256. Also appended to Bukhārī, *Ḍuʿafāʾ*, ed. Zāyid, 1–117. For MSS, *v. GAS* 1, 168–9, no. 3; Khalaf, *Istidrākāt*, 418–19.

29. Ibn Khayr, *Index*, no. 339 = *Fahrasah*, 177; Sakhāwī, *Bughyah*, 67.

30. I have inspected *Majmūʿat rasāʾil*, 15–17 *45–63*. Also appended to Bukhārī, *Ḍuʿafāʾ*, ed. Zāyid, 130–3.

31. Ibn Khayr, no. 358 = *Fahrasah*, 182.

32. Sakhāwī, *Bughyah*, 67.

al-Nasāʾī (more on this below) and are named among Muḥammad ibn Aḥmad ibn Mufarraj's Egyptian shaykhs.[33]

(19) *Al-Mujtabā.* Also sometimes referred to as *al-Sunan*, but several section titles within apparently refer to it as *al-Mujtabā*; e.g. *Kitāb Manāsik al-ḥajj* 134, *dhikr al-faḍl fī al-ṭawāf wa-huwa min* Kitāb al-Mujtabā *min al-ḥajj*. Many commercial editions are available, none of which may claim to be the standard edition, so it is best to cite *ḥadīth* from here not by volume and page but by *kitāb* and *bāb*, or at least the *kitāb* and the number of the *bāb* according to Wensinck's usage (indicated in Arabic as the numbering of *al-Muʿjam*). However, the numbering of individual *ḥadīth* reports in the 1950s edition of Muḥammad ʿAṭāʾ Allāh al-Amritsarī seems to be on the way to becoming standard, so if any number is cited, it should be from there.[34] As [383] electronic searching becomes usual, it may become best to quote the beginning of a cited *ḥadīth* report (its *ṭaraf*) in Arabic.

(20) *Musnad ʿAlī ibn Abī Ṭālib. Ḥadīth* from the fourth caliph (d. 40/661). Mentioned by, among others, al-Dhahabī and al-Sakhāwī.[35] Indexed by al-Mizzī, *Tahdhīb.*

(21) *Musnad ḥadīth Ibn Jurayj. Ḥadīth* from the Meccan client ʿAbd al-Malik ibn ʿAbd al-ʿAzīz (d. 150/767–8?). Mentioned by Ibn Khayr, who says it was transmitted from al-Nasāʾī by Saʿīd ibn Jābir.[36]

(22) *Musnad ḥadīth al-Zuhrī bi-ʿilalih wa-al-kalām ʿalayh.* Mentioned by Ibn Khayr.[37] Al-Sakhāwī mentions *Gharāʾib al-Zuhrī.*[38] Ibn Khayr says it was transmitted from al-Nasāʾī by Abū ʿAbd Allāh Muḥammad ibn Saʿīd ibn Nabāt ibn ʿAbbās ibn Aṣbagh, whom I have not been able to trace. However, this same Ibn Aṣbagh related no. 23 from Saʿīd ibn Jābir < al-Nasāʾī, so it seems likely that it was actually Saʿīd ibn Jābir who transmitted *Musnad ḥadīth al-Zuhrī* directly from al-Nasāʾī.

(23) *Musnad ḥadīth Sufyān ibn Saʿīd al-Thawrī. Ḥadīth* from the Kufan traditionist. Mentioned by Ibn Khayr, who says it was transmitted from al-Nasāʾī by Saʿīd ibn Jābir.[39]

33. Ibn al-Faraḍī, *Tārīkh ʿulamāʾ al-Andalus*, ed. Ibrāhīm al-Abyārī, 2 vols (n.p.: Dār al-Kutub al-Islāmīyah, Cairo and Beirut 1403/1983), 2, 771, no. 1358.

34. Al-Nasāʾī, *al-Sunan*, ed. Muḥammad ʿAṭāʾ Allāh al-Fūjayānī al-Amritsarī (Lahore 1376, repr. 1976). I have not seen a copy, myself. The numbering of this edition has been taken over by, among others, *Mawsūʿat al-sunnah: al-kutub al-sittah wa-shurūḥuhā*, ed. Shaʿbān Qawart, 23 vols (Istanbul, Tunis and Riyadh 1992), vols 15–16; *Sunan al-Nasāʾī al-sughrā*, ed. Ṣāliḥ ibn ʿAbd al-ʿAzīz ibn Muḥammad ibn Ibrāhīm Āl al-Shaykh (Riyadh 1420/1999); also *al-Kutub al-sittah*, Mawsūʿat al-ḥadīth al-sharīf (Riyadh 1420/1999); and *Sunan al-Nasāʾī* (Beirut 1420/1999). For MSS, *v. GAS* 1, 167–8, no. 1, and Khalaf, *Istidrākāt*, 412–16.

35. Al-Dhahabī, *Siyar aʿlām al-nubalāʾ*, ed. Shuʿayb al-Arnaʾūṭ, et al., 25 vols (Beirut 1401–9/1981–8), 14, 133; Sakhāwī, *Bughyah*, 67.

36. Ibn Khayr, no. 201 = *Fahrasah*, 124.

37. Ibn Khayr, no. 193 = *Fahrasah*, 122.

38. Sakhāwī, *Bughyah*, 67.

39. Ibn Khayr, *Index*, no. 196 = *Fahrasah*, 122.

(24) *Musnad ḥadīth Shuʿbah.* Mentioned by Ibn Khayr.[40] *Ḥadīth* from the Basran traditionist.

(25) *Musnad ḥadīth al-Fuḍayl ibn ʿIyāḍ wa-Dāwūd al-Ṭāʾī wa-Mufaḍḍal ibn Muhalhal al-Ḍabbī. Ḥadīth* from, respectively, the Khurasani renunciant (l. Mecca, d. 187/802–3?) and two Kufan worshippers (d. 166/782–3, 167/783–4). Mentioned by Ibn Khayr, who says it was transmitted from al-Nasāʾī by Ḥamzah al-Kinānī and Ibn Ḥayyawayh.[41] Al-Sakhāwī mentions *Ḥadīth al-Fuḍayl ibn ʿIyāḍ*.[42]

(26) *Musnad ḥadīth Mālik ibn Anas. Ḥadīth* from the Medinese jurisprudent (d. 179/795), evidently arranged not by Companion but by Mālik's shaykh, for Ibn Khayr had a version whose section from the *ḥadīth* of Ibn al-Munkadir to that of Nāfiʿ < Ibn ʿUmar came from Ibn Rashīq al-ʿAskarī < al-Nasāʾī. Ibn Khayr and al-Sakhāwī both mention [384] versions transmitted from al-Nasāʾī by Abū ʿAlī al-Suyūṭī and Ḥamzah al-Kinānī.[43]

(27) *Musnad ḥadīth Yaḥyā ibn Saʿīd al-Qaṭṭān. Ḥadīth* from the Basran *ḥadīth* critic (d. 198/813). Mentioned by Ibn Khayr, who says it comprised eight fascicles (*ajzāʾ*), also that it was transmitted from al-Nasāʾī by Ḥamzah al-Kinānī.[44]

(28) *Musnad Manṣūr ibn Zādhān al-Wāsiṭī.* Mentioned by al-Sakhāwī.[45] *Ḥadīth* from the Wasiti worshipper (d. 129/746–7?).

(29) *Muʿjam al-shuyūkh.* Names about half of al-Nasāʾī's shaykhs in *al-Mujtabā*, his sources for about 90 per cent of the *ḥadīth* there (along with a few traditionists from whom, he says, he wrote nothing). Published.[46]

(30) *Maʿrifat al-ikhwah wa-al-akhawāt.* Mentioned by al-Sakhāwī.[47] Presumably a list of brothers and sisters known for relating *ḥadīth*.

(31) *Man ḥaddatha ʿanhu Ibn Abī ʿArūbah wa-lam yasmaʿ minh.* Eight Followers from whom the Basran Saʿīd (d. 156/772–3?) related *ḥadīth* without naming his immediate source. Published.[48]

The list suggests that al-Nasāʾī devoted himself strictly to *ḥadīth*. The works of al-Bukhārī make a contrasting example, for they include collections of *ḥadīth* on specific issues of

40. Ibn Khayr, *Index*, no. 195 = *Fahrasah*, 122.
41. Ibn Khayr, *Index*, no. 203 = *Fahrasah*, 124.
42. Sakhāwī, *Bughyah*, 67.
43. Ibn Khayr, *Index*, no. 194 = *Fahrasah*, 122; Sakhāwī, *Bughyah*, 67.
44. Ibn Khayr, *Index*, no. 202 = *Fahrasah*, 124.
45. Sakhāwī, *Bughyah*, 67.
46. Al-Nasāʾī, *Tasmiyat al-shuyūkh*, ed. Qāsim ʿAlī Saʿd (Beirut 1424/2003).
47. Sakhāwī, *Bughyah*, 67.
48. Appended to Bukhārī, *Ḍuʿafāʾ*, ed. Zāyid, 122. For MSS, *v. GAS* 1, 169, no. 8, and Khalaf, *Istidrākāt*, 418–19.

law and theology: *Kitāb Rafʿ al-yadayn* and *al-Qirāʾah khalfa al-imām* on the ritual prayer, *Kitāb Khalq afʿāl al-ʿibād* on the metaphysical nature of acts.

Al-Sakhāwī (d. 902/1497) lists eleven who transmitted *al-Sunan al-kubrā* from al-Nasāʾī:[49]

(1) His son Abū Muḥammad (elsewhere Abū Mūsā) ʿAbd al-Karīm (d. Old Cairo, 344/955);[50]
(2) Abū Bakr Aḥmad ibn Muḥammad ibn Isḥāq al-Dīnawarī *ibn al-Sunnī* (d. 364/975);[51] [385]
(3) Abū al-Ḥasan Aḥmad ibn Muḥammad ibn Abī Tammām (was alive 353/964);
(4) Abū Bakr Aḥmad ibn Muḥammad ibn Ismāʿīl *ibn al-Muhandis* (d. 385/995–6);[52]
(5) *Abū ʿAlī* al-Ḥasan ibn al-Khaḍir ibn ʿAbd Allāh *al-Asyūṭī* (d. 361/971–2);[53]
(6) Abū Muḥammad al-Ḥasan *ibn Rashīq al-ʿAskarī* (d. 370/980–1);[54]
(7) Abū al-Qāsim *Ḥamzah* ibn Muḥammad. ibn ʿAlī ibn al-ʿAbbās *al-Kinānī* (d. 357/968);[55]
(8) ʿAlī ibn Abī Jaʿfar Aḥmad ibn Muḥammad ibn Salāmah al-Ṭaḥāwī. He was alive in Giza, 350/961–2, according to Ibn Abī al-Wafāʾ, *al-Jawāhir al-muḍīyah fī ṭabaqāt al-ḥanafīyah*, ed. ʿAbd al-Fattāḥ Muḥammad al-Ḥulw, 5 vols. (Cairo: Dār Iḥyāʾ al-Kutub al-ʿArabīyah, 1398–1408/1978–88, repr. Giza: Hajr, 1413/1993), 2:541–2;
(9) *Abū al-Ḥasan* Muḥammad ibn ʿAbd Allāh ibn Zakarīyāʾ *ibn Ḥayyawayh* al-Naysābūrī (d. 366/977);[56]
(10) Muḥammad ibn al-Qāsim ibn Muḥammad *ibn Sayyār* al-Qurṭubī (d. 327/939);[57]
(11) Abū Bakr Muḥammad ibn Muʿāwiyah al-Qurashī al-Andalusī *ibn al-Aḥmar* (d. 358/969).[58]

Most of these were Egyptians, but no. 9 was prominent in Khurasan, while nos. 10 and 11 took *al-Sunan al-kubrā* to Andalusia. Ibn Khayr al-Ishbīlī (d. Cordova, 575/1179) clearly distinguishes between *al-Sunan al-kubrā* and *al-Mujtabā*. He had all or parts of *al-Sunan*

49. Sakhāwī, *Bughyah*, 38–9. This account was evidently unavailable to Robson, who lists nos. 2, 4, 7, 9–11 and traces the further transmission of the *Sunan* from them: Robson, 'Transmission,' 40–57.

50. Dhahabī, *Tārīkh al-islām* 25 (331–50 H.), 299.

51. *GAS* 1, 198; Dhahabī, *Tārīkh al-islām* 26, 318–19 with further references. Al-Dhahabī himself alleges that Ibn al-Sunnī restricted himself to (*iqtaṣara ʿalā*) relating *al-Mujtabā*: Dhahabī, *Siyar* 16, 256.

52. Dhahabī, *Tārīkh al-islām* 27 (381–400 H.): 91–2 with further references.

53. Dhahabī, *Tārīkh* 26, 280 with further references.

54. *GAS* 1, 201–2; Dhahabī, *Tārīkh* 26, 437–8 with further references.

55. *GAS* 1, 192–3; Dhahabī, *Tārīkh* 26, 160–2 with further references.

56. *GAS* 1, 199; Dhahabī, *Tārīkh* 26, 365–6 with further references.

57. Dhahabī, *Tārīkh* 24, 216–7 with further references.

58. Dhahabī, *Tārīkh* 26, 184–5 with further references.

al-kubrā from nos. 1, 3–5, 7, and 9–11. He also had *Khaṣāʾiṣ ʿAlī*, no. 3 on the above list of al-Nasāʾī's works, from an Abū Aḥmad al-Ḥusayn ibn Jaʿfar ibn Muḥammad, of whom I have found no further trace. His name may be a distortion of no. 8 on al-Sakhāwī's list (or the other way around). Ibn Khayr adds one name to al-Sakhāwī's list, stating that he had *kitāb al-khayl* (book 30 of *al-Sunan al-kubrā*) from (ultimately) Abū Hurayrah < Abū al-ʿIṣām (as well as in Ibn Ḥayyawayh's recension).[59] This appears to be a copyist's error for one man whom al-Mizzī names among the transmitters from al-Nasāʾī, Aḥmad ibn ʿAbd Allāh ibn al-Ḥasan al-ʿAdawī, known as Abū Hurayrah ibn Abī al-ʿIṣām (d. 346/957).[60] Probably, then, he should be added to al-Sakhāwī's list as a twelfth transmitter of *al-Sunan al-kubrā* from al-Nasāʾī. Ibn Ḥajar himself had all or [386] parts of *al-Sunan al-kubrā* only from nos. 9 and 11, but he was aware of recensions from all of al-Sakhāwī's eleven except no. 3.[61]

There are two major puzzles concerning al-Nasāʾī's works. The first is who put together *al-Mujtabā*. It was known to subsequent generations in the recension of just one man, Ibn al-Sunnī (no. 2 on Sakhāwī's list of those who transmitted *al-Sunan al-kubrā*), whereas eleven or twelve recensions of *al-Sunan al-kubrā* were known a century later. That ours is the recension of Ibn al-Sunnī appears clearly from the beginning of *kitāb al-ashribah*: '< Abū Bakr Aḥmad ibn Muḥammad ibn Isḥāq al-Sunnī by reading to him for his approval in his house (*qirāʾatan ʿalayhi fī baytih*) < the imam Abū ʿAbd al-Raḥmān Aḥmad ibn Shuʿayb al-Nasāʾī . . . .' After no. 1542, Ibn al-Sunnī appears in the text, commenting on al-Zuhrī. After no. 5042, at the end of *kitāb al-īmān*, there appears a comment from 'al-Qāḍī, meaning Ibn al-Kassār' quoting an ʿAbd al-Ṣamad al-Bukhārī. Aḥmad ibn al-Ḥusayn al-Kassār is identified among those who related *ḥadīth*, evidently including *al-Mujtabā*, from Ibn al-Sunnī.[62] (I have not identified ʿAbd al-Ṣamad al-Bukhārī.) Al-Dhahabī (d. 748/1348?) and Ibn Nāṣir al-Dīn (d. 842/1439?) even take it that *al-Mujtabā* was selected from al-Nasāʾī's *ḥadīth* by Ibn al-Sunnī.[63] However, it appears from the beginning of *kitāb al-ṣayd wa-al-dhabāʾiḥ* that Ibn al-Sunnī heard the *Sunan* as one of several students: '< the imam Abū ʿAbd al-Raḥmān al-Nasāʾī in Old Cairo, being read to as I listened, < Suwayd ibn Naṣr . . . .' This implies a complete text assembled by al-Nasāʾī himself. Moreover, Ibn Khayr gives us the names of two others besides Ibn al-Sunnī who transmitted *al-Mujtabā* from al-Nasāʾī: his son ʿAbd al-Karīm ibn Aḥmad (no. 1 on Sakhāwī's list of those who transmitted *al-Sunan al-kubrā*) and a Walīd ibn al-Qāsim al-Ṣūfī. The recension

59. Ibn Khayr al-Ishbīlī, *Index*, no. 160 = *Fahrasah*, 93–6.

60. Mizzī, *Tahdhīb* 1, 330. On Abū Hurayrah ibn Abī al-ʿIṣām, *v.* Dhahabī, *Tārīkh* 25, 344–5 with further references.

61. Ibn Ḥajar, *al-Muʿjam al-mufahras*, ed. Muḥammad Shakūr Maḥmūd al-Ḥājjī Amīr al-Mayādīnī (Beirut 1418/1998), 34–5; idem, *Tahdhīb* 1, 6, 37.

62. Dhahabī, *Tārīkh* 26, 319.

63. Dhahabī, *Tārīkh* 26, 319; idem, *Siyar* 14, 133; Ibn Nāṣir al-Dīn, *apud* Ibn al-ʿImād, *Shadharāt al-dhahab*, 8 vols (Cairo 1350–1), 3, 48.

of the former was known in Andalusia.[64] Altogether, then, it seems fairly certain that it was al-Nasāʾī himself, near the end of his life, who came up with *al-Mujtabā*.[65]

The second, related puzzle concerns the relation between *al-Sunan al-kubrā* and *al-Mujtabā*. Whether by al-Nasāʾī or someone else, was *al-Mujtabā* extracted from *al-Sunan*? Both are collections of *ḥadīth* [387] arranged by topic. *Al-Mujtabā* has usually been counted the fifth of the Six Books; however, some medieval scholars who treated the Six Books (e.g. Ibn ʿAsākir and al-Mizzī) worked from *al-Sunan al-kubrā*. Moreover, confusingly, some scholars (notably Ibn al-Athīr) seem to have counted *al-Mujtabā* among the Six but referred to it as *al-Sunan*.[66] *Al-Mujtabā* comprises around 5,760 *ḥadīth* reports altogether, of which over half appear to be repeats, meaning reports that appear more than once under different headings, sometimes with different *isnāds*.[67] *Al-Sunan al-kubrā* comprises almost 12,000 *ḥadīth* reports, a little over twice as many as *al-Mujtabā* (but approximately the same number as Muslim's *Ṣaḥīḥ*). The two books sometimes differ in the distribution of *ḥadīth* among section headings, occasionally in the *isnāds* attached to particular *ḥadīth* reports. Some *ḥadīth* reports in *al-Mujtabā* have no parallel in *al-Sunan*.[68]

Ibn Khayr tells a story by which a certain governor (*amīr*) asked al-Nasāʾī whether all of his *Sunan* was sound. When al-Nasāʾī said 'No,' the governor charged him with writing down what was sound in it alone (reading *mujarradan* for *mujawwadan*).[69] Abū al-Faḍl al-ʿIrāqī (d. 806/1414) specifies the governor of al-Ramlah.[70] Ibn Khayr tells us that al-Nasāʾī 'omitted every *ḥadīth* report that he had brought out in the *Sunan* whose *isnād* had been aspersed as weak.' On the contrary, however, it appears from ratings of traditionists as synthesized by Ibn Ḥajar that there is no difference between *al-Sunan* and *al-Mujtabā* as to the soundness of *ḥadīth* included.[71] Moreover, *al-Mujtabā* is not merely an abridgement of *al-Sunan*. Besides sometimes including *ḥadīth* that are not in the *Sunan* or that are there but with alternative *isnāds*, it includes one whole book (47, *kitāb al-īmān wa-sharāʾiʿih*) not found in the *Sunan*. As noted above, several section titles expressly refer to *al-Mujtabā*. Notably, the title to the last section of *kitāb al-qiṣāṣ wa-al-qawad wa-al-diyāt* (45) runs *al-qiṣāṣ min* al-Mujtabā *mimmā laysa fī* al-Sunan, meaning '(the topic of) retaliation from *al-Mujtabā*, of what is not in the *Sunan*.' Titles are the part [388] of the text most

64. Ibn Khayr al-Ishbīlī, *Index*, no. 160 = *Fahrasah*, 97.

65. An overlapping but not identical case for al-Nasāʾī's assembling *al-Mujtabā* was earlier made by Fārūq Ḥamādah, introduction to Nasāʾī, *ʿAmal*, 65–70.

66. Abū Bakr, *al-Imām al-Nasāʾī*, 47, 52.

67. Abū Bakr, *al-Imām al-Nasāʾī*, 14, 76.

68. Abū Bakr, *al-Imām al-Nasāʾī*, 61–72.

69. Ibn Khayr, *Index*, no. 160 = *Fahrasah*, 97. Repeated by, among others, Ibn al-Athīr, *Jāmiʿ*, ed. al-Arnāʾūṭ and Jādir, 1, 197 = ed. Shaʿbān, 1, 131. Accepted by Robson, 'Transmission,' 39.

70. Al-ʿIrāqī, *apud* al-Suyūṭī, *Tadrīb al-rāwī, al-nawʿ al-awwal* = ed. Abū ʿAbd al-Raḥmān Ṣalāḥ ibn Muḥammad ibn ʿUwayḍah, 2 vols in 1 (Beirut 1417/1996), 1, 48.

71. Abū Bakr, *al-Imām al-Nasāʾī*, 74.

likely to be later interpolations. Whoever wrote this one, however, whether al-Nasāʾī or a later transmitter, was clearly aware of the two books, *al-Mujtabā* and *al-Sunan*, and expressly confirmed that the present one was not a mere abridgement of the earlier. If the story of the governor's charge is not a complete invention, it evidently distorts either that charge or al-Nasāʾī's response to it.

The *kitāb al-ṭahārah* at the beginning of *al-Mujtabā* is actually longer than the *kitāb al-ṭahārah* at the beginning of *al-Sunan al-kubrā*. It includes 275 topic headings as opposed to 185 in *al-Sunan al-kubrā*, 451 *ḥadīth* reports as opposed to 308. Later books of *al-Mujtabā* are shorter than the corresponding books of *al-Sunan al-kubrā*, as if al-Nasāʾī initially set out to make *al-Mujtabā* equally long (if not longer) but changed his mind.[72] Longer books in *al-Mujtabā* of course tell against the story that al-Nasāʾī came up with it by abridging *al-Sunan al-kubrā*. The inconsistency between a long initial book and shorter later books is an example of the unfinished feel of the *Mujtabā* as a whole. Another example is the way it includes a *kitāb al-jihād* (25), on making war, but never gets to the *jizyah* tax and other obligations of non-Muslim subjects, which take up the second half of *kitāb al-siyar* in *al-Sunan al-kubrā* (78). It includes a *kitāb qaṭʿ al-sāriq* (46), on the penalty for theft, but does not treat the remaining *ḥadd* penalties for adultery, unsupported accusation of adultery, drinking alcohol, and highway robbery. Occasional series of *ḥadīth* from single shaykhs suggest that al-Nasāʾī was copying directly from his own notebooks without taking time for rearrangement; e.g. seven in a row from the Homsi ʿAmr ibn Yaḥyā ibn al-Ḥārith at 4146–52, five in a row from the Basran Muḥammad ibn Bashshār at 5543–7. Both *al-Sunan al-kubrā* and *al-Mujtabā* have a *kitāb al-zīnah* on personal adornments. The one in *al-Mujtabā* (48) begins with the same *ḥadīth* reports as the one in *al-Sunan al-kubrā* (80), occasionally omitting one. Halfway through, however, it apparently starts over again, this time with *ḥadīth* reports not found in the *Sunan*: *dhikr al-fiṭrah* (no. 5227), *iḥfāʾ al-shawārib* (5228), and *ḥalq ruʾūs al-ṣibyān* (5229) correspond to the earlier sections *al-fiṭrah* (5043–7), *iḥfāʾ al-shārib* (5048–50), and *al-rukhṣah fī ḥalq al-raʾs* (5050). It looks as though additional *ḥadīth* were inserted in the wrong place.

It seems likely that al-Nasāʾī's work on the two books, *al-Sunan al-kubrā* and *al-Mujtabā*, overlapped in time. The inclusion of various books in some recensions but not others suggests that *al-Sunan al-kubrā* was a work in progress for some time. Ibn al-Aḥmar heard [389] it from al-Nasāʾī in Fusṭāṭ (Old Cairo) in the year 297/909–10.[73] Only one recension is known of *al-Mujtabā*. Ibn al-Sunnī is said to have heard it from al-Nasāʾī in 302/914–15.[74] It, too, was probably a work in progress for some time. Al-Bukhārī seems to have similarly left his *Ṣaḥīḥ* in an unfinished state.[75] This habit of continual revision was probably com-

72. Abū Bakr, *al-Imām al-Nasāʾī*, 68–9.
73. Ibn Khayr al-Ishbīlī, *Index*, no. 160 = *Fahrasah*, 93.
74. Sakhāwī, *Bughyah*, 39, citing Ibn al-Nuqṭah, *al-Taqyīd*.
75. V. Christopher Melchert, 'Bukhārī and his *Ṣaḥīḥ*,' *Le Muséon* 123 (2010), 425–54, at 445–6 [*HPL 4].

mon enough to help account for the marked tendency of the Islamic tradition to identify a writer's thought straitly with what he said at the end of his life, showing little interest in its evolution from early to middle to later periods.[76]

From percentages in *al-Mujtabā*, it can be roughly inferred how much time al-Nasāʾī spent in different regions. From 46 Khurasani shaykhs, he collected 1,895 *ḥadīth* reports, 33 per cent of the total. From 60 Basran shaykhs, he collected 1,479 *ḥadīth* reports, 26 per cent of the total; from 44 Baghdadi, 767 *ḥadīth* reports, 13 per cent; from twenty Kufan 146 *ḥadīth* reports, 3 per cent; from five Wasiti, seven *ḥadīth* reports, for a total of 129 shaykhs and 2,398 *ḥadīth* reports from Iraq, 42 per cent of the total. From twenty Egyptian shaykhs, he collected 660 *ḥadīth* reports, 11 per cent of the total. From 48 Mesopotamian (*jazarī*) shaykhs, he collected 530 *ḥadīth* reports, 9 per cent of the total. From 46 Syrian shaykhs, he collected [390] 474 *ḥadīth* reports, 8 per cent of the total. From five Meccan shaykhs, he collected 82 *ḥadīth* reports, somewhat more than 1 per cent of the total. Additionally, he collected a very few *ḥadīth* reports from Medinese and Jibali shaykhs, probably not in actual trips to Medina or the Jibal but in other places where he came across these shaykhs. (The chart below compares percentages of *ḥadīth* from shaykhs of different places in *al-Sunan al-kubrā*, based on a sample of 150 *ḥadīth* reports. Percentages here are similar although usually not identical.)

I recently came across an apparent reference by Bukhārī himself to his *Ṣaḥīḥ*: al-Bukhārī, *K. al-Tārīkh al-kabīr*, 4 vols in 8 (Hyderabad 1941–5, repr. Hyderabad 1377/1958, repr. with added index vol., Beirut n.d.), 7, 87. Bukhārī there quotes a *ḥadīth* report by which the Prophet said, 'One of God's servants will do the work of the people of Paradise for a long time. Then he will be exposed to one of the avenues of the Fire and he will act by it until he dies. This is according to what was decreed for him.' Bukhārī comments, 'We have made this clear in *K. al-Mukhtaṣar*.' This must refer to the *Ṣaḥīḥ*, whose full title was *al-Jāmiʿ al-musnad al-ṣaḥīḥ al-mukhtaṣar*. That collection has roughly the same statement from the Prophet (with very different *asānīd* from the one in the *Tārīkh*) at nos. 3208, 3332, 6594, and 7454. Bukhārī dictated *al-Tārīkh al-kabīr* to someone else in 246/860–1, although the extant version mentions persons who died in 252. The suggestion is still that Bukhārī had some version of the *Ṣaḥīḥ* going at least ten years before his death, probably more. Presumably, the *Mujtabā* would likewise have taken years to assemble.

76. The tendency is identified by Roy Mottahedeh, 'The Transmission of Learning: the Role of the Islamic Northeast,' *Madrasa: la transmission du savoir dans le monde musulman*, dir. N. Grandin and M. Gaborieau (Paris 1997), 63–72, at 64. Mottahedeh relates the phenomenon to an essentialist theory of knowledge and to 'the tendency of authors to present their works as expositions of the same message for different audiences.'

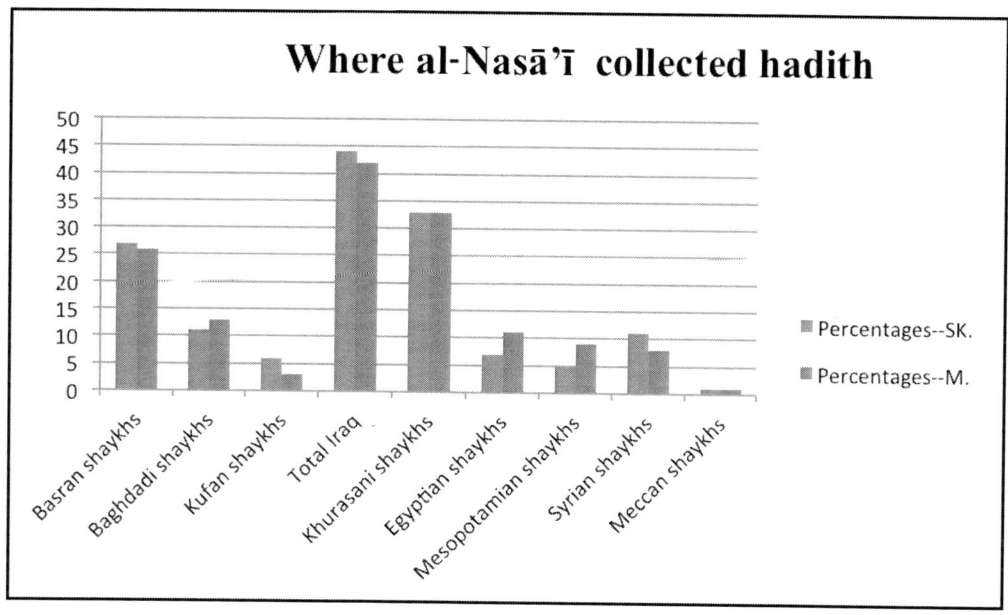

A digression on historical method: some scholars at the Juynboll memorial conference questioned whether we can know where al-Nasāʾī and others collected *ḥadīth*. The principal evidence is how his teachers are identified in the biographical sources. Identifications most often take the form *fulān al-baṣrī, al-kūfī*, and so on ('so-and-so the Basran,' 'the Kufan'), next most often *yuʿaddu min al-baṣrīyīn* ('he is counted among the Basrans'), then *ḥadīthuhū fī al-baṣrīyīn* ('his *ḥadīth* is among the Basrans'). I think these identifications are likely to tell us where al-Nasāʾī collected *ḥadīth* for several reasons. First, traditionists usually appear to have travelled in their youths, collecting *ḥadīth*. References to travelling in old age, dictating *ḥadīth*, do come up but are not usual. When someone is described as a Basran, for example, it will usually indicate where he dictated *ḥadīth* in his old age. Secondly, the early biographers evidently considered geographical provenance an important datum. Dates of death are very prominent in the modern secondary literature but much less in the primary; for example, 6 per cent of entries in al-Bukhārī, *al-Tārīkh al-kabīr*, include a date of death, less than 1 per cent of entries in Ibn [391] Abī Ḥātim, *al-Jarḥ wa-al-taʿdīl*, none at all in al-Nasāʾī, *Tasmiyat al-shuyūkh* (*Muʿjam al-shuyūkh*).[77] By contrast, 44 per cent of entries in al-Bukhārī, *al-Tārīkh al-kabīr*, include some indication of where someone was from, 43 per cent in Ibn Abī Ḥātim, *al-Jarḥ wa-al-taʿdīl*, and 72 per cent in al-Nasāʾī, *Tasmiyat al-shuyūkh*. (Ibn Ḥajar [d. 852/1449], synthesizing many early biographical collections, provides some indication of date, even so general as the caliphal

77. C. Melchert, 'Bukhārī and Early Hadith Criticism,' *Journal of the American Oriental Society* 121 (2001), 7–19, at 11, 16 [*HPL 2].

reign in which someone died, for about 40 per cent of all the men in the Six Books, an indication of geographical provenance for 70 per cent.[78]) I have found provenances for over 95 per cent of al-Nasāʾī's shaykhs, unsurprising inasmuch as they include few unknowns (*majāhīl*) such as fill up *al-Tārīkh al-kabīr* and *al-Jarḥ wa-al-taʿdīl*. The less we dare make of such geographical identifications, the more puzzling it becomes why early traditionists considered them so noteworthy.

Of al-Nasāʾī's own shaykhs, there is contradictory information about just one of any significance: Aḥmad ibn ʿUthmān ibn Ḥakīm, Abū al-Jawzāʾ al-Awdī (d. 261/874–5), source of 18 *ḥadīth* reports in *al-Mujtabā*. Al-Nasāʾī identifies him as Basran in *al-Mujtabā* itself (no. 2126) but as a Kufan in *Tasmiyat al-shuyūkh*. He is 'counted among the Kufans' according to Ibn Abī Ḥātim. This is evidently the identification that Ibn Ḥajar accepts.[79] There is evidence that a few of them moved about. Maḥmūd ibn Ghaylān, source of 74 *ḥadīth* reports in *al-Mujtabā*, is called 'al-Marwazī' in several sources.[80] Ibn Ḥajar identifies him as someone who settled in Baghdad (*nazīl Baghdād*), then quotes someone as saying that he made the pilgrimage in '46 (861), then went to Marv, where he died in 249 (863–4). Alternatively, there are two reports by which he died in 239/853–4. Stories associating him with Isḥāq ibn Rāhawayh do make it possible that al-Nasāʾī heard from him in Nishapur before he left Khurasan; on the other hand, the report that he was imprisoned over the Qurʾān suggests that he was in Baghdad in the 220s/835–45.[81] My guess is [392] that al-Nasāʾī heard *ḥadīth* from him in Baghdad. Similarly, Muḥammad ibn Manṣūr (d. 254/868?), source of 111 *ḥadīth* reports in *al-Mujtabā*, is called 'al-Ṭūsī' but also expressly said to have settled in Baghdad.[82] Unavoidable reliance on some guesswork means to be sure that I propose figures showing where al-Nasāʾī collected *ḥadīth* as approximate but reliable, not precise and certain.

One scholar at the Juynboll conference brought up the designation *min ahl kadhā* as a surer indication of where someone should be located, doubtless alluding to an article by Monique Bernards and John Nawas, who state that '"*min ahl*" has the clearest and

---

78. G.H.A. Juynboll justly draws attention to Ibn Ḥajar's usefulness in *Muslim Tradition* (Cambridge Studies in Islamic Civilization, Cambridge 1983), chap. 4.

79. Nasāʾī, *Tasmiyat al-shuyūkh*, 55; Ibn Abī Ḥātim, *K. al-Jarḥ wa-al-taʿdīl*, 9 vols (Hyderabad 1360–71, repr. Beirut n.d.), 2, 63; Ibn Ḥajar, *Tahdhīb* 1, 61. The *ḥadīth* report in question, *k. al-ṣiyām* 12, *dhikr al-ikhtilāf ʿalā ʿAmr ibn Dīnār*, is not shared with *al-Sunan al-kubrā*.

80. Notably Nasāʾī, *Tasmiyat al-shuyūkh*, 86, and Ibn Abī Ḥātim, *Jarḥ* 8, 291.

81. Ibn Ḥajar, *Tahdhīb* 10, 64–5; al-Khaṭīb al-Baghdādī, *Tārīkh Baghdād*, 14 vols (Cairo 1349/1931, repr. Cairo and Beirut n.d.), 13, 89–90 = *Tārīkh Madīnat al-Salām*, ed. Bashshār ʿAwwād Maʿrūf, 17 vols (Beirut 1422/2001), 15, 104–5; Aḥmad ibn Ḥanbal (attrib.), *al-ʿIlal wa-maʿrifat al-rijāl*, rec. of al-Tamīmī, in *K. al-Jāmiʿ fī al-ʿilal wa-maʿrifat al-rijāl*, ed. Muḥammad Ḥusām Bayḍūn, 2 vols (Beirut 1410/1990), 1, 15–68, at 40.

82. Nasāʾī, *Tasmiyat al-shuyūkh*, 38; Ibn Abī Ḥātim, *Jarḥ* 8, 94; Ibn Ḥajar, *Tahdhīb* 9, 472.

broadest range of associations with the adult life cycle of the *ʿulamāʾ*.'[83] This seems to me a doubtful generalization, for it is a rare expression in early biographical works except Ibn Saʿd (d. 230/845), *Kitāb al-Ṭabaqāt*, and Ibn Ḥibbān al-Bustī (d. 354/965), *al-Thiqāt* and *al-Majrūḥīn*. Ibn Saʿd's *Ṭabaqāt* is arranged geographically, so he most often uses *min ahl kadhā* within a section to specify a city. For example, of 55 persons in the section on Khurasan (excluding Companions), fourteen are said to be *min ahl Marw*, *min ahl Sarakhs*, or some other particular city of Khurasan. A few more, seventeen, are identified with a particular city of Khurasan by *nisbah*. I strongly doubt whether *min ahl Marw* tells us more than *al-Marwazī*. In five remaining cases, the expression *min ahl kadhā* definitely does not indicate where someone most likely transmitted *ḥadīth*. Rather, four men are identified as *min ahl al-Baṣrah*, having emigrated from there to Khurasan, one *min ahl Sijistān*, whose base of trade (*matjar*) was Nishapur.[84]

As for Ibn Ḥibbān, there is some indication of place in *al-Thiqāt* for a little over half of all entries (excluding Companions).[85] When there is an indication of place, it is *min ahl kadhā* for about two-thirds, a *nisbah* for about a fifth (these figures based on a random sample of 171). Occasionally, both expressions come up. I do not see [393] that *min ahl kadhā* is regularly the surer. For example, Rayḥān ibn Saʿīd al-Shāmī is described as *min ahl al-Baṣrah* (8:245). Accordingly, I would count him Basran, not Syrian (even apart from indications that he should more properly be called *al-Sāmī*[86]). To the contrary, however, Ismāʿīl ibn Jaʿfar ibn Abī Kathīr is described as *min ahl al-Madīnah* but *sakana Baghdād* (6:44), according to which I would count him Baghdadi, not Medinese; that is, transmitting *ḥadīth* mainly in Baghdad, not Medina.

It is more difficult to tell exactly when al-Nasāʾī visited most of these places. He recalled going to hear from Qutaybah ibn Saʿīd (d. 240/854) of Baghlān, Khurasan, in 230/844–5, and staying with him for a year and two months.[87] His study in Khurasan was relatively concentrated. Qutaybah ibn Saʿīd himself was the source of over a third of his *ḥadīth* from Khurasanis. In second and third place, respectively, are Isḥāq ibn Rāhawayh (Marwazi but lived in Nishapur, d. 238/853?) and Suwayd ibn Naṣr (Marwazi, d. 240/854–5?), al-Nasāʾī's source especially for *ḥadīth* from Ibn al-Mubārak. His top three Khurasani shaykhs were together the source of almost two-thirds of his *ḥadīth* from Khurasanis.[88] The

---

83. M. Bernards and J. Nawas, 'The Geographic Distribution of Muslim Jurists during the First Four Centuries AH,' *Islamic Law and Society* 10 (2003), 168–81, quotation from 172 fn.

84. Ibn Saʿd, *Biographien*, ed. Eduard Sachau, et al., 9 vols in 15 (Leiden: E. J. Brill, 1904–40), 7/2, 101–9 = *al-Ṭabaqāt al-kubrā*, 9 vols (Beirut 1957–68), 7, 368–79.

85. I have examined Ibn Ḥibbān, *K. al-Thiqāt*, ed. Muḥammad ʿAbd al-Muʿīd Khān, 7 vols (Hyderabad 1393–1403/1973–83).

86. V. Ibn Ḥajar, *Tahdhīb* 3:301fn.

87. Ibn al-Manẓūr, *Mukhtaṣar Tārīkh Dimashq*, 3, 100.

88. Top shaykhs with numbers of *ḥadīth* reports in *al-Mujtabā* are listed by Abū Bakr, *al-Imām al-Nasāʾī*, 13–14.

Meccan shaykhs from whom he related *ḥadīth* died between 248/862–3 and 256/869–70, inclusive, so it seems certain that he visited Mecca to collect *ḥadīth* before the earlier date, probably just once. He is said to have been constant in pilgrimage, which suggests that he normally did not combine *ḥadīth* collection with making the pilgrimage (else there should be *ḥadīth* in *al-Mujtabā* from shaykhs who died later than 256).[89] He must have come to Iraq before 239/853–4, for that is the earliest death date of any of his Iraqi shaykhs. On similar evidence, his earliest visits to Mesopotamia and Syria must have been within less than five years of this. We have his express statement that he entered Egypt when Ḥarmalah ibn Yaḥyā was ill, and did not write from him, implying that he entered Egypt for the first time not long before Ḥarmalah's death at the end of Shawwāl 243/mid-February 858.[90]

Some writers have made much of the precise terminology used for the transmission of *ḥadīth*. Al-Nasāʾī appears to be inconsistent. Mālik ibn Anas notoriously would not dictate *ḥadīth* but rather [394] insisted on having disciples read or recite for his approval.[91] But when al-Nasāʾī relates *ḥadīth* < al-Ḥārith ibn Miskīn < Ibn al-Qāsim < Mālik, the term for the last is sometimes *ḥaddathanī* (nos. 20, 1096, 1286, 1578, 1695, 1698, 1836, 2040, 2343, 2616), sometimes *ʿan* (nos. 1774, 3247, 3368, 3680), once each that I have remarked *qāla* (no. 3339) and *akhbaranī* (5036). Al-Nasāʾī's shaykh Qutaybah usually transmits from Mālik using *ʿan* (e.g. 1785, 2566, 4320) but sometimes instead *ḥaddathanī* (e.g. 1515, 1689, 3262). As reported in Bukhārī's *Ṣaḥīḥ*, by comparison, Qutaybah always uses *ʿan* for his transmission from Mālik. It is impossible to say, of course, whether the discrepancy goes back to al-Bukhārī or al-Nasāʾī in taking dictation or to Qutaybah himself in dictating on different occasions. (Al-Bukhārī is not completely self-consistent. For example, he almost always quotes his number-one source for *ḥadīth* from Mālik, ʿAbd Allāh ibn Yūsuf, as saying *akhbaranā* but occasionally *ʿan* or *ḥaddathanā*.)

G.H.A. Juynboll has proposed that 'Tradition collectors in early Islam may be visualized as always presenting virtually everything they had amassed on a certain legal or moral issue, provided, the *isnāds* . . . met their personal standards.'[92] Otherwise, he argued, collections of weak *ḥadīth* would have been much larger; also, the great collectors ought to have been more successful at eliminating contradictory *ḥadīth*. Certainly, al-Nasāʾī presents many contradictory *ḥadīth* reports. On the other hand, he certainly knew *ḥadīth* that he does not include in his main collections. If about half the *ḥadīth* reports in the extant part of *al-Ighrāb* are in *al-Sunan al-kubrā* or *al-Mujtabā*, half in neither, then we posit a pattern of his including half of what he knew in his major collections, we may extrapolate an upper boundary to his knowledge at around 30,000 prophetic *ḥadīth* reports.

---

89. Ibn al-Manẓūr, *Mukhtaṣar Tārīkh Dimashq* 3, 102.

90. Nasāʾī, *Tasmiyat al-shuyūkh*, 95.

91. E.g. Ibn Saʿd, *al-Ṭabaqāt al-kubrā: al-qism al-mutammim*, ed. Ziyād Muḥammad Manṣūr, Silsilat iḥyāʾ al-turāth 6 (Medina 1403/1983), 438.

92. G.H.A. Juynboll, 'Some *Isnād*-analytical Methods,' *al-Qanṭara* 10 (1989), 343–83, at 374.

Nasāʾī's *Ḥadīth* Criticism

Al-Nasāʾī acquired a considerable reputation for *ḥadīth* criticism. The critics most often mentioned by Ibn ʿAdī al-Qaṭṭān (d. Gurgan, 365/976?) in his encyclopaedia of weak transmitters, *al-Kāmil fī ḍuʿafāʾ al-rijāl*, are al-Bukhārī and Yaḥyā ibn Maʿīn, followed in descending order by al-Nasāʾī, Aḥmad ibn Ḥanbal, and the obscure [395] al-Saʿdī. What Ibn ʿAdī quotes of al-Nasāʾī is succinct characterizations of individual traditionists. The same characterizations are found in no. 16 on the list of his works, *al-Ḍuʿafāʾ wa-al-matrūkīn*. Other characterizations are found in no. 29 on the list of his works, *Muʿjam al-shuyūkh*, and in comments on particular *ḥadīth* reports in *al-Mujtabā*. A little less than 2 per cent of all entries in *al-Mujtabā* have comments from al-Nasāʾī, compared with a fifth of all entries in Abū Dāwūd's collection, 90 per cent of all entries in al-Tirmidhī's. (There are proportionately more comments in *al-Sunan al-kubrā*, but apparently less consequential, mostly pointing out that the following *ḥadīth* report disagrees with the one just past.) Some of these comments are on particular traditionists. For example, al-Nasāʾī declares after no. 1803, 'Fulayḥ ibn Sulaymān is not strong,' meaning a Medinese (d. 168/784–5) in the *isnād* to the preceding *ḥadīth* report. After no. 4983, he says, 'ʿUmar ibn Abī Salamah is not strong in *ḥadīth*,' meaning the Companion in the previous *ḥadīth* report (d. 83/702–3?). Other comments are on particular *ḥadīth* reports. For example, he points out additions contained in nos. 217 and 218 and declares of nos. 1666, 3495, 4134, 4137, and 4987 that they are actually *mursal*, meaning that someone has mistakenly supplied the name of the Companion who related this from the Prophet. He explains an obscure word in no. 3597, *shikāl*, the quality in horses of having either one or three legs marked by white, which the Prophet disliked. (Al-Nasāʾī is generally much less interested in philology than, for example, al-Bukhārī, as a comparison of their respective books of *tafsīr* will quickly show.) A few of his comments document the importance of writing in *ḥadīth* transmission, at least in his century. Of no. 2429, for example, he states that the correct version is from Abū Dharr (Companion, d. 32/652–3). 'It appears that *Dharr* was omitted from writing, while *Abū* became *Ubayy*.'

His comments suffice to show that al-Nasāʾī relied on the same basic method as other *ḥadīth* critics of the ninth century, namely to compare *isnāds*. If a *ḥadīth* report was supported by multiple, mutually corroborative *isnāds*, it must be sound. If a particular link was without parallels, one investigated whether the transmitter's *ḥadīth* were usually corroborated or not. If they were, he got the benefit of the doubt in this case; if not, then this uncorroborated report must be considered weak and the transmitter became suspect.[93] Of no. 58, [396] for example, he says that Yaʿqūb ibn Ibrāhīm (al-Dawraqī, Baghdadi, d. 252/866–7) would not relate this particular *ḥadīth* report concerning ritual

93. An excellent description is provided by E. Dickinson, *The Development of Early Sunnite* Ḥadīth *Criticism*, Islamic History and Civilization, Studies and Texts, 38 (Leiden: Brill, 2001), chap. 6.

purity except for a dinar. This must be an example of taking an uncorroborated *ḥadīth* report from someone whose *ḥadīth* normally were corroborated by other transmitters (al-Dawraqī appears in all of the Six Books; the *isnād* of the previous *ḥadīth* report agrees with al-Dawraqī's at the Follower level). Of no. 1288, for example, al-Nasāʾī comments, 'He related this to us from his book but it is a mistake.' This *ḥadīth* report has the link Sulaymān < ʿAmr ibn Murrah < ʿAbd al-Raḥmān ibn Abī Laylā, whereas the next one, which al-Nasāʾī prefers, has al-Ḥakam between Sulaymān and ʿAbd al-Raḥmān ibn Abī Laylā. Al-Nasāʾī's shaykh, who carefully related from his notebook, al-Nasāʾī elsewhere pronounces trustworthy.[94] Of no. 2258, for example, al-Nasāʾī comments, 'This is a mistake. What is correct is the one before. We know no one who corroborated (*tābaʿa*) Ibn Kathīr's version of this.' Of no. 3356, he says, 'I don't know anyone who said Aswad was involved with this *ḥadīth* report except Zāʾidah.' G.H.A. Juynboll has pointed out a significant quotation regarding the Kufan Nuʿaym ibn Ḥammād (d. 227/843?): 'He was often the only transmitter who transmitted a number of particular traditions on the authority of the well-known masters and thus he became one of those whose traditions may not be used as arguments.'[95] There is no evidence that al-Nasāʾī considered the criteria most often mentioned in the modern secondary literature on *ḥadīth* criticism, mainly the dates of birth and death and personal characteristics of traditionists. He cites only two earlier critics that I have noticed, once each Aḥmad ibn Ḥanbal (d. 241/855) and Abū Usāmah (the Kufan, d. 201/816–17).[96]

For a particular example of al-Nasāʾī's method, consider three *ḥadīth* reports in a row by which the Prophet listed the three most enormous sins (with references to how many of the Six Books [397] transmitters appear in and where they appear in Ibn Ḥajar, *Tahdhīb* al-Tahdhīb).

> 4018 < Muḥammad ibn Bashshār (Bundār, Basran, 6/6, d. 252/866, *IḤT* 9, 70–3) < ʿAbd al-Raḥmān (ibn Mahdī, Basran client, 6/6, d. 198/814, *IḤT* 6, 279–81) < Sufyān (al-Thawrī, Kufan, 6/6, d. 161/777? *IḤT* 4, 111–15) < Wāṣil (ibn Ḥayyān, Kufan, 6/6, d. 120/737–8? *IḤT* 11, 103) < Abū Wāʾil (Kufan, 6/6, d. after 82/701, *IḤT* 4, 361–3) < ʿAmr ibn Shuraḥbīl (Kufan, 5/6, d. bef. 63/682–3, *IḤT* 8, 47) < ʿAbd Allāh < Messenger of Θ.

94. The Kufan al-Qāsim ibn Zakarīyāʾ ibn Dīnār (d. *ca.* 250/864–5), al-Nasāʾī's source for 23 reports in *al-Mujtabā*, on whom *v.* Ibn Ḥajar, *Tahdhīb* 8, 313–14.

95. G.H.A. Juynboll, '(Re)appraisal of Some Technical Terms in *Ḥadīth* Science,' *Islamic Law and Society* 8 (2001), 303–49, at 312–13, citing Ibn Ḥajar, *Tahdhīb* 10, 461, where al-Nasāʾī is quoted through Abū ʿAlī al-Naysābūrī; i.e. al-Ḥusayn ibn ʿAlī (d. 349/960).

96. Nasāʾī, *Mujtabā*, *ashribah*, *dhikr al-akhbār allatī iʿtalla bihā man abāḥa sharāb al-muskir*, no. 5680; *ibid.*, *ashribah*, *dhikr al-ikhtilāf ʿalā Ibrāhīm fī al-nabīdh*, no. 5755. For casual over-emphasis on dates of birth and death and personal characteristics, *v.* for example *Encyclopaedia of Islam*, new edn, s.v. 'Ḥadīth,' by J. Robson.

4019 < ʿAmr ibn ʿAlī (Basran, 6/6, d. 249/864, *IḤT* 8, 80–2) < Yaḥyā (ibn Saʿīd al-Qaṭṭān, Basran, 6/6, d. 198/813–14, *IḤT* 11, 216–20) < Sufyān < Wāṣil < Abū Wāʾil < ʿAbd Allāh < Messenger of Θ.

4020 ʿAbdah (ibn ʿAbd Allāh, Basran, 5/6, d. 258/871–2, *IḤT* 6, 460–1) < Yazīd (ibn Hārūn, Wasiti cl., 6/6, d. 206/821) < Shuʿbah (ibn al-Ḥajjāj, Basran cl., 6/6, d. 160/776? *IḤT* 4, 338–46) < ʿĀṣim (ibn Sulaymān al-Aḥwal, Basran cl., 6/6, d. 141/758–9? *IḤT* 5, 42–3) < Abū Wāʾil < ʿAbd Allāh < Messenger of Θ.

Following the last of these, al-Nasāʾī comments, 'This is a mistake. The correct version is the previous one. This *ḥadīth* report from Yazīd is a mistake. It is from Wāṣil alone.'[97] In the first two versions, we have Wāṣil relating this report from Abū Wāʾil, in the third rather ʿĀṣim from Abū Wāʾil. What al-Nasāʾī lacks are parallel transmissions by Shuʿbah from ʿĀṣim (there are none in the Six Books, according to Mizzī). In effect, he blames Yazīd ibn Hārūn for spuriously diving to Abū Wāʾil, presumably because he was confused (it was only a mistake), not malicious. (*Diving* is a term coined by Juynboll for inventing a new chain of transmission between oneself and someone in an extant *ḥadīth* report. This is what Schacht calls 'the spread of *isnāds*,' 'that is the creation of additional authorities or transmitters for the same doctrine or tradition.'[98]) The three quotations of the Prophet are not identical, but the first two are almost so. By contrast, the third notably reorders the three most enormous sins: the first two rank them as polytheism, then infanticide for fear of poverty, then adultery with a neighbour's wife, the third polytheism, then adultery, then infanticide. This discrepancy al-Nasāʾī passes over in silence, confirming his faith in *isnād* comparison to detect false attributions.[99] [398] Another puzzle is the way the first version has Abū Wāʾil getting this report from Ibn Masʿūd through ʿAmr ibn Shuraḥbīl whereas the second and third agree on his getting it directly from Ibn Masʿūd. This discrepancy also al-Nasāʾī passes over in silence, perhaps because he considered all Companions sufficiently reliable that it hardly mattered.

How much corroboration was enough? The method is to some degree impressionistic and intuitive rather than systematic and rational. This accounts among other things for contradictory evaluations. Sometimes, it is al-Nasāʾī who contradicts himself, as in eight instances from a random sample of 184 of his collected evaluations, or about 4 per cent of the time. For example, of Fiṭr ibn Khalīfah (d. after 150/767–8), a Kufan client who

97. Nasāʾī, *Mujtabā*, *taḥrīm al-dam*, *dhikr aʿẓam al-dhanb*.

98. *V.* G.H.A. Juynboll, *Encyclopedia of Canonical Ḥadīth* (Leiden 2007), xxii-iii; Joseph Schacht, *The Origins of Muhammadan Jurisprudence* (Oxford 1950), 166.

99. Jonathan Brown has attributed avoidance of express *matn* criticism, such as pointing out this discrepancy in content, to traditionalist distaste for Muʿtazili rationalism: 'How we know early ḥadīth critics did *matn* criticism and why it's so hard to find,' *Islamic Law and Society* 15 (2008), 143–84. In this case, to be sure, the precise ranking could hardly be insisted on as essential. Is infanticide a lesser offence when its purpose is to cover up adultery? Is adultery a lesser offence when it involves the wife of someone who lives far away?

appears in all of the Six Books except Muslim's, al-Nasāʾī is quoted as saying both 'not bad' (a middling grade) and 'trustworthy' (a high one).[100] Qāsim ʿAlī Saʿd proposes that inconsistent evaluations reflect al-Nasāʾī's changing his mind over time, as he considered new evidence.[101] This is possible.

More often, al-Nasāʾī's evaluations disagree with those of other critics. Abū Ḥātim al-Rāzī (d. 277/890) is quoted as defending himself against the insinuation of relying on intuition by the evidence that his evaluations of individual *ḥadīth* reports agreed with those of Abū Zurʿah al-Rāzī (d. 264/878) without their communicating with each other.[102] (Abū Ḥātim likens his expertise to that of an assayer, which G.H.A. Juynboll took as a defence of intuition; however, I think Abū Ḥātim's insistence that this is *ʿilm*, not *mujāzafah*, indicates the contrary.)[103] It lays down disagreement among critics as an [399] indication of weakness in their method. Scott C. Lucas has taken up the challenge by comparing evaluations of traditionists from three sources: Ibn Saʿd, *al-Ṭabaqāt* (of which our text appears to be a composite of recensions by two men of the next generation); Yaḥyā ibn Maʿīn as reported by ʿAbbās al-Dūrī (d. 271/884), *al-Tārīkh*; and Aḥmad ibn Ḥanbal as reported by ʿAbd Allāh ibn Aḥmad (d. 290/903), *al-ʿIlal wa-maʿrifat al-rijāl*. Lucas finds little intersection among the three, such that only 7 per cent of the men evaluated by Ibn Saʿd are also evaluated by both Yaḥyā ibn Maʿīn and Aḥmad. However, classifying characterizations as positive, ambiguous, or negative, Lucas finds that when characterizations are reported of all three, they agree over 80 per cent of the time.[104] I have thought to take a random sample of Yaḥyā ibn Maʿīn's evaluations from al-Dūrī (308, reduced to 280 by the necessary subtraction of ambiguous names), then compare them with evaluations from

100. Ibn Ḥajar, *Tahdhīb* 8, 301.

101. Saʿd, *Manhaj* 4, 1833.

102. Ibn Abī Ḥātim, *Jarḥ* 1, 349–51. The passage is translated *apud* Dickinson, *Development*, 9–10. Abū Ḥātim's son admits that he has deliberately suppressed at least some contradictory evaluations: Ibn Abī Ḥātim, *Jarḥ* 2, 38.

103. Juynboll, *Muslim Tradition*, 161. There may be more stress on intuition (i.e. an undefinable method informed by vast experience) in someone's reported exchange with the earlier Basran critic ʿAbd al-Raḥmān ibn Mahdī (d. 198/814): 'How do you know what is false?' 'As the physician knows the madman': Ibn Abī Ḥātim, *Jarḥ* 1, 252; sim. with a different interlocutor *apud* Ibn ʿAdī al-Qaṭṭān, *al-Kāmil fī ḍuʿafāʾ al-rijāl*, ed. ʿĀdil Aḥmad ʿAbd al-Mawjūd and ʿAlī Muḥammad Muʿawwaḍ, 9 vols (Beirut 1418/1997), 1, 198, and al-Khalīlī, *al-Irshād*, ed. ʿĀmir Aḥmad Ḥaydar (Beirut 1993/1414), 147. ʿAbd al-Raḥmān ibn Mahdī is also quoted as saying 'It is nothing to me but a pastime (*ʿabath*), the way a man diverts himself with dogs or pigeons or something' and 'It is enough for the traditionist to sniff a *ḥadīth* report': Ibn ʿAdī al-Qaṭṭān, *Kāmil* 1, 208.

104. S.C. Lucas, *Constructive Critics,* Ḥadīth *Literature, and the Articulation of Sunnī Islam*, Islamic History and Civilization, Studies and Texts, 51 (Leiden 2004), chap. 7. Lucas was probably responding particularly to Juynboll, *Muslim tradition*, chap. 4, widely interpreted as exposing the randomness of evaluations from different critics.

new, comprehensive collections of Aḥmad's and al-Nasāʾī's evaluations.[105] Thirty-nine per cent of this sample is evaluated by all three. Classifying evaluations as high, middling, or low, after Lucas, I have found that, where all three evaluate the same man, they agree 60 per cent of the time.[106] (When they evaluate the same traditionist, Aḥmad individually agrees with Yaḥyā ibn Maʿīn 65 per cent of the time, al-Nasāʾī with Yaḥyā ibn Maʿīn 76 per cent of the time, and al-Nasāʾī with Aḥmad also 76 per cent of the time.) [400]

As a basis for investigating how ninth-century *ḥadīth* critics operated, I think my sample should be more reliable than Lucas's. The greatest difference between my sample and Lucas's is obviously my substitution of al-Nasāʾī for Ibn Saʿd. This is justified, I think, by their relative statures as critics of *ḥadīth*. Whereas Ibn ʿAdī al-Qaṭṭān, among others, often quotes al-Nasāʾī, no one, to my knowledge, quotes Ibn Saʿd's evaluations before al-Khaṭīb al-Baghdādī (d. 463/1071). Michael Cooperson has plausibly located his *Kitāb al-Ṭabaqāt al-kabīr* in the tradition of *adab* rather than *ḥadīth*.[107] Ibn Saʿd was not a *ḥadīth* collector like Yaḥyā ibn Maʿīn or Aḥmad ibn Ḥanbal and does not belong in their company. A second difference, perhaps due to their being equally expert, is that a particular traditionist is much more often evaluated by all of my three. They do not agree so often as Yaḥyā ibn Maʿīn and Aḥmad ibn Ḥanbal with Ibn Saʿd. Rather, they confirm how heavily the critics' method was intuitive, not scientific. It is harsh to speak of 'the overall impotence, inconsistency, and superficiality of medieval Muslim *isnād* appraisal,'[108] but complete agreement is the standard proposed by Abū Ḥātim, Lucas's 80 per cent is less than that, and 60 per cent significantly less still. The degree to which *ḥadīth* criticism avoided caprice may be estimated by the difference between 60-per cent agreement and the 11-per cent that pure chance would produce. (Chance would produce one-third agreement between two critics. Juynboll characterized his own method as based, in large measure, on speculation, often expressly acknowledged, as in the frequent appearance in his *Encyclopedia* of his abbreviation for 'seeming,' frequently enclosed by parentheses to indicate an intermediate degree of uncertainty.)

---

105. Yaḥyā ibn Maʿīn, *al-Tārīkh*, rec. of ʿAbbās al-Dūrī, ed. ʿAbd Allāh Aḥmad Ḥasan, 2 vols (Beirut n.d.); Aḥmad ibn Ḥanbal, *Mawsūʿat aqwāl al-imām Aḥmad ibn Ḥanbal*, coll. al-Sayyid Abū al-Maʿāṭī al-Nūrī, Aḥmad ʿAbd al-Razzāq ʿĪd, and Maḥmūd Muḥammad Khalīl, 4 vols (Beirut 1417/1997); Saʿd, *Manhaj* (v. n. 1). Another comprehensive collection of Yaḥyā ibn Maʿīn's evaluations and other comments has also now been published, although I have not used it here: *Mawsūʿat aqāwīl Yaḥyā ibn Maʿīn*, coll. Bashshār ʿAwwād Maʿrūf, Jihād Muḥammad Khalīl, and Maḥmūd Muḥammad Khalīl, 5 vols (Tunis 1430/2009).

106. When Aḥmad or al-Nasāʾī is quoted inconsistently, I have counted the evaluation that agrees with Yaḥyā ibn Maʿīn's, to give Lucas's thesis of consistency the fullest chance of confirmation.

107. M. Cooperson, *Classical Arabic Biography* (Cambridge Studies in Islamic Civilization, Cambridge 2000), 3–6; *idem*, 'Ibn Saʿd,' *Arabic Literary Culture, 500–925*, ed. M. Cooperson and S.M. Toorawa, *Dictionary of Literary Biography* 311 (Detroit 2005), 193–204, esp. 200; admittedly, *contra* Juynboll, *Muslim Tradition*, 134.

108. G.H.A. Juynboll, *Encyclopedia of Canonical Ḥadīth* (Leiden 2007), xxiv.

Al-Nasāʾī's reliance on evaluations of men can also be gauged by what he saw fit to include in his *ḥadīth* collections. He names 326 shaykhs of his in *al-Mujtabā*, by my count, with some probable duplication. The 156 of them named in his own separate list of his shaykhs, *Tasmiyat al-shuyūkh* (*Muʿjam al-shuyūkh*), were responsible for 90 per cent of all the *ḥadīth* in *al-Mujtabā*. Al-Nasāʾī himself pronounces trustworthy 77 of them, responsible for 3,685 *ḥadīth* reports in *al-Mujtabā*, 64 per cent of the total, an average of 48 reports [401] per shaykh. Al-Nasāʾī himself pronounces middling 79 of them, responsible for 1,469 *ḥadīth* reports in *al-Mujtabā*, 26 per cent of the total, an average of 19 reports per shaykh. What this bespeaks is a preference for relying on the trustworthy but a substantial willingness to rely on the middling. There would be two reasons for reliance on the middling: lack of anything better concerning a particular point of law and confidence in particular *ḥadīth* reports they related because they were corroborated by parallel transmissions from others.

Nasāʾī's Affiliation in Law

In law, al-Nasāʾī has been identified as a Shāfiʿi. Al-ʿAbbādī (d. 458/1066) includes him in the earliest extant biographical dictionary of the Shāfiʿi school.[109] Ibn al-Athīr alleges in particular that his collection of *manāsik* (rituals, especially at the pilgrimage) follows Shāfiʿi doctrine. It is difficult to isolate points where the Shāfiʿi school disagrees with all three of the other main Sunni schools. Ibn Rushd does identify it as a uniquely Shāfiʿi position that circumambulation is unexceptionable at all times.[110] Al-Nasāʾī offers one *ḥadīth* report in support of this position, none opposed (*kitāb manāsik al-ḥajj* 137, *ibāḥat al-ṭawāf fī kull al-awqāt*, no. 2927). Similarly, Ibn Rushd identifies it as a uniquely Shāfiʿi position that circumambulation is validly performed while riding, not walking.[111] Al-Nasāʾī offers one *ḥadīth* report in support of this position, none opposed (*kitāb manāsik al-ḥajj* 140, *al-ṭawāf bi-al-bayt ʿalā al-rāḥilah*, no. 2931). Unfortunately, most of the inter-school disagreements over the pilgrimage have to do with the atonements appropriate to various sorts of defective performance, which area of the law *al-Mujtabā* ignores.

A check of disagreements in other parts of the law indicates considerable independence. *Al-Mujtabā* 7, *al-adhān* 5, *kayfa al-adhān*, nos. 632–3, supports the Shāfiʿi pattern of lines the muezzin cries aloud and lines he repeats in a subdued voice, but *al-adhān* 15, *al-tathwīb*, supplies two *ḥadīth* reports (nos. 648–9) in support of [402] adding the line

109. Al-ʿAbbādī, *K. Ṭabaqāt al-fuqahāʾ aš-šāfiʿīya*, ed. Gösta Vitestam, Veröffentlichungen der 'De Goeje-Stiftung' 21 (Leiden 1964), 51.

110. Ibn Rushd, *Bidāyat al-mujtahid wa-nihāyat al-muqtaṣid, al-ḥajj, al-qawl bi-al-ṭawāf, al-qawl fī shurūṭih* = ed. ʿAbd al-Majīd Ṭuʿmah Ḥalabī, 4 vols in 2 (Beirut 1418/1997), 2, 135.

111. Ibn Rushd, *Bidāyah, al-ḥajj, al-qawl fī al-jins al-thālith, al-qawl fī al-kaffārāt al-maskūt ʿanhā* = ed. ʿAbd al-Majīd Ṭuʿmah Ḥalabī, 4 vols in 2 (Beirut 1418/1997), 2, 172.

al-ṣalāh khayr min al-nawm ('Prayer is better than sleep') at the call to the dawn prayer, against the Shāfiʿi school and in support of the other three. Concerning whether to raise the hands throughout the ritual prayer or only near the beginning, al-Nasāʾī begins with a *ḥadīth* report in support of raising the hands repeatedly, in support of the Shāfiʿi and Ḥanbali position, then another allowing one to raise them only at the beginning, in support of the Ḥanafi position (*al-Mujtabā* 12, *al-taṭbīq* 19, *bāb rafʿ al-yadayn ḥadhwa al-mankibayn ʿinda al-rafʿ*, no. 1058, and 20, *al-rukhṣah fī tark dhālik*, no. 1059).[112] In the section of the *Umm* on the *tashahhud* near the end of the ritual prayer, al-Shāfiʿī relates a *ḥadīth* report through al-Layth ibn Saʿd in which the first line is *al-taḥīyāt al-mubārakāt al-ṣalawāt al-ṭayyibāt lillāh*, then observes that various different versions have been related but that this is the form he likes best.[113] Al-Nasāʾī reports the same form but as the fourth of five variants, with no indication of special favour (*al-Mujtabā*, *al-taṭbīq* 103, *nawʿ ākhar min al-tashahhud*, no. 1175). This particular variant is not reported in *al-Sunan al-kubrā*, although several others are.[114]

It appears, then, that Ibn al-Athīr was right to remark agreement with Shāfiʿi doctrine in *kitāb al-manāsik* but probably not to extrapolate general agreement. In general, rather, al-Nasāʾī is most securely identified as an independent investigator of the traditionist-jurisprudents, the party that expected sound *ḥadīth* to indicate the law with little need for sophisticated reasoning or, for one knowing much *ḥadīth*, relying on the opinions of recent jurisprudents.[115] His *Tasmiyat fuqahāʾ al-amṣār* includes continual comments on *ḥadīth* transmission (e.g., of each of Ibn Abī Laylā and Abū Ḥanīfah, 'He was not strong in *ḥadīth*') and organizes jurisprudents geographically, casting doubt on whether he recognized personal schools.[116] Al-Shāfiʿī and his followers appear among the people of Mecca, doubtfully where al-Nasāʾī would have included himself. At the same time, al-Nasāʾī [403] evidently did not expect to define the law solely by letting *ḥadīth* reports speak for themselves, for *al-Mujtabā* includes long disquisitions by al-Nasāʾī himself on agricultural contracts and the division of booty.[117]

112. The Māliki school was divided on this question, although tending toward the Shāfiʿi position. V. M.I. Fierro, 'La polémique à propos de *rafʿ al-yadayn fī l-ṣalāt* dans al-Andalus,' *Studia Islamica*, no. 65 (1987), 69–90.

113. Shāfiʿī, *Umm* 1, 101 = ed. ʿAbd al-Muṭṭalib, 2, 269.

114. Nasāʾī, *al-Sunan al-kubrā*, *k. ṣifat al-ṣalāh* 76, 78–80, *ījāb al-tashahhud*, *al-tashahhud*, and *nawʿ ākhar min al-tashahhud*.

115. 'Traditionist-jurisprudents' (*fuqahāʾ aṣḥāb al-ḥadīth*) is Ibn al-Nadīm's term. V. further C. Melchert, 'Traditionist-jurisprudents and the Framing of Islamic Law,' *Islamic Law and Society* 8 (2001), 383–406 [*HPL 13].

116. Quotation at *Majmūʿat rasāʾil*, 8 32. Also appended to Bukhārī, *Ḍuʿafāʾ*, ed. Zāyid, 124.

117. Nasāʾī, *Mujtabā*, *al-muzāraʿah*, *dhikr ikhtilāf al-alfāẓ al-maʾthūrah*, after nos. 3959 and 3969; *qasm al-fay*,' nos. 4152–3. There is also a short statement from al-Nasāʾī after no. 5613 condemning all alcoholic drinks, attributing drunkenness to every drop, not just the last.

Al-Mujtabā includes over 90 Companion *ḥadīth* reports, almost 2 per cent of all items, eight opinions of Followers (but note that no. 3786 names four Follower opinions not separately numbered). By comparison, about 9 per cent of al-Bukhārī's *Ṣaḥīḥ* is given to Companion *ḥadīth*, 11 per cent of Abū Dāwūd's *Sunan*. The difference seems to reflect the increasing eclipse of Companion *ḥadīth* by Prophet across the ninth century. It need not be taken as evidence of loyalty to al-Shāfiʿī in particular, famous though he is for the promotion of Prophet *ḥadīth*, for the *Umm* cites Prophet and Companion *ḥadīth* in a ratio of only 3:2.

Several biographers have observed that al-Nasāʾī is sometimes referred to in *ḥadīth* collections as a qadi. Al-Ṭabarānī (d. 360/976) said in his *Muʿjam*, 'There related to us Abū ʿAbd al-Raḥmān al-Nasāʾī the qadi in Old Cairo . . . .' Abū ʿAwānah (d. 316/929) said in his *Ṣaḥīḥ*, 'There related to us Aḥmad ibn Shuʿayb al-Nasāʾī, qadi for Homs . . . .'[118] It seems possible that someone did name him qadi for Homs at some time, most likely as someone's deputy; however, I have seen no evidence of it from our usual sources for judicial appointments, which stress the main centres.

Nasāʾī's Shiʿism

Al-Nasāʾī is said to have died for his loyalty to ʿAlī and especially hostility toward Muʿāwiyah. The story is told that he professed to have composed a book on the virtues of ʿAlī in hopes that God would guide to the truth the many in Damascus who wrongly disparaged him. Later, he composed a book on the virtues of all the Companions. When someone asked him why he hadn't brought out *ḥadīth* praising Muʿāwiyah, he reportedly said, 'What might I bring [404] out? "May God not satisfy his belly"?'[119] (Later biographies place this exchange immediately before his fatal beating, but not *Tārīkh madīnat Dimashq*.) Al-Nasāʾī alludes here to a *ḥadīth* report, included by Muslim in his *Ṣaḥīḥ*, according to which the Prophet said 'May God not satisfy his belly' after he had three times asked a boy to bring out Muʿāwiyah and the boy had three times come back to say that Muʿāwiyah was eating (and so would not come).[120] There is some uncertainty over what the friends of Muʿāwiyah did to him. Al-Sakhāwī quotes Ibn Mandah the Isfahani traditionist (d. 395/1005) on al-Nasāʾī's beating, offering three pointings: they continued to press on his *ḥ*ḍʾayn* (meaning not found by me), his *ḥiḍnayn* (breast or sides), or his

118. Dhahabī, *Siyar* 14, 132. The editor of this volume, Akram al-Būshayyī, provides a reference to Ṭabarānī in an edition not available to me. Only the beginning of Abū ʿAwānah's collection has been published, which does not include any reference to al-Nasāʾī: Abū ʿAwānah, *al-Musnad*, 2 vols (Hyderabad 1362–3).

119. Ibn Manẓūr, *Mukhtaṣar Tārīkh Dimashq* 3, 101.

120. Muslim, *Ṣaḥīḥ*, *k. al-birr*, *bāb man laʿanahu al-nabī*, no. 2604.

khuṣyayn (testicles) until they had put him out of the mosque.[121] Altogether, it seems most likely that James Robson's interpretation was correct: 'he was kicked on the testicles and put out of the mosque.'[122]

Still, al-Nasāʾī's Shiʿism was moderate. He characterizes ʿAbd al-Salām ibn Ṣāliḥ al-Harawī (d. 236/851) as 'a foul Rāfiḍī.'[123] He deprecates the inclination of al-Jārūd ibn Muʿādh al-Tirmidhī (d. 244/858–9) towards Murjiʾism (which presumably included his refusing to choose between ʿAlī and Muʿāwiyah) but pronounces him trustworthy in *ḥadīth* and includes him in *al-Mujtabā*.[124] *Al-Sunan al-kubrā* includes some decidedly non-Shiʿi *ḥadīth* reports. For example, ʿĀʾishah is quoted as saying that the Prophet's favourite Companions were Abū Bakr, then ʿUmar, then Abū ʿUbaydah ibn al-Jarrāḥ, refusing to go any further (conspicuously mentioning neither ʿUthmān nor ʿAlī).[125] The *kitāb al-manāqib* there includes sections for Ṭalḥah, al-Zubayr, and ʿĀʾishah, who fought against ʿAlī in the First Civil War, although no section for Muʿāwiyah. (By comparison, al-Bukhārī's *Ṣaḥīḥ* includes sections on all of these, including Muʿāwiyah, while Muslim's includes *ḥadīth* praising the first three but not specifically Muʿāwiyah.) Although al-Nasāʾī is listed among Shiʿi writers in some modern compilations, Muḥammad al-Kāẓim, editor of *Khaṣāʾiṣ ʿAlī*, more credibly denies that he should be.[126] But [405] this is using the modern definition of 'Shiʿism.' Medieval writers, who distinguished between mild *tashayyuʿ* and severe *rafḍ*, validly applied the former term to al-Nasāʾī.[127]

Al-Nasāʾī's Significance

Al-Nasāʾī's principal significance for students of Islamic history is probably his *ḥadīth* criticism, which resembles that of other *ḥadīth* collectors and critics of the ninth century but of which he explains examples in more detail than most others. He also illustrates the tendency for Khurasan to produce notable *ḥadīth* collectors, although he collected the bulk of his *ḥadīth* and even settled elsewhere, by contrast with, among others, al-Bukhārī and Muslim, who likewise collected the bulk of their *ḥadīth* in Iraq and elsewhere but returned to the Northeast at the end of their lives. He illustrates the tendency over the ninth century for Prophet *ḥadīth* to eclipse Companion and later *ḥadīth* as the basis of Islamic law. He illustrates the persistence of purely traditionalist Sunni law, expecting *ḥadīth* reports to virtually speak for themselves and resisting identification with any of

121. Sakhāwī, *Bughyah*, 90.
122. Robson, 'Transmission,' 39.
123. Nasāʾī, *Tasmiyat al-shuyūkh*, 73.
124. Ibn Ḥajar, *Tahdhīb* 2, 53.
125. Nasāʾī, *al-Sunan al-kubrā*, *k. al-manāqib* 15, *Abū ʿUbaydah*, no. 8201.
126. Kāẓim, introd'n to *Khaṣāʾiṣ*, 33–4.
127. E.g. Ibn al-Jawzī, *Muntaẓam* 6, 132 = ed. ʿAṭā and ʿAṭā, 13, 156; Dhahabī, *Siyar* 14, 133.

the emerging schools of law. Finally, he illustrates the persistence of an unclear boundary between Sunnism and Shiʿism.

For present purposes, however, al-Nasāʾī's significance is most importantly whether examination of his works confirms or refutes some of the many theses with which G.H.A. Juynboll enriched the modern discussion of *ḥadīth* collection and criticism. I have proposed contradictory evaluations of traditionists from al-Nasāʾī and other acknowledged master critics as confirmation that the medieval method of *ḥadīth* criticism was substantially arbitrary, although far from completely so. Al-Nasāʾī evidently did not include every *ḥadīth* report he knew in his major collections, but medieval estimates of his total knowledge seem to be grossly exaggerated. On both of these points, it appears to me that Juynboll was essentially correct although probably overstating his case.

Juynboll's most important single articles on the methods of ninth-century traditionists were probably his translation of Muslim's introduction to *al-Jāmiʿ al-ṣaḥīḥ*, published in 1984, and '(Re)appraisal of Some Technical Terms in *Ḥadīth* Science,' published in 2001.[128] [406] I have already cited the latter article once and glossed as 'corroborated' one of the key terms that he analyses there, *tābaʿa*. As Juynboll recognizes, medieval *ḥadīth* critics normally used *tābaʿa* of what they considered a good thing, whereas he supposes that 'dives' are a sign of forgery or theft, categories recognized by the medieval critics (*waḍʿ* and *sariqah*, respectively) but sparingly applied. Juynboll has been specifically attacked on this point by Halit Ozkan, so far as I can tell to little effect.[129] Ranging rather unsystematically over the whole length of *ḥadīth* literature from the ninth century to the twentieth, Ozkan finds the patterns that Juynboll has made us familiar with, mainly *isnād* networks with common links, whom medieval *ḥadīth* critics commonly call *madār*s ('pivots'), alongside single strands of *akhbār al-āḥād* supporting the same reports. The difference between Juynboll and Ozkan is little more than its seeming obvious to Juynboll that the common links are the probable originators of *ḥadīth* reports, while single strands are to be disregarded, whereas it seems obvious to Ozkan and the medieval Sunni critics that *akhbār al-āḥād* may offer valuable corroboration and that *ḥadīth* reports are to be presumed authentic.[130] The authenticity debate is deadlocked, I tend to think, depending on initial assumptions, as forcefully argued by Herbert Berg.[131] I myself tend toward

128. G.H.A. Juynboll, 'Muslim's Introduction to his *Ṣaḥīḥ*,' *Jerusalem Studies in Arabic and Islam*, no. 5 (1984), 263–311.

129. H. Ozkan, 'The *Common Link* and its Relation to the *Madār*,' *Islamic Law and Society* 11 (2004), 42–77.

130. '"The burden of proof" rests upon scholars who regard the single strands as unhistorical': so Ozkan, '*Common Link*,' 47 n. The sceptical position since Goldziher has been that the extant body of *ḥadīth* is so replete with contradiction that back projection must be the scholarly presumption, genuine antiquity what needs demonstration. Ozkan avoids discussing theft and how to detect it.

131. H. Berg, *The Development of Exegesis in Early Islam*, Curzon Studies in the Qurʾān (Richmond, Surrey 2000), chap. 2. Cf. Michael Cook, who has said, 'The bottom line in the study of early Islamic traditions may well be that anyone can wriggle out of anything': 'Eschatology and the Dating of Traditions,'

the sceptical side, like Juynboll (although Berg classifies him among the 'sanguine' for thinking that *isnād* analysis can suggest probable dates of origin within the eighth century). As practised by al-Nasāʾī and his contemporaries, *isnād* comparison must have been much better at detecting clumsy back projection than clever, also better at detecting back projection of [407] aberrant views than of common wisdom. Both Juynboll's studies and Ozkan's are welcome as contributing to the shift among modern scholars from stress on the terminology of evaluations ('trustworthy,' 'weak,' and so on) to stress on *isnād* comparison.[132] It is certainly my impression that al-Nasaʾi consciously identified the reliable *ḥadīth* above all by *isnād* comparison.

Princeton Papers in Near Eastern Studies 1 (1992), 23–47, at 35. Harald Motzki has substantially conceded the importance of initial assumptions, saying 'concrete assumptions are needed: for instance, on the dimensions of fabrication and falsification in the field of *Ḥadīṯ*; on the ways how knowledge was transmitted in the first two centuries of Islam; on the nature of the common links and single strands': 'Dating Muslim Traditions,' *Arabica* 52 (2005), 204–53, at 253.

132. Dickinson, *Development*, made a major advance, esp. chap. 6. With J.A.C. Brown, *Hadīth* (Foundations of Islam, Oxford: Oneworld, 2009), the new stress on *isnād* comparison has moved into the textbooks. It also informs Ghassan Abdul-Jabbar, *Bukhari* (Makers of Islamic Civilization, London 2007), and seems to be making progress even in Arabophone ḥadīth scholarship: *v.* esp. Abū Bakr ibn Laṭīf Kāfī, *Manhaj al-imām Aḥmad fī al-taʿlīl wa-atharuhu fī al-jarḥ wa-al-taʿdīl*, supv. Muḥammad ʿAbd al-Nabī (Beirut 1426/2005).

PIETY

6

THE TRANSITION FROM ASCETICISM TO MYSTICISM AT THE MIDDLE OF THE NINTH CENTURY C.E.

Muslims seem to insist so strongly on divine transcendence, to stress so highly the element of morality in religion, that the development of an Islamic mystical tradition has sometimes been attributed to foreign influences.[1] Louis Massignon argued, largely on the evidence of terminology, that Islamic mysticism developed out of an earlier, thoroughly Islamic ascetical tradition.[2] A transition from Islamic asceticism to Islamic mysticism has now become a scholarly commonplace.[3] No one has gone further, though, by way of (1) precisely defining "ascetical" and "mystical" and (2) showing just where and when the transition took place. I think I can demonstrate that the extant record is overwhelmingly ascetical, not mystical, until Dhū al-Nūn al-Miṣrī. Thereafter, truly mystical schools emerged at about the same time in Khurasan (Abū Yazīd and especially the less famous

Kevin Reinhart commented helpfully on an earlier draft of this article.

1. See, for example, Reynold A. Nicholson, "A Historical Enquiry Concerning the Origin and Development of Sufiism," *Journal of the Royal Asiatic Society*, 1906, 303–348, esp. 306. It is accurate to equate Islamic mysticism with Sufism in discussing the perceptions of Western scholars early in this century; however, Jacqueline Chabbi has demonstrated that Sufism, by that name, was only one of several mystical traditions until at least the eleventh century C.E.: "Réflexions sur le soufisme iranien primitif," *Journal asiatique* 266 (1978):37–55.

2. See above all Louis Massignon, *Essai sur les origines du lexique technique de la mystique musulmane*, rev. edn. (Paris: J. Vrin, 1954).

3. E.g., see *The Encyclopedia of Religion*, ed. Mircea Eliade (New York: Macmillan, 1987), s.v. "Sufism," by Peter J. Awn.

Originally published in *Studia Islamica* 83 (1996): 51–70.

Abū Ḥafṣ al-Naysābūrī) and Baghdad (al-Kharrāz, al-Nūrī). There was soon trouble with old-style ascetics, and seventy-odd Sufis were arrested in the Inquisition of Ghulām Khalīl. Then Islamic mysticism found the apologist it needed in al-Junayd, who developed [52] a new language to treat mystical experience without unduly alarming ascetics.

I: The Emergence of Mysticism at the Middle of the Ninth Century

The opposition of ascetical to mystical religion goes back above all to Max Weber.[4] It has been developed by numerous others, notably the Neo-Orthodox theologian Paul Tillich, and skillfully summarized by Gert H. Mueller.[5] Schematically, ascetical piety emphasizes obedience to a transcendent God; imposing God's will on the natural world. Mystical piety, by contrast, is about communion with an immanent God; about finding God revealed in the objects of nature. God can be obeyed at any time, in any place (indeed, must be obeyed at all times and in all places); therefore, the ascetic will pay less regard than the mystic to special times and places. Ascetics characteristically perceive more personality in divinity than mystics, for whom divinity may seem very diffuse. Ascetics tend to be pessimists, and may alternate personally between fear and chosenness. Mystics, by contrast, tend to be optimists, confidant of abundant grace.

"Asceticism" is commonly used to denote a program of self-discipline and austerity, and as such may well characterize the practice of mystics;[6] however, that is emphatically not the sense in which I use it here. Rather, I use "asceticism" in contrast to "mysticism," as have Weber, Massignon, and the others who have bequeathed the term. Similarly, a Muslim need not be a Sufi for there to be distinctly mystical elements in his or her outlook. Neither will there be found a Muslim mystic whose piety is without strong ascetical elements. On the contrary, elements of both asceticism and mysticism will be found in every religion and every individual's worldview; however, note well, in different proportions that can be measured.

Islamicists in particular have often used "asceticism" to translate the Arabic *zuhd*, "mysticism" to translate "*taṣawwuf*." I use "asceticism" [53] rather than *zuhd* for the sake of precision, to indicate an ideal type identified by students of religion in the twentieth century rather than the conscious ethical ideal of medieval Muslims.[7] I use "mysticism"

4. Max Weber, *Economy and Society*, ed. Guenther Roth & Claus Wittich, 2 vols. (Berkeley: Univ. of Calif. Press, 1978), 544–551.

5. My debt to Mueller is great: "Asceticism and Mysticism. A Contribution Towards the Sociology of Faith," in *International Yearbook for the Sociology of Religion* 8: *Sociological Theories of Religion/Religion and Language*, ed. Günter Dux, Thomas Luckmann, & Joachim Matthes (Opladen: Westdeutscher Verlag, 1973), 68–132, with appendices summarizing earlier dichotomies by Nietzsche, Otto, Tillich, & al.

6. E.g., *Encyclopedia of Religion*, s.v. "Asceticism," by Walter O. Kaelber. Cf. Mueller, 97f.

7. For the ethical ideal of *zuhd*, see Leah Kinberg, "What Is Meant by *Zuhd*," *Studia Islamica*, no. 61 (1985), 27–44.

both for the sake of precision, as the opposite of "asceticism," and because it is now clear that classical Sufism, the *taṣawwuf* of the late ninth century and after, was not the only variety of Islamic mysticism.[8]

We may conveniently take our chronology of Islamic mysticism from the biographical dictionary of ʿAbd al-Raḥmān al-Sulamī (d. AH 412/AD 1021), *Ṭabaqāt al-ṣūfiyah.*[9] Al-Sulamī divides the Sufis up to his time into five generations each comprising twenty names. For each Sufi, he gives name, dates, a short characterization, a sample of the prophetic hadith reports he related, and then a collection of his sayings, usually attached to chains of transmitters. My method is to examine these figures' sayings, looking for evidence of the ascetical or mystical worldview. Further sayings can be found in other guides to Sufism like Abū Naṣr al-Sarrāj (d. 378/988), *Kitāb al-Lumaʿ fī al-taṣawwuf*, and Abū Nuʿaym al-Iṣbahānī (d. 430/1038), *Ḥilyat al-awliyā*ʾ, less often in other standard biographical dictionaries.[10]

One must always beware of later generations' having projected a given saying back onto a famous early figure. Fairly seldom does this appear to be a problem in the *Ṭabaqāt* of al-Sulamī. First, this biographical dictionary begins after the earliest period, where such projections seem to be thickest. (Contrast the earlier volumes of Abū Nuʿaym.) Second, al-Sulamī's chief tendency must have been to demonstrate continuity between the Sufis of his day and the ascetics with whom he begins: if the sayings of the earliest figures suggest rather discontinuity, it seems unlikely that he has projected the ideas of his own time back to theirs. Finally, quotations of the earlier figures do, for the most part, suggest coherent, individual outlooks, not mere literary types (although it is not the [54] main purpose of this essay to reconstruct those outlooks — rather, simply, to weigh their ascetical and mystical elements).[11]

Almost without exception, the earliest figures of al-Sulamī's first generation seem pronouncedly ascetical. The earliest of all is Ibrāhīm ibn Ad'ham (d. 163/779–780?), most of whose sayings indicate an other-worldly but ascetical outlook; for example, "Love of

8. Roughly contemporary with classical Sufism in Baghdad there developed the Karrāmīyah and Malāmatīyah in Khurasan, for whom see Jacqueline Chabbi, "Remarques sur le développement historique des mouvements ascétiques et mystiques au Khurâsân," *Studia Islamica*, no. 46 (1977), 5–72. Sahl al-Tustarī and after him the Sālimīyah constituted a rival movement in Basra. From the thirteenth century C.E., there developed rivals to Sufism of the Qalandari type, for whom see Ahmet T. Karamustafa, *God's Unruly Friends* (Salt Lake City: Univ. of Utah Press, 1994).

9. Al-Sulamī, *Ṭabaqāt al-ṣūfiyah*, ed. Johannes Pedersen (Leiden: E.J. Brill, 1960). Also available as edited by Nūr al-Dīn Sharībah (Cairo: Jamāʿat al-Azhar lil-Nashr wa-al-Ṭibāʿah, 1953).

10. Al-Sarrāj, *K. al-Lumaʿ fī al-taṣawwuf*, ed. Reynold A. Nicholson, E.J.W. Gibb Memorial Ser. 12 (London: Luzac, 1914); Abū Nuʿaym, *Ḥilyat al-awliyā*ʾ, 10 vols. (Cairo: Maṭbaʿat al-Saʿādah, 1932–1938).

11. For a sustained attempt to characterize the major figures of the early period, see Massignon, *Essai*. On the apologetic purposes of the tenth- and eleventh-century biographers, see Chabbi, "Réflexions," 55.

meeting people is part of the love of the world, while leaving them is part of leaving the world."[12] Reports of the way he lived further suggest an ascetical temperament: austerities like continual fasting, winter clothing of only a fur with no undershirt, and no shoes or headcover.[13] Likewise, his career as a frontier raider (by one account, he died fighting in Upper Mesopotamia) suggests a man of struggle — of action rather than contemplation.[14] When he speaks of coming close to God, he maintains an ascetical emphasis on God's personality: "It is impossible that you should become close to him (*an tuwāliyah*) without his becoming close to you."[15]

The piety of al-Fuḍayl ibn ʿIyāḍ (d. Mecca, 187/803), too, is overwhelmingly ascetical. His servant Ibrāhīm ibn al-Ashʿath said, "When he heard mention of God or . . . heard the Qurʾān, fear and sadness overcame him, his eyes filled up, and he wept."[16] Abū ʿAlī al-Rāzī declared,[17]

> I was disciple to al-Fuḍayl ibn ʿIyāḍ for thirty years and never saw him laugh or smile save the day his son ʿAlī died. I asked him about that, so he told me, "God (mighty and glorious is he) loved this matter, and I have loved what God loved."

Most of his recorded sayings drive at the cultivation of a serious and single-minded devotion; for example, "Blessèd is he who flees from people, keeps company with his Lord, and weeps over his sin."[18]

Shaqīq ibn Ibrāhīm (d. Kūlān, 184/810) was said to be the first to speak of the states (*aḥwāl*) in Transoxania, anticipating the usage of mystics.[19] However, actual quotations emphasize divine predestination, on the one [55] hand, mourning and insecurity, on the other, betraying a thoroughly ascetical outlook; for example,[20]

> One who is self-possessed (*ʿāqil*) never departs from these three particles: first, that he be afraid on account of sins that have gone before; second, that he know

12. Abū Nuʿaym, 8:19.
13. Abū Nuʿaym, 7:373.
14. Abū Nuʿaym, 8:9.
15. Abū Nuʿaym, 8:36. It is probable that the large collection of his sayings does include many inventions reflecting the piety of a later date. Especially dubious are circumspect attributions through later mystics like the series that al-Sulamī quotes from al-Kharrāz, 16–21 = Sharībah, ed., 31–35 (henceforward "Sh.").
16. Abū Nuʿaym, 8:84.
17. Abū Nuʿaym, 8:100.
18. Al-Sulamī, 12 = Sh., 14.
19. "States" and "stations" became Sufi technical terms for landmarks along the mystical path. Some masters assigned them a definite order, or distinguished between transient "states" and permanent "stations," but usage was not uniform. See *The Encyclopaedia of Islam*, new edn. (Leiden: E.J. Brill, 1960–), s.v. "Ḥāl," by L. Gardet.
20. Al-Sulamī, *Ṭabaqāt*, 55 = Sh., 63.

> not what will be made to come to him from one moment to the next; and third, that he fear the obscurity of the outcome.

Shaqīq died fighting the pagan Turks.[21]

Maʿrūf al-Karkhī (d. 200/815–816) was a prominent Baghdadi ascetic, concerned with al-Fuḍayl to devote himself wholly to God. For example, when Maʿrūf was asked about the hallmark of the friends (of God; *awliyāʾ*), he answered, "their concern for God, their preoccupation with him, and their flight to him."[22] He adds a definite and thoroughly ascetical emphasis on good works; for example, "Seeking paradise without works is one of the sins. Awaiting intercession without a cause is a species of delusion. Hoping for mercy from one who is disobeyed is ignorance and stupidity."[23] Equally ascetical appear to be the rest of the earlier names in al-Sulamī's first generation: the Basran preacher Manṣūr ibn ʿAmmār (d. Baghdad, early 200's/ca. 820?), the Kufan immigrant to Antioch ʿAbd Allāh ibn Khubayq (d. early 200's/ca. 820 or after?), the Syrian Abū Sulaymān al-Dārānī (d. 215/830–831), Aḥmad ibn ʿĀṣim al-Anṭākī (d. 220/835), the famous Baghdadi Bishr al-Ḥāfī (d. 227/841), and the Syrian traditionist Ibn Abī al-Ḥawārī (d. 230/844–845).

Around the middle of the ninth century, we see a change: some of the later figures in al-Sulamī's first generation are still predominantly ascetical, like the earlier, but an equal number are mystics. Al-Muḥāsibī (d. Baghdad, 243/857–858) pursued thorough self-purification with the object of knowing only God: "When love is made firm in the servant's heart, he has nothing left over for remembering man or jinn, heaven or hell — nothing but the recollection (*dhikr*) of the beloved."[24] In such oblivion there might seem to be something like a mystical transcendence of opposites; notice, however, that al-Muḥāsibī does not speak of God's loving the servant, but only of the servant's loving God.[25] Ascetical, too, [56] seems al-Muḥāsibī's attention to the external concomitants of inward purification: "Whoever has corrected his interior by means of self-observation and sincerity will ornament his exterior with striving and following the Sunnah (the precept and example of Muḥammad, leading source of Islamic law)."[26]

---

21. Abū Nuʿaym, 8:64.
22. Al-Sulamī, 79 = Sh., 90.
23. Al-Sulamī, 78 = Sh., 89.
24. Abū Nuʿaym, 10:78.
25. To be sure, the Qurʾān itself speaks of God's loving his creatures (5.55 is oft cited), and al-Muḥāsibī devoted a treatise to the love of God. The apparent extract in Abū Nuʿaym, 10:76–79, tends to press the difference, though, between God's love and the worshipper's. God loves in spite of having no need of the worshipper, whereas the worshipper's love springs from gratitude toward God (76). Moreover, quite in the ascetic tradition, love (*ḥubb*) is expressly equated with longing (*shawq*), a felt lack (79), which cannot be felt by God.
26. Abū Nuʿaym, 10:75. Josef van Ess, *Die Gedankenwelt des Ḥāriṯ al-Muḥāsibī*, Bonner orientalistische Studien, n.s., 12 (Bonn: Orientalischen Seminars, 1961), is thorough and reliable, and often refers to al-Muḥāsibī as a mystic; however, van Ess does not use the term to distinguish between al-Muḥāsibī's

Sarī al-Saqaṭī (d. 253/867?), another Baghdadi, appears to be closer the ascetical pole. As with others before him, his concern for pure devotion to God alone makes him anti-social: "Do not ask anything of anyone, do not take anything of anyone, and have nothing of which to give anything to anyone."[27] He seems anxious about impeccable performance of his ritual duties: "If part of my *wird* prayer escapes me, I can never make it up."[28] Perfectly ascetical seems his concern to complement good works with orthodoxy: "A little according to the Sunnah is better than much with heresy."[29]

Our early sources quote Abū Turāb al-Nakhshabī (d. Ḥijāz, 245/859–860) as giving advice like that of earlier and contemporary ascetics, directed mainly at paying attention to God, not men, yet ever preserving the gulf between the worshipper and God; for example, "True wealth is that you be able to do without one who is like you, while true poverty is that you want not one who is like you."[30] Later sources associate him with miracles, usually an indication of the mystical outlook; however, these stories seem to date from the tenth century.[31] [57]

Aḥmad ibn Khiḍrawayh (d. 240/854–855), originally of Balkh, seems to be a transition figure difficult to characterize. His program of single-minded devotion to God was probably similar to that of his ascetical contemporaries and predecessors: "The truth of knowing is love of him with the heart, recollection of him with the tongue, and cutting off concern for everything but him."[32] Yet Aḥmad also hints at confidence in abundant grace, a trait of mystics notably absent in ascetics like Shaqīq ibn Ibrāhīm: "The way is

---

piety and an ascetic's. I assert not that van Ess is wrong but only that the elements of al-Muḥāsibī's piety that justify calling him a mystic do not outweigh those that make him an ascetic.

27. Al-Sulamī, 42 = Sh., 49.

28. Al-Sulamī, 43 = Sh., 50; Abū Nuʿaym, 10:124. The *wird* is a private prayer to be performed at a specific time but outside the five daily prescribed prayers.

29. Al-Sulamī, 45 = Sh., 52. The Islamic tradition may, on the whole, stress orthodoxy less than orthopraxy, and "Sunnah" may be translated "orthopraxy"; however, I interpret Sarī's statement in the light of several by his older contemporary Aḥmad Ibn Ḥanbal; e.g., "Orthodox reprobates are the friends of God, while heretical ascetics are the enemies of God (*fussāq ahl al-sunnah awliyāʾ Allāh wa-zuhhād ahl al-bidʿah aʿdāʾ Allāh*)" (apud Ibn Abī Yaʿlá, *Ṭabaqāt al-ḥanābilah*, ed. Muḥammad Ḥāmid al-Fiqī, 2 vols. [Cairo: Maṭbaʿat al-Sunnah al-Muḥammadīyah, 1952], 1:184). The heresies that bothered Aḥmad were above all the propositions (1) that the Qurʾān was created and (2) that its pronunciation was — propositions he never connects with unconventional practice. For a sensible study of Sarī al-Saqaṭī, see Tawfīq ibn ʿĀmir, "Al-Sarī al-Saqaṭī wa-nashʾat al-madrasah al-baghdādīyah fī al-taṣawwuf," *Ḥawlīyāt al-jāmiʿah al-tūnisīyah* 16 (1978): 187–225. Tawfīq finds him a transitional figure between "pure asceticism" (*al-zuhd al-maḥḍ*) and "mysticism" (*al-taṣawwuf*; 214f).

30. Al-Sulamī, 139 = Sh., 150.

31. See al-Qushayrī, *al-Risālah*, *Bāb fa-mā al-ghālib* . . . = (Cairo: Muṣṭafá al-Bābī al-Ḥalabī, 1318), 200; al-Subkī, *Ṭabaqāt al-shāfiʿīyah al-kubrá*, ed. ʿAbd al-Fattāḥ Muḥammad al-Ḥulw and Maḥmūd Muḥammad al-Ṭanāḥī, 10 vols. (Cairo: ʿĪsá al-Bābī al-Ḥalabī, 1964–1976), 2:308. Al-Khaṭīb al-Baghdādī tells a similar story of Dhū al-Nūn: *Tārīkh Baghdād*, 14 vols. (Cairo: Maktabat al-Khānjī, 1931), 5:214.

32. Al-Sulamī, 96 = Sh., 105.

clear, the truth is shining, and the caller has been heard: what confusion can there be after this save from blindness?"[33]

The earliest to seem clearly from his own sayings more mystical than ascetical is the Nubian Dhū al-Nūn al-Miṣrī (d. Giza, 245/860–246/861). His advice to one who would be humble has all the characters of the mystical outlook[34]:

> let him direct his soul to the greatness of God, for then it will dissolve and become pure. Whoever regards the power of God, his own power goes away, for all souls are poor next to his awesomeness.

So has Dhū al-Nūn's advice to seek revelation by looking at finite things: "Knowing (*maʿrifah*) is gotten by three: regarding affairs, how he has administered them; things ordained, how he has ordained them; and things created, how he has created them."[35] Dhū al-Nūn's involvement with alchemy and, syncretistically, ancient wisdom, agree well with a mystical outlook.[36] It does not appear that Dhū al-Nūn applied the term "Sufi" to himself, but R.A. Nicholson seems justified in regarding Dhū al-Nūn as virtually the founder of theosophical Sufism.[37]

The preacher Yaḥyá ibn Muʿādh al-Rāzī (d. Nishapur, 258/872) might be interpreted as either an ascetic or a mystic. His practical advice to think only on God sounds not unlike that of earlier ascetics. On the other hand, [58] he also has also has much to say about spiritual hierarchies that sound mystical; for example, ranking lowest the *abdāl*, associated with miracles, next the people of love, associated with blessings, highest the knowers, in perpetual recollection (*dhikr*).[38]

Unquestionably mystical is Abū Yazīd al-Basṭāmī (d. 261/875?).[39] His celebrated *shaṭaḥāt* — such scandalous outbursts as "There is nothing in this garment but God" — are classic examples of the mystical sensibility.[40] With Abū Yazīd, at last, the servant is aware

33. Al-Sulamī, 96 = Sh., 105.

34. Al-Sulamī, 25f. = Sh., 20.

35. Abū Nuʿaym, 9:39.

36. Al-Qifṭī, *Tārīkh al-ḥukamā,*' ed. Julius Lippert (Leipzig: Dieterlich'sche Verlagsbuchhandlung, 1903), 185.

37. Nicholson, "Historical Enquiry," 309. A manuscript from the 7th/13th cent., *K. Miʿyār al-taṣawwuf*, Kastamonu 2713, does present definitions of Sufism from Dhū al-Nūn (122b, 123b), but equally from figures like Jaʿfar al-Ṣādiq (89b) and Abū Ḥanīfah (124b), casting doubt on the historicity of every attribution. On the ms., see Fuat Sezgin, *Geschichte des arabischen Schrifttums*, 9 vols. (Leiden: E.J. Brill, 1967–), 1:646. The attribution to al-Kharrāz is impossible.

38. Al-Sarrāj, *Lumaʿ*, 327. Contemporary traditionists (collectors of hadith reports) used the term *abdāl* ("substitutes") to indicate the most saintly traditionists. For later Sufi usage, see *Encyclopaedia of Islam*, new edn., s.v. "Abdāl," by I. Goldziher.

39. Often "Bisṭāmī," but see al-Samʿānī, *K. al-Ansāb*, E.J.W. Gibb Memorial Ser. 20 (Leiden: E.J. Brill, 1912), 81a.

40. See Carl W. Ernst, *Words of Ecstasy in Sufism* (Albany: State Univ. of NY Press, 1985), part I.

that God reciprocates his love: "The wonder is not my love for you, when I am a poor slave: the only wonder is your love for me, when you are a mighty king."[41]

Abū Ḥafṣ al-Naysābūrī (d. 270/883–884?) is presented as virtually the founder of classical Sufism in Khurasan. Characteristically mystical is his recognition of special times and places: "Sufism (*al-taṣawwuf*) is a matter of etiquette (*adab*). For every time there is an etiquette, for every state there is an etiquette, and for every station there is an etiquette."[42] Significantly, Abū Ḥafṣ is the first in al-Sulamī's collection to identify his way as "Sufism." Dhū al-Nūn speaks of the people of truth (*ahl al-ḥaqq*) and the lover of God (*muḥibb Allāh*), Abū Yazīd of the friends (of God; *awliyā*ʾ), but not of "Sufis." Earlier references to "Sufis" by figures in *Ṭabaqāt al-ṣūfiyah* tend to be depreciative; for example, Abū Sulaymān al-Dārānī, "I have seen only one Sufi who was any good, ʿAbd Allāh ibn Marzūq,"[43] and Yaḥyá ibn Muʿādh al-Rāzī, "unlike ignorant would-be [59] Sufis" (*al-mutaṣawwifah al-jāhilīn*).[44] In Abū Ḥafṣ, al-Sulamī recognized a mystic like himself.[45]

Al-Sulamī's second generation of Sufis comprises mainly mystics. The earliest of this generation are the brothers Ibn Abī al-Ward, whose other-worldliness is still ascetical. "Whose soul does not love the world," declared Muḥammad (d. Baghdad, 263/877?), "the people of the earth will love him. Whose heart does not love the world, the people of heaven will love him."[46]

---

41. Abū Nuʿaym, 10:34. Of course, as noted earlier, the Qurʾān speaks of God's love for his people, and earlier figures than Abū Yazīd did not fail to notice. According to al-Sulamī, Ibn Abī al-Ḥawārī said that God must have loved his servant before his servant can love God; yet, characteristically, the sign of loving God, Ibn Abī al-Ḥawārī begins, is obedience to God (al-Sulamī, *Ṭabaqāt*, 90 = Sh., 90).

42. Al-Sulamī, 110 = Sh., 119.

43. Abū Nuʿaym, 9:260. Cf. the remark of Yūnus ibn ʿAbd al-Aʿlá (d. 264/877), an Egyptian student of al-Shāfiʿī's: "I have seen no self-possessed man (*ʿāqil*) among the *ṣūfiyah* save Idrīs ibn Yaḥyá al-Khawlānī," apud al-Dhahabī, *Siyar aʿlām al-nubalāʾ*, 25 vols. (Beirut: Muʾassasat al-Risālah), 10 (ed. Muḥammad Nuʿaym al-ʿIrqasūsī, 1982): 166. Abū Nuʿaym does relate a story in which Dhū al-Nūn meets, in the mountains near Antioch, an apparent madwomen who is clad in wool, although not called *ṣūfiyah*. She enjoins disinterested obedience to God (Abū Nuʿaym, 9:340). The earliest *ṣūfiyah* in Egypt were rowdies in Alexandria who "enjoined the good" and rejected the governor's authority in the year 200/815–816, according to al-Kindī, *The Governors and Judges of Egypt*, ed. Rhuvon Guest, E.J.W. Gibb Memorial Ser. 19 (London: Luzac, 1912), 162. Louis Massignon cites early references to *ṣūf*, *ṣūfī*, and *ṣūfiyah* in *Essai*, 131–133.

44. Al-Sulamī, 104 = Sh., 113.

45. Chabbi observes that the biographer al-Ḥākim al-Naysābūrī applies the term "*ṣūfī*" to no one earlier than Abū Bakr al-Wāsiṭī (d. after 320/930), suggesting to her that Abū Ḥafṣ was a Malāmatī who would not have made such remarks about Sufism as al-Sulamī attributes to him: "Remarques," 31, 40f, 62–64. Al-Sulamī's attribution is justified by the story of Abū Ḥafṣ's travelling to Baghdad and meeting al-Junayd (for which see note 55). Whether or not we accept al-Sulamī's quotation of Abū Ḥafṣ, Iraqi mystics must have applied the term to themselves in about the 260's/873–883.

46. Al-Sulamī, 248 = Sh., 250.

Sahl al-Tustarī (d. Basra, 283/896?) likewise seems to fall mainly on the ascetical side of the spectrum, recommending avoidance of wrongdoing over active good works: "As for works of piety, the pious and the reprobate alike perform them, whereas no one avoids acts of rebellion save the righteous (*ṣiddīq*)."[47] He sees a constant danger of condemnation: "There is no heart or soul save that God is watching over it night and day. Any heart or soul in which he sees a need for other than him, he gives power over it to the devil."[48] Still, like al-Muḥāsibī, Sahl was led by his concentration on God alone towards something close to mystical communion; for example, "The heart will not deem anything greater than, preferable to, or more magnificent than its beholding God (mighty and glorious is he), its listening to him, and its talking with him."[49]

Al-Kharrāz (d. Baghdad, 277/890–891?) was disciple to Dhū al-Nūn in Egypt as well as to the Syrian Abū ʿUbayd al-Busrī, Sarī al-Saqaṭī, and other Iraqis. An experience he describes in his *Kitāb al-Sirr* seems clearly mystical[50]: [60]

> If one of them was asked, "What do you know?", he would say "God." When he talked he would say "God", when he looked he would say "God", and if his limbs spoke, they would say "God", for his members are filled with God.

It was he who first spoke of *fanāʾ* (annihilation) and *baqāʾ* (remaining) to describe the contemplative's first losing all consciousness of his own finitude, then subsisting in contemplation.[51]

Al-Nūrī (d. Baghdad, 295/907–908), the second name in al-Sulamī's second generation, is plainly in the mystical camp. Because it drew down persecution on him, he is famous for saying, "I love God and God loves me" (*aʿshaqu Allāh wa-Allāh yaʿshaqunī*).[52] Al-Sulamī's quotations tend to be clever rather than clear, but one of the most direct is typically mystical: "Joining with the Truth is parting from everything else, as parting with everything else is joining with it."[53] Al-Nūrī is the earliest figure in al-Sulamī's

---

47. Al-Sulamī, 202f = Sh., 209; cf. Abū Nuʿaym, 10:197. Cf. also Aḥmad Ibn Ḥanbal, apud Ibn Abī Yaʿlá, *Ṭabaqāt al-ḥanābilah* 1:325. When asked whether the Prophet's enjoining and forbidding (*amr*, *nahy*) were not the same, Aḥmad answered, "Yes, but his forbidding is more severe (*ashadd*)."

48. Al-Sulamī, 200f = Sh., 208; Abū Nuʿaym, 10:194.

49. Al-Ṣiqillī (d. ca. 423/1031–1032?), ed., *Kalām*, Köprülü (Istanbul) 727, 3a. The overall tone of al-Ṣiqillī's collections (Sezgin, 1:647) is fully as ascetical as the much smaller selections of al-Sulamī and Abū Nuʿaym. On al-Tustarī, see Gerhard Böwering, *The Mystical Vision of Existence in Classical Islam*, Studien zur Sprache, Geschichte u. Kultur des islamischen Orients, n.s. 9 (Berlin: Walter de Gruyter, 1980). Like van Ess concerning al-Muḥāsibī, Böwering often refers to al-Tustarī as a mystic, with like justification; that is, not to distinguish him from ascetics but rather on the basis of the mystical elements in his outlook.

50. Apud al-Khaṭīb al-Baghdādī, 4:277.

51. Al-Sulamī, 223 = Sh., 228.

52. Al-Sarrāj, *Pages From the "Kitāb al-Lumaʿ,"* ed. A.J. Arberry (London: Luzac, 1947), 5.

53. Al-Sulamī, *Ṭabaqāt*, 153 = Sh., 166.

Ṭabaqāt to speak of this joining (*jamʿ*): others might speak of longing for God, but al-Nūrī of substantial satisfaction.

Al-Junayd (d. Baghdad, 298/911?) was a disciple of Sarī al-Saqaṭī and al-Muḥāsibī, whom I have reckoned among the ascetics; however, al-Junayd lectured on the ecstatic *shaṭaḥʾāt* of Abū Yazīd[54] and entertained Abū Ḥafṣ al-Naysābūrī.[55] The extant writings of al-Junayd are many but difficult: as A.J. Arberry says, "His style is involved to the point of obscurity."[56] Still, he clearly refers to mystical experience when he speaks, for example, of being "transported by gnosis (*maʿrifah*) whither knowledge (*ʿilm*) never transported them — to an infinite aim."[57] He was once disabled by ecstasy in Mecca.[58] He always speaks respectfully of the law, yet did not require a high standard of all his associates: "I would rather be kept company by a good-natured debauchee than an ill-natured ascetic."[59]

It appears, then, that a transition from asceticism to mysticism took place at about the middle of the ninth century CE. This has been no exhaustive survey. Some notable figures are missing from al-Sulamī's list; [61] for example, the heresiarch Ibn Karrām (d. Palestine, 255/869), his teacher Aḥmad ibn Ḥarb before him (d. Nishapur, 235/849–850), and his followers after.[60] So are figures of the earlier ninth century who did call themselves Sufis. However, nothing suggests that it was part of al-Sulamī's and the other biographers' apologetic purpose to conceal early tendencies toward mysticism. Therefore, the absence of suspected heretics should not affect the location of a transition to mysticism.

In the *Ṭabaqāt*, al-Sulamī omits to mention any women, but his lost *Tārīkh al-ṣūfiyah* evidently mentioned a number, and an extract concerning them has recently been discovered and published.[61] There, he tells of notable female ascetics like Rābiʿah al-ʿAdawīyah (d. Basra, 185/801–802?), celebrated by Western scholars for many sayings about the love of God, Fāṭimah al-Naysābūrīyah (d. on the way to Mecca, 223/837–838), consulted by both Dhū al-Nūn and Abū Yazīd, and Rābiʿah al-Shāmīyah (d. Damascus, 229/843–844),

54. Al-Sarrāj, 346.

55. Al-Khaṭīb al-Baghdādī, 12:221f. On a session for trading definitions at which al-Junayd and Abū Ḥafṣ were the most prominent speakers, see al-Sulamī, 107f = Sh., 117f.

56. *Encyclopaedia of Islam*, new edn., s.v. "Djunayd," by A.J. Arberry.

57. Al-Junayd, "The Book of the Cure of Souls," ed. & tr. A.J. Arberry, *Journal of the Royal Asiatic Society*, 1937, 220 (Ar.), 226 (tr.).

58. Abū Nuʿaym, 10:270.

59. Al-Sarrāj, *Lumaʿ*, 177. On *qāriʾ* as "ascetic," see Ignác Goldziher, *Introduction to Islamic Theology and Law*, tr. Andras and Ruth Hamori (Princeton: Princeton Univ. Press, 1981), 127, n. 35. Roger Deladrière has pointed out the characteristic humor of al-Junayd's teachers in his introduction to al-Junayd, *Enseignement spirituel* (Paris: Sindbad, 1983), 26f.

60. See Massignon, *Essai*, 260–272, where Yaḥyá ibn Muʿādh is included among them; also Chabbi, "Remarques," 30.

61. Al-Sulamī, *Dhikr al-niswah al-mutaʿabbidāt al-ṣūfiyāt*, ed. Maḥmūd Muḥammad al-Ṭanāḥī (Cairo: Maktabat al-Khānjī, 1993).

who had visions of heaven. Were there mystics among them? Rābiʿah al-ʿAdawīyah has been cited as inventor of a new love mysticism. On sober examination, though, her sayings plainly express just the common, ascetical concern for single-minded devotion to God.[62] The reported sayings of Fāṭimah al-Naysābūrīyah are likewise entirely consistent with ascetical concern for single-minded devotion to God.[63]

Rābiʿah al-Shāmīyah, wife of Ibn Abī al-Ḥawārī, sounds the closest to mysticism. For example, there is the story of her apologizing to Ibn Abī al-Ḥawārī, "I was prevented from answering you by my heart's being filled with joy at God (be he exalted), so I was unable to answer you."[64] I have taken it as a sign of mysticism that al-Junayd was once disabled by rapture. However, Rābiʿah al-Shāmīyah never quite speaks, as a mystic would, of reciprocal love between herself and God, nor of close communion. Other sayings, like her being constantly reminded of the Last Judgement, are perfectly ascetical. In sum, neither she nor any other female ascetic sounds far in advance of her male contemporaries in developing an Islamic mysticism.[65] [62]

It may be objected that the very technical terms of later, full-blown Islamic mysticism appear very early, in the eighth century: "stations," "states," and so forth. Do these not indicate a mystical sensibility at the same early date? I would answer "Not necessarily." Mystics are well known for finding esoteric meaning in the given tradition.[66] Therefore, we must not assume that even terms like "stations" and "states," not used in the literature of jurisprudence, were always mystical. The Mamluk traditionist and biographer al-Dhahabī (d. Damascus, 748/1348) clearly remarked the difference[67]:

> The original Sufis meant by them (*fanāʾ* and *baqāʾ*) the forgetting of created things and leaving them, the lower soul's completely leaving pre-occupation with what is not God.

This is ascetical single-mindedness as opposed to mystical communion.[68]

62. See R. Caspar, "Râbiʿa et le pur amour de Dieu," *IBLA* (Tunis) 121 (1968): 71–95. Cf. Margaret P. Smith, *Rābiʿa the Mystic & Her Fellow-Saints in Islām* (London: Cambridge Univ. Press, 1928); David P. Brewster, "The Study of Sufism; Towards a Methodology," *Religion* 6 (1976): 31–47; *Encyclopedia of Religion*, s.v. "Sufism," by Peter J. Awn.

63. Al-Sulamī, *Dhikr al-niswah*, 61f.

64. Al-Sulamī, *Dhikr al-niswah*, 60.

65. Ruth Roded similarly finds these women outstandingly ascetical: *Women in Islamic Biographical Collections* (Boulder, Colo.: Lynne Rienner, 1994), 94f. For a discussion of the two Rābiʿahs as figures of legend, see Julian Baldick, "The Legend of Rābiʿa of Basra: Christian Antecedents, Muslim Counterparts," *Religion* 20 (1990): 233–247.

66. See Steven T. Katz, "The 'Conservative' Character of Mystical Experience," pp. 3–60 in Katz, ed., *Mysticism and Religious Traditions* (Oxford: Oxford Univ. Press, 1983).

67. Al-Dhahabī, *Siyar* 15 (ed. Ibrāhīm al-Zaybaq, 1983): 393.

68. Of course, ascetical single-mindedness never left Islam, or even (*pace* al-Dhahabī) Sufism. William Chittick has recently gone from here to assert that, "In most cases, Sufi life and practice have nothing

If a predominantly mystical Islamic piety did appear for the first time in the ninth century, it will be asked from where it came. An Indian connection has been proposed for Abū Yazīd, but seems untenable.[69] The idea of a Persian connection has recurred, but Massignon's dismissal remains persuasive[70]; moreover, it can hardly explain Dhū al-Nūn, or even al-Kharrāz. I would suggest that self-mortification at the individual level conduces to the experience of mystical states. As Abū Sulaymūn al-Dārānī said, "If the servant goes to an extreme in *zuhd* (renunciation), that will put him into *tawakkul* (reliance)"; that is, ultimately, the complete dependence that is arguably the essence of mystical religious experience.[71]

Finally, we should have a social explanation to account for the widespread expression of mystical experience at a certain time. The evidence [63] is exiguous, and the two suggestions I offer are admittedly tentative. First, concentration of arbitrary political power has often seemed to encourage mysticism, checks on the concentration of political power to encourage asceticism.[72] Probably, the increasing political power of soldiers over the ninth century encouraged a turn toward mysticism. Ḥamdūn al-Qaṣṣār (d. Nishapur, 271/884–885), who lived exactly at the turning point, expressly admonished a follower of his who was troubled by having to deal with soldiers, "If you know for certain that you are better than they, do not deal with them."[73] In other words, one normally ought to deal with them, as a sign of proper humility. Toleration of sinners and the mighty of this world, together with the cultivation of humility, are characteristic of the mystical outlook.

---

to do with mysticism." This is based on an excessively narrow identification of mysticism with passivity and "strange psychic phenomena": William Chittick, *Faith and Practice of Islam*, SUNY Series in Islam (Albany: State Univ. of New York Press, 1992), 168–173, esp. 173.

69. See, for example, Marijan Molé, *Les Mystiques musulmanes*, Mythes et religions (Paris: Presses Universitaires de France, 1965), 24f; Annemarie Schimmel, *Mystical Dimensions of Islam* (Chapel Hill: Univ. of North Carolina Press, 1975), 47f.

70. Massignon, 63–69. Cf., for example, Ḥusayn Murūwah, *al-Nazaʿāt al-māddīyah fī al-falsafah al-ʿarabīyah al-islāmīyah*, 2 vols. (Beirut: Dār al-Fārābī, 1979), 2:177.

71. Abū Nuʿaym, 9:256. Later, Abū Ḥamzah says, "If the heart is pure of the love of the world, *zuhd* will enter it, and if *zuhd* enters, that will bequeath to it *tawakkul*": he probably does mean *tawakkul* in the mystic's sense of unquestioning trust (al-Sulamī, *Ṭabaqāt*, 296 = Sh., 296). Richard Gramlich has made a full, careful collection of sayings by Abū Sulaymān: "Abū Sulaymūn al-Dārānī," *Oriens* 33 (1992): 22–85. Tor Andrae mentions Abū Sulaymān among Sufis who had transcended the earlier ascetic religion: *In the Garden of Myrtles*, tr. Birgitta Sharpe, Muslim Spirituality in South Asia (New York: State Univ. of New York Press, 1987): 57–60. His is a delightful book, but, like many treatments of Sufism and its antecedents, lacking rigor in chronology and terminology.

72. Cf. Guy Swanson, *Religion and Régime: A Sociological Account of the Reformation* (Ann Arbor: Univ. of Mich. Press, 1967).

73. Al-Sulamī, *Ṭabaqāt*, 116 = Sh., 125.

Second, it seems likely that the development of a fully mystical piety followed from the development of institutions for the material support of religious specialists. As Weber points out, the mystic characteristically relies on others' working in the world in order for him to leave it.[74] Already in a warning from Abū Turāb al-Nakhshabī (d. 245/859–860), the *khānqāh* appears as a special place for ascetics not only to meet but to receive alms[75]:

> Whoever of you has worn the *muraqqaʿah* (distinctive patched garment) has begged; whoever of you has sat in the *khānqāh* or the mosque has begged; whoever of you has read the Qurʾān from the (public) bound copy or so that people might hear has begged.

By the later ninth century, at least, the ascetics of Isfahan could expect regular stipends administered by the qadi.[76] [64]

II: Conflict Between Mysticism and Asceticism

Growing difficulty between ascetics and mystics confirms that something new was afoot by the middle of the ninth century. To be sure, difficulties there had been for some time. Abū Sulaymūn al-Dārānī was expelled from Damascus for saying that he had seen angels and been addressed by them. Ibn Abī al-Ḥawārī was later forced to flee from the same city for saying he preferred the friends (of God; *awliyāʾ*) to the prophets. Possibly led by a Māliki jurisprudent, the people of Old Cairo repudiated Dhū al-Nūn and accused him of secret unbelief.[77] Aḥmad Ibn Ḥanbal accused Sarī al-Saqaṭī of unbelief.[78] Abū Yazīd was expelled from Basṭām for saying that he had made a heavenly ascension like the Prophet's, and went into exile for several years.[79] Abū Ḥamzah (d. Baghdad, 269/882–883) was expelled from Tarsus for recognizing the voice of God in the cawing of a crow.[80]

74. Weber, *Economy and Society*, 547.

75. Abū Nuʿaym, 10:46; al-Qushayrī, *Risālah*, 20.

76. See al-Dhahabī, *Siyar* 13 (ed. ʿAlī Abū Zayd, 1983): 434.

77. Al-Sulamī, *Miḥan al-ṣūfiyah*, apud Ibn al-Jawzī, *Naqd al-ʿilm wa-al-ʿulamāʾ aw Talbīs Iblīs* (Cairo: al-Ṭibāʿah al-Munīrīyah, n.d.), 161 = *Talbīs Iblīs*, ed. Khayr al-Dīn ʿAlī (Beirut: Dār al-Waʿy al-ʿArabī, n.d.), 187. Ibn al-Jawzī names ʿAbd Allāh ibn ʿAbd al-Ḥakam as leader of the opposition to Dhū al-Nūn, but he seems very early (d. 214/829). Probably, his yet more prominent son, Muḥammad (d. 268/882), was the leader in question. Al-Suyūṭī, likewise drawing on al-Sulamī, names ʿAbd Allāh ibn ʿAbd al-Ḥakam but adds the detail that he denounced Dhū al-Nūn to the caliph al-Mutawakkil (r. 232–247/847–861), a plain anachronism: *Tārīkh al-khulafāʾ* (Beirut: Dār al-Thaqāfah, 1970?), 378.

78. Yaʿqūb al-Ḥanbalī, *K. al-Ḥurūf*, apud Ibn Ḥajar, *Lisān "al-Mīzān,"* 7 vols. (Hyderabad: Majlis Dāʾirat al-Maʿārif, 1329–1331), 3:14. Yaʿqūb may have been an associate of al-Muḥāsibī's: v. Ibn Abī Yaʿlā, *Ṭabaqāt al-ḥanābilah* 1:233, l. 2 from bottom.

79. Al-Sulamī (*Miḥan*), apud al-Dhahabī, *Mīzān al-iʿtidāl*, ed. ʿAlī Muḥammad al-Bijāwī, 4 vols. (Cairo: ʿĪsá al-Bābī al-Ḥalabī, 1963), 2:347.

80. Abū Nuʿaym, 10:321.

Al-Kharrāz was forced out of Old Cairo for writing of mystical experience, of Mecca for slighting the goodness of ordinary believers.[81] Even the usually ascetical Sahl al-Tustarī was forced to flee from Tustar to Basra, where he died, on account of relating conversations with angels, jinn, and devils.[82]

One indication of growing difficulty between ascetics and mystics is the appearance of warnings against antinomianism. "Whoever asserts that esoteric knowledge contradicts the exoteric rule," said Sarī al-Saqaṭī, "he is mistaken."[83] Most often, such warnings come from the early mystics themselves. "Every esoteric insight that contradicts an exoteric (rule) is null," proclaimed al-Kharrāz.[84] "Whom you see claiming a state [65] with God that pushes him outside the Law, do not go near," warned al-Nūrī.[85]

Difficulty between ascetics and mystics in Baghdad finally came to a head at the Inquisition of Ghulām Khalīl. Ghulām Khalīl (d. Baghdad, 275/888) was a traditionist and popular preacher who came from Wāsiṭ to Baghdad at the beginning of 264/Fall 877 and whose Inquisition took place the same year.[86] A conflict was already under way in Basra between traditionalist ascetics (*nussāk, ahl al-ḥadīth*), used to enjoining the good and forbidding the bad, and "the people of love" (*ahl al-maḥabbah*). The people of love asserted that their love of God was such that fear had fallen away from them.[87]

In Baghdad, Ghulām Khalīl began to preach against the people of love, asserting that one might love fellow creatures but that God must be feared. He appealed to both the court and the general, who admired him for his austerity.[88] At last, Ghulām Khalīl prevailed on the mother-in-law of the shadow caliph, al-Muwaffaq, to make the *muḥtasib* follow his orders, so he provided him with a list of seventy-odd Baghdadis to be arrested. Most of them hid, some were arrested and imprisoned. Stories are told of al-Nūrī's addressing the qadi so graciously that he became unwilling to execute them, then address-

81. For Egypt, see Ibn al-Jawzī, *Naqd* (Cairo), 164 = ed. ʿAlī, 190. For Mecca, see Ibn ʿAsākir, *Tahdhīb "Tārīkh Dimashq,"* abr. ʿAbd al-Qādir Badrān, 7 vols. (Damascus: Rawḍat al-Shām, n.d.), 1:429.

82. Ibn al-Jawzī, *Naqd* (Cairo), 162 = ʿAlī, 197; Böwering, *Mystical Vision*, 59–63.

83. Abū Nuʿaym, 10:121.

84. Al-Sulamī, *Ṭabaqāt*, 226 = Sh., 231.

85. Abū Nuʿaym, 10:252f.

86. Al-Dhahabī, *Siyar* 14 (ed. Akram Būshayyī, 1983): 71, quoting Abū Nuʿaym, although the date is not in *Ḥilyah* 10:250, nor the same passage as quoted by al-Khaṭīb al-Baghdādī, *Tārīkh Baghdād* 5:134.

87. This account of the Inquisition and its Basran antecedents based on Ibn al-Aʿrābī, *Ṭabaqāt al-nussāk*, apud al-Dhahabī, *Tārīkh al-islām wa-wafayāt al-mashāhīr wa-al-aʿlām*, ed. ʿUmar ʿAbd al-Salām Tadmurī, 40 vols. to date (Beirut: Dār al-Kitāb al-ʿArabī, 1987–), 20 (A.H. 261–280): 212, 277; cf. al-Dhahabī, *Siyar* 13:284.

88. Ibn al-Nadīm lists Ghulām Khalīl among the Sufis in his *Fihrist*, ed. Gustav Flügel, with Johannes Roediger and August Mueller (Leipzig: F. C. W. Vogel, 1872), 186, while al-Khaṭīb al-Baghdādī reports that he ate only vegetables, 5:80. "The general" is a good English term that works so well to translate *al-ʿāmmah* (recall "'Twas caviare to the general," Hamlet II.ii.465) that I will endeavor to revive it.

ing the caliph such that he released them altogether.[89] The happy ending is cast in doubt by al-Nūrī's leaving Baghdad to reside in al-Raqqah for fourteen years, as we shall see.

Carl Ernst has explained the Inquisition of Ghulām Khalīl by contemporary political crises like the Zanj rebellion, which presumably created a climate of fear.[90] Thus, he says, the Inquisition is not evidence of hostility toward mysticism. Destructive as these political crises were, though, our sources for the Inquisition do not mention them—only the religious issues. The religious issues alone can explain both the Inquisition [66] in Baghdad and the expulsions of Abū Sulaymān from Damascus, Abū Ḥamzah from Tarsus, and al-Kharrāz from Old Cairo and Mecca[91]; moreover, only the predominance of the religious issues can explain the central role played by ascetics, not policemen.[92] In all, it seems safer to stress religion than politics. If the 870's was about when full-blown mysticism first appeared in Iraq, it should not surprise us that numbers of older-style ascetics should be upset.

III: Al-Junayd's Reconciliation

One mystic who escaped arrest at the Inquisition was al-Junayd. He asserted that he was not a Sufi at all but a student of jurisprudence, specifically that of Abū Thawr.[93] Some scholars have credited him with going on to develop a Sufism of sobriety: the normal state of the Sufi was not *sukr* (drunkenness) but *ṣaḥw* (sobriety), and Abū Yazīd's drunken style was not to be imitated.[94] It seems dubious, though, to oppose al-Junayd to Abū Yazīd as proponents of fundamentally different paths, for al-Junayd admired Abū Yazīd and lectured on his *shaṭaḥāt*.[95] It would be more accurate to say that al-Junayd (and, no doubt, the circle around him) converted Abū Yazīd's mysticism into something unthreatening to ascetics.

---

89. Abū Nuʿaym, 10:250f. There are similar stories of Dhū al-Nūn before the caliph al-Mutawakkil; e.g., al-Khaṭīb al-Baghdādī, 8:393–395.

90. Ernst, *Words of Ecstasy*, 101.

91. Also, later, Muḥammad ibn al-Faḍl (d. 319/931–932) from Balkh (al-Dhahabī, *Siyar* 14:525), al-Ḥakīm al-Tirmidhī (d. after 318/930) from Tirmidh (Ibn Ḥajar, *Lisān* 5:308), & al.

92. Controversy in Basra; the Inquisition of Ghulām Khalīl; in Rayy, it was expressly the ascetics (*zuhhād*) who led the outcry against Yūsuf ibn al-Ḥusayn, according to al-Sulamī (probably *Miḥan al-ṣūfiyah*), apud al-Dhahabī, *Siyar* 14:250.

93. Ibn ʿAṭāʾ, apud Ibn al-Jawzī, *Naqd* (Cairo), 167 = ed. ʿAlī, 193.

94. The tradition goes back to Hujvīrī (d. Lahore, 465/1072–73?), *Kashf al-maḥjūb*, ed. Valentin A. Zhukovskii (Leningrad, 1926; repr. Tehran: Muʾassasah-i Maṭbūʿātī Amīr-i Kabīr, 1957), 230, 235 = tr. Reynold A. Nicholson, E.J.W. Gibb Memorial Ser. 17 (Leiden: E.J. Brill, 1911), 185, 189.

95. Al-Sarrāj, *Lumaʿ*, 346, noticed by Ernst, 11, 50.

What they did was, on the one hand, to develop a language to deal with mystical experience that would not offend. I have already mentioned the difficulty of al-Junayd's language. A leader of the Muʿtazilah could praise him[96]: [67]

> I have seen a shaykh for you in Baghdad. He is called al-Junayd, and my eyes have not seen his like. The *katabah* (writers[97]) go to him for his locutions (*alfāẓ*), the *falāsifah* (philosophers) for the subtlety of his concepts, the *mutakallimīn* (theologians) for the mastery of his learning.

The less sophisticated ascetics must often have found abstruseness to the point of impenetrability, hence al-Junayd became invulnerable to their criticism.

Moreover, al-Junayd and his school put a new stress on outwardly acceptable behaviour and self-description. Triads like separation-union-separation (*farq-jamʿ-farq*) and subsistence-annihilation-subsistence (*baqāʾ-fanāʾ-baqāʾ*) replaced the old dichotomies. Hence the Sufi might go so far, as before, as to lose consciousness of himself (an upsetting development to ascetics, used to emphasizing divine transcendence) but then return to a transformed consciousness of reality, now described (reassuringly to ascetics) as sobriety.

On the other hand, al-Junayd and his school seem to have pushed mysticism in an inward direction, offering a style of mystical piety that would not interfere so clearly with the collection of hadith reports, the study of jurisprudence, and so on.[98] Hence, for example, his five principles of right living begin with austerities but end with an inward attitude of trust: "to fast by day, to stay up by night (to pray), to act with total sincerity, to control one's actions by constant vigilance, and to commit oneself to God with confidence in all circumstances."[99] Here, *tawakkul* (reliance on God) has left behind both the stern purgation of the ascetics (e.g., Ibrāhīm ibn Ad'ham) and the foolish trust of the early mystics (e.g., Abū Ḥamzah, who refused to call for help when he had fallen into a well, waiting for a lion to rescue him[100]). It was now compatible with, say, supporting a family.[101] [68]

---

96. Al-Khaṭīb al-Baghdādī, 7:243. The Muʿtazili was Abū al-Qāsim al-Kaʿbī (d. Balkh, 319/931?), on whom see Sezgin, *GAS* 1:622f.

97. "I.e., the eloquent (*al-bulaghāʾ*)," glosses al-Dhahabī (*Siyar* 14:67); however, "state secretaries" seem more likely to have been meant.

98. On inner-worldly as opposed to other-worldly mysticism, see Mueller, "Asceticism," 74.

99. Al-Sarrāj, *Lumaʿ*, 288.

100. Abū Nuʿaym, *Ḥilyah* 10:320f. Also said to have befallen Abū Ḥamzah al-Khurāsānī (d. 290/902–903), for which see Ibn Manẓūr, *Mukhtaṣar "Tārīkh Dimashq,"* ed. Rawḥīyah al-Naḥḥās, & al., 29 vols. (Damascus: Dār al-Fikr, 1984–1989), 28:245.

101. Aḥmad Ibn Ḥanbal regretted only one feature of Bishr al-Ḥāfī's lifestyle, his failure to marry: al-Khaṭīb al-Baghdādī, 7:73. For the evolution of *tawakkul* from an outward, ascetical dependence on God to an inward, mystical dependence, see Benedikt Reinert, *Die Lehre vom* Tawakkul *in der klassischen Sufik*,

Not all the Sufis of Baghdad acclaimed al-Junayd's deferential style. Opposition from old-style mystics, unconcerned to mollify ascetics, seems to be crystallized in a number of stories about al-Nūrī. Al-Nūrī complained to al-Junayd, "You have cheated them, and so they have given you the place of honor. I counselled them, and so they threw stones at me."[102] Al-Junayd visited al-Nūrī when he was ill, later al-Nūrī visited al-Junayd when he was ill; however, al-Nūrī not only sat by his bedside, but cured his illness, as well.[103] The underlying issue was probably, as Massignon guesses, the contrast between the frankness of al-Nūrī's language and the disarming dissimulation of al-Junayd's.[104]

("Giving counsel" and "cheating" may have had special reference to condemning bad behaviour: the later Ḥanbali leader al-Barbahārī [d. 329/941], disciple at one time to Sahl al-Tustarī, asserts, "It is not licit for anyone to refrain from giving counsel [*naṣīḥah*] to any of the Muslims, righteous or otherwise, in the matter of faith. Whoever refrains has cheated [*ghashsha*] the Muslims."[105] Several stories associate al-Nūrī with daring acts like breaking wine jars bound for the caliphal palace. Therefore, he may have objected to al-Junayd's quietism as well as his evasive language.)

Indeed, al-Junayd and his circle spoke so different a language from that of al-Nūrī and the old-style mystics that al-Nūrī could scarcely communicate with them. The Sufi biographer Abū Saʿīd Ibn al-Aʿrābī (d. Mecca, 340/952?) relates a discussion of terminology that passed between him and al-Nūrī in 270/883–884, when al-Nūrī was still a refugee in al-Raqqah. Al-Nūrī asked about al-Junayd, so Ibn al-Aʿrābī told him of the new talk of second separation and sobriety. Al-Nūrī affirmed that the so-called second separation was really an aspect of joining. In other words, al-Junayd had merely coined new words to describe the familiar mystical experience.[106]

Eight years later, Ibn al-Aʿrābī and two friends spotted al-Nūrī in Baghdad. The older mystic was initially reluctant to associate with Sufis. Memories of betrayal at the Inquisition must have rankled. However, they [69] eventually persuaded him to come to their mosque, where they spent the night. On the next Friday, they took a boat to where

Studien zur Sprache, Geschichte u. Kultur des islamischen Orients, n.s. 3 (Berlin: W. de Gruyter, 1968), 226, 264–266. Reinert does not propose to locate a general transition from asceticism to mysticism, as I do, but his location of the change in *tawakkul* at the late ninth century, particularly in the circle around al-Junayd, confirms my location of a general transition.

102. Abū Nuʿaym, 10:251f.

103. Al-Khaṭīb al-Baghdādī, 5:132.

104. Louis Massignon, *The Passion of al-Hallāj*, tr. Herbert Mason, Bollingen ser. 98, 4 vols. (Princeton: Univ. Press, 1982), 1:79. A. J. Arberry's characterization of al-Junayd's prose has been quoted already: "involved to the point of obscurity." I have found similar obscurity in al-Sulamī's selection of the sayings of al-Nūrī; however, al-Nūrī's treatise *Maqāmāt al-qulūb* is far more lucid than anything of the sort we have from al-Junayd: Paul Nwyia, ed., "Textes mystiques inédits d'Abū-l-Ḥasan al-Nūrī (m.295/907)," *Mélanges de l'université Saint-Joseph* (Beirut) 44 (1968): 117–154.

105. *Sharḥ "Kitāb al-Sunnah,"* apud Ibn Abī Yaʿlá, *Ṭabaqāt al-ḥanābilah* 2:26.

106. This and the following based on Ibn al-Aʿrābī, *Ṭabaqāt al-nussāk*, apud al-Dhahabī, *Siyar* 14:74f.

al-Junayd was. At first, everyone welcomed al-Nūrī, and he and al-Junayd traded reminiscences and joked with each other. Then all the Sufis sat for a formal discussion. Al-Junayd urged al-Nūrī to address the first question, but al-Nūrī declined, saying "I am just come, and prefer to listen." Al-Junayd and the others spoke a while longer, then again pressed al-Nūrī to talk, but he said, "You have used terms (*alqāb*) that I do not know, and talk in a fashion I am not used to: let me listen and get to know what you mean." Al-Junayd's terminology was unfamiliar to him.

At last, someone asked him about the separation (*farq*) that comes after the joining (*jamʿ*), what its signs were, and what was the difference between it and the first separation. Al-Nūrī resorted to ambiguity: "It is not one aspect of joining," he said, "nor is it sobering up from joining, but they return to what they know." The Sufis Ruwaym and Ibn ʿAṭāʾ complained that al-Nūrī was asserting something and its contrary. Al-Junayd begged them not to be unkind to al-Nūrī, who might have become senile. In the upshot, concludes Ibn al-Aʿrābī,

> Abū al-Ḥusayn (al-Nūrī) withdrew from all of them and spurned them. He became ill and went blind. He stuck to the deserts and graveyards . . . . I have heard a number say that for anyone who had seen al-Nūrī since his return from al-Raqqah without having seen him before that might as well not have seen him at all, on account of his changing (God have mercy on him).

Such was the pitiful end of a mystic who could speak only of joining and drunkenness, not knowing how to speak the sophisticated new language of the second separation, the second sobriety, and so on.

Al-Junayd's new language mollified ascetical Muslims: it now remained to change the outlook of the mystics. That is, if ascetics were now appeased by a mystical language that stressed steadfastness and sobriety, the mystics would have to be shown some reason to respect ascetics. For example, al-Junayd may have taken over the new terminology of *fanāʾ* and the second *baqāʾ* from the mystic al-Kharrāz in the interest of appeasing ascetics, but he must have wished to discourage mystics from boasting as al-Kharrāz had, provoking his expulsion from Mecca: "The sins of those brought near are the good qualities of the pious."[107] He cannot have wished to provoke ill will. As a mystic, besides, he must have found it easy to overlook the obtuseness of the ascetics, to love them in spite of it.

In an unpublished work, the *Waṣāyā*, it appears that al-Junayd did come up with something for the mystics, mainly a tripartite division of [70] the Muslims that establishes a place for them alongside the others.[108] Al-Junayd distinguishes three groups. The first comprises those who have chosen ritual worship and fear (*al-ʿibādāt wa-al-takhaw-*

107. See above, note 77.

108. Rešit Efendi (Istanbul) 1218/1. See Sezgin, *GAS* 1:649, no. 19.

wuf); the second those who have chosen renunciation, longing, and austerity (*al-zuhd wa-al-shawq wa-al-taqashshuf*); the third, finally, those who have chosen poverty and Sufism (*al-faqr wa-al-taṣawwuf*). These last have had their hearts filled with love as the hearts of the servants have not been, and they speak of the truths of the unseen.[109] The three groups correspond precisely to the ordinary devout like Ghulām Khalīl, the earlier ascetics like al-Muḥāsibī and Sarī al-Saqaṭī, and finally the speculative mystics around al-Junayd. There is no doubt that the Sufis enjoy favors above the rest, but equally they are part of the same grand scheme, the same community of the faithful.

109. Al-Junayd, *al-Waṣāyā*, 1b, 2a.

7

EARLY RENUNCIANTS AS *ḤADĪTH* TRANSMITTERS

Classical Sufism crystallized in Baghdad in the last quarter of the ninth century C.E.[1] Biographers of the early eleventh century worked out a spiritual lineage for Sufism going back to the Companions of the Prophet. The immediate forbears of the Sufis they identified as eighth- and ninth-century renunciants known as *zuhhād*, *nussāk*, or *ʿubbād*.[2] They underwent austerities, devoted extraordinary amounts of time to qur'anic recitation and prayer, and generally cultivated a solemn attitude toward life.[3] Some spoke of thinking often and steadily of God, but the ideas of mutual love and mystical union were yet to come. A few wore wool, but express references to *ṣūfiyya* before the later ninth century usually have to do with marginal, disreputable figures not identified as forebears by the

1. Classical Sufism is here taken to be the quietist mysticism that crystallized around al-Junayd (d. 298/911?). For the late introduction of classical Sufism to Khurasan, see Jacqueline Chabbi, "Remarques sur le développement historique des mouvements ascétiques et mystiques au Khurasan." *Studia Islamica*, no. 46 (1977), 5–72. The situation elsewhere, as in Basra, has yet to be sorted out, but see now Alexander Knysh, *Islamic Mysticism: A Short History*, Themes in Islamic Studies 1 (Leiden: Brill, 2000). For leading figures, see also Richard Gramlich, *Alte Vorbilder des Sufitums* 1: *Scheiche des Westens* and 2: *Scheiche des Ostens* (Wiesbaden: Harrassowitz, 1995–96).

2. The most important extant biographical dictionaries are al-Sulamī (d. 412/1021), *Kitāb Ṭabaqāt al-ṣūfiyya*, ed. Johannes Pedersen (Leiden: E. J. Brill, 1960), and Abū Nuʿaym (d. 430/1038), *Ḥilyat al-awliyāʾ*, 10 vols. (Cairo: Matʾbaʿat al-Saʿāda and Maktabat al-Khānjī, 1352–57/1932–38).

3. A useful survey of the practices that distinguished the eighth-century *zuhhād*, *nussāk*, and *ʿubbād* is Ofer Livne-Kafri, "Early Muslim Ascetics and the World of Christian Monasticism," *Jerusalem Studies in Arabic and Islam*, no. 20 (1996), 105–29.

Originally published in *The Muslim World* 92 (2002): 407–18.

later Sufi biographers.[4] Modern research has largely confirmed that Sufism grew out of this earlier, ascetic tradition.[5]

According to the Sufi biographers, most of these earlier renunciants had been active transmitters of *Ḥadīth*. (For *zuhhād* and *nussāk*, I normally use "renunciants," suggested to me by Michael Cooperson, rather than "ascetics" in order to avoid implying the opposition of "mysticism" to "asceticism" as worked out by Max Weber.[6]) The piety of the ninth-century Traditionalists (those who would base their law and theology mainly on *Ḥadīth* as opposed to rational speculation), so far as we can reconstruct it, was identical to that of most eighth-century renunciants as the Sufi sources present them.[7] *Ḥadīth* and Sufism thus had origins in common (confirmed, incidentally, by the way *Ḥadīth* collectors identified certain ones of their own number as *abdāl*, later a favorite concept of the Sufis[8]). But when exactly did *Ḥadīth* and Sufism separate?

The voluminous literature of *rijāl* criticism shows us how *Ḥadīth* collectors and critics thought of their renunciant forebears and contemporaries. For the most part, it must be said, the great ninth-century *rijāl* critics (evaluators of *Ḥadīth* transmitters) ignored the renunciants of the later eighth century, at least as transmitters of *Ḥadīth*; however, they were inclined to respect as many as [408] they did comment on. They regarded the renunciants of their own century more suspiciously, depreciating more of their *Ḥadīth* transmission. Finally, with the advent of classical Sufism near the end of the ninth century, the mystical tradition went its own way. Although its adherents continued to transmit *Ḥadīth*, *Ḥadīth* specialists of the tenth century and after almost completely ignored them.

4. The earlier ascetics who were expressly called "Sufis" were seldom characterized by mysticism, often by ordering the good and prohibiting evil; e.g., certain Muʿtazila, on whom see A. J. Arberry, "New Material on the *Kitāb al-Fihrist* of Ibn al-Nadīm," *Islamic Research Association Miscellany*, IRA ser., no. 12, 1 (1948): 19–45, esp. 34. How the term "Sufi" was transferred to the mystics around Junayd remains unclear, as Bernd Radtke observes in his recent article for *The Encyclopaedia of Islam* (new edn., s.v. "taṣawwuf").

5. See Louis Massignon, *Essai sur les origines du lexique technique de la mystique musulmane*, rev. edn. (Paris: J. Vrin, 1954), now also available as *Essay on the Origins of the Technical Language of Islamic Mysticism*, trans. Benjamin Clark (Notre Dame, Ind.: Notre Dame Univ. Press, 1997).

6. Max Weber, *Economy and Society*, ed. Guenther Roth and Claus Wittich, 2 vols. (Berkeley: Univ. of Calif. Press, 1978), 544–51. The dichotomy of ascetical and mystical has been developed by numerous others, culminating in the skillful summary of Gert H. Mueller, "Asceticism and Mysticism," in *International Yearbook for the Sociology of Religion* 8, ed. Günter Dux, et al. (Opladen: Westdeutscher Verlag, 1973), 68–132.

7. For a start, see Jacqueline Chabbi, "Fuḍayl b. ʿIyâḍ, un précurseur du Ḥanbalisme," *Bulletin d'études orientales* 30 (1978): 331–45.

8. Cf. *Encyclopaedia of Islam*, new edn., s.v. "*abdāl*," by I. Goldziher, stressing the Sufi concept, and *Encyclopaedia Iranica*, s.v. "abdāl," by Jacqueline Chabbi, noticing the earlier association with *Ḥadīth*.

Renunciants in the *Rijāl* Books

Western scholars have commonly argued that there has never been any conflict between the transmission of *Ḥadīth* and the cultivation of ascetic and mystical vocations. (They often appear to be defending Islamic mysticism against modern Muslims, an argument in which I have no wish to obtrude.[9]) George Makdisi argues that Sufism had to be orthodox precisely inasmuch as most Sufis transmitted Ḥadīth.

> From the very beginning, *Ḥadīth* was the vehicle of instruction; Sufi biographies are replete with the names of tradition-experts. There was never a question of Sufism not being orthodox; it grew up as part and parcel of orthodox Islam in the security of the *Ḥadīth*, a most orthodox Islamic science.[10]

Makdisi is certainly right that early biographical dictionaries of renunciants and Sufis identify many as active transmitters of *Ḥadīth*. It should be possible to say exactly how many. Moreover, by looking up renunciants in directories of *Ḥadīth* transmitters, we should be able to tell how renunciant transmitters were regarded by specialists in *Ḥadīth*. With this search began the present study.

The most convenient history of Sufism is al-Sulamī (d. Nishapur, 412/1021), *Ṭabaqāt al-ṣūfiyya*, an abridgement of his lost *Tārīkh al-ṣūfiyya*. Whereas the *Tārīkh* covered a thousand names, the *Ṭabaqāt* covers one hundred, sorted into five generations of twenty apiece.[11] The first generation ranges chronologically from Ibrāhīm ibn Adham (d. Damascus, 163/779–80?) to Ḥamdūn al-Qaṣṣār (d. Nishapur, 271/884–85), which is to say it comprises mainly the renunciant precursors to the classical Sufis. The second generation ranges from Aḥmad Ibn Abī al-Ward (d. Baghdad, 263/877) to Abū ʿAlī al-Jūzajānī (d. *ca.* 320/932), and includes most of the first generation of Sufis properly speaking. The third generation ranges from Abū Ḥamza al-Baghdādī (who Sulamī says died in 289/901–2) to Abu al-Ḥasan Ibn al-Ṣāʾigh al-Dīnawarī (d. Old Cairo, 331/943). Here is how they rank as Ḥadīth transmitters. (If someone is counted here as "active," it means that Sulamī tells us he transmitted Ḥadīth; if "rated," that his reliability as a transmitter of Ḥadīth is characterized in one or more of these four works: al-Khaṭīb al-Baghdādī, [409] *Tārīkh Baghdād*, al-Dhahabī, *Tārīkh al-islām*, and Ibn Ḥajar, *Tahdhīb* al-Tahdhīb and *Lisān* al-Mīzān.[12])

9. On hostility to Sufism, see Frederick de Jong and Bernd Radtke, eds., *Islamic Mysticism Contested* (Leiden: Brill, 1999), Elizabeth Sirriyeh, *Sufis and Anti-Sufis* (Richmond: Curzon, 1999), and Alexander Knysh, *Ibn ʿArabī in the Later Islamic Tradition* (Albany: State Univ. of New York Press, 1999).

10. George Makdisi, "The Sunnī Revival," *Islamic Civilisation 950–1150*, ed. D. S. Richards (Oxford: Cassirer, 1973), 155–68, at 163.

11. On Sulamī's *Ṭabaqāt* and *Tārīkh*, see Pedersen's introduction, *Ṭabaqāt al-ṣūfiyya*, esp. 50–62, and now Jawid A. Mojaddedi, *The Biographical Tradition in Sufism*, Curzon Studies in Asian Religion (Richmond: Curzon, 2001), chap. 1.

12. Al-Khaṭīb al-Baghdādī (d. Baghdad, 463/1071), *Tārīkh Baghdād*, is a biographical dictionary of per-

Table 1. Subjects of al-Sulamī, *Ṭabaqāt*, as Ḥadīth Transmitters

Generation	Active	Rated	Unrated
1	17 (85%)	7 (35%)	13 (65%)
2	14 (70%)	2 (10%)	18 (90%)
3	3 (15%)	2 (10%)	18 (90%)

The downward trend is clear: fewer and fewer of the named Sufis are active in Ḥadīth transmission, especially in the fourth/tenth century, while there is an even sharper drop in the proportion of those active whom the *rijāl* critics deemed necessary to evaluate. Furthermore, whereas a majority of those in the first generation who received ratings were considered trustworthy (four against three), none in the second generation was found trustworthy.

Another important history of the Sufi tradition is Abū Nuᶜaym (d. Isfahan, 430/1038), *Ḥilyat al-awliyā*ʾ.[13] This work comprises biographies of Muslim renunciants, organized roughly in chronological order from the Rightly Guided Caliphs through famous Sufis of the tenth century. *Ḥilyat al-awliyā*ʾ stresses its subjects' activity as *Ḥadīth* transmitters, so that most biographies end with sample quotations of *Ḥadīth* their subjects transmitted. Indeed, Ibn al-Jawzī (d. Baghdad, 597/1201) indignantly complains that Abū Nuᶜaym should have restricted the *Ḥilya* to exemplary stories of his subjects' characters, omitting accounts of the *Ḥadīth* they related and omitting to quote from their commentaries on the Qur'an.[14] He complains, too, that Abū Nuᶜaym wrongly associated various early figures with Sufism: the first four caliphs, Sufyān al-Thawrī, al-Shāfiᶜī, Aḥmad ibn Ḥanbal, and others.[15] Modern critics have taken up his line, seeing in *Ḥilyat al-awliyā*ʾ a crafty justification of Sufism. As an example of modern scholarship, let me quote Hamid Dabashi:

---

sons who lived or at least passed through Baghdad, mainly *Ḥadīth* transmitters. Al-Dhahabī (d. Damascus, 748/1348?), *Tārīkh al-islām*, is a massive biographical dictionary of Muslims from all regions, mainly *Ḥadīth* transmitters. Ibn Ḥajar (d. Cairo, 852/1449), *Tahdhīb* al-Tahdhīb, is a biographical dictionary covering those *Ḥadith* transmitters who appear somewhere in the Six Books. It is a reworking of al-Mizzī (d. Damascus, 742/1341), *Tahdhīb* al-Kamāl. *Lisān* al-Mīzān is a reworking of Dhahabī, *Mīzān al-iᶜtidāl*, omitting those transmitters already covered in *Tahdhīb* al-Tahdhīb.

13. See Raif Georges Khoury, "Importance et authenticité des textes de *Ḥilyat al-awliyā*ʾ," *Studia Islamica*, no. 46 (1977), 73–113, and Mojaddedi, chap. 2.

14. Ibn al-Jawzī, *Ṣifat al-ṣafwa*, ed. Muḥammad ᶜAbd al-Muᶜād Khān, 4 vols., 2nd edn. (Hyderabad: Majlis Dāʾirat al-Maᶜārif al-ᶜUthmāniyya, 1355–56, 2nd edn., 1968), 1: 2 = ed. Ibrāhīm Ramaḍān and Saᶜīd al-Laḥḥām, 4 vols. in 2 (Beirut: Dār al-Kutub al-ᶜIlmiyya, 1409/1989), 1: 6f.

15. Ibn al-Jawzī, *Ṣifa* 1 (Hyderabad): 3 = 1 (Beirut): 9f.

> In opposition to [the Ḥallājian] Kharaqānī stands Abū Nuʿaym al-Iṣfahānī . . . whose monumental composition of the *Ḥilyat al-awliyāʾ* is a valiant attempt to renarrate and thus reconstruct a respectable and self-legitimizing genealogy for Islamic mysticism whereby the earliest generations of Muslim mystics are traced back to the Four "Rightly Guided" Caliphs . . . ; and thus Abū Bakr, ʿUmar, ʿUthmān, and ʿAlī are considered among the first Sufis.[16]

I have my doubts. Abū Nuʿaym was himself far more prominent as a *Ḥadīth* expert than as a Sufi.[17] Whether or not we suppose he had reliable data [410] at hand, should we not grant that he was genuinely interested in the piety of the Rightly Guided Caliphs? Moreover, Abū Nuʿaym did not invent these volumes of data about the renunciation of the Companions and Followers (*tābiʿūn*). Rather, we should take them as evidence of how the pious ancestors and later renunciants were remembered among *Ḥadīth* transmitters. Finally, we should beware of anachronism: the lines dividing *Ḥadīth* transmitters, Qur'an commentators, and Sufis may have been clear in Ibn al-Jawzī's day, but the *Ḥilya* is evidence that they were less so in Abū Nuʿaym's.

The overwhelming majority of the renunciants covered in the early volumes of the *Ḥilya* were also important *Ḥadīth* transmitters. For example, volume three, which finishes the review of the Followers of Basra, then goes on to the Followers of Medina and Mecca, comprises 50 separate biographies. Abū Nuʿaym identifies all fifty as active transmitters of *Ḥadīth*; forty-six also appear as transmitters somewhere in the Six Books, while only four do not; and of these remaining four, three are at least acknowledged and rated as transmitters by Ibn Abī Ḥātim.[18] In short, all were active, forty-nine out of fifty were "rated," and only one in fifty was "unrated." Later generations seem very different. Here is a summary for those who are covered in the last three printed volumes.

16. Hamid Dabashi, "Historical Conditions of Persian Sufism During the Seljuk Period," *Classical Persian Sufism*, ed. Leonard Lewisohn (New York: Khaniqahi Nimatullahi Publications, 1993), 137–74, at 142.

17. Consider the balance between *Ḥadīth* and Sufism in al-Dhahabī, *Tārīkh al-Islām*, ed. ʿUmar ʿAbd al-Salām Tadmurī, 52 vols. (Beirut: Dār al-Kitāb al-ʿArabī, 1407–21/1987–2000), 29 (A.H. 421–40): 274–80, with ref'ces. Cf. *Encyclopaedia of Islām*, new edn., s.v. "Abū Nuʿaym al-Iṣfahānī," by J. Pedersen, rather desperately collecting what little is known of his Sufism.

18. Ibn Abī Ḥātim (d. Ray, 327/938), *K. al-Jarḥ wa-al-taʿdīl*, lists some 19,000 early hadith transmitters with the names of those from whom and to whom they related *Ḥadīth*. It offers evaluations of the reliability of about half its subjects.

Table 2. Subjects of Abū Nuʿaym, *Ḥilyat al-awliyāʾ* 8–10, as *Ḥadīth* Transmitters

Date of death	Active	Rated	Unrated
A.H. 151–200	29 (62%)	24 (51%)	23
A.H. 201–250	31 (32%)	19 (19%)	79
A.H. 251–300	24 (41%)	4 (7%)	54
After A.H. 301	18 (31%)	4 (8%)	55

(Abū Nuʿaym reports no date of death for the majority of his subjects; therefore, most of these dates are my inferences from the length of the *isnād* up to Abū Nuʿaym.) Plainly, many more renunciants were remembered for their renunciation than as important *Ḥadīth* transmitters. More of Abū Nuʿaym's subjects are identified as *Ḥadīth* transmitters than Sulamī's, no doubt because Abū Nuʿaym was himself primarily a collector of *Ḥadīth* and filled his biographical dictionary with other collectors. Nevertheless, the trend is plainly downwards: a majority of the early renunciants were considered important enough as *Ḥadīth* transmitters to be rated by the great critics of the ninth century, but only a few of the ninth- and tenth-century renunciants were important enough as *Ḥadīth* transmitters to be rated. The actual ratings these early renunciant *Ḥadīth* transmitters receive likewise decline, on the whole: of [411] those who died A.H. 250 or before and are rated, about three times as many are rated favorably as unfavorably. For those few who died after A.H. 250 and who are rated, acceptance and rejection are about equally common.

Finally, here is a somewhat different table for comparison: renunciants in al-Khaṭīb al-Baghdādī, *Tārīkh Baghdād*, as appearing in either *Tahdhīb al-Tahdhīb* or *Lisān al-Mīzān*.

Table 3. Renunciants & Sufis in *Tārīkh Baghdād* as *Ḥadīth* Transmitters

Date of death	Active	Rated	Unrated
A.H. 151–200	5 (56%)	2 (40%)	3
A.H. 201–250	24 (71%)	6 (25%)	18
A.H. 251–300	22 (28%)	6 (27%)	18
A.H. 301–350	13 (25%)	3 (23%)	10

Like previous tables, this one shows decline over time, both in the proportion of renunciants who were demonstrably active as *Ḥadīth* transmitters and, even more steeply, in the proportion of renunciant *Ḥadīth* transmitters who caught the attention of *rijāl* critics.

The drop-off for attention from *Ḥadīth* transmitters is steepest at the early ninth century, for activity as *Ḥadīth* transmitters at the later.

Why Renunciants and *Ḥadīth* Transmitters Pulled Apart

It appears, then, that Makdisi's characterization of Sufism as growing up in the security of *Ḥadīth* must be qualified. First, by the time classical Sufism took shape in the late ninth century, fewer renunciants than formerly were active transmitters of *Ḥadīth*. Second, those Sufis and other renunciant contemporaries who did transmit *Ḥadīth* were notably less well regarded by mainstream *Ḥadīth* experts than renunciant transmitters of earlier generations. I have urged elsewhere that the ninth-century Ḥanābila in particular were hostile to crucial practices of the developing Sufi movement, such as special sessions for reciting the Qurʾān and recollecting God apart from the transmission of *Ḥadīth*.[19] Moreover, the tone of their piety was sometimes at significant variance with that of the early Sufis; for example, in the Traditionalists' cultivation of unremitting seriousness.[20]

Often, sheer lack of time probably made it difficult to pursue both *Ḥadīth* and renunciant vocations. According to Ibn Ḥibbān, Munkadir ibn Muḥammad (d. 180/796–97) was prevented from properly memorizing *Ḥadīth* by his devotion to ritual worship.[21] Someone told Aḥmad ibn Ḥanbal it was [412] impossible both to seek *Ḥadīth* and to worship at the mosque, although Aḥmad said both were incumbent.[22] Some quotations from Sarī al-Saqaṭī (d. Baghdad, 253/867?) suggest that he thought *Ḥadīth* and renunciation were compatible if one tackled them in the proper sequence: one should start with *Ḥadīth*, then go to *nusk* (renunciation), rather than the other way around.[23] Presumably, he thought to take advantage of youthful ability in memorization. However, the Nishapuran Muḥammad ibn Ibrāhīm ibn Ḥamsh (d. 353/964–65) heard *Ḥadīth* in his youth, then became preoccupied with Sufism, later returned to *Ḥadīth* but proved incompetent.[24] To maintain his memory of *Ḥadīth*, the Traditionist needed to review his notebooks daily. Sufism evidently took too much time to allow such review.

19. Ibn Abī Yaʿlā, *Ṭabaqāt al-ḥanābila*, ed. Muḥammad Ḥāmid al-Fiqī, 2 vols. (Cairo: Maṭbaʿat al-Sunna al-Muḥammadiyya, 1371/1952), 1: 255; more generally, Christopher Melchert, "The Ḥanābila and the Early Sufis," forthcoming in *Arabica* [48 (2001): 352–367].

20. Christopher Melchert, "The Piety of the Hadith Folk," forthcoming in *International Journal of Middle East Studies* [*HPL 7].

21. Ibn Ḥibbān, apud Ibn Ḥajar, *K. Tahdhīb* al-Tahdhīb, 12 vols. (Hyderabad: Majlis Dāʾirat al-Maʿārif al-Niẓāmiyya, 1325–27), 10: 318, ll. 3–5.

22. Ibn Abī Yaʿlā, *Ṭabaqāt* 1: 23.

23. Sulamī, *Ṭabaqāt*, 48.

24. Al-Ḥākim al-Naysābūrī, apud Ibn Ḥajar, *Lisān* al-Mīzān, 7 vols. (Hyderabad: Majlis Dāʾirat al-Maʿārif, 1329–31; repr. Beirut: Muʾassasat al-Aʿlamī, 1406/1986), 5: 25.

It is easy to see why the ninth century is when renunciants tended to leave *Ḥadīth* transmission, for this is just the century when renunciation became extreme, hence increased difficulty pursuing devotional exercises and *Ḥadīth* at the same time. The ninth century was the heroic age of *tawakkul*, relying on whatever came one's way for sustenance rather than actively earning a living.[25] Increasingly, then, one had to choose between normal family life and a life of renunciation. Abū Bakr al-Naysābūrī (d. 324/936) related that he could no longer live on five grains a day and stay up all night after his marriage.[26] Traditionalists were upset. Having heard of someone's saying that worry about one's provision for the morrow would be counted a sin, Aḥmad complained, "Who is so strong as this?"[27] He regretted that Bishr al-Ḥāfī (d. 227/841) had failed to marry.[28] By the tenth century, the Sufis around al-Junayd had renounced outward *tawakkul* in favor of an inward moral attitude. They left the complete rejection of earning a living, *inkār al-kasb*, to the Muʿtazili renunciants and their successors (in Khurasan) the Karrāmiyya.[29] In the tenth century, it presumably became easier again to pursue both Ḥadīth and renunciation. By now, however, the renunciant and *Ḥadīth* traditions had been separated for most of a century.

Ḥadīth may have become more demanding over the ninth century by an even greater margin. At the beginning of the century, famous traditionists are commended for having several thousand Ḥadīth reports by memory. For example, the Kufan Ḥafṣ ibn Ghiyāth (d. 194/810?) transmitted three or four thousand, the Meccan Sufyān ibn ʿUyayna (d. 198/814) had about seven thousand.[30] From later in the century, by contrast, Abū Zurʿa al-Rāzī (d. 264/878) is quoted as doubting whether anyone was qualified to rule on questions of marriage and divorce without knowing 100,000.[31] To be sure, it was easier to

25. See Benedikt Reinert, *Die Lehre vom* Tawakkul *in der klassischen Sufik*, Studien zur Sprache, Geschichte u. Kultur des islamischen Orients, n.s. 3 (Berlin: W. de Gruyter, 1968).

26. Al-Khaṭīb al-Baghdādī, *Tārīkh Baghdād*, 14 vols. (Cairo: Maktabat al-Khānjī, 1349/1931), 10: 122, ll. 4–7.

27. Aḥmad ibn Ḥanbal, *K. al-Waraʿ*, ed. Muḥyī al-Dīn Naṣr al-Kurdī (Cairo: Maṭbaʿat al-Saʿāda, 1340; repr. Alexandria: Dār al-Īmān, 1993), 80.

28. Al-Khaṭīb al-Baghdādī, *Tārīkh* 7: 73, ll. 2–6.

29. On the Muʿtazila and Karrāmiyya, see Josef van Ess, "Une Lecture à rebours de l'histoire du muʿtazilisme," *Revue des études islamiques* 46 (1978): 163–240, at 192. Abū ʿImrān al-Raqāshī (fl. 9th cent.) was a proto-Muʿtazili who disbelieved in *makāsib*: Ibn al-Murtaḍā, *Die Klassen der muʿtaziliten*, ed. Susanna Diwald-Wilzer, Bibliotheca Islamica 21 (Wiesbaden: Franz Steiner, 1961), 77. Among the classical Muctazila, al-Rummānī (d. 384/994) wrote a book on *Taḥrīm al-makāsib*: Sezgin, *GAS* 8: 114, no. 21. For Karrāmi rejection of *kasb*, see Josef van Ess, *Ungenützte Texte zur Karrāmīya*, Sitzungsberichte der heidelberger Akademie der Wissenschaften, philosophisch-historische Klasse; Jahrg. 1980, 6. Abhandlungen (Heidelberg, Winter 1980), 30–32; *idem*, "Lecture," 190; Louis Massignon, *The Passion of al-Hallāj*, trans. Herbert Mason, Bollingen Ser. 98, 4 vols. (Princeton: Univ. Press, 1982), 3: 227.

30. Al-Khaṭīb al-Baghdādī, *Tārīkh* 8: 195, ll. 5–9 (Ḥafṣ), 9: 179, ll. 5f (Sufyān).

31. Al-Dhahabī, *Siyar aʿlām al-nubalāʾ*, 25 vols. (Beirut: Muʾassasat al-Risāla), 13 (ed. ʿAlī Abū Zayd,

know 100,000 in Abū Zurʿa's time, since written notes were by then universally accepted, whereas Ḥafṣ and Sufyān had gotten by without them. In the tenth century, with the recognition of authoritative collections such as Bukhārī's and Muslim's, *Ḥadīth* science must have become somewhat easier. [413] But by now, again, the renunciant and *Ḥadīth* traditions had been separated for a century.

Moreover, despite what apologists will say, renunciants and Sufis did sometimes oppose outright the collection and transmission of *Ḥadīth*. Muḥammad ibn Yūsuf al-Iṣbahānī (d. *ca.* 200/815–16) and Bishr al-Ḥāfī buried their notebooks and related little *Ḥadīth*.[32] The famous Syrian *Ḥadīth* transmitter Ibn Abī al-Ḥawārī (d. 246/860) was said to have cast his books into the sea, saying they had been a necessary means but were necessary no longer.[33] Muḥammad ibn Muʿādh (d. 334/945–46) heard *Ḥadīth* reports from Abū al-Walīd al-Ṭayālisī (d. 224/838–39) and others, then became a Sufi and buried his books. He forgot all but one of his old *Ḥadīth* reports before resuming his collection.[34] Jaʿfar al-Khuldī (d. 348/959–60) reminisced that he had not gone to hear ʿAbbās al-Dūrī in his youth because a Sufi had discouraged him.[35] Ibn Khafīf (d. 371/982?) collected *Ḥadīth* in spite of discouragement from Sufis, hiding his paper and ink.[36]

We also have some direct quotations expressing renunciant hostility toward the collection of *Ḥadīth*. Al-Fuḍayl ibn ʿIyāḍ (d. 187/803) is quoted as saying, "When I hear the sound of the *Ḥadīth* transmitters, I am seized by the need to piss, taking me away from them."[37] He preferred being asked for money to being asked to relate *Ḥadīth*,[38] and insisted that the wise, not the learnèd (*ḥukamāʾ*, *ʿulamāʾ*), were heirs of the prophets.[39] When someone mentioned *Ḥadīth*, Sarī al-Saqaṭī warned that it was not the food of the tomb.[40] Sarī disparaged a meeting for trading *Ḥadīth* reports (*mudhākara*) as "a way-station for idlers (*munākhan lil-baṭṭālīn*)."[41] Abū Muḥammad al-Jarīrī (d. 312/924?) directly

---

1403/1983): 69.

32. Abū Nuʿaym, *Ḥilya* 8: 227 (Muḥammad); Ibn Ḥajar, *Tahdhīb* 1: 445 (Bishr). These examples have been briefly discussed by Franz Rosenthal, "Of Making Many Books There Is No End," *The Book in the Islamic World*, ed. George N. Atiyeh (Albany, 1995), 40f, 53.

33. Ibn Abī Yaʿlā, *Ṭabaqāt* 1: 78.

34. Ibn ʿAsākir, *Tārīkh Dimashq*, s.n. ʿAbd al-ʿAzīz ibn Muḥammad al-Yaḥsubī, apud Ibn Ḥajar, *Lisān* 5: 385.

35. Al-Khaṭīb al-Baghdādī, *Tārīkh* 7: 227.

36. Ibn ʿAsākir, *Tabyīn kadhib al-muftarī* (Damascus: al-Qudsī, 1347), 191.

37. Abū Nuʿaym, *Ḥilya* 8: 94.

38. *Ibid.* 8: 86f.

39. *Ibid.* 8: 92.

40. *Ibid.* 10: 126f. Similarly, Bishr al-Ḥāfī, apud al-Khaṭīb al-Baghdādī, *Tārīkh* 7: 70, ll. 6–8; 71, l. 12.

41. Al-Sarrāj, *The Kitáb al-Lumaʿ*, ed. Reynold Alleyne Nicholson, E. J. W. Gibb Memorial Ser. 22 (London: Luzac & Co., 1914), 180. For a useful survey of *mudhākara* as it appears in *Tārīkh Baghdād*, see Munir-ul-Din Ahmed, "The Institution of al-Mudhākara," *ZDMG* Suppl. 1, Teil 2 (1969), *17. Deutsche Orientalistentag Wurzburg 1968* (Wiesbaden: F. Steiner, 1983), 595–603.

condemned this central institution of Ḥadīth science: "Sitting for *mudhākara* is to close the gate of benefit, while sitting for *munāṣaḥa* (exchanging counsel) is to open the gate of benefit."[42]

What did the renunciants have against *Ḥadīth*? For one, *rijāl* criticism looked liked *ghība*, insulting absent Muslims. Aḥmad once said only Bishr could tell whether ʿĪsā ibn Yūnus (d. 191/806–7?) had related a particular *Ḥadīth* report. Bishr lamented that he was unqualified to judge next to such men.[43] The famous renunciant Abū Turāb al-Nakhshabī (d. 245/859–60) is said to have warned Aḥmad, "Do not slander the ulema (*lā taghtāb* [*sic*] *al-ʿulamāʾ*)." Aḥmad rejoined, "Beware—this is counsel, not slander (*naṣīḥa, ghība*)."[44] Muḥammad ibn Bundār (d. 292/904–5) complained that it was hard for him to say that so-and-so was weak, so-and-so a great liar. Aḥmad argued in reply that if he and other experts kept their silence, the ignorant would never be able to distinguish the sound from the weak.[45] Ibn Abī Ḥātim (d. 327/938) makes a point of saying that disparaging bad *Ḥadīth* transmitters does not constitute *ghība*.[46] Yet it is said that when someone related to him Yaḥyā ibn Maʿīn's admission that some whom the critics aspersed might have long since [414] put down their saddlebags in Paradise, Ibn Abī Ḥātim dropped the book he was holding and wept uncontrollably.[47]

Renunciants also took offense, it seems, at *Ḥadīth* transmitters' self-importance. This is probably the reason Bishr al-Ḥāfī prayed God to forgive every step he had taken in quest of *Ḥadīth*.[48] Bishr is directly quoted as explaining that he did not relate *Ḥadīth* because he desired to do so, "and whenever I desire something, I renounce it."[49] The memory contest (*mudhākara*) was presumably offensive as an occasion for showing off. Even more, it appears, renunciants were bothered by *Ḥadīth* transmitters' failing to practice what they preached. Bishr al-Ḥāfī, again, is famously quoted as telling some *Ḥadīth* transmitters,

> You may know that an alms tax on them is incumbent on you. If one of you has 200 dirhams, he owes five, and likewise if one of you has heard 200 *Ḥadīth* reports, he must put five of them into practice. Otherwise, beware of what will be incumbent on you tomorrow.[50]

42. Sarrāj, *Lumaʿ*, 179.
43. Al-Khaṭīb al-Baghdādī, *Tārīkh* 7: 77f.
44. *Ibid*., 12: 316.
45. Ibn Abī Yaʿlā, *Ṭabaqāt* 1: 287.
46. Ibn Abī Ḥātim, *K. al-Jarḥ wa-al-taʿdīl*, 9 vols. (Hyderabad: Jamʿiyyat Dāʾirat al-Maʿārif al-ʿUthmāniyya, 1360–71, repr. Beirut: Dār Iḥyāʾ al-Turāth al-ʿArabī, n.d.), 2: 23.
47. Dhahabī, *Siyar* 13: 268.
48. Al-Khaṭīb al-Baghdādī, *Tārīkh* 4: 344f.
49. *Ibid*. 7: 70, ll. 2–6; similarly, Abū Nuʿaym, *Ḥilya* 8: 355.
50. Al-Khaṭīb al-Baghdādī, *Tārīkh* 7: 69, ll. 14–20. Cited by Massignon to show that the conflict between Bishr and the *Ḥadīth* collectors was sharper than Ḥanbali sources admit, *Essai*, 231.

Renunciants were sometimes defended as the ones who put *Ḥadīth* into practice, as opposed to merely relating it. According to Abū Nuᶜaym, Maᶜrūf al-Karkhī (d. ca. 200/815–16) was distracted from relating much *ᶜilm* by his observing it.[51] According to Abū Bakr al-ᶜAṭṭār, Junayd knew *ᶜilm al-sharīᶜa*, but undertaking its truths prevented him from relating *Ḥadīth*.[52] These excuses are not necessarily reliable inasmuch as none that I have found is for a known contemporary; however, they would probably not have been offered had not those who offered them seen men in their own time whose devotions distracted them from *Ḥadīth* transmission.

To be sure, we must not exaggerate the enmity of *Ḥadīth* transmitters and renunciants. Many *Ḥadīth* transmitters also warned against self-importance and failure to practice what one preached. Jacqueline Chabbi has found no significant difference between the piety of al-Fuḍayl ibn ᶜIyāḍ, who disliked the company of *Ḥadīth* transmitters, and of the ninth- and tenth-century Ḥanābila.[53] Some of Bishr al-Ḥāfī's pronouncements against *Ḥadīth* transmitters and their mode of life come from Aḥmad ibn al-Ṣalt (d. 308/921), notorious for false attribution in aid of exalting the Ḥanafiyya and discrediting their traditionalist adversaries.[54] Furthermore, one continues to find, in the tenth century and after, persons identified as *zuhhād* who do not appear to have been Sufis in particular; for example, the famous Shāfiᶜi jurisprudent Abū Isḥāq al-Shīrāzī (d. Baghdad, 476/1083).[55] In all centuries, there were Muslims active in both renunciation and *Ḥadīth*.

In the end, it remains that outstanding renunciants of the eighth century were very often outstanding *Ḥadīth* transmitters as well, yet outstanding *Ḥadīth* transmitters from the tenth century onward were seldom outstanding [415] Sufis, and likewise outstanding Sufis were seldom outstanding experts in *Ḥadīth*. The transition took place across the

51. Abū Nuᶜaym, *Ḥilya* 8: 367.

52. Abū Bakr al-ᶜAṭṭār, apud al-Sulamī, *Ṭabaqāt*, 142.

53. Chabbi, "Fuḍayl," esp. 340–45.

54. Abū Nuᶜaym, *Ḥilya* 8: 344; al-Khaṭīb al-Baghdādī, *Tārīkh* 3: 157. On Aḥmad ibn al-Ṣalt, see Eerik Dickinson, "Aḥmad b. al-Ṣalt and His Biography of Abū Ḥanīfa," *Journal of the American Oriental Society* 116 (1996): 406–17. The relations between Aḥmad ibn Ḥanbal and Bishr al-Ḥāfī, or more precisely the evolving literary tradition of their relations, has been the subject of a brilliant study by Michael Cooperson: "Ibn Ḥanbal and Bishr al-Ḥāfī," *Studia Islamica*, no. 86 (1997), 71–101. I have suggested that disparaging quotations of Bishr have less to do with Sufi influence than Cooperson assumes and more to do with polemics among the *Ḥadīth* transmitters themselves.

55. Al-Dhahabī quotes al-Samᶜānī as calling him a *zāhid*, although I do not find the term in al-Samᶜānī, *K. al-Ansāb*, s.n. "*fīrūzābādhī*": see *Siyar aᶜlām al-nubalāʾ* 18 (ed. Muḥammad Nuᶜaym al-ᶜIrqasūsī, 1405/1984): 454. Ibn al-Jawzī describes him as *qashif al-ᶜaysh mutawarriᶜ*, living austerely and avoiding everything not unambiguously licit: *al-Muntaẓam*, 6 vols. (Hyderabad: Dāʾirat al-Maᶜārif al-ᶜUthmāniyya, 1357–60), 9: 7 = ed. Muḥammad ᶜAbd al-Qādir ᶜAṭā and Muṣṭafā ᶜAbd al-Qādir ᶜAṭā, w. Nuᶜaym Zurzūr, 18 vols. (Beirut: Dār al-Kutub al-ᶜIlmiyya, 1412/1992), 16: 230. Subkī mentions that he had the reputation of having his every prayer answered: *Ṭabaqāt al-shāfiᶜiyya al-kubrā*, ed. Maḥmūd Muḥammad al-Ṭanāḥī and ᶜAbd al-Fattāḥ al-Ḥulw, 10 vols. (Cairo: ᶜĪsā al-Bābī al-Ḥalabī, 1964–76), 4: 216.

ninth century, as can be demonstrated from the appearance and ratings of renunciants in books of *rijāl* criticism. As the century wore on, remembered renunciants were ever less likely to be active transmitters of *Ḥadīth* and even less likely to attract the notice of *Ḥadīth* specialists.

8
THE PIETY OF THE HADITH FOLK

One of the most remarkable surveys of Islamic history and civilization remains Marshall G. S. Hodgson's *The Venture of Islam*, published posthumously in 1974.[1] For an introductory text, it has some bad faults—notably, a very dense style. Moreover, it has inevitably fallen out of date at many points. For example, we may admire Hodgson for coming up with his own critique of modernization theory in volume 3, but modernization theory has fallen so completely before other critiques, we hardly need Hodgson any longer. On the other hand, Hodgson has had some permanent effects on the way scholars approach Islamic history. For example, we may not have adopted many of his neologisms, but he certainly has made us self-conscious when we use the traditional terminology. The mere mention of "Jamâ'i-Sunni," "Islamicate," "Arabist bias," and other special terms immediately alerts us to the dangers of some customary approaches to Islamic history.

One of Hodgson's most notable challenges was to the traditional periodization. Instead of dividing Islamic history according to Sunni dogmatic preferences—mainly the Rightly Guided Caliphs (to 661), then the Umayyads, excluding ʿUthman (to 750), then the ʿAbbasids (to 1258)—Hodgson proposed a primitive period running up to the advent of the Marwanids (685), then a Classical Period running up to the advent of the Buyids (945), then a High Middle Period to the Mongol conquest.[2] One of the main objects of this essay is to identify more precisely the elements that went into the Sunni synthesis that crystallized in the early 10th century—in particular, competing forms of piety.

Piety was important to Hodgson, for part of his enterprise was to show why it was fair to call a civilization "Islamic" (hence his subtitle, "Conscience and History in a World

1. Marshall G. S. Hodgson, *The Venture of Islam*, 3 vols. (Chicago: University of Chicago Press, 1974).
2. Ibid., 1:234.

Originally published in *International Journal of Middle East Studies* 34 (2002): 425–39.

Civilization"). As a Quaker, he assumed that Muslims also had their inner lights, which must be taken seriously. His description of what he calls the "Sharī'ah-minded" is unsurpassed as an account of one party's basic world view. These were the Muslims who elaborated and transmitted the revealed law and thought that the law, more than custom, good taste, personal experience, or anything else, should mold the lives of the faithful. Yet clearly Hodgson's own sympathies lay mainly with Sufi mystics, whom he treats at much greater length. Accordingly, further sympathetic attention to the "Sharī'ah-minded" seems in order, especially in the formative 9th [426] century. Can we be more precise about who constituted the "Sharī'ah-minded?" Can we say more precisely how their piety differed from other forms on offer, particularly Sufism and *adab* (narrowly, polite letters; more broadly, the culture of courtiers)?

The theological map of the 9th century has been sketched in some detail, now.[3] Important new attention has also been given to the evolution of Islamic law in that century.[4] The Sufis and their precursors have been the subject of much work, too, although we apparently still lack any widely accepted historical overview of the early period.[5] Yet one of the century's most influential juridical-theological movements has scarcely been studied at all from the side of piety, mainly what Marshall Hodgson called the "Ḥadîth folk."[6]

---

3. See W. Montgomery Watt, *The Formative Period of Islamic Thought* (Edinburgh: Edinburgh University Press, 1973), and above all, now, Josef van Ess, *Theologie und Gesellschaft im 2. und 3. Jahrhundert Hidschra*, 6 vols. (Berlin: de Gruyter, 1991–95).

4. To the classic work of Joseph Schacht, *The Origins of Muhammadan Jurisprudence* (Oxford: Clarendon Press, 1950), now add Norman Calder, *Studies in Early Islamic Jurisprudence* (New York: Clarendon Press, 1993); Wael B. Hallaq, "Was al-Shafiʿi the Master Architect of Islamic Jurisprudence?" *International Journal of Middle East Studies* 25 (1993): 587–605; George Makdisi, "*Ṭabaqāt*-Biography: Law and Orthodoxy in Classical Islam," *Islamic Studies* (Islamabad) 32 (1993): 371–96; Christopher Melchert, *The Formation of the Sunni Schools of Law*, Studies in Islamic Law and Society 4 (Leiden: Brill, 1997), and Jonathan E. Brockopp, "Early Islamic Jurisprudence in Egypt: Two Scholars and Their *Mukhtaṣars*," *International Journal of Middle East Studies* 30 (1998): 167–82.

5. See, most recently, Alexander Knysh, *Islamic Mysticism: A Short History*, Themes in Islamic Studies 1 (Leiden: E. J. Brill, 2000). Many of the most important figures have been surveyed by Richard Gramlich, *Altevorbilder des Sufitums*, Akademie der Wissenschaften und der Literatur, Mainz, Veröffentlichungen der Orientalischen Kommission 42, 2 vols. (Wiesbaden: Harrassowitz, 1995–96). On the Karrami and Malamati movements in Khurasan, the trail was blazed by Jacqueline Chabbi, "Remarques sur le développement historique des mouvements ascétiques et mystiques au Khurasan," *Studia Islamica* 46 (1977): 5–72, and further developed by Sara Sviri, "Ḥakīm Tirmidhī and the Malāmatī Movement in Early Sufism," in *Classical Persian Sufism*, ed. Leonard Lewisohn (New York: Khaniqahi Nimatullahi Publications, 1993), 583–613. The renunciants to whom the term *ṣūfī* was applied before the late 9th century were by and large not the ones acclaimed as their predecessors by the Sufis of the 10th and later centuries. How the term shifted from one group to another remains mysterious, observes *The Encyclopaedia of Islam*, new edn., s.v. "Taṣawwuf" (B. Radtke).

6. For Hodgson's treatment, see *Venture*, 1:315–409, esp. 386–92. Exceptionally, the asceticism of Ahmad b. Hanbal and his disciples has subsequently been treated by Nimrod Hurvitz, "Aḥmad Ibn Ḥanbal

Hodgson's "Sharî'ah-minded" comprised the "host of pious men and women who came to be called the 'ulamâ, the 'learnèd,'" gradually professionalized from the 8th century to the 10th or later and certainly cutting across multiple theological lines.[7] It is much easier to study the hadith folk than the "Sharî'ah-minded," for they were a self-conscious party, precisely identifiable, with distinctive programs in theology, law, and devotion.

Hodgson proposed "Ḥadîth folk" as a substitute for the older "traditionalists," and I use it here in tribute to him. "Ḥadîth" plainly indicates what they recognized as the chief source of religious authority alongside the Qurʾan.[8] "Ḥadîth folk" avoids the suggestion of "traditionalist" that their program was older than the programs of their adversaries, which is doubtful. I will nevertheless continue to use "traditionalist" because "hadith folk" does not have convenient singular and adjectival forms (although Hodgson tries "Hadithi"[9]). The Baghdadi hadith folk have sometimes appeared in modern scholarship as "Hanbalis," but I prefer to avoid that term in discussing the movement before the formation of a specific school of law in the next century.[10]

The 9th-century hadith folk's own preferred term for themselves was *ahl al-sunna*.[11] It is not convenient for us to call the hadith folk "Sunnis" because that term now calls to mind the great tripartite division of Sunnis, Shiʿis, and Kharijis. At least for the 9th century and earlier, a mere tripartite division is simplistic and practically impossible to

---

and the Formation of Islamic Orthodoxy" (Ph.D. diss., Princeton University, Princeton, N.J., 1994), chap. 6; and idem, "Biographies and Mild Asceticism: A Study of Islamic Moral Imagination," *Studia Islamica* 85 (1997): 41–65. Hurvitz stresses the moderateness of Ahmad's ascetic regime, its connection with *al-amr bi-'l-maʿrūf*, and its cohesive effect on the developing school of law and theology. My chief reservation is the thinness of Hurvitz' documentation, especially for Sufis and others outside Ahmad's circle.

7. Hodgson, *Venture*, 1:238.

8. Ibid., 1:386. "Hadith" is not unambiguous, for it is nowadays usually taken to mean, as Hodgson himself says, "ḥadîth reports about the Prophet," whereas in the 9th century it normally included reports about the companions and other early jurisprudents. On Ahmad's frequent resorting to the practice and opinions of Companions, see Susan A. Spectorsky, "Aḥmad Ibn Ḥanbal's *Fiqh*," *Journal of the American Oriental Society* 102 (1982): 461–65. The idea that Shafiʿi's polemics forced Muslims to distinguish sharply between *hadith* from the Prophet and *āthār* from the companions goes back mainly to Schacht, *Origins*. More recent studies have shown that one can hardly make out the effect of Shafiʿi's theories on wider legal thought before the last quarter of the 9th century. See most conveniently Hallaq, "Was al-Shafiʿi the Master Architect?"

9. Hodgson, *Venture*, 1:389.

10. Cf. Ira M. Lapidus, "The Separation of State and Religion in the Development of Early Islamic Society," *International Journal of Middle East Studies* 6 (1975): 363–85, esp. 382–84, assuming a Hanbali movement from the early 9th century; and Wilferd Madelung, "The Vigilante Movement of Sahl b. Salāma al-Khurāsānī and the Origins of Ḥanbalism Reconsidered," *Journal of Turkish Studies* 14 (1990): 331–37, showing that Hanbalism strictly speaking had different emphases and came later.

11. For example, in Ahmad, Creeds I, III, IV, VI, quoted by Ibn Abī Yaʿlā, *Ṭabaqāt al-ḥanābila*, ed. Muḥammad Ḥāmid al-Fiqī, 2 vols. (Cairo: Maṭbaʿat al-Sunna al-Muḥammadiyya, 1952), 1:24, 242, 294, 345.

document. To begin with, 9th-century definitions of Shiʿism were considerably different from those of later times; for example, traditionalist *rijāl* critics regularly distinguished between *tashayyuʿ*, a special regard for ʿAli and his house that the hadith folk were willing to overlook, and *rafḍ*, the rejection of Abu Bakr and ʿUmar that they thought put one outside the Muslim community. With equal emphasis, the 9th-century hadith folk distinguished themselves from Qadariyya, Murjiʾa, Muʿtazila, and other theological parties not accounted for by a simple, anachronistic dichotomy between Sunnis and Shiʿis. The polarity of Sunni and Shiʿi was not strong until the mid-10th century, while full Sunni mutual recognition and self-awareness appeared only in the 11th century. Finally, modern scholars should avoid endorsing the hadith folk's own estimate that they were the overwhelming majority, as calling them "Sunnis" might do.[12] The significance of their calling themselves *ahl al-sunna* is not that their views were identical to those of the later, great Sunni community, which they were not, but rather that the later community deliberately identified them as its forebears. We need to understand their piety.

Their adversaries preferred not to call them *ahl al-sunna* and proposed various other terms.[13] Al-Jahiz disparaged the *nābita*, those who sprouted up like weeds to extol the enemies of ʿAli and to promulgate such crass ideas as assigning God an [427] imaginable body (*tajsīm*, *taṣwīr*). Other writers attributed similar errors to the *ḥashwiyya* (vulgar). The hadith folk complained that the Murjiʾa called them *shukkāk* (doubters) for saying "I am a believer, God willing," while the Qadariyya called them *mujbira* or *jabriyya* for upholding divine predestination.[14] To use any of these terms for the hadith folk would mean to take sides as much as it would to call them *ahl al-sunna*, which is needless for modern scholars.

There were hadith folk in all the great centers of Islam. The traditionalist leader of Nishapur wrote traditionalist leaders in Ray and Baghdad to warn them against Dawud al-Zahiri, who alleged that the Qurʾan was *muḥdath* (i.e., there had been a time when the Qurʾan was not).[15] Hadith folk in Baghdad warned those of Nishapur against the famous

12. On the multiple meanings of "Sunni," cf. Hodgson, *Venture* 1:278 fn. On the formation of orthodoxies, see now John B. Henderson, *The Construction of Orthodoxy and Heresy: Neo-Confucian, Islamic, Jewish, and Early Christian Patterns* (Albany: State University of New York Press, 1998), esp. 41 (comparison with church history, where likewise later orthodoxy was earlier one minority position among many), 53 (chronology of Sunnism).

13. See the caliph al-Maʾmun's complaint that they illegitimately associate themselves with the sunna: al-Ṭabarī, *Annales*, ed. M. J. de Goeje, 3 vols. in 15 (Leiden: E. J. Brill, 1879–1901), 3:1114, equivalent to *Tārīkh al-Ṭabarī*, ed. Muḥammad Abu 'l-Faḍl Ibrāhīm, Dhakhāʾir al-ʿArab 30, 10 vols. (Cairo: Dār al-Maʿārif, 1960–69), 7:632.

14. For most of these terms, see A. S. Halkin, "The Ḥashwiyya," *Journal of the American Oriental Society* 54 (1934): 1–28, which needs remarkably little updating apart from editions cited (although Hodgson's criticism is just, *Venture*, 1:391 fn). See also *EI2*, s.v. "Nābita" (Ch. Pellat); and Wadād al-Qāḍī, "The Earliest 'Nābita' and the Paradigmatic 'Nawābit,'" *Studia Islamica* 78 (1993): 27–61. Ahmad protests the application of various terms at the conclusion of Creed I, quoted by Ibn Abī Yaʿlā, *Ṭabaqāt*, 1:35 f.

15. Al-Khaṭīb al-Baghdādī, *Tārīkh Baghdād*, 14 vols. (Cairo: al-Khānjī, 1931), 8:373 f; al-Dhahabī, *Tārīkh*

that salvation came by membership in the community, or that the primary significance of the law was to mark out the Islamic community. Yet Ahmad did insist that sins (violations of the law) do not put one outside the community, only wrong beliefs (rejecting the Qurʾan and hadith, in Watt's terms the markers of the community).[43]

Watt traces back the importance of the community to the Arab experience of tribalism. Hodgson allows that the needs of the early-Islamic militia decisively informed the developing shariʿa, alongside the needs of cosmopolitan merchants.[44] However, one now recognizes the preponderant influence of the urban setting in which classical Islamic culture evolved and doubts whether it was crucially influenced by memories of life in the desert.[45] The hadith folk in particular were no Rechabites. Ahmad himself rejected the nomadic life; for example, he recommended that one live in the city except when there was civil strife.[46] Watt's formula of the charismatic community does little, anyway, to characterize the Islamic community. For example, it does not predict the famous qualified communalism of Islamic ritual prayer: all face the same direction, make the same gestures and say the same words, with none standing for his fellows as a Christian priest would stand for the congregation, nor with any mystical joining of those at prayer, but only a salutation at the end.

The community as conceived by the hadith folk seems to have flowed mainly not from the exigencies of life in the desert but from a stress on obedience to a transcendent God as opposed to communion with an immanent God—that is, in Weber's terms of ideal types, an ascetical (moralistic) orientation rather than a mystical one.[47] For example, it has most of the earmarks of a contractual community, whose membership is voluntary and within which there is substantial equality. Voluntary membership and equality flow from a stress on morality, which continually makes the individual choose to do one thing and not another, which also tends to demand the same choices from all individuals. By contrast, mystics tend toward an organic conception of community, accepting hierarchy and specialization, for some will be found closer to God than others. Perhaps, to give

---

without knowing the meaning": al-Dhahabī, *Siyar aʿlām al-nubalāʾ*, 25 vols. (Beirut: Muʾassasat al-Risāla, 1981–88), ed. Shuʿayb al-Arnaʾūṭ and Ṣāliḥ al-Samr (1983), 61.

43. Ibn Abī Yaʿlā, *Ṭabaqāt*, 1:26, 27, 343.

44. For example, Hodgson, *Venture*, 1:346.

45. So, for example, Calder, *Studies*, chap. 8.

46. Ibn Abī Yaʿlā, *Ṭabaqāt* 1:409.

47. Max Weber, *Economy and Society*, ed. Guenther Roth and Claus Wittich, 2 vols. (Berkeley: Univ. of Calif. Press, 1978), 544–51. The dichotomy of ascetical and mystical has been developed by numerous others, culminating in the skillful summary of Gert H. Mueller, "Asceticism and Mysticism," in *International Yearbook for the Sociology of Religion* 8: *Sociological Theories of Religion/Religion and Language*, ed. Günter Dux, Thomas Luckmann, and Joachim Matthes (Opladen: Westdeutscher Verlag, 1973), 68–132. "Ascetical" as "moralistic," the opposite of "mystical," is easily confused with the more common usage of "ascetic" as "renunciant," perhaps the opposite of "self-indulgent." But "ascetical" is the term Weber chose, and we seem to be stuck with it.

Hodgson his due, it was indeed the exigencies of commercial life in cities that pushed the hadith folk in the direction of morality rather than mysticism—and he does speak of "the Sharî'ah-minded guardians of the single godly moralistic community."[48]

The ascetical (moralistic) character of the hadith folk's conception of community comes out clearly in their reaction to *tawakkul*, the endeavor to live entirely by what came without one's seeking it. Ahmad said, "*Tawakkul* is good; however, a man must not be a charge on others. He should work, in order that he make himself and his family independent."[49] Weber observes that the mystic depends on others' remaining in the world for him to leave it, provoking the ascetic's indignation. Weber was presumably thinking of early Protestant polemics against monasticism, but one could not find a clearer illustration than Ahmad's wariness of *tawakkul*. Likewise, indeed, the [430] examples of concern for the community quoted earlier from some who resisted at the Inquisition stress individual choice: it is not that the community must rise or fall as a body, but that Ahmad, Bakkar, and Buwayti were setting examples for other individuals to follow.

Concern to maintain community may often look like hostility to excellence. Hodgson says of the Sharî'ah as it was elaborated in early ʿAbbâsî times,

> Its heritage of respect for the cultural homogeneity of Medina and then of the Marwânî Arabs now became a pressure for all Muslims to conform to a bourgeois pattern of life, a pattern necessarily adapted to the average man. Shar'î Islam required no "religious athletes" and discouraged any other special callings. The bold experimenter was required to show, at least externally, the face of mediocre propriety.[50]

Hence, although the hadith folk admired deliberate austerity, they characteristically disapproved of extremes. Barefootedness is a convenient example, as Maher Jarrar has recently devoted a special study to it.[51] Barefootedness connoted humility, and was especially practiced in connection with collective pious enterprises such as seeking hadith and walking in funeral processions.[52] Bishr al-Hafi's barefootedness at all times and in all places connoted humility before God at all times and in all places.[53] But the hadith folk

48. Hodgson, *Venture*, 2:200.

49. Quoted by al-Khallāl, *K. al-Ḥathth ʿalā al-tijāra*, ed. Abū ʿAbd Allāh Maḥmūd b. Muḥammad al-Ḥaddād (Riyadh: Dār al-ʿĀṣima, 1407), 158; also quoted by Benedikt Reinert, *Die Lehre vom* tawakkul *in der klassischen Sufik*, Der Islam Studien zur Sprache, Geschichte und Kultur des islamischen Orients 3 (Berlin: Walter de Gruyter, 1968), 255, citing the edition of Damascus (a.h. 1348), 29. Al-Khallal's work includes many other quotations to the same effect. So do other works—for example, Aḥmad, *Waraʿ*, ed. Zaghlūl, 24.

50. Hodgson, *Venture*, 1:344.

51. Maher Jarrar, "Bišr al-Ḥāfī und die Barfüßigkeit im Islam," *Der Islam* 71 (1994): 191–240.

52. Ibid., 220.

53. Ibid., 231.

were mistrustful.[54] A lesser expression of humility—probably the one I have most frequently encountered in the sources—is going on foot as opposed to riding. For example, Ahmad b. Hanbal's five pilgrimages are counted separately, those he performed on foot and those he performed riding.[55] Thus, in common with the extreme ascetics, the hadith folk admired humility but favored a less extreme form of it.

A major concern was evidently to keep ideal decorum within everyone's range. As Ahmad complained, having heard of someone's saying that worry about one's provision for the morrow would be counted a sin, "Who is so strong as this?"[56] Against Hodgson, I tend to doubt whether the point was to preserve the cultural homogeneity of ideal Medina. How did they know it was homogeneous? More important, what made that feature so attractive to them? I would say the point was rather to respect the nature of moral demands. A moral demand is necessarily the same for everyone, in every place, at every time. For example, adultery is not sometimes forbidden, sometimes allowed, but always forbidden; supporting one's family is not sometimes required, sometimes omissible, but always required. If someone did something not everyone might do, such as never worrying about his provisions for the morrow, it was evidently not in response to a moral demand from God. It rather had the nature of a stunt: "look what I can do." As such, it necessarily appeared to the hadith folk as frivolity, a reprehensible distraction from the performance of universal religious duties. Ibn Kathir suggests as much in his explanation of Ahmad's and Abu Zurʿa al-Razi's disapproval of Muhasibi and his fellow proto-Sufis: "their talk of austerity . . . and far-reaching, minute self-observation was something concerning which no command had come."[57]

More positively, we might see traditionalist hostility to special callings as concern to promote well-roundedness. Someone told Ahmad that a man might work at Qurʾanic recitation, frequent the mosque, or seek hadith, but not two of these at once. Ahmad said it was incumbent on him both to frequent the mosque and to seek hadith.[58] [431]

It is something of a puzzle, then, why it was not easy to be expelled from the community as conceived by the hadith folk, and why their community did not split into competing sects. These, too, are regular features of the religious community whose basis is moral, not mystical. To the moralist, unpunished adultery, for example, seems a standing insult to God, and the adulterer has removed himself from the community. The mystic, by contrast, tends to see past the individual's adultery to, perhaps, the inner light.[59] The

54. Ibid., 200 f.

55. Two of the five on foot, according to al-Khallāl, *Ḥathth*, 138; three according to Ibn Abī Ḥātim, *Jarḥ*, 1:304, and Abū Nuʿaym, *Ḥilya*, 9:175.

56. Aḥmad, *Waraʿ*, ed. Muḥyī al-Dīn Naṣr al-Kurdī (Cairo: Maṭbaʿat al-Saʿāda, 1340), 80.

57. Ibn Kathīr, *al-Bidāya wa-ʾl-nihāya*, 14 vols. (Cairo: Maṭbaʿat al-Saʿāda, 1932–39), 10:330.

58. Ibn Abī Yaʿlā, *Ṭabaqāt*, 1:23.

59. See Mueller, "Asceticism and Mysticism," 104.

easy answer must be, of course, that every piety has both ascetical (moralistic) elements and mystical. A mystical element of traditionalist piety is its refusal to expel persons from the community for wrong actions, sins. More subtly, one also might say that the hadith folk managed to rank Muslims by the quality of their obedience (as Hodgson says, "the only true difference among the faithful was in degree of piety"), and so they managed to accept a degree of hierarchy by which it was not necessary to expel those who would not follow the rules, only to look condescendingly down on them. Finally, a combination of hierarchy with stress on individual obedience suggests that obedience to God, for the hadith folk, had a pronouncedly ritual character.[60] The law was about following everywhere a revealed pattern. Such seems to be, indeed, the precise sense of shariᶜa, although the word is as rare in the writings of 9th-century hadith folk as elsewhere.[61] Traditionalist resentment of rationalistic theology would then have had to do with its threat to break loose from the received pattern; likewise, indeed, traditionalist suspicion of Sufism and, to a degree, *adab*.

Contrast with Sufi Piety

The value of sketching the piety of the hadith folk will be clear if it turns out, by contrast, to identify more precisely the piety of other parties. The ascetic tradition until the mid-9th century was mainly devoted to singlemindedness, and in this wise the piety of early ascetics was similar to that of contemporary and slightly later hadith folk.[62] Yet strains were evident even before the emergence of classical Sufism under Junayd (d. 911?). The famous ascetic Bishr al-Hafi often appears in Hanbali works such as *Kitāb al-Waraᶜ* (eighteen entries there, against none for any other famous precursor to classical Sufism). However, Ahmad's praise was qualified by criticism: "If Bishr had married, his affair would have been perfect."[63] Massignon guesses that Ahmad's conflict with Bishr was sharper than the biographers admit.[64]

60. The Muslim's life as guided by the law and described again and again in the biographical dictionaries has most of the characters of what Catherine Bell has recently identified as "ritual-like activities": formalism, traditionalism, invariance, and rule governance. See Catherine Bell, *Ritual: Perspectives and Dimensions* (New York: Oxford University Press, 1997), chap. 5.

61. See A. Kevin Reinhart, "Islamic Law as Islamic Ethics," *Journal of Religious Ethics* 11 (1983): 188 f; Wilfred Cantwell Smith, "The Concept of Sharīᶜa Among Some Mutakallimūn," *Arabic and Islamic Studies in Honor of Hamilton A. R. Gibb*, ed. George Makdisi (Leiden: E. J. Brill, 1965), 585, 598 f.

62. Jacqueline Chabbi has found virtual identity between the piety of al-Fudayl b. ᶜIyad (d. Mecca, 803) and that of the 9th- and 10th-century Hanabila: "Fuḍayl b. ᶜIyāḍ, un précurseur du Ḥanbalisme," *Bulletin d'études orientales* 30 (1978): 331–45, esp. 340–45.

63. Aḥmad, *Waraᶜ*, ed. Zaghlūl, 94; al-Khaṭīb al-Baghdādī, *Tārīkh*, 7:73.

64. Louis Massignon, *Essai sur les origines du lexique technique de la mystique musulmane*, rev. ed. (Paris: J.

Ahmad's relations with Muhasibi (d. 857–58) were much worse, and Muhasibi was forced to go into hiding.[65] Ahmad was probably angered above all by Muhasibi's involvement in *kalām*, where he was close to Ibn Kullab[66]; however, Abu Zurʿa al-Razi (d. 878) expressly repudiated Muhasibi's ascetical works as well. It was enough, he said, to take warning from the Qurʾan and hadith.[67]

Not only was Ahmad hostile to crucially important precursors of the Sufis, he rejected principal Sufi practices. He rejected roaming from place to place, worshipping: "*Siyāḥa* has nothing to do with Islam."[68] Someone told Ahmad of a group that met to pray, recite the Qurʾan, and recollect God (*yadhkurūna Allāh*). Ahmad responded that it was enough to read from the (public) bound copy, to recollect God to oneself, and to seek hadith. Meeting in public for these purposes was an innovation to be condemned.[69] On the whole, the Sufism of Junayd, with its regular meetings for the exchange of definitions, must have pleased him very little. [432]

As for the two salient features of traditionalist piety that I have pointed out before, seriousness and a contractual, moralistic conception of community, the hadith folk were at odds with the Sufis on both points. As for seriousness, Junayd said, "I would rather be kept company by a good-natured debauchee than an ill-natured ascetic."[70] I do not recall reading of a Sufi who was never seen laughing or smiling. As for the contractual community, mystics tend toward an organic conception of community, accepting hierarchy and specialization. Junayd and his comrades clearly specialized to a greater degree than the hadith folk allowed. Although they still paid some attention to Qurʾanic recitation and hadith, for example, they clearly devoted most of their time to other disciplines, and sometimes expressly rejected the collection of hadith when it came into conflict with the

Vrin, 1954), 231. Massignon's comparison of Bishr to Muhasibi is inapt inasmuch as Muhasibi was clearly involved in *kalām* and *uṣūl al-fiqh*, in which fields no one accused Bishr of meddling.

65. Al-Khaṭīb al-Baghdādī, *Tārīkh*, 8:215 f. Earlier, it seems, Muhasibi had fled to Kufa, whence he sent back word to Ahmad that he had repented of what Ahmad had rejected, which repentance, too, Ahmad rejected: Dhahabī, *Tārīkh*, vol. 18 (a.h. 241–50), 209.

66. Ibn Abī Yaʿlā, *Ṭabaqāt*, 1:62 f, 233 f; Dhahabī, *Siyar*, ed. Ṣāliḥ al-Samr, 11:174 f; Josef van Ess, *Die Gedankenwelt des Ḥāriṯ al-Muḥāsibī*, Bonner orientalische Studien n. S. 12 (Bonn: Selbstverlag des orientalischen Seminars der Universität Bonn, 1961), 9.

67. Al-Khaṭīb al-Baghdādī, *Tārīkh*, 8:215.

68. Ibn Hāniʾ, *Masāʾil al-imām Aḥmad*, ed. Zuhayr al-Shāwīsh, 2 vols. (Beirut: al-Maktab al-Islāmī, a.h. 1394), 2:176.

69. Ibn Abī Yaʿlā, *Ṭabaqāt*, 1:255.

70. Al-Sarrāj, *The Kitáb al-Lumaʿ fi 'l-tasawwuf*, ed. Reynold Alleyne Nicholson, E. J. W. Gibb Memorial Series 22 (London: Luzac, 1914), 177. On *qāriʾ* as "ascetic," see Ignaz Goldziher, *Introduction to Islamic Theology and Law*, trans. Andras and Ruth Hamori (Princeton, N.J.: Princeton University Press, 1981), 127n. 35.

demands of Sufi devotion.[71] Junayd's argument for mystics to respect less enlightened ascetics clearly demonstrates a hierarchical notion of the Islamic community.[72]

However, it is clear that the classical Sufis were closer to the hadith folk than some of their predecessors had been. In particular, I think of Muʿtazili ascetics and the Karramiyya, who strongly disagreed with the hadith folk concerning *kasb* (gain). The Muʿtazila are most famous for their rationalistic theology, but they evidently began as an ascetic movement, the name signifying withdrawal from sinful society.[73] They were only gradually distinguished from the general ascetic tradition in the late 8th century, scarcely any earlier than the hadith folk themselves were distinguished from the general religious movement.[74] The term *ṣūfī* was applied to Muʿtazili ascetics before it was to Junayd and his circle. Early Muʿtazili ascetics and the later Karramiyya, who more or less absorbed Muʿtazili asceticism, sometimes exalted complete renunciation of normal gain, counting it best to live off alms.[75] The hadith folk, as noted, strongly urged that every man support

---

71. Although there is much insistence that Sufis were also good traditionists, there is abundant evidence that Sufism and the transmission of hadith were to some degree opposed. For example, Abu Nuʿaym al-Isbahani (d. 1038) was a prominent traditionist who is widely supposed to have written *Ḥilyat al-awliyāʾ* in part to demonstrate precisely that the great traditionists and the great ascetics and mystics were part of the same tradition. Yet he quotes Junayd's master, Sari al-Saqati (d. 867?), as saying, "If a man starts (with austerity) and then writes hadith, he will languish, whereas if a man starts with writing hadith and then takes up austerity (*tanassaka*), he will reach (his goal)": *Ḥilya*, 10:125. Evidently, *tanassuk* and collecting hadith were not to be practiced at once. A little later, Abu Nuʿaym actually quotes Sari as disparaging a hadith report someone has just recited—"This is not the food of the tomb"—and admits that he transmitted little himself: *Ḥilya*, 10: 127.

72. See Christopher Melchert, "The Transition from Asceticism to Mysticism," *Studia Islamica* 83 (1996): 51–70 [*HPL 9], at 69 f, based on Junayd, *al-Waṣāyā*, Reşit Efendi (Istanbul) 1218/1.

73. Cf. Qurʾan 19.48 f, where the verb *iʿtazala* describes Abraham's withdrawal from his father, his people, and their idolatry. The crucial study is Sarah Stroumsa, "The Beginnings of the Muʿtazilah, Reconsidered," *Jerusalem Studies in Arabic and Islam*, no. 13 (1990): 265–93.

74. Hence Ahmad b. Hanbal used to relate hadith of the Muʿtazili leader ʿAmr b. ʿUbayd (d. 761–62), then took to relating his hadith without naming him, and only at the end refused altogether to relate of him anything: al-Khaṭīb al-Baghdādī, *Tārīkh*, 12:184.

75. On the Muʿtazila and Karramiyya, see Josef van Ess, "Une Lecture à rebours de l'histoire du muʿtazilisme," *Revue des études islamiques* 46 (1978): 163–240, esp. 192; 47 (1979): 16–69. Abu ʿImran al-Raqashi (fl. 9th century) was a proto-Muʿtazili who disbelieved in *makāsib*: Ibn al-Murtaḍā, *Die Klassen der muʿtaziliten*, ed. Susanna Diwald-Wilzer, Bibliotheca Islamica 21 (Wiesbaden: Franz Steiner, 1961), 77. Among the classical Muʿtazila, al-Rummani (d. 994) wrote a book on *Taḥrīm al-makāsib*: Sezgin, *GAS* 8: 114, no. 21. For Karrami rejection of *kasb*, see Josef van Ess, *Ungenützte Texte zur Karrāmīya*, Sitzungsberichte der Heidelberger Akademie der Wissenschaften, philosophisch-historisch Klasse; Jahrg. 1980, 6, Abhandlungen (Heidelberg: C. Winter, 1980), 30–32; idem, "Lecture," 190; Massignon, *The Passion of al-Hallāj*, trans. Herbert Mason, Bollingen Series 98, 4 vols. (Princeton, N. J.: Princeton University Press, 1982), 3:227; Margaret Malamud, "The Politics of Heresy in Medieval Khurasan: The Karramiyya in Nishapur," *Iranian Studies* 27 (1994): 43 f. Note also the jibe of al-Maqdisī (Muqaddasī), that the Karamiyya were never free of piety, partisanship, humility, and begging: *Aḥsan al-taqāsīm*, ed. M. J. De Goeje, Bibliotheca

himself (and his family). The Sufis around Junayd compliantly rejected outward *tawakkul* in favor of inward renunciation.[76] Their position concerning *tawakkul* is then an example of the classical Sufis' having moved halfway to appease the hadith folk. (The Karramiyya were locally opposed, in Nishapur, by the mystics whom Sulami calls the Malamatiyya. The latter naturally took a position similar to that of the Sufis in Baghdad, to whom they were assimilated by the second quarter of the 11th century.[77] So far, affairs in Basra appear less clear-cut than in Nishapur; however, Sahl al-Tustari and the Salimiyya seem to have respected both classical *tawakkul* and working for a living.)

Contrast with the Piety of *ahl al-adab*

The piety of *ahl al-adab*, cultivators of belles-lettres, is another to be distinguished from that of the hadith folk. As a category, *zuhd* (asceticism in the sense of renunciation) was equally prominent in 9th-century books of *adab* and collections of hadith.[78] Perhaps no single conception of community prevailed in *adab*. Singlemindedness and unrelieved seriousness do seem to distinguish the piety of the hadith folk from that of *ahl al-adab*. As for singlemindedness, it was a favorite principle of the hadith folk that a good Muslim should leave what did not concern him. A hadith report to this effect was named by Abu Dawud al-Sijistani (d. 889), the one of the Six closest to the hadith folk, among the four reports that suffice for a man's religion.[79] The hadith folk may have understood "what does not concern him" to mean primarily *kalām* [433] (speculative theology).[80] Still, stories did circulate in Iraq implying that leaving what does not concern one applied to all idle curiosity. One man punished himself by fasting for a month after he had asked when a room had been constructed; that is, expressly, "asking about what does not concern you." Another man privately blamed himself at extravagant length for having asked what someone was doing, then reproached the man for napping; that is, expressly, "asking about what does not concern you and talking of what does not concern you."[81] In

geographorum Arabicorum 3, 2nd ed. (Leiden: E. J. Brill, 1906), 41. *Kasb* later became a technical term of Ashᶜari theology for the relation of humans to their actions, but that sense is clearly not at issue here.

76. The classic study is Reinert, *Die Lehre vom* tawakkul.

77. See al-Sulamī, *Risālat al-malāmatiyya*, in Abu 'l-ᶜAlāʾ al-ᶜAfīfī, *al-Malāmatiyya*, Muʾallafāt al-Jamᶜiyya al-Falsafiyya al-Miṣriyya 5 (Cairo: ᶜĪsā al-Bābī al-Ḥalabī, 1945), 86–120. The most important studies are those of Chabbi, "Remarques," and Sviri, "Ḥakīm Tirmidhī."

78. See Chabbi, "Remarques," 24. Chabbi observes that the *zuhd* sections of books of *adab* dwell on the miraculous more than do the comparable sections of books of hadith.

79. *Min ḥusni islāmi 'l-marʾi tarkuhu mā lā yaᶜnīh*. See al-Khaṭīb al-Baghdādī, *Tārīkh*, 9:57, ll. 4–9; Ibn Abī Yaᶜlā, *Ṭabaqāt*, 1:161.

80. See Abū Nuᶜaym, *Ḥilya*, 9:186, where Ahmad tells a man who has asked him "about what does not concern him" to consult rather Ibn Abi Duwad, the Muᶜtazili qadi.

81. Ibn Abī al-Dunyā, *Muḥāsabat al-nafs*, ed. Majdī al-Sayyid Ibrāhīm (Cairo: Maktabat al-Qurʾān, n.d.),

a broader sense, leaving what does not concern one must preclude the pursuit of encyclopedic knowledge so prominent in *adab*. Take the story of Abu Dawud, that he wore a garment with one sleeve wide and one narrow. Asked why, he explained, "The wide one is for (carrying) notebooks, whereas the other is not needed."[82] Someone this devoted to the necessary and nothing more could not have been amused by a *Kitāb al-Ḥayawān*.

Humor, then, was clearly an important category in *adab*, whereas to the hadith folk it betrayed a relaxation of one's moral attentiveness and reverence for God. The Basran philologist Abu Hatim al-Sijistani (d. 869?) was generally rejected as a traditionist. The *rijāl* critic Ibn Hibban al-Busti (d. 965), known for his lenience, admitted that Abu Hatim was much given to playfulness (*mudāʿaba*) but argued that his hadith was sound (*mustaqīm*), even if it included "that which *ahl al-adab* are never without."[83] Here is a clear indication, I think, that the constraints of *adab* were not fully compatible with the science of hadith. It is almost enough by itself to put the Qurʾan reciter Ibn Mujahid (d. 936) outside the ranks of traditionalism that he was given to playfulness (*kathīr al-mudāʿaba*).[84] Yaqut tells the story of Ibn Mujahid's entering an orchard with some men of religion. When someone commented on his refusing to talk seriously, he protested, "Self-restraint in an orchard is like dissipation in a mosque (*taʿāqul, takhāluʿ*)."[85] One could hardly ask for a clearer expression of respect for different rules in different places among *ahl al-adab*, as opposed to the hadith folk's insistence that obedience is equally demanded at all times and in all places. It is not surprising that *adab* came to be taught mainly in homes, not mosques, and that the hadith folk should not have embraced such figures as Ibn Qutayba (d. 889?) and Ibn Abi al-Dunya (d. 894).[86]

At the same time, 9th-century Muslims of different theological parties clearly had a great deal in common at the level of piety. For example, it was considered excellent manners among diverse parties not to lean. (What better illustration could be asked of Islamic dignity?) To start with the hadith folk, Ahmad, although ill, sat up straight when

---

42, 57 f. Cf. al-Ḥakīm al-Tirmidhī, *Nawādir al-uṣūl fī maʿrifat aḥādīth al-rasūl* (Istanbul, 1293; repr. Beirut: Dār Ṣādir, n.d.), 131, expressly relating this hadith report to renouncing superfluities of food, speech, and wealth along with all unnecessary actions.

82. Ibn Dasa, quoted by Dhahabī, *Tārīkh*, 20:362.

83. For evaluations of Abu Hatim, see Ibn Ḥajar, *Tahdhīb* 4:257 f.

84. Ibn al-Nadīm, *Kitâb al-Fihrist*, ed. Gustav Flügel with Johannes Roedigger and August Mueller (Leipzig: F. C. W. Vogel, 1872), 31; i.e., *fann* 3, *maqāla* 1.

85. Yāqūt, *The Irshád al-aríb ilá maʿrifat al-adíb*, ed. D. S. Margoliouth, E. J. W. Gibb Memorial Series 6, 7 vols. (Leiden: E. J. Brill, 1907–27), 2:119, equivalent to *Muʿjam al-udabāʾ*, ed. Iḥsān ʿAbbās, 7 vols. (Beirut: Dār al-Gharb al-Islāmī, 1993), 2:523.

86. *Pace* Gérard Lecomte, who has attributed the rejection of Ibn Qutayba to his having embraced traditionalism just when Mutawakkil had made it opportune: Lecomte, "Le problème d'Abū ʿUbayd," *Arabica* 12 (1965): 164; idem, *Ibn Qutayba* (Damascus: Institut Français de Damas, 1965), pt. 2, chap. 1. On confusion among modern scholars over Ibn Abi al-Dunya's status as an ascetic, see Chabbi, "Remarques," 24 n.

someone mentioned the Khurasani traditionist Ibrahim b. Tahman (d. 784–85?). He commented, "It is not meet to mention the pious while reclining."[87] Ahmad's successor, ʿAbd al-Wahhab, warned against leaning in the course of the ritual prayer; better that a man who feels weak should sit, then rise.[88] Abu Bakr b. ʿAyyash (d. 809?), as a minor traditionist and major Qurʾan reciter, stood on the border between hadith and *adab*.[89] Among other austerities, it is said, he did not put his side to the ground for forty years.[90] Salm b. Salim (d. 810?) was a Murjiʾ, hence not of the hadith folk, and they rejected his transmission of hadith.[91] He was never seen to lean.[92] Moving toward Sufism, Sari al-Saqati was never seen reclining save in his death illness.[93] The Sufi Ibrahim al-Khawwas (d. 903–04?) was invited to lean on a pillar but said, "I refuse to lean on something created."[94] To sit or stand straight without leaning was plainly good form across the Islamic spectrum. Little shared [434] habits such as this undergirded a sense of community that transcended theological divisions, from which the united Sunni community of later centuries eventually arose.

Conclusion

The hadith folk emerged as a distinct group at about the end of the 8th century. They lost importance in the 10th century. Chroniclers usually refer to their 10th-century successors in Baghdad as the Hanabila or simply *al-ʿāmma* (the general), periodically rioting against the Shiʿis. Meanwhile, their own name for themselves, *ahl al-sunna*, was claimed by virtually all parties except the Shiʿis. Even the Muʿtazila called themselves *ahl al-sunna wa-al-jamāʿa*, on the plea that if they were not actually the great majority, they ought to have been.[95] (I have not compared the piety of the hadith folk with that of 9th-century

87. Al-Khaṭīb al-Baghdādī, *Tārīkh*, 6:110.

88. Aḥmad ibn Ḥanbal, *Waraʿ*, ed. Zaynab Ibrāhīm al-Qārūṭ (Beirut: Dār al-Kutub al-ʿIlmiyya, 1983), 89.

89. His name appears in five of the Six Books, but the *rijāl* critics did not record many high evaluations of his reliability. For these, see Ibn Ḥajar, *Tahdhīb*, 12:34–37. He is quoted concerning the Qurʾan in Aḥmad, *Waraʿ*, ed. Zaghlūl, 70.

90. Al-Khaṭīb al-Baghdādī, *Tārīkh*, 14:380.

91. See ibid., 9:142–44.

92. Ibid., 5:141.

93. Al-Qushayrī, *al-Risāla* (Cairo: Muṣṭafā al-Bābī al-Ḥalabī, 1318), 12, equivalent to ed. ʿAbd al-Ḥalīm Maḥmūd and Maḥmūd ibn al-Sharīf, 2 vols. (Cairo: Dār al-Kutub al-Ḥadītha, 1972), 1:80.

94. Al-Rāfiʿī, *K. al-Tadwīn fī dhikr ahl al-ʿilm bi-Qazvīn*, Lâleli (Istanbul) 2010, 120b.

95. ʿAbd al-Jabbār (d. 1025?), *Faḍl al-iʿtizāl*, in *Faḍl al-iʿtizāl*, ed. Fuʾād Sayyid (Tunis: al-Dār al-Tūnisiyya lil-Nashr, 1974), 187; cf. Abu 'l-Qasim al-Balkhi (d. 931?), leader of the Baghdadi Muʿtazila, among whose works is a *Kitāb al-sunna wa-al-jamāʿa*: Johann Fück, "Neue Materialien zum Fihrist," *Zeitschrift der Deutschen Morgenländischen Gesellschaft* 90 (1936): 305. Thanks to Patricia Crone for pointing out these passages.

Shiʿis, rewarding though such a comparison would be. At least a wing of the Shiʿi movement probably had something very close, which ought to show up in Shiʿi hadith.)

For a time, however, the hadith folk's importance was great. The caliph Maʾmun undertook a major effort to break them, while most caliphs from Mutawakkil forward tried to attach at least a section of them to themselves.[96] It was in part because the program they articulated had such deep popular appeal that so many Muslim thinkers identified themselves with it. And although their program was an extreme form, insufficiently catholic to prevail in the long term, their piety did inform universally valid, ideal Islam ever after.[97]

Students of Islamic law and theology have commonly regarded the hadith folk with annoyance, considering only their dogged rejection of sophisticated theorizing. Likewise, students of Islamic mysticism have regarded them with annoyance, considering only distrust of esoterism, while students of *adab* may have regarded them mainly in terms of dourness. These students have therefore misunderstand not only why the hadith folk were not captivated by sophisticated theorizing, mysticism, and letters, but why jurisprudents, theologians, mystics, and littérateurs went on to adopt so much of the traditionalist program (for example, by redefining law and theology as primarily exegetical). One must be touched by the earnestness that makes a man wear asymmetrical clothing because strictly speaking he needs only one wide sleeve. One has to appreciate that earnestness to make sense of Islamic civilization.

---

96. See esp. *EI2*, s.v. "Miḥna," by M. Hinds, with further references, and Christopher Melchert, "Religious Policies of the Caliphs From al-Mutawakkil to al-Muqtadir," *Islamic Law and Society* 3 (1996): 316–42.

97. For "ideal," "normative," "valid," and "actual Islam," see J. D. J. Waardenburg, "Official and Popular Religion as a Problem in Islamic Studies," *Official and Popular Religion*, ed. Pieter Hendrik Vrijhof and Jacques Waardenburg, Religion and Society 19 (The Hague: Mouton, 1979), 340–86.

9

BAṢRAN ORIGINS OF CLASSICAL SUFISM

History is largely about rooting out anachronisms. One that bedevils the history of Sufism is an unsurprising tendency to project later forms backward. Our idea of who was a Sufi in the ninth century tends to come from the *Ṭabaqāt al-ṣūfiya* of the Naysābūran al-Sulamī (d. 412/1021) and a few other books, some dependent on his.[1] Sulamī begins his first generation with notices of al-Fuḍayl ibn ʿIyāḍ (d. Mecca, 187/803), Ibrāhīm ibn Adham (d. al-Ǧazīra, 163/779–80?), Ḏū l-Nūn (d. Ǧīza, 246/861?), Bišr al-Ḥāfī (d. Baghdad, 227/841?), Sarī al-Saqaṭī (d. Baghdad, 253/867?), and al-Muḥāsibī (d. Baghdad?, 243/857–58)—the usual big names for the late eighth century and, mainly, early ninth. Massignon's lineage of Sufism (leading up to al-Ḥallāǧ) stays almost entirely within this line, and indeed I have no serious quarrel with it as a lineage of classical Ǧunaydī Sufism.[2]

The trouble is that, so far as we know, not one of these persons was actually called a Sufi (*ṣūfī*) in his lifetime. (Admittedly, however, I have found Ibrāhīm ibn Adham associated with an attendant called Ibrāhīm ibn Baššār al-Ṣūfī.[3]) Meanwhile, certain contemporaries of theirs actually were called Sufis. Frustratingly for the modern historian, Sulamī's forebears and those actually called Sufis in their own time seem to have had much in common. Above all, both parties underwent austerities [222] (*zuhd*), devoted ex-

1. Al-Sulamī, *Ṭabaqāt al-ṣūfiyya*, ed. Johannes Pedersen (Leiden, 1960) = ed. Nūr al-Dīn Šarība (Cairo, 1953). On the Sufi biographical tradition, see now Jawid A. Mojaddedi, *The Biographical Tradition in Sufism* (Richmond, Surrey, 2001).

2. The foundational modern history of Sufism is Louis Massignon, *Essai sur les origines du lexique technique de la mystique musulmane* (Paris, 1922, rev. 1954), also now available as *Essay on the Origins of the Technical Language of Islamic Mysticism*, trans. Benjamin Clark (Notre Dame, 1997).

3. Abū Nuʿaym, *Ḥilyat al-awliyāʾ* (Cairo, 1352–57/1932–38), VII, 346. Also noticed by Massignon, *Essay*, 105.

Originally published in *Der Islam* 82 (2005): 221–40.

traordinary amounts of time to Qur'ānic recitation and prayer (*ṣalāt* and *ḏikr*), and generally cultivated a solemn attitude toward life. It is difficult to tell what distinguished them.

Our historical problem is then twofold: (1) to determine why some persons in the late eighth and earlier ninth centuries were called "Sufis" and (2) to discern how the term "Sufi" came to shift from them to the people described by Sulamī, et al. The earliest emergence of persons called Sufis has been studied before, and I have no previously undiscovered data to report here. The time seems to have been the last third of the eighth century.[4] Bernd Radtke has already noticed the second problem, of how the term "Sufi" seems to have shifted over time:

> As opposed to the *religiosi*, antinomian, anti-social and anti-governmental tendencies became noticeable among them . . . . Notwithstanding the fact that the *religiosi* in general rejected these practices [*ḏikr* and *samāʿ*], the word *Ṣūfī*, which in the 2nd/8th century still had been an expression for a somewhat disreputable fringe group, had been adopted for the entire mystical movement in the course of the 3rd/9th century for reasons which are not clear.[5]

(As will become clear, I accept little of Radtke's characterization of what separated the earliest Sufis from others; however, he is to be commended for clearly identifying the problem.) At least part of the solution, I now propose, is *ninth-century Baṣra*, particularly the circle of *Abū Ḥātim al-ʿAṭṭār*.

Eighth-century Baṣra seems to have led in the development of Islamic piety. "The legal discernment (*fiqh*) of a Kūfan and the worshipfulness (*ʿibāda*) of a Baṣran" seems to have been a proverbial expression.[6] In the *Ḥilyat al-awliyāʾ*, our greatest single source for the early renunciant tradition, Abū Nuʿaym (d. Iṣfahān, 430/1038) considers Baṣrans first after the Companions and the seven jurisprudents of Medina.[7] The [223] renunciant tradition in Syria seems to have been a branch of the Baṣran.[8] The Muʿtazila, a renunciant movement that became theological, first appeared in Baṣra and maintained a distinctive Baṣran branch through the ninth century.[9] Ǧunayd, under whom there crystallized

4. R. A. Nicholson, "An Historical Enquiry Concerning the Origin and Development of Sufism," *JRAS* 38 (1906), 303–48, esp. 305. *V.* also Massignon, *Essay*, 104–107.

5. *EI*², s.v. "Taṣawwuf," by B. Radtke.

6. Abū Nuʿaym, *Ḥilya*, II, 321.

7. Baṣrans: *Ḥilya*, II, 198–III, 133, VI, 149–315; Medinese: III, 133–266; Meccans: III, 266–381; Yemenis: IV, 4–81; Kūfans: IV, 82–V, 119; Syrians: V, 120–VI, 148. The term "renunciant" (for *zāhid* and *nāsik*), suggested by Michael Cooperson, is more convenient than "ascetic" inasmuch as it suggests no opposition to "mystic."

8. Josef van Ess, *Theologie und Gesellschaft im 2. und 3. Jahrhundert Hidschra* (Berlin, 1991–95), II, 102.

9. Sarah Stroumsa, "The Beginnings of the Muʿtazilah, Reconsidered," *JSAI* 13 (1990), 265–93.

classical, Sunnī Sufism, was thoroughly Baghdadi, but one of his principal teachers, al-Muḥāsibī, had important Baṣran connections and by one report died there.[10]

Abū Ḥātim al-ʿAṭṭār was personally connected with al-Ǧunayd, al-Ḫarrāz, and other important Baghdadis. He was allegedly the first to talk of *išārāt* ("allusions"). His followers were expressly called Sufis, and like earlier Sufis they were associated with *al-amr bi-l-maʿrūf wa-l-nahy ʿan al-munkar* ("ordering the good and prohibiting evil"). Contrary to many earlier Sufis, he did not reject normal gain. He seems to be the missing link between the earlier disreputable Sufism and the classical Sunnī Sufism of Ǧunayd and his circle.

Renunciation in the Earlier Eighth Century

The first to be called a "Sufi" was famously a Kūfan named Abū Hāšim (d. 150/767–68?).[11] Before then, renunciation (*zuhd*), the deliberate embrace of practical austerities, seems to have been common to all parts of the religious movement. The most obvious austerity is of course the one for which the Sufis were named, mainly wearing wool. Muslims may have taken it over from Christian renunciants.[12] An early Baṣran renunciant, Abū l-ʿĀliya (d. 90/709), is quoted as rebuking another for [224] wearing wool, "the dress of monks (*ruhbān*)."[13] Wool is more liable to tear than cotton and linen, so wearers of wool must have tended to look ragged.[14] Raggedness would be attractive to critics of customary ways. A prominent anthropologist has suggested that supporters of the status quo regularly prefer "smooth" to "shaggy," whereas malcontents regularly prefer "shaggy."[15] In our day, for example, we may think of prosperous lawyers in worsted wool suits as opposed to underpaid academics in tweed. It fits the pattern that Muslims characteristically engaged in *al-amr bi-l-maʿrūf* should prefer to wear shaggy wool. It was also the characteristic dress of the proletariat, for the Baṣran renunciant Mālik ibn Dīnār (d. *ca.* 130/747–48) urged the *qāriʾ* not to be impressed by vain praise but to wear a woolen gown (*dāriʿa*) and carry a shepherd's staff, while Muḥāsibī quotes persons who recommend

10. Al-ʿAbbādī, *K. Ṭabaqāt al-fuqahāʾ al-šāfiʿīya*, ed. Gösta Vitestam (Leiden, 1964), 27.

11. *V. supra*, n. 4.

12. *V.* Göran Ogén, "Did the Term "*ṣūfī*" Exist before the Sufis?," *Acta Orientalia* 43 (1983), 33–48, offering a philological argument from Syriac, with data on which Muslims were called "Sufis" probably too sparse for conclusiveness; also Tor Andræ, "Zuhd und Mönchtum," *Le Monde Oriental* (Uppsala) 25 (1931), 296–327, esp. 300. Ofer Livne-Kafri, "Early Muslim Ascetics and the World of Christian Monasticism," *JSAI* 20 (1996), 105–29, is fuller for the practice of early Muslim renunciants, of which it provides a good survey, than for continuity with Christian monasticism.

13. Abū Nuʿaym, *Ḥilya*, II, 217. Abū l-ʿĀliya is also quoted as admiringly attributing a woolen garment to ʿĪsā ibn Maryam, *ibid.*, 221. Cf. Massignon, *Essay*, 104, with similar examples.

14. Raggedness is expressly one reason to wear wool (*li-l-ḫurūq allatī taḥduṯu fīhi*) according to al-Muḥāsibī, *al-Masāʾil fī aʿmāl al-qulūb*, ed. ʿAbd al-Qādir ʿAṭā (Cairo, 1969), 104.

15. Mary Douglas, *Natural Symbols* (London, 1970), 72.

it as the dress of porters and sailors.[16] Al-Ṭabarī mentions someone begging in wool.[17] Compared with cotton and linen, wool had to be less comfortable during the hot season, which in Iraq means most of the year.[18] Also, *ḥadīṯ* reports indicate that wool might be smelly, especially when wet.[19] [225]

Finally, wool was uncomfortably scratchy. The prominent Medinese Successor Saʿīd ibn al-Musayyab (d. 94/712–13?) once suffered 30, 50, or 100 lashes for refusing to swear allegiance at once to both the new Umayyad caliph, ʿAbd al-Malik, and his sons al-Walīd and Sulaymān as designated successors. By one account, Ibn al-Musayyab was spitefully flogged on a cold day, then had cold water thrown over him and was dressed in a woolen cloak (*ǧubba*). Alternatively, he was said to have been clothed in a hair shirt (*musūḥ, tubbān min šaʿr*): clearly, wool meant discomfort.[20]

Radtke mentions antinomian, anti-social and anti-governmental tendencies as hallmarks of the earliest, pre-classical Sufis. They do not seem distinctive of any particular group in the eighth century. Actually, it is hard to find antinomianism at any time.[21] Re-

16. Abū Nuʿaym, *Ḥilya*, II, 364; Muḥāsibī, *Masāʾil*, 104. All the *aḥbār* of the Israelites had walked with staffs, according to a Syrian renunciant, *apud* Abū Nuʿaym, V, 238. Muḥāsibī's advocates of wool likewise identify it as the dress of pious persons (*ṣāliḥīn*) of previous nations (*loc. cit.*). Ibn Qutayba quotes a story in which someone asks an anonymous *ḥakīm* why he habitually carries a staff when he is neither old nor sick. The wise man answers: "To remind me that I am a traveller" (Ibn Qutayba, *ʿUyūn al-aḫbār* [Cairo, 1346/1928], II, 323).

17. Al-Ṭabarī, *Annales*, ed. M. J. De Goeje, et al. (Leiden, 1879–1901), II, 1452, noticed by Josef van Ess, *Theologie*, II, 88. V. index, s.v. "*ṣūf*," for many further examples of wool-wearing; similarly, Richard Gramlich, *Alte Vorbilder des Sufitums* (Wiesbaden, 1995–96), index, s.v. "Wolle."

18. V. Abū Dāwūd, *Sunan*, *ṭahāra* 128, *bāb al-ruḫṣa fī tark al-ġusl*, on profuse sweating by wearers of wool in a small mosque.

19. Ibn Abī Šayba, *al-Muṣannaf*, ed. Saʿīd al-Laḥḥām (Beirut, 1409/1989), VI, 39 = *k. al-libās*, *fī lubs al-ṣūf*; Abū Dāwūd, *Sunan* 31, *k. al-libās* 6, *bāb fī l-ṣūf wa-l-šaʿr*; Tirmiḏī, *Ǧāmiʿ* 35, *k. ṣifat al-qiyāma* 38; Ibn Māǧa, *Sunan* 32, *k. al-libās* 4, *bāb lubs al-ṣūf*.

20. Ibn Saʿd, *Biographien*, ed. Eduard Sachau, et al. (Leiden, 1904–40), V, 93–94 = *al-Ṭabaqāt al-kubrā* (Beirut, 1957–68), V, 125–28; Aḥmad, *al-Zuhd* (Mecca, A.H. 1357; repr. Beirut, 1403/1983), 459, 466; Abū Nuʿaym, *Ḥilya*, II, 168–72. Ibn Saʿd also relates that he was flogged by Ibn al-Zubayr's governor, either for refusing to swear allegiance to Ibn al-Zubayr as caliph or for criticizing the governor for marrying before his previous fourth wife had been properly divorced: *Biographien*, V, 90–91 = *Ṭabaqāt*, V, 122–23. A ninth-century Baghdadi renunciant was called Abū ʿAlī al-Musūḥī (d. 256/869–70?). For a conversation between him and Ǧunayd, *v.* al-Ḫaṭīb al-Baġdādī, *Tārīḫ Baġdād* (Cairo, 1349/1931; repr. Cairo and Beirut, n.d.), VII, 367. As a Sufi in Baghdad, Ḥallāǧ sometimes wore hair shirts (*musūḥ*), among other distinctive clothing (ibid., VIII, 112). For another early example of someone flogged, then dressed in wool, V. van Ess, *Theologie*, II, 88.

21. *EI*^{2}, s.v. "Ibāḥa" by W. Madelung (Shiism) and M. G. S. Hodgson (Sufism), asserts that "antinomian trends were strong among the more radical Shīʿī circles from an early date" but cites only the evidence of later heresiographies, doubtfully rising above the level of insults as historical sources, and that "Among Ṣūfīs, antinomianism seems to have been later in developing," with examples from the *ṭarīqa* period.

nunciants scorned rulers in the name not of freedom but of a superior moral standard. The only exception I have come across is the *rūḥānīya* denounced by the heresiographer al-Malaṭī (d. 377/987–88), perhaps quoting the earlier Egyptian heresiographer Ḫušayš ibn Aṣram (d. 253/867). He names two advocates of adultery and drinking alcohol, among other enormities: Rabāḥ and Kulayb.[22] The latter is presumably the same as the Kulayb on al-Ǧāḥiẓ's [226] short list of Sufi renunciants (*al-ṣūfīya min al-nussāk*).[23] One may doubt whether heresiographical invective is good evidence for their actual doctrine, but it is good evidence of Sufis in disrepute for antinomianism. However, "Rabāḥ" presumably indicates Riyāḥ ibn ʿAmr al-Qaysī (d. 170s/787–97?), a Baṣran traditionist and renunciant sometimes associated with Rābiʿa al-ʿAdawīya.[24] The critic Abū Zurʿa (d. Ray, 264/878) accepted him as a well-intentioned (*ṣadūq*) transmitter of *ḥadīṯ*, but Abū Dāwūd (d. Baṣra, 275/889) accused him of *zandaqa* (secret unbelief).[25] The trouble is that no one identifies him as a Sufi, whereas he appears in, if not Sulamī's *Ṭabaqāt*, at least Abū Nuʿaym's *Ḥilyat al-awliyāʾ* and some other surveys of the retrospectively legitimate precursors to the classical Sufis. Therefore, antinomianism does not distinguish pre-classical Sufis from the non-Sufi precursors to the classical Sufis around Ǧunayd.

By contrast, anti-social tendencies are not at all scarce in the sources. Mālik ibn Dīnār, mentioned above, recommended three actions as conducive to humility: restraint of the tongue, frequent pleas for forgiveness, and withdrawal from society (*ʿuzla*).[26] Sufyān al-Ṯawrī (d. Baṣra, 161/778?) wrote to another renunciant: "Incumbent on you is withdrawal and mixing little with people. It used to be that people benefitted from one another when they met, but that is gone today, and we think salvation is [227] to be found in leaving them."[27] Al-Fuḍayl ibn ʿIyāḍ stayed home when Sufyān ibn ʿUyayna (d. Mecca,

22. Al-Malaṭī, *Die Widerlegung der Irrgläubigen und Neuerer*, ed. Sven Dedering (Istanbul, 1936), 73–74 = *al-Tanbīh wa-l-radd ʿalā ahl al-ahwāʾ wa-l-bidaʿ*, ed. Muḥammad Zāhid ibn al-Ḥasan al-Kawtharī (Cairo, 1949; repr. 1418/1997), 93–94; also Louis Massignon, *Recueil de textes inédits concernant l'histoire de la mystique en pays d'Islam* (Paris, 1929), 7.

23. Al-Ǧāḥiẓ, *al-Bayān wal-tabyīn*, ed. ʿAbd al-Salām Muḥammad Hārūn (Cairo, 1467/1948), I, 366.

24. For the name, *v.* Ibn Mākūlā, *al-Ikmāl*, ed. ʿAbd al-Raḥmān ibn Yaḥyā al-Muʿallimī al-Yamāmī (Hyderabad, A.H. 1381–86), IV, 14, and Ibn Ḥağar, *Tabṣīr al-mushtabih bi-taḥrīr al-Muntabih*, ed. ʿAlī Muḥammad al-Biğāwī, rev. Muḥammad ʿAlī al-Naǧǧār (Beirut, n.d.), II, 588. For biographies, *v.* al-Ḏahabī, *Siyar aʿlām al-nubalāʾ* (Beirut, 1401–1409/1981–88), VIII (ed. Naḏīr Ḥamdān), 155–56, with references. Several sources expressly call him *al-baṣrī*, and Abū Nuʿaym lists him among the Baṣran Successors of the Successors, *Ḥilya*, VI, 192–97; however, he is identified as a Kūfan by Ibn Abī Ḥātim, *al-Ǧarḥ wal-taʿdīl* (Hyderabad, A.H. 1360–71; repr. Beirut, n.d.), III, 511, also by Ḏahabī, for which *v.* Ibn Ḥağar, *Lisān al-Mīzān* (Hyderabad, A.H. 1329–31; repr. Beirut, 1406/1986), II, 469, s.v. Riyāḥ ibn ʿAmr. Massignon takes the heresiographer's pointing to be correct, the *ḥadīṯ* collectors' "Riyāḥ" to be in error (*Essay*, 79–80).

25. Ibn Ḥağar, *Lisān*, II, 469.

26. Abū Nuʿaym, *Ḥilya*, II, 377. He is also said to have recommended living with dogs in refuse heaps, *ibid.*, II, 359, 369.

27. Ibid., VI, 376. One would apparently not like to have lived next to him, for among other anti-social

198/814) came to the mosque. When Ibn ʿUyayna called on him at home and asked when he would return to his place, al-Fuḍayl told him: "This is not the time for meeting."[28]

Finally, anti-governmental tendencies are also fairly easy to find in the eighth-century mainstream. Outright rebellion might actually be looked on favourably; for example, Saʿīd ibn Ǧubayr's rebellion against al-Ḥaǧǧāǧ and death at his hands count in his favour in the Sunnī biographical tradition.[29] The usual expression of anti-governmental tendencies was *al-amr bi-l-maʿrūf wa-l-nahy ʿan al-munkar*. The phrase is Qurʾānic (Q. 3:110, 7:157, 9:71, 22:41), so it could never become the exclusive property of a sect. In practice, it normally covered two related activities, rebuke of misbehaving rulers and private correction of misbehaviour where the ruler has failed to enforce the law.[30] From the *ḥadīṯ*, *naṣḥ* and *naṣīḥa*, "counsel," also cover telling Muslims what to do, while *taġyīr* is another term for actively correcting misbehaviour. In the eighth century, it was emphatically not only Sufis who were active in rebuking rulers. Mālik ibn Dīnār got a tax collector to release a merchant's boat and rebuked the governor of Baṣra.[31] There are a number of stories about the rudeness of Sufyān al-Ṯawrī toward some governor or even caliph.[32] Aḥmad ibn Ḥanbal (d. Baghdad, 241/855) asserted that Ibn Abī Ḏiʾb (d. 159/775–76?) was better than the famous jurisprudent Mālik (d. 179/795) because he commanded and forbade Abū Ǧaʿfar (al-Manṣūr, the caliph) whereas Mālik was silent.[33] [228]

Radtke also mentions *ḏikr* and *samāʿ* as characteristic, offensive activities of the early Sufis. It is not hard to find *ḏikr* associated with the eighth-century mainstream. Sometimes, of course, it is used non-technically to mean simply "recollection," as in the Qurʾān. However, it usually appears in renunciant literature with reference to reciting praises of God; for example, when the Kūfan Masrūq (d. 63/682–83?) asserts that whoever recollects God in his heart is in *ṣalāt* even if he is in the market, better yet if he moves his lips.[34]

---

sayings he is said to have declared: "When a renunciant's neighbours are pleased with him, he is a flatterer" (*ibid.*, VII, 50).

28. Al-Marrūḏī, *Kitab al-Waraʿ*, ed. Muḥammad Sayyid Basyūnī Zaġlūl (Beirut, 1409/1988), 13 = ed. Zaynab Ibrāhīm al-Qārūṭ (Beirut, 1403/1983), 8–9.

29. Johan Weststeijn and Alex De Voogt, "Saʿīd b. Ǧubayr: Piety, Chess and Rebellion," *Arabica* 49 (2002), 383–86.

30. For discussions of *al-amr bil-maʿrūf* in later Islamic legal literature, *v.* Michael Cook, *Commanding Right and Forbidding Wrong in Islamic Thought* (Cambridge, 2000).

31. Abū Nuʿaym, *Ḥilya*, II, 374, 384.

32. E.g. *ibid.*, VII, 42 (Abū Ǧaʿfar), 45 (Muḥammad ibn Ibrāhīm), 46–47 (Maʿn ibn Zāʾida), 49 (ʿAbd al-Ṣamad ibn ʿAlī and al-Mahdī). *V.* also now Steven C. Judd, "Competitive Hagiography in Biographies of al-Awzāʿī and Sufyān al-Thawrī," *JAOS* 122 (2002), 25–37, esp. 31–36.

33. Aḥmad, *K. al-ʿIlal wa-maʿrifat al-riǧāl*, ed. Waṣī Allāh ibn Muḥammad ʿAbbās (Beirut, 1988), I, 509, 539 = *K. al-Ǧāmiʿ fī l-ʿilal wa-maʿrifat al-riǧāl*, ed. Muḥammad Ḥusām Bayḍūn (Beirut, 1410/1990), I, 188, 198.

34. Aḥmad, *Zuhd*, 418; same attributed to one Hilāl ibn Abī ʿUbayda (ʿAbīda?), *ibid.*, 457; same attributed to another Kūfan, Abū ʿUbayda ibn ʿAbd Allāh ibn Masʿūd (d. after 80/699), Abū Nuʿaym, *Ḥilya*, IV,

It is often a formal, scheduled activity. Al-Ḥasan al-Baṣrī (d. Baṣra, 110/728) recalled how the pious predecessors had preferred to be in a state of ritual purity when they recollected God.[35] The Syrian jurisprudent al-Awzāʿī (d. 157/773–74?) would not speak to anyone after the dawn prayer until he had finished his *ḏikr Allāh*, although he would reply if spoken to.[36] Even group recitation was found in the mainstream; for example, the Baṣran Ṯābit al-Bunānī (d. 120s/738–48) would spend a tenth of every day with his *aṣḥāb* in *ḏikr*.[37]

Samāʿ, by contrast, seems to be rare in the eighth century. "In fact," says Jean During, "apart from Qurʾānic psalmody, the tradition of musical audition for spiritual purposes is not attested before the middle of the ninth century."[38] This is probably an overstatement. Ibn al-Ǧawzī reports indignantly that Saʿd ibn ʿAbd Allāh, a Damascene worshipper of the early eighth century, bought a slave girl who sang *qaṣāʾid* (presumably *zuhdīyāt*) to the *fuqarāʾ*, while the Kūfan ʿAwn ibn ʿAbd Allāh (d. before 120/737–38) had a slave girl preach and sing after he had finished his own [229] sermon.[39] But *samāʿ* is certainly not closely associated with Sufis, so-called, until the later ninth century. To sum up, then, what was supposed to be offensive in the early, pre-classical Sufis appears to have been characteristic either of eminently respectable figures of the earlier eighth century as well or of practically no one at all until the mid-ninth century.

The Estrangement of Pre-Classical *ṣūfīya* and Proto-Sunnīs

The story of pious, proto-Sunnī opposition to renunciation across the eighth century certainly needs to be told in detail, but here I shall attempt only the briefest sketch. Suspicion of renunciation for show has a very long history. Consider, for example: "Also it will come about in that day that the prophets will each be ashamed of his vision when he prophesies, and they will not put on a hairy robe in order to deceive."[40] Therefore, there is nothing inherently incredible about Abū l-ʿĀliya's stricture against wool. Sometimes

204, citing Aḥmad: *v.* Aḥmad, *Zuhd*, 381 (Mecca, 1357). For the edition available in the Middle Ages, *v.* Ibn Ḥaǧar, *Taʿǧīl al-manfaʿa bi-zawāʾid riǧāl al-aʾimma al-arbaʿa* (Hyderabad, A.H. 1324), 8 = ed. Ikrām Allāh Imdād al-Ḥaqq (Beirut, 1416/1996), I, 243.

35. Aḥmad, *Zuhd*, 315.

36. Abū Nuʿaym, *Ḥilya*, VI, 143.

37. *Ibid.*, II, 323.

38. Jean During, "Musique et rites: le *samāʿ*," in Alexandre Popovic and Gilles Veinstein, eds., *Les voies d'Allah: les ordres mystiques dans l'islam des origines à aujourd'hui* (Paris, 1996), 157–72, at 159. Similarly, Arthur Gribetz, "The *samāʿ* controversy: Sufi vs. legalist," *Studia Islamica* 74 (1991), 43–62, at 44; Massignon, *Essay*, 106.

39. Ibn al-Jawzī, *Talbīs Iblīs*, ed. ʿIṣām Fāris al-Ḥarastānī (Beirut, 1414/1994), 316–17. Abū Nuʿaym does not mention preaching, but he does describe a slave girl of ʿAwn's named Bišra who recited the Qurʾān so tunefully and sorrowfully that ʿAwn's associates all threw off their turbans and wept (*Ḥilya*, IV, 264).

40. Zechariah 13:4, NASB.

the same figure is quoted both for and against outward austerities. For example, al-Ḥasan is said to have identified wool with various paragons of piety, telling the caliph ʿUmar ibn ʿAbd al-ʿAzīz that Moses had worn wool, along with being emaciated and walking instead of riding, and that he had met 70 veterans of Badr who wore wool.[41] At the same time, we are told that he himself wore linen, and Sunnī and Muʿtazilī sources agree that he reproached wearers of wool for being proud of their outward humility.[42]

There seem to be signs of new tension in about the last third of the eighth century, just when there emerge persons called Sufis. Tension becomes visible between *ḥadīṯ* transmission and renunciation. Sufyān al-Ṯawrī is quoted by turns as calling for one to seek *ḥadīṯ* in complete sincerity (i.e. never for worldly ends), as admitting that he had started out [230] without a proper *nīya* but later acquired one, and lamenting that he had not sought *ḥadīṯ* for the sake of God and was now being punished for it.[43] Ibn al-Mubārak (d. Hīt, 181/797) once refused to relate *ḥadīṯ* in Mecca because Muḥammad ibn Yūsuf al-Iṣbahānī (d. *ca.* 200/815–16) had forbidden him to do so.[44] Someone else reproached him in Ṭarsūs for engaging in the innovation of sorting *ḥadīṯ* by topic. He managed to quit for twenty days before the love of *ḥadīṯ* drew him back to it.[45]

Sufyān ibn ʿUyayna, a Kūfan active mainly in Mecca, is the first Muslim authority who seems to have rejected outward austerity. Earlier renunciants such as al-Ḥasan al-Baṣrī had called for matching outward humility with inward, but this Sufyān went further: "Renunciation means shortness of hope, not eating poorly."[46] He defended the most modest renunciation by citing prophetic example:

> Renunciation (*zuhd*) concerns what God has forbidden. As for what God has pronounced licit, God has made it a matter of indifference for you (*abāḥakahu*). The

41. Abū Nuʿaym, *Ḥilya*, II, 134, 137; VI, 196; Ibn Saʿd, *Biographien*, VII/1, 123 = *Ṭabaqāt*, VII, 169; Ǧāḥiẓ, *Bayān*, III, 153; Ibn Qutayba, *ʿUyūn*, II, 372. *V.* also van Ess, *Theologie*, II, 65, for a report from al-Ḥasan that Solomon wore wool.

42. Ibn Saʿd, *Biographien*, VII/1, 123, 126 = *Ṭabaqāt*, VII, 169, 173. Similar comment on wool *apud* Ǧāḥiẓ *Bayān*, III, 153.

43. Abū Nuʿaym, *Ḥilya*, VI, 362 (for piety's sake), 367 (acquired proper intention), 371 (self-blame), 384 (reporting in someone's dream that God had forgiven him, "even my seeking *ḥadīṯ*"). *V.* also *ibid.*, VII, 64: "I have never reproached myself except when sitting for *ḥadīṯ*." Ibrāhīm ibn Adham is said to have reproached Sufyān for drawing attention to himself by *ḥaddaṯanā ḥaddaṯanā* (*ibid.*, VI, 34).

44. *Ibid.*, VIII, 230.

45. *Ibid.*, VIII, 165.

46. Ibn Qutayba, *ʿUyūn*, II, 356. Almost the same (with the addition of "or wearing the *ʿabāʾ*"), Wakīʿ ibn al-Ǧarrāḥ, *al-Zuhd*, ed. ʿAbd al-Raḥmān ʿAbd al-Ǧabbār al-Faryawāʾī (Riyadh, 1994), I, 222. Cf. Ibn Abī l-Dunyā, *al-Zuhd*, ed. Yāsīn Muḥammad Al-Sawwās (Damascus, 1420/1999), 63, and Abū Nuʿaym, *Ḥilya*, VI, 386, where it is attributed to Sufyān al-Ṯawrī. The sentiment is consonant with some of Ṯawrī's biography, such as his eating great quantities (*Ḥilya*, VI, 389) and saying: "I prefer that a man, when God has amply provided for him, amply provide for himself" (*ibid.*, VII, 80).

> prophets married, rode, and ate, but when God forbade them something, they accepted his forbidding and thus were renunciant with regard to it.[47]

He is a very early advocate of the famous interior *ǧihād* against one's soul.[48] [231]

At an earlier point in my researches, I expected at this point to identify what was offensive about the earliest Sufis as distinct from the non-Sufi renunciants whom Sulamī and others recognized as the precursors to the classical Sufis. I thought I could identify two doctrines that would distinguish the rejected Sufis from the proto-Sunnī mainstream better than "antinomian, anti-social and anti-governmental tendencies," likewise *ḏikr* and *samāʿ*: (1) the repudiation of normal gain, *inkār al-kasb*, in favour of living off whatever should come one's way (normally alms, we may presume), and (2) ordering the good and prohibiting evil, *al-amr bi-l-maʿrūf wa-l-nahy ʿan al-munkar*. Both are indeed associated with pre-classical Sufis of the late eighth and early ninth century and also with contemporary, non-Sunnī theological movements, outstandingly the Murǧiʾa and Muʿtazila.[49]

Unfortunately, it appears that these characteristics also are largely common to the earliest, pre-classical Sufis and to Sulamī's precursors to the classical Sufis. As for *inkār alkasb*, distrust of trading is attested early in the mainstream. Al-Ḥasan al-Baṣrī complained: "There is no good in the people of the market. I have heard that one of them will do his brother out of a *dirham*."[50] Mālik ibn Dīnār warned: "The market increases wealth but takes away religion."[51] (Al-Ḥasan lived off a pension, Mālik ibn Dīnār by copying the Qurʾān.) On the other hand, Muḥāsibī names two Sufis who repudiated buying and selling, ʿAbd Allāh ibn Yazīd and ʿAbdak, perhaps in particular at the time of the Fourth Civil War (Amīn *vs.* Maʾmūn, 195–98/810–13, much longer in Syria).[52] Certain Muʿtazila are likewise identified with the repudiation of normal gain; among others, Abū ʿImrān al-Raqāšī (*fl.* early 3rd/9th cent.) and al-Rummānī (d. 384/994).[53] And in the ninth century, the repudiation of normal gain became a distinctive doctrine of the Karrāmīya, who

47. Abū Nuʿaym, *Ḥilya*, VII, 297. The prophet ʿĪsā was famously celibate, but Sufyān explained that he simply had no desire for women on account of his special creation, without a human father (*ibid.*, VII, 299; sim., Aḥmad, *Zuhd*, 97).

48. "*Ǧihād* comprises ten [parts]: *ǧihād* against the enemy is one, your *ǧihād* against your self is nine" (Abū Nuʿaym, *Ḥilya*, VII, 284).

49. For Murǧiʾ devotion to *al-amr bi-l-maʿrūf*, *v.* Wilferd Madelung, "The Early Murjiʾa in Khurāsān and Transoxania and the Spread of Ḥanafism," *Der Islam* 59 (1982), 32–39, esp. 36–37. *Al-amr bi-l-maʿrūf* of course appeared among the five defining principles (*al-uṣūl al-ḫamsa*) of Muʿtazilism.

50. Aḥmad, *Zuhd*, 351; al-Fasawī, *K. al-Maʿrifa wal-tārīḫ*, ed. Akram Ḍiyāʾ al-ʿUmarī (Medina, 1410/1989), II, 42.

51. Abū Nuʿaym, *Ḥilya*, II, 385.

52. Muḥāsibī, *al-Makāsib*, *al-Masāʾil fī aʿmāl al-qulūb* (henceforth C), 212 = *al-Makāsib*, ed. ʿAbd al-Qādir ʿAṭā (Beirut, 1987; henceforth B), 64.

53. *V.* Ibn al-Murtaḍā, *Die Klassen der muʿtaziliten*, ed. Susanna Diwald-Wilzer (Wiesbaden, 1961), 77 (Abū ʿImrān); *GAS*, VIII, 114 (Rummānī, *Taḥrīm al-makāsib*).

tended to [232] absorb the Muʿtazilī renunciant tradition.[54] But Muḥāsibī attributes the doctrine above all to Šaqīq ibn Ibrāhīm al-Balḫī (d. Kūlān, Transoxania, 194/809–10): "According to what is related of him, Šaqīq asserted that effort (*ḥaraka*) in pursuit of gain is a sin."[55] Ibrāhīm ibn Adham is quoted as remonstrating with Šaqīq against his repudiation of gain.[56] Šaqīq does appear in Sulamī's *Ṭabaqāt al-ṣūfiya*. Thus, *inkār al-kasb* works no better than antinomianism, anti-social attitudes, and the rest to distinguish the unacceptable pre-classical Sufis from the acceptable precursors to the classical Sufis.

A previous article mentions several examples of early, pre-classical Sufis who undertook *al-amr bi-l-maʿrūf*: al-ʿAbbās ibn al-Muʾammal al-Ṣūfī, imprisoned by Hārūn for "ordering the good"; rowdies in Alexandria who "ordered the good" and rejected the governor's authority in the year 200/815–16; someone who rebuked al-Maʾmūn (who successfully defended himself rather than punish the man); and someone who rebuked Ibn Ṭūlūn (who did punish the man), among others.[57] To these might be added other Sufis in the entourage of the Egyptian *qāḍī* ʿĪsā ibn al-Munkadir (d. Baghdad, after 215/830–31), who was himself later taken away to Iraq to die in prison for defying the governor's authority, and the Sufis who, in alliance with the local Zaydīya, took over Kūfa for a few weeks on behalf of two Ḥasanids in 255/869.[58] Although he was not called a Sufi, [233] the ʿAlid ʿAbd Allāh ibn Muʿāwiya clothed himself in wool when he commenced his open rebellion against the Umayyads (127/744).[59] Again, however, several of Sulamī's precursors to the classical Sufis are also identified with *al-amr bi-l-maʿrūf* specifically in the sense of rebuking rulers; for example, Ibrāhīm ibn Adham and al-Nūrī.[60]

---

54. *V.* esp. Josef van Ess, "Une Lecture à rebours de l'histoire du muʿtazilisme," *REI* 46 (1978), 163–240, at 190, 192; idem, *Ungenützte Texte zur Karrāmīya* (Heidelberg, 1980), 30–32; Louis Massignon, *The Passion of al-Hallāj*, trans. Herbert Mason (Princeton, 1982), III, 227. "Karrāmīya" has become the conventional form, but some early poetry in praise of the movement's eponym requires "Kirām" to scan properly. *V.* Ibn Ḥağar, *Tabṣīr al-mushtabih*, III, 1191. Edmund Bosworth preferred yet another form in his initial article describing them: "The Rise of the Karāmiyyah in Khurasan," *Muslim World* 50 (1960), 5–14.

55. Muḥāsibī, *al-Makāsib*, C194 = B61; followed by Massignon, *Essay*, 173.

56. Abū Nuʿaym, *Ḥilya*, VIII, 37.

57. Christopher Melchert, "The Ḥanābila and the Early Sufis," *Arabica* 48 (2001), 352–67, esp. 354.

58. Wakīʿ, *Aḫbār al-quḍāt*, ed. ʿAbd al-ʿAzīz Muṣṭafā al-Marāġī (Cairo, 1366–69/1947–50), III, 240. As an example of anachronism, let me note Jonathan E. Brockopp, *Early Mālikī Law* (Leiden, 2000), 45, 47, which assumes that the Sufis around Ibn al-Munkadir were mystics and thinks it paradoxical that Ibn ʿAbd al-Ḥakam (d. 214/829), a close associate of Ibn al-Munkadir's, should have led the persecution of the early Egyptian mystic Ḏū l-Nūn (d. 245/860?; for the persecution, *v.* Ḏahabī, *Siyar*, XI [ed. Ṣāliḥ al-Samr]: 534, drawing on Sulamī, *Miḥan al-ṣūfiya*). The paradox dissolves as soon as one recognizes that "Sufi" had as yet no necessary connection with mysticism and that Ḏū l-Nūn was doubtfully known in his lifetime as a Sufi. On Kūfa, *v.* al-Ṣūlī, *Kniga listov* (i.e. *K. al-Awrāq*), ed. Anas Ḫalidov (St. Petersburg, 1998), 366.

59. Noticed by van Ess, *Theologie*, II, 88.

60. Abū Nuʿaym, *Ḥilya*, VIII, 10 (Ibn Adham); Ḏahabī, *Siyar*, XIV, 76 (Nūrī).

The Sunnī tradition is ambivalent when it comes to *al-amr bi-l-maʿrūf*. However much he believed in its opposition to the dogma of a create Qurʾān, Aḥmad ibn Ḥanbal would have nothing to do with the rebellion of Aḥmad ibn Naṣr carried out in the name of *al-amr bi-l-maʿrūf*) and told some Baghdadi jurisprudents that they were obliged to repudiate the caliph (al-Wāṯiq) in their hearts but should not disobey or cause strife among the Muslims.[61] Apparently, Aḥmad could admire Muslims of the previous centuries bold enough to rebuke rulers, yet recommended against rebuking in his own time. A Baghdadi follower asked him: "When must a man engage in ordering and prohibiting?" Aḥmad answered: "This is not the time for forbidding . . . . Do not oppose the ruler (*lā tataʿarraḍ li-l-sulṭān*), for his sword is drawn and his staff [is likewise ready]."[62]

We should not imagine, then, the two parties set up by Radtke: (1) the general, proto-Sunnī religious movement and (2) the disreputable Sufis. Rather, we seem to have (1) the proto-Sunnī religious movement, becoming suspicious in the later eighth century of all renunciants, (2) the precursors to the classical Sufis, not called Sufis in their lifetimes, and (3) the disreputable pre-classical Sufis themselves. Of course, there were borderline figures such as Bišr al-Ḥāfī, often quoted in the earliest Ḥanbalī tradition but also one of Sulamī's precursors (hence straddling 1 and 2), and Riyāḥ ibn ʿAmr al-Qaysī, apparently a precursor but also condemned along with a pre-classical Sufi (hence straddling 2 and 3). [234]

As for what divided the proto-Sunnī movement of the late eighth and early ninth centuries from renunciants, it seems most likely to me that it was above all proto-Sunnī determination to promote a style of piety available equally to all the Muslims. The proto-Sunnīs admired renunciants of the earlier eighth century, when the Muslims had been a small élite at the top of society, but now, with Muslims the clear majority, the style of an élite seemed less viable. In al-Ḥasan al-Baṣrī's day, one did not have to worry about having no clothes to wear or food to eat if all the Muslims should retire from economic activity in favour of religious exercises: there would still be the *ʿaṭāʾ* from (ultimately) *ḏimmī* taxpayers to pay for the products of *ḏimmī* labour. This was no longer so in the day of Sufyān ibn ʿUyayna or Aḥmad ibn Ḥanbal.[63] What separated Sulamī's precursors from

61. For the rebellion, 231/846, *v.* Ṣūlī, *apud* Ḏahabī, *Siyar*, XI, 167–68; Ḥanbal ibn Isḥāq, *Ḏikr miḥnat Aḥmad ibn Ḥanbal*, ed. Muḥammad Naġš (Cairo, 1397/1977), 81–83; Ibn Abī Yaʿlā, *Ṭabaqāt al-ḥanābila*, ed. Muḥammad Ḥāmid al-Fiqī (Cairo, 1371/1952), I, 145.

62. Ibn Hāniʾ, *Masāʾil al-imām Aḥmad ibn Ḥanbal*, ed. Zuhayr al-Šāwīš (Beirut, A.H. 1400), II, 175. For many quotations of Aḥmad cautioning against active correction of wrongdoing, *v.* al-Ḫallāl, *K. al-Amr bi-l-maʿrūf wa-l-nahy ʿan al-munkar*, ed. Ismāʿīl al-Anṣārī (Cairo, 1969).

63. Cf. Leah Kinberg: "Renunciation of worldly goods was always the main current in Islam, and traditions favoring property and wealth arose only as a concession to the ruling economic power of the bourgeoisie" ("Compromise of Commerce: A Study of Early Traditions Concerning Wealth and Poverty," *Der Islam* 66 [1989], 193–212, at 195); similarly, Shelomo Dov Goitein, "The Rise of the Near-Eastern Bourgeoisie in Early Islamic Times," *Journal of World History* 3 (1956), 583–604.

the Sufis of the late eighth and early ninth centuries is harder to say, since only meagre reports survive of the Sufis. Association with rejected theological movements (especially Muᶜtazilism) and unsuccessful politics (e.g. Egyptian independence) must have been a good part of it.

Abū Ḥātim al-ᶜAṭṭār

All three strands come together—the term "Sufi," recognition by Sulamī as a precursor, and emphatic Sunnism—with the Baṣran Abū Ḥātim al-ᶜAṭṭār (d. 260's/874–84). He evidently had an entry in the biographical dictionaries of the Baṣran Ibn al-Aᶜrābī (d. Mecca, 340/952?), *Ṭabaqāt al-nussāk*, and Sulamī, *Tārīḫ al-ṣūfiya*, but both these works survive only in scattered quotations.[64] He was omitted from Sulamī's short dictionary, *Ṭabaqāt al-ṣūfiya*, which is extant; also, oddly, from Abū Nuᶜaym, *Ḥilyat al-awliyāʾ*; however, he does have a short chapter in ᶜAbd Allāh Anṣārī's *Ṭabaqāt al-ṣūfiya*, probably based immediately on the entry in *Tārīḫ al-ṣūfiya* [235] and ultimately on Ibn al-Aᶜrābī.[65] What follows is based primarily on al-Ḏahabī's quotations from Ibn al-Aᶜrābī.

As for Abū Ḥātim's express doctrine, Ḏahabī relates eight short sayings. Their main thrust is to deprecate demonstrative renunciation. One should cultivate humility by making oneself inconspicuous in one's own eyes and in the eyes of others; for example: "Whoever remembers the grace of God forgets his work," and: "Woe betide you. How much you weep and wail. Correct [your behaviour] and relax."[66] To the same effect is his comment on obvious renunciants who prayed in skirts, cloaks, and wool (*fuwaṭ*, *abrād*, *ṣūf*): "You have published your emblems and beaten your drums. Would that I knew what sort of men you are."[67] I have argued elsewhere that a predominantly mystical piety first emerged about the time of Abū Ḥātim's death; that is, with the generation of his disciples.[68] Indeed, none of Abū Ḥātim's remembered sayings speaks distinctively of union with God, reciprocal love of God, or God's immanence in creatures, as a mystic would speak. Rather, as in the sayings of contemporaries, one sees the self-abnegation and concentration on God that would soon conduce to mysticism. Sulamī, on the other hand,

64. For Ibn al-Aᶜrābī, *v. GAS* 1:660–61; for al-Sulamī, *v. GAS*, I, 671–74. Numerous quotations by Ḏahabī from Ibn al-Aᶜrābī are indicated below. For quotations from Sulamī's *Tārīḫ*, *v. infra*, nn. 69, 91, 93.

65. ᶜAbd Allāh Anṣārī, *Ṭabaqāt al-ṣūfiya*, ed. Muḥammad Surūr Mawlāʾī (n.p., A. H. 1342), 93–94.

66. Al-Ḏahabī, *Tārīḫ al-islām*, ed. ᶜUmar ᶜAbd al-Salām Tadmurī (Beirut, 1407–21/1987–2000), XX (A.H. 261–80), 211–12.

67. Ḏahabī, *Tārīḫ al-islām*, XX (A.H. 261–80), 212. Hišām al-Fūṭī (Fuwaṭī) was a prominent Baṣran Muᶜtazilī of the early ninth century, on whom *v.* Johann Fück, "Neue Materialien zum Fihrist," *ZDMG* 90 (1936), 298–321, at 318 and n. His *nisba* plainly refers to a characteristic dress of the renunciants.

68. Christopher Melchert, "The Transition From Asceticism to Mysticism at the Middle of the Ninth Century C.E.," *Studia Islamica*, 83 (1996), 51–70 [*HPL 9].

asserts that Abū Ḥātim was the first to speak in Iraq of *ᶜulūm al-išārāt* (allusions to the ineffable), which sounds more in the line of Ǧunaydī mysticism.[69]

Abū Ḥātim al-ᶜAṭṭār did not renounce normal gain but seems to have made his living as a druggist and looked like any trader.[70] Ibn al-Aᶜrābī relates the reminiscence of his Baghdadi disciple Ruzayq al-Naffāṭ, who once saw Abū Ḥātim offering merchandise to a customer and asked him a question. He heard in return that there was a proper saying for every station, "but have patience until I am free."[71] [236]

Abū Ḥātim's followers were associated with moderate Sunnism. At least one of them was friendly towards *kalām*. Ibn al-Aᶜrābī names altogether seven Baṣrans who were close to Abū Ḥātim: Ibn al-Šuwayṭī, Abū Saᶜīd al-Ġanawī, al-Marzūqī, ᶜAbd al-Ǧabbār al-Sulamī, al-Ḥasan ibn al-Muṯannā, Aḥmad ibn ᶜAmr ibn Abī ᶜĀṣim, and al-Ǧuḏūᶜī. Ibn al-Aᶜrābī identifies the last four as "Sufis of the Mosque, of *ahl al-sunna wa-l-ḥadīṯ*, adhering to austerity (*nusuk*) and ordering the good and prohibiting evil (*al-amr bi-l-maᶜrūf wa-l-nahy ᶜan al-munkar*). They had weight and prestige in the city."[72] As *ahl al-sunna wa-l-ḥadīṯ*, these Sufis sound close to the Ḥanābila of Baghdad. Aḥmad ibn Ḥanbal identified his beliefs as those of *ahl al-sunna wa-l-ǧamāᶜa wa-l-āṯār*.[73] As orderers of the good and prohibiters of evil, however, they sound closer to the pre-classical Sufi tradition and more distant from the Ḥanābila, who did not take up the active ordering of the good until the tenth century.[74]

Concerning one of Abū Ḥātim's Baṣran followers, Abū Saᶜīd al-Ġanawī, Ibn al-Aᶜrābī adds that he "inclined towards something of *kalām* and knew it."[75] Again, this does not sound Ḥanbalī, for Aḥmad emphatically rejected all *kalām*. Given the emphatically Sunnī character of Abū Ḥātim's following, al-Ġanawī could hardly have been committed to any other tendency in *kalām* than what I have called the semi-rationalist, of which Muḥāsibī had been a leading adherent; that is, the defence and elaboration of traditionalist doctrines by the means of their rationalist adversaries.[76]

---

69. Sulamī, *apud* Ḏahabī, *Tārīḫ al-islām*, XV (A.H. 211–20), 212.

70. Ibn al-Aᶜrābī, *apud* Ḏahabī, *Tārīḫ al-islām*, XX (A.H. 261–80), 211–12.

71. Ḏahabī, *Tārīḫ al-islām*, XX (A.H. 261–80), 212.

72. *Ibid.*, XX (A.H. 261–80), 212. Editor Tadmurī counts two men, "Aḥmad ibn ᶜUmar" and "Ibn Abī ᶜĀṣim," where I count one. After my own notes from Köprülü 1071, I read "*yantaḥilūna al-nusuk*" where Tadmurī has rather *yattaḥilūna*.

73. Aḥmad, Creed I, *apud* Ibn Abī Yaᶜlā, *Ṭabaqāt*, I, 31. For the numbering of Aḥmad's creeds, *v.* Henri Laoust, *La profession de foi d'Ibn Baṭṭa* (Damascus, 1958), xv-xvi.

74. On one ninth-century example of ordering the good and prohibiting evil mistakenly taken to be the work of the Ḥanābila, *v.* Wilferd Madelung, "The Vigilante Movement of Sahl b. Salāma al-Khurāsānī and the Origins of Ḥanbalism Reconsidered," *Journal of Turkish Studies* 14 (1990), 331–37, *contra* Ira M. Lapidus, "The Separation of State and Religion in the Development of Early Islamic Society," *IJMES* 6 (1975), 363–85, esp. 382–84.

75. Ḏahabī, *Tārīḫ al-islām*, XX (A.H. 261–80), 212.

76. *V.* Christopher Melchert, "The Adversaries of Aḥmad Ibn Ḥanbal," *Arabica* 44 (1997), 234–53 [*HPL 1].

The only one of these Baṣrans I have been able to locate separately in the usual biographical sources is Aḥmad ibn ʿAmr ibn Abī ʿĀṣim, namely [237] the Baṣran traditionist, jurisprudent, and renunciant Abū Bakr ibn Abī ʿĀṣim al-Nabīl (d. Isfahan, 287/900).[77] Among his works now lost are reportedly a huge *Musnad* of 50,000 *ḥadīṯ* reports and two lesser collections each comprising 20,000.[78] Compare the *Musnad* of Aḥmad ibn Ḥanbal at about 28,000 reports, the *Ṣaḥīḥ* of al-Buḫārī at about 7,000. Early biographers Ibn al-Aʿrābī and Abū Nuʿaym al-Iṣbahānī report that he rejected analogy (*qiyās*) and adhered to the Ẓāhirī school of jurisprudence; however, Ḏahabī doubts this characterization, for Ibn Abī ʿĀṣim composed a book comprising 40 sound *ḥadīṯ* reports that Dāwūd had rejected.[79] One of his extant works is a collection of *ḥadīṯ* reports used by al-Šāfiʿī.[80] Probably, indeed, an actual adherent of the Ẓāhirī school before the eleventh century would have been called a *dāwūdī*, another indication that Ibn Abī ʿĀṣim was not one. But it matters little here, and it is not surprising that someone in this early period should have appeared sometimes a Ẓāhirī and sometimes a Šāfiʿī, inasmuch as Dāwūd al-Ẓāhirī himself was something of a Šāfiʿī.[81] What Ẓāhirism and Šāfiʿism bespeak at this point is the rational manipulation of *ḥadīṯ* and Qurʾān in jurisprudence, the rational defense of traditionalist doctrines in theology; that is, again, the semi-rationalist position.[82]

In theology, the *Kitāb al-Sunna* ascribed to Ibn Abī ʿĀṣim seems oddly inconclusive. It comprises mainly *ḥadīṯ* reports from the Prophet, as one might expect of a Šāfiʿī. It condemns the Qadarīya, Rawāfiḍ, and Murǧiʾa but is silent on the questions of *raʾy* (rational speculation as a basis of jurisprudence), the createdness of the Qur'ān and one's pronunciation of it (*lafẓ*), and whether faith comprises both word and deed. (There is one statement that faith increases but does not decrease, a position sometimes associated with Mālik ibn Anas.[83]) In other words, it seems consistent [238] with a semi-rationalist position but lacks distinctive tenets such as the create pronunciation.

---

77. *V. GAS*, I, 522 and Florian Sobieroj, *Ibn Ḫafīf aš-Šīrāzī* (Stuttgart, 1998), 113–19.

78. Ḏahabī, *Siyar*, XIII (ed. ʿAlī Abū Zayd, 1403/1983), 436.

79. *Ibid.*, XIII, 430–31.

80. *GAS*, I, 522, no. 7.

81. For example, Dāwūd al-Ẓāhirī was responsible for the first two biographies of Šāfiʿī: Abū Isḥāq al-Šīrāzī, *Ṭabaqāt al-fuqahāʾ*, ed. Iḥsān ʿAbbās (Beirut, 1970), 92.

82. On the Ẓāhirī school, *v.* Christopher Melchert, *The Formation of the Sunni Schools of Law* (Leiden, 1997), 178–90; Devin Stewart, "Muḥammad b. Dāʾūd al-Ẓāhirī's Manual of Jurisprudence," in Bernard Weiss, ed., *Studies in Islamic Legal Theory* (Leiden, 2002), 99–158.

83. Ibn Abī ʿĀṣim, *K. al-Sunna* (Beirut, 1980), II, 630. Mālik's position is variously reported: that faith increased, while he was reluctant to say whether it decreased (Ibn Wahb, *apud* Ibn ʿAbd al-Barr, *al-Intiqāʾ* [Cairo, A.H. 1350; repr. Beirut, n.d.], 33); that it increased, while he emphatically refused to talk of decrease (Ibn al-Qāsim, *apud* al-Qāḍī ʿIyāḍ, *Tartīb al-madārik*, ed. Aḥmad Bakīr Maḥmūd [Beirut, 1967–68?], I, 174); that it decreased but did not increase (Ibn Wahb, *apud* Ḏahabī, *Siyar*, VIII, 59); and, with the traditionalists, that faith was word and deed, increasing and decreasing (al-Qāḍī ʿIyāḍ, *Tartīb*, I, 173–74).

Ibn Abī ʿĀṣim al-Nabīl was appointed *qāḍī* for Iṣfahān in 269/883 by the caliph al-Muʿtamid.[84] His appointment fits a larger pattern of favour to semi-rationalist Baṣrans, which reached its height under al-Muʿtamid and his half-brother the shadow caliph al-Muwaffaq.[85] He was finally removed about 282/895–96 for imprisoning a local renunciant, ʿAlī ibn Mattawayh, who had insulted him in the course of a dispute over stipends to renunciants. (Presumably, Ibn Abī ʿĀṣim was in charge of disbursing them as supervisor of local *awqāf*.)[86] It is hard to say what he learnt from Abū Ḥātim al-ʿAṭṭār, though, as the biographies usually stress his discipleship to Abū Turāb al-Naḫšabī (d. Hijaz, 245/859–60).[87]

As for disciples from outside Baṣra, Ibn al-Aʿrābī also mentions three Baghdadis who came to Baṣra seeking Abū Ḥātim al-ʿAṭṭār: Muḥammad ibn Wahb, Yaʿqūb al-Zayyāt, and Ruzayq al-Naffāṭ.[88] The last I have been unable to identify further. Ǧunayd knew the second (d. 280s/894–903), who was disciple to Abū Turāb al-Naḫšabī as well as to Abū Ḥātim al-ʿAṭṭār and Abū ʿAlī ibn al-Ḏāriʿ.[89] The first (d. *ca.* 270/883–84) is recognizable as an associate of Ǧunayd's, Ǧunayd overseeing his burial next to Sarī al-Saqaṭī. He was a disciple to the same Abū ʿAlī (ibn) al-Ḏāriʿ as well as to Abū Ḥātim al-ʿAṭṭār.[90] Sulamī adds that another Baghdadi [239] with a similar name was disciple to Abū Ḥātim, mainly Abū Ǧaʿfar Aḥmad ibn Wahb *al-ṣūfī* (d. 270/883–84 or a little after), also associated with Ǧunayd in Baghdad.[91] One would guess that Muḥammad and Aḥmad were the same but that al-Ḫaṭīb devotes a separate biography to each of them. Additionally, Qušayrī describes Abū Turāb al-Naḫšabī as a disciple to Abū Ḥātim al-ʿAṭṭār.[92] The chronology is difficult, so *ṣaḥiba* here probably indicates no more than their meeting at some time; indeed, the same might be said of Ibn Abī ʿĀṣim al-Nabīl and Abū Turāb al-Naḫšabī.

Sulamī actually identifies Abū Ḥātim al-ʿAṭṭār as *ustāḏ* directly to Ǧunayd and Abū Saʿīd al-Ḫarrāz.[93] Al-Sarrāǧ quotes Ḫarrāz himself as saying:

---

84. Abū Nuʿaym, *Geschichte Isbahāns*, ed. Sven Dedering (Leiden, 1931–34), I, 82; Abū Mūsā al-Madīnī, *apud* Ḏahabī, *Siyar*, XIII, 435.

85. *V.* Christopher Melchert, "Religious Policies of the Caliphs from al-Mutawakkil to al-Muqtadir," *ILS* 3 (1996), 316–42, at 338–40.

86. Abu l-Šayḫ, *Ṭabaqāt al-muḥaddiṯīn bi-Iṣbahān*, ed. ʿAbd al-Ġafūr ʿAbd al-Ḥaqq Ḥusayn al-Balūshī (Beirut, 1412/1992), III, 380–81.

87. For biographies of Ibn Abī ʿĀṣim al-Nabīl, *v. GAS*, I, 522, also Ḏahabī, *Tārīḫ*, XXI (A.H. 281–90), 75n.

88. Ḏahabī, *Tārīḫ al-islām*, XX (A.H. 261–80), 211.

89. Al-Ḫaṭīb al-Baġdādī, *Tārīḫ*, XIV, 408; Ḏahabī, *Tārīḫ al-islām*, XXI (A.H. 281–90), 344. Apparently called *Abū* Yaʿqūb al-Zayyāt by Abū Nuʿaym, *Ḥilya*, X, 223–24, 342, although distinct from the Abū Yaʿqūb al-Zayyāt (d. 262/876) mentioned by Ḏahabī, *Tārīḫ al-islām*, XX (A.H. 261–80), 208.

90. Al-Ḫaṭīb al-Baġdādī, *Tārīḫ*, III, 333.

91. Sulamī, *apud* al-Ḫaṭīb al-Baġdādī, *Tārīḫ*, V, 190; Ḏahabī, *Tārīḫ al-islām*, XX (A.H. 261–80), 57.

92. Qušayrī, *al-Risāla* (Cairo, 1359/1940), 18. Cf. *Das Sendschriften al-Qušayris*, trans. Richard Gramlich (Wiesbaden, 1989), 61.

93. Sulamī, *apud* Ḏahabī, *Tārīḫ*, XV (A.H. 211–20), 212.

> I heard of Abū Ḥātim al-ʿAṭṭār and his virtue. He was in Baṣra, so I travelled to him from Old Cairo, continuing until I came to Baṣra and entered its Friday mosque, where I found him sitting with a number of his followers about him . . . .[94]

The saying he quotes praises God but mainly compliments Ḫarrāz as the one for whom Abū Ḥātim had been teaching. Abū Nuʿaym al-Iṣbahānī has no entry for Abū Ḥātim al-ʿAṭṭār, as for few ninth-century Baṣrans in general, but does say of Abū Turāb al-Naḫšabī that he met an otherwise unknown Abū Ḥamza al-ʿAṭṭār al-Baṣrī.[95] Textual confusion may have conflated Abū Ḥātim with some Abū Ḥamza.

Abū Ḥātim al-ʿAṭṭār was distant from Baṣran rivals to Ǧunaydī moderation in mysticism, notably certain "spirituals" and possibly Sahl al-Tustarī (d. Baṣra, 283/896?). By the former we may understand the erring minority of Baṣrans who asserted that their love of God had caused the fear of him to fall from them, provoking the rage of another Baṣran renunciant, Ġulām Ḫalīl (d. Baghdad, 275/888).[96] As for Sahl al-Tustarī, [240] it is possible that we have no record of his interacting with Abū Ḥātim merely because Sahl transferred to Baṣra only after his death; however, Sahl did have difficulty from some Baṣran adherents of the nascent Šāfiʿi school, which is to say the tendency of Abū Ḥātim's followers.[97]

To conclude, then, Abū Ḥātim al-ʿAṭṭār emerges as a figure close to Ǧunayd and the Sufis around him in Baghdad, known to some of them personally and teaching similarly. Like the generation of Baghdadis just before Ǧunayd, Abū Ḥātim himself preached a single-minded renunciation with elements that suggest incipient mysticism. Like Ǧunayd and the Sufis around him, Abū Ḥātim's Baṣran followers tended toward Šāfiʿī or Mālikī semi-rationalism rather than Ḥanbalī traditionalism. Whatever the personal connection between Ǧunayd and Abū Ḥātim, Ǧunayd certainly associated with a number of Baghdadis who were also at some point close to Abū Ḥātim.

Abū Ḥātim al-ʿAṭṭār and his circle also provide a thoroughly Sunnī basis for the activity of the Ḥanbalī al-Barbahārī in the next century, who led some active ordering the good and prohibiting evil in Baghdad in the 320s/930s, in contravention of the earlier Ḥanbalī tradition as represented by Abū Bakr al-Ḫallāl (d. Baghdad, 311/923).[98] Ordering the good

94. Abū Saʿīd al-Ḫarrāz, *apud* al-Sarrāǧ, *The Kitáb al-Lumaʿ*, ed. Reynold Alleyne Nicholson (Leiden, 1914; repr. London, 1963), 180.

95. Abū Nuʿaym, *Ḥilya*, X, 220.

96. For Ġulām Ḫalīl and his Sufi Inquisition in Baghdad, *v.* Massignon, *Passion*, index, s.v. Ghulām Khalīl; Carl Ernst, *Words of Ecstasy in Sufism* (Albany, 1985), 101; Melchert, "Transition," 65–66, based again on Ibn al-Aʿrābī as quoted by Ḏahabī; also Gramlich, *Alte Vorbilder*, II, 384–85, s.v. Abū lḤusayn al-Nūrī.

97. *EI*², s.v. "Sahl al-Tustarī," by G. Böwering.

98. On Barbahārī, *v.* *EI*², s.v., by H. Laoust, and Ḏahabī, *Siyar*, XIV, 90–93, with references. Cf. Christopher Melchert, "Ḥanābila," esp. 366–67, which explains Barbahārī's distinctiveness by his discipleship

and prohibiting evil is no longer a defining character of Sufis in the Ǧunaydī tradition, but it would never entirely disappear; for example, the Ḥanbalī ʿIzz al-Dīn Ibrāhīm ibn ʿAbd Allāh (d. Damascus, 666/1267) was blessed with *aḥwāl* (mystical states) and *karāmāt* (miracles) but was also an active *āmir bi-l-maʿrūf* (orderer of the good).[99]

---

to Sahl al-Tustarī, overlooking Abū Ḥātim al-ʿAṭṭār. That article is also to be corrected as to the identification of Ġulām Ḫalīl with Ḥanbalism, not alleged by Wilferd Madelung but by Louis Massignon (e.g. *Passion*, I, 80). It has also been alleged anew by Maher Jarrar and Sebastian Günther, "Ġulām Ḫalīl und das *Kitāb Šarḥ as-sunna*," *ZDMG* 153 (2003), 11–36.

99. Ibn Raǧab, *K. al-Ḏayl ʿalā Ṭabaqāt al-ḥanābila*, ed. Muḥammad Ḥāmid al-Fiqī (Cairo, 1952–53; repr. Beirut, n.d.), II, 278.

10
EXAGGERATED FEAR IN THE EARLY ISLAMIC RENUNCIANT TRADITION

The Qurʾan

The Qurʾan is presumably our earliest secure evidence of Islamic piety. It is difficult not to read it anachronistically, through the lens of ninth-century and later conceptions, but its principal theme seems to be the call to be heedful; in particular, to live in fear of God. Toshihiko Izutsu states that fear of the Last Judgement and the Lord of the Day is "the most fundamental motive of this new religion and underlies all its aspects and determines its basic mood," since "to believe in God means, briefly, to fear Him."[1] Fazlur Rahman has called *taqwá*, meaning fear of God, "perhaps the most important single term in the Qurʾān."[2]

Erik S. Ohlander has provided us with a useful, more detailed survey of qurʾanic texts relating to fear.[3] *Taqwá* seems to him the most important. Etymologically, it has to do with self-protection by interposing something between oneself and what one fears. Ohlander

---

The writing of this article was made possible by a research leave extension grant from the Arts and Humanities Research Council. E-mail: christopher.melchert@orinst.ox.ac.uk

1. Toshihiko Izutsu, *The Structure of the Ethical Terms in the Koran*, Keio University Studies in the Humanities and Social Relations 2 (Tokyo, 1959), p. 62, apud Erik S. Ohlander, "Fear of God (*taqwā*) in the Qurʾān: some notes on semantic shift and thematic context," *Journal of Semitic Studies*, L (2005), pp. 137–152, at p. 147.

2. Fazlur Rahman, *Major Themes of the Qurʾān*, 2nd edn (Minneapolis, 1989), p. 28, apud Ohlander, 'Fear of God,' p. 137.

3. Ohlander, 'Fear of God.'

Originally published in *Journal of the Royal Asiatic Society*, ser. 3, 21 (2011): 283–300.

finds [284] that it evolves from a state to be cultivated, in verses conventionally identified as coming from the late Meccan period, to a fully developed concern with not only eschatological but legal, moral, cultic, spiritual, and mundane matters. This evolution is interesting for various reasons but doubtfully, to my mind, explains how early Muslims understood the Qurʾan. They did not hear the Qurʾan recited in chronological order, and I have come across no report of early renunciants paying attention to the order of revelation in their glosses on particular words and phrases, whether having to do with fear or other things. On the contrary, they tend to suggest that words are interchangeable. For example, Abū al-Dardāʾ (d. early 30s AH/650s CE?) is quoted as saying, "Perfect *taqwá* is that the servant fear God until he fears him over a measure of corn; until he leaves some of what he considers licit for fear (*khashyah*) that it be forbidden, to be a screen between himself and the forbidden."[4] Similarly, the Kufan Saʿīd ibn Jubayr (d. 95 AH /714 CE?) is quoted as saying, "Fear (*khashyah*) is that you fear God so as to put your fear between you and sin."[5] These sayings seem to treat other words for "fear' as sharing the peculiar sense of *taqwá* mentioned above. Al-Ḥasan al-Baṣrī (d. 110AH/728CE) commented thus on Q. 21:90 (on Zakarīyāʾ and his wife), "They ... used to call to Us in longing and fear (*rahab*), and they used to humble themselves to Us": "Fear is constant in the heart (*al-khawf dāʾim fī al-qalb*)."[6] He is unconcerned by the difference between *rahab* and *khawf*. As in early exegesis generally, the word for 'fear' in the Qurʾan is taken to point to something, which another word can point to as well. (This is the justification for the supposition that the seven versions of the revealed Qurʾan, referred to in the famous hadith report about seven *aḥruf*, differed in substituting synonyms.[7])

The Qurʾan attributes fear of earthly enemies to various prophets; for example, Moses at Q. 28:21, when he flees for fear of being murdered. Abel disavows any intention of attacking Cain, even if Cain should attack him, from fear of God (*innī akhāfu Allāh rabbī*) at Q. 5:28. *Taqwá* and related forms are usually about fear of supernatural phenomena (e.g. the Fire at 2:24, the Last Day at 2:123 and 281) but not always, as when one form (*tattaqū*) is applied to fear of unbelievers as an acceptable excuse for making alliances with them (Q. 3:28). As Ohlander says, *khawf* and related forms are applied most generally, as for fear of the enemy (Q. 2:239, 4:101), poverty (Q. 9:28), and the Last Judgement (Q. 24:37, 40:32). *Khashyah* and related forms are likewise reactions to both supernatural and natural phe-

4. Ibn al-Mubārak, *al-Zuhd wa-al-raqāʾiq*, (ed.) Ḥabīb al-Raḥmān al-Aʿẓamī (Malegaon, 1386; reprint with different pagination Beirut, 1419AH/1998CE), no. 79 among additions from Nuʿaym ibn Ḥammād.

5. Ibn al-Mubārak, *Zuhd*, no. 138 < N.

6. Ibn al-Mubārak, *Zuhd*, no. 168. The same gloss is attributed to Sufyān al-Thawrī (Kufan, d. 161/777?) by Abū Nuʿaym, *Ḥilyat al-awliyāʾ*, 10 vols. (Cairo, 1352–57AH/1932–38CE), VII, p. 77. Here and henceforth, translations of the Qurʾan follow Alan Jones's translation unless otherwise noted.

7. V. al-Ṭabarī, *Jāmiʿ al-bayān*, 31 vols. (Cairo, 1321), 1:20–2 = ed. Maḥmūd Shākir with ʿAlī ʿĀshūr, 30 vols. in 16 (Beirut, 1421AH/2001CE), I, pp. 25–31.

nomena; for example, fear of people, it being better to fear God (Q. 3:173, 33:37), fear of ill fortune (Q. 5:52), and fear of sexual immorality (Q. 4:25).

Scott C. Alexander may be cited as an example of those who wish to assure us that the fear enjoined by the Qurʾan is not an unhealthy, debilitating state of anxiety. He says, for example,[8] [285]

> In terms of the dominant qurʾānic paradigm for the human-divine relationship, the individual who cultivates *taqwā* is the human "servant" (*ʿabd*) who perfectly "fears" his or her divine "master" (*rabb*), not by cowering in terror at the prospect of punishment for dereliction of duty, but rather by remaining ever watchful and steadfast in his or her respect for and devotion to the Master .... In order to evoke more effectively this important sense of the concept as well as to avoid English readers' misinterpreting *taqwā* as an ordinary type of "fear," one recent English translation of the Qurʾān deftly renders *taqwā* as "God-consciousness" (Asad, *passim*).

It is not my argument that 'God-consciousness' is an incorrect interpretation of qurʾanic *taqwá*.[9] It is my argument, rather, that this is not a necessary interpretation of qurʾanic *taqwá* and that this was not the predominant interpretation of qurʾanic *taqwá* and other words for 'fear' in the first two or three centuries of Islam. On the contrary, precisely "terror at the prospect of punishment" was commonly recommended as the proper deportment of the faithful.

Early Piety

Inscriptions from the seventh century such as graffiti and funerary monuments so stress appeal for divine forgiveness and hope of entering Paradise that virtually no other character of the new religion can be discerned. Official inscriptions likewise stress piety, such that it must have been the central means of political legitimation in the later seventh century.[10]

8. *Encyclopædia of the Qurʾān*, s.v. 'Fear,' by Scott C. Alexander, referring at the end to Muhammad Asad, *The Message of the Qurʾan* (Gibraltar, 1980).

9. *Taqwá* is likewise glossed as 'God-consciousness' by Abdelkader Tayob, *Islam: a short introduction* (Oxford: Oneworld, 1999), p. 55, although he shortly goes on to describe it more plausibly as 'a concept [that] connotes a sense of fear, awe and reverence in the presence of God.'

10. Solange Ory, 'Aspects religieux des texts épigraphiques du début de l'Islam,' *Les premières écritures islamiques*, dir. Alfred-Louis de Prémare, Revue du monde Musulman et de la Méditerranée 58 (Aix-en-Provence, 1990), pp. 30–39; Fred Donner, *Narratives of Islamic Origins*, Studies in Late Antiquity and Early Islam 14 (Princeton, 1998). Donner has been challenged by Amikam Elad, 'Community of believers of "holy men" and "saints" or community of Muslims?' *Journal of Semitic Studies*, XLVII (2002), pp. 241–308.

Our principal sources for the early history of piety belong to three traditions: *adab*, or polite letters; Sufism; and hadith. The *adab* tradition is distinguished by its attraction to elegant locutions, more subtly to humour and miracles. From the ninth century CE, the *zuhd* sections of al-Jāḥiẓ (d. 255AH/868–9CE), *al-Bayān*, and Ibn Qutaybah (d. 276AH/889CE?), *ʿUyūn al-akhbār*, are examples of this tradition, along with the many works of Ibn Abī al-Dunyā (d. 281AH/894CE), which apparently have the most overlap with the hadith tradition.[11] The Sufi tradition probably begins with two collections of sayings and stories from the earlier tenth century, those of Ibn al-Aʿrābī (d. 341AH/952CE?) and Jaʿfar al-Khuldī (d. 348AH/959CE), mostly lost except in quotation. It is characterized by a tendency to present renunciation as a precursor to Sufism (anticipating the standard view among historians today), perhaps a necessary early step in the formation of a Sufi, also to project a mystical outlook onto early figures. The hadith tradition is distinguished by attention to *asānīd*. To it belong [286] our most voluminous sources for early piety, mainly Abū Nuʿaym (d. 430AH/1038CE), *Ḥilyat al-awliyāʾ*, Aḥmad ibn Ḥanbal (d. 241AH/855CE), *al-Zuhd*, Ibn al-Mubārak (d. 181AD/797CE), *al-Zuhd*, the *zuhd* and other sections of Ibn Abī Shaybah (d. 235AD/849CE), *al-Muṣannaf*, and Hannād ibn al-Sarī (d. 243AH/857CE), *al-Zuhd*.[12] All of these provide more sayings than any source in the traditions of *adab* and Sufism. These also include most of our earliest sources. Moreover, traditionists (collectors of hadith) seem to have been the most inclined to quote accounts of a piety that contradicted their own. Altogether, then, literature in the hadith tradition seems generally the least likely to reflect back projection from the ninth and later centuries.

It is admittedly a separate question how far back we may expect that insulation against back projection to extend. The principle of dissimilarity—roughly, what sounds most like current orthodoxy is most likely a back projection from that time, what is contrary to it is most likely to be a genuine relic of an earlier time—notoriously gives us a relative chronology, not an absolute. My own inclination is to consider attributions to figures of the early eighth century normally reliable, at least at the level of paraphrase

---

It seems to me the question comes down to how early political and religious authority were differentiated, with Elad complacently projecting back a later division of labour.

11. As for the first two, the preferred editions remain, to my knowledge, Jāḥiẓ, *al-Bayān wa-al-tabyīn*, (ed.) ʿAbd al-Salām Muḥammad Hārūn, 4 vols. (Cairo, 1367–69AH/1948–50CE), and Ibn Qutaybah, *ʿUyūn al-akhbār*, 4 vols. (Cairo, 1343–49AH/1925–30CE). As for the last, *v.* Reinhard Weipert and Stefan Weninger, 'Die erhaltene Werke des Ibn Abī d-Dunyā. Eine vorläufige Bestandsaufnahme,' *Zeitschrift der Deutschen Morgenländischen Gesellschaft*, CXLVI (1996), pp. 415–455.

12. Abū Nuʿaym, *Ḥilyah* (*v.* n. 6); Aḥmad ibn Ḥanbal, *al-Zuhd* (Mecca, 1357, repr. Beirut, 1396AH/1976CE, also reprint with different pagination [Beirut, 1403AH/1983CE]—references to this edn. henceforth in *italic*); Ibn al-Mubārak, *al-Zuhd* (*v.* n. 4); Ibn Abī Shaybah, *al-Muṣannaf*, (ed.) Ḥamad ibn ʿAbd Allāh al-Jumʿah and Muḥammad ibn Ibrāhīm al-Luḥaydān, 16 vols. (Riyadh, 1425AH/2004CE); Hannād ibn al-Sarī, *Kitāb al-Zuhd*, (ed.) ʿAbd al-Raḥmān ibn ʿAbd al-Jabbār al-Faryawāʾī, 2 vols. (Kuwait, 1406AH/1985CE). For a list of over 60 early works on renunciation, including many not extant, *v.* ʿĀmir Aḥmad Ḥaydar, introduction to al-Bayhaqī, *K. al-Zuhd al-kabīr* (Beirut, 1408AH/1987CE), pp. 47–56.

and with some allowance for the tendency of sayings (possibly old) to float from one speaker to another. Attributions to figures of the seventh century seem more dubious. However, I would maintain that the renunciant tradition is at least as reliable as the legal. The tendency for the Prophet to call for markedly more modest austerities than renunciants of the early eighth century—austerities whose modesty is more closely in line with Sunni piety of the late eighth and early ninth centuries—, has clear parallels in legal hadith. Schacht's perception that attributions to Followers are presumptively older than attributions to the Prophet would work equally well for renunciation.[13] Even when it comes to Companions, I would argue that a good measure of their power probably did depend on reputations for piety. Nomads are notoriously difficult to coerce. Presumably, the first charisma that kept them loyal to the early caliphs was military success, but the piety of those caliphs and other leaders seems likely to have been a vital reinforcement.[14] Abū Nuᶜaym is especially often the object of scorn for beginning his history of the pure with the first four caliphs.[15] Actually, his biographical dictionary seems on close examination to make a very credible history of Sufism and the Sunni tradition. For example, the term 'Sufi,' which would plainly be anachronistic if he applied it to early caliphs, first comes up there in biographies of the later eighth century and moves into the mainstream only in biographies [287] of the later ninth century.[16] Our earliest extensive biographies of the first four caliphs, those of Ibn Saᶜd (d. 230AH/845CE), confirm that they had significant reputations for piety by the early ninth century. I see no reason to suppose that their reputations for juridical acuity were earlier than their reputations for piety.

(On the other side are those who tend to believe reports of what the Prophet said concerning the law, at least when they appear in famous Sunni collections, while discounting reports of what he and others said about renunciation. They often cite the principle that traditionists maintained higher standards of proof when it came to reports establishing rules than reports encouraging piety. To some extent, of course, this takes us to issues beyond the scope of this article, which is the evolution of Islamic piety across

---

13. Joseph Schacht, *The Origins of Muhammadan Jurisprudence* (Oxford, 1950), p. 156.

14. For the prophet Muḥammad as a holy man whose chief charisma was military success, *v.* Chase Robinson, 'Prophecy and holy men,' *The Cult of Saints in Late Antiquity and the Middle Ages: Essays on the Contribution of Peter Brown*, ed. James Howard-Johnson and Paul Antony Howard (Oxford, 1999), pp. 241–62. Compare the degree to which the temporal authority of Late Antique bishops depended on their reputations for piety, as developed by Rosemarie Nürnberg, *Askese als sozialer Impuls*, Hereditas: Studien zur alten Kirchengeschichte 2 (Bonn, 1988), and Andrea Sterk, *Renouncing the World yet Leading the Church* (Cambridge, Mass., 2004).

15. A tradition that admittedly goes back as far as Ibn al-Jawzī (d. 597AH/1201CE), *K. Ṣifat al-ṣafwah*, 4 vols. (Hyderabad: Maṭbaᶜat Majlis Dāᵓirat al-Maᶜārif al-ᶜUthmānīyah, 1355–6), I, p. 3.

16. For the terminological history of 'Sufism' (*taṣawwuf*), *v.* Louis Massignon, *Essay on the Origins of the Technical Language of Islamic Mysticism*, trans. Benjamin Clark (Notre Dame, Indiana, 1997), and *The Encyclopaedia of Islam*, new edn., s.v. '*taṣawwuf*,' by B. Radtke.

the eighth and ninth centuries, not the evolution of Islamic law from the seventh. But this distinction between legal and other hadith is also one that modern research has not, to my knowledge, confirmed.[17])

Hadith attributes fear of God to many prophets. God is quoted as telling Job, "O Ayyūb, have you not learnt that I have worshipping ulema, wise men (*ḥukamāʾ*), and persons who relate what I say (*nuṭaqāʾ*) whom I have made to live in fear of me (*askantuhum khashyatī*)?"[18] Moses is quoted as saying to God, "My Lord, which of your worshippers most fears you (*akhshá lak*)?" God answers him, "The one who knows me best (*aʿlamuhum bī*)."[19] ʿĪsá ibn Maryam would cry out like a woman on anyone's mentioning the Last Judgement before him.[20]

Many stories also ascribe fear to virtuous early Muslims. Kaʿb al-Aḥbār (d. 32AH/652–653CE?) plainly thought prophets were at risk (and so much more other mortals): "If a man had to his credit the work of 70 prophets, he would still fear (*khashiya*) not to escape the evil of Resurrection Day."[21] Ibn Masʿūd (d. 32AH/652–3CE?) passed some people working a forge and fell down on the spot (reminded of the Fire).[22] The Companion Shaddād ibn Aws (d. *ca.* 60AH/679–680CE) on his bed was said to be like a grain of wheat on a frying pan. He would say, "O God, the Fire has prevented me from sleeping," then get up for supererogatory ritual prayer.[23] Al-Rabīʿ ibn Khuthaym told his daughter he did not sleep [288] like other men because he feared sins (*yakhāfu al-sayyiʾāt*), meaning the punishment due for them.[24] One night in Ramadan, the Kufan ʿUmar ibn Dharr (d. 153AH/770CE?) spoke at his session on the Last Judgement, particularly interrogation by angels, such

17. Cf. Christopher Melchert, 'The *Musnad* of Aḥmad ibn Ḥanbal,' *Der Islam*, LXXXII (2005), pp. 32–51, at pp. 45–47 [*HPL 3].

18. Ibn al-Mubārak, *Zuhd*, no. 1473.

19. Ibid., no. 223.

20. Ibid., no. 229; Aḥmad, *Zuhd*, pp. 57–58 *p. 75*. It will be indicated where items in the *Zuhd* came not through Aḥmad but only through its compiler, his son ʿAbd Allāh (d. 290AH/903CE).

21. Ibn al-Mubārak, *Zuhd*, no. 159.

22. Ibn Abī Shaybah, *Muṣannaf*, *zuhd* 73, XII, p. 371; Aḥmad, *Zuhd*, p. 160 *p. 200*. Alternatively, he wept on seeing a hot iron in the forge: Ibn Abī Shaybah, *Muṣannaf*, *zuhd* 92, XII, p. 423; Aḥmad, *Zuhd*, p. 163 *p. 202*. Also said of Uways al-Qaranī (d. 37AH/657CE): Ibn Abī al-Dunyā, *al-Riqqah wa-al-bukāʾ*, ed. Muḥammad Khayr Ramaḍān Yūsuf (Beirut, 1416AH/1996CE), p. 63 = ed. Musʿad ʿAbd al-Ḥamīd Muḥammad al-Saʿdānī (Cairo: Maktabat al-Qurʾān, n.d.), p. 28 (references to this edn. henceforth in *italic*). An anonymous worshipper gazed at a smith's bellows, gave a sob, and died: Ibn Abī Shaybah, *Muṣannaf*, *zuhd* 92, XII, p. 425; Ibn Abī al-Dunyā, *Riqqah*, p. 63 *p. 28*. Al-Aʿmash (d. 148AH/765CE?) related that the earlier Kufan al-Rabīʿ ibn Khuthaym (d. 63AH/682–3CE) had sobbed on seeing a hot iron, then passed by the smiths himself to do the same but "there was no good in me"; that is, he did not weep himself (a good thing, though, inasmuch as it showed that he did not weep at will, for show): Aḥmad, *Zuhd*, p. 338 *p. 407*.

23. Aḥmad, *Zuhd* p. 195 *p. 243*.

24. Ibid., *Zuhd*, p. 337 *p. 406*.

that a youth leapt up shrieking and shaking till he died.[25] The famous Egyptian traditionist Ibn Wahb (d. 197/813) is said to have heard a book on the terrors of the Resurrection read aloud, fainted, and died three days later.[26]

Some figures are expressly identified in the biographical literature as *khāʾifīn*, 'fearers.' The Meccan Wuhayb ibn al-Ward (*fl.* mid-2nd/8th c.), on seeing people laughing the day after Ramadan, commented, "This is not the practice of the *khāʾifīn*."[27] Muḥammad ibn Maymūn (d. 167AH/783–784CE) was described as one of the *khāʾifīn lillāh*. "He used to perform the ritual prayer, then weep, until the pebbles were often soaked by his tears."[28] When 'Abd al-ʿAzīz ibn Salmān (*fl.* later 2nd/8th c.) of Basra would cry out in the mosque, other *khāʾifūn* would cry out from the sides of the mosque.[29] A *khāʾif* died when Manṣūr ibn ʿAmmār (*fl.* early 3rd/9th c.) recited some verses about the Fire.[30] Some of the same things (crying out, falling dead from terror of the Afterlife) are said of other renunciants not expressly called *khāʾifīn*, so this is evidently not an established technical term distinguishing some renunciants from others.

The express connection of fear with weeping is fairly common. Dāwūd the prophet was reproached for much weeping but said, "Leave me to weep before the day of weeping; before the burning of bones and the blazing of beards...."[31] A prophetic hadith promises, "There will not enter the Fire a man who has wept from fear of God unless the milk can re-enter the teat, nor will there combine dust on the path of God (in the holy war) and the smoke of Gehenna."[32] Another, similarly, promises that "Two eyes will not be touched by the Fire: an eye that has wept from the fear of God and an eye that has spent the night keeping watch on the path of God."[33] ʿAbd Allāh ibn Rawāḥah al-Anṣārī (d. 8AH/629CE) wept on being called out to *jihād*. He explained to his wife, "By God, I have not wept from fear of death ... but rather on account of God's saying, 'There is none of you who will not go down to it [Q. 19:71].' I am sure I am going down to it, but I do not

25. Aḥmad, *Zuhd*, p. 356 *p. 427* (< ʿAl.).

26. Abū Nuʿaym, *Ḥilyah*, VIII, p. 324.

27. *Ibid.*, VIII, p. 149.

28. Ibn Abī al-Dunyā, *Riqqah*, p. 120 *p. 50*.

29. Abū Nuʿaym, *Ḥilyah*, VI, p. 243.

30. *Ibid.*, IX, pp. 328–9.

31. Aḥmad, *Zuhd* (< ʿAl.), p. 69 *p. 88*.

32. Tirmidhī, *Jāmiʿ*, *faḍāʾil al-jihād* 8, *bāb mā jāʾa fī faḍl al-ghubār fī sabīl Allāh*, no. 1633, and *al-zuhd* 8, *bāb mā jāʾa fī faḍl al-bukāʾ min khashyat Allāh*, no. 2311; Nasāʾī, *Mujtabá*, *jihād* 8, *faḍl man ʿamila fī sabīl Allāh ʿalá qadamih*, no. 3109; Aḥmad ibn Ḥanbal, *al-Musnad*, 6 vols. (Cairo, 1313AH/1895CE), II, p. 505 = (ed.) Shuʿayb al-Arnaʾūṭ, & al., 50 vols. (Beirut, 1413–21AH/1993–2001CE), XVI, pp. 330–331 (references to the latter edition henceforth in *italic*).

33. Tirmidhī, *Jāmiʿ*, *faḍāʾil al-jihād*, *bāb mā jāʾa fī faḍl al-ḥars fī sabīl Allāh*, no. 1639. Sim. from Ibn Abī Shaybah, *Muṣannaf*, *jihād* 1, *mā dhukira fī faḍl al-jihād*, VII, p. 67; Aḥmad, *Musnad*, IV, p. 134 *XXVIII, p. 445–448*; al-Dārimī, *al-Sunan*, *k. al-jihād*, *bāb fī alladhī yas'haru fī sabīl Allāh ḥārisan* = 2 vols. (Damascus: al-Maṭbaʿah al-Ḥadīthīyah, 1349), II, p. 203.

know whether I shall escape or not."[34] Kaᶜb al-Aḥbār said, "I should prefer weeping from fear (*khashyah*) of God (be he exalted) [289] until the tears flow down my cheeks to giving as alms my weight in gold."[35] Seen weeping, ᶜAbd Allāh ibn ᶜAmr (d. 77AH/696–697CE?) explained, "Do you wonder that I should weep from fear (*khashyah*) of God? If you are not weeping, pretend to weep, until one of you says *ayh, ayh*."[36] Al-Ḥasan al-Baṣrī is often quoted as commending sadness; for example, "By God, O son of Adam, if you have read the Qurʾan and then believed in it, let your sadness in the world be prolonged, let your fear in the world be severe, and let your weeping in the world be plentiful."[37] Yazīd ibn Abān (d. bef. 120AH/737–738CE) made himself thirsty in the Basran heat for 40 years (that is, continuously fasted by day for that long), then said to his *aṣḥāb*, "Come, let us weep over cold water" (presumably contemplating the torment of Hell).[38] ᶜAbd al-Wāḥid ibn Zayd (*fl.* early 2nd/8th c.) explained that he wept from fear of the Fire.[39] The Damascene Saᶜīd ibn ᶜAbd al-ᶜAzīz (d. 168AH/784–785CE?) continually wept at prayer, explaining that hell was always then represented to him.[40]

In a book devoted to examples of weeping and tenderheartedness, Ibn Abī al-Dunyā gives us sections devoted to weeping in the course of preaching, mostly from the mimbar (ten examples) and in the course of ritual prayer (fifteen examples).[41] If weeping at the ritual prayer and in listening to sermons is strongly associated with fear, there is probably also a strong element of fear in the widely-reported custom of weeping at the recitation of the Qurʾan. The Qurʾan itself refers to weeping as a proper response to its own recitation; e.g., Q. 5:83, "When they hear what has been sent down to the messenger, you can see their eyes overflow with tears." The Prophet himself wept on hearing the Qurʾan, if not in fear for himself then presumably in pity for his followers.[42] Ghazālī presents ten

34. Wakīᶜ, *Zuhd*, I, p. 260–261; Aḥmad, *Zuhd*, p. 200 *p. 249*; Hannād, *Zuhd*, I, p. 163; sim., Ibn al-Mubārak, *Zuhd*, no. 310; Abū Nuᶜaym, *Ḥilyah*, I, pp. 118–119.

35. Ibn Abī Shaybah, *Muṣannaf*, *zuhd* 92, *mā qālū fī al-bukāʾ min khashyat Allāh*, XII, p. 427; Abū Nuᶜaym, *Ḥilyah*, V, p. 366.

36. Ibn Abī Shaybah, *Muṣannaf*, *zuhd* 92, *mā qālū fī al-bukāʾ*, XII, p. 425. Sim. exhortation to weep from the Prophet, apud Ibn Mājah, *Zuhd* 19, *bāb al-ḥuzn wa-al-bukāʾ*, no. 4196; from Abū Bakr, apud Ibn Abī Shaybah, *Muṣannaf*, *zuhd* 92, *mā qālū fī al-bukāʾ*, XII, p. 424, and Aḥmad, *Zuhd*, p. 108 *p. 135*; from Abū Mūsá al-Ashᶜarī (d. 50/670–671?), apud Aḥmad, *Zuhd*, p. 199 *p. 247*.

37. Aḥmad, *Zuhd*, p. 259 *p. 317* (< ᶜAl.).

38. Abū Nuʾaym, *Ḥilyah*, III, p. 50.

39. Ibid., VI, pp. 160–161.

40. *Ibid.*, VIII, p. 274.

41. Ibn Abī al-Dunyā, *Riqqah*, pp. 97–103, 117–20 *pp. 41–4, 48–51*.

42. Ibn al-Mubārak, *Zuhd*, no 110, mentioning Q.4:41 in particular; also apud Bukhārī, *al-Jāmiᶜ al-ṣaḥīḥ*, *tafsīr*, *bāb fa-kayfa idhā jiʾnā min kull ummah*, no. 4082, *faḍāʾil al-Qurʾān*, *bāb qawl al-muqriʾ lil-qāriʾ ḥasbuk*, no. 5050, and *faḍāʾil al-Qurʾān*, *bāb a-bukāʾ ᶜinda qirāʾat al-Qurʾān*, no. 5055; cf. Aḥmad, *Zuhd*, p. 27 *p. 36*, mentioning Q. 73:12 in particular.

rules for outward deportment in reciting the Qurʾan, including as number six that one weep.[43]

To this day, tears are seen welling up in the eyes of audiences for qurʾanic recitation. Like references to fear in the Qurʾan, this has disturbed some observers. For example, Kristina Nelson is at pains to dissociate these tears from fear and sadness; e.g. "it is a response to spiritual and aesthetic stimuli (truth and beauty, if you will). It is clear that *bukāʾ* [weeping] in this context is not the weeping triggered by grief."[44] I cannot disprove this as a description of present-day Egyptians' emotions at recitation of the Qurʾan, and I will readily concede that physical reactions from tears to seasickness may well proceed from experiences of sublimity. Howbeit, it seems clear from the renunciant literature that the expected sadness on hearing the Qurʾan was, in the early centuries, very like normal sadness. Ibn ʿUmar [290] (d. 73AH/692–693CE?) began to recite Q. 83. When he reached *yawma yaqūmu al-nās li-rabb al-ʿālamīn* (Q. 83:6), he began to weep until he fell down and refused to recite what came after.[45] Here, weeping is specifically associated with verses about the terrors of the Last Judgement. ʿAbd Allāh ibn Masʿūd is quoted as saying that the bearer of the Qurʾan (meaning one who has memorized and recites it) should be known by his night when people are sleeping (that is, he gets up to recite the Qurʾan after sleeping only part of the night), his day when people are breakfasting (that is, he fasts not only during Ramadan but throughout the year), his sadness when people are joyful, and his weeping when people are laughing.[46] If special kinds of sadness and weeping were envisaged, they would be contrasted with normal sadness and weeping, not normal joy and laughter.

I have never remarked any attempt in the renunciant literature to dissociate sadness on contemplating spiritual things from sadness in the face of setbacks in the world. On the contrary, many sayings stress their similarity. The Kufan al-Aʿmash said, "When I saw Mujāhid, I used to think that his ass had strayed and he was worried about it," referring to the Meccan Qurʾan commentator Mujāhid ibn Jabr (d. 103AH/721–722CE?).[47] When someone asked what al-Ḥasan al-Baṣrī had been like, an early Muʿtazili responded, "When you saw him, it was as if he had just buried his mother. When he sat, it was as a prisoner sits who is about to have his head struck off. When he talked, he talked the talk of a man who has been condemned to the Fire."[48] A Kufan Follower on campaign came across someone sleeping in a thicket while his horse paced. They wakened him and asked whether he was

---

43. Ghazālī, *Iḥyāʾ ʿulūm al-dīn* 8, *k. ādāb tilāwat al-Qurʾān* 2, *fī ẓāhir ādāb al-tilāwah*.

44. Kristina Nelson, *The Art of Reciting the Qurʾan*, Modern Middle East Series 11 (Austin, 1985), p. 93.

45. Wakīʿ, *Zuhd*, I, pp. 252–253.

46. Aḥmad, *Zuhd*, p. 162 *pp. 201–202*.

47. Ibn Abī Shaybah, *Muṣannaf*, *zuhd* 86, *kalām Mujāhid*, XII, p. 408; also Abū Nuʿaym, *Ḥilyah*, III, p. 279, quoting a lost section of Aḥmad, *Zuhd*.

48. Aḥmad, *K. al-Jāmiʿ fī al-ʿilal wa-maʿrifat al-rijāl*, (ed.) Muḥammad Ḥusām Bayḍūn, 2 vols. (Beirut, 1410/1990), I, pp. 65–66; sim., al-Jāḥiẓ, *Bayān*, III, p. 171.

not afraid of wild beasts in such a place. He answered, "I should be ashamed before my Lord for him to learn that I feared anything short of him."[49] The answer would make no sense if there were envisaged one sort of fear appropriate to mundane threats, another sort of fear, possibly serene 'God-consciousness,' appropriate to God.

Preference to Avoid the Last Judgement

One of the most striking examples of exaggerated fear in the early renunciant tradition is preferring not to see the Last Judgement, no matter what the outcome. Here are examples I have collected, in chronological order of attribution:

> Abū Bakr the caliph (d. 13/634): "I wish I were this tree, eaten and cut down" (Basran *isnād*).[50]
>
> Abū Bakr saw a bird on a tree and said, "Blessed are you, O bird. You eat the fruit and alight on the tree. I wish I were a fruit pecked at by birds" (Kufan/Basran *isnād*).[51] [291]
>
> Abū Bakr passed by a bird alighting on a tree. He said, "Blessed are you, O bird. You alight on a tree, eat the fruit, then fly away. There is no accounting or torment (*ḥisāb*, *ʿadhāb*) for you. Would that I were like you. By God, I wish that God had created me a tree by the way, such that a camel would pass by me, take me, put it in its mouth, chew me, swallow me, then expel me as dung, and I had not been a human" (Kufan *isnād*).[52]
>
> Abū Bakr saw a bird alighting on a tree. He said, "Blessed are you, O bird. By God, I wish that I were like you. You alight on a tree, eat the fruit, then fly away. There is no accounting or torment (*ḥisāb*, *ʿadhāb*) for you. By God, I wish I were a tree by the way, such that a camel would pass by me, take me, put it in its mouth, chew me, swallow me, then expel me as manure, and I had not been a human"" (Kufan *isnād*).[53]

---

49. Ibn al-Mubārak, *Zuhd*, no. 982; Abū Nuʿaym, *Ḥilyah*, IV, p. 101. Sim. quoted of ʿAmr ibn ʿUtbah (d. 23–35AH/644–656CE) when he refused to flee from a lion, Aḥmad, *Zuhd*, p. 353 *pp. 432–434*; of an anonymous man discovered by Zayd ibn Wahb (d. 96AH/714–15CE?), Abū Nuʿaym, *Ḥilyah*, IV, pp. 171–172, quoting a lost section of Aḥmad, *Zuhd* (< ʿAl.); of an anonymous *sāʾiḥ* described by Wahb ibn Munabbih (d. 114AH/732CE?), Aḥmad, *Zuhd*, p. 101 *p. 126*.

50. Aḥmad, *Zuhd*, p. 112 *p. 139*.

51. Ibn al-Mubārak, *Zuhd*, no. 240.

52. Hannād, *Zuhd*, I, p. 258.

53. Ibn Abī Shaybah, *Muṣannaf*, *k. al-zuhd*, *kalām Abī Bakr*, XII, p. 184; first half without *isnād* apud Aḥmad, *Zuhd*, p. 138 *p. 172*; another short version, Wakīʿ, *Zuhd*, I, 398.

Abū Bakr: "I wish I were some herbage so that animals would eat me' (Basran *isnād*).[54]

Abū ʿUbaydah ibn al-Jarrāḥ (d. 18AH/639–640CE), one of the ten promised Paradise: "I wish I were a ram for my family to slaughter and eat my flesh and make soup (of the bones)" (Basran *isnād*).[55]

ʿUmar the caliph (d. 23/644): "Would that I were a ram for my family to fatten as long as they liked, until I was as fat as possible. There would visit them someone they loved, so they would grill some of me, cut some of me into strips, then eat me and expel me as excrement, and I should not have been a human" (Kufan *isnād*).[56]

"I saw ʿUmar take a straw from the ground and say, "Would that I were this straw. Would that I had not been a thing. Would that my mother had not given birth to me. Would that I had become something totally forgotten" (Basran/Medinese *isnād*).[57]

Kaʿb: "I wish I were my family's ram, so that would take me, fatten me, slaughter me, eat me, and feed their guests" (Kufan *isnād*).[58]

"Harim ibn Ḥayyān [Basran, d. after 26/647] and ʿAbd Allāh ibn ʿĀmir [d. after 80/700–701] went out seeking the land of the Hijaz. As they were going, they passed a place where there was pasture and herbiage .... Their mounts began to worry (? *yukhālijān*) the shrub. Ibn Ḥayyān said to Ibn ʿĀmir, "Would it please you to be one of these bushes, for this mount to eat, so that you would be expelled as dung and taken as dung?" He said, "No, by God, for what I hope for of the mercy of God is dearer to me than that." Harim ibn Ḥayyān said, "But I, by God, do wish I were one of these bushes for this camel to eat so that she would expel me as dung and I should be taken as dung and I did not have to endure the Reckoning on Resurrection Day, whether to Paradise or [292] the Fire. Woe to

54. Aḥmad, *Zuhd*, p. 112 *p. 139*.

55. Ibn al-Mubārak, *Zuhd*, no. 241; ʿAbd al-Razzāq, *al-Muṣannaf*, ed. Ḥabīb al-Raḥmān al-Aʿẓamī, Manshūrāt al-Majlis al-ʿIlmī 39, 11 vols. (Beirut, 1390–92AH/1970–72CE), XI, p. 307; sim., Ibn Saʿd, *Biographien*, ed. Eduard Sachau, & al., 9 vols. in 15 (Leiden, 1904–40), III/1, p. 300 = repr. with different pagination as *al-Ṭabaqāt al-kubrá*, 9 vols. (Beirut: Dār Ṣādir, 1957–68), III, p. 413—references to this edn. henceforth in *italic*; Aḥmad, *Zuhd*, p. 185 *p. 230*.

56. Hannād, *Zuhd*, I, p. 258; Abū Nuʿaym, *Ḥilyah*, I, p. 52.

57. Ibn Abī Shaybah, *zuhd* 10, *kalām ʿUmar ibn al-Khaṭṭāb*, XII, p. 196; Ibn al-Mubārak, *Zuhd*, no. 234; Ibn Saʿd, *Biographien*, III, p. 262 *III, p. 360*. 'Something totally forgotten (*nasyan mansīyan*)' alludes to Q. 19:23, where Maryam makes the same wish. I depart from Jones's translation in substituting 'something' for 'someone.'

58. Hannād, *Zuhd*, I, p. 259; sim., Aḥmad, *Zuhd*, pp. 204, 233 *pp. 253, 284*.

you, Ibn ʿĀmir: I fear the greatest calamity."" Al-Ḥasan said, "By God, he was the more discerning and knowledgeable of God of the two of them" (Basran *isnād*).[59]

Ibn Masʿūd: "Would that, when I die, I should not be raised" (Kufan *isnād*).[60]

Ibn Masʿūd: "If I were between Paradise and the Fire and given a choice between having my works accepted and being nothing, I should choose to be nothing" (Basran *isnād*).[61]

ʿAbd Allāh ibn Masʿūd: "If I were standing between Paradise and Hell and told, "Choose—you may choose to be in whichever of them you like or you may become ashes," I should like to be ashes" (Basran *isnād*).[62]

ʿAbd Allāh (ibn Masʿūd): "I wish I were a bird with feathers on my shoulders" (Kufan *isnād*).[63]

ʿAbd Allāh (ibn Masʿūd): "Would that I were a tree cut down" (Kufan *isnād*).[64]

Abū Dharr (d. 32/652–653): "I wish I were a tree and cut down. I wish I had never been created" (Kufan *isnād*).[65]

Abū Dharr < the Messenger of God: "I see what you do not see and hear what you do not hear. The heavens have brayed and well may they bray. There is no place there of four inches but that an angel is prostrating himself on it. If you knew what I know, you would laugh little and weep much. You would not enjoy yourselves with your wives on your beds but go out to the heights to supplicate God (mighty and glorious is he)." At this, Abū Dharr said, "By God, I wish I were a tree cut down" (Kufan *isnād*).[66]

---

59. Aḥmad, *Zuhd*, p. 233 *pp. 284–285*; sim., *ibid*., p. 233 *pp. 284*; Hannād, *Zuhd*, I, p. 260; Ibn al-Mubārak, *Zuhd*, no. 237; also *Ḥilyah*, II, pp. 119–120, quoting a lost section of Aḥmad, *al-Zuhd* (< ʿAl.).

60. Wakīʿ, *Zuhd*, I, p. 396; Aḥmad, *Zuhd*, p. 156 *p. 195*; Ibn Abī Shaybah, *Muṣannaf*, *zuhd* 12, *kalām Ibn Masʿūd*, XII, p. 209.

61. Aḥmad, *Zuhd*, p. 161 *p. 200*.

62. Abū Nuʿaym, *Ḥilyah*, I, p. 133 (sim., VI, p. 271); Ibn Abī Shaybah, *Muṣannaf*, *zuhd* 12, *kalām Ibn Masʿūd*, XII, p. 209.

63. Wakīʿ, *Zuhd*, I, p. 395; Ibn Abī Shaybah, *Muṣannaf*, *zuhd* 12, *kalām Ibn Masʿūd*, XII, p. 205; Aḥmad, *Zuhd*, p. 156 *p. 195*.

64. Ibn Abī Shaybah, *Muṣannaf*, *zuhd* 12, *kalām Ibn Masʿūd*, XII, p. 205.

65. Aḥmad, *Zuhd*, p. 146 *p. 182*; Wakīʿ, I, pp. 159, 161.

66. Aḥmad, *Musnad*, V, p. 173 *XXXV, pp. 405–406*. Sim., Aḥmad, *Zuhd*, pp. 145–6 *p. 182* (< ʿAl.). Also sim. in Tirmidhī, *Jāmiʿ*, *zuhd* 9, *fī qawl al-nabī ... law taʿlamūna mā aʿlam*, no. 2312, and Ibn Mājah, *al-Sunan*, *zuhd* 19, *al-ḥuzn wa-al-bukāʾ*, no. 4190, where the last words appear to be those of the Prophet himself. Tirmidhī comments that they are also attributed to Abū Dharr.

Abū Dharr: "By God, I wish that on the day when God created me, he had created me as a tree cut down, its fruits eaten" (Kufan *isnād*).[67]

Abū al-Dardāʾ: "I wish I were a ram belonging to my family, by whom a guest would pass, so they would order my throat cut and eat and give to eat" (Basran *isnād*).[68]

Abū al-Dardāʾ: "If you knew what you were to see after death, you would not eat food with appetite or drink anything with appetite. You would not enter any house to be shaded by it but go out to the heights to strike your breasts and weep for yourselves. I wish I were a tree cut down, then eaten" (Kufan/Basran *isnād*).[69] [293]

ʿUthmān (d. 35/56): "If I were between Paradise and the Fire, not knowing to which I should be commanded (to go), I should prefer to be ashes before learning to which of them I was to go" (Basran *isnād*).[70]

ʿImrān ibn al-Ḥuṣayn (d. 52/672): "I wish I were ashes to be scattered by the wind on a foul, stormy day" (Basran *isnād*).[71]

ʿImrān ibn al-Ḥuṣayn: "I wish I were ashes to be scattered by the wind" (Basran *isnād*).[72]

ʿĀʾishah (d. 57/676–677?), passing by a tree: "I wish I were one of the leaves of this tree" (Kufan/Medinese *isnād*).[73]

ʿĀʾishah: "Would that when I die, I should be something totally forgotten (*nasyan mansīyan*)" (Kufan/Medinese *isnād*).[74]

ʿĀʾishah: "Would that I were something totally forgotten," meaning a menstrual rag (*ḥīḍah*) (Medinese/Meccan *isnād*).[75]

67. Hannād, *Zuhd*, I, p. 259.

68. Ibn al-Mubārak, *Zuhd*, no. 238.

69. Aḥmad, *Zuhd*, p. 138 *pp. 171–172* (< ʿAl.).

70. Aḥmad, *Zuhd*, p. 129 *p. 160*.

71. Ibn al-Mubārak, *Zuhd*, no. 241; ʿAbd al-Razzāq, *Muṣannaf*, XI, p. 307; Ibn Saʿd, *Biographien*, IV/2, p. 26 *IV, p. 287*.

72. Aḥmad, *Zuhd*, p. 149 *p. 186*.

73. Aḥmad, *Zuhd*, p. 165 *p. 206*.

74. Hannād, *Zuhd*, I, p. 260; Aḥmad, *Zuhd*, p. 164 *p. 205*.

75. ʿAbd al-Razzāq, *Muṣannaf*, XI, p. 307. Al-Ṭabarī explains that a *nasy mansī* is something unwanted, discarded, and totally forgotten *such as* a menstrual rag: *Jāmiʿ al-bayān*, *ad* Q. 19:23. The gloss of 'menstrual rag' from ʿAbd al-Razzāq (or a later reader if it is a marginal note that has moved into the text) is one of five alternative definitions of *nasy* given by al-Māwardī, *al-Nukat wa-al-ʿuyūn*, *ad* Q. 19:23, who attributes it to ʿIkrimah (d. 107AH/725–726CE?); one of two definitions offered by al-Qurṭubī, *al-Jāmiʿ fī*

ʿĀ'ishah, on passing a tree: "Would that I were a leaf on this tree" (Kufan *isnād*).[76]

ʿĀ'ishah: "I wish I were a tree and cut down. I wish I had never been created" (Kufan *isnād*).[77]

ʿAbd Allāh ibn ʿAmr: "I wish I were this tree" (Kufan *isnād*).[78]

Muṭarrif ibn al-Shikhkhir (Basran, d. 95/713–714): "If I were poised between Paradise and Hell, then a voice cried to me "O Muṭarrif, would you like us to tell you in which of them you are to be?" I should prefer to be cold ashes to being told in which of them I was to be" (Basran *isnād*).[79]

Muṭarrif: "If a being came to me from my Lord and gave me the choice between informing me whether I was among the People of Paradise or among the People of Hell or that I should become dust, I would choose to become dust" (Basran *isnād*).[80]

Ṣāliḥ al-Murrī (Basran, d. 172AH/788–9CE?): "I asked ʿAṭāʾ al-Salīmī [Basran, *fl.* first half, 2nd/8th cent.], "What do you desire?" He wept and said, "I wish, by God, Abū Bishr, that I were ashes, of which not a handful (*suffah*) would ever be gathered in this world or the last." He [294] made me weep, by God. I knew that he wanted only to escape from the distress of the Day of Reckoning" (Basran *isnād*).[81]

Al-Fuḍayl (ibn ʿIyāḍ, d. Mecca, 187/803?): "If I were given the choice between being revived and entering Paradise and not being revived, I should choose not to be revived." Ibn Abī al-Ḥawārī: "I asked Muḥammad ibn Ḥātim whether this was from shyness (*ḥayāʾ*). He said, 'This is from shyness before God (mighty and glorious is he)'" (Syrian *isnād*).[82]

---

aḥkām al-Qurʾān, ad Q. 19:23, who quotes for it the lexicographer al-Farrāʾ (d. 207AH/822–823CE). The previous quotation, in which ʿĀʾishah wishes to become this thing after death, obviously presupposes the more general definition of *something forgotten*.

76. Ibn al-Mubārak, *Zuhd*, no. 239; Ibn Abī Shaybah, *Muṣannaf, zuhd* 28, *kalām ʿĀʾishah*, XII, p. 260.
77. Aḥmad, *Zuhd*, p. 164 *p. 206*.
78. Ibn Abī Shaybah, *Muṣannaf, zuhd* 24, *kalām ʿAbd Allāh ibn ʿAmr*, XII, p. 255.
79. Aḥmad, *Zuhd*, p. 241 *p. 295*.
80. Aḥmad, *Zuhd*, p. 238 *p. 292* (< ʿAl.); sim., Ibn Abī Shaybah, *Muṣannaf, zuhd* 66, *Muṭarrif ibn al-Shikhkhīr*, XII, p. 343, also apud Abū Nuʿaym, *Ḥilyah*, II, 199.
81. Abū Nuʿaym, *Ḥilyah*, VI, p. 224.
82. *Ibid.*, VIII, p. 84.

> Al-Fuḍayl ibn ʿIyāḍ: "If I were given the choice of living as a dog, dying as a dog, and not seeing Resurrection Day, I should prefer living as a dog, dying as a dog, and not seeing Resurrection Day" (Basran/Khurasani *isnād*).[83]

> Ḥudhayfah (ibn Qatādah al-Marʿashī, d. 207AH/822–823CE): "If there came down to me an angel from heaven to inform me that I should not see the Fire with my eye and that I should go to Paradise but that I should stand before my lord (be he exalted) to interrogate me, then go to Paradise, I would say, 'I do not want Paradise or to stand at that place'" (Mesopotamian *isnād*).[84]

This surprising sentiment is attributed in our principal biographical sources mainly to figures of the seventh and early eighth centuries, suggesting that the sentiment is genuinely early (if it were merely a back projection from later on, it would presumably be found equally in all generations to the time of our sources), although not necessarily as early as the Companions. *Isnād* analysis suggests that it was prevalent in all the major centres. The dominant mood here is plainly *ascetical*; that is, it has to do with the piety of obedience to a transcendent God, not communion with an immanent God.[85] Far from rejoicing in communion with God, these pious Muslims are depicted as finding so little comfort in the thought of God's presence that they would rather vanish and never be judged than go the Last Judgement and be saved.

Hope and Fear

These wishes to vanish and never be judged are surprising partly because they seem to bespeak terrible uncertainty, if not despair, about the chances of one's salvation. Muslims today do not seem characteristically anxious about their salvation, and it is a tenet of Sunni theology that all Muslims will be saved, against the Muʿtazilah, Khawārij, and others, who held that qurʾanic and other threats of eternal punishment applied to deserving Muslims as well as non-Muslims. Expressions of deep uncertainty are also not rare in early renunciant literature. Abū Maysarah (Kufan, d. 63AH/682–683CE) took to his bed and said, "Would that my mother had never borne me." His wife said, "Abū Maysarah: God has done well by you, having guided you to Islam." He said, "Yes, but God has made it clear to us that we are bound for the Fire, without making clear to us that we are going out of it."[86] Abū [295] Hurayrah (d. 58AH/677–678CE) wept in his death illness not over

83. *Ibid.*, VIII, p. 84.

84. *Ibid.*, VIII, p. 268.

85. The most useful definitions of *asceticism* and *mysticism* are, to my mind, those proposed by Gert H. Mueller, 'Asceticism and Mysticism. A Contribution Towards the Sociology of Faith,' *International Yearbook for the Sociology of Religion 8: Sociological Theories of Religion/Religion and Language*, (ed.) Günter Dux, Thomas Luckmann, and Joachim Matthes (Opladen, 1973), pp. 68–132.

86. With allusion again to Q. 19:71: Ibn al-Mubārak, *Zuhd*, no. 312; Ibn Abī Shaybah, *Muṣannaf*, *zuhd* 45,

the world but uncertainty whether he would be sent to Paradise or the Fire.[87] The Kufan Ibrāhīm al-Nakhaʿī (d. 96AH/714CE?), found weeping, explained that he was uncertain whether the angel of death would announce he was heading for Paradise or the Fire.[88] In another version, it was specifically on his deathbed that he explained, "How could I not weep when I await a messenger bearing news (*yubashshirunī*) of either this or that?"[89]

Also not rare in early renunciant literature (and abundant in prophetic hadith) are expressions of hopefulness. ʿĀʾishah is quoted as saying, "If any of you wishes, let him do it plentifully, for he is asking only his lord."[90] The Damascene Yūnus ibn Maysarah (d. 132AH/750CE) reported that God had an inscription before him saying, "I am God, than whom there is no other god; I am the Merciful, the Compassionate; I have mercy and enjoin mercy (*arḥam wa-ataraḥḥam*); my mercy precedes my anger, my pardon my punishment; I permit him who brings one 330th part to enter Paradise."[91] There is abundant testimony that performing the ritual prayers erases sin; for example, from the Prophet, Salmān (d. 34AH/654–655CE), and Ibn Masʿūd.[92] Sometimes, it appears that hope should outweigh fear. The Yemeni Ṭāwūs (d. 106/724–725?) recommended, "Fear God until there is nothing you fear more than him and hope even more than you fear him."[93]

Other times, it appears to be safer for fear to outweigh hope. Al-Ḥasan al-Baṣrī is quoted as saying, "Faith is not by decoration (*taḥallī*) or wishing (*tamallī*). Faith settles in the heart and is confirmed by works (*ʿamal*)."[94] The Kufan ʿAwn ibn ʿAbd Allāh (d. bef. 120AH/737–738CE) is quoted as saying, "How many who have looked forward to the end of a day have not completed it; who have waited for the morrow but not reached it. If you looked at your lifespan and its going, you would despise hope (*amal*) and its delusions."[95] But it appears that keeping hope and fear in balance is the predominant ideal. The prophet (or wise man) Luqmān is quoted as telling his son, "Hope (*urju*) in God without feeling safe from his trickery (*makr*). Fear God without despairing of his mercy." His son asked, "How can I do that, father, when I have only one heart?" Luqmān answered, "My son, the believer is like someone with two hearts, one with which to hope and one with which to

XII, p. 296; Aḥmad, *Zuhd*, p. 363 *p. 435* (< ʿAl.); Abū Nuʿaym, *Ḥilyah*, IV, p. 141.

87. Ibn al-Mubārak, *Zuhd*, no. 154 < N.; Aḥmad, *Zuhd*, p. 153 *p. 192* (< ʿAl.); Ibn Saʿd, *Biographien*, IV/2, pp. 62–63 *IV, p. 339*.

88. Aḥmad, *Zuhd*, p. 364 *p. 437*; by another *isnād*, Ibn al-Mubārak, *Zuhd*, no. 437; by yet another, Abū Nuʿaym, *Ḥilyah*, IV, p. 224.

89. Ibn Abī Shaybah, *Muṣannaf*, *zuhd* 83, *ḥadīth Ibrāhīm*, XII, p. 397.

90. *Ibid.*, *zuhd* 28, *kalām ʿĀʾishah*, XII, p. 260.

91. Aḥmad, *Zuhd*, p. 168 *p. 210* (< ʿAl.).

92. Ibn al-Mubārak, *Zuhd*, nos. 905–908, 916. *V.* further Marion H. Katz, 'The study of Islamic ritual and the meaning of *wuḍūʾ*,' *Der Islam*, LXXXII (2005), pp. 106–145, esp. pp. 118–132 on the minor ritual ablution as erasing sin.

93. Hannād, *Zuhd*, I, p. 305.

94. Ibn Abī Shaybah, *Muṣannaf*, *zuhd* 72, *kalām al-Ḥasan al-Baṣrī*, XII, p. 363; Aḥmad, *Zuhd*, p. 263 *p. 322*.

95. Ibn al-Mubārak, *Zuhd*, no. 10.

fear."[96] (There is a tendency, although not a strict rule, to use *rajāʾ* for approved hope, *amal* and *tamannī* for delusory.) Muṭarrif ibn al-Shikhkhīr said, "If the believer's fear and hope were weighed, neither would outweigh the other."[97] "Hope and fear are the believer's two mounts," said [296] al-Ḥasan.[98] The Kufan Ibrāhīm al-Taymī (d. 92AH/710–711CE) considered himself unusually hopeful, yet hoped to just barely squeeze through: "No one who recollects is more hopeful for my soul that it should be saved than itself, but I wish just a sufficiency of salvation, neither against it nor for it."[99] The Yemeni Wahb ibn Munabbih apparently called for alternation: "When the friends of God are taken down the path of hardship, they hope; when down the path of ease, they fear."[100]

More precisely, the predominant ideal seems to be fearfulness on this side of the Last Judgement in hope of salvation thereafter. God himself is quoted as saying, "By my glory, I will not join together two fears against my servant, nor join together two safeties for him: if he feels safe from me (*law aminanī*) in the world, I will make him fear on Resurrection Day, while if he fears me in the world, I shall give him safety on Resurrection Day."[101] The Prophet prayed, "O God, provide me with two eyes that rain down torrents of tears, curing me of your fear before the tears become blood and the molars hot coals."[102] Many sayings stress that there can be no let-up of activity before the Last Judgement. Ibn Masʿūd is quoted as saying, "The believer has no rest (*rāḥah*) short of meeting God."[103] Muṭarrif ibn al-Shikhkhīr, told by someone that he depended on asking God's forgiveness and turning to him, warned him that he might not live to act so.[104] To quote al-Ḥasan again, "The believers are quick to fear in the world so that God will give them security on Resurrection Day, while the hypocrites put off fear so that God will make them fear on Resurrection Day."[105] Al-Ḥasan is also quoted as saying, "O people: constancy, constancy (*al-mudāwamah*)! God has not established a term to the believer's work short of death."[106] Fear to the last minute would keep them at their devotions to the last minute, as well.

96. *Ibid.*, no. 912; Aḥmad, *Zuhd*, pp. 106–107 *p. 132* (shorter version at p. 105 *p. 130*).

97. Aḥmad, *Zuhd*, 238–239 *p. 293*; Ibn Abī Shaybah, *Muṣannaf, zuhd* 66, *Muṭarrif ibn al-Shikhkhīr*, XII, p. 344; sim. attributed to another Basran, Maṭar ibn Ṭahmān (d. 125AH/742–743CE?), Abū Nuʿaym, *Ḥilyah*, III, p. 76.

98. Aḥmad, *Zuhd*, p. 265 *p. 324* (< ʿAl.).

99. Ibid., p. 215 *p. 265*.

100. *Ibid.*, p. 374 *p. 447*.

101. Ibn al-Mubārak, *Zuhd*, nos. 157–158.

102. *Ibid.*, no. 480; Aḥmad, *Zuhd*, p. 10 *p. 15*.

103. Wakīʿ, *Zuhd*, I, p. 311; Aḥmad, *Zuhd*, p. 156 *p. 194*. With an addition ('Whosever rest is in meeting God, it is as if he already had') apud Ibn al-Mubārak, *Zuhd*, no. 17.

104. Aḥmad, *Zuhd*, p. 239 *p. 293*.

105. Ibn Abī Shaybah, *Muṣannaf, zuhd* 72, *kalām al-Ḥasan al-Baṣrī*, XII, p. 364.

106. Ibn al-Mubārak, *Zuhd*, no. 18.

Michael Cooperson brilliantly interprets al-Jāḥiẓ' book of misers as a satire on renunciants.[107] The man who is indignant that his father would touch his bread to pieces of cheese, rather than merely waving them in its proximity, is like Bishr al-Ḥāfī, desiring a particular dish and continually exposing himself to it but never permitting himself to eat it. There are many similar stories of earlier renunciants. For example, the Basran Mālik ibn Dīnār (d. *ca.* 130AH/747–748CE) once remarked to one of his fellows that he desired bread with curdled milk (*raghīf bi-laban rāʾib*, presumably something like yoghurt). The fellow procured some and brought it to him but Mālik turned over the loaf (spilling the curdled milk), telling it "I have desired you for forty years but I have defeated you until today. Now you want to defeat me. Get away from me!"[108] To my mind, this is why our early renunciants cultivated exaggerated fear. They liked to maintain a constant state of excitation. Unremitting fear was their safeguard against complacency, while reminders to hope would keep them from slipping into despairing inaction. [297]

It may seem that wishing one had not been created bespeaks lack of faith in God. Indeed, the literature of renunciation often encourages acceptance of God's decree. Abū al-Dardāʾ is quoted as saying not only "I wish I were a tree cut down" but also "I hope that when God decrees something, we are satisfied with his decree."[109] Ibn Masʿūd is quoted as saying not only "Would that I were a tree cut down" but also "I do not care, when I return to my family, in what state I see them, whether prosperous or afflicted. I have never begun the day in such a condition that I wished for another."[110] Apparently contradictory attributions suggest opposed parties projecting backward their preferred doctrines. Alternatively, one might infer from the contradictions that renunciant thought was somewhat incoherent, a possibility that seems the more likely inasmuch as the same persons seem to have quoted them in contradiction to themselves. The famous renunciants were not theologians; many were not even intellectuals. Maintaining a certain mood, warding off complacency, was more important to them than logical consistency.

The Attenuation of Fear

Exaggerated fear of God is attested in books of the ninth century but not often ascribed to pious figures of the ninth century itself. It seems to me this comes from several main forces at work. First, if early Muslim renunciants cultivated anxious fear to keep them at their devotions, this sounds reminiscent of the role that Max Weber proposed for anxie-

107. Michael Cooperson, 'Al-Jāḥiẓ, the Misers, and the Proto-Sunnī Ascetics,' *Al-Jāḥiẓ: A Muslim humanist for our time*, (ed.) Arnim Heinemann, John L. Meloy, Tarif Khalidi & Manfred Kropp, Beiruter Texte und Studien 119 (Würzburg-Beirut, 2009), pp. 197–219.

108. Aḥmad, *Zuhd*, p. 322 *p. 389*.

109. Ibn al-Mubārak, *Zuhd*, no. 124 < N.

110. *Ibid.*, no. 125 < N.

ty about one's salvation among predestinarian Protestants.[111] A major difference is that Weber stressed the innovative Protestant encouragement of activity in a worldly calling, whereas the otherworldly early Muslim renunciants encouraged activity in ritual. (For example, consider the quotation above of Kaᶜb al-Aḥbār, contrasting generous almsgiving with weeping from fear of God. The Kufan Abū ᶜUbaydah ibn ᶜAbd Allāh ibn Masᶜūd [d. after 80AH/699–700CE] is quoted as saying there is less reward for standing in the road, giving a dinar to everyone who comes, than for standing there saying *Allāh akbar*.[112]) Early renunciant literature is distinctly pessimistic about combining worldly activity with the pious life. Abū al-Dardāᵓ is expressly identified as having found trade and worship incompatible.[113] The Basran Muwarriq al-ᶜIjlī (d. after 100/718–719) did trade, but lived on very little and distributed his profits among the poor, saying, "If not for the poor, I would not expose myself to trade."[114] The Kufan Ṭalḥah ibn Muṣarrif (d. 112AH/730–731CE or after) disliked to make a profit off Muslims by selling food.[115] The Syrian ᶜAbd Allāh ibn Zakarīyāᵓ (d. 119AH/717CE) never touched money.[116] [298] Zubayd al-Yāmī of Kufa (d. 122AH/739–740CE or after) likened dirhams to dung.[117] Mālik ibn Dīnār said, "The market increases wealth but takes away religion (*dīn*)."[118] When al-Aᶜmash is quoted as saying, "We used to count the people of the market the worst of us but today we count them the best of us,"[119] he is understood as lamenting the decadence of the age, not praising traders. This had to change when Muslims ceased to be a small élite at the top of society, living off tribute, and became the majority, most of them necessarily working for a living. Extreme forms of self-mortification such as sleeping only two or three hours a night and living on garbage heaps made sense if exaggerated fear of the Last Judgement was to be the governing emotion, but as they became harder to practise, so also it made less sense to cultivate exaggerated fear. Sufism, which took off in the later ninth century, is famously compatible with practising a trade. (Possibly, exaggerated fear of God and

111. Max Weber, *The Protestant Ethic and the Spirit of Capitalism*, trans. Talcott Parsons, Unwin University Books 19 (London, 1930).

112. Aḥmad, *Zuhd*, p. 393 *p. 470* (< ᶜAl.). Sim. attrib. to the Damascene Abū al-Dardāᵓ, *ibid.*, p. 137 *p. 170*; somewhat less sim. attrib. to the Khurasani Abū Barzah al-Aslamī (d. after 65/684–5), *ibid.*, p. 187 *p. 233* (< ᶜAl.).

113. Ibn Saᶜd, *Biographien*, VII/2, p. 117 VII, pp. 391–392; Ibn Abī Shaybah, *Muṣannaf*, *zuhd* 12, *kalām Abī al-Dardāᵓ*, XII, p. 226; Aḥmad, *Zuhd*, p. 138 *p. 172*; Hannād, *Zuhd*, II, p. 353.

114. Two reports, Aḥmad, *Zuhd*, p. 314 *p. 381* (< ᶜAl.). His fellow Basran Ḥassān ibn Abī Sinān (*fl.* earlier 2nd/8th cent.) likewise traded for the sake of the poor: Abū Nuᶜaym, *Ḥilyah*, III, pp. 115–116. Cf. Eph. 4:28, calling for the repentant thief to work in order to be able to give to the poor.

115. Aḥmad, *Zuhd*, p. 365 *p. 438* (< ᶜAl.). Similarly, the Damascene Yazīd ibn Maysarah (*fl.* earlier 2nd/8th cent.), according to Abū Nuᶜaym, *Ḥilyah*, V, p. 235, quoting a lost sec. of Aḥmad, *Zuhd*.

116. Abū Nuᶜaym, *Ḥilyah*, V, p. 151.

117. Abū Nuᶜaym, *Ḥilyah*, V, p. 31.

118. *Ibid.*, II, p. 385.

119. *Ibid.*, V, p. 50.

extreme self-mortification also became less attractive as expectations of imminent apocalypse diminished.)

Second is the theological struggle between the Sunni party and their adversaries. The controversy over *al-istithnā*ʾ, meaning whether it was righteous to say "I am a believer, God willing," was about the acceptability of fear for one's salvation. The Ḥanābilah scorned the Murjiʾah for their complacency, presuming to be as faithful as the angels and the prophets.[120] According to Aḥmad ibn Ḥanbal, "One says "I am a believer, God willing" out of fear and precaution (*makhāfatan wa-iḥtiyāṭan*)," whereas refusing to say it is a sign of self-satisfaction (*taʿajjub*).[121] On the other hand, against the Khawārij and Shiʿah, they believed in the *jamāʿah*, the necessity of cleaving to the community. This seemed to entail not doubting the faith of ordinary Muslims. Sufyān al-Thawrī is quoted as summarizing their doctrine: "In our view, the people are believers when it comes to rulings and inheritances. We hope they really are that without knowing our status in God's view."[122] Against the Khawārij in particular, they refused to call anyone an unbeliever on account of a sin (except for the sin of refusing to perform the ritual prayer).[123] Against the Murjiʾah, then, they found themselves denying that any doubt was implied in saying "I am a believer, God willing." For example, Sufyān ibn ʿUyaynah (d. 198/814) is quoted as explaining that if someone asks him whether he is a believer, he answers, "I do not doubt my faith. Your asking me is an innovation. I do not know what I am in the view of God, whether happy (saved)—whether my work is accepted—, or otherwise."[124] Sufyān ibn ʿUyaynah was also a major advocate of moderate austerity as opposed to severe. If it had become necessary to profess certainty in one's own faith, it had to have become difficult to maintain the radical uncertainty expressed in wishing one had never been, deathbed tears, and so on. In time, Sunnis united around the tenet that [299] all Muslims would be saved, although possibly having to undergo some torment before the Last Judgement.[125]

Thirdly, there also arose across the ninth century a new, mystical piety. The ascetical mood characteristically swings between hope and fear, confidence and anxiety. Accordingly, our early literature of renunciation includes expressions of despair, such as wishing one were a tree cut down, alongside assurances of God's willingness to overlook sins.

---

120. Al-Khallāl, *al-Sunnah*, ed. Abū ʿĀṣim al-Ḥasan ibn ʿAbbās ibn Quṭb, 2 vols. (Cairo, 1428/2007), I, pp. 480, 482; Ibn Abī Yaʿlá, *Ṭabaqāt al-ḥanābilah*, ed. Muḥammad Ḥāmid al-Fiqī, 2 vols. (Cairo, 1371/1952), I, p. 25 (Creed I).

121. Khallāl, *Sunnah*, I, p. 475.

122. ʿAbd Allāh ibn Aḥmad, *al-Sunnah* (Mecca, 1349), p. 73 = (ed.) Abū Hājir Muḥammad al-Saʿīd ibn Basyūnī Zaghlūl (Beirut, 1414/1994), p. 83—references to this edn. henceforth in *italic*.

123. Ibn Abī Yaʿlá, *Ṭabaqāt*, I, pp. 27, 130–1, 246, 294, 311–12, 344 (Creeds I-VI).

124. ʿAbd Allāh, *Sunnah*, p. 85 *p. 95*; *v.* also Khallāl, *Sunnah*, I, p. 478.

125. *V.* Patricia Crone and Fritz Zimmermann, *The Epistle of Sālim ibn Dhakwān*, Oxford Oriental Monographs (Oxford, 2001), pp. 231–236, which mostly supersedes W. Montgomery Watt, *The Formative Period of Islamic Thought* (Edinburgh, 1973), pp. 136–143.

Mystics are characteristically optimistic. Accordingly, although Sufi literature refers to fear, it looks different from fear in the earlier, ascetical, renunciant literature. For example, the Baghdadi Sufi al-Nūrī (d. 295AH/907–908CE) declaimed at the end of a poem, "My weeping is from fear that I should not see You," very different from the fear of condemnation or just divine awesomeness reported of earlier figures.[126] Al-Ḥakīm al-Tirmidhī (d. *ca.* 295/907–908?), on being asked whether those to whom God spoke (*al-muḥaddathūn*) need fear a bad end, said, "Fear (*khawf*), terror (*hawl*), and anxiety (*qalaq*) are like stray thoughts (*khaṭarāt*). They pass. God does not like them to roil his bounties."[127] At most, alternating fear and hope appear in Sufi literature as early stages in the Sufi's mystical progress.[128] Sufism may not have dominated Islamic piety until the twelfth century, but it was clearly on the ascendant from the tenth century.

Conclusions

The cultivation of anxious fear seems to have characterized the piety of all major centres. Inasmuch as this commonality suggests early diffusion from one point of origin, it confirms that renunciant piety is relatively old by comparison with Islamic legal culture, in which many disagreements have a clear regional character; for example, Kufa against Basra, Iraq against Medina. (Grammar and the qurʾanic readings are two other disciplines where the tradition itself makes out strong regional patterns.) Some of the compilers of our early collections of renunciant sayings collected more material in their home towns than elsewhere, of which Hannād ibn al-Sarī of Kufa is the extreme example. However, I am not aware of a book that expressly classifies renunciant sayings by region before Abū Nuʿaym, *Ḥilyat al-awliyāʾ*, which devotes roughly equal space to all major regions one after another. At about the same time, Khargūshī, *Tahdhīb al-asrār* expressly contrasts Sufi practice in Iraq with Malāmati practice in Khurasan. Abū Nuʿaym may have got the idea of organizing renunciant sayings by region from the Sufis, although there are also sufficient earlier precedents in hadith literature. Significantly, he does not take over from Khargūshī the idea of identifying characteristic differences of doctrine and practice in different regions.

The attraction of anxious fear seems to have been its power to keep renunciants to their devotions, more generally to subordinating their worldly interests to their salva-

126. Al-Kharkūshī, *K. Tahdhīb al-asrār*, (ed.) Bassām Muḥammad Bārūd (Abu Dhabi, 1999), p. 502 = (ed.) Sayyid Muḥammad ʿAlī (Beirut, 1427AH/2006CE), p. 461.

127. Al-Sulamī, *Kitāb Ṭabaqāt al-ṣūfiyya*, ed. Johannes Pedersen (Leiden, 1960), p. 215.

128. For much more on fear and hope in classical Sufi thought, *v.* Sara Sviri, 'Between fear and hope: on the coincidence of opposites in Islamic mysticism,' *Jerusalem studies in Arabic and Islam*, no. 9 (1987), pp. 316–349; also Franz Rosenthal, *"Sweeter than hope": Complaint and Hope in Medieval Islam* (Leiden, 1983), pp. 141–147.

tion in the [300] Afterlife. The argument here is not that abject fear of God is a feature of original, qur'anic Islam, from which more confident pieties are a deviation. It is the argument here to see that the deliberate cultivation of anxious fear was one historical response to the challenge of the Qur'an, for a time rather the prevailing one. It ceased to prevail as the subordination of worldly interests became impractical for most Muslims, as theological polemic forced the nascent Sunni party to affirm their confidence in the salvation of all Muslims, and as optimistic Sufi piety eclipsed pessimistic renunciant. In Gert H. Mueller's terminology, the prevailing Islamic piety moved in the ninth century from the ascetical pole towards the mystical. In John B. Carman's, perhaps, the polarity of majesty and meekness, justice and mercy shifted for Muslims from coinciding with their experiences of divinity in present and (expected) future to being equally present, equally to be the objects of contemplation for believers now.[129] There seems little doubt that Islamic thought came to be more subtle and to accommodate a wider range of religious temperaments. But I find something attractive about the way these pious figures of the early eighth century determinedly resisted temptations to complacency—temptations perhaps underestimated by too many later figures.

129. Mueller, 'Asceticism and mysticism,' with appendices summarising earlier dichotomies by Nietzsche, Otto, Tillich, & al.; John B. Carman, *Majesty and Meekness: A Comparative Study of Contrast and Harmony in the Concept of God* (Grand Rapids, 1994).

11
RENUNCIATION (*ZUHD*) IN THE EARLY SHIʿI TRADITION

Both the Sunni and Shiʿi parties will tend to see themselves as coherent bodies from the time of the First Civil War (35–40/656–661). Actually, the people who called themselves *ahl al-sunna wa-'l-jamāʿa* were one party among many till the later 9th century. Indeed, as Marshall Hodgson has observed, the term *sunnī* continued to have multiple applications (opposition to Shiʿism, *kalām* and Sufism) long after it became the majority party in the later 9th century, each of these multiple applications a vestige of its time as a minority party before then.[1] Shiʿism, on the other hand, had a natural principle of self-identification according to which Imam any group supported. Here as well, though, lines were much blurred compared with later; for example, consider the ʿAbbāsids' various tacks, first supporting ʿAbd Allāh b. Muʿāwiya on the Zaydī principle that the proper ruler was whichever member of the House was militarily successful, then themselves on the same principle, later still invoking rather the Rāfiḍī principle of *naṣṣ* designation.[2]

1. Marshall G. S. Hodgson, *The Venture of Islam* (Chicago, 1973), vol. 1, p. 278fn. The formation of Sunnism across the 9th century still awaits a specialist monograph, but see, provisionally, John B. Henderson, *The Construction of Orthodoxy and Heresy: Neo-Confucian, Islamic, Jewish, and Early Christian Patterns* (Albany, NY, 1998), esp. p. 53 on the chronology of Sunnism.

2. See Patricia Crone, 'On the Meaning of the ʿAbbasid Call to *al-Riḍā*,' in C. E. Bosworth, et al., ed., *The Islamic World: From Classical to Modern Times. Essays in Honor of Bernard Lewis* (Princeton, 1989), pp. 95–111, and Claude Cahen, 'Points de vue sur la révolution ʿAbbāside,' *Revue Historique*, 230 (1963), pp. 295–338.

Originally published in *The Study of Shiʿi Islam: History, Theology and Law*. Edited by Farhad Daftary and Gurdofarid Miskinzoda. The Institute of Ismaili Studies Shi'i Heritage Series 2 (London: I. B. Tauris, 2014), 271–94.

From the 11th century AD, Sunni-Shiʿi interaction takes the familiar form of the Sunni majority ignoring the Shiʿi minority while the minority pays wary attention to the majority.[3] Again, however, there was much blurring of lines before then. The depth of support for the House of the Prophet forced mature Sunnism to recognise ʿAlī as the fourth caliph and fourth best Companion, an impressive list of Sunni heroes were [272] remembered as preferring ʿAlī to ʿUthmān, and Sunni *rijāl* criticism did not rely on a single category of 'Shiʿi' but distinguished between *tashayyuʿ*, which had to be overlooked, and *rafḍ*, which usually rendered someone's testimony unacceptable.[4] Not only is the 9th century split between traditionalists and semi-rationalists observable within both Sunni and Shiʿi camps, it appears to be continuous with 10th-century Ḥanbali-Shiʿi strife, at least in Baghdad.[5]

The present study is concerned with the early development of Islamic piety, particularly renunciation (*zuhd*).[6] In the later 9th century, this issued into classical Sufism, which the Shiʿis were slow to take up.[7] The traditional explanation has been that Shiʿis were reluctant to recognise the Sufi master as a charismatic figure for fear that he would rival the Imam. That is why the present volume has sections for Law, Qurʾan, and *Ḥadīth* but not Sufism, as a survey of Sunni Islam surely would. The present study will mainly address not Shiʿi attitudes toward classical Sufism, rather toward the renunciation that went before. My principal finding is that this also is an area where lines were blurred. There is little to distinguish professed Shiʿi ideas of renunciation from early Sunni ideas.

3. For example, Sunni views are included in al-Ṭūsī Shaykh al-Ṭāʾifa (d. 460/1067?), *al-Khilāf*, ed. ʿAlī al-Khurāsānī, et al. (Qumm, 1416–1421/1995–2000), but Shiʿi views are not in, among others, al-Qaffāl al-Shāshī (d. 507/1114), *Ḥilyat al-ʿulamāʾ fī maʿrifat madhāhib al-fuqahāʾ*, ed. Yāsīn Aḥmad Ibrāhīm Darādaka (Amman, 1988).

4. On ʿAlī as fourth best, see Christopher Melchert, *Ahmad ibn Hanbal* (Oxford, 2006), pp. 94–98. Ibn Qutayba provides a long list of Sunni heroes remembered as Shiʿa (i.e., preferring ʿAlī to ʿUthmān): *al-Maʿārif*, ed. Tharwat ʿUkāsha (6th ed., Cairo, 1992), p. 624. On *rijāl* criticism, see among other studies Liyakatali Takim, 'Evolution in the Biographical Profiles of Two ḥadīth Transmitters,' in L. Clarke, ed., *Shīʿite heritage* (Binghamton, NY, 2001), pp. 285–299. Aḥmad ibn Ḥanbal said that all Kufans had preferred ʿAlī to ʿUthmān except two: Ṭalḥa ibn Muṣarrif (d. 112/730–731?) and ʿAbd Allāh ibn Idrīs (d. 192/807–808): Aḥmad, *Kitāb al-ʿilal wa-maʿrifat al-rijāl*, ed. Waṣī Allāh ibn Muḥammad ʿAbbās (Beirut, 1988), vol. 2, p. 535; *Kitāb al-jāmiʿ fī'l-ʿilal wa-maʿrifat al-rijāl*, ed. Muḥammad Ḥusām Bayḍūn (Beirut, 1410/1990), vol. 2, p. 47 (references to the latter ed. henceforth in *italic*). Kufans comprise a little more than two-thirds of the names on Ibn Qutayba's list.

5. Christopher Melchert, 'The Imāmīs between Rationalism and Traditionalism,' in Clarke, ed., *Shīʿite heritage*, pp. 273–283.

6. I prefer 'renunciation,' proposed by Michael Cooperson, to the more conventional 'asceticism' because I consider it useful to maintain a consistent distinction between *asceticism* and *mysticism*, as sketched in Christopher Melchert, 'The Transition from Asceticism to Mysticism at the Middle of the Ninth Century C.E.,' *SI*, 83 (1996), pp. 51–70 [*HPL 9]. Actually, it is Arabic *ijtihād* that corresponds most closely to Greek *askēsis*, while Arabic *zuhd* corresponds most closely to Greek *apatheia*.

7. For an up-to-date historical survey, see Ahmet T. Karamustafa, *Sufism* (Edinburgh, 2007).

It is only with the Sufi era in Sunnism, from the late 9th century forward, that Sunni and Shiʿi ideas about piety appear to significantly diverge.

Sources

My main source on the Shiʿi side is al-Kulaynī (d. 329/941?), *al-Kāfī*, the first large Twelver collection of *ḥadīth*, secondarily al-Qāḍī al-Nuʿmān (d. 363/974), *Daʿāʾim* [273] *al-islām*, the principal handbook of Ismaili law.[8] My main sources on the Sunni side are Ibn al-Mubārak (d. 181/797), *al-Zuhd*, in the recension of al-Ḥasan b. al-Ḥusayn (d. 246/860–861); Ibn Abī Shayba (d. 235/849), *al-Muṣannaf*, in the recension of Baqī b. Makhlad (d. 276/889) but without additions from him; Aḥmad b. Ḥanbal (d. 241/855), *al-Zuhd*, in the recension of his son ʿAbd Allāh; and Abū Nuʿaym al-Iṣbahānī (d. 430/1038), *Ḥilyat al-awliyāʾ*. The first three obviously predate my main Shiʿi sources by one to three generations. The last is from a century later. However, Abū Nuʿaym always names his sources and frequently quotes these earlier collectors, along with a few others such as Wakīʿ b. al-Jarrāḥ, which quotations can be checked and continually prove accurate. Therefore, I am inclined to consider Abū Nuʿaym a faithful transmitter of earlier knowledge, as reliable a guide to renunciation as it was remembered in the 9th century as the 9th-century collectors themselves whose works are extant. How reliably he and our 9th-century sources represent renunciation as it was thought of and practised in the early 8th century and before is of course a separate question.

It is regrettable that we have so little Shiʿi material from the 9th century. I have consulted two collections specifically of renunciant sayings, al-Ḥusayn b. Saʿīd al-Ahwāzī (fl. earlier 3rd/9th century), *al-Muʾmin*, and Muḥammad b. Hammām al-Iskāfī (d. 336/947–948), *al-Tamḥīṣ*.[9] Both are short and specialised (Ahwāzī offers encouragements of fraternal love, Ibn Hammām disparagements of this world) and will not be further cited. They do both confirm that the Twelver tradition attributed renunciant sayings especially to Jaʿfar al-Ṣādiq. From Kāmil Muṣṭafā al-Shaybī we have two modern studies with very interesting titles: *al-Fikr al-shīʿī wa'l-nazaʿāt al-ṣūfiyya* ('Shiʿi thought and Sufi tendencies') and *al-Ṣila bayna al-taṣawwuf wa'l-tashayyuʿ* ('the relation between Sufism and Shiʿism').[10] For the most part, I have found him to offer interesting although often doubtful charac-

8. Citation of this source may justify inclusion of this chapter in the part on Law. Furthermore, juridical handbooks such as the *Daʿāʾim* are concerned mainly with identifying actions as required, recommended, indifferent, discouraged, or forbidden. Inasmuch as renunciant literature is about identifying the recommended and discouraged, it also is juridical.

9. Al-Ahwāzī, *al-Muʾmin* (Qum, 1404/1984) and Ibn Hammām, *al-Tamḥīṣ* (Qum, n.d.).

10. Kāmil Muṣṭafā al-Shaybī, *al-Fikr al-shīʿī wa'l-nazaʿāt al-ṣūfiyya* (Baghdad, 1386/1966); *al-Ṣila bayna al-taṣawwuf wa'l-tashayyuʿ* (Baghdad, 1382–1383/1963–1964).

terizations of Sufism and its antecedents (for example, valiant attempts to identify styles of renunciation peculiar to Syria, Kūfa and Baṣra) but little on early Shiʿism.

The Community Defined by Piety

The early Shīʿa certainly professed themselves to be interested in piety. They were defined, of course, by their recognising the correct Imam. 'He who dies without knowing the Imam of his time dies a Jāhili death' was a leading principle of theirs, although [274] one that Sunni Muslims might also accept.[11] But we are also told that Muḥammad al-Bāqir declared, 'Our party (*shīʿa*) is nothing but whoever obeys God (mighty and glorious is He).'[12] More elaborately, he is given as explaining:[13]

> Does it suffice for one who adheres to *tashayyuʿ* that he speak of his love for the people of the house? By God, our party is nothing but whoever fears God and obeys him. They are known by humility, submissiveness, honesty, much recollecting God, fasting, prayer, filial piety, keeping faith with poor neighbours and the indigent, debt-ridden, and orphans, truthful speech, reciting the Qurʾan, and speaking only good of people ... Whoever is obedient to God is our friend and whoever is rebellious toward God is our enemy.

This is actually going a little further than definitions of Sunnism. Before Sunni and Shiʿi were distinct, 'the Muslims' and 'the pious' might be identified, as in a saying ascribed to al-Ḥasan al-Baṣrī (d. 110/728): 'The good has gone and the bad remains. Whoever is left of the Muslims is dejected.'[14] Even more often, 'believer' is equated with 'pious'; for example, when the Companion Ibn Masʿūd (d. 32/652–653?) is quoted as saying, 'The believer (*muʾmin*) sees his sins as if he were sitting at the foot of a mountain, fearing that it should fall over onto him, whereas the reprobate (*fājir*) thinks his sins are like a fly that

---

11. Hodgson, *Venture*, vol. 2, p. 348. See al-Kulaynī, *al-Kāfī, kitāb al-rawḍa*, ed. ʿAlī Akbar al-Ghaffārī, corr. Muḥammad al-Ākhūndī (Tehran, 1389–1391), 8:146, and Aḥmad ibn Ḥanbal, *Musnad imām al-muḥaddithīn* (Cairo, 1313/1895), vol. 4, p. 96; *Musnad al-imām*, ed. Shuʿayb al-Arnaʾūṭ, et al. (Beirut, 1413–1421/1993–2001), vol. 28, pp. 88–89 (references to the latter ed. henceforth in *italic*). Admittedly, Sunni collections usually stress versions that warn 'whoever dies apart from the *jamāʿa* dies a Jāhilī death'; e.g. Aḥmad, *Musnad*, vol. 1, pp. 275, 297, vol. 2, p. 70, vol. 3, pp. 445–446, vol. 5, p. 387 *vol. 4, pp. 290–291, vol. 9, pp. 284–286, vol. 24, pp. 452, 459–463, vol. 38, pp. 319–320, 324–325.* Aḥmad himself glossed 'the Imam of his time' as 'he of whom all the Muslims say "This is an Imam"': Ibn Hāniʾ, *Masāʾil al-imām Aḥmad b. Ḥanbal*, ed. Zuhayr al-Shāwīsh (Beirut, 1400), vol. 2, p. 185.

12. Al-Kulaynī, *Kāfī, kitāb al-īmān wa'l-kufr, bāb al-ṭāʿa wa'l-taqwā* , vol. 2, p. 73.

13. Ibid., vol. 2, pp. 74–5.

14. Aḥmad, *al-Zuhd*, ed. ʿAbd al-Raḥmān ibn Qāsim (Mecca, 1357), p. 258 (= repr. Beirut, 1403/1983), p. *316* (references to the latter ed. henceforth in *italic*).

passes by his nose.'[15] But note also express reluctance to identify Sunnism with a renunciant lifestyle, also anxiety over heretical renunciants; for example, in another saying attributed to Ibn Masʿūd: 'Moderate exertion (*iqtiṣād*) in the Sunna is better than strenuous exertion (*ijtihād*) in innovation.'[16] [275] Sunnism crystallised in the late 8th century and across the 9th, by which time the Muslims were no longer a tiny minority at the top of society living off tribute, hence by which time no majoritarian party could demand a style of life that would interfere with making a living or, indeed, that would disqualify ordinary persons. On this point, Al-Kulaynī apparently preserves the outlook of an earlier generation of Muslims better than his Sunni contemporaries. He could afford to when Shiʿism remained safely minoritarian.

Fear of God

Muḥammad al-Bāqir begins his definition of the righteous Shīʿa by describing them as those who fear God. According to Jaʿfar al-Ṣādiq, 'God spoke to Moses saying, "My servants have not approached me by anything that I like better than three characters."' Moses said, 'O my lord, what are they?' He said, 'Moses, renunciation of the world, precaution regarding sins, and weeping from fear (*khashya*) of Me.'[17] The literary form is certainly familiar. As for dialogue between God and an early prophet, I might mention a typical report from Abū Fazāra Rāshid b. Kaysān, a late Kūfan Follower: 'I have heard that Dāwūd asked his Lord, "My Lord, indicate to me a work that will bring me into Paradise." He said, "Prefer my fancy (*hawā*) to yours."'[18] As for the number three, Muḥammad b. Kaʿb al-Quraẓī (Medinese, also Kūfa, d. 120/737–738 or before) said, 'If God wishes well for a servant, he puts three characters in him: discernment in the faith, renunciation of the world, and sightedness concerning his faults.'[19] There are many Sunni descriptions of weeping from fear of God. Sometimes the Prophet, sometimes Abū Hurayra (d. 58/677–

---

15. Ibn al-Mubārak, *al-Zuhd wa'l-raqāʾiq*, ed. Ḥabīb al-Raḥmān al-Aʿẓamī (Malegaon, 1386; repr. with different pagination Beirut, 1419/1998), no. 69; also in Bukhārī, *al-Jāmiʿ al-ṣaḥīḥ*, *Kitāb al-daʿawāt* 4, *bāb al-tawba*, no. 6308; Ibn Masʿūd < Prophet in Aḥmad, *Musnad*, vol. 1, p. 383 *vol. 6, pp. 131–132*.

16. Aḥmad, *Zuhd*, p. 159 *198*. *Iqtiṣād* means literally sticking to the middle of the road. A similar statement is attributed to another Companion, Ubayy ibn Kaʿb (d. 32/652–653?), in Ibn al-Mubārak, *Zuhd*, no. 8 among additions from Nuʿaym ibn Ḥammād, also Abū Nuʿaym, *Ḥilyat al-awliyāʾ* (Cairo, 1352–1357/1932–1938), vol. 1, p. 252. An Ismaili source admittedly attributes a similar statement to Jaʿfar al-Ṣādiq: 'A little work in the *sunna* is better than much work in innovation.' See al-Qāḍī al-Nuʿmān, *Daʿāʾim al-islām*, *kitāb al-ṣalāt* 24, *dhikr ṣalāt al-sunna wa'l-nāfila*, ed. Asaf Ali Asghar Fyzee (Cairo, 1379–1383/1960–1963, repr. Damascus, n.d.), vol. 1, 216.

17. Al-Kulaynī, *Kāfī*, *kitāb al-duʿāʾ*, *bāb al-bukāʾ*, vol. 2, pp. 482–483.

18. Al-Khuttalī, *Kitāb al-maḥabba lillāh*, in Bernd Radtke, ed., *Materialien zur alten islamischen Frömmigkeit* (Leiden, 2009), pp. 108–109; sim., Ibn Qutayba, *ʿUyūn al-akhbār* (Cairo, 1343–1349/1925–1930), vol. 2, p. 263.

19. Ibn al-Mubārak, *Zuhd*, no. 282.

678?), is quoted as saying, 'He will not enter the Fire who weeps from fear (*khashya*) of God, until the milk returns into the teat.'[20] ʿAbd Allāh b. ʿAmr (d. Mecca, 63/683?), seen weeping, said, 'Do you wonder that I should weep from fear of God? If you are not weeping, pretend to weep, until [276] one of you says *ayh, ayh*. This moon weeps from fear of God (be he exalted).'[21] Many more such quotations could be cited in addition to these.

Both Shiʿi and Sunni literatures are concerned with balancing hope and fear. Al-Kulaynī quotes Jaʿfar al-Ṣādiq as saying the believer has both hope and fear in his heart. 'If this were weighed, it would not outweigh that, and if that were weighed, it would not outweigh this.'[22] Compare Muṭarrif b. ʿAbd Allāh b. al-Shikhkhīr (Basran, d. 95/713–714): 'If the believer's fear and hope were weighed, neither would outweigh the other.'[23] Similarly, Maṭar b. Ṭahmān (Basran, d. 125/742–743?) is quoted as saying, 'If the believer's fear and hope were weighed in the balance, neither would be found to exceed the other at all.'[24] The Sunni literature provides some sayings in favour of letting fear outweigh hope, more in favour of letting hope outweigh fear, but the predominant sentiment seems to be that hope and fear should be evenly balanced. The wise man Luqmān is quoted as saying to his son, 'Hope in God without feeling safe from His trickery (*makr*). Fear God without despairing of His mercy.' His son said, 'How can I do that, father, when I have only one heart?' Luqmān replied, 'My son, the believer is like one with two hearts, one heart with which to wish and one heart with which to fear.'[25] The Prophet is quoted as saying, 'If the unbeliever knew all that God has of mercy, he would not despair of Paradise, while if the Muslim knew all that God has of torment, he would not feel safe from Hell-fire.'[26]

Weeping, No Laughing

To this day, weeping is a prominent feature of Shiʿi devotions. Jaʿfar al-Ṣādiq is quoted as saying, 'If you are not weeping, pretend to weep.'[27] He is also quoted as approving a specif-

20. From the Prophet: Aḥmad, *Musnad*, vol. 2, p. 505 *vol. 16, pp. 330–331*; Hannād, *Kitāb al-zuhd*, ed. ʿAbd al-Raḥmān b. ʿAbd al-Jabbār al-Faryawāʾī (Kuwait, 1406/1985), vol. 1, p. 268, Tirmidhī, *al-Jāmiʿ al-ṣaḥīḥ*, *kitāb al-zuhd* 8, *bāb mā jāʾa fī faḍl al-bukāʾ min khashyat Allāh*, no. 2311. From Abū Hurayrah: Wakīʿ, *Kitāb al-zuhd*, ed. ʿAbd al-Raḥmān ʿAbd al-Jabbār al-Faryawāʾī (Riyadh, 1415/1994), vol. 1, pp. 249–250; Aḥmad, *Zuhd*, p. 178 *222–223*; al-Nasāʾī, *al-Mujtabā*, *bāb faḍl man ʿamila fī sabīl Allāh ʿalā qadamih*.

21. Ibn Abī Shayba, *al-Muṣannaf*, *kitāb al-zuhd* 92, *mā qālū fī'l-bukāʾ min khashyat Allāh*; ed. Ḥamad ʿAbd Allāh al-Jumʿa and Muḥammad Ibrāhīm al-Luḥaydān (Riyadh, 1425/2004), vol. 12, p. 425.

22. Al-Kulaynī, *Kāfī*, *kitāb al-īmān wa'l-kufr*, *bāb al-khawf wa'l-rajāʾ*, vol. 2, p. 67.

23. Aḥmad, *Zuhd*, pp. 238–239 *293*; Ibn Abī Shayba, *Muṣannaf*, *kitāb al-zuhd* 66, *Muṭarrif b. al-Shikhkhīr*, vol. 12, p. 344.

24. Abū Nuʿaym, *Ḥilya*, vol. 3, p. 76.

25. Ibn al-Mubārak, *Zuhd*, no. 912; Aḥmad, *Zuhd*, pp. 106–107, *132*.

26. Bukhārī, *Ṣaḥīḥ*, *kitāb al-riqāq* 19, *bāb al-rajāʾ wa'l-khawf*, no. 6469.

27. Al-Kulaynī, *Kāfī*, *kitāb al-duʿāʾ*, *bāb al-raghba wa'l-rahba*, vol. 2, p. 483.

ic technique to stimulate weeping. One Isḥāq b. ʿAmmār told him, 'It happens that I pray and wish to weep but it does not come. Often, I have recollected some of my family who have died. Then I soften and weep. Is that permissible?' Jaʿfar answered, 'Yes, remember them, and if you have softening, then weep and pray to your Lord (blessed and exalted is He).'[28] In Sunni literature, the Prophet is quoted as saying, 'Weep. And if you do not weep, pretend to weep (*fa-in lam tabkū* [277] *fa-tabākaw*).'[29] So is Abū Bakr (d. 13/34): 'Weep! And if you are not weeping, pretend to weep.'[30] Another Companion, Abū Mūsā al-Ashʿarī (d. 50/670–671?), is quoted as saying the same with an explanation: 'O people, weep. If you do not weep, pretend to weep. The people of the Fire are weeping tears till they are cut off, then they weep blood such that if boats were sent among them, they would float.'[31]

To the contrary, the Sunni tradition also records doubts about demonstrative weeping. In a book devoted to weeping, Ibn Abī al-Dunyā cites nine examples of disapproval of weeping in public.[32] The Companion Abū Umāma (d. 100/718–719) reproached someone for weeping and praying in prostration (i.e., in the course of the ritual prayer in the mosque): 'If only this were in your house.'[33] Al-Ḥasan al-Baṣrī was notable for looking always sad, but when a man began to weep loudly in his session, he said, 'Satan is now making this one weep.'[34] He warned a man who sobbed at a sermon of his, 'God will surely ask you what you meant by this.'[35] A number of other sayings are directed against de/liberately induced weeping. Ibrāhīm b. ʿAbd Allāh al-Kattānī (fl. early 2nd/8th century) said, 'I have heard that weeping is nine-tenths hypocrisy, one-tenth for God, so if it comes to someone for God once a year, that is a lot.'[36] Shuʿayb al-Jubbāʾī (Yemeni, fl. 1st/8th century?) said, 'When a man's reprobation is complete, he gains control of his eyes so that whenever he wishes to weep, he weeps.'[37] Muḥammad b. Sīrīn (Basran, d. 110/729), on being asked about those who sobbed on hearing the Qurʾan, proposed a test: 'If they were to sit on a wall and the Qurʾan was recited to them from beginning to end, if they fell off,

---

28. Ibid., vol. 2, p. 483.

29. Ibn Māja, *al-Sunan, kitāb al-zuhd* 19, *bāb al-ḥuzn wa'l-bukāʾ*, no. 4196; Abū ʿUbayd, *Faḍāʾil al-Qurʾān*, ed. Marwān al-ʿAṭiyya, Muḥsin Kharāba and Wafāʾ Taqī al-Dīn (Damascus, 1415/1995), p. 135; Hannād, *Zuhd*, vol. 1, p. 270; Aḥmad, *Zuhd*, p. 27, *36*.

30. Ibn al-Mubārak, *Zuhd*, no. 131; Wakīʿ, *Zuhd*, vol. 1, p. 254; Aḥmad, *Zuhd*, p. 108 *135*; Ibn Abī Shayba, *Muṣannaf, kitāb al-zuhd* 92, *mā qālū fi'l-bukāʾ*, vol. 12, p. 424.

31. Aḥmad, *Zuhd*, p. 199 *247*; sim., Abū Nuʿaym, *Ḥilya*, vol. 1, p. 261.

32. Ibn Abī al-Dunyā, *al-Riqqa wa'l-bukāʾ*, ed. Muḥammad Khayr Ramaḍān Yūsuf (Beirut, 1416/1996), pp. 53–54.

33. Ibn al-Mubārak, *Zuhd*, no. 156.

34. Aḥmad, *Zuhd*, p. 274 *334*.

35. Abū Nuʿaym, *Ḥilya*, vol. 6, p. 305, quoting a lost section of Aḥmad, *Zuhd* (< ʿAl. = abbreviation for ʿAbd Allāh).

36. Aḥmad, *Zuhd*, p. 229 *279* (< ʿAl.).

37. Ibn al-Mubārak, *Zuhd*, no. 129; Wakīʿ, *Zuhd*, vol. 2, p. 788.

then they would be as they say.'[38] ʿĪsā b. Zādhān (fl. earlier 2nd/8th century) predicted, 'There will befall the people a time when Satan lives in people's eyes and whoever wishes to weep will weep.'[39] Mālik b. Dīnār (Basran, d. 130/747–748?) said, 'When a slave has reached perfection in debauchery, he gains control of his eyes.'[40] This is explained in an extension attributed to Sufyān al-Thawrī (Kufan, d. 161/777?): 'When a slave has perfected debauchery, he gains control of his eyes so that he weeps with [278] them whenever he wills.'[41] Weeping at the recitation of the Qurʾan is still considered appropriate in Sunni circles today, but weeping is of course much more conspicuous in the course of Shiʿi ceremonies such as visiting tombs.

Unsurprisingly, the early Shiʿi and Sunni traditions are both sceptical of laughter. In the former, Jaʿfar al-Ṣādiq is quoted as saying, 'The believer's laughter is smiling.'[42] There are many Sunni parallels. Abū Sulaymān al-Dārānī (Syrian, d. 215/830–831) said, 'The laughter of the knower (*ʿārif*) is smiling.'[43] Jābir b. Samura is remembered as saying of the Prophet after the dawn prayer, 'They would converse, taking up the matter of the Jāhiliyya. They would laugh while he would smile.'[44] In the Shiʿi tradition, again, Jaʿfar al-Ṣādiq is quoted again as saying, 'Much laughter kills the heart,' also, 'Much laughter dissolves faith as water dissolves salt.'[45] Compare, in the Sunni tradition, the saying of the Prophet: 'Do not laugh much, for much laughter kills the heart.'[46] There are many other discouragements of laughing in the Sunni tradition similar to Jaʿfar's discouragement in

38. Abū Nuʿaym, *Ḥilya*, vol. 2, p. 265.

39. Aḥmad, *Zuhd*, p. 275 *335*.

40. Ibid., pp. 322–323 *390*.

41. Abū Nuʿaym, *Ḥilya*, vol. 7, p. 72.

42. Al-Kulaynī, *Kāfī*, *kitāb al-ʿishra*, *bāb al-duʿāba wa'l-ḍaḥik*, vol. 2, p. 664.

43. Abū Nuʿaym, *Ḥilya*, vol. 9, p. 267.

44. Muslim, *Ṣaḥīḥ*, *kitāb al-masājid* 52, *bāb faḍl al-julūs fī muṣallāh*, no. 1525, Kufan *isnād*; ibid., *kitāb al-faḍāʾil* 17, *bāb tabassumuh*, no. 2322; Aḥmad, *Musnad*, vol. 5, p. 91 *vol. 34, p. 431*. G. H. A. Juynboll ascribes this to Simāk ibn Ḥarb (Kufan, d. 123/740–41): Juynboll, *Encyclopedia of Canonical Ḥadīth* (Leiden, 2007), p. 566. Jābir b. Samura is also quoted as describing the Prophet so: 'He would be long silent and laugh little. His companions would mention before him things of poetry and their affairs. They would laugh, while he would often smile'; Tirmidhī, *Jāmiʿ*, *al-adab* 70, *bāb mā jāʾa fī inshāʾ al-shiʿr*, no. 2850; Abū Dāwūd al-Ṭayālisī, *Musnad Abī Dāwūd al-Ṭayālisī* (Hyderabad, 1321, repr. Beirut, n.d.), no. 771; Aḥmad, *Musnad*, vol. 5, p. 86 *vol. 34, pp. 405–406*. And again from Jābir b. Samura: 'The Messenger of God's thighs were slender. He did not laugh, only smile'; Tirmidhī, *Jāmiʿ*, *al-zuhd* 12, *bāb qawl Ibn Samura*, no. 3645; Aḥmad, *Musnad*, vol. 5, pp. 97, 105 *vol. 34, pp. 466–467, 511*. See also Wakīʿ, *Zuhd*, vol. 1, pp. 266–267.

45. Al-Kulaynī, *Kāfī*, *kitāb al-ʿishra*, *bāb al-duʿāba wa'l-ḍaḥik*, vol. 2, p. 664.

46. Hannād, *Zuhd*, vol. 2, pp. 501, 553 (shortened version of same), Basran *isnād*; Tirmidhī, *Jāmiʿ*, *kitāb al-zuhd* 2, *man ittaqā al-maḥārim*, no. 2305, Basran *isnād*, different from Hannād's; Ibn Māja, *Sunan*, *kitāb al-zuhd* 19, *bāb al-ḥuzn wa'l-bukāʾ*, no. 4193, Medinese *isnād*, also *Kitāb al-zuhd* 24, *bāb al-waraʿ wa'l-taqwā*, no. 4217; Aḥmad, *Musnad*, vol. 2, p. 310 *vol. 13, pp. 458–459* with *isnād* like Tirmidhī's; Abū Nuʿaym, *Ḥilya*, vol. 1, p. 167.

the Shiʿi. Al-Ḥasan al-Baṣrī said, 'Much laughter kills the heart.'[47] Sufyān al-Thawrī said, 'Do not overeat, for it hardens the heart; suppress laughter and do not laugh much, for it kills hearts.'[48]

Al-Kulaynī balances sayings against laughter with encouragements of moderate laughing. Jaʿfar al-Ṣādiq asked Yūnus al-Shaybānī how their jesting (*mudāʿabah*) was. He said, 'Little.' Jaʿfar said, 'Do not do it. Jesting is part of goodnaturedness (*ḥusn al-khuluq*). It conveys pleasure to your brother. The Messenger of God . . . would jest with a man he wished to please.'[49] Muḥammad al-Jawād said, 'God (mighty and [279] glorious is He) likes jesting in a group without indecency (*rafath*).'[50] According to Mūsā al-Kāẓim, 'Yaḥyā b. Zakarīyāʾ would weep but not laugh, while ʿĪsā b. Maryam would laugh and weep.' The narrator's comment is preserved: 'It was as if what ʿĪsā did was better than what Yaḥyā did.'[51] Similarly in the Sunni tradition is to be found praise of laughter over some things. Al-Ḥasan quoted the Prophet as saying,[52]

> There are two kinds of laughter, laughter that God loves and laughter that God despises. As for the laughter that God loves, it is that a man bare his teeth in the face of his brother on first recognising him, from longing to see him. As for the laughter that God despises, it is that a man speak harshly or meaninglessly, to laugh or to provoke laughter.

Likewise, there is Sunni praise for alternate laughing and weeping. Muḥammad b. Sīrīn was heard weeping by night, laughing by day.[53] He would laugh over poetry he recited, then blanch on hearing *ḥadīth* about the Sunna.[54] He often laughed until tears ran.[55] Ibn al-Mubārak reports a Companion's observation, 'I never saw anyone who smiled more than the Messenger of God,' although also observations that the Prophet never laughed, only smiled.[56] Sometimes, to be sure, the emphasis is on secret weeping, presumptively sincere. Muʿāwiya b. Qurra (Basran, d. 113/731–732) said, 'Who will lead me to one who weeps by night but smiles by day?'[57] Muḥammad b. Wāsiʿ (Basran, d. 123/740–741) would weep by night, then grin in his friends's faces in the morning.[58]

---

47. Abū Nuʿaym, *Ḥilya*, vol. 2, p. 152.
48. Ibid., vol. 7, p. 36.
49. Al-Kulaynī, *Kāfī, kitāb al-ʿishra, bāb al-duʿāba wa'l-ḍaḥik*, vol. 2, p. 663.
50. Ibid.
51. Ibid., vol. 2, p. 665.
52. Hannād, *Zuhd*, vol. 2, p. 552.
53. Abū Nuʿaym, *Ḥilya*, vol. 2, p. 272.
54. Ibid., vol. 2, p. 274, quoting a lost § of Aḥmad, *Zuhd* (< ʿAl.).
55. Abū Nuʿaym, *Ḥilya*, vol. 2, p. 274.
56. Ibn al-Mubārak, *Zuhd*, nos. 145, 146, 148.
57. Abū Nuʿaym, *Ḥilya*, vol. 2, p. 299.
58. Ibn Abī al-Dunyā, *Riqqa*, p. 70.

Recollection

The devotional exercises that Muḥammad al-Bāqir describes begin with 'much recollecting God, fasting, prayer.' 'Recollection' (*dhikr*), so regularly appears in early renunciant literature as something audible that it seems this ought to be taken as its primary meaning. Al-Kulaynī quotes Jaʿfar al-Ṣādiq as saying, 'Lightning will not strike one who recollects (*al-dhākir*).' On being asked, 'What is a *dhākir*?,' he said, 'One who recites one-hundred verses.'[59] More often, *dhikr* refers to reciting not the Qurʾan but short phrases. For example, Jaʿfar al-Ṣādiq reports that the Prophet would say [280] *astaghfiru 'llāh* seventy times a day and *atūbu ilā 'llāh* seventy times a day.[60] ʿAlī al-Riḍā said 100 times after the morning prayer and again 100 times after the sunset, 'In the name of God, the Merciful, the Compassionate, there is no power or strength save by God, the High, the Great.' He urged that no one quit sunset prayer till he had said this 100 times.[61] According to Jaʿfar al-Ṣādiq, Fāṭima would say on going to bed *Allāhu akbar* thirty-four times, *al-ḥamdu lillāh* thirty-three times, *subḥāna 'llāh* thirty-three times, then recite the throne verse, the last two chapters of the Qurʾan, and the first and last ten verses of Q.37 (*al-Ṣāffāt*).[62] Jaʿfar quoted the Prophet as saying that 'The one who recollects God among the neglectful (*al-dhākir lillāh, al-ghāfilīn*) is like the one who fights to protect the ones fleeing (*al-muqātil ʿan al-fārrīn*).'[63] It is easy to find Sunni parallels. The Prophet is quoted as saying, 'I ask God's forgiveness and repent to him 100 times a day.'[64] A Kufan Follower, ʿAwn b. ʿAbd Allāh (d. bef. 120/738), is credited with saying, 'The one who recollects God among the neglectful (*al-dhākir Allāh, al-ghāfilīn*) is like the fighter behind the fleers (*al-fārrīn*).'[65] Almost the same statement, 'The one who recollects God among the indifferent is like the fighter behind those who have turned to flee (*al-mudbirīn*),' is also attributed to the Basran Ḥassān b. Abī Sinān (fl. first half 2nd/8th century).[66]

The Shiʿi tradition expects believers to pray in groups, probably repeating verbal formulae. Jaʿfar al-Ṣādiq is quoted as saying,[67]

> There is no group of forty men who meet and pray to God (mighty and glorious is he) concerning a matter save that God will answer them. If they are not forty,

59. Al-Kulaynī, *Kāfī, kitāb al-duʿāʾ, bāb anna al-ṣāʿiqa lā tuṣību dhākiran*, vol. 2, p. 500.
60. Ibid., *bāb al-istighfār*, vol. 2, p. 505.
61. Ibid., *kitāb al-duʿāʾ, bāb al-qawl ʿinda al-iṣbāḥ wa-al-imsāʾ*, vol. 2, pp. 531–532.
62. Ibid., *Kāfī, bāb al-duʿāʾ ʿinda al-nawm*, vol. 2, p. 536.
63. Ibid., *Kāfī, kitāb al-duʿāʾ, bāb dhikr Allāh . . . fi'l-ghāfilīn*, vol. 2, p. 502. A slightly different version on the same page is attributed to Jaʿfar.
64. Ibn Abī Shayba, *Muṣannaf, Kitāb al-duʿāʾ* 49, *mā dhukira fi'l-istighfār*, vol. 10, p. 87.
65. Ibn al-Mubārak, *Zuhd*, no. 357; Abū Nuʿaym, *Ḥilya*, vol. 4, p. 241, quoting a lost section of Aḥmad, *Zuhd*; Ibn Abī Shayba, *Muṣannaf, kitāb al-zuhd* 54, *kalām ʿAwn b. ʿAl.*, 12, p. 307.
66. Aḥmad, *Zuhd*, p. 328 *396*.
67. Al-Kulaynī, *Kāfī, kitāb al-duʿāʾ, bāb al-ijtimāʿ*, vol. 2, p. 487.

> then four will not pray to God ten times (mighty and glorious is he) save that God will answer them. If they are not four, then one will not pray to God forty times save that God the mighty and all-powerful will answer him.

He foresees prayer by a designated leader, with his followers to respond by 'Amen' at the end: 'The one who prays and the one who says *āmīn* share in the reward.'[68]

We have abundant evidence from the Sunni tradition of a similar expectation of group prayer. The Prophet is supposed to have said, 'There is no group who have met to recollect God, desiring by that nothing but his face, save that a crier from Heaven cries "Arise forgiven: your bad characters have been replaced by good (*sayyiʾāt*, [281] *ḥasanāt*).'[69] Al-Ḥasan al-Baṣrī related from the Messenger of God, 'When a group gather to recollect God (mighty and glorious is He), God tells his angels, "I have forgiven them, so wrap them with mercy." The angels say, "Our Lord, among them is so-and-so." God says, "They are a group who will not be lost by one sitting with them."'[70] Khulayd al-ʿAṣarī (Basran, fl. early 2nd/8th century) said that the adornment of mosques is men who help one another at recollecting God (*dhikr Allāh*).[71]

At the same time, the Sunni tradition also reports considerable suspicion and disparagement of group chanting. ʿAbd Allāh b. Masʿūd (d. Medina, 32/652–653) reproached someone for sitting in the mosque, having his circle repeat *Allāhu akbar, subḥān Allāh*, and so on, for set numbers of times.[72] People came to al-Rabīʿ b. Khuthaym (Kufan, d. 63/682–683?) 'for you to praise God and for us to praise him with you, and for you to recollect God and for us to recollect him with you.' He told them, 'God be praised — why don't you come to us saying "We have come for you to drink and for us to drink with you and for you to commit adultery and for us to commit adultery with you"?'[73] Aḥmad (d. 241/855) was himself asked whether it was discouraged for a group to meet to pray to God and raise their hands: 'I do not dislike it for brothers so long as they have not met deliberately, unless they are many.' Isḥāq b. Rāhawayh's gloss shows the reason: '"Unless they are many" means that they should not make a habit of it such that they become known for it.'[74] Devotions should be directed toward pleasing God, not the people.

68. Ibid., vol. 2, p. 487.

69. Aḥmad, *Musnad*, vol. 3, p. 142 *vol. 19, p. 437*; Abū Nuʿaym, *Ḥilya*, vol. 3, p. 108. Similar attributed to Sahl b. Ḥanẓala, Companion, by Ibn Abī Shayba, *Muṣannaf, kitāb al-duʿāʾ* 50, *fī thawāb dhikr Allāh*, vol. 10, p. 95; Aḥmad, *Zuhd*, p. 205 *254*.

70. Aḥmad, *Zuhd*, p. 395 *472*.

71. Ibid., p. 237 *291* (< ʿAl.); Abū Nuʿaym, *Ḥilya*, vol. 2, p. 233 (quoting a lost section of Aḥmad, *Zuhd*, < Aḥmad).

72. Aḥmad, *Zuhd*, p. 358 *428–429* (< ʿAl.).

73. Ibid., p. 331 *399* (< ʿAl.).

74. Al-Kawsaj, *Masāʾil al-imām Aḥmad b. Ḥanbal wa-Isḥāq b. Rāhawayh*, ed. Abū al-Ḥusayn Khālid b. Maḥmūd al-Rabāṭ, Wiʾām al-Ḥawshī, and Jumʿa Fatḥī (Riyadh, 1425/2004), vol. 2, p. 598, no. 3499.

The Shiʿi tradition certainly shows concern that devotions be practised for the sake of God alone. Jaʿfar al-Ṣādiq is quoted as saying, 'Our *shīʿa* are those who, when they are alone, recollect God often.'[75] ʿAlī al-Riḍā is quoted as saying, 'The servant's prayer in secret is worth seventy in public.'[76] Compare some sayings in the Sunni tradition. The Prophet himself is quoted as saying, 'The best recollection is the hidden, the best provision that which suffices.'[77] ʿĀ'isha (d. 57/676–677?) is quoted as saying, 'The hidden recollection that the guardian angels do not record is multiplied over other prayers seventy times.'[78] 'The hidden recollection (*al-dhikr al-khafī*)' is evidently the one spoken in such a subdued voice that the guardian angels do not notice. ʿUqba b. [282] ʿAbd al-Ghāfir (Basran, d. 83/702–703) said, 'One prayer (*daʿwa*) in secret is preferable to seventy in public.'[79] Ḥassān b. ʿAṭiyya (Damascene, d. 120s/738–748) said, 'A secret prayer (*duʿāʾ*) is seventy times preferred over a public.'[80] Al-Ḥasan al-Baṣrī is quoted as saying, 'There is no Muslim who resorts to his bed to recollect God save that his bed becomes a mosque for God and he is written in God's view among those who recollect (*al-dhākirīn*).'[81]

In a leading early Ismaili work, I have found a number of recommendations of recollecting not exactly God but death. Here, it seems that 'recollection' must refer to something like 'contemplation' rather than the repetition of phrases. The Prophet is said to have told one of the *anṣār*, 'I commend to you the recollection of death, for it will make you forget the matter of the world.'[82] Likewise, the Prophet commented that 'the one who most recollects death is the readiest for it.'[83] Muḥammad al-Bāqir is quoted as saying, 'Recollect death often, for no man recollects death often without renouncing the world.'[84] There is much talk of contemplating death in Sunni renunciant sources, as well. Al-ʿAlāʾ b. Ziyād (Basran, d. 94/712–713) recommended imagining oneself on the point of death, hence acting in obedience to God.[85] Shumayṭ b. ʿAjlān (Basran, fl. early 2nd/8th century) said, 'Whoever sets up death before his eyes will not care about the narrowness or wideness of the world.'[86] Al-Rabīʿ b. Abī Rāshid (Kufan, fl. early 2nd/8th century) said, 'If the recollection of death departs from me for an hour, it corrupts my heart.'[87]

75. Al-Kulaynī, *Kāfī, kitāb al-duʿāʾ, bāb dhikr Allāh kathīran*, vol. 2, p. 499.
76. Al-Kulaynī, *Kāfī, kitāb al-duʿāʾ, bāb ikhfāʾ al-duʿā*, vol. 2, p. 476.
77. Aḥmad, *Musnad*,vol. 1, pp. 72, 180, 187 *vol. 3, pp. 76, 131–132, 168–169*.
78. Ibn Abī Shayba, *Muṣannaf, kitāb al-duʿāʾ* 94, *fī rafʿ al-ṣawt bi'l-duʿāʾ* 2, vol. 10, p. 143.
79. Aḥmad, *Zuhd*, p. 311 *377*.
80. Abū Nuʿaym, *Ḥilya*, vol. 6, p. 73.
81. Ibid., vol. 6, p. 271.
82. Al-Qāḍī al-Nuʿmān, *Daʿāʾim*, vol. 1, p. 224 = ed. ʿĀrif Tāmir (Beirut, 1416/1995), vol. 1, 264.
83. Ibid., vol. 1, p. 224; ed. Tāmir, vol. 1, p. 264.
84. Ibid., vol. 1, p. 224; ed. Tāmir, vol. 1, p. 264.
85. Aḥmad, *Zuhd*, p. 255 *312*.
86. Abū Nuʿaym, *Ḥilya*, vol. 3, p. 129.
87. Ibn al-Mubārak, *Zuhd*, no. 266; Ibn Abī Shayba, *Muṣannaf, kitāb al-zuhd* 84, *bāb al-Shaʿbī*, vol. 12, p.

'Recollection' in this sense more often goes by the name of *tafakkur*. Jaʿfar al-Ṣādiq says, 'The best worship is prolonged contemplation (*tafakkur*) of God and his power.'[88] Jaʿfar is told, and evidently approves, contemplation for an hour is better than staying up all night (in ritual prayer and Qurʾanic recitation).[89] This is exactly what Abu'l-Dardāʾ and al-Ḥasan al-Baṣrī are quoted as saying: 'Contemplation for an hour is better than staying up all night.'[90] The Companion Ibn ʿAbbās is quoted as saying, 'Two moderate sets of bowings (*rakʿatān muqtaṣidatān*) with [283] contemplation are better than staying up all night with a straying mind (*wa'l-qalb sāhīn*).'[91] Umm al-Dardāʾ (Syrian, d. after 81/700–701) is often quoted as saying *tafakkur* and *iʿtibār* (observing things and taking warning) had been the best work of her husband, Abu'l-Dardāʾ (d. early 30s/650s?).[92]

Restricted Eating and Drinking

Second among the devotional exercises that Muḥammad al-Bāqir describes is fasting. Fasting during Ramaḍān is a duty for all Muslims, likewise as atonement for various offences. Apart from encouragements of formal fasting, al-Kulaynī also reports many injunctions to eat little. He quotes Jaʿfar al-Ṣādiq as saying, 'Much eating is hateful,' 'The servant is closest to God when his stomach is light, while the servant is most despised by God when his stomach has been filled,' 'The servant is closest to God when his stomach is light, while the servant is most despised by God when his stomach has been filled,' and 'God despises much eating,' and 'There is nothing God despises more than a full stomach.'[93] Adding to a tradition going back to Christian renunciants centuries earlier, Jaʿfar is quoted as observing, 'The son of Adam has no alternative to eating in order to maintain his body. When one of you eats food, let him make a third of his stomach for food, a third of his stomach for drink, and a third of his stomach for his soul. Do not fatten yourselves as swine are fattened for slaughtering.'[94]

Many recommendations and examples of eating little are to be found in the Sunni tradition. Al-Qāsim b. Mukhaymira, who lived in Syria (d. 100/718–719), quoted the advice

---

405; Abū Nuʿaym, *Ḥilya*, vol. 5, pp. 75–76. Also attributed to Ṣāliḥ al-Murrī (Basran, d. 172/788–789?), p. Ibn al-Mubārak, *Zuhd*, no. 260.

88. Al-Kulaynī, *Kāfī, kitāb al-īmān wa'l-kufr, bāb al-tafakkur*, vol. 2, p. 55.

89. Ibid., vol. 2, p. 54.

90. Ibn Abī Shayba, *Muṣannaf, kitāb al-zuhd* 13, *kalām Abi'l-Dardāʾ*, and *kitāb al-zuhd* 72, *kalām al-Ḥasan al-Baṣrī*, vol. 12, pp. 219, 365; also Aḥmad, *Zuhd*, p. 272 *332* (al-Ḥasan).

91. Ibn al-Mubārak, *Zuhd*, no. 288, with 'moderate' presumably referring to their length.

92. Ibid., no. 286; Aḥmad, *Zuhd*, p. 135 *168*; Abū Nuʿaym, *Ḥilya*, vol. 1, p. 208, vol. 4, p. 253, vol. 7, p. 300; *tafakkur* alone apud Ibn Abī Shayba, *Muṣannaf, kitāb al-zuhd* 13, *kalām Abi'l-Dardāʾ*, vol. 12, p. 219.

93. All al-Kulaynī, *Kāfī, kitāb al-aṭʿima, bāb karāhiyat kathrat al-akl*, vol. 6, p. 269, except the last, vol. 6, p. 270.

94. Ibid., vol. 6, pp. 269–270.

of Luqmān to his son: 'My son, beware of satiety, for it betrays you by night and humiliates by day.'[95] ʿUmar (d. 23/644) is said to have reproached ʿĀṣim b. ʿAmr, a Hijazi Follower, for gnawing on a piece of meat. 'It is excess enough that a man should eat everything he desires.'[96] Samura b. Jundub, a Companion who settled in Basra (d. 58/677–678), was told that his son had not slept the night. He asked, 'Is it overeating (*basham*)?' Told that it was, he said, 'If he died, I would not pray over him,' suggesting that overeating was virtual apostasy.[97] The Kufan al-Aswad b. Yazīd al-Nakhaʿī (d. 75/694–695?) fasted till he had turned green and yellow and [284] lost an eye.[98] Al-ʿAlāʾ b. Ziyād (d. 94/712–713) was a Basran who lived on one loaf a day and fasted till he had turned green.[99] Al-Ḥasan al-Baṣrī said that a Muslim did not eat with all his belly.[100]

More generally, we have the theme of licit eating. Early Muslims seem to have been deeply concerned not to take into their bodies what had not been rightly purchased. A man told Abū Jaʿfar (Muḥammad al-Bāqir) that he was weak of work (worship) but hoped to eat only what was licit. The Imam commented, 'What devotion (*ijtihād*) is better than chastity of the belly and genitals?'[101] Sunni sources often report concern for eating only what is licit. For example, ʿĀmir b. ʿAbd Qays (*fl.* 1st/7th century) would eat fat (*samn*) only from *arḍ al-ʿarab*, the pre-conquest territory of the Arabs, since it was unknown what other fat had been mixed with anything from elsewhere.[102] Yūsuf b. Asbāṭ, a Kufan who lived in Antioch (d. 195/810–811), would eat only what was licit and make do with dust if he found none.[103] But this concern for eating only the licit seems to have died out in the early 9th century. Wakīʿ (Kufan, d. 197/812?) declared, 'If a man swore to eat nothing but the licit, wear nothing but the licit, and not walk except in the licit, we would tell him, "Take off your

95. Abū Nuʿaym, *Ḥilya*, vol. 6, p. 82.

96. Ibn al-Mubārak, *Zuhd*, no. 769.

97. Wakīʿ, *Zuhd*, vol. 1, p. 302; Aḥmad, *Zuhd*, p. 199 *248*; Aḥmad b. Ḥanbal (attrib.), *Kitāb al-waraʿ*, ed. Zaynab Ibrāhīm al-Qārūṭ (Beirut, 1403/1983), p. 102; ed. Muḥammad Sayyid Basyūnī Zaghlūl (Beirut, 1409/1988), p. 84.

98. Ibn Abī Shayba, *Muṣannaf*, *kitāb al-zuhd* 43, *kalām al-Aswad*, vol. 12, p. 294; multiple reports, Abū Nuʿaym, *Ḥilya*, vol. 2, pp. 103–104.

99. Ibn al-Mubārak, *Zuhd*, no. 965; Abū Nuʿaym, *Ḥilya*, vol. 2, p. 243.

100. Ibn al-Mubārak, *Zuhd*, no. 271.

101. Al-Kulaynī, *Kāfī*, *kitāb al-īmān wa'l-kufr*, *bāb al-ʿiffa*, vol. 2, p. 79. Comment repeated twice, ibid., vol. 2, p. 80.

102. Aḥmad, *Zuhd*, p. 220 *270*. *Cf.* Ibn al-Mubārak, *Zuhd*, no. 866, where he says he eats fat from some places but not others, and Ibn Saʿd, *Biographien*, ed. Eduard Sachau et al. (Leiden, 1904–1940), vol. 7, pp. 74–5; *al-Ṭabaqāt al-kubrā* (Beirut, 1957–68), vol. 7/1, pp. 104–105, where he says that he eats fat from the desert.

103. Ibn Ḥibbān, *Kitāb al-thiqāt*, ed. Muḥammad ʿAbd al-Muʿīd Khān (Hyderabad, 1393–1403/1973–1983), vol. 7, p. 638; Ibn Ḥajar, *Tahdhīb al-tahdhīb* (Hyderabad, 1325–1327, repr. Beirut, n.d), vol. 11, p. 408.

clothes and throw yourself in the Euphrates." . . . The purely licit we do not know today . . . . The world has the status of carrion: take from it what will sustain you.'[104]

Al-Kulaynī encourages eating cold food over hot. Jaʿfar al-Ṣādiq quotes ʿAlī as saying, 'Lay by what is hot in order for it to cool off, for the Messenger of God . . . had some hot food brought near him but said, "Lay it by for it to cool off. God has not fed us what is hot. Blessing is in the cold.'[105] Then we are told:[106]

> Supper was brought for Abū ʿAbd Allāh (Jaʿfar al-Ṣādiq) in the summertime. A table was brought with bread on it. He was also brought some soup and meat. He said, 'Let me have this food' and approached, then put his hand on it but raised it again, saying, 'I take refuge with God from the Fire; I appeal to God to preserve me [285] from the Fire; I appeal to God to preserve me from the Fire. We have no patience for this, so how the Fire? We are not strong enough for this, so how the Fire? We cannot bear this, so how the Fire?' He kept on saying that until the food had cooled. Then he ate and we with him.

The idea is evidently that hot food is akin to Hellfire — better, then, to avoid it. There is no Sunni parallel that I have remarked, except for the archaic discussion of calling for ritual ablutions after touching anything touched by fire.[107]

Supererogatory Ritual Prayer

Third among the devotional exercises that Muḥammad al-Bāqir describes is the ritual prayer. This refers, of course, not to the required five daily prayers but to additional, supererogatory prayer. *Ijtihād* in renunciant literature refers especially to ritual worship (corresponding more closely than other terms to Greek *askēsis*). This is what Jaʿfar al-Ṣādiq refers to when he warns that ritual performance must be accompanied by right action: 'I enjoin on you fear of God, *waraʿ*, and *ijtihād*. Know that there is no benefit to *ijtihād* without scrupulosity.'[108] Scrupulosity (*waraʿ*) means avoiding not only what is plainly forbidden but anything remotely likely to be forbidden. In the Sunni tradition, it is said of ʿAbd al-Raḥmān b. al-Aswad (Kufan, d. 99/717–718) that he would pray 700 bowings a day. 'They used to say he was the least of the people of his house in *ijtihād*. I have heard that he became bone and skin. They used to say the Aswad family were among the people

104. Abū Nuʿaym, *Ḥilya*, vol. 8, p. 370.

105. Al-Kulaynī, *kitāb al-aṭʿima, bāb al-ṭaʿām al-ḥārr*, vol. 6, pp. 321–632, followed by three more prophetic *ḥadīth* reports with almost the same words, vol. 6, p. 322.

106. Ibid., vol. 6, p. 322.

107. For which see Marion Holmes Katz, *Body of text: the emergence of the Sunnī law of ritual purity* (Albany, 2002), pp. 102–123.

108. Al-Kulaynī, *Kāfī, kitāb al-īmān wa'l-kufr, bāb al-waraʿ*, vol. 2, p. 76.

of Paradise.'[109] Recalling the heightened piety of an earlier generation, al-Ḥasan al-Baṣrī is quoted as saying, 'They used to exert themselves (*yajtahidūna*) in prayer (*duʿāʾ*), and you would hear nothing but whispering.'[110]

Unsurprisingly, the Shiʿi tradition recommends supererogatory ritual prayer. According to an Ismaili source, ʿAlī b. al-Ḥusayn (d. Medina, 95/714) would pray 1,000 sets of supererogatory prayer per day.[111] There are very many reports in the Sunni literature of prodigious routines of supererogatory prayer. For example, the Kufan *mukhaḍram* Murra b. Sharāḥīl (d. 76/695–696) is said to have prayed 500 bowings a day in his youth, 250 in old age.[112] ʿAlī b. ʿAbd Allāh b. al-ʿAbbās [286] (Medinese, d. 118/736–737) prayed over 500 bowings a day.[113] The Palestinian Rajāʾ b. Abī Salama (d. 161/777–778) prayed a thousand prostrations a day.[114]

Al-Kulaynī also reports advice on how to pray apart from the ritual prayer. Jaʿfar al-Ṣādiq demonstrated gestures: 'Mention of a desire [at this he showed the insides of his palms to heaven]; thus is fear (*rahba*) [at this he put the backs of his hands to heaven]; thus is self-abasement (*taḍarruʿ*) [at this he moved his fingers right and left]; thus is chastity (*tabattul*) [at this he raised his fingers once and put them down once]; thus is supplication (*ibtihāl*) [at this he extended his hand before his face to the *qibla*]. One does not supplicate until a tear flows.'[115] Someone once presumed to correct the Imam:[116]

> A man passed by me as I was praying in the course of my ritual prayer with my left. He said, 'Abū ʿAbd Allāh, with your right.' I said, 'O servant of God, God (be He blessed and exalted) has a claim on this as he has on this.' Desire is that you extend your hands and show their insides. Fear is that you extend your hands and show their backs. Self-abasement is that you move the right pointing finger to right and left. Chastity is that you move the left pointing finger and raise it to heaven slowly (*rislan*), then put it down. Supplication is that you extend your hands and arms to heaven, supplication coming when you see the occasions of weeping.

---

109. Aḥmad, *Zuhd*, p. 360 *430*.

110. Ibn Abī Shayba, *Muṣannaf*, *kitāb al-duʿāʾ* 94, *fī rafʿ al-ṣawt bi'l-duʿāʾ*, vol. 10, p. 144; Wakīʿ, *Zuhd*, vol. 2, p. 616.

111. Al-Qāḍī al-Nuʿmān, *Daʿāʾim*, ed. Fyzee, vol. 1, p. 211; ed. Tāmir, vol. 1, p. 261.

112. Al-ʿIjlī, *Ta'rīkh al-thiqāt*, arr. Ibn Ḥajar al-Haythamī, ed. ʿAbd al-Muʿṭī Qalʿajī (Beirut, 1405/1984), p. 424; al-Jāḥiẓ, *al-Bayān wa'l-tabyīn*, ed. ʿAbd al-Salām Muḥammad Hārūn (Cairo, 1367–1369/1948–1950), vol. 3, p. 129.

113. Abū Nuʿaym, *Ḥilya*, vol. 3, p. 207; *cf.* Abū Dāwūd, *Kitāb al-zuhd*, ed. Muṣṭafā Maḥmūd Ḥusayn (Tanta, 1424/2003), p. 231, nos. 451–452.

114. Abū Nuʿaym, *Ḥilya*, vol. 6, p. 91.

115. Al-Kulaynī, *Kāfī*, *kitāb al-duʿāʾ*, *bāb al-raghba wa'l-rahba*, vol. 2, p. 480.

116. Ibid., vol. 2, p. 480. Also, '*Masʾala* is extending the palms; *istiʿādha* is raising (*ifḍāʾ*) the palms; chastity is indicating with the finger; self-abasement is moving the finger; supplication is extending both of one's hands' (ibid., vol. 2, p. 481).

Compare the Prophet from the Sunni tradition: 'If you ask God (for something), ask him with the palms of your hands; do not ask him with their backs.'[117] Shahr b. Ḥawshab (Syrian, d. 112/730–731) gave this recommendation: spread the hands toward the face for *masʾala* (asking for a good), palms reversed for *taʿawwudh* (taking refuge with God from some danger).[118]

Concern for the Poor

Muḥammad al-Bāqir's recommendation of filial piety seems completely unremarkable, so that there can be no need to demonstrate Sunni parallels. As for the next on his list, 'keeping faith with poor neighbours and the indigent, debt-ridden, and orphans,' it is not particularly prominent in the rest of al-Kulaynī's collection of pious [287] recommendations and it has some but not very numerous parallels in the Sunni literature. The Kufan Khaythama b. ʿAbd al-Raḥmān (d. after 80/699–700), willed that he be buried in the cemetery of the poor of his tribe.[119] The Basran Muṭarrif b. ʿAbd Allāh (d. 95/713–714) wore wool and sat with the poor for the sake of humility.[120] People attended the session of the Kufan Sufyān al-Thawrī in rags, and the rich there were said to be humbled, the poor exalted.[121]

Qurʾanic Recitation

Next on Muḥammad al-Bāqir's list is truthful speech, again unremarkable. 'Reciting the Qurʾan' overlaps with recollection, as observed above. This devotional form is apparently more prominent in Sunni renunciant literature than Shiʿi. It is sometimes described as being superior to participation in the Holy War or other pious activities. ʿAbd Allāh b. Masʿūd said that one who recollects God, glossed as 'a man who recites the Book of God' (*rajul yatlū kitāb Allāh*) is better than a man who rides on the Holy War.[122] Salmān (d. Medina, 34/654–655) said, 'If one man stayed up all night giving eggs to slave girls (*qaynāt*) while another stayed up reciting the Qurʾan and recollecting God, I think the one recollecting God would be the better.'[123] Sufyān al-Thawrī said it was better to re-

117. Ibn Abī Shayba, *Muṣannaf*, *kitāb al-duʿāʾ* 45, *al-rajul idhā daʿā bi-baṭn kaffih*, vol. 10, p. 78; *isnād* Kufan in lower part, Basran upper.

118. Ibid., vol. 10, p. 79.

119. Ibn Abī Shayba, *Muṣannaf*, *kitāb al-zuhd* 60, *Khaythama b. ʿAr.*, vol. 12, p. 321; Aḥmad, *Zuhd*, p. 359 *429* (< ʿAl.).

120. Abū Nuʿaym, *Ḥilya*, vol. 2, p. 200.

121. Ibid., vol. 6, pp. 364–365.

122. Ibn Abī Shayba, *Muṣannaf*, *kitāb faḍāʾil al-Qurʾān* 29, *man qāla qirāʾat al-Qurʾān afḍal min siwāh*, vol. 10, p. 241.

123. Ibid., vol. 10, pp. 241–242.

cite the Qurʾan than to go frontier raiding.[124] There are as many reports in the Sunni literature of prodigious routines of Qurʾanic recitation as there are of supererogatory prayer. ʿUthmān would recite the Qurʾan in a single *rakʿa* by night.[125] ʿAlqama (Kufan, d. after 70/689–690?), recited the whole Qurʾan in a night around the Kaʿbah.[126] Murra b. Sharāḥīl recited the Qurʾan daily and so was safe from the *fitna* of Ibn al-Zubayr.[127] Saʿīd b. Jubayr (Kufan, d. 95/714) entered the Kaʿba and recited the entire Qurʾan in a single *rakʿa*, also daily during Ramadan, every three days during the rest of the year.[128] Al-Zuhrī (d. 124/742?) recited the Qurʾan before breakfasting on the 21st, 23rd, 25th, 27th, and [288] 29th of Ramadan.[129] Thābit al-Bunānī (Basran, d. 127/744–745?) recited the Qurʾan daily as well as fasting perpetually.[130] And so on and so on.

Other Austerities

Nighttime devotions are recommended in a saying from Jaʿfar al-Ṣādiq in the Ismaili tradition: 'I despise that a servant should recite the Qurʾan, then awaken in the night and not get up until morning is near, only then getting up and beginning to pray.'[131] The idea is that he should rather recite the Qurʾan after the evening prayer, go to bed, then get up for further devotions as soon as he wakes up, whenever that is. Compare the example of Abū Isḥāq al-Sabīʿī (Kufan, d. 129/746–747?), who would not go back to sleep if he awoke at night.[132] Sufyān al-Thawrī told his disciples it was all right to sleep at any length but not to go back to sleep after one had once woken up.[133]

Hostility to music is a common theme of pious literature, Sunni and Shiʿi. Jaʿfar al-Ṣādiq is said to have glossed Q.22:30, 'Avoid the abomination of idols, and avoid the speaking of falsehood,' as 'Singing'; likewise Q.6:31, 'Among the people are those who buy diverting tales to lead [people] away from the path of God without any knowledge'; and likewise Q.25:72, 'And those who will not bear false witness.'[134] He said, 'Playing lutes

124. Abū Nuʿaym, *Ḥilya*, vol. 7, p. 65.

125. Ibn Saʿd, *Biographien*, vol. 3, p. 153 = *Ṭabaqāt*, vol. 3, pp. 75–76; Aḥmad, *Zuhd*, p. 127 *158*; Abū Nuʿaym, *Ḥilya*, vol. 1, p. 57.

126. Ibn Abī Shayba, *Muṣannaf*, *kitāb ṣalāh* 851, *man kāna yuḥibbu idhā qadima an yaqraʾa al-Qurʾān*, vol. 3/1, p. 618–619. Also, 'He recited the Qurʾan in a night': ibid., *kitāb al-zuhd* 44, *kalām ʿAlqama*, vol. 12, p. 295.

127. Abū Nuʿaym, *Ḥilya*, vol. 4, pp. 162–163.

128. Ibid., vol. 4, p. 273.

129. Ibid., vol. 3, p. 170.

130. ʿAbd Allāh b. Aḥmad, *ʿIlal*, vol. 1, p. 486 *vol. 1, p. 181.*

131. Al-Qāḍī al-Nuʿmān, *Daʿāʾim*, ed. Fyzee, vol. 1, p. 213; ed. Tāmir, vol. 1, p. 264.

132. Abū Nuʿaym, *Ḥilya*, vol. 4, p. 340, quoting a lost section of Aḥmad, *Zuhd*.

133. Ibid., vol. 7, p. 60.

134. Al-Kulaynī, *Kāfī*, *kitāb al-ashriba*, *bāb al-ghināʾ*, vol, 6, pp. 431–433.

(*ḍarb al-ᶜīdān*) makes hypocrisy spring up in the heart as water makes verdure spring up'; alternatively, 'Listening to singing and idle talk (*lahw*) makes hypocrisy spring up in the heart as water makes plants spring up.'[135] And he said, 'Whoever strikes strings (*rubṭ*) in his house for forty days, God gives a devil power over him . . . . When he is in that state, the life drops from him and he does not care what he says or what is said of him.'[136] On the other side, Sunni denunciations of music are plentiful. The Prophet is quoted as saying, 'Singing plants hypocrisy in the heart.'[137] Pouring out wine and smashing musical instruments are often paired as prime examples of *al-amr bi'l-maᶜrūf wa'l-nahy ᶜan al-munkar*.[138] Zubayd al-Yāmī, a Kufan worshipper (d. 122/739–740 or after), seized and broke the reed flute he saw one slave girl carrying, the tambourine [289] of another.[139] Aḥmad b. Ḥanbal (d. Baghdad, 241/855) said of singing, 'It establishes hypocrisy in the heart. I dislike it.'[140] He approved of breaking a lute or mandolin and denied that the breaker owed anything to the owner in compensation.[141]

Al-Kulaynī quotes Jaᶜfar al-Ṣādiq as relating of the Messenger of God, 'Leaning in the mosque is the monasticism (*rahbāniyya*) of the Arabs. The believer's session is his mosque and his cell is his house.'[142] The Sunni tradition more often recommends the Holy War as the new monasticism; for example, the Companion Abū Saᶜīd al-Khudrī (d. Medina, 64/683–684) is quoted as saying, 'I enjoin you to fear God, for it is the chief of everything. Incumbent on you is *jihād*, for it is the *rahbāniyya* of Islam.'[143] But sitting in the mosque is certainly encouraged in the Sunni tradition and sometimes identified with monasticism. ᶜUthmān b. Maẓᶜūn came to the Prophet and asked, among other things, 'O Messenger of God, permit us monasticism (*tarahhub*).' He said, 'The *tarahhub* of my community is sitting in the mosque waiting for the ritual prayer.'[144] Abū Idrīs al-Khawlānī (Syrian, d. 80/699–700) is quoted as saying, 'The mosques are the nobles' places of sitting (*majālis al-kirām*).'[145] Note how, similarly to Jaᶜfar with Arabism, he conflates concepts of right re-

135. Ibid., vol. 6, p. 434.

136. Ibid., vol. 6, p. 434.

137. Abū Dāwūd, *Sunan*, *kitāb al-adab* 60, *bāb karāhiyat al-ghināʾ wa'l-zamr*, no. 4927. Further examples apud al-Ājurrī, *Taḥrīm al-nard wa'l-shaṭranj wa'l-malāhī*, ed. Muṣṭafā ᶜAbd al-Qādir ᶜAṭā (Beirut, 1408/1988), pp. 93–102.

138. As in Ghazālī's exemplary discussion of the duty, *Iḥyāʾ ᶜulūm al-dīn*, book 19. Many examples are cited by Michael Cook, *Commanding Right and Forbidding Wrong in Islamic Thought* (Cambridge, 2000).

139. Abū Nuᶜaym, *Ḥilya*, vol. 5, p. 32.

140. ᶜAbd Allāh b. Aḥmad, *Masāʾil al-imām Aḥmad b. Ḥanbal*, ed. Zuhayr al-Shāwīsh (Beirut, 1401/1981), p. 316.

141. Abū Dāwūd, *Kitāb masāʾil al-imām Aḥmad*, ed. Muḥammad Bahja al-Bayṭār (Cairo, 1353/1934, repr. Beirut, n.d.), p. 279.

142. Al-Kulaynī, *Kāfī*, *kitāb al-ᶜishra*, *bāb al-ittikāʾ wa'l-iḥtibāʾ*, vol. 2, p. 662.

143. Ibn al-Mubārak, *Zuhd*, no. 840.

144. Ibid., no. 845.

145. Aḥmad, *Zuhd*, p. 380 *455*.

ligion and social status. The Muslim's house is identified with a monk's cell in a number of sayings in the Sunni tradition. Abu'l-Dardāʾ is supposed to have said, 'What a good cell for a man is his house. In it, he restrains his sight and tongue. Beware of the market, for it negates and distracts (*tulghī, tulhī*).'[146] Al-Ḥasan al-Baṣrī said, 'The believers' cells are their houses.'[147]

Some Shiʿi advice on clothing is very similar to Sunni. Al-Kulaynī quotes the Prophet as saying, 'Wear white, for it is better and purer. Shroud your dead in it.'[148] Sunni *ḥadīth* collections report exactly the same words.[149] But al-Kulaynī's repeated [290] discouragement of wool seems unlike the Sunni tradition. He reports that Jaʿfar said, 'Linen (*kattān*) is the dress of the prophets and makes the flesh grow.'[150] He reports that Jaʿfar said, 'Do not wear wool or hair save in illness (*min ʿilla*).'[151] He reports that ʿAlī said, 'Wear clothes of cotton (*quṭn*), for it is the dress of the Messenger of God and our dress. He did not wear wool or hair save from illness (*min ʿilla*).'[152] A section of *ḥadīth* relating to clothing comprises only encouragement to wear the best clothing one can.[153]

The contrary tendency can also be found. Al-Kulaynī quotes someone as saying,[154]

> I saw Abū ʿAbd Allāh (Jaʿfar al-Ṣādiq) wearing a rough shirt under his clothes, on top of it a woollen *jubba*, on top of it a rough shirt. I felt it and said, 'God make me your ransom: the people dislike to wear wool.' He said, 'On the contrary: Abū Muḥammad b. ʿAlī (al-Ḥasan) wore it and ʿAlī b. al-Ḥusayn (Zayn al-ʿĀbidīn) wore it. They would wear their roughest clothing when they got up to perform the ritual prayer. That is what we do.'

---

146. Wakīʿ, *Zuhd*, vol. 2, p. 516; Aḥmad, *Zuhd*, p. 135 *168*; Ibn al-Mubārak, *Zuhd*, no. 14 among additions < N.; Jāḥiẓ, *Bayān*, vol. 3, p. 132.

147. Ibn al-Mubārak, *Zuhd*, no. 15 among additions < N.; Ibn Abī Shayba, *Muṣannaf*, *kitāb al-zuhd* 72, *kalām al-Ḥasan al-Baṣrī*, vol. 12, p. 380; Abū Nuʿaym, *Ḥilya*, vol. 3, p. 19, quoting a lost section of Aḥmad, *Zuhd*.

148. Two versions: al-Kulaynī, *Kāfī*, *kitāb al-zī wa'l-tajammul*, *bāb al-libās*, vol. 6, p. 445.

149. Tirmidhī, *Jāmiʿ*, *kitāb al-adab* 46, *bāb mā jāʾa fī lubs al-bayāḍ*, no. 2810; Aḥmad, *Musnad*, vol. 5, pp. 10, 12, 13, 17, 18, 19, 20–21 *vol. 33, pp. 297, 318–319, 327–328, 354–355, 364, 372–373, 381–382*; ʿAbd al-Razzāq, *Muṣannaf*, ed. Ḥabīb al-Raḥmān al-Aʿẓamī (Johannesburg, 1390–1392/1970–1972), vol. 3, pp. 428–429 (3 versions). Similar advice is to be found apud Abū Dāwūd, *Sunan*, *kitāb al-ṭibb* 14, *bāb fi'l-amr bi'l-kuḥl*, no. 3878, repeated *kitāb al-libās* 13, *bāb fi'l-bayāḍ*, no. 4061; Tirmidhī, *Jāmiʿ*, *kitāb al-janāʾiz* 18, *bāb mā yustaḥabbu min al-akfān*, no. 994; Ibn Māja, *Sunan*, *kitāb al-libās* 5, *bāb al-bayāḍ min al-thiyāb*, no. 3567; Aḥmad, *Musnad*, vol. 1, pp. 247, 274, 328, 355, 363 *vol. 4, pp. 94, 282, vol. 5, pp. 161–162, 352–353, 398.*

150. Al-Kulaynī, *Kāfī*, *kitāb al-zī wa'l-tajammul*, *bāb al-kattān*, vol. 6, p. 449.

151. Ibid., *bāb lubs al-ṣūf wa-al-shaʿr*, vol. 6, p. 445.

152. Ibid., vol. 6, p. 450.

153. Ibid., *Kāfī*, *kitāb al-zī wal-tajammul*, *bāb al-libās*, vol. 6, pp. 441–444.

154. Ibid., *bāb lubs al-ṣūf wa'l-shaʿr*, vol. 6, p. 450.

A Sunni source reports in rough conformity with this last report that Sufyān al-Thawrī discovered Jaʿfar al-Ṣādiq to be wearing wool underneath a silken *jubba*.[155] More generally, the Sunni tradition seems overwhelmingly friendly to the wearing of wool. Mūsā never wore anything but wool, likewise ʿĪsā.[156] Ibn Masʿūd (d. 32/652–653?) said, 'The prophets milked sheep, rode asses, and wore wool.'[157] According to al-Ḥasan al-Baṣrī, the Prophet Muhammad rode an ass (not a horse), wore wool, licked his fingers, and ate on the floor.'[158] It was a mark of humility.[159] Strictures against wearing wool are also to be found, but they belong to the category of sayings against outward humility and inward pride; for express example, al-Ḥasan al-Baṣrī, quoted as saying of those who wear wool, 'They have hidden pride in their hearts [291] while outwardly showing humility in their clothing. By God, one of them is more proud of his dress than the wearer of a silken robe in his.'[160] Jaʿfar al-Ṣādiq is not alone in being reported to have worn wool underneath more comfortable clothing, hence to avoid making any show of humility; likewise, among others, the Basran Hārūn b. Rabāb (fl. early 2nd/8th century), the Kufan ʿAbd al-Wāḥid b. Zayd (fl. early 2nd/8th century), and the Mesopotamian Maymūn b. Mihrān (d. 117/735–736) wore wool under other clothes to hide their renunciation.[161]

Al-Kulaynī also reports various encouragements of notably modest austerity. One is a long story of Jaʿfar al-Ṣādiq's being approached by Sufis who bid others to join them. He tells them that it is best to give away some of one's wealth but not all of it. It would be impossible for everyone to join them, lest women, the elderly, and the sickly perish. And if everyone joined them, no one would be left to receive charity as atonement or *zakāt*.[162] Jaʿfar is also quoted as identifying proper renunciation not with outward austerity but

155. Abū Nuʿaym, *Ḥilya*, vol. 3, p. 193.

156. Al-Ḥasan al-Baṣrī on Moses, Abū Nuʿaym, *Ḥilya*, vol. 2, p. 137; Zuhrī on ʿĪsā, Abū ʿUbayd, *al-Khuṭab wa-al-mawāʿiẓ*, ed. Ramaḍān ʿAbd al-Tawwāb (Cairo, 1406/1986), p. 163; also Khaythama b. ʿAbd al-Raḥmān (d. after 80/699), Abū Nuʿaym, *Ḥilya*, vol. 4, p. 117.

157. Kufan *isnād*; Aḥmad, *Zuhd*, p. 60 *78*.

158. Ibn al-Mubārak, *Zuhd*, no. 995 (not < Ibn al-Mubārak).

159. For further discussion and examples, see Christopher Melchert, 'Baṣran origins of Classical Sufism,' *Der Islam*, 82 (2005), pp. 223–225 [*HPL 8]. Shaybī believes that wool-wearing originated with Kufan renunciants who took it up as a sign of their opposition to al-Ḥajjāj (*Ṣila*, vol. 1, pp. 280–286), but I believe there is equal evidence of it in other centres, most notably (in the generation of the Followers) Basra.

160. Ibn Saʿd, *Biographien* vol. 7/1, p. 123 = *Ṭabaqāt*, vol. 7, p. 169; Jāḥiẓ, *Bayān*, vol. 3, p. 153; Ibn Qutayba, *ʿUyūn*, vol. 2, p. 372.

161. Hārūn b. Rabāb, Abū Nuʿaym, *Ḥilya*, vol. 3, p. 55; ʿAbd al-Wāḥid b. Zayd, ibid., vol. 6, p. 232; Maymūn b. Mihrān, ibid., vol. 4, pp. 91–92.

162. Al-Kulaynī, *Kāfī, kitāb al-maʿīsha, bāb dakhala al-ṣūfiyya ʿalā Abī ʿAbd Allāh*, vol. 5, pp. 65–70. The express reference to Sufis is probably anachronistic, inasmuch as the first to be called a Sufi was an Iraqi contemporary of Jaʿfar's—perhaps, though, not by much, for the term was used to designate disreputably extreme renunciants before about the mid-9th century. See further Melchert, 'Baṣran origins,' pp. 229–230.

entirely an inward attitude: 'Renunciation of the world is not wasting money or forbidding what is licit. Rather, renunciation of the world is that you be no more sure of what is in your hand than of what God has.'[163] Al-Kulaynī quotes ʿAlī to similar effect: 'Renunciation of the world is shortness of hope, thankfulness for every blessing, and scruple before everything God (mighty and glorious is He) has forbidden.'[164]

Sunni parallels can be found. ʿAbd Allāh b. Masʿūd went to some Kufans who had withdrawn and established themselves somewhere in the vicinity to worship: 'What induced you to do what you have done?' They said, 'We wished to go away from the crowd (*ghumār al-nās*).' Ibn Masʿūd told them, 'If the people did what you have done, who would fight the enemy? I will not go away till you return.'[165] ʿAlī is quoted as saying that he was most fearful of length of hope and following fancies (referring especially to heresy), since length of hope makes one forget the Afterworld, while following fancy turns one away from the truth.[166] Sufyān b. ʿUyayna (d. Mecca, 198/814) said, 'Renunciation of the world is shortness of hope, not eating what is [292] rough or wearing a hood (*ʿabāya*).'[167] I have provisionally located this inward redefinition of renunciation (emphatically not the same thing as calling for inward attitudes to match outward appearances) in the last third of the 8th century AD (just the time of Sufyān b. ʿUyayna). The Imāmiyya seem to have embraced exactly this tendency, presumably for similar reasons: that they now included Muslims of all social classes, so that the rich among them needed to be shielded from complaints from the middling while the middling had to be offered a style of piety that would not prevent them from earning a living.[168]

Comments in Twelver literature on Sufis are uncommon. I have mentioned the Sufis whose call for withdrawal from society is rejected by Jaʿfar al-Ṣādiq. In the biographical literature, I have remarked Aḥmad b. Hilāl al-ʿAbartānī (fl. early 3rd/9th century), an Imāmī, who made fifty-four pilgrimages, twenty on foot, but whom the Imam nonetheless denounced as a deceiving Sufi (*ṣūfī mutaṣanniʿ*).[169] Wool-wearing occasionally turns up also in the record of early non-Imāmī Shiʿism. I have earlier mentioned the Sufis who, in alliance with the local Zaydiyya, took over Kufa for a few weeks on behalf of two Ḥasanids in 255/869.[170] Although he was not called a Sufi, the ʿAlid ʿAbd Allāh b. Muʿāwiya

163. Al-Kulaynī, *Kāfī, kitāb al-maʿīsha, bāb maʿnā al-zuhd*, vol. 5, pp. 70–71.

164. Ibid., vol. 5, p. 71.

165. Ibn al-Mubārak, *Zuhd*, no. 1104 (not < Ibn al-Mubārak).

166. Wakīʿ, *Zuhd*, vol. 2, pp. 439–441; Ibn al-Mubārak, *Zuhd*, no. 255; Aḥmad, *Zuhd*, pp. 130, *162–163*; Hannād, *Zuhd*, vol. 1, p. 291; Ibn Abī Shayba. *Muṣannaf, kitāb al-zuhd* 11, *kalām ʿAlī b. Abī Ṭālib*, vol. 12, p. 200.

167. Wakīʿ, *Zuhd*, vol. 1, p. 222; also Abū Nuʿaym, *Ḥilya*, vol. 6, p. 386, citing Ibn Abī Shayba, with 'wearing wool' instead of 'wearing a hood.'

168. Melchert, 'Baṣran origins,' pp. 230, 234.

169. Al-Kashshī, *Rijāl al-Kashshī*, ed. Aḥmad al-Ḥusaynī (Karbala, n.d.), pp. 449–450.

170. Al-Ṣūlī, *Kniga listov* (i.e., *Kitāb al-awrāq*), ed. Anas Khalidov (St. Petersburg, 1998), p. 366; Melchert,

clothed himself in wool when he commenced his open rebellion against the Umayyads (127/744).[171] Ḥallāj, executed in 309/922, sometimes identified himself with the Shiᶜa and is included among them by, among others, Ibn al-Nadīm.[172] Provisionally, I propose that al-Kulaynī is markedly more hostile to wool-wearing than Sunni *ḥadīth* collectors in part because it was the badge of non-Imāmī Shīᶜa.

Conclusion

There is evidently considerable overlap between reported Shiᶜi and Sunni sayings about renunciation. The Sunni sayings are attested earlier. Moreover, reattributions seem more likely to cluster around a few very prominent figures (such as the Imams on the Shiᶜi side, the Prophet on both Shiᶜi and Sunni) than be dispersed among many individuals. On both counts, *it seems probable that the Sunni literary tradition is the* [293] *earlier, and that influence ran primarily from the Sunni side to the Shiᶜi rather than the other way around.* At the same time, sayings seem to float from person to person in the Sunni literature, so that it seems more certain that these sayings were current among proto-Sunnis of the 8th century than that they must be attributed to exactly the individuals to which our sources of the 9th century attribute them. Whichever way influence flowed, overlap between Sunni and Shiᶜi sayings about renunciation seems to indicate a common piety. I have looked for evidence of geographical specialisation in the Sunni record without success — this is in contrast to the record of opinions about law, where evidence of geographical specialisation is abundant. This suggests to me that the renunciant tradition has its origin at an earlier point than the legal tradition. It must have continued in the Shiᶜi tradition as much as the Sunni, so that although Shiᶜi tradition attributes all sayings to Imams, Shiᶜi opinions and practices concerning renunciation must have been similar to Sunni throughout the 8th and 9th centuries.

Of special interest, then, are the parts of the Sunni renunciant tradition that do not appear in the Shiᶜi record, such as preference for wearing wool. Divergence between Sunni and Shiᶜi attitudes toward renunciation constitutes further evidence of Sunni-Shiᶜi differentiation, presumably in the course of the 9th century. It may be that sayings about wool were not taken into the Shiᶜi tradition as documented by al-Kulaynī just because of Shiᶜi resistance in the late 9th and early 10th centuries to taking up the Junaydi Sufi syn-

---

'Baṣran origins,' p. 232.

171. Noticed by Josef van Ess, *Theologie und Gesellschaft* (Berlin, 1991–1995), vol. 2, p. 88. This and three other examples from the next century noticed by Shaybī, *Fikr*, p. 68 and *Ṣila*, vol. 2, pp. 12–13.

172. Ibn al-Nadīm, *Fihrist, fann* 5, *maqāla* 5; *Kitâb al-Fihrist*, ed. Gustav Flügel, with Johannes Roedigger and August Mueller (Leipzig, 1872), 190–192. For Ḥallāj interpreted principally as a Shiᶜi rather than Sufi, see Said Amir Arjomand, 'The Crisis of the Imamate and the Institution of Occultation in Twelver Shiᶜism,' *International Journal of Middle East Studies*, 28 (1996), pp. 506–508.

thesis. This is the usual argument for the long-delayed development of Sufism in the Shiʿi tradition, namely that loyalty to the Imams, the defining character of Shiʿism, conflicted with loyalty to the *awliyāʾ*, a defining character of Sufism.[173] However, it appears also that *the Imāmī rejection of wool-wearing reflects earlier disquiet with non-Imāmī Shiʿi wool-wearers.*

Two questions concerning the development of Sufism seem most salient. First is the degree to which the emergence of Sunni Sufism reflects Shiʿi influence. This has often been alleged, as by Annemarie Schimmel: 'The thoughts of Jaʿfar and other early mystical thinkers must have been at work beneath the surface, permeating the mystical life until they appeared in the sayings of a number of Sufis.'[174] But this depends on taking attributions to Jaʿfar al-Ṣādiq at face value, a rash move for any scholar today. More modestly, with better documentation, Sara Sviri has characterised quotations of Shiʿi Imams in Sufi sources of the 10th century as 'Shīʿī material that became included in Ṣūfī literature.'[175] I am inclined to doubt whether much of the material to which Sviri refers, none of which is distinctly Shiʿi, actually has Shiʿi origins. More likely, like sayings about renunciation that al-Kulaynī attributes to various Imams, earlier Sunni collectors to various renunciants of the early 8th century and before, it had circulated from the start among proto-Sunnis. The thesis that Shiʿi [294] esoterism, looking for Qurʾanic allusions to the house of the Prophet, gave rise to Sufi esoterism depends also on supposing that the esoterism of 10th-century Shiʿi texts such as (above all) *Rasāʾil Ikhwān al-Ṣafāʾ* was not a development of the 10th century but already a character of 8th-century Shiʿism. I doubt this can ever be more than a supposition in the absence of 8th-century Shiʿi texts, or at least 9th-century. Inasmuch as it is a matter of 10th-century attributions to famous Imams, not a multitude of lesser names, it doubtfully deserves the presumption of greater reliability than Sunni attributions. *The present study of renunciant sayings weakly supports the larger argument that Sufism did not flow from an earlier Shiʿi tradition.*

The second great question is why Sufism was for so long exclusively Sunni. Although I offer here no answer, the absence of sayings about wool in al-Kulaynī's collection of renunciant sayings seems likely to document active resistance in his generation and the one before to the Junaydi synthesis. Among the Sunnis, 'Sufi' moved from a term for disreputable marginal figures to one for respectable orthodox ones at about the middle of the 9th century.[176] Shiʿa of some sort had worked closely with primitive Sufis, just before Sufism became respectable, but the Twelvers seem to have been opposed to them from

173. See Karamustafa, *Sufism*, pp. 18, 20.

174. Annemarie Schimmel, *Mystical Dimensions of Islam* (Chapel Hill, NC, 1975), p. 42.

175. Sara Sviri, 'The Early Mystical Schools of Baghdad and Nīshāpūr,' *JSAI*, 30 (2005), pp. 457–462 (quotation from p. 457). See Christopher Melchert, 'Khargūshī, *Tahdhīb al-asrār*,' *BSOAS*, 73 (2010), pp. 33–34.

176. B. Radtke, 'Taṣawwuf,' *EI2*, vol. 9, pp. 313–314; Melchert, 'Baṣran origins,' esp. pp. 222–223, 234–240.

the start. As, then, there seems to be a measure of continuity between Ḥanbali opposition to would-be Sunni *mutakallimīn* in the 9th century and to Shiʿa in the 10th, *there seems to be a measure of continuity between Imāmī opposition to would-be Shiʿi Sufis in the 9th century to a refusal to develop a form of Sufism in the 10th*. It was a part of Twelver consolidation and an important aspect of conscious Sunni-Shiʿi differentiation in the 10th century.

LAW

12
HOW ḤANAFISM CAME TO ORIGINATE IN KUFA AND TRADITIONALISM IN MEDINA

The surviving Sunni schools of law are named after jurisprudents of the eighth and ninth centuries C.E.: Abū Ḥanīfa (d. 150/767), Mālik (d. 179/795), al-Shāfiʿī (d. 204/820), and Aḥmad ibn Ḥanbal (d. 241/855). Dāwūd al-Ẓāhirī (d. 270/884) and Ibn Jarīr al-Ṭabarī (d. 310/923) also had important schools named after them, although the Dāwūdi school was sometimes called the Ẓāhiri after its outstanding principle of literalism.[1] Largely following earlier Muslim historians of Islamic law, Joseph Schacht characterized these schools as succeeding local, regional schools, the jurisprudence of Kufa surviving as Ḥanafism, of Medina as Mālikism.[2] More recently, George [319] Makdisi has pointed out three distinct stages in the evolution of the schools of law, first that of regional schools (when jurisprudents consciously identified their practice with that of some city or province), then personal schools (when jurisprudents identified their practice with that of some person),

The research behind this article was made possible by a fellowship from the Social Science Research Council, largely funded by the United States Information Agency.

1. Its first biographical dictionary, by Ibn al-Akhḍar (d. 429/1038), was titled *Akhbār ahl al-ẓāhir*, and Abū Isḥāq al-Shīrāzī, *Ṭabaqāt al-fuqahāʾ*, devotes a section to the Ẓāhirīya. References in the previous century are usually to the Dāwūdīya or *aṣḥāb Dāwūd*; e.g., in Ibn al-Nadīm, *al-Fihrist*, al-Khwārizmī, *Mafātīḥ al-ʿulūm*, and al-Maqdisī, *Aḥsan al-taqāsīm*. Early figures identified in jurisprudence with *al-ẓāhir* may or may not be connected directly with Dāwūd and his followers; e.g., the Isfahani qadi and ascetic writer Ibn Abī ʿĀṣim al-Nabīl (d. 287/900), the Sufi Ibn al-Aʿrābī (d. 341/952?).

2. See most conveniently Joseph Schacht, "The Schools of Law and Later Developments of Jurisprudence," 57–84 in *Law in the Middle East*, vol. 1: *Origin and Development of Islamic Law*, ed. Majid Khadduri & Herbert J. Liebesny (Washington, D.C.: Middle East Institute, 1955); also, idem, *The Origins of Muhammadan Jurisprudence* (Oxford: Clarendon Press, 1950), 239, 248, 306.

Originally published in *Islamic Law and Society* 6.3 (1999): 318–47.

finally guild schools (still personal but now having recognized local chiefs and claiming exclusive authority to regulate the teaching and practice of law).[3] But were there really regional groupings with identifiable doctrines or did every major center simply have its individual jurisprudents with individual circles of disciples without larger features in common with other local jurisprudents such that we may speak of schools? The regional schools of Arabic grammar certainly appear to have been projections backward. Why not the regional schools of law as well?

The extent to which we may identify early Islamic doctrine on the basis of the surviving juridical literature remains a vexed question. Harald Motzki has been a notable optimist, reconstructing very early Meccan jurisprudence on the basis of ʿAbd al-Razzāq's *Muṣannaf*.[4] At the other extreme, Norman Calder has asserted that the actual doctrines of Abū Ḥanīfa, al-Shāfiʿī, and other early figures are virtually irrecoverable.[5] The more persuasive arguments against Calder have had to do with the transmission of the *Muwaṭṭāʾ* as reconstructed from extant manuscripts and from the other extant recensions of the *Muwaṭṭaʾ* not discussed by Calder.[6] Less persuasive have been arguments that infer from *isnāds* integral transmission without editing and other sorts of feedback along the way. One also misses a direct, nondogmatic answer to Calder's literary-historical argument for locating the *Muwaṭṭaʾ* after the *Mudawwana*, mainly that its focus on Mālik and respect for Prophetic hadith are more plausibly located after [320] than before the *Mudawwana*'s more diffuse appeal to the opinions of Medinese jurisprudents.[7] We are still in suspense when it comes to early Ḥanafī and Shāfiʿī works, concerning which the prevailing response to Calder seems to be wishing him away.[8]

3. George Makdisi, "*Ṭabaqāt*-Biography: Law and Orthodoxy in Classical Islam," *Islamic Studies* (Islamabad), xxxii (1993), 371–396.

4. Harald Motzki, *Die Anfänge der islamischen Jurisprudenz: Ihre Entwicklung in Mekka bis zur Mitte des 2./8. Jahrhunderts* (Stuttgart: Franz Steiner, 1991); idem, "The *Musannaf* of ʿAbd al-Razzāq al-Ṣanʿānī as a Source of Authentic *aḥādīth* of the First Century A.H.," *Journal of Near Eastern Studies*, l (1991), 1–21.

5. Norman Calder, *Studies in Early Muslim Jurisprudence* (Oxford: Clarendon Press, 1993).

6. Most prominently, Miklos Muranyi, "Die frühe Rechtsliteratur zwischen Quellenanalyse und Fiktion," *Islamic Law and Society*, iv (1997), 224–41. Calder admits the bearing of manuscripts on dating, *Studies*, 38. See also Yasin Dutton, "*ʿAmal* v. *ḥadīth* in Islamic Law: The Case of *sadl al-yadayn* (Holding One's Hands by One's Sides) When Doing the Prayer," *Islamic Law and Society*, iii (1996), 13–40, esp. 28–33.

7. Calder, *Studies*, 36–37. A start on these lines has been made by Abdel-Magid Turki, "Le *Muwaṭṭaʾ* de Mâlik, ouvrage de *fiqh*, entre le *ḥadīt* et le *raʾy*, ou Comment aborder l'étude du Mâlikisme Kairouanais au IV/Xe siècle," *Studia Islamica*, no. 86 (1997), 5–35.

8. For example, Jonathan Brockopp patiently demonstrates by triangulation with the *Mukhtaṣar* of ʿAbd Allāh ibn ʿAbd al-Ḥakam that some doctrines in the *Muwaṭṭaʾ* must go back to Mālik; yet he assumes without argument that the *Risāla* goes back to Shāfiʿī and explains that Muzanī simply felt free to disregard his teacher's methodology: Jonathan E. Brockopp, "Early Islamic Jurisprudence in Egypt: Two Scholars and Their *Mukhtaṣars*," *International Journal of Middle East Studies*, 30 (1998), 167–182. Cf. Schacht's comment on Goldziher's skeptical regard for prophetic hadith: "This brilliant discovery be-

The history of early Islamic doctrine is naturally complicated by the very uneven survival of texts. We are relatively well informed when it comes to the nascent Mālikī school, particularly as it developed in Egypt and the West. On the basis of the *Mudawwana* of Saḥnūn, for example, Norman Calder has clearly identified a stage in the formation of Mālikī doctrine that focuses on Hijazi experts of the eighth century, by contrast with the sharp focus of the *Muwaṭṭa'* of Mālik (particularly the recension of Yaḥyā ibn Yaḥyā) on (1) hadith, Prophetic valued above Companion, and (2) Mālik as their authoritative interpreter.[9] For the Mālikī school, then, Schacht's theory of a regional stage seems to be confirmed.

Unfortunately, there is no book of Ḥanafī doctrine corresponding to the *Mudawwana* stage of Mālikī: that is, the books of Shaybānī and other extant Ḥanafī works of the mid-ninth century already focus almost exclusively on Abū Ḥanīfa, Abū Yūsuf, and Shaybānī. Had Ḥanafī doctrine an earlier, Kufan stage corresponding to the Hijazi stage of Mālikī doctrine? Schacht's theory of regional schools assumes there was; however, proof seems unavailable from the purely juridical literature, for the key works on the Iraqi side are lost or, occasionally, extant but unpublished. (Will someone go to Istanbul and tell us about al-Muᶜallā ibn Manṣūr, *Kitāb al-Nawādir?*[10])

For now, further evidence may be available in another body of literature, mainly biographical dictionaries. Whereas very little Ḥanafī [321] literature from the early ninth century is available to us, three biographical dictionaries from jurisprudents of that period have been edited and published: *al-Ṭabaqāt al-kubrā* of Ibn Saᶜd (d. 230/845) and the *Tārīkh* and *Ṭabaqāt* of Khalīfa ibn Khayyāṭ (d. 240/854–855?). Some collections of ninth-century Iraqi *rijāl* criticism seem insufficiently coherent to be called "biographical dictionaries," but I will check them as controls so far as possible. From later in the century, *al-Tārīkh al-kabīr* of al-Bukhārī (d. 256/870) turns out on examination to be mainly about identifying traditionists by name, not characterizing them, so let me leave it aside for review elsewhere. I shall also leave aside several less coherent works such as the *Ḍuᶜafā'* of Abū Zurᶜa al-Rāzī (d. 264/878) and the *Tārīkh* of Abū Zurᶜa al-Dimashqī (d. 281/894).[11]

---

came the corner-stone of all serious investigation of early Muhammadan law and jurisprudence, even if some later authors, while accepting Goldziher's method in principle, in their natural desire for positive results were inclined to minimize it in practice": Schacht, *Origins*, 4.

9. Calder, *Studies*, 11f, 16f, 21–24.

10. Fuat Sezgin, *Geschichte des arabischen Schrifttums*, 9 vols. to date (Leiden: E. J. Brill, 1967–), vol. 1, 434.

11. Saᶜdī al-Hāshimī, *Abū Zurᶜa al-Rāzī wa-juhūduhu fī al-sunna al-nabawīya*, al-Jāmiᶜa al-islāmīya bi-al-Madīna al-munawwara, al-Majlis al-ᶜilmī, Iḥyā' al-turāth al-islāmī 3, 3 vols. (n.p., 1402/1982), of which volume 2 includes editions of *Kitāb al-Ḍuᶜafā'* (317–555) and *Kitāb Asmā' al-ḍuᶜafā'* (557–778); Abū Zurᶜa al-Dimashqī, *Tārīkh*, ed. Shukr Allāh Niᶜmat Allāh al-Qūjānī, 2 vols. (Damascus: Majmaᶜ al-Lugha al-ᶜArabīya, 1980), repr. with new pagination and new introduction and notes by Khalīl Manṣūr (Beirut: Dār al-Kutub al-ᶜIlmīya, 1996).

Complicating comparisons, these latter works presumably do not express an Iraqi point of view anyway. But al-Fasawī (d. 277/890), *Kitāb al-Maʿrifa wa-al-tārīkh*, is another ninth-century biographical work from a specifically Basran point of view that should make a good supplementary witness to the state of Iraqi jurisprudence in that century.

My plan is to examine each of these books in turn, first looking for adherents of the Ḥanafi, Māliki, and Shāfiʿi schools, both as identified in later biographical dictionaries and as identified in these early works themselves; second looking for other evident divisions among the men of religion. (My basic list of Ḥanafīya comes from al-Ṣaymarī [d. 436/1045], *Akhbār Abī Ḥanīfa*,[12] of Mālikīya and Shāfiʿīya from Ibn ʿAbd al-Barr [d. 463/1071], *al-Intiqāʾ*.[13]) Together, I shall argue, these works suggest that the Ḥanafī school was originally Baghdadi; furthermore, that the notion of Ḥanafī origins in a regional Kufan school developed *pari passu* with a Basran tradition of opposing Medinese *ḥadīth* to Kufan *raʾy*. [322]

Khalīfa ibn Khayyāṭ

Khalīfa ibn Khayyāṭ was a minor Basran traditionist disparaged by the great *rijāl* critics of his century.[14] His *Tārīkh* is a concise chronology of Islamic history comprising mainly lists of names with some dates of birth and more of death. Under the names of caliphs are often listed their qadis. The last year covered is 232/846–847. Khalīfa ibn Khayyāṭ died when texts were still characteristically unstable, but I have observed no internal evidence by which to assign the *Tārīkh* to a later date.

Concerning the Ḥanafī school of law, the *Tārīkh* mentions both Abū Ḥanīfa himself, sub anno 150, and a considerable number of men listed by al-Ṣaymarī among the leading *aṣḥāb* of Abū Ḥanīfa and of his closest disciples. By date of death are listed Zāʾida (s.a. 161), Ḥibbān ibn ʿAlī (171), Abū Yūsuf (182), al-Fuḍayl ibn ʿIyāḍ (187), Muḥammad al-Shaybānī (189), Yūsuf ibn Khālid al-Samtī (190), Ḥafṣ ibn Ghiyāth (194), Wakīʿ ibn al-Jarrāḥ (197), Yaḥyā ibn Saʿīd al-Qaṭṭān (198), Muʿallā ibn Manṣūr al-Rāzī (211), Abū ʿĀṣim al-Ḍaḥḥāk ibn Makhlad (212), ʿAbd Allāh ibn Dāwūd al-Khuraybī (213), Muḥammad ibn ʿAbd Allāh al-Anṣārī (215), and ʿĪsā ibn Abān (221). In lists of different caliphs' qadis and governors, it additionally mentions al-Qāsim ibn Maʿn, al-Ḥasan ibn Ziyād al-Luʾluʾī, Ismāʿīl ibn Ḥammād ibn Abī Ḥanīfa, and Muḥammad ibn Muqātil al-Rāzī. Terse as it is, however, the *Tārīkh* never mentions schools of law nor even connections among the tra-

12. Al-Ṣaymarī, *Akhbār Abī Ḥanīfa wa-aṣḥābih*, Silsilat al-Maṭbūʿāt 13 (Hyderabad: Maṭbaʿat al-Maʿārif al-Sharqīya, 1394/1974; repr. Beirut: Dār al-Kitāb al-ʿArabī, 1976).

13. Ibn ʿAbd al-Barr (d. 463/1071), *al-Intiqāʾ fī faḍāʾil al-thalātha al-aʾimma al-fuqahāʾ* (Cairo: Maktabat al-Qudsī, 1350), 48–63, 104–115.

14. Ibn Ḥajar, *Tahdhīb "al-Tahdhīb,"* 12 vols. (Hyderabad: Majlis Dāʾirat al-Maʿārif al-Niẓāmīya, 1325–27), vol. 3, 160–61.

ditionists and qadis it lists. Therefore, we cannot tell whether Khalīfa associated any of these men with Abū Ḥanīfa.

As for the Mālikī school, Mālik's birth is noted under the name of the Umayyad caliph Sulaymān, his death s.a. 179.[15] Of those men whom Ibn ʿAbd al-Barr counts among the leading *aṣḥāb* of Mālik, the *Tārīkh* mentions only two: Maʿn ibn ʿĪsā (s.a. 198) and ʿAbd Allāh al-Qaʿnabī (220). Neither, as expected, is expressly connected with Mālik. Al-Shāfiʿī does not appear in the *Tārīkh*, nor any of his leading *aṣḥāb*.

Khalīfa's *Ṭabaqāt* appears to come from slightly later than the *Tārīkh*, for the last express date of death it mentions is 236/850–851.[16] [323] The *Ṭabaqāt* presents much the same information as the *Tārīkh* but is interested primarily in genealogy, hence is organized by family as well as date. Among the Companions, al-ʿAbbās and then the rest of the Hāshimids come first, then the Umayyads, and so forth. Next are listed the various metropoleis in which the Companions settled: Kufa, Basra, Medina, Mecca, Egypt, Syria, and so forth. The Companions within each region are still arranged according to genealogy, specifically nearness to the Prophet. Khalīfa ignores order of conversion.[17] The Followers and later generations are listed only according to geography, and some *mawālī* are admitted. Along with names, Khalīfa often provides dates and places of death but little more. Despite the universal absence of the familiar evaluations ("trustworthy," "weak," etc.), Khalīfa's interest as a traditionist (*muḥaddith*) emerges at such points as sections on who related hadith from the Prophet. An interest in hadith emerges also in his identification of succeeding *ṭabaqāt* not according to birth or death dates but, plainly, the evidence of *asānīd*, the chains of authorities supporting hadith reports.[18]

Abū Ḥanīfa appears twice in the *Ṭabaqāt*, once as a Kufan, once among those who settled in Baghdad. The *Ṭabaqāt* also mentions a number of men later listed among the leading *aṣḥāb* of Abū Ḥanīfa: among the Kufans, al-Qāsim ibn Maʿn, Mindal (or Mandal) ibn ʿAlī, Zāʾida ibn Qudāma, Ḥafṣ ibn Ghiyāth, and Wakīʿ ibn al-Jarrāḥ; among those who settled in Baghdad, Abū Yūsuf, Muḥammad al-Shaybānī, Yūsuf ibn Abī Yūsuf, and

15. Khalīfa ibn Khayyāṭ, *Tārīkh*, ed. Akram Ḍiyāʾ al-ʿUmarī (2nd ed., Damascus: Dār al-Qalam & Beirut: Muʾassasat al-Risāla, 1977), 318, 451.

16. Khalīfa ibn Khayyāṭ, *K. al-Ṭabaqāt riwāyat Abī ʿImrān Mūsā al-Tustarī*, ed. Akram Ḍiyāʾ al-ʿUmarī (Baghdad: Maṭbaʿat al-ʿĀnī, 1387/1967), 229 = *K. al-Ṭabaqāt*, ed. Suhayl Zakkār (2nd ed., Beirut: Dār al-Fikr, 1414/1993), 400. This latter is apparently the same text as Zakkār's first edition (Damascus: Wizārat al-Thaqāfa, 1967), unfortunately with altered pagination. The names referred to can easily be found in the indexes. Otherwise, "U" will precede references to al-ʿUmarī's first edition, "Z" references to Zakkār's second.

17. Akram Ḍiyāʾ al-ʿUmarī, "Introduction," *K. al-Ṭabaqāt* by Khalīfa ibn Khayyāṭ, ed. al-ʿUmarī, 38.

18. ʿUmarī, "Introduction," 45. Eerik Dickinson has now established that reported dates of death were of secondary interest to the great *rijāl* critics of the ninth century, who preferred to rely precisely on the evidence of *asānīd*: "The Development of Early Muslim Ḥadīth Criticism," Ph.D. diss., Yale Univ., 1992, chap. 6, esp. 165–169. Ibn al-Nadīm lists Khalīfa ibn Khayyāṭ and his works not among the historians but traditionist-jurisprudents: *K. al-Fihrist*, ed. Riḍā Tajaddud (n.p., n.d.), 111 = *fann* 6, *maqāla* 6.

al-Muʿallā ibn Manṣūr al-Rāzī; among the Basrans, Yūsuf ibn Khālid al-Samtī and Abū ʿĀṣim al-Ḍaḥḥāk ibn Makhlad; and among the Khurasanis, Ibn al-Mubārak. They are fewer than those mentioned in the *Ṭārīkh*, lacking chiefly those who appeared in the earlier work in lists of qadis and governors. The traditionist and ascetic Ibn al-Mubārak (d. Hit, 181/797?) is the only new name on the list, the only Ḥanafi (by later identification) found only in the *Ṭabaqāt*. Like the *Tārīkh*, the *Ṭabaqāt* never mentions connections among the [324] men it lists; therefore, again, we cannot tell whether Khalīfa himself connected any of these men with Abū Ḥanīfa.

Mālik ibn Anas appears in the *Ṭabaqāt* of Khalīfa ibn Khayyāṭ where one would expect, among the Medinese. Likewise, the *Ṭabaqāt* mentions a number of men later listed among Mālik's leading *aṣḥāb*: among the Medinese, ʿAbd al-ʿAzīz ibn Abī Ḥāzim, Maʿn ibn ʿĪsā, and ʿAbd Allāh ibn Nāfiʿ al-Ṣāʾigh; among the Basrans, Qaʿnabī; and among the people of the Maghrib (which for Khalīfa stretches from Egypt to Andalusia), Ibn Wahb. There are still some striking omissions; yet the *Ṭabaqāt* does name twice as many Mālikīya as does the *Tārīkh*. Neither work connects any of these men to Mālik. Al-Shāfiʿī does not appear in the *Ṭabaqāt*, and neither do any of his leading *aṣḥāb*.

A striking feature of the *Ṭabaqāt* and *Tārīkh* of Khalīfa ibn Khayyāṭ is their geographical unevenness. In the *Ṭabaqāt*, the last death recorded among the Kufans is 229 (U173, Z295), among the Basrans 236 (U229, Z400), with plenty more from the 220's; among the Medinese, by contrast, the last recorded death is 199 (U276, Z483), among the Meccans 214 (U284, Z505), among the Maghribis 223—but the previous entry is for 196 or 197 (U297, corrected, Z545); among the Syrians, finally, it is 202 (U317, Z581). Khalīfa thus appears to be up to date concerning Iraq, a little less so concerning the Hijaz, and only sketchily informed of developments in Syria and North Africa. Presumably, this is a good part of the reason so many fewer Mālikīya appear in his works than Ḥanafīya, and no Shāfiʿīya whatever. However, his interest in the Ḥanafīya (at least as they would be identified in retrospect) appears to have decreased between the writing of the *Tārīkh* and the *Ṭabaqāt*, whereas his interest in the Mālikīya appears to have increased.

Ibn Saʿd

Muḥammad ibn Saʿd was a *mawlā* of Basran origin.[19] He was known as Kātib al-Wāqidī on account of his discipleship to Muḥammad ibn ʿUmar al-Wāqidī (d. Baghdad, 207/823), an historian and jurisprudent who moved from Medina to Baghdad in 180/796–797 at the age of 50 [325] or so.[20] Ibn Saʿd was sufficiently prominent to be one of the first half-dozen

19. Al-Khaṭīb al-Baghdādī, *Tārīkh Baghdād*, 14 vols. (Cairo: Maktabat al-Khānjī, 1931), vol. 5, 321; Ibn Khallikān, *Wafayāt al-aʿyān*, ed. Iḥsān ʿAbbās, 7 vols. + index (Beirut: Dār al-Thaqāfa, 1968, 1973; repr. Dār Ṣādir, n.d.), vol. 4, 351.

20. Al-Khaṭīb al-Baghdādī, *Tārīkh*, vol. 3, 4.

jurisprudents summoned by Maʾmūn in 218/833 to testify in public that the Qurʾan was create.[21] His reputation as a traditionist was a little better than Khalīfa's.[22]

Ibn Saʿd's *Ṭabaqāt* is essentially, as al-Khaṭīb al-Baghdādī says, "a large book on the layers of the Companions, the Followers, and those who came after them until his own time."[23] It is certainly fullest for the first Islamic century. It begins with a biography of the Prophet, occupying about a quarter of the whole, then relates stories of the Companions in the period of the Medinese caliphate, another quarter or so of the whole. The second half, of interest here, describes the jurisprudents and traditionists of each major metropolis, except for a large section at the end describing female Companions.

Unlike the *Tārīkh* and *Ṭabaqāt* of Khalīfa ibn Khayyāṭ, we cannot plausibly assign the *Ṭabaqāt* of Ibn Saʿd entirely to its reputed author: although Ibn Saʿd died in 230/845, his dictionary includes an entry for himself[24] and for many other persons who died in the 230's. The latest death it expressly notices is that of Aḥmad ibn Ḥanbal in 241/855 (L7/2:92, B7:354f), indicating about when it was finished. (Of all its subjects, the last to die, so far as I have noticed, is Abū Saʿīd al-Ashajj. All that appears of him in the *Ṭabaqāt* is that "his name is ʿAbd Allāh ibn Saʿīd al-Kindī," without further information: it seems likely that it was set down before his death, which other sources tell us was in 257/871 [L6:289, B6:415]. Nearby, someone is referred to in the present tense ["he lives in al-Maṭmūra in Kufa near the house of Abū Usāma"] who other sources tell us died in 248/862 [L6:289, B6:414]. Conventions such as not to mention the names of contemporaries were doubtfully well-established already in the mid-ninth century.) The interpolator seems to have been al-Ḥusayn ibn Fahm (d. 289/901–902).[25] Comparison with the works of Khalīfa ibn

21. Al-Ṭabarī, *Annales*, ed. M. J. de Goeje, 3 vols. in 15 (Leiden: E. J. Brill, 1879–1901), vol. 3, 1116 = *Tārīkh al-Ṭabarī*, ed. Muḥammad Abū al-Faḍl Ibrāhīm, Dhakhāʾir al-ʿArab 30, 10 vols. (Cairo: Dār al-Maʿārif, 1960–69), vol. 8, 634.

22. See Ibn Ḥajar, *Tahdhīb*, vol. 9, 182–83.

23. Al-Khaṭīb al-Baghdādī, *Tārīkh*, vol. 5, 321.

24. Ibn Saʿd, *Biographien*, ed. Eduard Sachau, & al., 9 vols. in 15 (Leiden: E. J. Brill, 1904–40), vol. 7/2, 99 = *al-Ṭabaqāt al-kubrā*, 8 vols. + index (Beirut: Dār Ṣādir, 1957–68; repr. 1418/1998), vol. 7, 364. Henceforward, "L" will precede references to the Leiden edition, "B" to the Beirut, which is almost exactly the same text but shorn of introductions and notes.

25. So *Encyclopaedia of Islam*, new ed., s.v. "Ibn Saʿd," by J. W. Fück; *contra* Fuat Sezgin, who names al-Ḥārith ibn Abī Usāma al-Tamīmī (d. 282/896): *GAS*, vol. 1, 300. One of our manuscripts of the *Ṭabaqāt* is said to combine the recensions of Ibn Fahm and al-Ḥārith ibn Abī Usāma: Ibn Saʿd, *Biographien*, vol. 5, ix. The evidence for Fück's view is that many apparent interpolations in the *Ṭabaqāt* are quoted in *Tārīkh Baghdād* as coming from al-Ḥusayn ibn Fahm; e.g., concerning Muṣʿab al-Zubayrī (d. 236/851), L7/2:84, B7:344 = al-Khaṭīb al-Baghdādī, *Tārīkh*, vol. 13, 114, ll. 12–16. Cf. *Tārīkh Baghdād*, vol. 12, 415, ll. 12–17, where information about Abū ʿUbayd (d. 224/839?) comes < al-Ḥusayn ibn Fahm < Muḥammad ibn Saʿd = L7/2:93, B7:355. Admittedly, one sometimes finds confusion between Ibn Fahm's knowledge and Ibn Saʿd's; e.g., *Tārīkh Baghdād*, vol. 7, 83, ll. 9–16, where information about the 230's comes < Ibn Fahm < Ibn Saʿd (L7/2:93, B7:355). Ibn Fahm is apparently credited with a separate work, *Tasmiyat man*

Khayyāṭ on the one [326] hand and of Fasawī on the other suggests that the *Ṭabaqāt* of Ibn Saʿd does belong somewhere between them; that is (as I shall develop further below), its perspective fits what else is firm about the rivalry of different schools at the third quarter of the ninth century.

Strikingly, Ibn Saʿd presents the Ḥanafīya as a phenomenon of Baghdad, not Kufa. Abū Ḥanīfa himself has two entries, one among the traditionists and jurisprudents of Kufa (L6:256, B6:368f), another among those of Baghdad (L7/2:67, B7:322). No subsequent Kufan is connected with him, and only one, Zufar ibn al-Hudhayl (L6:270, B6:387f), is even associated with *raʾy*. One later Basran is connected with *raʾy*, Yūsuf ibn Khālid al-Samtī (L7/2:47, B7:292f), but likewise not with Abū Ḥanīfa himself.

On the contrary, nearly all those whom Ibn Saʿd points out as transmitting the opinions of Abū Ḥanīfa or of his disciples appear as Baghdadis: Abū Yūsuf (L7/2:73f, B7:330f), Asad ibn ʿAmr al-Bajalī (L7/2:74, B7:331), ʿĀfiya ibn Yazīd al-Awdī (L7/2:74, B7:331), Muḥammad al-Shaybānī (L7/2:78, B7:336f), Yūsuf ibn Abī Yūsuf (L7/2:78f, B7:337), al-Ḥusayn ibn Ibrāhīm ibn al-Ḥurr (L7/2:87f, B7:348), and Bishr ibn al-Walīd al-Kindī (L7/2:93, B7:355f). Al-Muʿallā ibn Manṣūr is associated with *raʾy* but not specifically Abū Ḥanīfa's (L7/2:82, B7:341), in contrast to the later tradition that puts him among the early *aṣḥāb*.[26] The only non-Baghdadi whom Ibn Saʿd identifies as among the *aṣḥāb* of Abū Ḥanīfa is al-Naḍr ibn Muḥammad al-Marwazī, listed among the jurisprudents and traditionists of Khurasan (L7/2:105, B7:373). [327]

Ibn Saʿd's characterization of Ḥanafism as a Baghdadi phenomenon agrees with Nurit Tsafrir's finding, mainly from the evidence of judicial appointments in Wakīʿ, *Akhbār al-quḍāh*, that Ḥanafism did not effectively take over jurisprudence in Kufa and Basra until well into the third Islamic century.[27] It would have come as an outside force equally to each city.

Actually, we should have missed early Kufan Ḥanafism long ago. The Ḥanafi biographer al-Ṣaymarī, whose *Akhbār Abī Ḥanīfa wa-aṣḥābih* is the earliest extant biographical treatment of the Ḥanafi school, goes on from listing the supposed *aṣḥāb* of Abū Ḥanīfa to listing twenty-four other leading lights of the school up to Abū al-Ḥasan al-Karkhī (d. 340/952), beginning with the *aṣḥāb* of Abū Yūsuf, Zufar, and Shaybānī.[28] Only one of the twenty-four seems to have been Kufan, an Egyptian qadi said to have learnt jurispru-

kāna bi-Baghdād min al-ʿulamāʾ, at *Tārīkh Baghdād*, vol. 10, 448, l. 22, Ibn Fahm and Ibn Saʿd together with a *Tasmiyat man kāna bi-Baghdād min al-muḥaddithīn* at *Tārīkh Baghdād*, vol. 12, 229, ll. 5–6. Possibly, the various geographic components of the *Ṭabaqāt* sometimes circulated independently. His name appears as "Ḥusayn ibn al-Fahm" in the *Ṭabaqāt* itself: L7/2:94, B7:357.

26. Ṣaymarī, *Akhbār*, 154.

27. Nurit Tsafrir, "The Spread of the Ḥanafī School in the Western Regions of the ʿAbbāsid Caliphate Up to the End of the Third Century A.H.," " Ph.D. diss., Princeton, 1993, chaps. 2, 3.

28. Ṣaymarī, *Akhbār*, 154–162.

dence from Abū Yūsuf (therefore very likely, in fact, Baghdadi in formation).[29] Otherwise, they comprise ten figures from Baghdad, seven from the Jibal, four from Basra, and one from Old Cairo, with two others of whom almost nothing is known.[30] Kufan Ḥanafīya are not missing only from Ibn Saᶜd, then, for not even Ḥanafi sources indicate a flourishing Ḥanafi school in Kufa.

Mālik has a prominent place in Ibn Saᶜd's treatment of the Medinese, at the head of his *ṭabaqa*.[31] Of his *aṣḥāb* (as identified by Ibn ᶜAbd al-Barr), there appear among the Medinese ᶜAbd al-ᶜAzīz ibn Abī Ḥāzim (L5:313f, B5:424), Maᶜn ibn ᶜĪsā (L5:324, B5:437), ᶜAbd Allāh ibn Nāfiᶜ al-Ṣāᵓigh (L5:324, B5:438),ᶜAbd Allāh ibn Nāfiᶜ al-Zubayrī (L5:325, B5:439), and ᶜAbd al-Malik ibn al-Mājashūn [328] (L5:327, B5:442); among the Basrans, Qaᶜnabī (L7/2:302, B7:302); and among the Egyptians, Ibn Wahb (L7/2:205, B7:518) and ᶜAbd Allāh ibn ᶜAbd al-Ḥakam (L7/2:205, B7:518). This is three more than appear in the *Ṭabaqāt* of Khalīfa ibn Khayyāṭ.

The list of those whom Ibn Saᶜd himself expressly identifies as *aṣḥāb* of Mālik or as having stuck to him is rather different: in Medina, ᶜAbd Allāh ibn Nāfiᶜ al-Ṣāᵓigh (d. 206/821–822; L5:324, B5:438), Muṭarrif ibn ᶜAbd Allāh (d. 220/835, L5:325, B5:438f), ᶜAtīq ibn Yaᶜqūb (d. 227 or 228/ca. 842; L5:326, B5:439f), and ᶜAbd al-Malik ibn al-Mājashūn (L5:327, B5:442). Among the Basrans, Bishr ibn ᶜUmar al-Zahrānī (d. 209/824; L7/2:52, B7:300) and Qaᶜnabī (L7/2:54, B7:302) are described as relating much from Mālik but not precisely as *aṣḥāb*; similarly, in Baghdad, Muṣᶜab al-Zubayrī (d. 236/851; L7/2:84, B7:344), who related the *Muwaṭṭaᵓ*. Mālik is not mentioned in connection with anyone in Khurasan or Egypt. It would be unreasonable to conclude from Ibn Saᶜd's omitting to mention something, such as Egyptian Mālikism, that it did not exist. Independent evidence sometimes proves otherwise, as surviving juridical texts such as the *Mudawwana* prove that Egyptian learning from Medina was considerable. It does seem reasonable to conclude that Egyptian Mālikism was scarcely known in Baghdad in the later 240's/earlier 860's. As from the works of Khalīfa ibn Khayyāṭ, Shāfiᶜī and his Egyptian *aṣḥāb* are completely absent from the *Ṭabaqāt* of Ibn Saᶜd (with the single exception of al-Ḥumaydī,

29. Ibrāhīm ibn al-Jarrāḥ (d. Old Cairo, 217/832?), on whom see Ibn Abī al-Wafāᵓ, *al-Jawāhir al-muḍīya fī ṭabaqāt al-ḥanafīya*, ed. ᶜAbd al-Fattāḥ Muḥammad al-Ḥulw, 5 vols. (Cairo: Dār Iḥyāᵓ al-Kutub al-ᶜArabīya, 1398–1408/1978–88; repr. Giza: Hajr, 1413/1993), vol. 1, 75–77, with references to other sources.

30. Al-Ḥasan ibn Abī Mālik (d. 204/819–820) and Sulaymān ibn Shuᶜayb al-Kaysānī, the latter evidently confused by Ibn Abī al-Wafāᵓ with a later Egyptian of the same name: see *Jawāhir*, vol. 2, 234–35; Samᶜānī, *Ansāb*, s.v. "Kaysānī" = 5 vols. (Beirut: Dār al-Janān, 1408/1988), vol. 5, 123. Ṣaymarī expressly observes that he has omitted to list the Ḥanafīya of Khurasan: *Akhbār*, 168.

31. The Leiden edition of Ibn Saᶜd, *Ṭabaqāt* (also in turn the Beirut edition), is missing several generations of Medinese, including the first half of Mālik's. This gap is now filled by Ibn Saᶜd, *al-Ṭabaqāt al-kubrā: al-Qism al-mutammim li-tābiᶜī ahl al-Madīna wa-man baᶜdahum, min rubᶜ al-ṭabaqa al-thālitha ilā muntaṣaf al-ṭabaqa al-sādisa*, ed. Ziyād Muḥammad Manṣūr, Silsilat iḥyāᵓ al-turāth 6 (Medina: al-Jāmiᶜa al-Islāmīya & al-Majlis al-ᶜIlmī, 1403/1983).

L5:368, B5:502, without express connection to Shāfiʿī). Therefore, we may venture to say also that Egyptian Shāfiʿism was yet unknown in Baghdad.

Ibn Saʿd's arrangement of the Companions differs from that of Khalīfa in that he does pay attention to dates of conversion.[32] His arrangement of the great metropoleis differs, as well: not Kufa, Basra, Medina, Mecca, but Medina, Mecca, Kufa, Basra. As the Hijaz seems to have become more important from the *Tārīkh* of Khalīfa to his *Ṭabaqāt*, so also it has become more important from the *Ṭabaqāt* of Khalīfa to the *Ṭabaqāt* of Ibn Saʿd. Fasawī continues the trend, on which more below.

It is not evident from Ibn Saʿd's comments on individual traditionists and jurisprudents that he favors one city over another. He does report a higher proportion of weak transmitters in Kufa and Medina, the smallest proportion of weak transmitters in Basra. His comments on individual traditionists and jurisprudents suggest two other important [329] oppositions: first, *ḥadīth* and *athar* (transmitted material) against *raʾy* (original speculation); second, *sunna* (here, orthodoxy) against various heresies.

As for *ḥadīth* against *raʾy*, Ibn Saʿd apparently accepts that some of the pious early figures engaged in speculative jurisprudence, *raʾy*. The prominent Meccan jurisprudent Ibn Jurayj is quoted as saying of ʿAṭāʾ ibn Abī Rabāḥ (d. 114 or 115/*ca.* 733), "When he related something and I asked whether it was *ʿilm* or *raʾy*, he would tell me it was *ʿilm* if it was transmitted (*in kāna atharan*), whereas if it was *raʾy* he would say it was *raʾy*" (L5:345, B5:469). Ibn Saʿd actually refers to "the hadith of the *raʾy* of al-Shaʿbī" (L6:243, B6:349), elsewhere says that had al-Ḥasan al-Baṣrī met the Companions as an adult, they would have needed his *raʾy* (L7/1:117, B7:161). This positive appraisal of *raʾy* is in line with the word's original signification. It is also in line with the respect of Ibn Saʿd's traditionalist contemporaries for the opinions of the earliest generations of Muslims (as opposed to the opinions of later jurisprudents) evident in the juridical work of Aḥmad ibn Ḥanbal.[33]

Nevertheless, Ibn Saʿd plainly prefers that one stick to transmission rather than answering speculatively. The prominent Basran traditionist Ḥammād ibn Zayd is quoted as saying of Ayyūb al-Sakhtiyānī (d. 131/748–749), "Ayyūb was asked about something, to which he said, 'Nothing has reached me concerning it.' He said, 'Answer with your opinion.' He said there had reached him nothing of opinion" (L7/2:14, B7:247). A similar exchange with the Basran al-Shaʿbī (d. 105/723–724?) concludes more colorfully with al-Shaʿbī's saying, "What will you do with my opinion? Piss on my opinion" (L6/174, B6:250).

The way Ibn Saʿd describes more recent figures' engagement with *raʾy* likewise bespeaks distaste. Of Abū Yūsuf, for example, he says,

32. ʿUmarī, "Introduction," 38–39.

33. See Susan A. Spectorsky, "Aḥmad Ibn Ḥanbal's *Fiqh*," *Journal of the American Oriental Society*, 102 (1982), 461–65.

> He used to go to the traditionist and memorize fifty or sixty hadith reports, then go and dictate them to the people. Then he stuck to Abū Ḥanīfa al-Nuʿmān ibn Thābit and learnt jurisprudence. He was won over by *raʾy* and turned from hadith (L7/2:74, B7:330).

"Jurisprudence" (*fiqh*) appears as a special category not reducible to either hadith or *raʾy*. For example, Ibn Saʿd describes al-Muʿallā ibn Manṣūr as a master of *ḥadīth*, *raʾy*, and *fiqh*. "Some traditionists (*aṣḥāb al-ḥadīth*) relate (all sorts of learning) from him, while some of them do not relate *raʾy* from him" (L7/2:82, B7:341). And whereas *raʾy* is accepted in early figures, rejected in later, *fiqh* seems to be accepted [330] even in near-contemporaries. For example, the Māliki ʿAbd al-Malik ibn al-Mājashūn is credited with having both *fiqh* and *riwāya*, jurisprudence and relation (of hadith; L5:327, B5:442).

As for *sunna* against heresy, the principal enemies seem to be the Murjiʾa, Qadarīya, and Shīʿa. A majority of the named Murjiʾa are Kufan, but others are found in Mecca, Basra, al-Madaʾin, and Khurasan, and the doctrine was allegedly invented by a Medinese, al-Ḥasan ibn al-Ḥanafīya (B5:328). It was possible to be both a Murjiʾ and a trustworthy traditionist; e.g., Shabāba ibn Sawwār of al-Madaʾin (L7/2:66, B7:320). The Qadarīya are fewer, either Basrans or Damascenes. Again, it was possible to talk of *qadar* and remain a trustworthy traditionist; e.g., Hishām ibn ʿAbd Allāh (d. 152/769–770?) of Basra (L7/2:37, B7:279). Shiʿism, too, was sometimes compatible with trustworthiness in hadith; e.g., ʿAbbād ibn al-ʿAwwām (d. 185/801–802), a Wasiti who settled in Baghdad after a period of imprisonment there at the hands of Hārūn (L7/2:73, B7:330). Shīʿism admits of degrees (*shadīd*, *mufriṭ*), but no one is accused of *rafḍ*. Of course, sectaries might sometimes recommend themselves by attacking other sectaries; e.g., ʿAwf ibn Abī Jamīla (d. 146/763–764), a Basran Shiʿi who exposed the lying of the Muʿtazili ʿAmr ibn ʿUbayd (L7/2:22, B7:258). ʿAmr is the only Muʿtazili to whom a biography is devoted (L7/2:33, B7:273).

Remarkably, although a number of Baghdadis are noted for advocating *waqf*, refusal to declare the Qur'an either create or increate, Ibn Saʿd accuses no one of holding outright that the Qurʾan was create. Neither is anyone identified for any other reason as a Jahmī, the usual word in Aḥmad ibn Ḥanbal's parlance for someone who said the Qurʾan was create, denied that hell would last forever, and so on. As one would expect, the post-Inquisition controversies over the createdness of faith and of the pronunciation (*lafẓ*) of the Qur'an make no appearance. More surprisingly, although *ṣāḥib raʾy* is fairly common, *ṣāḥib kalām* never appears at all. Ibn Saʿd and his redactor write as traditionalists but do not use precisely the language of the ninth-century Ḥanābila.

On the positive side, Ibn Saʿd identifies a number of men as *ṣāḥib sunna*, others as *ṣāḥib sunna wa-jamāʿa*. The stress of the addition is presumably on anti-Shiʿism but not every sort of anti-Shiʿism, for several Basrans are also given the label "ʿUthmānī." *Aṣḥāb sunna* are more numerous in Kufa than any other metropolis, presumably because it was a locus of controversy and positions were declared more [331] emphatically. There is no necessary connection between being *ṣāḥib sunna* and being a prolific or trustworthy traditionist; e.g., Ibrāhīm ibn Abī al-Layth of Baghdad, considered weak (L7/2:97, B7:360).

Al-Fasawī

Another biographical source from the ninth century itself is *Kitāb al-Maʿrifa wa-al-tārīkh* of Abū Yūsuf Yaʿqūb ibn Sufyān al-Fasawī. Fasawī's *shuhra* refers to Fasā, a city in the province of Fars.[34] He collected hadith in Basra, the Hijaz, Egypt, Syria, and Mesopotamia. He was back in Fars by 237/851–852 and reached Balkh in 240/854–855.[35] However, he died back in Basra, 277/890. He was a respected traditionist, appearing in two of the Six Books.[36]

Only some of his book, *Kitāb al-Maʿrifa wa-al-tārīkh* (henceforward *KMT*), has survived in manuscript. The greater part has been edited by Akram Ḍiyāʾ al-ʿUmarī, whose third edition is the fullest and to which citations in this article refer.[37] He includes at the end some quotations by other writers that may represent lost portions of *KMT* (3:248–576).

On the evidence of dates alone, Fasawī's *KMT* is about as old as Ibn Saʿd's *Ṭabaqāt*, the last recorded death in *KMT* being likewise that of Aḥmad ibn Ḥanbal in 241/855 (1:213). The editor of *KMT* considers Fasawī to have composed it in the first half of the third century (i.e., before 251/866), which seems likely for the chronological section but less so for what follows.[38] For one, Fasawī is often expressly named at the head of its chains of authorities and occasionally talked about in the third person; e.g., "He passed Ibn Ṭāwūs and another whom al-Ḥumaydī named but whose name Abū Yūsuf [al-Fasawī] forgot" (2:691). For another, *KMT* is a strangely disordered book. Only the introductory chronology, the *tārīkh* of the title, looks like a deliberate composition, running up to the death of Aḥmad A.H. 241 and Fasawī's own activities A.H. 242. From there it proceeds to discussions of the Companions by order of name, first the ʿAbādila (1:238), then the [332] ʿUthmāns (1:271), etc. This sequence suggests the beginning of a biographical dictionary not unlike the *Ṭabaqāt* of Ibn Saʿd and might indeed have been written by Fasawī in the first half of the century.

Before going on to the Followers of Medina, though, Fasawī presents a letter from the Egyptian al-Layth ibn Saʿd to Mālik, then Mālik's reply, which the editor has removed to another spot (1:346, 687–695). The letters in their original position would have made only one of very many digressions to come. For example, a section on *kunyas* (3:67–85) turns into a list of persons from whom Sufyān ibn ʿUyayna related hadith, with comments,

34. Samʿānī, *Ansāb*, s.v. "Fasawī" = (Beirut) vol. 4, 384.

35. See the résumé in al-ʿUmarī, "Introduction," *K. al-Maʿrifa wa-al-tārīkh* by al-Fasawī, ed. Akram Ḍiyāʾ al-ʿUmarī, 4 vols. (3rd ed., Medina: Maktabat al-Dār, 1410/1989), vol. 1, 8–11, based mainly on remarks in *K. al-Maʿrifa wa-al-Tārīkh* itself.

36. Ibn Ḥajar, *Tahdhīb*, vol. 11, 385–388.

37. I have been unable to consult Miklòs Muranyi, *Beiträge zur Geschichte der Ḥadīt- und Rechtsgelehrsamkeit der Mālikiyya bis zum 5. Jh. d. H.*, Bio-bibliographische Notizen aus der Moscheebibliothek von Qairawān (Wiesbaden: Otto Harrassowitz, 1996).

38. ʿUmarī, "Introduction," *KMT*, vol. 1, 42.

goes on to comments from Ḥumaydī on some others (114f), goes back to *kunyas* for a few pages (117f, 123), then miscellany, back to Sufyān ibn ʿUyayna's shaykhs (151–153), back to Ḥumaydī's shaykhs, finally back to *kunyas* with further digressions (168–174, 203–207, 210f, 231–245). The image it suggests is of Fasawī reading off his notes to one or more students. *KMT*'s development of certain themes just barely visible in the books of Khalīfa ibn Khayyāṭ and Ibn Saʿd, as well as what we know of Ḥanafi-Māliki conflict in ninth-century Baghdad, also suggest a date near the time of Fasawī's death, on which more below.

To begin as usual with the leading Ḥanafiya, as remembered by Ṣaymarī in the eleventh century, Fasawī mentions fewer than either Khalīfa ibn Khayyāṭ or Ibn Saʿd. This must be partly because he himself apparently never travelled to either Baghdad or Kufa. More, however, it must be due to his clear hostility toward the Ḥanafi school. Those whom he expressly connects with Abū Ḥanīfa are Abū Yūsuf, Ḥafṣ ibn Ghiyāth, al-Qāsim ibn Maʿn, Wakīʿ ibn al-Jarrāḥ, Yaḥyā ibn Saʿīd al-Qaṭṭān, Abū ʿĀṣim al-Ḍaḥḥāk ibn Makhlad, and Ibn al-Mubārak, most of whom Ibn Saʿd mentions without a Ḥanafi connection. Fasawī characterizes most of them as outright hostile to Abū Ḥanīfa. Ḥafṣ ibn Ghiyāth complains that Abū Ḥanīfa would endorse five different positions in one day concerning a single problem (2:789). Wakīʿ ibn al-Jarrāḥ quotes Abū Ḥanīfa as saying (incriminating himself), "Some analogies are uglier than pissing in a mosque" (1:673). (The terminology does not imply direct transmission, and Wakīʿ has just quoted the Medinese Rabīʿat al-Raʾy [d. 136/753–754], as well, against analogy.) Yaḥyā ibn Saʿīd al-Qaṭṭān quotes Sufyān al-Thawrī as saying that Abū Ḥanīfa was twice asked to repent of *kufr* (2:786). Abū ʿĀṣim al-Ḍaḥḥāk ibn Makhlad confirms that Abū Ḥanīfa misrepresented the position of Ibn ʿAbbās, as al-Thawrī had accused him of doing (3:14). Ibn al-Mubārak is quoted as saying that Abū [333] Ḥanīfa was a Murjiʾ (2:783). He is also made to disparage Abū Yūsuf, advising that someone repeat any prayers he has prayed behind him (implying that Abū Yūsuf was an unbeliever) and expressing disgust for the mention of his name (2:789). Abū Yūsuf does not sound hostile, but he is quoted as admitting that Abū Ḥanīfa had been a Jahmī and a Murjiʾ (2:782, again 783). Another Kufan reproaches al-Qāsim ibn Maʿn for going to sit with Abū Ḥanīfa. "He will give you mastery over as much *raʾy* as you can chew, but you will go back home without *fiqh*" (2:790).

(Al-Khaṭīb al-Baghdādī quotes the same reproach from the same Kufan but has it directed either to "a man" [one *isnād*, not including Fasawī] or to "a group" [two *isnād*s, neither including Fasawī].[39] Some traditionalist may have tried to whitewash al-Qāsim ibn Maʿn's reputation by suppressing his association with Abū Ḥanīfa; alternatively, someone

39. Al-Khaṭīb al-Baghdādī, *Tārīkh*, vol. 13, 416 (446 of rev. ed. with pro-Ḥanafi footnotes). A garbled version without al-Qāsim appears in Aḥmad ibn Ḥanbal, *K. al-ʿIlal wa-maʿrifat al-rijāl*, ed. Waṣī Allāh ibn Muḥammad ʿAbbās, 4 vols. (Beirut: al-Maktab al-Islāmī, 1988), vol. 1), 387 = idem, *K. al-Jāmiʿ fī al-ʿilal wa-maʿrifat al-rijāl*, ed. Muḥammad Ḥusām Bayḍūn, 2 vols. (Beirut: Muʾassasat al-Kutub al-Thaqāfīyah, 1410/1990), vol. 1, 150.

tried to blacken it by adding al-Qāsim's name to the story. The different versions surely constitute a warning that witticisms were more easily remembered than individuals, and that we should not presume a secure documentary record behind any of these polemics.)

Most of these expressly anti-Ḥanafi sayings are from a section headed "What has come down concerning Kufa, Abū Ḥanīfa al-Nuʿmān ibn Thābit and his *aṣḥāb*, al-Aʿmash, and others" (2:746–795). The section begins with reports concerning the End Times. By my count, it includes thirty-three items derogatory of Abū Ḥanīfa, five of Ḥammād ibn Abī Sulaymān, four of Abū Yūsuf, and one or two of half a dozen others (including once Shaybānī, 2:791). Fasawī's hostility toward Abū Ḥanīfa and his followers is notably sharper than Ibn Saʿd's. Fasawī's consideration of Abū Ḥanīfa next to earlier Kufan jurisprudents (even more the section title, although it admittedly might have been added by some later copyist) is a major shift from Ibn Saʿd's identification of Abū Ḥanīfa and his followers with Baghdad.

As for the Mālikīya, somewhat more appear in *KMT*, and more are connected with Mālik. The Egyptian Ibn Wahb appears in more than 150 *isnāds*, of which about a third go back to Mālik himself, the rest to various other Egyptian and Hijazi forebears. Ibn al-Qāsim is noted at his death s.a. 191, otherwise twice, both times quoting Mālik. Ashhab [334] is noted at his death s.a. 204, otherwise four times quoting Mālik. Muḥammad ibn Ibrāhīm ibn Dīnār appears once, as quoted by Ibn Wahb, relating that the early Medinese jurisprudent Ibn Hurmuz respected *sunna* over *raʾy* (1:652). ʿAbd Allāh ibn Nāfiʿ al-Ṣāʾigh appears in one *isnād* going back ultimately to the Companion Zayd ibn Thābit, who proposes that one may deduce the *sunna* from the practice of the people of Medina (1:438). ʿAbd al-Malik ibn al-Mājashūn is quoted once as transmitting from Mālik the story of a conversation between two Companions on the difference between ʿUmar's ruling and the Prophet's (1:363). ʿAbd Allāh ibn Ghānim al-Ifrīqī appears once as a transmitter from Mālik (2:504). Maʿn ibn ʿĪsā appears a dozen times, twice as a transmitter from Mālik. Qaʿnabī appears over sixty times, in the majority as a transmitter from Mālik. Yaḥyā ibn Yaḥyā al-Naysābūrī appears as a direct informant, also once as a transmitter from Mālik. Mālik himself is quoted through various transmitters 166 times.[40]

Mālik thus appears as by far the most illustrious jurisprudent of Medina; yet *KMT*'s coverage of the Mālikī school appears oddly lopsided. Fasawī's chief Meccan informant is Abū Bakr al-Ḥumaydī (d. 219/834), famous mainly as a traditionist. Fasawī's chief Egyptian informant is Ibn Wahb, famous in later Mālikī tradition precisely for his loyalty to hadith. (Recall the story of Asad's collecting his *Mudawwana* from Ibn al-Qāsim, Ibn Wahb having stubbornly refused to relate the *raʾy* that Asad needed.[41]) His chief Basran

---

40. ʿUmarī, "Introduction," *KMT*, vol. 1, 46.

41. Abū Bakr al-Mālikī, *K. Riyāḍ al-nufūs*, ed. Bashīr al-Bakkūsh, 2 vols. (Beirut: Dār al-Gharb al-Islāmī, 1983), vol. 1, 261; M. Talbi, "Kairouan et le mālikisme espagnol," *Etudes d'orientalisme dédiées à la mémoire de Lévi-Provençal*, 2 vols. (Paris: G.-P. Maisonneuve et Larose, 1957), vol. 1, 322.

transmitter from Mālik is ʿAbd Allāh al-Qaʿnabī, who appears to have been the Basran Māliki most loyal to hadith; whose recension of the *Muwaṭṭaʾ* will give a proof from hadith where Yaḥyā ibn Yaḥyā's is satisfied with *raʾy*.[42] By contrast, leading exponents of Māliki *jurisprudence* appear seldom or never. In Medina, ʿUthmān ibn ʿĪsā ibn Kināna (d. 185/801–802) was later known for sitting in Mālik's place after him yet never appears in *KMT*.[43] The most famous Egyptian exponents of Māliki jurisprudence are represented weakly (Ibn al-Qāsim and Ashhab; Yūnus ibn ʿAbd al-Aʿlā appears more often, transmitting from Ibn Wahb and [335] Ashhab) or not at all (ʿAbd Allāh ibn ʿAbd al-Ḥakam, not to mention the transmitters of Māliki doctrine to the West). Finally, one misses Aḥmad ibn al-Muʿadhdhal (d. *ca.* 240/854–855), said to have introduced Māliki *raʾy* to Basra.[44] Fasawī once mentions the *Muwaṭṭaʾ* of Mālik, but only to comment that all but one of the traditionists mentioned in it are trustworthy (1:425); that is, he treats it as a collection of hadith. In short, *KMT* presents a Māliki school devoted to hadith, not the school of jurisprudence familiar from the North African and Andalusian traditions.

Shāfiʿī is still elusive. At the end of the chronological section, Fasawī relates a conversation with the Damascene traditionist and Qurʾan reciter Hishām ibn ʿAmmār (d. 245/859?) concerning whom he had met in Egypt. After relating that al-Layth ibn Saʿd and Ibn Lahīʿa had died before he got there, Hishām goes on say, "I ate with al-Shāfiʿī. I talked to him and he talked to me (or debated; *kallamtuhu wa-kallamanī*) in Old Cairo" (1:213). Aḥmad ibn Ḥanbal condemned Hishām for declaring that his pronunciation of the Qurʾan was create.[45] Aḥmad has been quoted depreciating Shāfiʿī for devotion to *kalām*, an accusation apparently confirmed by Hishām's associating Shāfiʿī not with law or hadith but, precisely, *kalām*.[46]

The second time Shāfiʿī appears in *KMT*, his disciple Ḥarmala (d. 243/857) quotes him as punning, "Relation from Ḥirām is *ḥarām*" (3:138), referring to the rejected Medinese traditionist Ḥirām ibn ʿUthmān (d. 149/766–767?).[47] It is very exceptional to find Shāfiʿī quoted as a *rijāl* critic. Fasawī quotes Ḥarmala about ten other times, but almost always relating something from Ibn Wahb, never from Shāfiʿī. Abū Bakr al-Ḥumaydī counts as one of Fasawī's chief informants, yet never to relate anything of Shāfiʿī, even though

42. Turki, "Muwaṭṭaʾ," 10. See also Christopher Melchert, *The Formation of the Sunni Schools of Law*, Studies in Islamic Law and Society 4 (Leiden: Brill, 1997), 168–69.

43. Ibn ʿAbd al-Barr, *Intiqāʾ*, 55.

44. Ibn Ḥazm, *al-Iḥkām fī uṣūl al-aḥkām*, ed. Aḥmad Muḥammad Shākir, 8 vols. in 1 (Cairo: Maktabat al-Khānjī, 1925), vol. 5, 98 = 8 vols. in 2 (Beirut: Dār al-Kutub al-ʿIlmīya, n.d.), vol. 2, 94.

45. See al-Dhahabī, *Tārīkh al-islām*, vol. 18 (A.H. 241–250), 520–28; Ibn Ḥajar, *Tahdhīb*, vol. 11, 52–54; also al-Khallāl, *Musnad min masāʾil Abī ʿAbd Allāh Aḥmad ibn Muḥammad ibn Ḥanbal*, ed. Ẓiyāʾuddīn Aḥmad, Asiatic Society of Bangladesh Publication 29 (Dacca: Asiatic Society of Bangladesh, 1975), 556.

46. Al-Qāḍī ʿIyāḍ, *Tartīb al-madārik wa-taqrīb al-masālik li-maʿrifat aʿlām madhhab Mālik*, ed. Aḥmad Bakīr Maḥmūd, 5 vols. in 3 (Beirut: Maktabat al-Ḥayāh, 1967–68?), vol. 1, 389, l. 11; 390, l. 9.

47. See al-Khaṭīb al-Baghdādī, *Tārīkh*, vol. 8, 277–280.

Ḥumaydī would appear at the head of Ibn ʿAbd al-Barr's list of the disciples of Shāfiʿī.[48] Shāfiʿī's most famous disciples, Buwayṭī, Muzanī, and Rabīʿ al-Murādī, are completely absent. It seems safe to say that Fasawī was [336] at least uninterested in Egyptian Shāfiʿism, despite his repeated visits to Egypt between 216/832 and 230/845. His lack of interest does not prove but is certainly consistent with Calder's contention that the voluminous, sophisticated works attributed to Shāfiʿī were actually built up across the century after his death.

Aḥmad ibn Ḥanbal appears very often, although nearly always through a named intermediary, usually Salama ibn Shabīb al-Naysābūrī, al-Faḍl ibn Ziyād, or Abū Ṭālib. All three are well known in the Ḥanbali tradition.[49] Ibn Abī Yaʿlā includes an item from Faḍl not found in *KMT* to the effect that Aḥmad sat with Shāfiʿī in Mecca and learnt from him Qurashi Arabic, whereas Shāfiʿī learnt from Aḥmad hadith.[50] Fasawī's overriding concern with Mālik and Medina apparently made him uninterested in establishing the relation between Aḥmad and Shāfiʿī, on which the Ḥanbali and Shāfiʿi traditions were obviously at odds. Fasawī uses Aḥmad almost entirely as a *rijāl* critic, in very much the style of other ninth-century collectors of his answers to questions.[51] In Fasawī's view of things, as in contemporary Ḥanābila's, it would probably not have seemed complimentary to present Aḥmad as an innovative jurisprudent.

As for the balance among the regions, Fasawī is a much stronger, open partisan of the Medinese tradition than Ibn Saʿd. Some examples have already come up. Medinese preeminence comes at the expense of Iraq, particularly Kufa. Half a dozen pages in a row are devoted to depreciations of Iraqi hadith science. ʿĀ'isha is quoted as saying,

> O people of Iraq, the people of Syria are better than you. A large number of the Companions of the Prophet . . . went out to them and related to them hadith that we recognize, whereas a small number of the Companions of the Prophet . . . went out to you, and you have related to us such hadith as we sometimes recognize and sometimes do not (2:756f).

The Yemeni Follower Ṭāwūs is quoted, "If an Iraqi relates to you 100 hadith reports, toss out 99 of them" (2:757). The Meccan Companion [337] Saʿd ibn Abī Waqqāṣ is quoted as telling someone, "I hate to give you a hadith report for you to turn into 100" (2:759).

48. Ibn ʿAbd al-Barr, *Intiqā'*, 104.

49. For Salama, see Ibn Abī Yaʿlā, *Ṭabaqāt al-ḥanābila*, ed. Muḥammad Ḥāmid al-Fiqī, 2 vols. (Cairo: Maṭbaʿat al-Sunna al-Muḥammadīya, 1952), vol. 1, 168–170; for Faḍl, see *ibid.*, vol. 1, 251–253; for Abū Ṭālib, see *ibid.*, vol. 1, 39–40 (assuming that Fasawī's informant is Aḥmad ibn Aḥmad, not the Zayd ibn Akhram identified by ʿUmarī, "Introduction," *KMT*, vol. 1, 89).

50. Ibn Abī Yaʿlā, *Ṭabaqāt*, vol. 1, 252.

51. E.g., Aḥmad, *ʿIlal* (ed. ʿAbbās) = *ʿIlal* (ed. Bayḍūn); Abū Dāwūd, *Su'ālāt Abī Dāwūd . . . lil-imām Aḥmad*, ed. Ziyād Muḥammad Manṣūr (Medina: Maktabat al-ʿUlūm wa-al-Ḥikam, 1414/1994).

Sometimes, criticism of Iraq is lightened by expressions of respect for Basra. Ibn ʿUmar is quoted as telling a Basran, "The people of Basra are better than the people of Kufa," of telling a Kufan, "How miserable a people [you are], either prisoners or Kharijites" (*sibāʾī*, *ḥarūrī*; 2:758). As to "prisoners" (i.e., non-Arab converts), among whom Fasawī would presumably have had to include himself, there are compensations. Aḥmad ibn Ḥanbal is quoted as saying,

> Knowledge (*ʿilm*) is in storehouses, and God distributes it to whomever he pleases. If he especially favored anyone with knowledge, the people of the house of the Prophet . . . would be most suitable. Yet ʿAṭāʾ ibn Abī Rabāḥ was an Abyssinian, Yazīd ibn Abī Ḥabīb was a black Nubian, al-Ḥasan al-Baṣrī was a client to the Anṣār, and Ibn Sīrīn was a client to the Anṣār (1:639).

But plainly Fasawī's self-esteem depends on loyalty to Mālik and the Medinese tradition more than on the virtues of the Basrans.

As for the struggle of hadith against *raʾy*, Fasawī is even more strongly committed than Ibn Saʿd. He tells almost the same story as Ibn Saʿd from Ḥammād of Ayyūb's refusing to answer according to *raʾy* (2:236),[52] and many more to similar effect. He associates more names with blameworthy *raʾy*, and seems less tolerant of early examples. He relates a comment from Shuʿba, "Al-Ḥakam was greater as to hadith while Ḥammād was the more excellent of them as to *raʾy*," but then nervously adds his own comment (a rare occurrence), "By Abū Bisṭām's (i.e., Shuʿba's) statement, al-Ḥakam was above Ḥammād in every way" (2:16f).[53]

Many of Fasawī's quotations implicitly concede that the Iraqis have more hadith than the Medinese and the adherents of *raʾy* more impressive juridical reasoning than the adherents of hadith. One defense, then, is to contrast knowledge of hadith and fancy reasoning in Iraq with faithful practice in Medina. The early Kufan jurisprudent Ibn Shubruma is quoted as saying, "There are some questions that do credit to neither the one who asks them nor the one who answers" (2:611f). The Companion Abū al-Dardāʾ complains, "I never saw a people more [338] given to questions about *ʿilm* nor more given to leaving it than you, O people of Iraq" (2:772). Another defense is to present *raʾy* as derivative. Shaʿbī says of Ibrāhīm al-Nakhaʿī, "Aren't you amazed by this one-eyed man who comes to me by night and asks me questions, then gives juridical opinions by day" (2:603)? Someone says,

52. Fasawī's version explicitly makes it "a certain ruler (*amīr*)" who requests Ayyūb's opinion. Fasawī is typically more interested than Ibn Saʿd in relations with rulers: ʿUmarī, "Introduction," *KMT*, vol. 1, 53.

53. The men in question are the Basran Shuʿba (d. 160/776) and the Kufan Followers al-Ḥakam ibn ʿUtayba (d. 113/731–732) and Ḥammād ibn Abī Sulaymān.

> Al-Qāsim scarcely replied to anyone in his session or reproached him for (what he had said). One day, Rabīʿa spoke in al-Qāsim's session and went on at length. When al-Qāsim went away, he leaned on me, turned to me, and said, "I would not say this to anyone else, but do you think the people did not know what our comrade here was saying" (1:547)?

The traditionists knew what the masters of abstruse reasoning knew—they just did not chatter about it.

It is harder to find expressions of respect for *fiqh* in *KMT* than in the *Ṭabaqāt* of Ibn Saʿd. ʿAlī ibn al-Madīnī expresses a distaste for *fiqh*, which he evidently equates with *raʾy* (perhaps Fasawī's own gloss, 2:135f). Praise of men for their *fiqh* (perspicacity) seems limited to fairly early figures, the same as *raʾy*; for example, someone praises Ibn Abī Najīḥ (d. 131/748–749?) as the most perspicacious (*afqah*) of the Meccans after ʿAṭāʾ (1:702).

Outright heresy seems less prominent in *KMT* than in the *Ṭabaqāt* of Ibn Saʿd, although the heretics are the same: Murjiʾa, Qadarīya, and Shīʿa, plus the one Muʿtazili, ʿAmr ibn ʿUbayd. As noted above, Abū Yūsuf is made to admit that Abū Ḥanīfa was a Jahmī; however, the term is never explained and there is no other express reference to the doctrine of the create Qur'an. Fasawī occasionally mentions the Inquisition, but it is not a major issue. Neither its institution nor its major turning points appear in the opening chronology. Aḥmad is quoted as pronouncing the Medinese Ibn Abī Uways and the Baghdadi ʿAffān above suspicion on account of their having occupied distinguished positions at the Inquisition (2:177f).[54] Outside *KMT*, Fasawī appears in one chain of transmitters for Aḥmad's disparaging al-Karābīsī and his fellow semi-rationalists (3:494), but nowhere in what is certainly from *KMT* itself.[55] Unlike Aḥmad and his followers in Baghdad, [339] Fasawī is unconcerned with the danger of *kalām*. He quotes Mālik as praising the earlier Medinese Ibn Hurmuz, "He knew *kalām* and would refute the people of fancies" (i.e., heretics; 1:652, similarly 653).

Khalīfa, Ibn Saʿd, Fasawī, and Ninth-Century Caliphal Policy

From the *Tārīkh* of Khalīfa ibn Khayyāṭ to his *Ṭabaqāt*, from Khalīfa to Ibn Saʿd, and again from Ibn Saʿd to Fasawī, one finds a marked shift of focus from Iraq and rationalistic jurisprudence toward Medina and traditionalism. This is a matter first of who gets named, Iraqis or Medinese, Ḥanafīya or Mālikīya, with Ibn Saʿd paying more attention to the

---

54. Abū Bakr ibn Abī Uways suffered house arrest: see Abū al-ʿArab, *K. al-Miḥan*, ed. Yaḥyā Wahīb al-Jabūrī (Beirut: Dār al-Gharb al-Islāmī, 1403/1983; repr. 1408/1988), 446. ʿAffān was deprived of his stipend: see al-Khaṭīb al-Baghdādī, *Tārīkh*, vol. 12, 270–72.

55. For the semi-rationalists (alternatively *ahl al-ithbāt* or *mutakallimī ahl al-sunna*) and Ḥanbali polemics against them, see Christopher Melchert, "The Adversaries of Aḥmad Ibn Ḥanbal," *Arabica*, xliv (1997), 234–53 [*HPL 1].

Medinese and Mālikīya than Khalīfa and Fasawī more than Ibn Saʿd. It is also a matter of which cities have pride of place, Kufa and Basra with Khalīfa or Mecca and Medina with Ibn Saʿd and Fasawī. As all three authors were Basran, it seems reasonable to make out behind this shift of focus a growing school within Basra devoted to Medina and Mālik, yet Mālik in the mold of moderate Iraqi traditionalism, not Mālik as he appears in the familiar early Māliki texts of Egypt and the West.

This shift of focus corresponds also to a shift in caliphal patronage. Remember that dates within the *Tārīkh* of Khalīfa suggest that it was finished about the time of Mutawakkil's accession in Dhū al-Ḥijja 232/August 847. His *Ṭabaqāt* should have been finished shortly after the death of Hudba ibn Khālid in 236/850. In 234/848–849, Mutawakkil publicly forbade talk of the Qur'ān (i.e., debate over it) and summoned numbers of jurisprudents and traditionists to Baghdad and Samarra to preach. The most prominent of these traditionists were Muṣʿab al-Zubayrī and the Kufan brothers Abū Bakr (d. 235/849) and ʿUthmān ibn Abī Shayba (d. 239/853).[56] In 236/850–851 (or possibly 238/852–853), Mutawakkil razed the tomb of al-Ḥusayn and the buildings around it.[57] The stress of the *Ṭabaqāt* on nearness to the Prophet, beginning with al-ʿAbbās, not order of conversion, agrees well with what is reported of Abū Bakr ibn Abī Shayba's preaching, likewise stressing loyalty to al-ʿAbbās.[58] Its placing ʿAbbās and his progeny [340] first, not ʿAlī and his, agrees with Mutawakkil's hostility toward the Shīʿa. Khalīfa's inclusion of the brothers Ibn Abī Shayba in their own *ṭabaqa* at the end of the section on Kufa (U173, Z296) also seems to point toward Mutawakkil's patronage. Finally, Khalīfa's increasing attention to Medina and decreasing attention to Iraqi Ḥanafīya from the *Tārīkh* to the *Ṭabaqāt* likewise agree with a shift in caliphal patronage: Maʾmūn and his two immediate successors had tended to favor the Ḥanafīya (the Inquisition may be read as the establishment of a particularly Ḥanafī theological doctrine), whereas Mutawakkil favored Basrans and Qurashis.[59]

---

56. Al-Khaṭīb al-Baghdādī, *Tārīkh*, vol. 2, 344, ll. 17–20 (from al-Ṣūlī); vol. 10, 67, ll. 9–19 (from Muḥammad ibn ʿArafa, i.e., Nifṭawayh). Muṣʿab al-Zubayrī and the brothers Ibn Abī Shayba are the intersection of the two lists.

57. Ibn al-Jawzī, *al-Muntaẓam*, ed. Muḥammad ʿAbd al-Qādir ʿAṭā & Muṣṭafā ʿAbd al-Qādir ʿAṭā, with Nuʿaym Zurzūr, 18 vols. (Beirut: Dār al-Kutub al-ʿIlmīya, 1992), vol. 11, 237.

58. Al-Khaṭīb al-Baghdādī, *Tārīkh*, vol. 10, 68. ʿUthmān ibn Abī Shayba was also known for relating hadith favorable to the ʿAbbāsids, while the two other traditionists on Ṣūlī's list of those called to preach in 234, Ibrāhīm al-Taymī and Muḥammad ibn Abī al-Shawārib, were both known for exalting Mutawakkil in particular: see al-Khaṭīb al-Baghdādī, *Tārīkh*, vol. 2, 345, vol. 13, 151; Wakīʿ, *Akhbār al-quḍāh*, ed. ʿAbd al-ʿAzīz Muṣṭafā al-Marāghī, 3 vols. (Cairo: Maṭbaʿat al-Istiqāma, 1947–50), vol. 2, 179–181. Although Nifṭawayh states that Mutawakkil ordered these traditionists to preach against the Muʿtazila and Jahmīya, the main point may have been rather to preach in favor of the ʿAbbāsids in general and Mutawakkil in particular. Mutawakkil would not sack his Muʿtazili chief qadi until three years later.

59. On the Inquisition and the Ḥanafīya, see *Encyclopaedia of Islam*, new ed., s.v. "Miḥna," by M. Hinds.

The *Ṭabaqāt* of Ibn Saʿd fits less tightly with the policies of any one caliph. The last years of Mutawakkil's reign (he was assassinated in 247/861) fit reasonably well. The Mālikī school one makes out from his work is mainly Medinese, with branches in Basra and Baghdad. It appears to be known from the transmission of hadith (not yet restricted, in the 240's, to reports from the Prophet) rather than books of Mālikī jurisprudence such as the *Asadīya* of Asad ibn al-Furāt, the *Mukhtaṣar* of Ibn ʿAbd al-Ḥakam, and the *Mudawwana* of Saḥnūn by which it was spread in the West.

The most crucial event in Iraq for dating both the *Ṭabaqāt* of Ibn Saʿd and *KMT* of Fasawī looks like the rise of Ismāʿīl ibn Isḥāq al-Jahḍamī (d. 282/896). Having studied Mālikī jurisprudence in Basra under ʿAlī ibn al-Muʿadhdhal, he was appointed qadi for the East Side of Baghdad in 246/860–861.[60] The Muʿtazili caliph Muhtadī removed him in 255/869, but Muhtadī was murdered after less than a year and Ismāʿīl was restored to the East Side. Soon, he won over the shadow caliph Muwaffaq and with Muwaffaq's support gained the judgeships of the West Side of Baghdad and al-Sharqīya in 258/871–872, the [341] whole of Baghdad in 262/875–876.[61] The chief qadi at this time was ʿAlī ibn Abī al-Shawārib, apparently a Ḥanafī, but he became powerless.[62]

These are the years when Ḥanafī-Mālikī rivalry must have become most intense. Muhtadī's reaction in favor of rationalist jurisprudence and theology had to alarm the more traditionalist Mālikīya of Iraq, and the qāḍī Ismāʿīl was known for his polemics against the Ḥanafīya. The important Ḥanafi jurisprudent Abū Khāzim (d. 292/905) would complain that Ismāʿīl had striven for forty years to kill the memory of Abū Ḥanīfa in Iraq.[63] Ismāʿīl made collections of hadith[64] and was remarkable (among ninth-century Māliki jurisprudents, presumably) for supporting his opinions with hadith reports, complete with chains of transmitters.[65] He also prided himself on his knowledge of Medinese jurisprudence. He told the story of his visiting the Basran Yaḥyā ibn Aktham (d. 242/857?), chief qadi for Mutawakkil from the end of the Inquisition (237–239/851–853). "There were a number of people with him debating jurisprudence, saying 'The people of Medina say . . . .' When he saw me approaching, he said, 'Here comes Medina.'"[66] Here in the qadi Ismāʿīl is almost exactly the outlook we see in *KMT*: respect for hadith, respect

On the religious policies of the caliphs, see Christopher Melchert, "Religious Policies of the Caliphs From al-Mutawakkil to al-Muqtadir," *Islamic Law and Society*, 3 (1996), 316–42.

60. Al-Khaṭīb al-Baghdādī, *Tārīkh*, vol. 6, 287.

61. Ṭalḥa ibn Muḥammad, apud al-Khaṭīb al-Baghdādī, *Tārīkh*, vol. 6, 288.

62. For a somewhat fuller treatment of these developments, see Melchert, "Religious Policies," 329–30, 334–40.

63. Al-Qāḍī ʿIyāḍ, *Tartīb*, vol. 3, 170.

64. Sezgin, *GAS*, vol. 1, 475, 476; al-Qāḍī ʿIyāḍ, *Tartīb*, vol. 3, 180.

65. Kātib Çelebī, *Keşf-el-zunun*, ed. Şerefettin Yaltkaya & Rifat Bilge, 2 vols. (Istanbul: Maarif Matbaası, 1941, 1943), 1279, s.v. *Faḍl al-ṣalāh ʿalā al-nabī*.

66. Al-Khaṭīb al-Baghdādī, *Tārīkh*, vol. 6, 286, ll. 15–19.

for Medina, respect for Mālik, but hostility toward Abū Ḥanīfa and his school—all points shared with the *Ṭabaqāt* of Ibn Saʿd but in notably sharper form.

A striking difference between the *Ṭabaqāt* of Ibn Saʿd and *KMT* of Fasawī is that whereas the former looks on Ḥanafism as a Baghdadi phenomenon, the latter associates it with Kufa. For Ibn Saʿd, Kufa is still the locus of important activity in hadith. For Fasawī, Kufa's glory days are long in the past, rather overshadowed by Kufan shame. Long sections devoted to abusing Abū Ḥanīfa and his *aṣḥāb* in Kufa (2:746–795) and to listing weak transmitters from Kufa (3:34–46, 52–66) have been mentioned already. Whereas Ibn Saʿd sees ideological struggles within most metropoleis between hadith and *raʾy*, *sunna* and heresy, Fasawī tends to see a geographical struggle between Medina and Kufa, with Basra redeemed inasmuch as it has aligned itself with [342] Medina. As a Medinese background has materialized for traditionalist jurisprudence, so a Kufan background has materialized for Ḥanafi.

From where came this Kufan background to Ḥanafi jurisprudence, invisible in Ibn Saʿd? It does not seem likely that Mālikī polemists invented it. Fasawī and others should have been happy to identify the Ḥanafī school with Baghdad, a city whose jurisprudents could boast no illustrious forebears of the Umawi period. More likely, it seems, a Kufan background should have been invented by ninth-century Ḥanafī apologists to confront the Medinese background claimed by moderate Basran traditionalists. We should be able to check by finding out on whose authority various Kufans were identified with the Ḥanafī school after Ibn Saʿd. This is the method of Nurit Tsafrir, who has applied it to a slightly different list with similar results.[67] For three out of eight Kufans identified by Ṣaymarī as *aṣḥāb* to Abū Ḥanīfa whom Ibn Saʿd mentions with no Ḥanafi connection, no source is mentioned by Ṣaymarī, al-Khaṭīb al-Baghdādī, or Ibn Abī al-Wafāʾ.[68] That is, Ṣaymarī himself seems to be our earliest source for these three. One of the eight is connected with Abū Ḥanīfa in *Tārīkh Baghdād* in an item from the tenth-century Ḥanafī biographer Ibn Kās.[69] One is connected with Abū Ḥanīfa by the Egyptian al-Ṭaḥāwī (d. 321/933) and one through al-Ṭaḥāwī by his teacher, Ibn Abī ʿImrān (d. 280/893).[70] Finally, two are connected with Abū Ḥanīfa by the Baghdadi Ibn al-Thaljī (d. 266/880).[71] Similar results come of examining forty-odd early Kufans associated with Abū Ḥanīfa

67. Nurit Tsafrir, "Semi-Ḥanafis and Ḥanafī Biographical Sources," *Studia Islamica*, no. 84 (1996), 67–85, esp. 80–83.

68. Zāʾida (d. 160 or 161/*ca.* 777), Mindal ibn ʿAlī (d. 167 or 168/*ca.* 784), and Ḥafṣ ibn Ghiyāth (d. 194/809–810?). Al-Khaṭīb al-Baghdādī seems to have known a fuller version of Ṣaymarī's work than what we have independently.

69. Wakīʿ ibn al-Jarrāḥ (d. 197/812?).

70. Zufar (d. 158/774–775), also connected to Abū Ḥanīfa by Ibn al-Thaljī, and al-Qāsim ibn Maʿn (d. 175/791–792).

71. Zufar and Ḥibbān ibn ʿAlī (d. 171/787–788).

by Ibn Abī al-Wafāʾ: where Ibn Abī al-Wafāʾ names any source (not most of the time), he most often names Ṣaymarī, followed in decreasing order by Ibn al-Thaljī, Ibn Abī ʿImrān, and Ṭaḥāwī. (Sometimes, Ibn Abī al-Wafāʾ has evidently taken names from books of jurisprudence rather than biographical collections. The history of the Ḥanafi tradition in Khurasan seems especially dependent on citations in books of jurisprudence.)

Tsafrir is more inclined to trust these connections than I am.

> The Ḥanafī connections of the semi-Ḥanafīs were probably secondary to their affiliation with the Traditionist party, and were documented and [343] preserved only by Ḥanafī authors, who were interested in this detail in particular.[72]

Decisive proof is unlikely to emerge, but most of various Kufans' condemnations of Abū Ḥanīfa are attested earlier (as in *KMT*) than the same Kufans' praises of him (as in Ṣaymarī and his sources). Will we see documentation behind the Ḥanafī tradition but only invention behind the anti-Ḥanafī? Concerning another Kufan, Yaḥyā ibn Abī Zāʾida, Tsafrir says,

> The traditions in *Ta'rīkh Baghdād* and the *Akhbār* were handed down through Ibn Kaʾs, the one in the *Jawāhir* through al-Ṭaḥāwī. Ibn Kaʾs worked in Baghdad, al-Ṭaḥāwī in Egypt, and they transmitted Ḥanafī material independently of each other.[73]

Ṭaḥāwī's disciple Abū Bakr al-Dāmaghānī (d. 350s/960s) was active in Baghdad so his work did get back to Baghdad and presumably his books were available to Ibn Kās. Moreover, Ṭaḥāwī was connected with the Baghdadi tradition through his teacher Ibn Abī ʿImrān, who had learnt Ḥanafi jurisprudence in Baghdad and even transmitted biographical material from Ibn al-Thaljī.[74] Thus the Egyptian and Baghdadi traditions had a common origin.

Ibn al-Thaljī was known independently for attaching hadith to the jurisprudence of Abū Ḥanīfa and otherwise rebutting traditionalist attacks. He would have been just the one to develop a rich Kufan background for Ḥanafi jurisprudence to counterbalance the Medinese background now increasingly claimed for traditionalism.[75] Along with his work in hadith, a biographical reconstruction of Ḥanafism must have seemed the logical

72. Tsafrir, "Semi-Ḥanafīs," 85.

73. Tsafrir, "Semi-Ḥanafīs," 83. In this particular case, the tradition from Ibn Kās is merely that Ibn Abī Zāʾida was among *muḥaddithī ahl al-Kūfa*, which to my mind implies no Ḥanafi connection at all (al-Khaṭīb al-Baghdādī, *Tārīkh*, vol. 14, 118, ll. 9–15).

74. Ṣaymarī, *Akhbār*, 158–59; Ibn Abī al-Wafāʾ, *Jawāhir*, vol. 2, 90, s.n. al-Ḥasan ibn Abī Mālik; vol. 2, 285, s.n. ʿAbbād ibn Ṣuhayb.

75. On the fitting of Ḥanafi jurisprudence with hadith at this time and Ibn al-Thaljī's work in particular, see further Melchert, *Formation*, 49, 51–53.

next step if we accept Calder's proposal that the works of Shaybānī reached their present form at about A.H. 250.[76] The Ḥanafi biographical tradition was then further developed by Ṭaḥāwī, Aḥmad ibn al-Ṣalt, Mukram ibn Aḥmad, Ibn Kās, and Ṣaymarī.[77] [344]

The progressive invention of a Kufan background for Ḥanafī jurisprudence, as of an ancient Medinese tradition of devotion to hadith, should be demonstrable from the Ḥanafī and Mālikī juridical literature, as well. Unfortunately, we have the old problem of dating that juridical literature. For example, if we assume that the *Āthār* of Shaybānī go straight back to Shaybānī (d. 189/805), it must appear that Ibn Saᶜd is of limited value in describing the contemporary schools of law, whereas if we assume that Ibn Saᶜd is reliable, then the attribution of the *Āthār* is thrown into question. The best test should be those juridical works whose dating has not been strongly questioned, such as the book on *waqf* of Hilāl al-Raʾy (d. 245/859–860) and the *Mudawwana* of Saḥnūn (d. 240/854).[78] The former does not quote a broad range of Kufan authorities, rather Abū Ḥanīfa and (less often) his immediate disciples, Abū Yūsuf and Shaybānī. Thus, it confirms what Ibn Saᶜd suggests, that a Kufan background for Ḥanafī jurisprudence was worked out some time after the mid-240's/late 850's.

As for the early Mālikī school, the *Mudawwana* suggests that its devotion to hadith was still fairly new at that time, continually relying as it does on the opinions of various Medinese and Egyptian jurisprudents rather than hadith reports including chains of transmitters: thus far, it confirms the observed shift in emphasis between Ibn Saᶜd and Fasawī. On the other hand, the *Mudawwana* makes an unsatisfactory witness inasmuch as it comes of the Western Mālikī tradition that Ibn Saᶜd and Fasawī more or less ignore. The *Muwaṭṭaʾ* in the recension of Qaᶜnabī at least confirms a stronger devotion to hadith among the Mālikīya of Iraq than of the West.

Finally, then, what of other ninth-century biographical literature? None is so easy to read as Ibn Saᶜd. Aḥmad ibn Ḥanbal, *al-ᶜIlal wa-maᶜrifat al-rijāl*, was collected by ᶜAbd Allāh ibn Aḥmad (d. 290/903). It usually associates Abū Ḥanīfa with Kufa; e.g., the invention of jurisprudence by *raʾy* is blamed on ᶜUthmān al-Battī in Basra, Rabīᶜat al-Raʾy in Medina, and Abū Ḥanīfa in Kufa.[79] Mālik is quoted as disparaging both Kufa and Basra for sheltering or heeding Abū Ḥanīfa.[80] At one point, Aḥmad complains of retrojected Ḥanafism,

76. Calder, *Studies*, 66.

77. Our knowledge of all these has been enriched by Nurit Tsafrir, "Semi-Ḥanafīs," esp. 80–84, and Eerik Dickinson, "Aḥmad b. al-Ṣalt and His Biography of Abū Ḥanīfa," *Journal of the American Oriental Society* 116 (1996):406–417.

78. Calder raises no objection to *K. Aḥkām al-waqf* of Hilāl al-Raʾy: *Studies*, 50–51, 146. It posits no Kufan background for Ḥanafi jurisprudence. He does question the attribution of the *Mudawwana* personally to Saḥnūn, but moves the date of its final redaction to only about ten years after his death: *Studies*, 19.

79. Aḥmad, *ᶜIlal*, vol. 3 (ed. ᶜAbbās), 137, 156 = vol. 2 (ed. Bayḍūn), 133, 141.

80. Aḥmad, *ᶜIlal*, vol. 1 (ed. ᶜAbbās), 486, vol. 2, 373, 547, vol. 3, 164 = vol. 1 (ed. Bayḍūn), 181, 332, vol. 2, 52, 144.

[345] charging Isḥāq ibn Najīḥ (*fl.* late 2nd/8th cent.) with ascribing the *ra'y* of Abū Ḥanīfa to ʿUthmān al-Battī of Basra.[81] Alleging entire invention by Abū Ḥanīfa himself, *ʿIlal* certainly does not depict Ḥanīfism as developing out of earlier Kufan jurisprudence; however, showing no interest in the followers of Abū Ḥanīfa, it sheds no light on whether Ḥanāfism further developed in Baghdad or Kufa. As for the identification of hadith with the Hijaz, Aḥmad usually speaks respectfully of Mālik as a traditionist, but I find no suggestion, as in *KMT*, that the Hijazi tradition is generally reliable, the Iraqi corrupt.

The collected sayings of Yaḥyā ibn Maʿīn are even harder to apply to the problem of Ḥanafi origins. Similarly to the *Ṭabaqāt* of Ibn Saʿd, Yaḥyā's *Tārīkh* is loosely organized by city: first Mecca and Medina, then Kufa, Basra, Baghdad, etc. Abū Ḥanīfa and Abū Yūsuf are most often mentioned among the Kufans; however, this classification cannot be assigned with confidence to Yaḥyā but only to the compiler, ʿAbbās al-Dūrī (d. 271/884). Yaḥyā's comments on Abū Ḥanīfa, Zufar, and Abū Yūsuf are notably friendlier than Aḥmad's, being usually neutral but sometimes even positive; e.g., "Zufar, *ṣāḥib ra'y*, was highly trustworthy."[82] No comment betrays where Yaḥyā thought the followers of Abū Ḥanīfa were concentrated, nor suggests that he identified hadith with Medina, *ra'y* with Iraq.

Ibn Qutayba (d. 276/889) has been characterized as an arch-traditionalist, but this is a mistake, for the traditionalists themselves did not embrace him, and he sometimes endorsed semi-rationalist positions.[83] His *Kitāb al-Maʿārif* does not mention Aḥmad ibn Ḥanbal, and Gérard Lecomte proposes that the first version of it was finished before 252/866 but that our text includes revisions from a little before 266/879 or even later.[84] It includes a famous chapter naming *aṣḥāb al-ra'y*: the Kufan Ibn Abī Laylā (d. 148/765–766), Abū Ḥanīfa, the Medinese Rabīʿat al-Ra'y, the Basran Zufar, the Syrian Awzāʿī (d. 157/774), the Kufan Sufyān al-Thawrī (d. 161/778), Mālik ibn Anas, Abū Yūsuf, and Muḥammad al-Shaybānī.[85] (Ibn Qutayba nowhere mentions [346] Shāfiʿī.) To identify Awzāʿī, Sufyān al-Thawrī, and especially Mālik with *ra'y* is completely opposed to the tendency of *KMT*

81. Aḥmad, *ʿIlal*, vol. 2 (ed. ʿAbbās), 30 = vol. 1 (ed. Bayḍūn), 216.

82. Yaḥyā ibn Maʿīn, *al-Tārīkh*, ed. ʿAbd Allāh Aḥmad Ḥasan, 2 vols. (Beirut: Dār al-Qalam, n.d.), vol. 1, 365. I have also consulted idem, *Maʿrifat al-rijāl*, vol. 1, ed. Muḥammad Kāmil al-Qaṣṣār, Maṭbūʿāt Majmaʿ al-Lugha al-ʿArabīya (Damascus: Dār al-Fikr, 1405/1985); idem, *Maʿrifat al-rijāl*, vol. 2, ed. Muḥammad Muṭīʿ al-Ḥāfiẓ' and Ghazwa Budayr, Maṭbūʿāt Majmaʿ al-Lugha al-ʿArabīya (Damascus: Dār al-Maʿārif, n.d.).

83. See discussions in Ibn Ḥajar, *Lisān "al-Mīzān,"* 7 vols. (Hyderabad: Maṭbaʿat Majlis Dā'irat al-Maʿārif, 1325–27), vol. 3, 357–359, and Gérard Lecomte, *Ibn Qutayba* (Damascus: Institut Français de Damas, 1965), pt. 2, chap. 1. For semi-rationalist positions, see notably Ibn Qutayba, *al-Ikhtilāf fī al-lafẓ wa-al-radd ʿalā al-jahmīya wa-al-mushabbiha*, ed. Muḥammad Zāhid al-Kawtharī (Cairo: Maktabat al-Qudsī, 1349).

84. Gérard Lecomte, *Ibn Qutayba* (Damascus: Institut Français de Damas, 1965), 90.

85. Ibn Qutayba, *al-Maʿārif*, ed. Tharwat ʿUkāsha (6th ed., Cairo: al-Hay'a al-ʿĀmma lil-Kitāb, 1992), 494–500.

yet consistent with the sayings of Aḥmad ibn Ḥanbal and Yaḥyā ibn Maʿīn, who also refer to their *raʾy*.[86] *Maʿārif* tells us nothing about the identification of Ḥanafism with Kufa, while the shifting reputations of Mālik and Shāfiʿī among the Ḥanābila and others in the later ninth century is a subtle problem requiring far more extended treatment than is possible here. Certainly, though, the sayings of Aḥmad and Yaḥyā ibn Maʿīn suggest that the identification of Medina with hadith, while strong in Basra (particularly, one presumes, among moderate traditionalists there), was weak in Baghdad.

To sum up, the ninth-century biographical dictionaries seem to make untenable at least two older postulates about the early history of Islamic law. First is *the opposition of* raʾy *and Iraq to* ḥadīth *and the Hijaz*. Schacht questioned it on the ground that Mālik depended on *raʾy* quite as much as the Ḥanafīya (Mālikī and Shāfiʿī polemics to the contrary).[87] I myself have objected that it makes a puzzle of where Iraqi traditionalism came from, as no one has proposed that exposure to Medinese methods is what led Aḥmad and his fellows to take up *ḥadīth*. Moreover, it is now plain that Khalīfa ibn Khayyāṭ and Ibn Saʿd saw flourishing schools of hadith in Kufa and Basra as well as Mecca and Medina. The opposition of *raʾy* and Iraq to *ḥadīth* and the Hijaz comes only later in the ninth century, with Fasawī.

A second untenable postulate is *the origin of the Ḥanafi school in a personalization of Kufan jurisprudence* (my own phrase although based on the analyses of Schacht and Makdisi[88]). There surely did exist "semi-Ḥanafīs," men who "adopted just a few Ḥanafī legal precepts."[89] Abū Ḥanīfa may have taken much Kufan doctrine to Baghdad, and others may have taken Kufan doctrine from him to other cities.[90] But much of the connection between Ḥanafi learning and the Kufan tradition must have come from Ḥanafīya such as Ibn al-Thaljī [347] of the later ninth century when they looked for the precedents on which Abū Ḥanīfa must, in their view, have based his opinions. Specifically Ḥanafi doctrine was developed in Baghdad (and Basra), not Kufa, while the native Ḥanafi tradition in Kufa was negligible.

86. E.g., Abū Dāwūd, *Suʾālāt Abī Dāwūd*, 226, where Aḥmad is quoted as saying ʿAbd Allāh ibn Nāfiʿ was not good at hadith, rather knew the *raʾy* of Mālik; Yaḥyā ibn Maʿīn, *Tārīkh*, vol. 2, 325, in favor of recording the *raʾy* of Sufyān al-Thawrī, Mālik, Ḥasan ibn Ṣāliḥ, and Awzāʿī.

87. Schacht, *Origins*, 21, 27, 114–15.

88. See Melchert, *Formation*, 32–38.

89. Tsafrir, "Semi-Ḥanafīs," 73.

90. As Nurit Tsafrir has more recently demonstrated in "The Beginnings of the Ḥanafī School in Iṣfahān," *Islamic Law and Society*, v (1998), 1–34. Perhaps she lacks control against back-projection: much of her evidence is from a family notebook rediscovered by a grandson after, presumably, Abū Ḥanīfa had become famous.

13
TRADITIONIST-JURISPRUDENTS AND THE FRAMING OF ISLAMIC LAW

At the level of theory, Joseph Schacht makes out two chief contenders in the eighth- and early-ninth-century struggle to frame Islamic law: on the one hand, *aṣḥāb al-raʾy*, the rationalistic jurisprudents; on the other hand, *aṣḥāb al-ḥadīth*, their adversaries the traditionists. Al-Shāfiʿī, he says, tried to steer a middle course between them, accepting the traditionists' stress on hadith but rejecting the crudeness of their legal thought.[1] One might therefore expect subsequent historians of Islamic law to have paid equal attention to both parties. In fact, they have tended to ignore the traditionist-jurisprudents. For example, Norman Calder scrutinizes works of the nascent Mālikī, Shāfiʿī, and Ḥanafī traditions but ignores the early Ḥanbalī.[2] [384]

Are the traditionist-jurisprudents indeed irrelevant to the broad history of Islamic law across the ninth century? This seems impossible. We should recognize that the

This article was largely written at the Institute for Advanced Study, Princeton, New Jersey, on a grant from the National Endowment for the Humanities.

1. Joseph Schacht, *The Origins of Muhammadan Jurisprudence* (Oxford: Clarendon Press, 1950), esp. 36, 56–57. Shāfiʿī's middle course is further developed by Christopher Melchert, "The Formation of the Sunni Schools of Law," Ph.D. diss., Univ. of Pennsylvania, 1992, chap. 3, and Wael B. Hallaq, "Was al-Shafiʿi the Master Architect of Islamic Jurisprudence?" *International Journal of Middle East Studies*, xxv (1993), 587–605, and idem, *A History of Islamic Legal Theories* (Cambridge: Univ. Press, 1997), chap. 1, esp. 18–19, 30–35.

2. Norman Calder, *Studies in Early Muslim Jurisprudence* (New York: Clarendon Press, 1993). Calder has come in for harsh criticism, but none of the dozen or so reviews listed in *Index Islamicus* complains of his neglecting traditionist-jurisprudents.

Originally published in *Islamic Law and Society* 8.3 (2001): 383–406.

traditionist-jurisprudents were crucial to the rise of hadith as the primary material of Islamic law and of *isnād* criticism as the primary method of dealing with contradictory hadith. The attractiveness of a systematic work like the *Risāla* of Shāfiʿī is undeniable, and scholars are not to be blamed for spending time with it. Neither should we be surprised if the taste that relishes the *Risāla* should be repelled by an unsystematic work like *al-ʿIlal wa-maʿrifat al-rijāl* of Aḥmad ibn Ḥanbal. But scholars should not go from reading the *Risāla* and similar works because they are attractive to dismissing the *ʿIlal* and the movement behind it as unimportant. It takes a little work for a modern Western academic to see, but enough ninth-century Muslims found something religiously attractive in the intellectually self-abnegating, unsystematic approach of *al-ʿIlal wa-maʿrifat al-rijāl* to give some decisive political advantages to the traditionist-jurisprudents behind it. Had the traditionist-jurisprudents lacked such support, Islamic law must have taken a very different form.

The first object of this article is to show that there was a distinct party of traditionist-jurisprudents and to bring it back onto the stage. It proposes some indications of how to place a given juridical work of the ninth century on the spectrum running from extreme traditionalists at one end to rationalists at the other. Its conclusion is that by about the last quarter of the century, once the mainstream, rationalistic jurisprudents of the nascent Mālikī, Shāfiʿī, and Ḥanafī schools had taken up hadith as the basic material of jurisprudence and hadith criticism as the principal means of dealing with contradictions, the traditionist-jurisprudents could hardly help but adjust their practice in the opposite direction. From the later ninth century, we may observe them seeking to join the rationalistic mainstream either as necessary auxiliaries (pure traditionists) or as practicing jurisprudents fully capable of dialectic as needed. Ever since, it has been in the interest of Ḥanafīya and Ḥanābila alike to minimize differences between Ḥanafi and Ḥanbali practice in the ninth century; to make out that the Ḥanafīya had always relied on hadith and hadith criticism, that the Ḥanābila and their allies had always deliberately followed the procedures of *uṣūl al-fiqh*. Scholars today may look directly at the evidence of the ninth century and see [385] how the later synthesis of rationalist and traditionalist methods was effected only gradually, in spite of serious resistance on both sides.

The Two Parties

It needs to be demonstrated that *aṣḥāb al-raʾy*, the rationalistic jurisprudents, and *aṣḥāb al-ḥadīth*, traditionist-jurisprudents, were indeed distinct parties. Certainly, contemporaries recognized distinct parties. Already in the eighth century (to disregard retrospective accounts), Ibn al-Muqaffaʿ (d. 139/756 or later) observes that one party claims to follow the *sunna*, although he chides them for actually, on examination, tending to follow earlier *raʾy*.[3] Implicitly, other jurisprudents did openly follow *raʾy*. In the earlier ninth

3. Ibn al-Muqaffaʿ, *Risālat al-ṣaḥāba*, ed. Yūsuf Abū Ḥalqa, 2nd printing (Beirut: Maktabat al-Bayān, 1960), 167.

century, Ibn Saʿd (d. 230/845) concludes notices for various men with the label *ṣāḥib raʾy*. A generation later, at mid-century, Ibn Qutayba (d. 276/889?) expressly names the leading parties *aṣḥāb al-raʾy* and *aṣḥāb al-ḥadīth*.[4] In the later tenth century, Ibn al-Nadīm (*fl.* 377/987–88) classifies jurisprudents as follows:

1) the Mālikīyīn;
2) Abū Ḥanīfa and his followers, the Iraqis or *aṣḥāb al-raʾy*;
3) al-Shāfiʿī and his followers;
4) Dāwūd al-Ẓāhirī and his followers;
5) Shiʿi jurisprudents;
6) traditionists (*aṣḥāb al-ḥadīth*) and traditionist-jurisprudents (*fuqahāʾ al-muḥaddithīn*);
7) al-Ṭabarī and his followers; and finally
8) Khāriji jurisprudents (*shurāt*).[5]

This is not the simple dichotomy sketched by Schacht (for an earlier period), but it clearly distinguishes hadith as jurisprudence (category six) from what these various others practiced (including, note, Ẓāhirism, whose identification with traditionalism is a mistake we should put behind us). In sum, the distinction between rationalistic jurisprudents and traditionist-jurisprudents is no mere modern projection on the past.

Terminology still presents difficulties. A relatively trivial one is that the words "traditionist" and "traditionalist" are hard to keep straight. [386] As established by George Makdisi, "traditionist" indicates a *muḥaddith*, someone who studies and transmits hadith, whatever his theological inclination, whereas "traditionalist" indicates someone who systematically prefers to base his law and theology on textual sources as opposed to speculative reasoning.[6] Writing before Makdisi, Schacht referred only to "traditionists," and for the early period that concerned him, before 204/820, reputable traditionists almost invariably were traditionalists. In the later ninth century, however, there emerged outstanding traditionists whose orthodoxy traditionalists did not recognize; e.g., Bukhārī and Ṭabarī.[7] The contrast between, say, Shāfiʿī's passive use of hadith criticism (he was

4. Ibn Qutayba, *al-Maʿārif*, ed. Tharwat ʿUkāsha (6th edn., Cairo: al-Hayʾa al-ʿĀmma li'l-Kitāb, 1992), 494–500.

5. Ibn al-Nadīm, *Fihrist*, *maqāla* 6.

6. George Makdisi, "Ashʿarî and the Ashʿarites in Islamic Religious History," *Studia Islamica*, no. 17 (1962), 37–80, at 49.

7. Traditionalists drove Bukhārī from Nishapur over the question of *lafẓ al-Qurʾān*, for which see al-Khaṭīb al-Baghdādī, *Tārīkh Baghdād*, 14 vols. (Cairo: Maktabat al-Khānjī, 1349/1931, repr. Cairo:

not a traditionist-jurisprudent) and Ṭabarī's active practice of it (he helped synthesize the two approaches) is one of the occasions for this article. At any rate, however, I refer here to "traditionist-jurisprudents," after Ibn al-Nadīm, rather than "traditionalists."

More seriously, some have doubted whether we should speak of *aṣḥāb al-raʾy*. Is this not to endorse a pejorative term coined by their adversaries? As Schacht says, "There never was a school of thought in religious law that called itself, or consented to be called, *aṣḥāb al-raʾy*, and the distinction between *ahl al-ḥadīth* and *aṣḥāb al-raʾy* is to a great extent artificial."[8] Similarly, one might add, although there certainly was a school of thought that called itself *aṣḥāb al-ḥadīth*, precisely who adhered to this school was in some doubt, for it was not a guild school with enforceable boundaries. Moreover, it was sometimes polemically useful to include persons who had earlier been excluded (more below on the example of Ibn Qutayba).

We should remember, though, that *raʾy* originally had a positive connotation, as observed by Joseph Schacht: "*Raʾy* originally meant 'sound opinion,' and was used of the element of human reasoning, whether strictly systematic [referring to *qiyās*] or more personal and arbitrary [referring to *istiḥsān*]."[9] It may have acquired the negative [387] connotation of "(mere) opinion" because of traditionalist polemics against it. Till some time in the ninth century, actual jurisprudents by *raʾy* may well have accepted it as an honorable description of how they arrived at their doctrine. The continual introduction of arguments by *a-lam tara*, *a-raʾayta*, and the like (with qurʾanic precedent, even), suggests a positive construction of *raʾy*. A certain example is the mystic al-Ḥakīm al-Tirmidhī (d. *ca.* 295/907–8?), who unashamedly states in his autobiography that in his youth, he studied *ʿilm al-āthār*, meaning hadith, and *ʿilm al-raʾy*, meaning jurisprudence.[10] In political contexts, *raʾy* retains an entirely positive meaning. It is a considered judgement, not whimsy. For example, Ibn Ḥibbān (d. 354/965) mentions uprightness and sound opinion (*ʿafāf*, *raʾy*) as the defining qualities of a good vizier.[11]

Moreover, we continue to see the positive use of *raʾy* in the North African Māliki tradition. Al-Khushanī (d. Cordoba, 371/981?) states of Mūsā ibn ʿAbd al-Raḥmān (*fl.* later 3rd/9th cent.), "He was good at juridical problems and debating (*masāʾil*, *takallum*)

Maktabat al-Khānjī and Beirut: Dār al-Fikr, n.d.), vol. 2, 30–32. The Ḥanābila blockaded Ṭabarī in his house, for which affair see Franz Rosenthal, *The History of al-Ṭabarī* 1: *General Introduction and From the Creation to the Flood*, Bibliotheca Persica and SUNY Ser. in Near Eastern Studies (Albany: State Univ. of New York Press, 1989), 69–78, with references.

8. *Encyclopaedia of Islam* (new edn.), s.v. "Aṣḥāb al-raʾy," by J. Schacht.

9. *Loc. cit.*

10. Al-Ḥakīm al-Tirmidhī, *The Beginning of the Affair of . . . al-Ḥakīm al-Tirmidhī*, in *The Concept of Sainthood in Early Islamic Mysticism: Two Works by al-Ḥakīm al-Tirmidhī*, trans. with notes by Bernd Radtke and John O'Kane, Curzon Sufi Series (Richmond: Curzon, 1996), 15–36, at 15.

11. Ibn Ḥibbān, *Rawḍat al-ʿuqalāʾ wa-nuzhat al-fuḍalāʾ*, ed. Muḥammad Muḥyī al-Dīn ʿAbd al-Ḥamīd, et al. (Cairo: Maṭbaʿat al-Sunna al-Muḥammadīya, 1949), 268–69.

with regard to *raʾy* after the doctrine of Mālik and his *aṣḥāb*."[12] Ibn al-Faraḍī (d. Cordoba, 403/1012) uses it often.[13] Ibn Farḥūn (d. Medina, 799/1397) relates of Ibn al-Qāsim that Mālik said, "I may think on a question for ten-odd years without there occurring to me a sound opinion (*raʾy*) concerning it."[14]

Occasionally, *raʾy* even appears in a positive sense outside North Africa. Writing about 375/985, the geographer al-Maqdisī (Muqaddasī), a Ḥanafi, uses it as a synonym for "legal reasoning," something the Ḥanafīya and Shāfiʿīya evidently share but not the Ḥanābila.[15] [388] Al-Ḥākim al-Naysābūrī (d. Nishapur, 405/1014) says of the Shāfiʿi Abū Bakr al-Ṣibghī (d. 342/954) that his *ʿaql* and *raʾy* were proverbial.[16] In somewhat the same way, "opinion" may often have a negative connotation with us ("That's just your opinion") but retains a positive one in some contexts ("Today, the Supreme Court issued its opinion . . . "). Altogether, then, although we have a few self-descriptions from traditionist-jurisprudents as *aṣḥāb al-ḥadīth* but none from rationalistic jurisprudents as *aṣḥāb al-raʾy*, actual ninth-century use of *raʾy* suggests that they must have been slow to perceive it as a term of abuse. I have never noticed, either (against Schacht), that any early jurisprudent identified his doctrine with any of *al-madhāhib al-qadīma*, as I suppose one would translate Schacht's "ancient schools." We need feel little more compunction about identifying the rationalists as *aṣḥāb al-raʾy* than about identifying the Society of Friends as "Quakers."

How Traditionist And Rationalistic Jurisprudents Used Hadith

What distinguished the traditionist-jurisprudents is above all, of course, the way they used hadith. When ninth-century traditionist-jurisprudents wrote about the law, they simply assembled collections of hadith or, at least, quoted huge numbers of hadith reports. For example, the *Muṣannafs* of ʿAbd al-Razzāq (d. 211/827) and Ibn Abī Shayba (d. 235/849) simply announce juridical positions, then relate the hadith (mostly post-prophetic) that support them. They often enough present contradictory reports in

12. Al-Khushanī, *Ṭabaqāt ʿulamāʾ Ifrīqiya*, printed with Abū al-ʿArab, *Classes des savants de l'Ifriqiya*, ed. Mohammed ben Cheneb, Publications de la Facultée des lettres d'Alger, Bulletin de correspondance africaine 51 (Paris: Leroux, 1915), 159.

13. Ibn al-Faraḍī, *Historia virorum doctorum Andalusiæ*, ed. Francisco Codera, Bibliotheca arabico-hispana 7, 8, 2 vols. (Madrid: La Guirnalda, 1890–92). In the first fifty pages, I notice half a dozen references to *raʾy*, usually *ʿalā madhhab Mālik*.

14. Ibn Farḥūn, *al-Dībāj al-mudhahhab fī maʿrifat aʿyān ʿulamāʾ al-madhhab* (Cairo: ʿAbbās ibn ʿAbd al-Salām ibn Shaqrūn, 1351), 23.

15. E.g., al-Maqdisī, *Descriptio imperii moslemici*, ed. M. J. De Goeje, Bibliotheca geographorum Arabicorum, vol. 3, 2nd edn. (Leiden: E. J. Brill, 1906), 142, ll. 11–12, discussing Mesopotamia, where there is no *raʾy* save that of Abū Ḥanīfa and Shāfiʿī, although it also has Ḥanābila and a Shiʿi presence.

16. Al-Ḥākim al-Naysābūrī, apud al-Dhahabī, *Siyar aʿlām al-nubalāʾ*, 25 vols. (Beirut: Muʾassasat al-Risāla, 1401–9/1981–88), vol. 15 (ed. Ibrāhīm al-Zaybaq), 485–86.

succession: first, say, those who advocated a woman's leading other women in the ritual prayer, then those who rejected it.

Some have inferred that these are not, then, books of jurisprudence but collections of hadith in the spirit of the familiar Six Books; that is, not presentations of rules but the raw material from which jurisprudents are expected to infer rules. But this is wrong on two counts. First, it projects backwards later orthodoxy, assuming a division of labor between traditionists and jurisprudents not endorsed by traditionist-jurisprudents of the early ninth century. Traditionist-jurisprudents did not distinguish between the study of hadith and the study of jurisprudence. Second, one should recall that such indeterminacy was a feature of legal handbooks even in the classical period, when we see [389] jurisprudents such as al-Nawawī (d. 676/1271) frequently lay out contradictory positions without identifying any one as correct.[17]

Not every position in the *masāʾil* collections of Aḥmad ibn Ḥanbal is followed by quotation of hadith, but hadith reports are produced whenever there is disagreement. An example chosen almost at random gives Aḥmad's position concerning laughter during the ritual prayer:

> It does not require repetition of the ritual ablution. The hadith report from Abū al-ʿĀliya is weak. It is related from Abū Mūsā and Jābir that one repeats the prayer but not the ritual ablution. Al-Shaʿbī also took that position.[18]

As Susan Spectorsky has summarized Aḥmad's practice,

> Ibn Ḥanbal readily answers questions on non-controversial matters, but whenever he knows of conflicting traditions or conflicting opinion, he refuses to risk allowing his own answer to become authoritative. In fact, he answers all questions in terms of traditional criticism. If he cannot answer a question satisfactorily within the framework of traditions, he prefers not to answer at all.[19]

Hadith reports are not just authorities corroborating his opinions, they practically are his opinions. No Ḥanbali juridical work fails to quote hadith extensively until the *Mukhtaṣar* of al-Khiraqī (d. 334/945–46).[20]

---

17. Al-Nawawī's most detailed juridical work is the first half of *al-Majmūʿ*, ed. Zakarīyāʾ ʿAlī Yūsuf, 18 vols. (Cairo: Maṭbaʿat al-ʿĀṣima [1–7], Maṭbaʿat al-Imām [8–18], 1966–).

18. Ṣāliḥ ibn Aḥmad, *Masāʾil al-imām Aḥmad ibn Ḥanbal*, ed. Ṭāriq ibn ʿAwaḍ Allāh ibn Muḥammad (Riyadh: Dār al-Waṭan, 1420/1999), 264.

19. Susan Spectorsky, "Aḥmad ibn Ḥanbal's *Fiqh*," *Journal of the American Oriental Society*, cii (1982), 461–65, at 461.

20. Al-Khiraqī, *Mukhtaṣar al-Khiraqī*, ed. Muḥammad Zuhayr al-Shāwīsh (Damascus: Muʾassasat Dār al-Salām, 1378) = *Matn al-Khiraqī*, ed. Abū Ḥudhayfa Ibrāhīm ibn Muḥammad, Silsilat Mutūn al-Fiqh (Tanta: Dār al-Ṣaḥāba li'l-Turāth, 1413/1993).

It would be going too far to assert that the ninth-century *aṣḥāb al-raʾy*, by contrast, relied exclusively on rational speculation to determine the law. As far back as the sources will take us, on the contrary, it is plain that *aṣḥāb al-raʾy* did use hadith, at least to corroborate the results of their speculation. As Schacht observed (following Shāfiʿī), they did not consistently prefer hadith from the Prophet to hadith from Companions[21]; however, the notion that hadith constituted superior evidence for one or another rule one easily finds in their controversial literature. In *Ikhtilāf Abī Ḥanīfa wa-Ibn Abī Laylā*, for example, Abū Yūsuf normally just quotes the opinion of Abū Ḥanīfa, with which he agrees. This is the usual form of early rationalistic jurisprudence. [390] Sometimes, though, he will adduce in support of his position the practice or precept of either the Prophet or Companions.[22] In *Kitāb al-Ḥujja ʿalā ahl al-Madīna* and his edition of the *Muwaṭṭaʾ*, Shaybānī cites hadith more extensively: practically every time he disagrees (purportedly with the Medinese in *al-Ḥujja*, with Mālik in the *Muwaṭṭaʾ*), he offers a list of contrary hadith reports.

Sometimes, Shaybānī suggests that one hadith report may be superior to another; for example, when the Medinese cite hadith reports from al-Qāsim ibn Muḥammad, ʿUrwa ibn al-Zubayr, Nāfiʿ ibn Jubayr ibn Muṭʿim, and Ibn Shihāb al-Zuhrī, Shaybānī counters, "It is said to them, 'Do you hold those to be more trustworthy or ʿAbd Allāh ibn ʿUmar and Jābir ibn ʿAbd Allāh?' They said, "ʿAbd Allāh and Jābir, of course.'" Companions Ibn ʿUmar and Jābir are then quoted in favor of the Ḥanafi position.[23]

At the same time, there were significant differences between the use of hadith by early Ḥanafīya and by traditionist-jurisprudents. One is that the Ḥanafīya tended to use hadith only occasionally, in controversy with their opponents. In didactic works for internal, Ḥanafī consumption, hadith seldom appears. For example, there is practically no hadith in *al-Jāmiʿ al-kabīr* and *al-Jāmiʿ al-ṣaghīr*, the principal Ḥanafī teaching texts of the ninth and tenth centuries. There is more hadith in the work of al-Khaṣṣāf (d. 261/874) on *waqf* than in the earlier work of Hilāl al-Raʾy (d. 245/859–60); however, both works in fact elaborate the law of *waqf* by speculation, without much reference to hadith.[24] Contemporary Mālikī practice is similar. For example, the *Mukhtaṣar* of Ibn ʿAbd al-Ḥakam (d. 214/829), evidently a didactic work for internal, Māliki consumption, cites no hadith whatever, while the *Mudawwana* of Saḥnūn (d. 240/854) certainly cites hadith but apparently relies more often on the opinions of recent jurisprudents.[25] [391]

---

21. Schacht, *Origins*, chap. 4.

22. Abū Yūsuf, *Ikhtilāf Abī Ḥanīfa wa-Ibn Abī Laylā*, ed. Abū al-Wafāʾ al-Afghānī (Cairo: Maṭbaʿat al-Wafāʾ, 1357), 84, 88, 144, 182, 218.

23. Shaybānī, *K. al-Ḥujja ʿalā ahl al-Madīna*, ed. Abū al-Wafāʾ al-Afghānī, et al., 4 vols., Silsilat al-Maṭbūʿāt 1 (Hyderabad: Maṭbaʿat al-Maʿārif al-Sharqīya, 1385/1965), vol. 1, 116.

24. Peter Charles Hennigan, "The Birth of a Legal Institution: The Formation of the *waqf* in Third Century A.H. Ḥanafī Legal Discourse," Ph.D. diss., Cornell Univ., 1999, esp. 39–42, 96–109.

25. For the *Mukhtaṣar* of Ibn ʿAbd al-Ḥakam, see Jonathan E. Brockopp, "Early Islamic Jurisprudence in Egypt: Two Scholars and Their *Mukhtaṣars*," *International Journal of Middle East Studies*, xxx (1998),

The *Muwaṭṭaʾ* of Mālik seems anomalous. About one *bāb* in four evidently lets hadith reports speak for themselves in the manner of traditionist-jurisprudents, yet we never see precisely the traditionalist form of argument, "The rule is X on account of hadith reports A and B, discounting C because . . . ." Moreover, roughly one *bāb* in five presents Mālik's unsupported opinion, in the manner of rationalistic jurisprudents. Usually, a *bāb* comprises some mixture of hadith and opinion. One might read all these points as signs of primitiveness, the *Muwaṭṭaʾ* being published only at about the same time as there emerged a self-aware, assertive party of traditionist-jurisprudents. Abdel-Magid Turki has detected their influence in the increasing resort to hadith from the earliest to the latest extant recensions of the *Muwaṭṭaʾ* roughly across the last third of the eighth century.[26] It would have been natural from such a basis for some later Mālikīya to stress the side of juristic acumen (*raʾy*), others to stress hadith. Yet the rules propounded often seem fairly independent of the hadith, so that one suspects extensive interpolation. Norman Calder's explanation of the anomalous form, that the hadith was inserted almost a century after Mālik's death, seems to be untenable; however, his critics have yet to come up with a fully satisfying alternative explanation.[27] The latest extensive treatment of the *Muwaṭṭaʾ*, from Yasin Dutton, does argue strongly that the last word regularly goes not to hadith but to the practice of Medina.[28]

A second major difference between the rationalists' use of hadith and the traditionist-jurisprudents' is in the treatment of the *isnād* (pl. *asānīd*), the chain of its transmitters we expect to precede a hadith report. Five quotations of hadith reports by Abū Yūsuf have been mentioned already as evidence that he did use hadith.[29] In three of these [392] instances, Abū Yūsuf offers no *isnād* at all; in each of the other two (88, 144), his proffered *isnād* is incomplete. The *Muwaṭṭaʾ* of Mālik offers relatively fewer hadith reports with

---

167–82; now also *Early Mālikī Law: Ibn ʿAbd al-Ḥakam and his Major Compendium of Jurisprudence*, Studies in Islamic Law and Society 14 (Brill: Leiden, 2000). For the style of argument in the *Mudawwana*, see Calder, *Studies*, chap. 1.

26. Abdel-Magid Turki, "Le *Muwaṭṭaʾ* de Mâlik, ouvrage de *fiqh*, entre le *ḥadīṯ* et le *raʾy*," *Studia Islamica*, no. 86 (1997), 5–35. For the emergence of a self-aware party of traditionist-jurisprudents in about the last quarter of the eighth century, see provisionally Melchert, *Formation of the Sunni Schools of Law*, Islamic Law and Society 4 (Leiden: Brill, 1997), 1–8.

27. Calder, *Studies*, chap. 2, esp. 34–38; largely refuted by Miklos Muranyi, "Die frühe Rechtsliteratur zwischen Quellenanalyse und Fiktion," *Islamic Law and Society*, iv (1997), 224–41, also Yasin Dutton, "*ʿAmal* v. *ḥadīth* in Islamic Law: The Case of *sadl al-yadayn* (Holding One's Hands by One's Sides) When Doing the Prayer," *Islamic Law and Society*, iii (1996), 13–40, esp. 28–33. Harald Motzki, "The Prophet and the Cat," *Jerusalem Studies in Arabic and Islam*, no. 22 (1998), 18–83, shows that the particular hadith report in question was attributed to Mālik well before Calder allowed but does not generalize on the relation between hadith and legal doctrine in the *Muwaṭṭaʾ*.

28. Yasin Dutton, *The Origins of Islamic Law: The Qurʾan, the* Muwaṭṭaʾ *and Madinan* ʿAmal, Culture and Civilization in the Middle East (Richmond, Surrey: Curzon, 1999).

29. See note 22.

incomplete *asānīd*, but there are still many, and differences among the recensions raise the possibility that some *asānīd* were completed posthumously.[30] By contrast, traditionist-jurisprudents normally quoted hadith reports with full *asānīd*; for example, again, ʿAbd al-Razzāq and Ibn Abī Shayba. (In the sample quoted earlier, Aḥmad admittedly quotes incomplete *asānīd*. This is the sort of lapse that justifies Schacht's complaint that the distinction between *ahl al-ḥadīth* and *aṣḥāb al-raʾy* is to a great extent artificial. Be it noted, however, that the quotation comes from what reads almost like a transcription of Aḥmad's conversation at the mosque. Like most of the *masāʾil* collections from Aḥmad, it is much more casual than *Ikhtilāf Abī Ḥanīfa wa-Ibn Abī Laylā* and the two *Jāmiʿ*s of Shaybānī. The most formal of the *masāʾil* collections from Aḥmad is apparently the one from Abū Dāwūd, studied by Spectorsky. It regularly offers full *asānīd*.[31] Note, also, that even in the sample quoted, Aḥmad relies on hadith criticism as Abū Yūsuf and Shaybānī do not.)

Finally, although these early rationalist works may refute opposing hadith with better hadith, they do not actually practice hadith criticism after the fashion of the traditionist-jurisprudents. In the example just given, from *Kitāb al-ḥujja ʿalā ahl al-Madīna*, Shaybānī speaks of his two authorities as "more trustworthy" than those of the Medinese. "Trustworthy," "veracious," and so on are terms of *rijāl* criticism, and Iraqi traditionists seem to have used them regularly by the first half of the ninth century.[32] However, this does not mean that Shaybānī has compared *asānīd* and found that his two authorities more regularly agreed with others in their transmission from particular authorities (the usual method of hadith criticism to determine whether someone was trustworthy).[33] Rather, Shaybānī uses "more trustworthy" simply to [393] indicate that they are higher authorities; mainly, Companions who had met the Prophet as opposed to mere Followers born after the Prophet's death.

Meeting in the Middle

It would be safest to posit that "rationalist" and "traditionist" approaches to jurisprudence were *ideal types*, to which the actual, nascent Ḥanafi and Ḥanbali traditions of

30. Citing Zurqānī, Goldziher tells us the *Muwaṭṭaʾ* (in the recension of Yaḥyā ibn Yaḥyā) comprises 1,720 hadith reports, of which 600 with full *isnād*, 222 *mursal*, and 613 *mawqūf*: Ignaz Goldziher, *Muslim Studies*, ed. S. M. Stern, trans. C. R. Barber and S. M. Stern, 2 vols. (Chicago: Aldine Atherton, 1968–71), vol. 2, 202.

31. Abū Dāwūd, *K. Masāʾil al-imām Aḥmad*, ed. Muḥammad Bahja al-Bayṭār (Cairo: Dār al-Manār, 1353/1934; repr. Beirut: Muḥammad Amīn Damaj, n.d.). Spectorsky examined the fuller MS in Damascus.

32. For *rijāl* criticism, the effort to sift out the reliable hadith by knowing the men, see G. H. A. Juynboll, *Muslim Tradition*, Cambridge Studies in Islamic Civilization (Cambridge: Univ. Press, 1983), chap. 5.

33. For the comparison of *asānīd* to sift out the reliable hadith, see esp. Eerik Nael Dickinson, "The Development of Early Muslim *ḥadīth* Criticism," Ph.D. diss., Yale Univ., 1992, chap. 6.

the ninth century respectively approached. Certainly, we should expect to find a spectrum, with some jurisprudents lining up closer the middle than either extreme. Isḥāq ibn Rāhawayh (d. 238/853?) is probably an example of a traditionist-jurisprudent who tended toward the middle.[34]

Shāfiʿī is the best-known compromiser. By contrast to Abū Yūsuf and Shaybānī, Shāfiʿī does refer to traditionalist methods of sorting hadith. In the *Risāla*, for example, "more trustworthy" clearly indicates not, as for Shaybānī, an earlier authority, but rather someone whose reliability has been demonstrated by comparison of *asānīd*.[35] In other words, the *Risāla* does use the terminology of hadith criticism in the same way the traditionist-jurisprudents do. But there is still a gap between Shāfiʿī's practice and, say, Aḥmad's. Going through a random sample of seventy pages from *Kitāb al-Umm*, I found a fair number of hadith reports from the Prophet but only one instance of criticism, where Shāfiʿī oppugns the hadith report on which his adversary relies. Rather than telling us just what is wrong with the *isnād*, though, he states that "a number of qualified hadith scholars (*ahl al-ʿilm bi-'l-ḥadīth*)" were present when he heard the report and all said it was mistaken.[36] In another work, Shāfiʿī even calls on *ahl al-ḥadīth* to [394] distinguish those having *fiqh* ("discernment," especially juridical acumen), hence to be counted in determining consensus.[37] In short, Shāfiʿī calls on traditionists as outside experts rather than engaging directly, himself, in hadith criticism.

The early Ḥanbalī tradition ignores much of Shāfiʿī's putative teaching, such as the dispensability of hadith from Companions, confirming Calder's suggestion that the *Risāla* as we know it comes from later than Shāfiʿī's lifetime.[38] (Wael Hallaq offers the alternative suggestion that Shāfiʿī's *Risāla* was simply too far ahead of its time for anyone to heed it until a century later.[39] Such precise anticipation of later theory seems unlikely to me, but it is hard to see what could disprove Hallaq's thesis.) However, the Ḥanbalī tradition does recall of Shāfiʿī something like what the *Risāla* says about traditionists' helping jurisprudents. For example, Shāfiʿī is said to have told Aḥmad, "Abū ʿAbd Allāh, if you find a

34. See studies by Susan Spectorsky elsewhere in *Islamic Law and Society* 8.3 and in Bernard G. Weiss, ed., *Studies in Islamic Legal Theory*, Islamic Law and Society 15 (Leiden: Brill, 2002); also her introduction to *Chapters on Marriage and Divorce* (Austin: Univ. of Texas Press, 1993), esp. 7.

35. See Shāfiʿī, *al-Risāla*, ed. Aḥmad Muḥammad Shākir (Cairo: Matʾbaʿat Muṣṭafā al-Ḥalabī wa-Awlādih, 1358/1940; repr. Beirut: n.p., n.d.), ¶ 1251. For Shāfiʿī and qualified hadith critics, see also the discussion in Joseph Lowry, "The Legal-Theoretical Content of the *Risāla* of Muḥammad b. Idrīs al-Shāfiʿī," Ph.D. diss., Univ. of Pennsylvania, 1999, esp. 378–81.

36. Shāfiʿī, *K. al-Umm*, 7 vols. in 4 (Bulaq: al-Maṭbaʿa al-Kubrā al-Amīrīya, 1321–25, repr. Cairo: Kitāb al-Shaʿb, 1388/1968), vol. 6, 160, concerning whether to kill or merely imprison the female apostate. There is a parallel in Shāfiʿī, *Ikhtilaf al-ḥadith*, *Umm*, vol. 7, 32, where *ahl al-ḥadith* sit in judgement of transmitters, identifying the reliable.

37. Shāfiʿī, *K. Jimāʿ al-ʿilm*, *Umm*, vol. 7, 256, last l.

38. Calder, *Studies*, chap. 9, esp. 242, provisionally suggesting the date A.H. 300.

39. Hallaq, *History*, 31–32, 34.

hadith report of the Messenger of God . . . to be sound, inform us, and we will go back to it."[40] Aḥmad is said to have preferred Shāfiʿī's Iraqi work because there he made sure his hadith was sound, whereas he did not check the hadith he used in the Egyptian work.[41] Whatever the date of the *Risāla* as we know it (I myself incline toward the late 250s/early 870s), this characterization of the traditionists as helping the jurisprudents probably goes back all the way to Shāfiʿī's teaching in the early ninth century.

Besides flattering the traditionists that they were necessary assistants to the most perspicacious jurisprudents, the *Risāla* of Shāfiʿī shows why the traditionists needed to know jurisprudence themselves. Mālik is frequently quoted to the effect that one must know jurisprudence for one's hadith transmission to be worthy of attention.[42] This is the more [395] or less rationalist position, against which the traditionist-jurisprudents related the hadith report that many a man transmits knowledge to one more learnèd than he.[43] Yasin Dutton proposes that Mālik's concern was pious, mainly to distinguish between those worthy and unworthy of instruction in the law; between those to whom a particular piece of learning should be offered and whom not.[44] Shāfiʿī makes the same requirement but expressly for a technical reason: the *Risāla* explains succinctly that a transmitter must know the juridical significance of any change in wording, lest he overlook it and transmit wrongly.[45] In other words, transmission by paraphrase (*al-riwāya bi-'l-maʿnā*), although plainly widespread, had to stop at changes that would entail unforeseen juridical consequences. Only expertise in jurisprudence would ensure that a transmitter made only harmless changes. Similarly, Ibn Mujāhid (d. 324/936) would in-

40. Ibn Abī Yaʿlā, *Ṭabaqāt al-Ḥanābila*, ed. Muḥammad Ḥāmid al-Fiqī, 2 vols. (Cairo: Maṭbaʿat al-Sunna al-Muḥammadīya, 1371/1952), vol. 2, 51; similarly, vol. 1, 6 (two reports), 181, 252.

41. Abū Nuʿaym, *Ḥilyat al-awliyāʾ*, 10 vols. (Cairo: Matʾbaʿat al-Saʿāda and Maktabat al-Khānjī, 1352–57/1932–38), vol. 9, 97. For the contrary Shāfiʿī tradition by which Aḥmad preferred the Egyptian books (for exactly the same reason, that Shāfiʿī more carefully checked the hadith in them), see Ibn Abī Ḥātim, *Ādāb al-Shāfiʿī wa-manāqibuh*, ed. ʿAbd al-Ghanī ʿAbd al-Khāliq and ʿIzzat ʿAṭṭār (Cairo: Maktabat al-Khānjī, 1953; repr. Aleppo: Maktabat al-Turāth al-Islāmī, 1954), 60; al-Bayhaqī, *Manāqib al-Shāfiʿī*, ed. Aḥmad Ṣaqr, 2 vols. (Cairo: Dār al-Turāth, 1970–71), vol. 1, 263.

42. Dutton, *Origins*, 17–18, with references, to which add Aḥmad ibn Ḥanbal (et al.), *al-ʿIlal wa-maʿrifat al-rijāl* (Ẓāhirīya 40/1), in *al-Jāmiʿ fī al-ʿilal wa-maʿrifat al-rijāl*, ed. Muḥammad Ḥusām Bayḍūn, 2 vols. (Beirut: Muʾassasat al-Kutub al-Thaqāfīya, 1410/1990), vol. 1, 15–68, at 44.

43. See Schacht, *Origins*, 54. For the classic hadith report, *rubba ḥāmili fiqhin laysa bi-faqīh*, &c., see Abū Dāwūd, *al-Sunan*, *k. al-ʿilm*, 15.

44. Dutton, *Origins*, 17–18.

45. Shāfiʿī, *Risāla*, ¶ 1001. The passage is directly quoted by Ibn Abī Ḥātim, *K. al-Jarḥ wa-al-taʿdīl*, Introduction + 4 vols. in 8 (Hyderabad: Jamʿīyat Dāʾirat al-Maʿārif al-ʿUthmānīya, 1360–71, repr. 9 vols., Beirut: Dār Iḥyāʾ al-Turāth al-ʿArabī, n.d.), vol. 2, 29–30, indicating acceptance in the next century by experts in hadith.

sist that the Qur'an reciter know grammar, in order that he maintain the correct vowels.[46] Sheer rote memorization was not enough.

In nearly the opposite direction, mainly the fringe of the Ḥanbali tradition, we may see the great hadith collector Abū Dāwūd al-Sijistānī (d. 275/889) reaching out toward the rationalistic jurisprudents. A generation earlier, Aḥmad had denied that there was any division of labor between traditionists who knew hadith and jurisprudents who knew *fiqh*, so that the books of Mālik and Shāfiʿī were entirely dispensable.[47] On the contrary, Abū Dāwūd proudly tells us that his *Sunan* documents their doctrine. "As for these juridical questions, mainly the questions of al-Thawrī, Mālik, and al-Shāfiʿī, these hadith [396] reports are their basis."[48] The point is not that Abū Dāwūd had gone through the books of al-Thawrī, Mālik, and Shāfiʿī, and collected the hadith quoted there; rather, he had taken their juridical opinions and collected the hadith to back them up. This is just the division of labor between jurisprudents and traditionists called for in Shāfiʿī's *Risāla*. Abū Dāwūd transmitted also from Shāfiʿī's Egyptian disciple al-Rabīʿ ibn Sulaymān, by the way.[49] (In the next century, traditionists would extend the same treatment to the opinions of Abū Ḥanīfa. Of eight tenth-century collections called *Musnad Abī Ḥanīfa*, only one was by an identifiable Ḥanafī. Most of the rest evidently came from traditionists who took it as their duty to name the hadith that would support the opinions of a famous jurisprudent.[50])

Perhaps controversy was another mechanism by which traditionist-jurisprudents came to see the usefulness of a rationalistic jurisprudence distinct from hadith. Ninth-century traditionist-jurisprudents were usually hostile to formal debate. For example, the Ḥanbalī tradition is obviously proud of Aḥmad's refusal to debate before the caliph al-Muʿtaṣim at the Inquisition.[51] Well into the tenth century, the Ḥanbalī leader al-Barbahārī (d. 329/941) declares in his creed,

46. Ibn Mujāhid, *K. al-Sabʿa fī al-qirāʾāt*, ed. Shawqī Ḍayf (Cairo: Dār al-Maʿārif, 1972), 45.

47. Ibn Abī Yaʿlā, *Ṭabaqāt*, vol. 1, 207, vol. 2, 15; (against Mālik); Ibn Abī Yaʿlā, *Ṭabaqāt*, vol. 1, 38, 57, 318 (against Shāfiʿī); see also Abū Dāwūd, *Masāʾil*, 275 (against Mālik), and Ibn Hāniʾ, *Masāʾil al-imām Aḥmad ibn Ḥanbal*, ed. Zuhayr al-Shāwīsh, 2 vols. (Beirut: al-Maktab al-Islāmī, 1400), 2:164 (for Shāfiʿī against Mālik). Quotations in favor of Mālik and Shāfiʿī are also to be found, mostly in books by Mālikīya and Shāfiʿīya. Disparaging quotations seem more credible on the principle that what contradicts later orthodoxy is presumptively more reliable than what confirms it.

48. Abū Dāwūd, *Risāla . . . ilā ahl Makka*, in *Thalāth rasāʾil fī ʿilm muṣṭalaḥ al-ḥadīth*, ed. ʿAbd al-Fattāḥ Abū Ghuddah (Aleppo: Maktab al-Maṭbūʿāt al-Islāmīya, 1417/1997), 27–54, at 46.

49. E.g., Abū Dāwūd, *Masāʾil*, 268.

50. Six tenth-century *musnads* used by Muḥammad ibn Maḥmūd al-Khwārizmī, *Jāmiʿ masānīd al-imām al-aʿẓam*, 2 vols. (Hyderabad: Maṭbaʿat Dāʾirat al-Maʿārif, 1332), two more listed by Fuat Sezgin, *Geschichte des arabischen Schrifttums*, 11 vols. to date (Leiden: E. J. Brill, 1967–), vol. 1, 415. The one collector who appears in the comprehensive Ḥanafī biographical dictionary of Ibn Abī al-Wafā,' *al-Jawāhir al-muḍīya*, is al-Ustādh al-Subadhmūnī (d. 340/952), a leader of the Transoxanian Ḥanafīya.

51. The fact of his refusal comes out in both Ḥanbalī and Muʿtazili accounts, but naturally with dif-

> Stop at what is ambiguous in the Qurʾān and hadith. Explain nothing (*lā tufassir shayʾan*). Do not look for any device with which to refute heretics, for you have been enjoined to silence before them. Do not give them power over you.[52]

[397] But his contemporary Ibn Abī Ḥātim (d. 327/938) quotes stories whereby Aḥmad praises Shāfiʿī and his learning precisely because they allow him to refute rationalistic jurisprudents; for example, "Our napes, as *aṣḥāb al-ḥadīth*, were in the hands of Abū Ḥanīfa and not to be wrested away until we saw Shāfiʿī."[53] If even so excellent a traditionist as Ibn Abī Ḥātim liked the way rationalist methods enabled traditionalists to win debates, the days of the old intransigence had to be numbered. Polemical works in the prevailing style of *kalām* soon did appear even in the Ḥanbalī tradition.[54]

Once the majority had adopted textual sources and hadith criticism, it was difficult for the traditionist-jurisprudents not to discontinue their offensive and seek to take their place among the more rationalistic jurisprudents. Hence, for example, the Ḥanābila allegedly attacked al-Ṭabarī near the end of his life for dismissing Aḥmad ibn Ḥanbal as a traditionist, not a jurisprudent.[55] Aḥmad's actual practice suggests that (for him) one could not be one without also being the other. One supposes that he and his contemporaries would not have disputed Ṭabarī's identifying Aḥmad as one but not the other; rather, they would have disputed his proposing to distinguish at all between mastery of hadith and mastery of jurisprudence. The old equation of jurisprudence with hadith, expecting hadith reports to speak for themselves, survived only as a rhetorical pose among the Ḥanābila; for example, with Ibn Qudāma (d. 620/1223), who continually reviews the positions of each rival school, then concludes "As for the Ḥanbalī position, hadith says . . . ."[56]

---

ferent connotations. Ḥanbal ibn Isḥāq, *Dhikr miḥnat al-imām Aḥmad ibn Ḥanbal*, ed. Muḥammad Naghash (Cairo: Dār Nashr al-Thaqāfa, 1397/1977), 48–50, stresses the rationalists' inability to come up with arguments from Qurʾan and hadith, whereas Ibn al-Murtaḍā, *Die Klassen der Muʿtaziliten*, ed. Susanna Diwald-Wilzer, Bibliotheca Islamica, vol. 21 (Wiesbaden: Franz Steiner, 1961), 125, stresses Aḥmad's admitted incompetence in *kalām*.

52. Al-Barbahārī, *Sharḥ al-sunna*, ed. Muḥammad ibn Saʿīd al-Qaḥṭānī, 3rd printing (Cairo: Maktabat al-Sunna, 1416/1996), 65; same text apud Ibn Abī Yaʿlā, *Ṭabaqāt*, vol. 2, 18–43, at 39.

53. Ibn Abī Ḥātim, *Jarḥ*, vol. 7, 203 (preferring marginal *aqfiyatunā* to *aqḍiyatunā* of the text). Same apud Ibn Abī Ḥātim, *Ādāb al-Shāfiʿī wa-manāqibuh*, ed. ʿAbd al-Ghanī ʿAbd al-Khāliq and ʿIzzat ʿAṭṭār (Cairo: Maktabat al-Khānjī, 1953, repr. Aleppo: Maktabat al-Turāth al-Islāmī, 1954), 55.

54. Notably *K. al-Radd ʿalā al-zanādiqa wa-al-jahmīya*, available in various editions, of which the best may be Aḥmad ibn Ḥanbal (attrib.), *K. al-Radd ʿalā al-jahmīya wa-al-zanādiqa*, ed. ʿAbd al-Raḥmān ʿUmayra (Riyadh: Dār al-Liwā', 1397/1977). I suggest it goes back to Ghulām al-Khallāl (d. 363/974). Certainly, the *isnād* for the work becomes confused before him.

55. Yāqūt, *Irshād al-arīb ilā maʿrifat al-adīb*, ed. Iḥsān ʿAbbās, 7 vols. (Beirut: Dār al-Gharb al-Islāmī, 1993), vol. 6, 2450–51, s.n. Muḥammad ibn Jarīr al-Ṭabarī.

56. Ibn Qudāma al-Maqdisī, *al-Mughnī*, ed. Ṭāhā Muḥammad al-Zaynī, 10 vols. (Cairo: Maktabat al-Qāhira, 1388–90); also ed. ʿAbd Allāh ibn ʿAbd al-Muḥsin al-Turkī and ʿAbd al-Fattāḥ Muḥammad al-Ḥulw, 15 vols. (Cairo: Hajr, 1406/1986).

On the rationalist side, of course, there was a movement toward the middle in the form of fitting out traditional Ḥanafī positions with a basis in hadith. Ibn Shujāʿ al-Thaljī (d. 266/880) seems to have been [398] the crucial figure in Iraq.[57] The first Ḥanafī to expressly take up the traditionists' methods of hadith criticism was apparently al-Ṭaḥāwī (d. 321/933) in Egypt. "I have seen you in the evening with the jurisprudents (*fuqahāʾ*) in their place," someone told him, "and I have seen you among the traditionists (*ahl al-ḥadīth*) in theirs: how few are they who combine the two."[58] In *Bayān mushkil al-ḥadīth*, Ṭaḥāwī harmonizes contradictory hadith reports in the manner of Shāfiʿī, without attempting hadith criticism himself, but in *Kitāb Maʿānī al-āthār*, by contrast, Ṭaḥāwī does presume to distinguish sound from unsound hadith reports. His *isnād* criticism might look capricious to a specialist in hadith, but it is by and large the method of the traditionist-jurisprudents of the earlier ninth century that Ṭaḥāwī had taken over.

Ibn Ḥibbān (d. 354/965) gives us our earliest systematic description from a traditionist of how to sort hadith by comparing *asānīd*. He distinguishes clearly between the jurisprudent and the traditionist: the jurisprudent is someone who knows only *mutūn*, the traditionist someone who knows only *asānīd*. The former is not to be relied upon to relate an *isnād* by memory, only from his written notes, while the latter is not to be relied upon to relate a *matn* by memory, only from his written notes. Moreover, though, he requires five conditions of its transmitters for a hadith report to be considered sound: probity in religion, truthfulness in hadith, understanding (*ʿaql*) of the hadith he has transmitted, knowledge (*ʿilm*) of what is ruled out by what he transmits, and avoidance of *tadlīs*.[59] Understanding and knowledge of what one is transmitting (in spite of the famous hadith report by which many a man bore knowledge to one more discerning than he) amount to jurisprudence. As for Shāfiʿī earlier, they were necessary to establish the reliability of any addition. So here at last is a traditionist who himself admits that the traditionists need the jurisprudents.

Where the Traditionist-Jurisprudents Were Not Important

As systematic works like the *Risāla* of Shāfiʿī were not alone responsible for all development in the theory and practice of Islamic law, so it must be admitted that the traditionist-jurisprudents were also not [399] responsible for all development. These, I take it, are

57. See Melchert, *Formation*, 51–3; *idem*, "How Ḥanafism Came to Originate in Kufa and Traditionalism in Medina," *Islamic Law and Society*, vi (1999), 318–47, at 342–43 [*HPL 12].

58. Al-Dhahabī, *Siyar* 15:30. *Cf.* Ibn Ḥajar, *Lisān al-Mīzān*, 7 vols. (Hyderabad: Majlis Dāʾirat al-Maʿārif, 1329–31), vol. 1, 279.

59. Ibn Ḥibbān, *Ṣaḥīḥ Ibn Ḥibbān bi-tartīb Ibn Balbān*, ed. Shuʿayb al-Arnaʾūṭ, 18 vols., 3rd printing (Beirut: Muʾassasat al-Risāla, 1414/1993), vol. 1, 151.

the most important transformations of mainstream jurisprudence in the leading centers over the course of the ninth century:

(1) Textual sources (Qurʾan and hadith) eclipsed rational speculation as the formal basis of the law.
(2) Hadith reports from the Prophet eclipsed reports from Companions and later authorities (but reports from Imams remained important for Shiʿi jurisprudence);
(3) Experts sifted hadith reports primarily by comparison of their *asānīd*, secondarily by examination of *rijāl*, the personal qualities of their transmitters.
(4) Personal schools eclipsed regional, such that jurisprudents came to be identified primarily with one or another teacher of the past rather than one or another region.
(5) Texts stabilized and some became the literary bases of personal schools.
(6) Jurisprudence and hadith were professionalized, each becoming increasingly distinct from the other and each the province of specialists distinct from interested laymen.

Of the main features of Islamic jurisprudence as we know it from the eleventh century forwards, only *guild schools*, which certified jurisprudents, and perhaps the science of *uṣūl al-fiqh* were yet to come, mainly in the first half of the tenth century.[60]

No one has proposed that traditionist-jurisprudents had much to do with the last two of these transformations, numbers 5 and 6: on the contrary, they unsuccessfully opposed them. Traditionist-jurisprudents looked for guidance to hadith, which is to say authoritative rulings from the Prophet and his Companions, not to the opinions of some recent jurisprudent. In principle, anyone should be able to add more and better hadith reports to an authoritative collection. This is just what we see in compilations such as the *Musnad* of Aḥmad ibn Ḥanbal, as many as a third of whose hadith reports, by some estimates, reflect improvements from ʿAbd Allāh ibn Aḥmad.[61]

Transformation 4 on the list has become controversial, as doubt has been cast on whether there ever existed regional schools before [400] personal. The conventional scholarly view has gone back to Joseph Schacht, who proposed that before Shāfiʿī, Muslim jurisprudents were grouped in the schools of Kufa and Medina with secondary schools in Damascus and Mecca.[62] Thanks mainly to the literary activity of the disciples of Abū

60. For the three-stage scheme of regional, personal, finally guild schools, see esp. George Makdisi, "*Ṭabaqāt*-Biography: Law and Orthodoxy in Classical Islam," *Islamic Studies* (Islamabad), xxxii (1993), 371–96. For the emergence of classical *uṣūl al-fiqh* only in the tenth century, see Hallaq, "Was al-Shafiʿi the Master Architect?" esp. 588–91.

61. See Melchert, *Formation*, 139.

62. Schacht, *Origins*, esp. chap. 2.

Ḥanīfa, Kufan jurisprudence survived after the mid-third century of the Hijra as Ḥanafī, while North African writers effected the survival of Medinese jurisprudence as Mālikī.[63] George Makdisi has identified a third stage after the initial establishment of personal schools, mainly "guild schools," which is to say institutions for certifying jurisprudents.[64] These are the classical schools of Islamic law, familiar from the eleventh century and forward, which took recognizable form at the beginning of the tenth century. With guild schools, there can be no question whether one is, say, a Ḥanafi or a Shāfiʿī, whereas characterizations for the period before the guild schools are necessarily less certain.

The latest and by far strongest critique of Schacht's scheme has come from Wael Hallaq, who points out that eighth-century doctrine is seldom anonymous, that it is easy to find disagreement within regions, and that jurisprudents personally chose what doctrines to follow with remarkable freedom. There never were, then, regional schools, nor afterwards personal if that is taken to mean that one was bound by the imam's personal opinions. However many common regional doctrines the sources may point to, they are not qualitatively different from such common doctrines as characterized regions in later centuries.[65] I am inclined to think that Hallaq works too hard to refute propositions no one has ever made, such as the thorough anonymity of doctrine in the regional stage, while addressing too little of the evidence that eighth-century jurisprudents were characteristically divided along regional lines. Concerning the business of this article, however, I will now [401] retract an earlier argument of my own, mainly that the traditionist-jurisprudents provoked the rationalists to stress the antiquity of their own doctrines, as by assigning them to venerable jurisprudents such as Abū Ḥanīfa and Mālik instead of to local opinion and practice.[66] It was not traditionist-jurisprudents who complained that the consensus of Medina was no fit basis of legal obligation, rather Shāfiʿī and later adherents of his school.[67] In short, the traditionist-jurisprudents probably had little to do with the rise of "Ḥanafī" and "Mālikī" schools in the place of "Kufan" and "Medinese."

63. Joseph Schacht, "The Schools of Law and Later Developments of Jurisprudence," *Law in the Middle East* 1: *Origin and Development of Islamic Law*, ed. Majid Khadduri and Herbert J. Liebesny (Washington, D.C.: Middle East Institute, 1955), 57–84, esp. 63.

64. Makdisi, "*Ṭabaqāt*-Biography."

65. Wael B. Hallaq, "From Regional to Personal Schools of Law? A Reevaluation," *Islamic Law and Society*, viii (2001), 1–26. Earlier denials that there was ever a regional stage include M. Mustafa al-Azami, *On Schacht's* Origins of Muhammadan Jurisprudence (Riyadh: King Saud University, 1985, repr. Oxford: Oxford Centre for Islamic Studies and Cambridge: Islamic Texts Society, 1996), chap. 4, and Nimrod Hurvitz, "Schools of Law and Historical Context: Re-examining the Formation of the Ḥanbalī *madhhab*," *Islamic Law and Society*, vii (2000), 37–64, esp. 42–46, 63.

66. Melchert, *Formation*, chap. 2; cf. Hallaq, "Regional," 2–5, similarly Eric Chaumont, review of *Formation*, *Bulletin critique des Annales islamologiques*, xvi (2000), 71–72.

67. See mainly Shāfiʿī, *K. Ikhtilāf Mālik wa-al-Shāfiʿī*, *Umm*, vol. 7, 177–249. Denial that Medina enjoyed any special privilege became a staple of *uṣūl al-fiqh* in the Shāfiʿī tradition, for which see most conveniently Bernard G. Weiss, *The Search for God's Law* (Salt Lake City: Univ. of Utah Press, 1992), 220–21.

Another of these transformations, mainly number 2, has been attributed to the traditionist-jurisprudents by mistake. Schacht took Shāfiʿī at his word, that he spoke for the traditionists. If we examine actual works from traditionist-jurisprudents in the earlier ninth century (few so easily available to Schacht as to us), we can see that they did not heed Shāfiʿī's case for relying only on hadith from the Prophet, never on conflicting hadith from the Companions and later authorities. For example, scarcely one in five items in the *Muṣannaf* of ʿAbd al-Razzāq goes back to the Prophet, about one in four items in the *Muṣannaf* of Abū Bakr Ibn Abī Shayba. Collections of Aḥmad ibn Ḥanbal's juridical opinions likewise point to an unembarrassed reliance on Companion hadith.[68] As for systematically preferring hadith from the Prophet, the traditionist-jurisprudents amended their practice across the ninth century at about the same rate as others. An express statement of method from Aḥmad goes so far as to identify the authoritative *sunna* with hadith from the Prophet and the first four caliphs, a wider canon than what Shāfiʿī calls for in his polemics against the Mālikīya but implicitly excluding most Companion hadith.[69]

By contrast, transformation number 1 seems inconceivable without pressure from traditionist-jurisprudents. It was precisely their program to rely on textual sources (mainly Qurʾan and hadith) to the exclusion [402] of rational speculation. Number 3 also can hardly be explained without pressure from traditionist-jurisprudents. It was they, not the rationalistic jurisprudents, who developed the methods of hadith criticism early in the ninth century that became standard for all jurisprudents by the end of it. (According to later tradition, of course, perspicuous hadith criticism was practiced well before the ninth century by famous jurisprudents such as Mālik; however, their methods are practically impossible to document.[70])

The Decline of Companion and Later Hadith

The use of hadith reports from Companions and later authorities was not an issue dividing traditionist-jurisprudents from rationalistic. Schacht sometimes ranged Shāfiʿī with the traditionist-jurisprudents, since he argued against irresponsible speculation (*raʾy*,

68. In Abū Dāwūd, *Masāʾil*, 277, he expressly identifies the binding *sunna* as that of the Prophet and the Rightly Guided caliphs, not of the Prophet alone, adding that he dislikes to disagree with any of the other Companions.

69. Abū Dāwūd, *Masāʾil*, 277. Ibn Māja includes three prophetic hadith reports for the inclusion of the Rightly Guided Caliphs, *Sunan*, Introduction, 6, *bāb ittibāʿ sunnat al-khulafāʾ al-rāshidīn al-mahdīyīn*.

70. "All the traditionists in the *Muwaṭṭaʾ* are trustworthy save one," according to al-Fasawī, *K. al-Maʿrifa wa-al-tārīkh*, ed. Akram Ḍiyāʾ al-ʿUmarī, 3rd edn., 4 vols. (Medina: Maktabat al-Dār, 1410/1989), vol. 1, 425; "Mālik would relate hadith reports only from the trustworthy": so Sufyān ibn ʿUyayna, apud al-Qāḍī ʿIyāḍ, *Tartīb al-madārik*, ed. Aḥmad Bakīr Maḥmūd, 4 vols. in 2 + index (Beirut: Maktabat al-Ḥayāt, 1967–), vol. 1, 130, 150, also apud Dutton, *Origins*, 17. Ibn Abī Ḥātim presents a small collection of Mālik's comments on traditionists, *Jarḥ*, vol. 1, 19–25.

istiḥsān). In consequence, Shāfiʿī's advocacy of hadith from the Prophet against hadith from Companions has sometimes seemed to express the opinion of traditionist-jurisprudents. But this is wrong. First, traditionist-jurisprudents of the earlier ninth century were willing to rely heavily on hadith from Companions. For example, again, the overwhelming majority of entries in the *Muṣannafs* of ʿAbd al-Razzāq and Abū Bakr Ibn Abī Shayba are not from the Prophet but from later authorities. Insofar as Shāfiʿī argued against hadith from Companions and Followers, he did not act as spokesman for the traditionist-jurisprudents of the earlier ninth century. Second, Shāfiʿī argued only occasionally for the superiority of hadith from the Prophet to hadith from other figures. In the *Risāla*, to the contrary, the equation of "hadith" with reports from the Prophet is everywhere assumed, never argued.[71]

Hadith was controversial, but the traditionist-jurisprudents were not prominent in either of the two controversies that led to the abandonment of hadith from Companions and later figures. To explain the rise of [403] prophetic hadith alone, Joseph Schacht pointed to one area of controversy, mainly between adherents of the different regional schools of the eighth century. Thus jurisprudents of Kufa, for example, would cite hadith from the Prophet to trump the hadith from the Companions cited by their Medinese opponents. An example whereby Shaybānī appeals to Companions against Followers has already come up. Shaybānī's preference for hadith from Companions to hadith from Followers is roughly in line with opinion among traditionist-jurisprudents of the early ninth century. Aḥmad's recognition of the Rightly Guided Caliphs as establishing the authoritative *sunna* has been noted already. We can hardly explain the rise of expressly prophetic hadith and the decline of hadith from Companions by pressure from traditionist-jurisprudents.

A second controversy evidently pitted what John Burton has called *ahl al-fiqh* (that is, jurisprudents as distinct from traditionists) against *ahl al-Qurʾān*. These last were rationalists who proposed to throw out rules based on hadith whenever they contradicted the Qurʾan.[72] This controversy is harder to document than that among the regional schools inasmuch as nothing survives from the Qurʾan-only side of the debate. However, the controversy may be inferred from such works as the *Risāla* of Shāfiʿī and *Taʾwīl mukhtalif al-ḥadīth* of Ibn Qutayba. Burton identifies the chief polemical tendency of the *Risāla* precisely as the defense of prophetic hadith against the Qur'an.[73] Where centrists

71. See Schacht, *Origins*, chaps. 3, 4, esp. 11–12, where Schacht develops Shāfiʿī's advocacy of hadith from the Prophet on the basis not of the *Risāla* but of *K. Ikhtilāf Mālik wa-al-Shāfiʿī*.

72. John Burton, *The Sources of Islamic Law* (Edinburgh: Univ. Press, 1990), 22–23. Qurʾan-only scripturalism has been documented most carefully by Michael Cook, "ʿAnan and Islam: The Origins of Karaite Scripturalism," *Jerusalem Studies in Arabic and Islam*, no. 9 (1987), 161–82, esp. 165–74. The attitude is found among Khawārij as well as Muʿtazila and fellow travellers, but Khāriji ideas evidently seemed hardly worth refuting in the ninth century.

73. Burton, *Sources*, 11, 22–25.

of the earlier ninth century such as Abū ʿUbayd (d. 224/838–39?) and al-Muḥāsibī (d. 243/857–58) conceded that the Prophet's word reflected a lower degree of inspiration than the Qurʾan did, the *Risāla* of Shāfiʿī argues emphatically that the Prophet's word and the Qur'an are equally inspired and equally to be obeyed.[74] Similarly, Ibn Qutayba's *Taʾwīl mukhtalif al-ḥadith* again and again justifies hadith reports contradicted by the Qurʾan, plainly to refute rationalists who would simply dismiss the hadith in question and go by the Qur'an alone. Like the *Risāla* of Shāfiʿī, it expressly asserts the equal inspiration of the Prophet's word [404] and the Qurʾan.[75] It was necessary to elevate the Prophet's authority this way in order to defend the authority of hadith-based rules against Qurʾan-only rationalists. Of course, the same argument required that hadith from Companions be quietly discarded as a basis of the law, inasmuch as it was hard to argue that hadith from Companions was also equally inspired with the Qurʾan.

Contemporary traditionist-jurisprudents made similar adjustments at about the same rate (or fifty years later, if we accept the traditional dating of Shāfiʿī's *Risāla* and other works). In the introduction to his *Sunan*, al-Dārimi (d. 255/869) argues vigorously for the equal inspiration of Qurʾan and prophetic *sunna*. He cites some of the same hadith as Shāfiʿī.[76] The Six Books (earliest attributed to Bukhārī [d. 256/870], latest to Nasāʾī [d. 303/915?]) implicitly endorse the same exclusive dependence on hadith from the Prophet to support every rule.

As traditionist-jurisprudents closed ranks with the moderate rationalists to resist the yet more dangerous Qurʾan-only rationalists, they came to embrace adherents of rationalistic jurisprudence whom their forebears had regarded with more reserve. In one case, it is possible to date precisely a traditionalist's embrace of at least some rationalistic jurisprudents. Ibn Qutayba's lists of traditionist-jurisprudents and rationalistic jurisprudents, respectively, have been mentioned already.[77] In the *Maʿārif*, the first version

74. Shāfiʿī, *Risāla*, ¶¶ 282–87, where such qurʾanic phrases as *mā unzila ilayk* and *awḥaynā ilayka min amrinā* are applied to the prophetic *sunna*. I treat Abū ʿUbayd and Muḥāsibī in "Qurʾanic Abrogation Across the Ninth Century," in Weiss (ed.), *Studies*, 75–98.

75. Ibn Qutayba, *Taʾwīl mukhtalif al-ḥadīth*, ed. Muḥammad Zuhrī al-Najjār (Cairo: Maktabat al-Kullīyāt al-Azharīya, 1386/1966), 166 (the *sunna* brought by Gabriel), 195 (likewise, and identified with *waḥy*) = *Le traité des divergences du ḥadīṯ d'Ibn Qutayba*, trans. Gérard Lecomte (Damascus: Institut Français de Damas, 1962), 184, 217.

76. "There will come a time when a man will recline on his couch (*arīka*), relating my words (*ḥadīth*), and will say, 'Between us and you is the Book of God. Whatever we have found it to permit, we have considered it permissible. Whatever we have found it to forbid, we have considered forbidden.' Is not what the Messenger of God has forbidden like what God has?" Dārimī, *Sunan*, Introduction, § 49 (48 according to Wensinck's reckoning); Shāfiʿī, *Risāla*, ¶ 295; also *idem*, *Bayān farāʾiḍ Allāh*, *K. al-Umm*, vol. 7, 264, ll. 13–15, 265, ll. 5–8. Quoted from Ibn Māja and pointed out in the *Risāla* by Burton, *Sources*, 24–25; earlier still by Schacht, *Origins*, 46.

77. See note 4.

of which of was finished before 252/866,[78] Mālik, Awzāʿī, and Sufyān al-Thawrī all appear among *aṣḥāb al-raʾy*. Ibn Qutayba wrote *Taʾwīl mukhtalif al-ḥadīth* a few years later, in the late 250s/early 870s,[79] and there also he lists traditionist-jurisprudents and rationalistic jurisprudents. Now, however, Mālik, Awzāʿī, and [405] Sufyān al-Thawrī have shifted columns, all appearing as exemplars of devotion to hadith (*aṣḥāb al-ḥadīth*) alongside Aḥmad ibn Ḥanbal. Only Abū Ḥanīfa and his followers continue to be disparaged as adherents of contemptible *raʾy*.[80] Ibn Qutayba's change of opinion probably reflects more closely the changing views of his patron the shadow-caliph al-Muwaffaq than the views of Baghdadi traditionist-jurisprudents in general.[81] One could hardly ask for a clearer illustration of how the traditionist-jurisprudents and the rationalists, once sharply divided, came to meet in the middle.

Conclusion

My thesis has been that the traditionist-jurisprudents are crucial to the development of Islamic law in the ninth century. They proposed to infer the law as directly as possible from Qurʾan and hadith, Companion or later hadith if prophetic was unavailable. If hadith reports appeared to contradict one another, they preferred to search out the correct solution by comparing *asānīd* to find the one report most reliably attested. They disliked excessive sophistication, clever argumentation, and speculation about cases that had not come up in real life. Their unremitting solemnity was religiously attractive, and over the course of the century, jurisprudents of virtually all parties conceded their insistence on a basis in hadith. Perhaps the Inquisition (218–37/833–52) was the turning point, for it showed decisively that winning abstruse theological arguments was not the way to establish one party as arbiter of Islamic orthodoxy.

78. Gérard Lecomte, *Ibn Qutayba* (Damascus: Institut Français de Damas, 1965), 90.

79. Lecomte, *Ibn Qutayba*, 90.

80. Ibn Qutayba, *Mukhtalif*, ed. al-Najjār, 17, 51–52 = *Traité*, 18–19, 56–57.

81. For Muwaffaq and his sponsorship of traditionalist Mālikism, see Christopher Melchert, "Religious Policies of the Caliphs From al-Mutawakkil to al-Muqtadir," *Islamic Law and Society*, iii (1996), 316–42, at 329–30, 334–40; *idem*, "How Ḥanafism," 340–41. Modern scholarship often refers to Ibn Qutayba as an arch-traditionalist, but some of his known theological positions were certainly closer to the rationalist pole than contemporary traditionist-jurisprudents. See Ibn Qutayba, *al-Ikhtilāf fī al-lafẓ*, ed. Muḥammad Zāhid al-Kawtharī (Cairo: Maktabat al-Qudsī, 1349), 71 (the Qurʾan increate but not one's pronunciation of it); also Ibn Qutayba, *Mukhtalif*, ed. al-Najjār, 80 = *Traité*, 90 (traditionists will collect twenty versions of a hadith report where two would suffice, similar to Dāwīd al-Ẓāhirī's complaint, indignantly quoted by Abū Ḥātim, apud Ibn Abī Ḥātim, *Jarḥ*, vol. 3, 410–11). Traditionalist unease with Ibn Qutayba is documented by Ibn Ḥajar, *Lisān*, vol. 3, 357–59, and Gérard Lecomte, *Ibn Qutayba* (Damascus: Institut Français de Damas, 1965), pt. 2, chap. 1.

Over the rest of the century, the traditionist-jurisprudents were able to watch the adherents of Abū Ḥanīfa, Mālik, and others take up their [406] own reliance on hadith as opposed to local custom, rational speculation, and so on, and their methods of sorting reliable from unreliable hadith reports. However, they did not watch them entirely give up their old sophistication, clever argumentation, and speculation about cases that had not come up in real life. On the contrary, as they watched their erstwhile adversaries take up hadith, it seemed increasingly imperative that the traditionalists themselves become more sophisticated. It no longer sufficed for a man to know prodigious amounts of hadith. Whether announcing that their work was fully complementary with the work of previous experts in jurisprudence not necessarily experts in hadith or insisting that their imam had been a great expert in jurisprudence as well as hadith, they had clearly conceded something to the rationalists. They were probably predisposed toward concessions by their theological position in favor of the majority, *al-jamāʿa*, against splinter movements.

The beginning of the fourth Islamic century (early 910s C.E.) was widely acknowledged in later tradition as a watershed, the dividing line between the ancients and the moderns, *al-mutaqaddimīn* and *al-mutaʾakhkhirīn*. After this point, the old enmity between rationalists and traditionalists continued fierce at the level of theology but scarcely any longer at the level of jurisprudence. Islamic law would henceforth be compounded of elements from each side. The Muslims gained a system demonstrably based on revelation but penetrable at multiple levels, affording the widest scope for intellectual play.[82] What they lost was the purity and power of simply letting hadith speak for itself; also, on the other side, a certain frankness about the importance of local tradition and personal speculation in the development of Islamic law.

82. See Norman Calder, "The Law," *History of Islamic Philosophy*, ed. Seyyed Hossein Nasr and Oliver Leaman, Routledge Hist. of World Philosophies 1, 2 vols. (London: Routledge, 1996), 979–98.

14

THE MEANING OF *QĀLA 'L-SHĀFIʿĪ* IN NINTH CENTURY SOURCES

How was al-Shāfiʿī's doctrine made known in the ninth century CE? The traditional story has Muḥammad b. Idrīs al-Shāfiʿī born, probably in Ashkelon, about 150/767–768. He grew up in Mecca and northern Arabia. He is said to have studied under Mālik (d. 179/795) in Medina for as long as ten years and later debated with al-Shaybānī (d. 189/804–805) in Baghdad. Four Baghdadis are customarily named as the leading transmitters of *al-qadīm*, al-Shāfiʿī's Baghdadi teaching:

> al-Ḥusayn b. ʿAlī al-Karābīsī (d. 245/859–860?),
> al-Ḥasan b. Muḥammad al-Zaʿfarānī (d. 260/874?),
> Abū Thawr (d. 240/854), and
> Aḥmad b. Ḥanbal (d. 241/855),

listed here in descending order of importance.[1]

Al-Shāfiʿī lived in Old Cairo for about six years before his death in 204/820. Here, his leading disciples and the transmitters of *al-jadīd*, his Egyptian teaching, were

> al-Muzanī (d. Old Cairo, 264/877?),
> al-Rabīʿ b. Sulaymān al-Jīzī (d. 256/870),
> al-Rabīʿ b. Sulaymān al-Murādī (d. Old Cairo, 270/884),
> al-Buwayṭī (d. Baghdad, 231/846?),

1. Al-Nawawī, *Tahdhīb al-asmāʾ wa-l-Lughāt*, II, Cairo: Idārat al-Ṭibāʿa al-Munīrīya, 1927 (reprint; Beirut: Dār al-Kutub al-ʿIlmīya, n.d.), p. 284.

Originally published in *Abbasid Studies: Occasional Papers of the School of Abbasid Studies, Cambridge, 6-10 July 2002*. Edited by James E. Montgomery. OLA 135. Leuven: Peeters, 2004), 277–301.

Ḥarmala (d. Old Cairo, 243/858?), and
Yūnus b. ʿAbd al-ʿAlāʾ (d. Old Cairo, 264/877).[2]

Al-Rabīʿ (traditionally identified as al-Murādī, not al-Jīzī) appears as the transmitter and to some extent the compiler of the following works:

K. al-Radd ʿalā Muḥammad b. al-Ḥasan;
Ikhtilāf ʿAlī wa-ʿAbd Allāh b. Masʿūd;
K. Ikhtilāf al-ʿIrāqīyayn;
K. Ibṭāl al-Istiḥsān;
K. Siyar al-Awzāʿī;
al-Risāla; [278]
Bayān Farāʾiḍ Allāh;
K. Jimāʿ al-ʿIlm;
K. Ikhtilāf Mālik wa-l-Shāfiʿī;
K. al-Umm; and
K. Ikhtilāf al-Ḥadīth,

listed here in chronological order as proposed by Schacht, who considered the *Risāla* the last of the Iraqi works, dating from 198/814 or before.[3] Al-Bayhaqī (d. Nishapur, 458/1066) lists the short works separately from the *Umm*;[4] however, al-Nawawī (d. Nawā, 676/1277) evidently considered some (perhaps all) of the short works part of the *Umm*, for he once remarks:

> He mentioned this *naṣṣ* (express position) in *al-Umm* in *Bāb Ṣalāt al-Jumʿa wa-l-ʿĪdayn*, from *Kitāb Ikhtilāf ʿAlī b. Abī Ṭālib wa-ʿAbd Allāh b. Masʿūd* . . . , it being among the last books of *al-Umm* before *Kitāb Siyar al-Wāqidī*.[5]

2. Al-Nawawī, *Tahdhīb*, II, p. 284.

3. J. Schacht, *The Origins of Muhammadan Jurisprudence*, Oxford, 1950, p. 330. All these works were printed together, along with the *Mukhtaṣar* of al-Muzanī, the *Musnad*, and the very short *K. Ṣifat Nahy Rasūl Allāh*, as Al-Shāfiʿī, *Kitāb al-Umm*, Bulaq: al-Maṭbaʿa al-Kubrā al-Amīrīya, 1321–1325 (reprint, without *al-Risāla*: Cairo: Kitāb al-Shaʿb, 1388/1968). Subsequent editions from Cairo and Beirut have been mere resettings of the Bulaq edition and are to be avoided, with the exception of *Mawsūʿat al-imām al-Shāfiʿī: Kitāb al-Umm*, ed. A.B.D. Ḥassūn, Beirut: Dār Qutayba, 1416/1996, which draws on manuscripts from Dublin and Berlin as well as Cairo, although, it appears, sparingly and unsystematically (besides ignoring the Istanbul manuscripts, for which see F. Sezgin, *Geschichte des arabischen Schrifttums*, I, Leiden, 1967, p. 487). This is not yet the scientific edition we need. Marginal numbers refer to the Bulaq pagination. It does not include the *Mukhtaṣar* of al-Muzanī.

4. Al-Bayhaqī, *Manāqib al-Shāfiʿī*, ed. S.A. Ṣaqr, Cairo: Dār al-Turāth, 1390–1391/1970–1971), I, p. 246 f.

5. Al-Nawawī et al., *al-Majmūʿ. Sharḥ al-Muhadhdhab*, III, Cairo: Maṭbaʿat al-ʿĀṣima and Maṭbaʿat al-Imām, 1966–1969, p. 504.

Yet Nawawī does not describe quite the *Umm* that we have: *Ikhtilāf ʿAlī wa-ʿAbd Allāh b. Masʿūd* is only the second of eight short works printed at the end of the Bulaq edition, and it seems that no copy of *Siyar al-Wāqidī* is extant.[6] Modern scholars have relied chiefly on the *Risāla* for al-Shāfiʿī's legal theory (although Schacht used mainly *Ikhtilāf Mālik wa-l-Shāfiʿī* and *Ikhtilāf al-Ḥadīth* for al-Shāfiʿī's arguments against reliance on custom and Companion *ḥadīth* whenever prophetic *ḥadīth* could be found).[7] The *Umm* appears to be the leading [279] compendium of al-Shāfiʿī's doctrine concerning the rules themselves, *Furūʿ al-Fiqh*. Modern scholars have also looked to the *Mukhtaṣar* of al-Muzanī for an account of al-Shāfiʿī's doctrine in *Furūʿ*. I shall henceforth refer to Muzanī's *Mukhtaṣar* and all of what al-Rabīʿ transmitted from al-Shāfiʿī as 'the Egyptian works.'

I once assumed that al-Muzanī and al-Rabīʿ straightforwardly presented the *jadīd*, but al-Muzanī's *Mukhtaṣar* expressly draws on the *qadīm* at points.[8] Moreover, express interpolations from al-Rabīʿ in some of the works mentioned above suggest compilation from multiple written sources, without apparent distinction between *qadīm* and *jadīd*. For example, al-Rabīʿ comments, in *Ikhtilāf al-ʿIrāqīyayn*, 'There is another dictum concerning this (question),' which he then presents, adding at the end, 'This is the meaning of al-Shāfiʿī's dictum (*maʿnā qawl al-Shāfiʿī*),' an expression that normally indicates paraphrase (*Umm* VII, p. 105.11–13). Although I have not come across any express references to *jadīd* and *qadīm* in *al-Umm*, al-Rabīʿ does refer periodically to 'the latter of his two dicta (*ākhir qawlay-hi*).'[9] None of al-Shāfiʿī's Baghdadi disciples is said to have visited Egypt, nor any of his Egyptian disciples Baghdad; however, al-Zaʿfarānī and al-Rabīʿ al-Murādī are

6. See Sezgin, *GAS*, I, p. 487–490. Al-Shāfiʿī is credited with a *K. Siyar al-Wāqidī*, distinct from *K. al-Radd ʿalā Muḥammad b. al-Ḥasan* and *K. Siyar al-Awzāʿī*, by Ibn al-Nadīm, *Fihrist*, *Fann* 3, *Maqāla* 6 = *Kitāb al-Fihrist*, ed. G. Flügel et al., Leipzig, 1872, p. 210.26. It seems a part of it is in Al-Shāfiʿī, *Umm*, IV, pp. 176–194, presumably placed there in the revision of al-Bulqīnī. The text there does not mention Wāqidī, so that Wāqidī doubtfully provided more than the order of topics.

7. J.E. Lowry, *The Legal-Theoretical Content of the* Risala, Ph.D. dissertation, University of Pennsylvania, 1999; W.B. Hallaq, *A History of Islamic Legal Theories*, Cambridge, 1997, Chapter 1; *La Risāla*, trans. L. Souami, Paris, 1997; N. Calder, *Ikhtilâf and Ijmâʿ in Shâfiʿî's Risâla*, in: *Studia Islamica* 58 (1983), p. 39–47; M. Khadduri (translator), *Islamic Jurisprudence: Shāfiʿī's Risāla*, Baltimore, 1961; Schacht, *Origins*.

8. E.g., on margin of Al-Shāfiʿī, *Umm*, I, p. 61: 'Al-Muzanī said, He said in the *qadīm* that he means concerning the *tathwīb* in the call to the dawn prayer, which is to say twice "*al-ṣalāh khayr min al-nawm*." He related it [the *ḥadīth* report in question] from Bilāl the *muʾadhdhin* of the Prophet . . . and from ʿAlī . . . . He considered it discouraged (*karihahu*) in the *jadīd* because Abū Maḥdhūra did not relate it from the Prophet.' Similarly, *Umm*, I, p. 138 marg., 'He said in the *qadīm* (that) he does not offer good wishes [to one who has sneezed, in the course of praying], nor does he return a salutation save by a sign. Al-Muzanī said . . . , I say that the *jadīd* has priority because returning (a salutation) is *farḍ* while silence is *sunna*, and *farḍ* has priority over *sunna*.' (Note in this last instance that the *jadīd* does not take precedence simply for being *jadīd*.) See also references in section headings; e.g., a section said to be abridged from, among other sources, '*K. al-Īlāʾ qadīm wa-jadīd*,' *Umm*, IV, p. 93–94 marg.

9. E.g., *Umm*, I, p. 58.17, similarly at *Umm*, VII, p. 131.12 from bottom (reading *ākhir qawlay al-Shāfiʿī*).

said to have met in Mecca at the pilgrimage of the year 240/855.[10] We evidently see an example of interference between the Baghdadi and Egyptian traditions in Ibn al-Nadīm's statement that al-Zaʿfarānī related *al-Mabsūṭ* from al-Shāfiʿī according to the order in which al-Rabīʿ related it, in it some discrepancy (*khilf yasīr*).[11] [280]

In the Middle Ages, adherents of the Shāfiʿī school looked for al-Shāfiʿī's opinions in a large number of sources. When al-Bayhaqī lists transmitters from al-Shāfiʿī, he includes ten men in addition to those named by al-Nawawī.[12] For example, in the third volume of *al-Majmūʿ*, a monumental collection of Shāfiʿī opinions, al-Nawawī certainly quotes al-Shāfiʿī's own doctrine most often from the *Umm* (about three times as often as from either al-Buwayṭī or al-Muzanī, the next most common among named sources); however, I have noticed twenty-eight additional named sources, here listed in chronological order:

> Al-Buwayṭī (III, p. 413); his *Mukhtaṣar*, where Shāfiʿī *naṣṣa ʿalay-hi* (expressly declared his opinion; III, p. 511);
>
> Ḥarmala, *al-Sunan*, pointing out the opposite in al-Buwayṭī (III, p. 228); where Shāfiʿī *naṣṣa ʿalay-hi* (III, p. 511);
>
> Al-Muzanī, *al-Mukhtaṣar* (III, p. 535);
>
> Al-Tirmidhī (d. Tirmidh, Transoxania, 279/892), *al-Jāmiʿ* (III, p. 323);
>
> [Manṣūr ibn] Ismāʿīl al-Ḍarīr (d. Old Cairo, 306/918–919), his *Tafsīr* (III, p. 561);
>
> al-Sājī (d. Basra, 307/919–920; III, p. 27);

10. Al-Bayhaqī, *Manāqib al-Shāfiʿī*, apud Al-Nawawī, *Tahdhīb*, I, p. 189.

11. Ibn Al-Nadīm, *al-Fihrist*, *Fann* 3, *Maqāla* 6 = *al-Fihrist*, ed. Flügel, p. 210–211. *Al-Mabsūṭ* has also been identified with Al-Muzanī, *al-Mukhtaṣar al-Kabīr*: Ibn Ḥajar, *Tawālī al-Taʾsīs*, Bulaq: al-Maṭbaʿa al-Mīrīya, 1301, p. 78 (= ed. A.F.ʿA.A. Al-Qāḍī, Beirut: Dār al-Kutub al-ʿIlmīya, 1406/1986, p. 155), followed by Heffening, 'al-Shāfiʿī,' in: *EI1*, IV, p. 252–254. Ibn al-Nadīm's Mālikī contemporary Ibn al-Qaṣṣār (d. Baghdad, 397/1007) refers to *al-Kitāb* of al-Rabīʿ alongside *al-Muwaṭṭaʾ* of Mālik and *al-Jāmiʿ* of al-Thawrī: Ibn Al-Qaṣṣār, *al-Muqaddima fī Uṣūl al-Fiqh*, ed. M.Ḥ. Al-Sulaymānī (*Dirāsāt wa-Nuṣūṣ fī Uṣūl al-Fiqh al-Mālikī*, 1), Beirut: Dār al-Gharb al-Islāmī, 1996, p. 36. One also finds al-Shāfiʿī's Iraqi book identified as a refutation of al-Shaybānī with the title *al-Ḥujja*: e.g., Ibn Ḥajar, *Tawālī*, Bulaq, p. 76 = Beirut, p. 147. The confusion of titles points to lingering textual instability in the later Tenth Century. Three-quarters of a century later, al-Bayhaqī presents the *Umm* as the main statement of al-Shāfiʿī's doctrine in *Furūʿ*, although his list of its contents still diverges from what we find in our printed edition: *Manāqib*, I, p. 247–254.

12. Al-Bayhaqī, *Manāqib*, I, p. 255–257. The ten include two whose transmission from al-Shāfiʿī includes many additions (*ziyādāt*) to what is known from *al-Umm*, mainly the Muʿtazilī Abū ʿAbd al-Raḥmān al-Shāfiʿī, on whom see Al-Dhahabī, *Taʾrīkh al-Islām*, ed. ʿU.ʿA.S. Tadmurī, XVII, Beirut: Dār al-Kitāb al-ʿArabī, 1407–1421/1987–2000, p. 427–428 (231–40 AH), and Abū 'l-Walīd al-Makkī, on whom more below.

Ibn al-Mundhir (d. Mecca, 310/922–923?), transmitting both directly from al-Shāfiᶜī and from Abū Thawr (III, p. 159);

al-Dāraquṭnī (d. Baghdad, 385/995), quoting Abū Bakr al-Naysābūrī (Baghdadi, d. 324/936), quoting in turn al-Rabīᶜ, quoting in turn al-Shāfiᶜī (III, p. 306);

Ibn Kajj (d. Dinawar, 405/1015), quoting al-Shāfiᶜī's *naṣṣ* (III, p. 239); quoting from *al-Umm* (III, p. 438);

Abū Ḥāmid al-Isfarāyinī (d. Baghdad, 406/1016), *al-Taᶜlīq* (III, p. 9); quoting al-Shāfiᶜī in *al-qadīm* and *al-jadīd* (III, p. 30); quoting al-Shāfiᶜī in *al-Umm* and *al-Imlā*ʾ (III, p. 174); quoting Shāfiᶜī in *al-qadīm* and *al-Imlā*ʾ, the latter identified as part of *al-jadīd* (III, p. 322); quoting Ibn Surayj (d. Baghdad, 306/918) quoting al-Shāfiᶜī in turn (III, p. 256);

al-Maḥāmilī (d. 407/1016), Baghdadi, *al-Majmū*ᶜ (III, p. 131); [281]

al-Qaffāl al-Ṣaghīr al-Marwazī (d. 417/1026), *Sharḥ al-Talkhīṣ*, quoting Abū Bakr al-Fārisī (d. Balkh? 305/917–918?), quoting al-Shāfiᶜī in turn from *Bāb Istiqbāl al-Qiblah* (III, p. 42);

al-Bandanījī (d. Bandanījīn, 425/1034), quoting *al-qadīm*, *al-Imlā*ʾ, and *Bāb Ṣalāt al-Jumᶜa* in *al-jadīd* (III, p. 322);

Abū Muḥammad al-Juwaynī (d. Nishapur, 438/1047), *al-Furū*ᶜ (III, p. 95);

al-Māwardī (d. Baghdad, 450/1058), *al-Ḥāwī*, quoting Abū Thawr, quoting al-Shāfiᶜī in turn (III, p. 33);

Abū 'l-Ṭayyib al-Ṭabarī (d. Baghdad, 450/1058), *al-Taᶜlīq* (III, p. 264); *Istiḥbāb al-Sūra* (III, p. 352);

al-Bayhaqī (d. Nishapur, 458/1066), quoting al-Shāfiᶜī in al-Buwayṭī (III, p. 183); quoting al-Zaᶜfarānī, quoting al-Shāfiᶜī in turn (III, p. 372); in al-Rabīᶜ (III, p. 373);

Abū ᶜAmr (i.e., ᶜUmar) b. ᶜAbd al-Barr (d. Jativa, 463/1071; III, p. 292);

al-Qāḍī Ḥusayn (d. Marv, 462/1069), quoting Aḥmad al-Bayhaqī, quoting al-Shāfiᶜī in turn (III, p. 33); also quoting al-Shāfiᶜī directly (III, p. 202); in his *Taᶜlīq*, quoting al-Shāfiᶜī's *naṣṣ* in *al-jadīd* somewhere else than in *al-Umm* (III, p. 332);

Abū Isḥāq al-Shīrāzī (d. Baghdad, 476/1083), quoting *al-qadīm* (III, p. 98); quoting *al-qadīm* and *al-jadīd*, but the latter erroneously, or else this is a copyist's error (III, p. 332);

Ibn al-Ṣabbāgh (d. Baghdad, 477/1083), *ṣāḥib al-Shāmil* (III, p. 99 f);

Imām al-Ḥaramayn (d. Bushtaniqān, 478/1085), including a dictum usually ascribed to Abū Ḥanīfa and *gharīb* as coming from al-Shāfiʿī (III, p. 265);

al-Mutawallī al-Naysābūrī (d. Baghdad, 478/1086), *ṣāḥib al-Tatimmah* (III, p. 202);

al-Ghazālī (d. Tus, 505/1111), specifying the *riwāya* of al-Rabīʿ (III, p. 458);

al-Baghawī (d. Marw-i Rudh, 510/1117?), *ṣāḥib al-Tahdhīb* (III, p. 79);

al-Ṣaydalānī (d. *ca.* 517/1123–1124), quoting from *al-Umm* (III, p. 438);

al-ʿImrānī (d. Yemen, 558/1163), *al-Bayān* (III, p. 9), quoting *K. al-Ṣalāh*; quoting Abū Yazīd (i.e., Zayd) al-Marwazī (d. 371/982), quoting al-Shāfiʿī in turn, an opinion that is *gharīb fī 'l-madhhab* (III, p. 98); and

al-Rāfiʿī (d. Qazvin, 623/1226), quoting both *al-qadīm* and *al-jadīd* (III, p. 141); quoting al-Shāfiʿī's *naṣṣ*, a *gharīb* transmission (III, p. 215).

Knowing al-Shāfiʿī's opinions was certainly not so simple for al-Nawawī as looking it up in the Egyptian works. The length of the list (which would presumably grow if one inspected other volumes of the *Majmūʿ*) indicates considerable fluidity. Quotations not of the *Umm* directly but of others than al-Rabīʿ of the *Umm* indicate a non-uniform text; that is, these jurisprudents had drawn on different versions from what was available to al-Nawawī himself. Note also that only three or four of al-Shāfiʿī's actual auditors are named, whereas al-Bayhaqī names sixteen as transmitting variants, al-Nawawī himself ten as the leading transmitters. It is certainly conceivable that the earliest Shāfiʿīya [282] cultivated precise accuracy in their transmission from al-Shāfiʿī, never disguising the source of their information or going beyond what they had heard directly, whereas later Shāfiʿīya became more careless about how they knew things. However, it seems unlikely.[13]

This study began with a survey of al-Shāfiʿī's doctrine as it is presented in three works of the later Ninth Century, Abū ʿĪsā al-Tirmidhī, *al-Jāmiʿ al-Ṣaḥīḥ*,[14] and Muḥammad

13. Later indifference to authenticating what was transmitted from al-Shāfiʿī is noticed by B.G. Weiss, *The Search for God's Law*, Salt Lake City, 1992, p. 268. For the derivation of the law not from primary sources but from textbooks of the school, see N. Calder, *The ʿUqūd Rasm al-Muftī of Ibn ʿĀbidīn*, in: *Bulletin of the School of Oriental and African Studies* 63 (2000), p. 215–228, and W.B. Hallaq, *Authority, Continuity and Change in Islamic Law*, Cambridge, 2001, esp. Chapter 3.

14. There are several leading editions of the *Jāmiʿ*: *al-Jāmiʿ al-Ṣaḥīḥ*, ed. A.M. Shākir, M.F. ʿAbd Al-Bāqī and K.Y. Al-Ḥūt, Beirut: Dār al-Kutub al-ʿIlmīya, n.d.; *Sunan al-Tirmidhī*, ed. ʿA.W.ʿA. Laṭīf and ʿA.R.M. ʿUthmān, Medina: al-Maktaba al-Salafīya, 1383–1387/1964–1967; and *Sunan al-Tirmidhī*, commentary by ʿI.ʿU. Al-Daʿʿās, Homs: Maktabat Dār al-Daʿwa, 1385–1388/1965–1968. The first has the advantage of being cross-referenced with both Wensinck's *Concordance* and Al-Mizzī's *Tuḥfat al-Ashrāf*, and partly for that reason it is the one I cite. However, its first three volumes, originally published in 1937 (ed. Shākir) and 1956 (ed. ʿAbd Al-Bāqī), are much better edited than the last two.

b. Naṣr al-Marwazī (d. Samarqand, 294/906), *Ikhtilāf al-ʿUlamāʾ* and *al-Sunna.*[15] My object was to see how al-Shāfiʿī's doctrine had spread. For example, did al-Tirmidhī systematically report the *qadīm* but al-Marwazī, who travelled to Egypt and heard some of al-Shāfiʿī's disciples there, only the *jadīd*?

Al-Tirmidhī's Testimony

Al-Tirmidhī collected *Ḥadīth* in Iraq and the Hijaz, but we are informed that he never went to Syria or Egypt.[16] Therefore, he cannot have learnt the doctrine of al-Shāfiʿī directly from the usual Egyptian disciples, al-Rabīʿ and al-Muzanī. Al-Tirmidhī refers to al-Shāfiʿī's doctrine in Baghdad and Old Cairo, respectively, without ever using the terms *al-qadīm* and *al-jadīd*.[17] Al-Tirmidhī himself states that he has the doctrine of al-Shāfiʿī from these sources: [283]

> al-Zaʿfarānī;
>
> Abū ʾl-Walīd al-Makkī (d. 230s/845–855?), concerning ablutions and prayer;
>
> and
>
> Abū Ismāʿīl al-Tirmidhī (d. Baghdad, 280/893) from al-Buwayṭī.[18]

Al-Zaʿfarānī was later reputed to be the foremost transmitter of the *qadīm*.[19]

Abū ʾl-Walīd al-Makkī, al-Tirmidhī's second source, was Mūsā b. Abī ʾl-Jārūd. According to Ibn ʿAbd al-Barr, he was among those who studied under al-Shāfiʿī in Mecca, before he left for Baghdad.[20] Aḥmad b. Ḥanbal is supposed to have recommended his transmission of al-Shāfiʿī's opinions (*raʾy*) after al-Buwayṭī's.[21] However, al-Khaṭīb al-Baghdādī reports al-Rabīʿ b. Sulaymān as quoting Ibn Abī 'l-Jārūd, 'Abū Yaʿqūb al-Buwayṭī was my

---

15. Al-Marwazī, *Ikhtilāf al-ʿUlamāʾ*, ed. Ṣ. Al-Sāmarrāʾī, Beirut: ʿĀlam al-Kutub, 1405/1985; Al-Marwazī, *al-Sunna*, ed. A.M.S.A. Al-Salafī, Beirut: Muʾassasat al-Kutub al-Thaqāfīya, 1408/1988.

16. Al-Dhahabī, *Siyar Aʿlām al-Nubalāʾ*, ed. ʿA. Abū Zayd, XIII, Beirut, 1403/1983, p. 271; confirmed by a random sample of 100 *Ḥadīth* reports from *al-Jāmiʿ al-Ṣaḥīḥ*, none of which was transmitted to al-Tirmidhī by an Egyptian and just one by a Syrian, al-Jūzajānī, presumably when he was sojourning in Mecca or Basra, for which see Al-Dhahabī, *Taʾrīkh al-islām*, XIX, p. 72 (251–260 AH).

17. Al-Tirmidhī, *Jāmiʿ*, III, p. 145–146, *K. al-Ṣawm*, 60.

18. Al-Tirmidhī, *Jāmiʿ*, V, p. 693, *K. al-ʿIlal*.

19. Al-Nawawī, *Tahdhīb*, I, p. 48 (*atqanu-hum fī riwāyati-hi*); Al-Nawawī, *Majmūʿ*, III, p. 33 (*athbat aṣḥāb al-qadīm*). Presumably, this estimate ignores al-Karābīsī, elsewhere ranked higher, because al-Nawawī had never come across an example of transmission from him.

20. Ibn ʿAbd Al-Barr, *al-Intiqāʾ*, Cairo: Maktabat al-Qudsī, 1350 (reprint Beirut: Dār al-Kutub al-ʿIlmīya, n.d.), p. 105.

21. Ibn ʿAbd Al-Barr, *al-Intiqāʾ*, p. 76.

neighbour. I was never awake for any hour of the night without hearing him reciting the Qurʾan and praying.'[22] Al-Buwayṭī died in Baghdad, where he was imprisoned for resisting the Inquisition, but had been al-Shāfiʿī's leading disciple in Egypt. His transmission should represent entirely *al-jadīd*.[23] Among those who transmitted from Ibn Abī 'l-Jārūd, Ibn Ḥajar mentions al-Rabīʿ b. Sulaymān and al-Zaʿfarānī.[24] Hence, we evidently see interference not only between the Baghdadi teaching, *al-qadīm*, and the Egyptian, *al-jadīd*, but between the Meccan and the Baghdadi and Egyptian. (The biographical data, such as al-Rabīʿ's transmitting from Ibn Abī 'l-Jārūd, may have arisen as inferences from observed interference in the remembered doctrines).[25]

As for Abū Ismāʿīl al-Tirmidhī, who settled in Baghdad, Abū ʿĪsā 'l-Tirmidhī states that he related al-Shāfiʿī's doctrine both from al-Buwaytī [284] and al-Rabīʿ b. Sulaymān al-Murādī, who then permitted al-Tirmidhī (presumably Abū ʿĪsā) in writing to transmit it.[26] Abū Ismāʿīl is quoted as saying that al-Rabīʿ transmitted the works of al-Shāfiʿī to some two-hundred men from all directions.[27] His transmission should represent the *jadīd* inasmuch as that is what al-Buwayṭī and al-Rabīʿ taught.

Looking through *al-Jāmiʿ al-Ṣaḥīḥ*, I have found thirty-two evident quotations of al-Shāfiʿī, besides many more reports that he took one or another position (e.g., 'This is the dictum of Mālik, al-Shāfiʿī, Aḥmad, and Isḥāq'). I have not discovered that any quotation actually contradicts the opinions recorded in the extant works of al-Shāfiʿī and al-Muzanī's *Mukhtaṣar*. About a third of the time, al-Tirmidhī quotes an opinion entirely without any parallel in the Egyptian works (and *al-Mukhtaṣar*). For example, al-Tirmidhī quotes al-Shāfiʿī as saying, of *al-maḍmaḍa bi-kaff wāḥid* (taking water into the mouth at the ritual ablution), 'If he combines them in one handful, that is permissible. If he sepa-

22. Al-Khaṭīb Al-Baghdādī, *Taʾrīkh Baghdād*, XIV. Cairo: Maktabat al-Khānjī, 1349/1931 (reprint: Cairo: Maktabat al-Khānjī & Beirut: Dār al-Fikr, n.d.), p. 300.

23. Abū Ismāʿīl al-Tirmidhī is said to have quoted al-Buwayṭī as quoting al-Shāfiʿī, 'I do not absolve anyone who relates from me the Iraqi book (*lā ajʿalu fī ḥill man rawā ʿannī al-kitāb al-ʿirāqī*)': Al-ʿAbbādī, *K. Ṭabaqāt al-Fuqahāʾ al-Shāfiʿīya*, ed. G. Vitestam (*Veröffentlichungen der 'De Goeje Stiftung,'* 21), Leiden, 1964, p. 57.

24. Ibn Ḥajar, *K. Tahdhīb al-Tahdhīb*, X, Hyderabad: Majlis Dāʾirat al-Maʿārif al-Nizʾāmīya, 1325–1327, p. 339.

25. Calder alleges the inference of biographical data from legal texts in *Studies in Early Muslim Jurisprudence*, Oxford, 1993, p. 88–89.

26. Al-Tirmidhī, *Jāmiʿ*, V, p. 693, *K. al-ʿIlal*; Ibn Ḥajar, *Tahdhīb*, III, p. 246, IX, p. 62–63. For the standard *rijāl* works, which oddly do not list al-Rabīʿ among Abū Ismāʿīl's authorities, see Ibn Abī Ḥātim, *K. al-Jarḥ wa-l-Taʿdīl*, VII, Hyderabad: Jamʿīyat Dāʾirat al-Maʿārif al-ʿUthmānīya, 1360–1371 (reprint: Beirut, n.d.), p. 190–191; Al-Khaṭīb Al-Baghdādī, *Taʾrīkh Baghdād*, IX, p. 62–63; Ibn Abī Yaʿlā, *Ṭabaqāt al-Ḥanābila*, ed. M.Ḥ. Al-Fiqī, I, Cairo, 1371/1952, p. 279–280.

27. Ibn ʿAbd Al-Barr, *Intiqāʾ*, p. 115.

rates them, that is preferable to me.'[28] I have not found any pronouncement on this detail in the Egyptian works.

The usual case is for al-Tirmidhī and the Egyptian works to agree but in different words. Al-Tirmidhī and the *Umm* clearly report the same opinion, but just as clearly, al-Tirmidhī had not before him the text with which we are familiar. In no instance have I found al-Tirmidhī's quotation to agree exactly with the words that are found in the Egyptian works. Here is what seems to me the closest parallel:

> Al-Tirmidhī, *Jāmiʿ*, II, p. 16, *Ṣalāh*, 68:
>
> Its meaning is that they would begin by reciting the *fātiḥa* of the Book before the *sūra*. The meaning is not that they did not use to recite *bi-ism Allāh al-Raḥmān al-Raḥīm.*
>
> *Umm*, I, p. 93:
>
> This means that they used to begin with reciting *umm al-Qurʾān* before reciting after it, God (be He exalted!) knowing best. It does not mean that they would leave *bi-ism Allāh al-Raḥmān al-Raḥīm.*

Al-Tirmidhī's report of al-Shāfiʿī's teaching is much closer at the level of identifying the *ḥadīth* reports by which al-Shāfiʿī argued: of [285] twenty-one identifications by al-Tirmidhī, I have found the same *ḥadīth* report in the Egyptian works sixteen times. This does not always mean the *Umm*: several times, the *ḥadīth* report that al-Tirmidhī tells us al-Shāfiʿī used appears only in the *Mukhtaṣar*, not the *Umm.*[29] Aḥmad Muḥammad Shākir suggests at one point that al-Tirmidhī has paraphrased al-Shāfiʿī, for the expression of his quotation lacks the power and elevation of the parallel passage in the *Risāla.*[30] This is possible, but of course it presumes that the power and elevation of the *Risāla* are the work of al-Shāfiʿī himself, not a superior paraphraser or elaborator.

It seems safer to observe two parallels with the doctrine of Mālik. First, the *Muwaṭṭaʾ* was demonstrably sharpened up by different transmitters:[31] al-Shāfiʿī's dicta must have

28. Al-Tirmidhī, *Jāmiʿ*, I, p. 41–43, *K. al-Ṭahārah*, 21.

29. Al-Tirmidhī, *Jāmiʿ*, II, p. 236, *Ṣalāh*, 171, *mā jāʾa fī sajdatay al-sahw qabla 'l-taslīm* = *Umm*, I, p. 85 marg.; Al-Tirmidhī, III, p. 316, *Janāʾiz*, 15, *mā jāʾa fī ghasl al-mayyit* = *Umm*, I, p. 170 marg.; Al-Tirmidhī, III, p. 451, *Nikāḥ*, 43, *mā jāʾa fī 'l-rajul yatazawwaju 'l-mar'ah fa-yamūtu ʿanhā qabla an yafriḍa lahā* = *Umm*, IV, p. 29 marg.; Al-Tirmidhī, IV, p. 86, *K. al-Aḍāḥī*, 24, *tark akhdh al-shaʿr li-man arāda an yuḍaḥḥiya* = *Umm*, V, p. 211 marg.

30. Al-Tirmidhī, II, p. 369n, *K. al-Jumʿa* 5, *mā jāʾa fī 'l-wuḍūʾ yawm al-jumʿa*; Al-Shāfiʿī, *al-Risāla*, ed. A.M. Shākir (Cairo: Maṭbaʿat Muṣṭafā al-Bābī al-Ḥalabī wa-Awlādi-hi, 1358/1940, §844; Al-Shāfiʿī, *Ikhtilāf al-Ḥadīth*, at *Umm*, VII, p. 177–181 marg.

31. J.E. Brockopp, *Early Mālikī Law* (*Studies in Islamic Law and Society*, 14), Leiden, 2000, p. 73–77. Some of the sharpening may have been the work of Mālik himself over the last thirty years or so of his life, as

been likewise susceptible to sharpening (or dulling). If al-Tirmidhī never quotes al-Shāfiʿī the same way as the *Umm* but usually cites the same *ḥadīth* reports as the *Umm*, it appears that, contrary to the impression one gets from Calder, the evidence of *ḥadīth* was less liable to change than the formulation of inferences from it (perhaps confirming Schacht's suggestion that the great age of manufacturing *ḥadīth* ended in the mid-Third/Ninth century, before the deaths of al-Muzanī, the two al-Rabīʿs, and al-Tirmidhī).[32] Second, Calder once proposed to account for discrepancies between al-Muzanī and al-Rabīʿ by their each drawing on a larger body of al-Shāfiʿī's dicta not otherwise extant.[33] Jonathan Brockopp has similarly [286] proposed to account for differences among the *Muwaṭṭaʾ*, Saḥnūn's *Mudawwana*, and *al-Mukhtaṣar al-kabīr* of Ibn ʿAbd al-Ḥakam by their each drawing on a larger, fourth body of Mālik's dicta not otherwise extant.[34] Discrepancies between al-Tirmidhī's wording of al-Shāfiʿī's position and that of the *Umm* might be put down to al-Tirmidhī's carelessness, but his agreeing sometimes with the *Umm*, sometimes with only *al-Mukhtaṣar* (even though no biographical source connects al-Tirmidhī with al-Muzanī), and occasionally with only *Ikhtilāf Mālik wa-l-Shāfiʿī* seems to demonstrate clearly that there was a larger body of Shāfiʿī doctrine for al-Rabīʿ, al-Muzanī, and al-Tirmidhī to draw on.

Al-Marwazī's Testimony

Muḥammad b. Naṣr al-Marwazī was born in Baghdad and grew up in Nishapur but collected *Ḥadīth* in Ray, Iraq, Syria, the Hijaz, and Egypt as well as Khurasan.[35] His second *Riḥla*, before he settled for a time in Nishapur, is said to have ended in 260/873–874.[36] His chief authorities in Egypt were Yūnus b. ʿAbd al-Aʿlā, Abū ʿAbd Allāh Ibn ʿAbd al-Ḥakam (d. Old Cairo, 268/882), and al-Rabīʿ b. Sulaymān al-Murādī, all of whom are sometimes characterized as disciples to al-Shāfiʿī, except that Yūnus and Abū ʿAbd Allāh were

---

urged by Y. Dutton, *The Origins of Islamic Law* (*Culture and Civilization in the Middle East*), Richmond, 1999, p. 22. However, the most famous transmitter of all, Yaḥyā b. Yaḥyā, now seems not to have met Mālik himself: M. Fierro, *El alfaquí beréber Yaḥyà b. Yaḥyà al-Layṯī (m. 234/848)*, in: M.L. Ávila and M. Marín (edd.), *Estudios onomástico-biográficos de al-Andalus* 8: *Biografías y género biográfico en el occidente islámico*, Madrid, 1997, p. 269–344, esp. p. 285–288. Therefore, his recension at least must reflect editing by others than Mālik.

32. Calder, *Studies*, p. 57, arguing that *K. al-Ḥujja ʿalā ahl al-Madīna* must be earlier than the *Mudawwana* and the *Muwaṭṭaʾ* of Yaḥyā b. Yaḥyā (in the forms in which we now have them) because it fails to cite the same *ḥadīth* reports.

33. Calder, *Studies*, p. 92.

34. Brockopp, *Early Mālikī Law*, p. 95–98.

35. See Sezgin, *GAS*, I, p. 494, with references, to which add al-Dhahabī, *Taʾrīkh al-Islām*, XXII, p. 295–299 (291–300 AH), with further references, and Ibn al-Ṣalāḥ, *Ṭabaqāt al-Shāfiʿīya*, ed. al-Nawawī, al-Mizzī, and M.D.ʿA. Najīb, I, Beirut: Dār al-Bashāʾir al-Islāmīya, 1413/1992, p. 277–282.

36. Al-Dhahabī, *Taʾrīkh al-islām*, XXII, p. 297 (291–300 AH).

more closely associated with the Mālikī school than the Shāfiʿī, and might therefore have transmitted slightly different opinions from what al-Rabīʿ did.[37] Oddly missing from the list is al-Muzanī. Additionally, however, al-Marwazī seems to have had some access to Baghdadi Shāfiʿī doctrine, for he quotes Abū Thawr concerning *Furūʿ* and *Uṣūl* and at least once reports al-Shāfiʿī's Baghdadi doctrine rather than his Egyptian.[38] Al-Marwazī was reputed to be an adherent of the Shāfiʿī school in the [287] loosest sense, as someone capable of a considerable degree of independent *ijtihād*.[39]

Only one incomplete manuscript is extant of al-Marwazī's *Ikhtilāf al-ʿulamāʾ*, missing the beginning and running from *ṭahāra* to *shahādāt* and *siyar* at the end. Al-Shāfiʿī's opinion is cited often but, unlike in al-Tirmidhī's *Jāmiʿ*, we seldom see here what purports to be a direct quotation. I have chosen at random 30 examples for examination, probably about a tenth of the opinions attributed to al-Shāfiʿī in the whole book. Whereas al-Tirmidhī's quotations agreed two-thirds of the time, al-Marwazī's statements of al-Shāfiʿī's positions agree with what the Egyptian works present only about 40 percent of the time. Another one example in seven agrees in part with the Egyptian works. For example, both al-Marwazī and al-Muzanī report that al-Shāfiʿī distinguished between menstruation (*ḥayḍ*) and other issues of blood (*istiḥāḍa*), only the former of which would prevent prayer. However, only Marwazī describes this refinement, which he attributes alike to al-Shāfiʿī and Abū Thawr: that if the two issues cannot be visually distinguished, the woman may nevertheless resume praying at a certain point if she knows from past observation that her period normally ends there.[40]

Against partial agreement, I find equally many examples of partial disagreement, where al-Marwazī describes as required what the Egyptian works identify merely as recommended; for example, al-Marwazī reports that al-Shāfiʿī required the minor ritual ablution of one who falls asleep sitting, whereas the *Umm* merely recommends it.[41] Moreover, I find several examples of outright contradiction; for example, al-Marwazī reports that, according to al-Shāfiʿī (among others), the *ʿidda* of a slave woman freed on her master's death is one menstrual period for the freeing and death together, whereas the *Umm* quotes al-Shāfiʿī as stating that her *ʿidda* is two months and five days.[42] In one instance, as

37. For examples of discrepancies between Mālikī and Shāfiʿī versions of Shāfiʿī's doctrine, see S.A. Jackson, *Setting the Record Straight: Ibn al-Labbād's Refutation of al-Shāfiʿī*, in: *Journal of Islamic Studies* 11 (2000), p. 121–146 (p. 128 & 139).

38. For Abū Thawr on questions of *Furūʿ*, see Al-Marwazī, *Ikhtilāf*, *passim*; on a question of *Uṣūl*, see Al-Marwazī, *Sunna*, p. 110; for a quotation of al-Shāfiʿī's Baghdadī definition of *ribā*, see Al-Marwazī, *Ikhtilāf*, p. 247; cf. *Umm* III, p. 12–13, and J. Schacht, *Ribā*, in: *EI2*, VIII, p. 491–493.

39. Ibn Al-Ṣalāḥ, *Ṭabaqāt*, I, p. 277; Al-Subkī, *Ṭabaqāt al-Shāfiʿīyah al-Kubrā*, ed. M.M. Al-Ṭanāḥī and ʿA.F. Al-Ḥulw, III, Cairo: ʿĪsā Bābī al-Ḥalabī, 1964–1976, p. 102. See also Hallaq, *Authority*, p. 59–61.

40. Al-Marwazī, *Ikhtilāf*, p. 36; Al-Muzanī, *Mukhtaṣar*, at *Umm*, I, p. 53 marg.

41. Al-Marwazī, *Ikhtilāf*, p. 28; *Umm*, I, p. 11.

42. Al-Marwazī, *Ikhtilāf*, p. 163; *Umm*, V. p. 199. Cf. also Al-Marwazī, p. 164–165 (Jewish or Christian

noted, al-Marwazī apparently reports al-Shāfiʿī's opinion concerning what counts as *ribā* as it stood in the *qadīm*. At the same time, there seem to [288] be two exact quotations, where al-Marwazī and al-Rabīʿ quote al-Shāfiʿī in identical words.[43]

Altogether, then, it seems clear that Marwazī did hear from al-Rabīʿ, as the biographies say, and that he supplemented al-Rabīʿ's transmission to a considerable extent with other, lost sources, on which also al-Muzanī drew. It seems probable that he also continually added to or outright distorted what his sources told him. Some addition was evidently expected in his time and for centuries afterwards. Wael Hallaq has recently identified as *takhrīj* the process by which later jurisprudents attributed new opinions to the eponyms of their schools, justifying the misattribution on the ground that if they were not actually quoting the eponym, they were faithfully following his theoretical procedure.[44] We may see a great deal of this in al-Marwazī, as we certainly do in al-Muzanī ('certainly' because he expressly tells us this is what he is up to, on which more below).

The classical Shāfiʿī school evidently goes back to the writing and especially teaching activity of Ibn Surayj (d. Baghdad, 306/918). Al-Qāḍī ʿAbd al-Jabbār (d. al-Rayy, 415/1024?) and some students of his were the last major Shāfiʿī jurisprudents who did not trace their intellectual lineages back through him. However, al-Marwazī's teaching activity in Khurāsān seems to have been similar.[45] If Ibn Surayj's works were extant, we might well discover that his version of al-Shāfiʿī's doctrine was as different from the Egyptian as al-Marwazī's version in *Ikhtilāf*, since Abū Ḥāmid al-Isfarāyinī famously commented, "We go along with Ibn Surayj concerning the broad outlines of jurisprudence, not the details."[46]

A very different sort of book is al-Marwazī's *al-Sunna*: not a collection of disputed rules but a rambling meditation on the status of the *Sunna* vis à vis the Qurʾān. Again, although much of what al-Marwazī attributes to al-Shāfiʿī has parallels in the Egyptian works, it seems clear that al-Marwazī did not work with the Egyptian works before him, or at least not all of them. Near the end, for example, he quotes al-Shāfiʿī to the effect that *al-ḥikma* means the *Sunna* of the Messenger of God and that *al-ḥikma* is paired with the Book of God. Therefore, the *Sunna* of [289] the Messenger is *mubayyina ʿan Allāh* (p. 108). This is the same argument but not the same words as we find in the *Risāla* (§§ 96–103, 245–53).[47]

---

wife who commits adultery stoned), with *Umm*, VI, p. 125 (up to the judge whether to stone her or hand her over to her own community).

43. Al-Marwazī, *Ikhtilāf*, p. 117 = *Umm*, II, p. 29; Al-Marwazī, 119 = *Umm*, II, p. 46.12–13 from bottom.

44. Hallaq, *Authority*, p. 43–56.

45. See C. Melchert, *The Formation of the Sunni Schools of Law* (*Studies in Islamic Law and Society*, 4), Leiden, 1997, Chapter 5.

46. Abū Isḥāq Al-Shīrāzī, *Ṭabaqāt al-fuqahāʾ*, ed. I. ʿAbbās, Beirut: Dār al-Rāʾid al-ʿArabī, 1970, p. 109.

47. The same equation is argued in *Jimāʿ al-ʿIlm* at *Umm*, VII, p. 251.

Over half the book is devoted to the problem of whether *Sunna* and Qurʾān may abrogate each other.[48] Al-Shāfiʿī's position in the *Risāla* is emphatic: *Sunna* may abrogate *Sunna*, Qurʾān may abrogate Qurʾān, but never may *Sunna* abrogate Qurʾān or Qurʾān abrogate *Sunna* (§§312–420, esp. 314). Al-Marwazī first presents al-Shāfiʿī's position anonymously:

> Some say, 'It abrogates one of the *aḥkām* of the Qurʾān', while some say, 'No, rather it makes clear what in the Qurʾān is particular and what is general. It is not abrogating, for the *Sunna* does not abrogate the Qurʾān but rather makes clear its particular and general and explains its *mujmal* and *mubham*' (al-Marwazī, *Sunna*, p. 35).

He later makes it explicit: it is al-Shāfiʿī's doctrine that when the *Sunna* allows what is forbidden by a verse of the Qurʾān, or forbids something allowed by a verse of the Qurʾān, these are to be understood as cases of generality (the Qurʾān) and particularity (the Sunnaic exception), not contradiction and abrogation (p. 92–93).

The most famous example of contradiction between Qurʾān and *Sunna* is the penalty for adultery.[49] The usual theory is that Q. 24:2, which calls for 100 lashes, was partially abrogated by *āyat al-rajm*, a verse remembered by the Caliph ʿUmar that called for stoning some (by interpretation, adulterers who were free, Muslim, and previously married). Its rule evidently remained in force even though the verse itself had been dropped from the Qurʾān as recited.

In the *Risāla*, al-Shāfiʿī once avoids talking of abrogation by declaring that the Qurʾanic call for flogging is a general command, with the *Sunna* showing by way of explanation that only never-married fornicators were intended, hence an example not of abrogation but particularization (§§225–227). Somewhat incoherently, however, the *Risāla* elsewhere refers to parts of the Qurʾanic penalty for adultery as having been abrogated, although without ever stating what has done the abrogating (*mansūkh* at §§380, 688, *naskh* at §§382, 694).[50] *Ikhtilāf al-ḥadīth* comes [290] close to embracing the explanation by *āyat al-rajm*, for al-Shāfiʿī there quotes it (through Mālik) and states that the *ḥadīth* report of the Prophet's stoning an adulterer tends to confirm ʿUmar's story.[51]

---

48. For discussions before al-Marwazī, see C. Melchert, *Qurʾanic Abrogation Across the Ninth Century*, in: B.G. Weiss (ed.), *Studies in Islamic Legal Theory* (*Islamic Law and Society*, 15), Leiden, 2002, p. 75–98; for abrogation more generally, see J. Burton, *The Sources of Islamic Law: Islamic Theories of Abrogation*, Edinburgh, 1990.

49. See Burton, *Sources*, Chapter 7.

50. Also noticed by Burton, *Sources*, p. 145.

51. *Ikhtilāf al-Ḥadīth, Bāb al-ʿUqūbāt fī 'l-Zinā*, at *Umm*, VII, p. 251 marg. Cf. *Umm*, VI, p. 119, 143, where al-Shāfiʿī justifies stoning by appeal to ʿUmar's example without expressly quoting *āyat al-rajm*; *K. Siyar al-Awzāʿī* at *Umm*, VII, p. 322.5 from bottom, where al-Shāfiʿī quotes the Qurʾanic call for flogging, then

Al-Marwazī departs most notably from the Egyptian presentation with regard to flogging as an additional penalty to stoning. He quotes of al-Shāfiʿī some of the same words as one of the Egyptian works:

> There were nondescript punishments for sins until the *ḥadd* punishments were revealed. Then the *ḥadd* punishments were revealed and the nondescript punishments were abrogated so far as there were relevant *ḥadd* punishments (*kānat al-ʿuqūbāt fī 'l-maʿāṣī qabla an yunazzala 'l-ḥadd thumma nuzzilat al-ḥudūd wa-nusikhat al-ʿuqūbāt fī-mā fī-hi 'l-ḥudūd*).[52]

According to al-Marwazī, al-Shāfiʿī held that the adulterer was earlier, on the basis of the Qurʾān, both flogged and stoned. Some jurisprudents held that the penalty for adultery continued to comprise both flogging and stoning.[53] According to al-Shāfiʿī, though, flogging was then removed on the basis of the Prophet's dictum (p. 96–97, with more close parallels to *Ikhtilāf al-Ḥadīth*). But whereas the Egyptian works do not quote al-Shāfiʿī as going on to identify abrogation of the Qurʾān by the *Sunna*, al-Marwazī does: 'Thus,' he concludes, 'al-Shāfiʿī affirmed concerning this question the abrogation of the Book by the *Sunna*' (p. 97).

Eventually, most of the Shāfiʿīya did hold (against the *Risāla*) that the *Sunna* might abrogate the Qurʾān.[54] It looks as though al-Marwazī was one of the first of the Shāfiʿīya to see that the express position of the *Risāla* was untenable and therefore asserted the opposite; however, because the *Risāla* had not yet its later stature as primary statement of Shāfiʿī *Uṣūl*, he tried to attribute his understanding directly to al-Shāfiʿī. If we take it, with Calder, that *al-Risāla* was the work not of al-Shāfiʿī personally but of later followers using his name, we may consider *al-Sunna* and *al-Risāla* as rival attempts to define Shāfiʿī doctrine. [291]

Al-Muzanī's Testimony

Al-Muzanī makes it quite clear that he has drawn on diverse written sources to compile his *Mukhtaṣar*. The *Mukhtaṣar* alternates between sections of al-Shāfiʿī's opinion, usually introduced by *qāla 'l-Shāfiʿī*, and sections of al-Muzanī's opinion, usually introduced by *qāla 'l-Muzanī*. From time to time, al-Muzanī expressly identifies his source, especially

says that the Prophet laid down (*sanna*) stoning for the *thayyib*, without explaining whether by particularity, abrogation of the Qurʾān by the *Sunna*, or confirmation of an unnamed, abrogating Qurʾanic verse.

52. Al-Shāfiʿī, *Ikhtilāf al-Ḥadīth*, at *Umm*, VII, p. 249–250; almost identical apud Al-Marwazī, *Sunna*, p. 95.

53. Al-Marwazī reviews their chief arguments, *Sunna*, p. 97–98. According to Ibn Rushd, they were al-Ḥasan al-Baṣrī, Isḥāq b. Rāhawayh, Aḥmad b. Ḥanbal, and Dāwūd al-Ẓāhirī: Ibn Rushd, *Bidāyat al-Mujtahid, K. fī Aḥkām al-Zinā, Bāb* 2 = ed. ʿA.M.Ṭ. Ḥalabī, IV, Beirut: Dār al-Maʿrifa, 1418/1997, p. 273.

54. Ibn Al-Ṣalāḥ, *Ṭabaqāt*, II, p. 553, s.n. ʿAbd al-Qāhir b. Ṭāhir.

at the beginning of a section. His sources fall into four categories. First come books that have survived to our day (examples from the margins of *Umm*, III):

> *K. Ikhtilāf Abī Ḥanīfah wa-bn Abī Laylā* (III, p. 174); cf. *Umm*, VII, p. 87–150;
> *Ikhtilāf al-Aḥādīth* (III, p. 47); *Ikhtilāf al-Ḥadīth* (III, p. 256); cf. *Umm* 7, margin;
> *Ikhtilāf al-Shāfiʿī wa-Mālik* (III, p. 120); cf. *Umm* 7:177–249;
> *al-Risāla* (III, p. 138, 256).

Kitāb al-Umm is referred to elsewhere (e.g., IV, p. 22 marg.), likewise oral transmission from al-Rabīʿ (e.g., I, p. 181 marg.). However, the books as al-Muzanī knew them were apparently not identical to what we have before us today. Sometimes he expressly names a section of the *Umm*, yet it cannot be found in our text; e.g., at *Umm*, IV, p. 22 marg., where al-Muzanī says, "This is analogous to his dictum (*qawl*) at the beginning of *Bāb mā Jāʾa fī 'l-Ṣadāq* in *Kitāb al-Umm*. It is his dictum but it is a mistake (as an extension from) its textual basis (*hādhā khaṭa' ʿalā aṣli-hi*)." Perhaps this is the reason al-Nawawī occasionally refers to al-Buwayṭī's *Umm* as distinct from al-Rabīʿ's. Likewise *Kitāb Ikhtilāf Abī Ḥanīfa wa-bn Abī Laylā*: al-Muzanī says he has drawn on its section *Taḍmīn al-Ijrāʾ min al-Ijāra* (III, p. 85 marg.), but this does not obviously correspond to anything in our text of *Ikhtilāf Abī Ḥanīfa*. And likewise *Ikhtilāf al-Shāfiʿī wa-Mālik*: al-Muzanī purports to quote two hadith reports from it, yet only one of them is found in our text (*Umm* III, p. 120 marg., VII, p. 201).

The second category of al-Muzanī's citations is to lost books named elsewhere (again, examples from *Umm*, III marg.):

> *Aḥkām al-Qurʾān* (III, p. 256, 293); cf. *Risāla*, § 416;
> *al-Imlāʾ ʿalā Masāʾil Mālik* (III, p. 255); cf. al-Nawawī, *Majmūʿ*, III, p. 322, where Abū Ḥāmid cites *al-Imlāʾ* and al-Nawawī comments that it is part of *al-jadīd*.

The most difficult category comprises fairly specific references to books, sometimes overlapping with sections of the *Umm* (examples from *Umm*, III marg.): [292]

> *K. al-ʿĀriya* (III, p. 101);
> *K. al-Daʿwā wa-l-Bayyināt* (III, p. 62);
> *K. ʿIshrat al-Nisāʾ* (III, p. 292, 293);
> *al-Jāmiʿ* (III, p. 255, 282);
> *K. al-Jizya* (III, p. 292);
> *K. Mā Yuḥramu 'l-Jamʿ bayna-hu* (III, p. 271, 292);
> *K. al-Murtadd* (III, p. 292);
> *K. al-Muzāraʿa wa-Kirāʾ al-Arḍ wa-l-Sharika fī 'l-Zarʿ wa-mā Dakhala fī-hi* (III, p. 91);
> *K. al-Nikāḥ jadīd wa-qadīm* (III, p. 255); *al-Nikāḥ al-qadīm* (III, p. 263);
> *K. Qasm al-Fayʾ wa-Qasm al-Ghanāʾim* (III, p. 179);
> *al-Riḍāʿ* (III, p. 278);
> *K. al-Ṣadaqāt min Kitābayn qadīm wa-jadīd* (III, p. 219);
> *K. al-Taʿrīḍ bi-'l-Khuṭba* (III, p. 271);
> *K. al-Waṣāyā* (III, p. 159);

al-Yamīn maʿa ʾl-Shāhid (III, p. 280).

Here are fifteen different documents, which number would be multiplied if one looked in further volumes of the *Umm*. *Al-Jāmiʿ* is presumably another work usually ascribed to al-Muzanī, of which the two *Mukhtaṣars* (only the smaller extant) are said to be abridgements.[55] A few of these expressly reached al-Muzanī in written form. He comments of the copy of *Kitāb al-Waṣāyā* that he was using, 'al-Shāfiʿī put it down in his own hand (*waḍaʿa-hu bi-khaṭṭi-hi*). I do not know that it was heard from him' (III, p. 159 marg.). Some of these named sources correspond to sections of the *Umm* (e.g., III, p. 292 marg., *K. Mā Yuḥramu ʾl-Jamʿ bayna-hu*, for which see *Umm*, V, p. 2), but not all.

The last category of al-Muzanī's sources comprises the vaguest citations, with no express indication of title (from the margins of *Umm*, III, once more):

> *ʿalā qawli-hi wa-qiyāsi-hi* (III, p. 69);
> *al-jadīd* (III, p. 229, 238);
> *kitāb ākhar* (III, p. 168, 293);
> *kitāb waḍaʿa-hu bi-khaṭṭi-hi* (III, p. 102, 131);
> *makān ākhar*, where he gave the opposite opinion (III, p. 82);
> *masāʾil* heard by al-Muzanī in these words (III, p. 92, 120);
> *al-qadīm* (III, p. 285);
> *wa-qāla fī mawḍiʿ ākhar* (III, p. 44, 290; with contradiction at III, p. 137, 289);
> *masāʾil ajabtu fī-hā ʿalā maʿnā qawl al-Shāfiʿī* (III, p. 54).

When he expressly remarks differences between *al-qadīm* and *al-jadīd* (III, p. 263–264 marg.), it seems fairly certain that he relies on written [293] texts before him. *Qiyās* and *maʿnā* (first and last items) presumably refer to extension (*takhrīj*) and paraphrase (*al-riwāya bi-l-maʿnā*) of al-Shāfiʿī's known teaching, although the paraphrased passages are still introduced by *qāla ʾl-Shāfiʿī* (e.g., III, p. 66–69 marg.).

Calder discusses such section headings in a similar context, but decides to disregard them as too likely to be interpolations.

> Analysis of the contents of the *Mukhtaṣar* had produced the assumption that Muzanī worked from known works by Shāfiʿī. These have been partly identified by the creation and interpolation of chapter-headings which aspire, not always successfully, to distinguish and order the component materials.[56]

Al-Muzanī's *Mukhtaṣar* was certainly subject to posthumous editing, for Ibn al-Nadīm expressly tells us of differing recensions.[57] Still, Calder does not persuade me to disregard

55. E.g., Al-Dhahabī, *Taʾrīkh al-islām*, XX, p. 66 (261–280 AH).
56. Calder, *Studies*, p. 88.
57. Ibn Al-Nadīm, *Fihrist*, *Fann* 3, *Maqāla* 6 = ed. Flügel, et al., p. 212.

al-Muzanī's chapter headings. First, these headings are more subtly varied than Calder takes the time to discuss. Second, most of the works that al-Muzanī cites hardly qualify as 'known works by Shāfiʿī.' Third, many such references to divergent written sources are found within the texts, not just in chapter headings. For example, al-Muzanī reports that al-Shāfiʿī said that if a man who is married to both a woman and her daughter should convert to Islam, both become forbidden to him if he has gone into both of them; however, al-Shāfiʿī goes on, if he has not gone into them, then he chooses whichever one he wishes and separates from the other. 'He said in another place,' al-Muzanī continues, 'that he takes hold of the daughter and leaves the mother.' Then we have 'al-Muzanī said,' then, 'This is closer to his position, in my opinion (*awlā bi-qawli-hi ʿindī*), and thus he said in *K. al-Taʿrīḍ bi-'l-Khuṭba*' (*Umm* III, p. 289 marg.). This sounds like more than some later editor's merely aspiring to distinguish and order the component materials. (The section of the *Umm* headed *K. al-Taʿrīḍ bi-'l-Khuṭba* does cover this situation. There, al-Shāfiʿī is quoted as saying something in between al-Muzanī's two quotations: that, if the man has not gone into either of them, he may take the daughter if he pleases but may not take the mother [*Umm*, V, p. 45.1].)

Occasionally, al-Muzanī refers directly to oral transmission from al-Shāfiʿī (*masāʾil* heard by him *lafẓan*). However, most references surely indicate written sources. Moreover, when he states that his source is something he literally heard al-Shāfiʿī say, is it not likely that, strictly [294] speaking, he is still working from a written source, mainly his notes from fifty years earlier? Occasional stylistic shifts, such as breaking into dialogue, are hardly explicable except as reproducing what al-Muzanī found in written sources (e.g., *Umm*, V, p. 251 marg., a section on *khilāf* without named sources simply beginning *qāla 'l-Shāfiʿī*). Once, I have noticed, al-Muzanī expresses disbelief of his source, surely written (despite its being introduced, as usual, by *qāla 'l-Shāfiʿī*): 'This must be a mistake on the part of someone else than al-Shāfiʿī, for the well-known gist (*maʿnā*) of his dictum is . . . ' (*Umm*, V, p. 259–260 marg.). Occasionally, al-Muzanī refers to what might be group discussions after Calder's hypothesis; e.g., where he begins 'our *aṣḥāb* say that al-Shāfiʿī says . . . ' (I, p. 102 marg.). However, the section introduced in this example is so long and involved, it must be fair to say that al-Muzanī worked mainly as we do, collating written sources and synthesizing them in more writing. As for the nature of al-Muzanī's written sources, the books referred to might well be *ajzāʾ* (fascicles) after Miklos Muranyi's model of the transmission of the works of Saḥnūn in Qayrawān.[58] Muranyi's terms are missing, *rizma* (a bundle of related fascicles) as well as *ajzāʾ*; however, they are also missing from the texts themselves that Muranyi examines, which continually refer rather to *kutub*, just as al-Muzanī does.

58. M. Muranyi, *Die Rechtsbücher des Qairawāners Saḥnūn b. Saʿīd* (*Abhandlungen für die Kunde des Morgenlandes*, 52/3), Stuttgart, 1999), p. xi, 2–3.

Al-Rabīʿ's Testimony

Kitāb al-Umm appears at a cursory reading to be the simplest case, mainly direct transmission from al-Shāfiʿī with occasional, expressly identified comments from al-Rabīʿ b. Sulaymān. On close examination, however, it appears that al-Rabīʿ worked much the same way as al-Muzanī, cobbling together from notes of various sorts and discussions with other Shāfiʿīya his own version of what the school's position ought to be. The leading modern account of the problem is that of Zakī Mubārak, who argues that *al-Umm* is composite on four chief grounds: its lack of an introduction such as a deliberately authored book ought to have (compare *al-Risāla* and *Ibṭāl al-Istiḥsān*); the way it sometimes quotes al-Shāfiʿī directly (*qāla 'l-Shāfiʿī*), sometimes by means of al-Rabīʿ (e.g., *ḥaddatha-nā 'l-Rabīʿ akhbara-nā 'l-Shāfiʿī imlāʾan*); stylistic shifts, especially the way dialogue sometimes alternates with simple [295] prose; and finally al-Rabīʿ's editorial comments. Comments from al-Rabīʿ sometimes take the form, like comments from al-Muzanī in the *Mukhtaṣar*, of pointing out alternative positions attributed to al-Shāfiʿī (e.g., *Umm* III, p. 53, ll. 7–8 from bottom, *li-l-Shāfiʿī fī-hi qawl thālith*; V, p. 144–45, *hādhā aṣaḥḥ al-qawlayn wa-huwa ākhir qawlay al-Shāfiʿī*) and sources (e.g., *al-Imlāʾ*, cited at *Umm*, I, p. 192.13 from bottom). Once, there is even mentioned a date of dictation, 207 AH, when al-Rabīʿ transmitted what al-Shāfiʿī had said (to whom is unclear; *Umm*, II, p. 93, beg. of *Bāb*). Finally, there are many interpolated comments from al-Rabīʿ, sometimes apparently arguing with other formulations of al-Shāfiʿī's position (e.g., *Umm*, V, p. 260.2–4, 'what *I* remember from al-Shāfiʿī'). Altogether, then, the *Umm* must be a posthumous collection, not al-Shāfiʿī's own deliberate work.[59]

I would point also to repetition from one nearby section to another as suggesting compilation from various written sources (e.g., *Umm*, VI, p. 119.4–11, repeated lines 10–14 from bottom). Comparison with al-Muzanī's *Mukhtaṣar* further suggests that al-Rabīʿ was working from written texts. For example, let me point to the section on *ityān al-ḥāʾiḍ* in al-Muzanī's *Mukhtaṣar* (*Umm*, III, p. 293 marg.). First, al-Muzanī states that he has based this section on something called *Waṭʾ Ithnayn qabla 'l-Ghusl* and *Kitāb ʿIshrat al-Nisāʾ*. Second, al-Muzanī's presentation includes some of the very words of the *Umm* (V, p. 161.4–5 from bottom), which are found there in a section introduced simply by *qalā 'l-Shāfiʿī*, without mention of *Waṭʾ Ithnayn qabla 'l-Ghusl*, *ʿIshrat al-Nisāʾ*, or any other written source. It seems most economical to suppose, again, that al-Muzanī and al-Rabīʿ drew on similar sources, and that al-Muzanī, who died several years before al-Rabīʿ, sometimes reported his sources whereas al-Rabīʿ very seldom reported his.

59. Z. Mubārak, *Iṣlāḥ Ashnaʿ Khaṭaʾ fī Taʾrīkh al-Tashrīʿ al-Islāmī*, Cairo: al-Maktaba al-Tijārīya al-Kubrā, 1352/1934 (reprint: Cairo: Dār Miṣr, 1991), esp. p. 23–28, 33–66.

Finally, occasional disagreements between al-Rabīʿ and al-Shāfiʿī point toward written sources and posthumous elaboration and away from a literal interpretion of *qawl al-Shāfiʿī*. For example, al-Shāfiʿī is quoted as saying,

> Our associates (*aṣḥābu-nā*) disagree over whether the adulterous male or female slave is to be banished, saying he or she is not, just as he or she is not stoned. If they are banished, it is for half a year. This is one of those things we must leave for God to know (*ustukhīra Allāh fī-hi*).' [296]

Then al-Rabīʿ comments, 'al-Shāfiʿī's dictum is that the male and female slaves are banished for half a year' (*Umm*, VI, p. 144.10–12). It seems a good guess that (1) this has not actually been al-Shāfiʿī speaking whose associates are in disagreement but rather a later adherent of his school and (2) al-Rabīʿ disagrees with this adherent and asserts a contrary position as that of the nascent school. In the *Umm*, then, *qawl al-Shāfiʿī* normally means what in later parlance would be called *al-madhhab*.

The biographical sources tell us al-Rabīʿ al-Murādī was a blockhead without imagination, able only to repeat what he had heard. However, this is probably no more than (1) an inference from the occasional obtuseness of al-Rabīʿs express comments in the received texts and (2) justification of a prior decision by the Tenth Century Shāfiʿī school to prefer al-Rabīʿ's version of Shāfiʿī doctrine to others,' hence wishing to present it as most directly al-Shāfiʿī's, without the reworking so often announced by al-Muzanī. (The later Shāfiʿīya also seem to have been offended by al-Muzanī's expressly taking issue with al-Shāfiʿī from time to time, which they blamed on either his misreading of Ḥarmala's and al-Rabīʿ's notes or his seizing on a short statement of al-Shāfiʿī's position where another, fuller statement of it elsewhere was above criticism.[60]) It is not to be taken as documentary evidence that al-Rabīʿ's transmission from al-Shāfiʿī should be taken at face value, as his very words. Occasionally, the *Umm* does refer directly to oral transmission. For example, before relating a hadith report he had heard from al-Shāfiʿī, al-Rabīʿ says, 'I doubted it after I had read it (*anā shakaktu baʿda mā qaraʾtu-hu*),' meaning read aloud from his doubtful transcript of al-Shāfiʿī's words for al-Shāfiʿī to approve (*Umm*, III, p. 12.3). More passages than these alone probably come of direct transmission, but it would be reckless to say most of the *Umm* does.

Al-Muzanī and al-Rabīʿ were effectively contemporaries to al-Tirmidhī. If we accept the biographical literature, we have to consider them as having been taught directly by al-Shāfiʿī when they were in their late twenties.[61] However, this must mean that they died in their late eighties and early nineties, respectively, which raises suspicions—suspicions that are reinforced by al-Buwayṭī's dismissive remark, on being asked about al-Muzanī's

60. Al-Bayhaqī, *Manāqib*, II, p. 347.

61. They were born six months apart in the year 174/790–91, according to al-Ṭaḥāwī, admittedly an early authority, apud Ibn Ḥajar, *Tahdhīb*, III, p. 246.

hearing from al-Shāfiʿī, 'He was a weak boy (*kāna ṣabīyan ḍaʿīfan*),' which suggests something much younger than the late [297] twenties.[62] More importantly, inasmuch as al-Muzanī and al-Rabīʿ worked mainly from what others had set down as al-Shāfiʿī's doctrine, then al-Tirmidhī's witness, likewise from what others had set down, has an equal presumption of reliability. For that matter, even what al-Muzanī and al-Rabīʿ set down themselves from al-Shāfiʿī's own talk is little more reliable than what al-Tirmidhī's teachers set down and doubtfully a full and reliable transcript of what he said. After all, writing was fairly new to the transmission of Islamic law, and there is no reason to suppose that Muslim jurisprudents became very good at it very swiftly. We have no report of shorthand transcription, for example, except inasmuch as Arabic writing, without vowels or diacritics, is necessarily a shorthand.[63] The Egyptian works have probably been overvalued as testimonies to what al-Shāfiʿī taught.

Conclusion

Al-Nawawī's approach appears to be the sensible one. First, the doctrine of al-Shāfiʿī is to be known from many sources. None is to be allowed systematically to overrule any other. This is because, second, their relation to al-Shāfiʿī himself is usually impossible to determine with certainty and precision. Al-Muzanī, al-Rabīʿ, al-Tirmidhī, and al-Marwazī all introduce statements of al-Shāfiʿī's doctrine by *qāla 'l-Shāfiʿī* and refer to his position as *qawl al-Shāfiʿī*; however, it is clear from internal evidence and from comparing each of them with the others that *qāla 'l-Shāfiʿī* might actually mean any of the following:

> 'al-Shāfiʿī said (in my hearing)';
> 'al-Shāfiʿī said (in someone else's hearing)';
> 'al-Shāfiʿī wrote';
> 'an adherent of al-Shāfiʿī said'; and
> 'if al-Shāfiʿī were here to answer our questions, I am sure he would say.'

This list should be doubled by prefixing each possibility with 'this is the gist of what.'

[298] The writing of express commentaries on the works of the eponyms is one feature among others distinguishing the classical, guild schools of law, which first appeared in the early Tenth Century.[64] The eponyms themselves died a century or more before

62. Al-Bayhaqī, *Manāqib*, II, p. 347.

63. See G. Schoeler, *Die Frage der schriftlichen oder mündlichen Überlieferung der Wissenschaften im frühen Islam*, in: *Der Islam* 62 (1985), p. 201–230; *Mündliche Thora und Ḥadīṯ*, in: *Der Islam* 66 (1989), p. 213–251; *Writing and Publishing on the Use and Function of Writing in the First Centuries of Islam*, *Arabica* 44 (1997), p. 423–434, trans. P. Butler, from *Schreiben und Veröffentlichen*, in: *Der Islam* 69 (1992), p. 1–43; M. Cook, *The Opponents of the Writing of Tradition in Early Islam*, in: *Arabica* 44 (1997), p. 437–530.

64. See G. Makdisi, Ṭabaqāt-*Biography: Law and Orthodoxy in Classical Islam*, in: *Islamic Studies* (Islam-

the emergence of the corresponding guild schools. What went on in that intervening century? Evidently, there did go on elaboration of the eponyms' doctrines (in the case of the Ḥanafī school, the doctrine of the eponyms' most famous followers as well); however, mostly unlike the commentators of the classical schools, Ninth Century commentators customarily ascribed their elaborations directly to the eponym (*qāla 'l-Shāfiʿī* with variants in Shāfiʿī works, *qāla Muḥammad* with variants in Ḥanafī). Much of the *Umm* presumably goes back to al-Shāfiʿī, some even in its very wording; however, there seldom seems to be any reliable way to tell which statements are verbatim quotations and which are any of the other possibilities just listed. Al-Muzanī's *Mukhtaṣar* is transitional, usually quoting al-Shāfiʿī directly but also unsystematically indicating the synthetic and extrapolative nature of its quotations.

Calder is to be commended, then, for one major, irreversible advance, mainly forcing us to reckon with the fluidity of texts throughout the ninth century. Perhaps Calder went too far in two respects. First, the extent of posthumous reworking may be less than he suggested. Al-Tirmidhī's formulation of al-Shāfiʿī's doctrine is never identical to what we see in the Egyptian works, but it is seldom in contradiction to it. It may be a fairly accurate transmission from a larger body of Shāfiʿī doctrine. Second, a much higher proportion of al-Marwazī's citations of al-Shāfiʿī's opinions seem to have no parallels whatever in the Egyptian works, and I have sometimes discovered them in blatant contradiction to the Egyptian works. Hallaq's theory of expansion by *takhrīj* seems to fit al-Marwazī (and the others) somewhat better than Calder's theory (after Schacht) of competing groups continually provoking one another to sharpen their arguments by introducing better evidence; however, the two are not mutually exclusive.

Appendix

I have referred above to a lively booklet by the Egyptian *adīb*, Zakī Mubārak (d. Cairo, 1952). I myself was led to it by the reference in Fuat Sezgin, *Geschichte des arabischen Schrifttums*. It has been unduly [299] neglected in the recent scholarly tradition; for example, there is no sign of Mubārak in Calder's discussion of *al-Umm*, nor any of the critiques of it that I have seen.[65] It would have saved me some trouble had I been able to read it before I made my presentation to the School of Abbasid Studies in July 2002—there seems to be no copy in the libraries of Oxford, London, or Cambridge. (A kind scholar in California finally supplied my want). I should like to devote some additional space to an evaluation of Mubārak's booklet just because it has been unduly neglected.

abad) 32 (1993), p. 371–396; Melchert, *Formation*, esp. p. 60–67, 102.

65. Calder, *Studies*, Chapter 4. To his credit, Joe Lowry has pointed out Mubārak in a note: J.E. Lowry, *Does Shāfiʿī Have a Theory of 'Four Sources' of Law?*' in: Weiss, *Studies*, p. 23–50 (24n).

Mubārak's starting point is the allegation from Abū Ṭālib al-Makkī (d. Baghdad, 386/996?) that al-Buwayṭī had anonymously assembled the *Umm* now attributed to al-Rabīᶜ. Al-Rabīᶜ took it from him, made additions with his name attached, and published it as his own.[66] Mubārak's full title is *Iṣlāḥ Ashnaᶜ Khaṭa' fī Taʾrīkh al-Tashrīᶜ al-Islāmī: Kitāb al-Umm lam Yuʾallif-hu 'l-Shāfiᶜī wa-inna-mā Allafa-hu 'l-Buwayṭī wa-Taṣarrafa fīhi 'l-Rabīᶜ b. Sulaymān*, by interpretation 'Correction of the Most Shameful Mistake in the History of Islamic Lawmaking: *K. al-Umm* was not Compiled by al-Shāfiᶜī but rather by al-Buwayṭī, then Appropriated by al-Rabīᶜ b. Sulaymān.' As for who collected the *Umm*, Mubārak observes that quotations of al-Shāfiᶜī and interpolated comments are attributed to (1) 'Abū Muḥammad' (no more than twenty times in the whole work), (2) 'Abū Yaᶜqūb,' and (3) 'al-Rabīᶜ' or 'al-Rabīᶜ b. Sulaymān.' The second plainly indicates al-Buwayṭī, but the first and third might refer equally to al-Rabīᶜ b. Sulaymān al-Murādī or al-Jīzī. As a concession to the biographical literature, perhaps, Mubārak proposes that the al-Rabīᶜ who appears at the heads of *asānīd* ('al-Rabīᶜ b. Sulaymān < al-Shāfiᶜī < Sufyān' and the like) is al-Murādī. Since ᶜAbū Muḥammad' and 'al-Rabīᶜ' are sometimes credited with separate comments on the same page or even concerning the same question (e.g., *Umm*, III, p. 29, VI, p. 226), Mubārak infers that they are two different persons and supposes that here, 'Abū Muḥammad' indicates al-Murādī, 'al-Rabīᶜ' al-Jīzī. He is uncertain whether al-Murādī's rare comments were collected by al-Buwayṭī or al-Jīzī (Mubārak, p. 73–77).

Mubārak's argument that the *Umm* was assembled by Shāfiᶜī's [300] disciples, not by Shāfiᶜī himself, seems very strong, supported by many quotations from the text. Aḥmad Muḥammad Shākir's refutation, endorsed by Sezgin, is that *akhbara-nā* must indicate verbatim quotation: if we take it to mean anything else, all attributions are in question, we accuse unquestionably upright men of lying, and so forth.[67] Between Shākir's dogmatic assertions and Mubārak's inferences from documentary evidence, we as scholars must choose the latter.

Unfortunately, Mubārak's main concern is not how Islamic law developed but whether Abū Ṭālib al-Makkī was right about al-Buwayṭī and al-Rabīᶜ, a secondary question on which, from lack of evidence, he has a poorer purchase. Abū Ṭālib al-Makkī's allegation and a similar one from al-Ghazālī seem only a little more presumptively reliable than assertions in the biographical literature that al-Rabīᶜ al-Murādī was the main transmitter of Shāfiᶜī's books.[68] They are hard to reconcile with al-Rabīᶜ's expressly transmitting

---

66. Abū Ṭālib Al-Makkī, *Qūt al-Qulūb*, ed. S.N. Makārim, II, Beirut, 1995, p. 438–439 = Cairo, 1310, II, p. 228. Cf. R. Gramlich, trans., *Die Nahrung der Herzen* (*Freiburger Islamstudien*, 16), III, Stuttgart, 1992–1995, p. 509; also Ibn Ḥajar, *Tahdhīb*, III, p. 246, quoting the allegation of one Yūsuf b. Yazīd (probably Syrian) that al-Rabīᶜ took most of al-Shāfiᶜī's books from al-Buwayṭī's family after his death.

67. A.M. Shākir, introduction to Al-Shāfiᶜī, *Risāla*, p. 9–10; Sezgin, *GAS*, I, p. 487.

68. E.g., 'He was the transmitter (*nāqil*) of *Kitāb al-Umm*': Al-ᶜAbbādī (d. 458/1066), *Ṭabaqāt*, 12; 'He is the one meant in the books of the school when "al-Rabīᶜ" is referred to, for if they mean al-Jīzī, they expressly restrict it (to him)': Al-Nawawī, *Tahdhīb*, I, p. 188.

some material from al-Buwayṭī (e.g., *Umm*, I, p. 96–97): why should he have acknowledged relying on al-Buwayṭī here if he had taken almost all the rest of the *Umm* from al-Buwayṭī, as well? They are hard to reconcile with the frequency with which, as we see in al-Nawawī, *al-Majmūʿ*, medieval Shāfiʿī jurists did expressly cite al-Buwayṭī for the opinion of al-Shāfiʿī (although presumably quoting al-Buwayṭī's *Mukhtaṣar*, still extant in the late Mamluk period, for which see *Umm*, I, p. 157.12–13 from bottom).

As for Mubārak's tentative identification of 'al-Rabīʿ' in the *Umm* with al-Rabīʿ b. Sulaymān al-Jīzī, it rests on, first, very few citations and, second, the assumption that authorities will always be referred to by one name. In a roughly contemporary encyclopaedia of traditionists, *al-Taʾrīkh al-kabīr* of al-Bukhārī (d. 256/870), I have noticed 'Abū ʿAbd Allāh said,' 'Muḥammad said,' and 'al-Bukhārī said' in apparently random alternation; likewise, in the same work, Aḥmad b. Ḥanbal is quoted by turns as 'Aḥmad,' 'Ibn Ḥanbal,' and 'Aḥmad b. Ḥanbal.' A more likely explanation of alternation between 'Abū Muḥammad' and 'al-Rabīʿ' in referring to the same person is the one that Mubārak himself offers for occasional alternation between 'Abū ʿAbd Allāh' and 'al-Shāfiʿī' in referring to the eponym of the school, [301] mainly that it betrays assemblage from different sources (Mubārak, p. 44–45).

Mubārak's identification of al-Jīzī as the compiler of the *Umm* does have the advantage of explaining, for once, why the work seems to have come so late into the Shāfiʿī legal tradition. The literary basis of Ibn Surayj's school was al-Muzanī's *Mukhtaṣar* (the small version, evidently, not the lost large version). Those who travelled to Egypt to learn al-Shāfiʿī's doctrine almost all went to al-Muzanī and al-Murādī, the biographical sources say, hence might have ignored al-Jīzī and his *Umm*. But why should they have ignored al-Jīzī and his *Umm*? It seems more economical to suppose (with Calder) that al-Shāfiʿī's doctrine circulated in the form of multiple discreet texts and recollections for most of the ninth century, and was not actually fixed until a century after his death.

15

MĀWARDĪ, ABŪ YAᶜLÁ, AND THE SUNNI REVIVAL

The most famous medieval work of Islamic political theory is *al-Aḥkām al-sulṭānīyah* of the Shāfiᶜi jurisprudent al-Māwardī (d. Baghdad, 450/1058). It was edited in Germany in the nineteenth century, translated into French in the early twentieth, and into English twice in the 1990s.[1] As for historical scholarship, it was made the subject of a celebrated essay by H. A. R. Gibb in 1937, which situated its description of the caliph's powers in the context of the Sunni Revival as Būyid power waned and powerful new Sunni dynasts waxed in Ghaznah and Transoxania.[2] Henri Laoust followed Gibb's lead by developing [38] Māwardī's biography, especially his personal involvement in politics.[3] Meanwhile, however, another work by the same title from exactly the same place and time had been edited: *al-Aḥkām al-sulṭānīyah* by the Ḥanbali jurisprudent Abū Yaᶜlá ibn al-Farrāʾ (d.

1. Al-Māwardī, *Maverdii Constitutiones politicae*, ed. Max Enger (Bonn: Adolphum Marcum, 1853); idem, *Les statuts gouvernementaux*, trans. E. Fagnan (Algiers: Adolphe Jourdan, 1915); idem, *The Laws of Islamic Governance*, trans. Asadullah Yate (London : Ta-Ha, 1996); idem, *The Ordinances of Government*, trans. Wafaa H. Wahba, Great books of Islamic civilisation (Reading: Garnet, 1996).

2. H. A. R. Gibb, 'Al-Māwardī's Theory of the Khilāfah,' *Islamic Culture* (Hyderabad) 11 (1937): 291–302; repr. idem, *Studies on the Civilization of Islam*, ed. Stanford J. Shaw and William R. Polk (London: Routledge and Kegan Paul, 1962), 151–165. For the Sunni Revival, *v.* Makdisi, *Ibn ᶜAqīl* (Damascus: Institut Français de Damas, 1963), chaps. 2, 4; idem, "The Sunnī Revival," *Islamic Civilization 950-1150*, ed. D. S. Richards, Papers on Islamic History 3 (Oxford: Cassirer, 1973), 155–168; and Erika Glassen, *Der mittlere Weg: Studien zur Religionspolitik und Religiosität der späteren Abbasiden-Zeit*, Freiburger Islamstudien 8 (Wiesbaden: Franz Steiner, 1981), chap. 2.

3. Henri Laoust, "La pensée et l'action politiques d'al-Māwardī (364–450/974–1058)," *Revue des études islamiques* 36 (1968): 11–92.

Originally published in *Prosperity and Stagnation: Some Cultural and Social Aspects of the Abbasid Period (750-1258)*. Edited by Krzystof Kościelniak. Orientalia Christiana Cracoviensia, Monographiae 1 (Cracow: UNUM, 2010), 37–61.

Baghdad, 458/1065).[4] In 1974, there appeared both a brief comparison of the two by Donald Little and a dissertation at al-Azhar on Abū Yaᶜlá's book (later published in Beirut) by the Jordanian scholar and political activist Abū Fāris.[5] Unfortunately, neither of these studies seems to have had much effect on subsequent scholarly use of Māwardī, which has by and large ignored the comparison with Abū Yaᶜlá.[6] I shall argue that Abū Yaᶜlá's version more likely preceded Māwardī's than the other way around. I think I can develop more fully than earlier writers the context of the two books in the establishment of four Sunni schools of law. I once thought that a comparison should help us above all to distinguish between what was generally believed at that time and what is peculiar to Māwardī. But now I am more inclined to remind scholars that these are only incidentally works of political thought, overwhelmingly works of Islamic law. [39]

The Sunni Revival

Roughly, ᶜAbbāsid power declined from the Fourth Civil War, 195–198/810–813, till the accession of al-Muᶜtamid in 256/870, under whom at least some measure of political stability was restored, then again from the accession of al-Muqtadir in 295/908. Politically, this meant instability at the centre, as military leaders increasingly dictated policy to caliphs and from time to time deposed and replaced them, also the rise of new dynasties on the periphery (e.g. Sistan conquered by Yaᶜqūb al-Ṣaffār in 251/865, Egypt effectively independent from at least 263/877) that of course refused to transfer tribute to the centre. Economically, this meant the decline of revenues from both the provinces and from Iraq itself, whose population probably declined from the later ninth century and plunged from the eleventh.[7] The warlord Ibn Rāʾiq was formally recognized as *amīr al-umarāʾ* in 324/936. In 334/945, the title was bestowed on Muᶜizz al-Dawlah Aḥmad, leader of a Daylami family, the Būyids (alternatively, "Buwayhids"), who was formally not even Sunni

4. Abū Yaᶜlá ibn al-Farrāʾ, *al-Aḥkām al-sulṭānīyah*, ed. Muḥammad Ḥāmid al-Fiqī (Cairo: Maktabat Muṣṭafá al-Bābī al-Ḥalabī, 1356/1938; repr. with continuous pagination 1386/1966; repr. Beirut: Dār al-Kutub al-ᶜIlmīyah, 1403/1983). Henceforward, citations will be of the reprint of the 1966 edition.

5. Donald P. Little, "A New Look at *al-Aḥkām al-sulṭāniyya*," *Muslim World* 64 (1974): 1–15, with a fuller review than mine of previous European scholarship at 1–5; Muḥammad ᶜAbd al-Qādir Abū Fāris, *al-Qāḍī Abū Yaᶜlá al-Farrāʾ wa-kitābuhu* al-Aḥkām al-sulṭānīyah (Beirut: Muʾassasat al-Risālah, 1403/1983). Abū Fāris' dissertation was submitted and accepted in 1394/1974, while it was first published as a book in 1400/1980.

6. e.g. Eric J. Hanne, "Abbasid Politics and the Classical Theory of the Caliphate," *Writers and Rulers: Perspectives on their Relationship from Abbasid to Safavid Times*, ed. Beatrice Gruendlier and Louise Marlow, Literaturen im Kontext: Arabisch-Persich-Türkisch 16 (Wiesbaden: Reichert, 2004), 49–71. Let me acknowledge here the influence on me of an unpublished seminar paper by fellow Makdisi student Sherman Jackson, arguing for the priority of Abū Yaᶜlá's version on the ground that he ought to have met Māwardī's arguments much better had he come second.

7. Robert McC. Adams, *Land behind Baghdad* (London: Univ. of Chicago Press, 1965), 84–85, 115.

but a Twelver Shiʿi. Having occupied Baghdad itself, the Būyids continued to rule until 447/1055.

Religiously, the ninth century saw the triumph and consolidation of Sunnism. In the early ninth century, *ahl al-sunnah wa-al-jamāʿah* were one party among others, distinguished by their insisting on revelation and especially hadith as the sole basis of theology and law. Al-Maʾmūn instituted the Inquisition in 218/833 to establish that the caliph dictated orthodoxy, not traditionists (collectors and critics of hadith), but his successor al-Mutawakkil gave up the fight over the first five years of his caliphate, 232–237/847–852.[8] By the beginning of the tenth century, the familiar Sunni schools of law were beginning to form, distinguished from the earlier personal schools by their devotion to commentaries on the works of the eponyms and their disciples and by a regular system of forming students.[9] [40] Sunnism became the great default category for all but Shiʿi Muslims and the remaining Muʿtazilah.

Even though they were Shiʿi, the Būyids did not abolish the ʿAbbāsid caliphate, since the last of the Twelver Imams had gone into occultation by then and it was politically convenient to maintain a subordinate ʿAbbāsid, especially *vis à vis* the Fāṭimids in North Africa and Egypt.[10] But Būyid overlordship did mean a measure of protection for the Twelver Shiʿah in their realm. The classical period of Twelver Shiʿism runs from the work of the traditionist al-Kulaynī (d. 329/941?) to the jurisprudents Ibn Bābawayh al-Ṣadūq (d. 381/991–992), al-Shaykh al-Mufīd (d. 413/1022), and al-Ṭūsī Shaykh al-Ṭāʾifah (d. 458/1065–1066?). It also meant patronage for Persian and Hellenistic learning in addition to Arabo-Islamic.[11]

Būyid power waned from the later tenth century, as intestine rivalries weakened the dynasty and the rise of new dynasties to the East, especially those of Maḥmūd ibn Sebüktegin of Ghaznah (d. 421/1030), then the Selchūqids of Transoxania, threatened to supplant them in their core territories of the Jibal (ancient Media), Fars (ancient Persia), and Iraq. The caliph had no military power at his command, but he could threaten to recognize someone else than the leading Būyid as overlord—as, for example, al-Qādir not

8. *V. The Encyclopaedia of Islam*, new edn., s.v. "Miḥna," by M. Hinds.

9. *V.* Christopher Melchert, "The Formation of the Sunnī Schools of Law," *The Formation of Islamic Law*, ed. Wael B. Hallaq, The Formation of the Classical Islamic World 27 (Aldershot: Ashgate, 2004), 351–366.

10. On the evolution of Shiʿism in the earlier tenth century, *v.* Verena Klemm, "The Four Sufarāʾ of the Twelfth Imām," trans. Gwendolyn Goldbloom, *Shīʿism*, ed. Etan Kohlberg, The Formation of The Classical Islamic World 33 (Aldershot: Ashgate, 2003), 135–152. On the evolution of Twelver law over the next century, *v.* Devin J. Stewart, *Islamic Legal Orthodoxy: Twelver Shiite Responses to the Sunni Legal System* (Salt Lake City: Univ. of Utah Press, 1998), and Robert Gleave, "Between *ḥadīth* and *fiqh*: The "Canonical" Imāmī Collections of *akhbār*," *Islamic Law and Society* 8 (2001): 350–382.

11. A classic survey is Adam Mez, *The Renaissance of Islam*, trans. Salahuddin Khuda Bukhsh and D. S. Margoliouth (London: Luzac and Co., 1937).

only appointed Maḥmūd of Ghaznah governor of Khurasan and Ghaznah, in place of the Sāmānids, but gave him the titles Yamīn al-Dawlah and Amīn al-Millah. Here, the turning point seems to have been, ironically, Abū Kālījār's demand in about 429/1038 to be recognized as *shāhanshāh*, "king of kings," which implicitly recognized the Būyids' dependence on the caliph for [41] their title.[12] As the Būyids weakened, the caliphs increasingly played up their devotion to Sunnism.

Al-Māwardī

Abū al-Ḥasan ʿAlī ibn Muḥammad ibn Ḥabīb al-Māwardī was a Muslim polymath. He was born in Basra, 364/974, and died in Baghdad, 30 Rabīʿ I 450/27 May 1058.[13] The *nisbah* by which he is famous refers to the preparation and sale of rose-water;[14] however, it is not known when this had last been the occupation of our Māwardī's family. Māwardī studied Shāfiʿi law in Basra under Abū al-Qāsim al-Ṣaymarī (d. after 386/996–7) and in Baghdad under the reputed renewer (*mujaddid*) of the turn of the century, Abū Ḥāmid al-Isfarāyinī (d. Baghdad, 406/1016).[15] Both teachers connect him with the sequence of teachers and students that begins with Ibn Surayj (d. Baghdad, 306/918), reputed renewer of the turn of the previous century, who [42] effectively founded the classical Shāfiʿi school by developing a regular curriculum for the formation of Shāfiʿi jurisprudents.[16]

12. Wilferd Madelung, "The Assumption of the Title Shāhanshāh by the Būyids," *Journal of Near Eastern Studies* 28 (1969): 84–108, 168–183, esp. 181–183.

13. For pre-modern biographies, v. mainly al-Khaṭīb al-Baghdādī, *Tārīkh Baghdād*, 14 vols. (Cairo: Maktabat al-Khānjī, 1349/1931; repr. Cairo: Maktabat al-Khānjī and Beirut: Dār al-fikr, n.d.), 12 : 102–103; *Tārīkh Madīnat al-Salām*, ed. Bashshār ʿAwwād Maʿrūf, 17 vols. (Beirut: Dār al-Gharb al-Islāmī, 1422/2001), 13 : 587 (henceforward, citations of this edn. in *italics*), and Yāqūt, *Irshād al-arīb ilá maʿrifat al-adīb*, ed. D. S. Margoliouth, E. J. W. Gibb Memorial Series 6, 7 vols. (Leiden: E. J. Brill, 1907–27), 5 : 407–409; ed. Iḥsān ʿAbbās, 7 vols. (Beirut: Dār al-Gharb al-Islāmī, 1993), 5 : 1955–1957. The last includes further references in a note. Among modern biographies in Arabic, I have been able to consult Muḥammad Sulaymān Dāwūd and Fuʾād ʿAbd al-Munʿim Aḥmad, *al-Imām Abū al-Ḥasan al-Māwardī* (Alexandria: Muʾassasat Shabāb al-Jāmiʿah, 1978), which collects many useful facts but is not always reliable in detail. For example, it confuses Māwardī's honorary title *aqḍá al-quḍāh* with the post *qāḍī al-quḍāh* (17).

14. Al-Samʿānī, *al-Ansāb*, s.v.

15. On al-Ṣaymarī (ʿAbd al-Wāḥid ibn al-Ḥusayn), *v.* al-Dhahabī, *Siyar aʿlām al-nubalāʾ*, ed. Shuʿayb al-Arnaʾūṭ, & al., 25 vols. (Beirut: Muʾassasat al-Risālah, 1401–9/1981–8), 17 : 14–15; on Abū Ḥāmid al-Isfarāyinī (Aḥmad ibn Muḥammad ibn Aḥmad), *v. ibid.*, 193–197, with further references.

16. Christopher Melchert, *The Formation of the Sunni Schools of Law*, Studies in Islamic Law and Society 4 (Leiden: Brill, 1997), chap. 5.

Chiefs of the Baghdadi Shāfiʿi School and Their Teachers

1. Abū al-ʿAbbās Aḥmad ibn ʿUmar *ibn Surayj*[17];

2. *Abū Isḥāq* Ibrāhīm ibn Aḥmad *al-Marwazī* (d. Ḥulwān, Egypt, 340/951),[18] learnt jurisprudence < 1;

3. Abū ʿAlī al-Ḥasan ibn al-Ḥusayn *ibn Abī Hurayrah* (d. 345/956),[19] < 1 and 2;

4. *Abū ʿAlī* al-Ḥusayn ibn al-Qāsim *al-Ṭabarī* (d. 350/960–961),[20] < 3;

5. Abū al-Ḥusayn Aḥmad ibn Muḥammad ibn Aḥmad *Ibn al-Qaṭṭān al-Baghdādī* (d. 359/970),[21] < 1 and 2;

6. Abū al-Ḥasan ʿAlī ibn Aḥmad *ibn al-Marzubān* (d. 366/977),[22] < 5;

7. Abū al-Qāsim ʿAbd al-ʿAzīz ibn ʿAbd Allāh *al-Dārakī* (d. 375/986),[23] < 2;

8. *Abū Ḥāmid* Aḥmad ibn Muḥammad *al-Isfarāyinī*, < 6 and 7.

9. *Abū al-Ṭayyib* Ṭāhir ibn ʿAbd Allāh *al-Ṭabarī* (d. 450/1058),[24] < Abū ʿAlī al-Zujājī (d. *ca.* 400/1009–10)[25] in Āmul, < Abū Saʿd (Saʿīd) al-Ismāʿīlī (d. 396/1006)[26] and Ibn al-Kajj (d. 405/1015)[27] in [43] Gurgan, < Abū al-Ḥasan al-Māsarjisī (d. 384/994)[28] in Nishapur, and < Abū Muḥammad al-Bāfī (d. 398/1007)[29] and 8 in Baghdad.

The Intellectual Lineage of Abū al-Qāsim al-Ṣaymarī

1. *Abū Ḥāmid* Aḥmad ibn Bishr *al-Marwarrūdhī* (d. 362/972–973),[30] learnt jurisprudence < Abū Isḥāq al-Marwazī and Abū ʿAlī al-Ḥusayn ibn Ṣāliḥ *ibn Khayrān* (d. 320/932?)[31];

2. *Abū al-Fayyāḍ* Muḥammad ibn al-Ḥusayn *al-Baṣrī* (d. *ca.* 375/985–6?),[32] < 1;

---

17. Al-Subkī, *Ṭabaqāt al-shāfiʿīyah al-kubrá*, ed. Maḥmūd Muḥammad al-Ṭanāḥī and ʿAbd al-Fattāḥ al-Ḥulw, 10 vols. (Cairo: ʿĪsá al-Bābī al-Ḥalabī, 1964–1976), 3 : 21–39.

18. V. Dhahabī, *Siyar* 15 : 429–430, with further references.

19. Subkī, *Ṭabaqāt* 3 : 256–263.

20. Subkī, *Ṭabaqāt* 3 : 280–281.

21. Dhahabī, *Siyar* 16 : 159.

22. Subkī, *Ṭabaqāt* 3 : 346.

23. Subkī, *Ṭabaqāt* 3 : 330–333.

24. Dhahabī, *Siyar* 16 : 429–430, with further references.

25. Subkī, *Ṭabaqāt* 4 : 331–332.

26. Dhahabī, *Siyar* 17 : 87–88, with further references.

27. Subkī, *Ṭabaqāt* 5 : 359–361.

28. Dhahabī, *Siyar* 16 : 446–447, with further references.

29. Subkī, *Ṭabaqāt* 3 : 317–320.

30. Subkī, *Ṭabaqāt* 3 : 12–13.

31. On whom *v.* Subkī, *Ṭabaqāt* 3 : 271–274 (who surmises that he learnt jurisprudence from the same shaykhs as Ibn Surayj and also sat before Ibn Surayj himself, 273).

32. Al-Isnawī, *Ṭabaqāt al-shāfiʿīyah*, ed. ʿAbd Allāh al-Jābūrī, Iḥyāʾ al-Turāth al-Islāmī, 2 vols. (Baghdad: Riʾāsat Dīwān al-Awqāf, 1390-1391/1970–1971), 1 : 193.

3. *Abū al-Qāsim* ᶜAbd al-Wāḥid ibn al-Ḥusayn *al-Ṣaymarī*, < 2;

Not Māwardī but his contemporary Abū al-Ṭayyib al-Ṭabarī (d. 450/1058) became chief of the Baghdadi Shāfiᶜīyah.[33] Neither had Māwardī any illustrious disciples in Islamic law. Still, he was a major figure in the elaboration of Shāfiᶜi doctrine, especially at the level of positive law (*furūᶜ*). In a highly detailed survey of Shāfiᶜi law, the *Majmūᶜ* of al-Nawawī (d. Nawa, 676/1277), Māwardī is the fourth most often-cited authority, behind Imām al-Ḥaramayn but ahead of al-Ghazālī.[34]

Al-Khaṭīb al-Baghdādī, followed by all later biographers, declares that Māwardī was appointed to many judgeships, but no one lists them.[35] There is nothing particularly surprising about this, for we [44] usually lack information concerning qadis outside the major centres.[36] He probably had deputies do most of the actual work.

Māwardī was close to some of the Būyid warlords who controlled Iraq and Iran, especially earlier in his career. He sometimes negotiated on their behalf with their neighbours. Better known is his involvement in negotiations with the Būyids on behalf of two caliphs, al-Qādir (*r.* 381–422/991–1031) and al-Qāʾim (*r.* 422–467/1031–1074). He once headed a diplomatic mission from the caliph to the Būyids' rivals, the Selchūqids.[37] In 429/1037–1038, al-Qāʾim named him *aqḍá al-quḍāh*, literally "the most decisive of the judges." Some contemporary jurisprudents objected, such as Abū al-Ṭayyib al-Ṭabarī of the Shāfiᶜi school and al-Ṣaymarī (d. 436/1045) of the Ḥanafi, but they were ignored.[38] In Ramadan of the same year (June-July 1038), al-Qāʾim promoted Jalāl al-Dawlah from *amīr al-umarāʾ*, "commander of commanders," to *malik al-mulūk*, "king of kings."[39] Abū al-Ṭayyib al-Ṭabarī, al-Ṣaymarī the Ḥanafi, and a certain Tamīmī of the Ḥanbali school issued opinions in favour of the new title, arguing that it was intended to refer only to earthly kings (that is, did not slight God *al-malik*).[40] Reports differ as to what Māwardī

33. For that sequence, *v.* Makdisi, *Ibn ᶜAqīl* 194–219.

34. Al-Nawawī, *al-Majmūᶜ*, ed. Zakarīyāʾ ᶜAlī Yūsuf, 18 vols. (Cairo: Maṭbaᶜat al-ᶜĀṣimah or Maṭbaᶜat al-Imām, 1966–1969). Vols. 1–9 are by al-Nawawī, the rest by various continuators. I have counted citations in the first three volumes.

35. Al-Khaṭīb al-Baghdādī, *Tārīkh* 12 : 102 *13 : 587*.

36. *V.* Heinz Halm, *Die Ausbreitung der šāfiᶜitischen Rechtsschule*, Beihefte zum tübinger Atlas des vorderen Orients, B (Geisteswissenschaften), 4 (Wiesbaden: Ludwig Reichert, 1974), 12–14, for the Shāfiᶜi school in particular.

37. For Māwardī's career, *v.* above all Laoust, "Pensée."

38. Yāqūt, *Irshād*, ed. Margoliouth, 5 : 407; ed. ᶜAbbās, 5 : 1955.

39. For Jalāl al-Dawlah's long struggle for supremacy, *v.* Laoust, "Pensée," 73–79.

40. Al-Ṣaymarī is particularly important to modern scholarship on account of his biography of Abū Ḥanīfah and his leading followers. For biographies, *v.* Dhahabī, *Siyar* 17 : 615–616. The Ḥanbali, Tamīmī, is more obscure. My guess is that it was Abū ᶜAlī ibn al-Mudhhib (d. 444/1052), on whom *v.* al-Khaṭīb al-Baghdādī, *Tārīkh* 7 : 390–392 *8 : 393–395*, but Laoust ("Pensée," 80) thinks it was rather Abū Muḥammad al-Tamīmī (d. 488/1095–1096), on whom *v.* Ibn Abī Yaᶜlá, *Ṭabaqāt al-ḥanābilah*, ed. Muḥammad Ḥāmid

said: that he argued similarly to Abū al-Ṭayyib al-Ṭabarī and that he denounced the title [45] as impious, for which he feared to be punished but ended up being complimented by Jalāl al-Dawlah.[41]

Caliphal interest in Māwardī 's works is indicated especially by the commissioning from him of an epitome of Shāfiᶜi law. Yāqūt mentions that the caliph al-Qādir requested exposés of the particular ordinances of each of what shortly became the four Sunni schools of law. Māwardī wrote *al-Iqnāᶜ*. The famous *Mukhtaṣar* of al-Qudūrī (d. 428/1037) is its Ḥanafi counterpart, while ᶜAbd al-Wahhāb al-Thaᶜlabī (d. 422/1031) prepared an epitome of Māliki law.[42] Yāqūt states that he does not know who wrote an epitome of Ḥanbali law on this occasion. One likely candidate would be Ibn Ḥāmid (d. 403/1012–1013), chief of the Ḥanbali school in Baghdad and close to the caliph al-Qādir. More likely, though, a Ḥanbali epitome came from the successor Ibn Ḥāmid himself designated, Abū Yaᶜlá, probably *al-Mujarrad*, no longer extant but named among his books by biographers and important in the later Ḥanbali school. The system of four mutually respectful Sunni schools of law goes back to about the turn of the eleventh century. Yaᶜakov Meron has asserted that it was the rise of *uṣūl al-fiqh*, resolutely probabilistic, that persuaded Muslim jurisprudents from then on to renounce the search for the one correct answer to every question, which is to say to prove that every other school was wrong.[43] This caliphal commissioning of parallel books from four schools presumably had something to do with the [46] predictability of judicial rulings. A Shāfiᶜi epitome would tell how a Shāfiᶜi qadi would rule, a Ḥanafi how a Ḥanafi, and so on. The issue was certainly current, for Māwardī and Abū Yaᶜlá both comment on the problem of whether one may validly appoint a qadi and require him to rule according to a particular school, his own or another.[44] Whatever its judicial connection, the commissioning sounds like another decisive impulse toward mu-

al-Fiqī, 2 vols. (Cairo: Maṭbaᶜat al-Sunnah al-Muḥammadīyah, 1371/1952), 2 : 250–251; likewise Glassen, *Mittlere Weg*, 12, but she has misinterpreted the passage cited in Ibn al-Jawzī, *al-Muntaẓam*, actually s.a. 442, in which this Tamīmī prayed over Abū al-Ḥasan al-Qazwīnī, not the caliph al-Qādir.

41. Ibn al-Jawzī, *al-Muntaẓam*, 6 vols. (Hyderabad: Dāᵓirat al-Maᶜārif al-ᶜUthmānīyah, 1357–60), 8 : 97–98; ed. Muḥammad ᶜAbd al-Qādir ᶜAṭā and Muṣṭafá ᶜAbd al-Qādir ᶜAṭā, with Nuᶜaym Zurzūr, 18 vols. (Beirut: Dār al-Kutub al-ᶜIlmīyah, 1412/1992), 15 : 264–265; Laoust, "Pensée," 79–80.

42. Al-Māwardī, *al-Iqnāᶜ fī al-fiqh al-shāfiᶜī*, ed. Khiḍr Muḥammad Khiḍr (Kuwait: Maktabat Dār al-ᶜUrūbah, 1402/1982). For the story of the commissioning, *v.* Yāqūt, *Irshād*, ed. Margoliouth, 5 : 408; ed. ᶜAbbās, 5 : 1956. Yāqūt names the Māliki qadi "ᶜAbd al-Wahhāb ibn Muḥammad ibn Naṣr," but other sources make him the son of ᶜAlī; e.g. al-Khaṭīb al-Baghdādī, *Tārīkh* 11 : 31–32 *12 : 292*; Abū Isḥāq al-Shīrāzī, *Ṭabaqāt al-fuqahāᵓ*, ed. Iḥsān ᶜAbbās (Beirut: Dār al-Rāᵓid al-ᶜArabī, 1970), 168–169; al-Qāḍī ᶜIyāḍ, *Tartīb al-madārik*, ed. Muḥammad ibn Tāwīt al-Ṭanjī and Saᶜīd Aḥmad Aᶜrāb, 8 vols. (Rabat and elsewhere: Maṭbaᶜat Faḍālah and others, 1966–1983), 7 : 220–222. On Ibn Ḥāmid and al-Qādir, *v.* Ibn Abī Yaᶜlá, *Ṭabaqāt* 2 : 177.

43. Yaᶜakov Meron, *L'obligation alimentaire entre époux en droit musulman hanéfite*, Bibliothèque de droit privé 114 (Paris: R. Pichon and R. Durand-Auzias, 1971).

44. Māwardī, *al-Aḥkām al-sulṭānīyah*, ed. ᶜIṣām Fāris al-Ḥarastānī and Muḥammad Ibrāhīm al-Zughlī

tual recognition and respect among the Sunni schools. It also sounds like a signal rebuke from the caliph to the Ẓāhiri school, still holding on at the time in Baghdad and Fars but under Būyid patronage and replete with Muᶜtazilah.

Māwardī often espouses Muᶜtazili views. Pre-modern Muslim critics pointed especially to some passages in his Qurʾan commentary, such as rejection of predestination.[45] Other examples can be found. One is the capacity of reason to tell that an imam is necessary (on which more below).[46] Michael Cook has pointed out agreements between Māwardī's presentation of commanding the right and forbidding the wrong (*al-amr bi-al-maᶜrūf wa-al-nahy ᶜan al-munkar*) and that of the Muᶜtazili tradition.[47] However, pre-modern critics exculpated Māwardī of advocating Muᶜtazili views systematically.[48] (Lester Little [47] detects rationalism in Māwardī's continually presenting different positions but refusing to choose among them.[49] I am more inclined to consider it an example of normal Islamic legal writing, which is often indeterminate in detail. Abū Yaᶜlá's *Aḥkām* is equally indeterminate when there is more than one version of Aḥmad's doctrine to report. Alternatively, it shows how Māwardī's *Aḥkām* falls under the category of *ikhtilāf*, a survey of the different schools's positions, as opposed to an exposition of his own Shāfiᶜi school's positions.) So far, no one has uncovered evidence in his writing of Ashᶜarism.[50]

In addition to Shāfiᶜi law, Māwardī is known to have written about the Qurʾan, Arabic grammar, personal ethics and deportment, political theory, and administration. Most of

---

(Beirut: al-Maktab al-Islāmī, 1416/1996), 111–113; trans. Wahba, 75–7 (henceforward, citations of this translation in *italics*). Abū Yaᶜlá, *Aḥkām*, 63–64.

45. E.g. Ibn al-Ṣalāḥ, *Ṭabaqāt al-fuqahāʾ al-shāfiᶜīyah*, ed. al-Nawawī, al-Mizzī, and Muḥyī al-Dīn ᶜAlī Najīb, 2 vols. (Beirut: Dār al-Bashāʾir al-Islāmīyah, 1413/1992), 2 : 638–640, 642, followed by Subkī, *Ṭabaqāt* 5 : 270.

46. For Muᶜtazili faith in reason to answer questions of right and wrong, *v.* George F. Hourani, *Reason and Tradition in Islamic Ethics* (Cambridge: Univ. Press, 1985), and A. Kevin Reinhart, *Before Revelation: The Boundaries of Muslim Moral Thought*, SUNY Series in Middle Eastern Studies (Albany: State Univ. of New York Press, 1995).

47. Michael Cook, *Commanding Right and Forbidding Wrong in Islamic Thought* (Cambridge: Univ. Press, 2000), 344, 401fn.

48. The final anecdote in Yāqūt's biography makes the point that Māwardī's own *ijtihād* occasionally led him to agree with the Muᶜtazilah: *Irshād*, ed. Margoliouth, 5 : 408–409; ed. ᶜAbbās, 5 : 1956–1957. Besides agreement, Ibn al-Ṣalāḥ also points out an instance of disagreement with the Muᶜtazilah, *Ṭabaqāt*, 642. Cf. al-Dhahabī, *Mīzān al-iᶜtidāl*, s.n. ᶜAlī ibn Muḥammad ibn Ḥabīb, affirming that Māwardī's own reasoning (*ijtihād*) sometimes led him to agree with the Muᶜtazilah on particular doctrines without his becoming an adherent of their party in general.

49. Little, "A New Look," 10–11.

50. Cook has deliberately looked for it and found none: *Commanding*, 344, n. 41. For some undemonstrated characterizations of Māwardī as an Ashᶜari, *v.* H. A. R. Gibb, "Some Considerations of the Sunni Theory of the Caliphate," *Studies*, 141–150 (originally in *Archives d'histoire du droit oriental* 3 [1939]: 401–410), at 142, and Riḍwān al-Sayyid, introduction to Māwardī, *Tas'hīl al-naẓar*, ed. al-Sayyid (Beirut: al-Markaz al-Islāmī lil-Buḥūth and Dār al-ᶜUlūm al-ᶜArabīyah, 1987; repr. n.d.), 31.

his known works are extant, and most of them draw heavily on the Persian and Hellenistic traditions. Others, however, notably *al-Aḥkām al-sulṭānīyah*, his qurʾanic commentary *al-Nukat wa-al-ʿuyūn*, and the monumental *al-Ḥāwī al-kabīr* on Shāfiʿi law, hew strictly to the Arabo-Islamic tradition. I am inclined to suppose that Māwardī put away the Persian and Hellenistic traditions as the Sunni revival progressed and he transferred his principal loyalties from the Būyids to the caliph.

As for Māwardī's personal character, we have just one report from a close associate, who apparently taught law as his deputy (*darrasa makānah*) for five years: "I never saw anyone more sedate than he. I never heard from him any jest and I never saw his forearm from the time I became close to him until he departed from this world."[51] Nothing indicates that he was a Sufi, but he admired renunciation. In *Adab al-dunyā wa-al-dīn*, he observes with pride that it was the rule among Shāfiʿī's followers that if someone willed a third of his [48] property to *aʿqal al-nās*, those best under the control of reason, it would have to go to the renunciants (*zuhhād*).[52]

Abū Yaʿlá ibn al-Farrāʾ

Abū Yaʿlá ibn al-Farrāʾ, Muḥammad ibn al-Ḥusayn, was the son and grandson of jurisprudents, although his grandfather Muḥammad (d. 390/999–1000) had adhered to the Ḥanafi school of law, being a disciple to al-Jaṣṣāṣ al-Rāzī (d. 370/981), chief of the Ḥanafi school in Baghdad in his day. (Brockelmann suggests that his *ʿurf* be *Ibn al-Farrāʾ*, but I refer to him rather as *Abū Yaʿlá*, first because this is far more usual in Ḥanbali literature, secondly because modern Arabophone scholarship sometimes makes him out to be simply *al-Farrāʾ*.) His father had transferred to the Ḥanbali school under Ibn Ḥāmid.[53] He was born on 28 Muḥarram 380/27 April 990 and died on 19 Ramaḍān 458/14 August 1066.[54]

Abū Yaʿlá's principal teacher in law was Ibn Ḥāmid. Elsewhere, I have counted references to earlier jurisprudents in a highly detailed survey of disagreements within the Ḥanbali school, the *Inṣāf* of al-Mardāwī (d. Damascus, 885/1480).[55] Abū Yaʿlá is there the seventh most often-cited authority, the only one in the top twenty who died in the elev-

51. Yāqūt, *Irshād*, ed. Margoliouth, 5 : 408; ed. ʿAbbās, 5 : 1956.

52. Māwardī, *Adab al-dunyā wa-al-dīn*, ed. Muḥammad Karīm Rājiḥ (Beirut: Dār Iqraʾ, 1401/1981), 19; ed. ʿAbd Allāh Aḥmad Abū Zīnah, 3 vols. (Cairo: Muʾassasat Dār al-Shaʿb, 1979–1980), 1 : 34.

53. For the Ḥanbali school in this period, *v.* Henri Laoust, "Le Hanbalisme sous le califat de Bagdad (241/855–656/1258)," *Revue des études islamiques* 27 (1959): 67–128. On Ibn Ḥāmid, *v.* Laoust, "Califat," 93–94, to whose references add Dhahabī, *Siyar* 17 : 203–204.

54. The principal pre-modern biography is Ibn Abī Yaʿlá, *Ṭabaqāt* 2 : 171–177. The principal modern studies are Makdisi, *Ibn ʿAqīl*, 232–237, and Abū Fāris, *al-Qāḍī Abū Yaʿlá*.

55. Christopher Melchert, "The Relation of Ibn Taymiyya and Ibn Qayyim al-Jawziyya to the Ḥanbali School of Law," forthcoming in a collection edited by Birgit Krawietz and Georges Tamer [*HPL 16]; al-Mardāwī, *al-Inṣāf fī maʿrifat al-rājiḥ min al-khilāf*, ed. Muḥammad Ḥāmid al-Fiqī, 12 vols. (Cairo: Maṭbaʿat

enth century CE and second to only one earlier authority, Aḥmad ibn Ḥanbal himself. His students Abū al-Khaṭṭāb [49] al-Kalwadhānī (d. Baghdad, 510/1116) and Ibn ʿAqīl (d. Baghdad, 513/1119) come in eighth and fourteenth, respectively. His significance for the Ḥanbali school seems to be even greater in *uṣūl al-fiqh* than in *furūʿ*, for there was virtually no tradition of writing *uṣūl al-fiqh* in the Ḥanbali school before him. From his time forward, there was such a tradition. Somewhat like his younger contemporary al-Bājī (d. Almeria, 474/1081), who started the Māliki tradition of *uṣūl al-fiqh*, he seems to have derived his idea of how to write *uṣūl* from the Shāfiʿi tradition rather than the Ḥanafi.[56]

In theology, Abū Yaʿlá composed refutations of the Ashʿarīyah, Karāmīyah, Sālimīyah, incarnationists, and an Ibn al-Labbān, meaning probably ʿAbd Allāh ibn Muḥammad (d. Isfahan, 446/1054), a Shāfiʿi in law but a disciple in theology to the leading Ashʿari Abū Bakr al-Bāqillānī (d. Baghdad, 403/1013).[57] However, it appears that further research is needed to determine Abū Yaʿlá's theological inclination, for despite reports of his refuting Ashʿarīyah, also of his inserting occasional Ḥanbali positions into an essentially Muʿtazili framework, some of his theological writings appear to advocate characteristically Ashʿari positions.[58] My guess is that, like Māwardī, he was fundamentally eclectic but inclined towards Muʿtazilism more than Ashʿarism.

As discussed above, Abū Yaʿlá may have written an epitome of Ḥanbali law for the caliph al-Qādir. He certainly came to that caliph's attention when he published his theological treatise *Ibṭāl taʾwīl al-ṣifāt*, which piled up hadith against non-literal interpretations of [50] apparently anthropomorphic hadith. Against Ashʿari and Muʿtazili practice, he called for relating such hadith reports just as they had come without explanation.[59] It pleased al-Qādir but aroused violent opposition, which the vizier Ibn al-Maslamah intervened to

al-Sunnah al-Muḥammadīyah, 1955–1958, repr. with new pagination Beirut: Dār Iḥyāʾ al-Turāth al-ʿArabī, 1419/1998).

56. On the Shāfiʿi and Ḥanafi traditions of *uṣūl al-fiqh*, *v.* A. Kevin Reinhart, "«Like the Difference Between Heaven and Earth:» Ḥanafī and Shāfiʿī Discussions of *farḍ* and *wājib* in Theology and Uṣūl," *Studies in Islamic Legal Theory*, ed. Bernard Weiss, Islamic Law and Society 15 (Leiden: Brill, 2002), 205–234, esp. 205–206.

57. Abū Yaʿlá's works are listed by Ibn Abī Yaʿlá, *Ṭabaqāt* 2 : 205–206. On Ibn al-Labbān, *v.* Dhahabī, *Siyar* 17 : 653 with further references. A hostile source reports that Abū Yaʿlá and another leading Ḥanbali read *uṣūl* for a time under Ibn al-Labbān's direction: Ibn ʿAsākir, *Tabyīn kadhib al-muftarī* (Damascus: Maṭbaʿat al-Tawfīq, 1347), 262.

58. On Muʿtazilism, *v.* Cook, *Commanding*, 130–138. For one essentially Ashʿari position, *v.* Daniel Gimaret, "Théories de l'acte humain dans l'école Ḥanbalite," *Revues d'études orientales* 29 (1977): 157–178, at 161–165.

59. Said to have been published as Abū Yaʿlá, *Ibṭāl al-taʾwīlāt li-akhbār al-ṣifāt*, ed. Abū ʿAbd Allāh Muḥammad ibn Ḥamd al-Ḥamūd al-Najdī (Kuwait: Dār Īlāf al-Dawlah, 1410/1989); available also as ed. Muḥammad ʿUthmān (Beirut: Dār al-Kutub al-ʿIlmīyah, 2009).

quiet. The caliph subsequently appointed Abū Yaʿlá qadi for the caliphal palace and its quarters for women, also Ḥarrān and Ḥulwān in Mesopotamia (modern northern Iraq).[60]

Like Māwardī, Abū Yaʿlá was involved in more than law. The list of his works includes treatments of the Qurʾan, Arabic, theology, piety, and history. A larger proportion of his works have been lost than of Māwardī's, but the list of titles surely indicates that he wrote always within the Arabo-Islamic tradition without venturing into Persian and Hellenistic wisdom.

Al-Aḥkām al-sulṭānīyah

Māwardī's *Aḥkām* and Abū Yaʿlá's are so close that either one must be a rewriting of the other or each must be a rewriting of some unknown original. (I shall henceforth refer to Māwardī's version as *MAS*, Abū Yaʿlá's as *YAS*.) They are very nearly the same length. The significance of the parallel is twofold. First, of course, it would diminish Māwardī's modern reputation if Abū Yaʿlá turned out to have written his version first, Māwardī on its pattern. Secondly, and regardless of which came first, agreement between the two texts ought to show us which ideas were widely held in eleventh-century Baghdad (at least in the Sunni community), while disagreement shows us which ideas were disputed.

To show how close the two versions are, here are some sample parallels. This first concerns the removal of a caliph (*MAS*, 31 *17* [but these are my own translations];*YAS*, 28): [51]

When the imam has undertaken [to satisfy] the claims (*ḥuqūq*) of the community such as we have mentioned, he renders the claim of God (be he exalted) as to what is for and against them. He has two claims on them: obedience and aid, so long as his state has not changed. What makes his state change and puts him out of the imamate are two things. One is some moral derangement (*jarḥ fī ʿadālatih*). The second is bodily weakness. As for moral derangement, meaning viciousness (*fisq*), it is of two kinds: one is that he indulges desire, the second is what depends on an ambiguity.

When the imam has undertaken [to satisfy] the claims (*ḥuqūq*) of the community, he has two claims on them: obedience and aid, so long as there is not found on his part what puts him out of the imamate. What puts him out of the imamate are two things: moral derangement (*jarḥ fī ʿadālatih*) and bodily weakness, which we have already explained. As for religious derangement (*al-jarḥ fī dīnih*), we have related the talk of Aḥmad (God—be he exalted—have mercy on him) concerning that, meaning what the soundness of the imamate involves.

60. Dhahabī, *Siyar* 18 : 90.

Māwardī explains shortly that 'ambiguity' refers to heterodox belief based on some ambiguity in Scripture. As often, Māwardī does not here seem committed to any one school of law whereas Abū Yaᶜlá plainly writes as a Ḥanbali.

Here they are on the problem, mentioned above, of whether one may require a qadi to rule according to a particular school (*MAS* 111 *75*; *YAS*, 63):

It is permissible for one who believes in the doctrine of al-Shāfiᶜī (God have mercy on him) to bestow the judgeship on one who believes in the doctrine of Abū Ḥanīfah, for the qadi may exercise his judgement (*lil-qāḍī an yajtahida bi-raʾyih*) in his decision. He is not bound to follow, in his cases and rulings, one to whose school he adheres.

It is permissible for one who believes in the doctrine of Aḥmad to bestow the judgeship on one who believes in the doctrine of al-Shāfiᶜī, for the qadi must exercise his judgement (*ᶜalá al-qāḍī an yajtahida bi-raʾyih*) in his decision. He is not bound to follow, in his cases and rulings, one to whose school he adheres.

In this instance, the legal discussion is almost identical with only the names changed. Māwardī, as usual, has avoided mentioning Aḥmad.

Finally, here they are on the problem of what to do with conquered territory (*MAS* 217 *152*; *YAS*, 146): [52]

As for territories that the Muslims have conquered, they fall into three divisions. The first is what has been taken by force and violence, such that they have departed from it by death, capture, or evacuation. The jurisprudents have disagreed over the legal category to which it belongs after the Muslims' conquering it. Al-Shāfiᶜī (God be pleased with him) taught that it is spoil like chattel, to be divided amongst its spoilers unless they prefer to leave it, in which case it becomes a trust (*tūqafu*) for the benefit of the Muslims. Mālik held that it becomes a trust for the Muslims at the time it is spoiled and that it is not permissible to divide it among the spoilers. Abū Ḥanīfah held that the leader has the choice whether to divide it among the spoilers, so that it becomes tithe land, to return it to the protected people, or to make it a trust (*yaqifahā*) for all the Muslims. It becomes the House of Islam whether the Muslims inhabit it or the polytheists are returned to it.

As for territories that the Muslims have conquered, they fall into three divisions. The first is what has been taken by force and violence, such that they have departed from it by death, capture, or evacuation. Concerning it there are two versions. One is that it becomes spoil like chattel, to be divided amongst its spoilers unless they prefer to leave it, in which case it becomes a trust (*tūqafu*) for the benefit of the Muslims. Aḥmad's (God, be he exalted, have mercy on him) exact words are "Every territory taken by force belongs to whoever fought for it, as with chattel: four shares are for whoever fought for it and one share for God and his Messenger and those near and the orphans and poor, as with chattel." This was transmitted by al-Khallāl in *al-Amwāl*. The second is that the leader has the choice whether to divide it among the spoilers, so that it becomes tithe land, to make it a trust (*yaqifahā*) for all the Muslims. It becomes the House of Islam whether the Muslims inhabit it or the polytheists are returned to it. Aḥmad's exact words concerning that are "The land, if it is taken by force, belongs to whoever fought for it unless the one who conquered it made it a trust (*waqafahā*) for the Muslims, as ʿUmar did to Lower Iraq and imposed on it the *kharāj*."

Abū Yaʿlá goes on to relate two other versions of what Aḥmad said, both of them expressly attributed, and quotes the earlier Ḥanbali Abū Bakr ibn ʿAbd al-ʿAzīz, better known as Ghulām al-Khallāl (d. 363/974).[61] In this passage, again, Abū Yaʿlá plainly writes as a Ḥanbali, whereas Māwardī seems only weakly committed to the Shāfiʿi school (he does put it first) and mainly concerned to present the spectrum of non-Ḥanbali opinion.

[53] The most striking difference between the two books is to me that *YAS* reads as a conventional exposé of Ḥanbali law. Inasmuch as *MAS* systematically surveys the positions of the three non-Ḥanbali schools, it is unconventional. Presumably, this unconventionality has not struck earlier writers first because they have not been specialists in Islamic law, secondly because they have been looking not for law but political theory. Māwardī also quotes poetry from time to time, unlike Abū Yaʿlá, and retells stories from the lifetime of the Prophet sometimes, it appears, in the spirit of *adab*, prizing miscellany and out-of-the-way knowledge.

As for which work is earlier, Ibn Rajab (d. 795/1393) has been noticed quoting Abū Yaʿlá as saying something "following Māwardī (*mutābaʿatan lil-Māwardī*)"; that is, acknowledging Māwardī's priority.[62] Actually, though, *mutābaʿah* in hadith science indicates corroboration, quoting somebody the same way from another source, which does not imply priority one way or the other. Among modern writers, Laoust and Little are neutral, merely calling for further, deeper study. So is Muḥammad Ḥāmid al-Fiqī, editor of *YAS*.

The fullest discussion of the question has been that of Abū Fāris.[63] He observes that ʿAbd Allāh Muṣṭafá al-Marāghī held that Abū Yaʿlá must have written first, Ṣubḥī al-Ṣāliḥ that Māwardī must have, although tentatively and without presenting his evidence.[64]

61. On whom *v.* Laoust, "Califat," 90.

62. Ibn Rajab, *al-Istikhrāj li-aḥkām al-kharāj* (Cairo: al-Maṭbaʿah al-Islāmīyah, 1932), 116, cited by Fuʾād ʿAbd al-Munʿim, introduction to Māwardī (attrib.), *al-Tuḥfah al-mulūkīyah fī al-ādāb al-siyāsīyah* (Alexandria: Muʾassasat Shabāb al-Jāmiʿah, 1978), 27.

63. Abū Fāris, *al-Qāḍī Abū Yaʿlá*, esp. 499–540.

64. Abū Fārīs, *al-Qāḍī*, 517, 520–521, citing ʿAbd Allāh Muṣṭafá al-Marāghī, *al-Fatḥ al-mubīn fī ṭabaqāt al-uṣūlīyīn*, 3 vols. in 1 (Beirut: Muḥammad Amīn Damj wa-Shurakāʾuh, 1974), 1 : 253, and Ṣubḥī al-Ṣāliḥ, *al-Nuẓum al-islāmīyah* (Beirut: Dār al-ʿIlm lil-Malāyīn, 1965), 520–521.

Abū Fāris himself thinks Māwardī wrote first. He interprets Māwardī's introduction to *MAS* as implying that it was commissioned by the caliph, who he thinks must have been al-Qādir, which means it was written in 422/1031 or before, when Māwardī was mature but not Abū Yaʿlá (522). Māwardī's political involvements must have equipped him to write such a book, and he wrote another called *Qawānīn al-wizārah* [54] (522–523). He disbelieves that the caliph would have benefitted from an exposition of the rules of just one school, which is all the Abū Yaʿlá furnishes (524). Finally, *YAS* continually says "It has been said" and what follows is more or less exactly what *MAS* says (527–537).

I would argue rather for the priority of Abū Yaʿlá's version. The first reason is that Abū Yaʿlá states in his introduction that the basis for *al-Aḥkām al-sulṭānīyah* was his own earlier work, *al-Muʿtamad*. Māwardī states in his introduction that he thought to write a book for the benefit of the subject, mainly the caliph, that he may know the jurists' doctrines (*madhāhib al-fuqahāʾ*). If Abū Yaʿlá wrote first, it is possible to believe both of these statements, whereas if he actually wrote his book mainly on the basis of Māwardī's, we must accuse him of serious dissimulation. Abū Yaʿlá's *Muʿtamad* is no longer extant, but an abridgement by Abū Yaʿlá himself is extant and has been published. It does include a substantial section on the imamate, although its structure and wording are admittedly different from those of *al-Aḥkām al-sulṭānīyah*.[65]

Secondly, I would point to al-Qādir's active endorsement of a system of four Sunni schools, overlooked (to my knowledge) by all previous writers on *MAS*. It seems doubtful whether he would have welcomed an account of just three schools unless it complemented an account he already had of the fourth. Thirdly, we know that the renascent caliphate was particularly allied with the Ḥanābilah. The Qādiri creed, publicly reaffirmed by al-Qāʾim, sometimes endorses not just Sunni but peculiarly Ḥanbali positions. For example, with the Ḥanābilah, it states that one who willingly omits to pray thereby becomes an apostate, liable to capital punishment. This is to disagree with the Ḥanafīyah, who do not consider it a capital offence, and the Mālikīyah and Shāfiʿīyah, who do call for capital punishment but consider it a *ḥadd* penalty, the offender never ceasing to be a Muslim.[66] [55] Contrary to what Abū Fāris thinks, it is thus easy to see why Abū Yaʿlá should have written an account of the Ḥanbali law of governance for al-Qādir, who promulgated a specifically Ḥanbali creed, even more for al-Qāʾim, who publicly endorsed the same creed and was so well impressed by Abū Yaʿlá's *Ibṭāl taʾwīl al-ṣifāt*. It is likewise easy to see why either caliph might have actively solicited an account of Ḥanbali law from Abū Yaʿlá. It is

65. Abū Yaʿlá, *Kitāb al-Muʿtamad fī uṣūl al-dīn*, ed. Wadi Z. Haddad, Recherches, n.s., A. Langue arabe et pensée islamique, 8 (Beirut: Dar el-Machreq, 1974), 222–255.

66. For the Qādiri creed, *v.* Ibn al-Jawzī, *Muntaẓam*, s.a. 433; for the positions of the different schools on *tārik al-ṣalāh*, *v.* most conveniently Ibn Rushd, *Bidāyat al-mujtahid wa-nihāyat al-muqtaṣid*, *k. al-ṣalāh*, *al-jumlah al-ūlá*, *al-masʾalah al-rābiʿah*, also *MAS*, 339 *241*, and *YAS*, 261.

harder, again, to see why Māwardī should have thought either caliph wanted an account of the three non-Ḥanbali schools unless he already had one of the Ḥanbali.

The usual modern argument for Māwardī is that *MAS* is more consistent with what else is known of his work. Abū Yaʿlá wrote no other work treating the vizierate, for example, whereas Māwardī did.[67] To the contrary, however, one might argue that *MAS* is no closer to the rest of Māwardī's works than *YAS* is to the rest of Abū Yaʿlá's, for Māwardī's other works on politics frequently draw on the Hellenistic and imperial Persian traditions, whereas *MAS* is entirely Arabo-Islamic. Māwardī periodically cites the opinions of anonymous *ʿulamāʾ* (scholars, especially jurisprudents) and *mutakallimīn* (theologians) of Basra, suggesting that the *Aḥkām* is a relatively early work, from when he was new to Baghdad. The earlier in life Māwardī wrote his version, the more likely it is that his was first, since he was born about 16 years before Abū Yaʿlá. On the other hand, *contra* Abū Fāris, its stress on the caliph and his claims fits better the latter part of Māwardī's life, when he himself was close to the caliph and when the caliph was reasserting his authority, especially to name deputies. Its neglect of the Hellenistic and Persian traditions also fits better the latter part of his life, when the Sunni reaction was more advanced. I would follow Laoust in supposing that Māwardī wrote it between 437 and 450 (1045–1058).[68]

As for the crucial question of whether it was like Māwardī to ignore the Ḥanbali school, comparison with *al-Ḥāwī al-kabīr* suggests not, although I cannot say it does overwhelmingly. Admittedly, that is, the *Ḥāwī* often does ignore Ḥanbali views. For example, *MAS* states that it is recommended but not required to perform all five [56] daily ritual prayers in assembly according to all the jurisprudents except Dāwūd (al-Ẓāhirī, d. 270/884), who alone required them unless there was some excuse (*MAS*, 158 *112*). *YAS* states that it is recommended but not required to perform all five daily ritual prayers in assembly according to many of the jurisprudents but required by Aḥmad and Dāwūd (*YAS*, 94). In the *Ḥāwī*, Māwardī states that it is recommended but not required to perform all five daily ritual prayers in assembly according to all the jurisprudents except Dāwūd ibn ʿAlī, the traditionists (*aṣḥāb al-ḥadīth*), and the Meccan Follower ʿAṭāʾ (d. 114/732–733?).[69] Aḥmad is included here in the category of "the traditionists," but Māwardī does not expressly name him.

67. For example, this is the opinion of Wilferd Madelung: "The priority between the books on the rules of government (*aḥkām sulṭāniyya*) by the Shāfiʿī al-Māwardī and the Ḥanbalī Abū Yaʿlā al-Farrāʾ is not disputed.... Al-Māwardī's is generally recognized as his own work, composed by him in line with other related books by him. Abū Yaʿlā largely plagiarized al-Māwardī's book in order to match it with a parallel version reflecting Ḥanbalī doctrine" (review of Frank Griffel, *Apostasie und Toleranz*, *Journal of the American Oriental Society* 123 [2003]: 177–179, at 178).

68. Laoust, "Pensée," 15.

69. Māwardī, *al-Ḥāwī al-kabīr*, ed. Maḥmūd al-Maṭrajī, & al., 24 vols. (Beirut: Dār al-Fikr, 1414/1994), 2 : 378; ed. ʿAlī Muḥammad Muʿawwaḍ and ʿĀdil Aḥmad ʿAbd al-Mawjūd, 20 vols. (Beirut: Dār al-Kutub al-ʿIlmīyah, 1414/1994), 2 : 297 (henceforward, citations of this edn. in *italics*).

Elsewhere, Māwardī even more obviously omits to mention Ḥanbali opinions. *MAS* explains that land taken by force is divided up among its conquerors according to Shāfiʿī, like other booty; becomes *waqf* for the Muslims according to Mālik; and may be divided or become *waqf* at the discretion of the *imām* according to Abū Ḥanīfah (*MAS*, 217 *152*). *YAS* quotes two versions of what Aḥmad said, one in favour of division, the other in favour of *waqf* (*YAS*, 146–7). In the *Ḥāwī*, Māwardī first gives the Shāfiʿi rule, that land taken by force is divided up among its conquerors, then later states that it is divided like other booty according to Shāfiʿī; becomes *waqf* for all the Muslims according to Mālik and al-Awzāʿī (d. 157/773–4?); and may be divided or become *waqf* at the discretion of the *imām* according to Abū Ḥanīfah.[70] I have found that the *Ḥāwī* often provides more detail in this way than *MAS* (e.g. the positions of ʿAṭā and Awzāʿī) while still overlooking the Ḥanbali position, which confirms that *MAS* is unusually focused on the three non-Ḥanbali schools, ignoring earlier, non-affiliated jurisprudents.[71] But it would admittedly be more [57] convenient for my argument if I found that the *Ḥāwī* regularly mentions Ḥanbali positions where *MAS* overlooks them.

On the other hand, Māwardī certainly does mention Ḥanbali positions much more often in the *Ḥāwī* than in *MAS*. In a sample of 122 pages from *MAS*, here are the authorities most often cited:

Prophet	54 times.
Qurʾan	43 times.
Abū Ḥanīfah	38 times.
Companions	21 times.
Shāfiʿī	21 times.
Mālik	13 times.
Followers	12 times.

Aḥmad does not appear once in the sample. (In the whole of *MAS*, to judge by Wahba's index, he appears three times.) Here, by contrast, are the authorities most often cited in a sample of 128 pages from *al-Ḥāwī al-kabīr*:

Shāfiʿī	90 times.
Prophet	76 times.
Abū Ḥanīfah	33 times.

70. Māwardī, *Ḥāwī* 18 : 240, 301 *14 : 209, 260*.

71. e.g. Māwardī, *Ḥāwī* 3 : 114 *2 : 489–90*, on the number of extra *takbīrahs* in the two festival prayers (cf. *MAS* 165 *117*); *Ḥāwī* 4 : 161–2 *3 : 188*, on the *zakāh* owed on chattel (cf. *MAS* 181 *129*); *Ḥāwī* 9 : 321–2 *7 : 477–8*, on the ownership of reclaimed land (cf. *MAS*, 294 *208–9*); *Ḥāwī* 18 : 345–6 *14 : 299*, on the amount of the *jizyah* (cf. *MAS*, 229 *160*).

Qurʾan	29 times.
Companions	26 times.
Mālik	20 times.
Abū ʿAlī ibn Abī Hurayrah	8 times.
Aḥmad ibn Ḥanbal	7 times.

In the sample, Aḥmad is named a little less often than one of Māwardī's Shāfiʿi forebears, only a little more often than several others: Abū Isḥāq al-Marwazī (five times), Ibn Surayj (five times), al-Muzanī (three times), and others mentioned only once or twice. Still, he is not conspicuously absent as in *MAS*. Moreover, the *Ḥāwī* is an expressly Shāfiʿi work, a commentary on the *Mukhtaṣar* of al-Muzanī presumably intended first of all to train Shāfiʿi jurisprudents. This is why Māwardī names Shāfiʿī almost three times as often in the *Ḥāwī* as in *MAS*. By contrast, [58] *MAS* is expressly about the doctrines of the jurisprudents in general (*madhāhib al-fuqahāʾ*), with Abū Ḥanīfah named considerably more often than Shāfiʿī, which makes it all the harder to see why Ḥanbali opinions should there be systematically overlooked, unless they had already been expounded to the caliph in *YAS*.

Concerning politics, some specific disagreements can be found. For example, Māwardī is neutral as to whether the necessity of the imamate is known by reason or revelation (*ʿaql, sharʿ*), whereas Abū Yaʿlá is certain that it comes by revelation (*samʿ*) alone, since reason cannot determine whether something is required or merely allowable (*MAS*, 13 *3*; *YAS*, 19). It is easy to see why Abū Yaʿlá's position might have been preferable to the caliph. On the other hand, Māwardī emphatically rejects the title *khalīfat Allāh*, adducing the overwhelming majority of jurisprudents (*jumhūr al-ʿulamāʾ*) who think it outrageous to call oneself "the deputy of God," whereas Abū Yaʿlá is neutral, merely laying out the two opposing views (*MAS*, 28–29 *15–16*; *YAS*, 27).[72] That Abū Yaʿlá should disagree with Māwardī on this point, despite Māwardī's talk of an overwhelming majority, probably indicates that modern scholars have emphasized it too heavily. Again, one supposes that the caliph would have preferred Abū Yaʿlá's position.

72. To the contrary, Māwardī quotes someone else (both Aristotle and Anūshirvān are credited with the saying elsewhere in the tradition) as saying "The king is the deputy of God in his country" without adverse comment in *Tasʾhīl al-naẓar wa-taʿjīl al-ẓafar fī akhlāq al-malik wa-siyāsat al-mulūk*, ed. Muḥyī Hilāl al-Sirḥān with Ḥasan al-Sāʿātī (Beirut: Dār al-Nahḍah al-ʿArabīyah, 1401/1981), 151; ed. Riḍwān al-Sayyid, 202; pointed out by Paul L. Heck, "Law in ʿAbbasid Political Thought," *ʿAbbasid Studies*, ed. James E. Montgomery, Orientalia Lovaniensia Analecta 135 (Leuven: Peeters, 2004), 83–109, at 91, 95fn. *V.* esp. 87–94 for Heck's discussion of Māwardī, which unfortunately does not extend to *MAS*. I take it Māwardī's willingness in the *Tasʾhīl* to speak of the ruler as God's deputy, unwillingness in the *MAS*, shows mainly how incomplete, yet, was his integration of the Hellenistic wisdom tradition with the Islamic. It also seems an additional reason to doubt whether *MAS* was written early in Māwardī's career and to be cautious about the argument that *MAS* is more consistent with Māwardī's other works than *YAS* with Abū Yaʿlā's.

However, the most significant difference between the *MAS* and *YAS* for political theory seems to me to be what Little remarked 35 years ago, namely that Māwardī seems less reluctant than Abū Yaʿlá to countenance the removal of a wicked caliph.[73] Māwardī has a full section on removal, beginning with the declaration translated above. He goes on to, for example, the caliph's disqualifying himself by giving himself over to gross carnal appetite such that he does what is forbidden. According to some *mutakallimīn* (dialectical theologians), he becomes caliph again as soon as he returns to uprightness without needing any renewed investiture (*MAS*, 31–36 *17–21*). Māwardī's younger Shāfiʿi contemporary Imām al-Ḥaramayn (d. 478/1085) would suggest still more strongly that a warlord might legitimately depose a caliph.[74] Living in Khurasan, he presumably had more to gain than Māwardī by flattering the Selchūqids and less to lose by offending the caliph.

Abū Yaʿlá makes virtually the same declaration, as we have seen. Instead of going on to a full explanation, though, he refers to his previous discussion, which actually, in the main, treats what to do if the caliph has been made prisoner by unbelievers or Muslim rebels. He also states just after reviewing the requisite characters of the imam that depravity (*fisq*) does not bar continuation in the imamate, whether this be a matter of external actions, such as drinking intoxicants, or erroneous belief, such as the doctrine that the Qurʾan is create (*YAS*, 20).[75] This reluctance to discuss removal is in line with a long tradition of Ḥanbali quietism and loyalty to the reigning caliph, as when Aḥmad ibn Ḥanbal refused to join Aḥmad ibn Naṣr al-Khuzāʿī's rebellion against al-Wāthiq in 231/846.[76] Abū Yaʿlá's version is significantly more convenient for the caliph and presumptively closer to the caliph's own thinking.

The theme of this colloquium is *prosperity and stagnation*. Māwardī and Abū Yaʿlá are both examples of personal prosperity. Māwardī was [60] the provincial who met major success at the capital (like his Shāfiʿi rival Abū al-Ṭayyib al-Ṭabarī). *MAS* directs the caliph's attention to the wider world, where Ḥanbalism is not established. Abū Yaʿlá's prosperity is that of the Baghdadi Ḥanbali school, loyally supporting the caliph against the pretensions of warlords from the provinces and elevated to special favour in return.

To my mind, the durability of Islamic law as taught by the four Sunni schools represents prosperity, too, for the larger Sunni community. *YAS* and the rest of Abū Yaʿlá's work effected the arrival of the Ḥanbali school, recognized by the caliph and at last comparable to the Ḥanafi, Māliki, and Shāfiʿi in having a comprehensive code and a theory of

73. Little, "A New Look," 13–14.

74. Wael B. Hallaq, "Caliphs, Jurists and the Saljūqs in the Political Thought of Juwaynī," *Muslim World* 74 (1984): 26–41.

75. *V.* also Abū Yaʿlá, *Muʿtamad*, 242–245, 249, where wickedness such as wrongful expropriation of property and maltreatment of persons is emphatically rejected as a justification for removing an imam.

76. On Aḥmad ibn Naṣr, *v. EI2*, s.v. "Miḥna," by M. Hinds, to whose references add Dhahabī, *Siyar* 11 : 166, with further references. On Ḥanbali quietism, *v.* Cook, *Commanding Right*, chaps. 5, 6.

how it was generated (that is, a Ḥanbali version of *uṣūl al-fiqh*). *MAS*, by insisting on three schools while ignoring alternatives (e.g. Awzāʿī, Sufyān al-Thawrī, and Abū Thawr), likewise marks the triumph of the caliphal model of four Sunni schools. The schools endured caliphal indifference in the early tenth century, caliphal decline in the rest of the tenth, caliphal revival in the eleventh and twelfth, then even the extinction of the caliphate at the Mongol conquest. The system of revealed law, maintained by the schools, was the principal institution holding together Islamic cities in the High Middle Ages.[77] Dynasties came and went, but society continued as shaped by the law. The schools are much attenuated today, but no alternative has come to take their place.

On the other hand, if the Sunni Revival prospered the schools of law, it also apparently constricted the range of accepted cultural styles. Māwardī's turn away from the Persian and Hellenistic wisdom literature he had so often exploited in his earlier works is an example of this constriction. That the most famous work of medieval political thought should be not a treatise on the theory of government but a work of law, reviewing the rules to be followed in various government bureaux with practically no concern to expound either basic principles or the possibility of new ways, is perhaps a sign that stagnation had [61] already set in. Māwardī's and Abū Yaʿlá's defence is that, after all, it was not until early modern times that anyone thought of stagnation as anything but the preferable alternative to degeneration and decline. A work laying down the customary rules was just the thing to delay unwelcome change.

77. Marshall G. S. Hodgson, *The Venture of Islam*, 3 vols. (Chicago: Univ. Press, 1973), 2 : 119. "The other two integrative institutions," he goes on, "the waqf foundations and the Ṣûfî ṭarîqahs, were themselves finally dependent on Sharʿî norms for their social viability."

16

THE RELATION OF IBN TAYMIYYA AND IBN QAYYIM AL-JAWZIYYA TO THE ḤANBALI SCHOOL OF LAW

Ibn Taymiyya and Ibn Qayyim al-Jawziyya were famously adherents of the Ḥanbalī school of law. Abdul Hakim Al-Matroudi has published a book on what the Ḥanbalī school meant to Ibn Taymiyya.[1] My first project here is to determine what Ibn Taymiyya and Ibn Qayyim al-Jawziyya meant to the late-medieval Ḥanbalī school itself, especially as concerns its characteristic rules. My second project is to characterize Ibn al-Qayyim's jurisprudence, especially what the Ḥanbalī school meant to him. Like the other Sunni schools of law (the Ḥanafī, Shāfiʿī, and Mālikī), the Ḥanbalī school was partly an institution for forming jurisprudents. Being Ḥanbalī meant that Ibn Taymiyya and Ibn al-Qayyim had studied under Ḥanbalī teachers who in time had certified them as competent to issue juridical opinions (fatwas) in the Ḥanbalī tradition. In their day, no attention would be paid to opinions from anyone who had not been so certified as competent in one or another of the Ḥanafī, Shāfiʿī, Mālikī, and Ḥanbalī traditions.[2] Those discursive traditions are the second main

1. Al-Matroudi, Abdul Hakim I.: *The Ḥanbalī School of Law and Ibn Taymiyyah. Culture and Civilization in the Middle East*, London 2006.

2. On the school of law as an institution for forming and certifying jurisprudents, see above all Makdisi, George: *The Rise of Colleges. Institutions of Learning in Islam and the West*, Edinburgh 1981, chapters 1–3, pp. 1–223, esp. pp. 1–9.

Originally published as "The Relation of Ibn Taymiyya and Ibn Qayyim al-Jawziyya and the Ḥanbali School of Law." In *Islamic Theology, Philosophy and Law: Debating Ibn Taymiyya and Ibn Qayyim al-Jawziyya.* Edited by Birgit Krawietz and Georges Tamer with Alina Kokoschka. Studien zur Geschichte des islamischen Orients, n.F. 27 (Berlin: de Gruyter, 2013), 146–61.

constitutive element of the Sunni school of laws. The theory of Islamic law that prevailed from at least 1000 CE is that God has revealed his will for mankind through the Koran and the word and deed of the Prophet. On some points, God has deigned to make the evidence is so clear that no dissent is allowed; e.g. the requirement to perform the ritual prayer five times a day. On most points, God has given us more ambiguous evidence of his will, admitting of multiple legitimate interpretations. Sometimes a school will agree on some point in opposition to all the rest; for example, the [147] Ḥanafiyya (adherents of the Ḥanafī school) raise their hands only at the beginning of the ritual prayer, adherents of the other Sunni schools at multiple other points in the course of it as well. More often, there will be disagreement within the school; for example, at those points of the prayer where one needs to recite the Koran aloud, the Ḥanafiyya disagree whether it suffices to recite loudly enough to hear oneself or only if someone else can hear, too. A full treatment of the rules of Islamic law (a book of many volumes) will normally provide arguments in favour of the rules identified by the author's own school, also review disagreement within that school, sometimes expressing a preference for one or another position but sometimes leaving internal disagreements unresolved. Being Ḥanbalī also meant, then, that Ibn Taymiyya and Ibn al-Qayyim wrote books identifying the range of opinion within the Ḥanbalī school and expressing their preferences.[3]

To judge by how often he is cited in an encyclopaedia of Ḥanbalī opinions from the late fifteenth century, it appears that the Ḥanbalī school after him regarded Ibn Taymiyya as a significant figure but less than some others. Numerous other Ḥanbalī jurisprudents, both earlier and later than he, effectively did more to shape the peculiar range of opinions that defined the school. By contrast, Ibn al-Qayyim attracted little attention from later Ḥanbalī jurisprudents, even with regard to juridical problems that he treated at length with special stress on Ḥanbalī positions. The reason for the difference in their effects on the Ḥanbalī tradition, respectively modest and negligible, seems to be that Ibn Taymiyya made a greater show of respecting the Ḥanbalī discursive tradition, whereas Ibn al-Qayyim too often ignored it in favour of what he took to be the positions of the school's eponym, Aḥmad b. Ḥanbal (d. 241/855).

The chief means I propose to measure the importance of Ibn Taymiyya and Ibn al-Qayyim to the Ḥanbalī school is to count citations of earlier Ḥanābila (adherents of that school) in an encyclopaedia of disagreement [148] within the school by ʿAlāʾ al-Dīn ʿAlī

3. For certain and uncertain questions in Islamic law, see Weiss, Bernard G.: *The Spirit of Islamic Law. The Spirit of the Laws*, Athens 1998. For the schools of law as discursive traditions, see Calder, Norman: The Law (in History of Islamic Philosophy), in: Seyyed Hossein Nasr and Oliver Leaman (eds.): *History of Islamic Philosophy*, London 1996, vol. 2, pp. 979–998, and Hallaq, Wael B.: *Authority, Continuity and Change in Islamic Law*, Cambridge 2001, chapter 2; also, for adherence to schools in Damascus a century or two before Ibn Taymiyya and Ibn al-Qayyim, Talmon-Heller, Daniella: Fidelity, Cohesion, and Conformity within Madhhabs in Zangid and Ayyubid Syria, in: Peri Bearman, Rudolph Peters, and Frank E. Vogel (eds.): *The Islamic School of Law*, Cambridge 2005, pp. 94–116.

b. Sulaymān al-Mardāwī (d. Damascus, 885/1480), *al-Inṣāf fī maʿrifat al-rājiḥ min al-khilāf ʿalā madhhab al-imām Aḥmad ibn Ḥanbal* (Doing Justice Concerning the Knowledge of What Predominates by Way of Disagreement in the School of Aḥmad b. Ḥanbal). This is formally a detailed commentary on Ibn Qudāma al-Maqdisī (d. Damascus, 620/1223), *al-Muqniʿ* (The Convincing).[4] I chose a sample of ten pages per volume (except for the last, of which about a third is given over to other texts), 116 altogether. The more someone is cited, the more important he presumptively was to the evolution of the Ḥanbalī juridical discourse.

Here is a summary of what I found, mainly the twenty-one authorities most often cited, with notes indicating names of books cited and references of first resort for biographical information.

1) Ibn Mufliḥ al-Qāqūnī, Muḥammad (d. Damascus, 763/1362).

256 citations, mostly of *al-Furūʿ* (The Branches). For biographical information, see Laoust, Henri: Le Hanbalisme sous les mamlouks bahrides (658–784/1260–1382), in: *Revue des études islamiques* 28 (1960), pp. 1–71, at pp. 68–69.

2) Ibn Qudāma, ʿAbd Allāh b. Aḥmad (d. Damascus, 620/1223).

225 citations, of *al-Mughnī* (That Which Relieves of Want), *al-Kāfī* (The Sufficient), etc., often as *al-Muṣannif* (the Author; since he wrote the book on which *al-Inṣāf* is a commentary). For biographical information, see Laoust, Henri: Le Hanbalisme sous le califat de Bagdad (241/855–656/1258), in: *Revue des études islamiques* 27 (1959), pp. 67–128, at pp. 124–125. [149]

3) Ibn Ḥamdān, Aḥmad (d. Cairo, 695/1295).

192 citations, of *al-Riʿāya al-kubrā* (The Greater Consideration) and *al-ṣughrā* (The Lesser Consideration). For biographical information, see Laoust, Bahrides, pp. 53–54.

4) Ibn Abī ʿUmar, ʿAbd al-Raḥmān (d. Damascus, 682/1283).

141 citations as *al-Shāriḥ* (The Commentator) or of *al-Sharḥ al-kabīr* (The Great Commentary on Ibn Qudāma, *al-Muqniʿ*). For biographical information, see Laoust, Bahrides, pp. 40–1.

4. I use al-Mardāwī, ʿAlāʾ al-Dīn ʿAlī b. Sulaymān: *al-Inṣāf fī maʿrifat al-rājiḥ min al-khilāf ʿalā madhhab al-imām Aḥmad ibn Ḥanbal*, ed. by Muḥammad Ḥāmid al-Fiqī, Cairo 1955–1958, as anonymously reworked and reprinted; Beirut 1419/1998. The edition of Abū ʿAbd Allāh Muḥammad Ḥasan Muḥammad Ḥasan Ismāʿīl al-Shāfiʿī, Beirut 1418/1997, seems to be superior, but not so as to affect my count of citations.

5) Ibn Ḥanbal, Aḥmad (d. Baghdad, 241/855).

135 citations, of which 51 (38 percent) with multiple, contradictory versions (*riwāyāt*) of what Ibn Ḥanbal said. For more on his jurisprudence, see Melchert, Christopher: *Ahmad ibn Hanbal*, Oxford 2006, chapter 3.

6) Al-Majd, Majd al-Dīn ʿAbd al-Salām b. ʿAbd Allāh (d. Harran, 652/1254?).

129 citations, of *al-Muḥarrar* (The Clarifier). For biographical information, see Laoust, Califat, p. 126.

7) Al-Qāḍī Abū Yaʿlā b. al-Farrāʾ, Muḥammad b. al-Ḥusayn (d. Baghdad, 458/1065).

111 citations, of *al-Mujarrad* (The Stripped Down) more than any other work but usually as *al-Qāḍī*. For more biographical information, see Laoust, Califat, pp. 96–98.

8) Abū al-Khaṭṭāb al-Kalwadhānī, Maḥfūẓ b. Aḥmad (d. Baghdad, 510/1116).

109 citations, of *al-Hidāya* (The Guidance), *al-Intiṣār* (Giving Victory), etc. For biographical information, see Laoust, Califat, pp. 102–103. [150]

9) ʿAbd al-Raḥmān b. Abī al-Qāsim, Basran (d. 684/1285).

95 citations, of *al-Ḥāwī al-ṣaghīr* (The Lesser Comprehensive) and *al-kabīr* (The Greater). For biographical information, see Ibn Rajab, ʿAbd al-Raḥmān b. Aḥmad: *K. al-Dhayl ʿalā tabaqāt al-ḥanābila*, ed. by Muḥammad Ḥāmid al-Fiqī, Cairo 1372/1952–53, reprint Beirut n.d., vol. 2, pp. 313–315.

10) Ibn Munajjā, Asʿad (Muḥammad?) (d. Damascus, 606/1209).

86 citations, of *al-Khulāṣa* (The Summary") and *Sharḥ* al-Hidāya (The Commentary on *al-Hidāya*). For biographical information, see Ibn Rajab, *al-Dhayl*, vol. 2, pp. 49–51.

11) Ibn al-Sarī al-Dujaylī, al-Ḥasan (Ḥusayn?) b. Yūsuf, Baghdadi (d. 732/1331).

81 citations, of *al-Wajīz* (The Concise). For biographical information, see Ibn Rajab, *Dhayl*, vol. 2, pp. 417–418.

12) ʿIzz al-Dīn al-Maqdisī, Muḥammad b. ʿAlī (d. Damascus, 820/1413).

67 citations, usually of *Naẓm al-mufradāt* (The Versification of *the Peculiar*), also as

shaykhunā (our Master). For biographical information, see al-ʿUlaymī, ʿAbd al-Raḥmān (d. Jerusalem, 927/1520–1521?): *al-Manhaj al-aḥmad fī tarājim aṣḥāb al-imām Aḥmad* (The Most Praiseworthy Way Concerning the Biographies of the Followers of the Leader Aḥmad), ed. by Riyāḍ ʿAbd al-Ḥamīd Murād, ʿAbd al-Qādir al-Arnaʾūṭ, Maḥmūd al-Arnaʾūṭ, Muḥyī al-Dīn Najīb, Ibrāhīm Ṣāliḥ, Ḥasan Ismāʿīl Muruwwa, Yāsīn Maḥmūd al-Khaṭīb and Walīd Yūsuf al-ʿĀnī, Beirut 1997, vol. 5, p. 203. Also adequate, to my knowledge, is the edition of *al-Manhaj al-aḥmad* by Muṣṭafā ʿAbd al-Qādir Aḥmad ʿAṭā, Beirut 1420/1999. Two earlier, two-volume editions by Muḥammad Muḥyī al-Dīn ʿAbd al-Ḥamīd, Cairo 1383/1963 and Beirut (ʿĀlam al-Kutub) 1403/1983, present only the first half of al-ʿUlaymī's work. [151]

13) Al-Sāmarrī, Muḥammad b. ʿAbd Allāh (d. Baghdad, 616/1219).

66 citations, of *al-Mustawʿib* (The Inclusive). For biographical information, see Laoust, Califat, p. 119.

14) Ibn ʿAqīl, ʿAlī (d. Baghdad, 513/1119).

63 citations, of *al-Funūn* (The Varieties), *al-Wāḍiḥ* (The Explainer), *al-Tadhkira* (The Reminder), etc., but usually by name. For biographical information, see Makdisi, George: *Ibn ʿAqīl et la résurgence de l'Islam traditionaliste au XIe siècle (Ve siècle de l'Hégire)*, Damascus 1963.

15) Ibn Qāḍī al-Jabal, Aḥmad b. al-Ḥasan (d. Damascus, 771/1370).

53 citations, of *al-Fāʾiq* (The Surpasser). For biographical information, see al-ʿUlaymī, *al-Manhaj al-aḥmad*, vol. 5, pp. 135–137.

16) Al-Zarkashī, Muḥammad b. ʿAbd Allāh (d. Cairo, 772/1370?).

47 citations, all by name. For biographical information, see al-ʿUlaymī, *al-Manhaj al-aḥmad*, vol. 5, pp. 137–138.

17) Fakhr al-Dīn b. Taymiyya, Muḥammad b. al-Khaḍir (d. Harran, 622/1225).

41 citations, of *al-Talkhīṣ* (The Summarizing). For biographical information, see Ibn Rajab, *al-Dhayl*, vol. 2, pp. 151–162.

18) Ibn Tamīm al-Ḥarrānī, Muḥammad (d. *ca.* 675/1276–1277).

39 citations, sometimes of *al-Mukhtaṣar* (The Epitome), but usually by name. For biographical information, see Ibn Rajab, *Dhayl*, vol. 2, p. 290. [152]

19) Ibn Taymiyya, Aḥmad b. ᶜAbd al-Ḥalīm (d. Damascus, 728/1328).

38 citations, always as *al-Shaykh Taqī al-Dīn*. For biographical information, see Al-Matroudi, *The Ḥanbalī School.*

20) Ibn Rajab, Abd al-Raḥmān b. Aḥmad (d. Damascus, 795/1393).

31 citations, of *al-Qawāᶜid al-fiqhiyya* (The Juristic Principles). For biographical information, see al-ᶜUlaymī, *al-Manhaj al-aḥmad*, vol. 5, pp. 168–171.

20) Al-Ādamī, Aḥmad b. Muḥammad al-Baghdādī (8th/14th?).

31 citations, of *al-Muntakhab* (The Selected), *al-Munawwar* (The Illuminated). For biographical information, see al-ᶜUlaymī, *al-Manhaj al-aḥmad*, vol. 5, p. 72.

As for the history of the Ḥanbalī school, the list suggests who were its most important figures, at least as expounders of Ḥanbalī law and from the viewpoint of the later 15th century. There are other ways of getting at who were the most important. Writing in the early twentieth century, Ibn Badrān states that the most important works of the Ḥanbalī school have been three: al-Khiraqī (d. Damascus, 334/945–946), *al-Mukhtaṣar* (The Epitome); ᶜAlāᵓ al-Dīn al-Mardāwī, *al-Tanqīḥ al-mushbiᶜ* (The Satiating Revision); and al-Futūḥī (d. Cairo, 972/1564–65?), *Muntahā al-irādāt* (The Ultimate of Wishes). From this point forward, people devoted themselves to this last and, from laziness and oblivion, abandoned other books. Then along came Mūsā al-Ḥujāwī (d. Cairo, 1051/1641), who wrote *al-Iqnāᶜ* (The Convincing). Ḥanbalī writers henceforward depended on these two books, by al-Futūḥī and al-Ḥujāwī.[5] This seems to be a list of leading textbooks for teach-

5. Ibn Badrān, ᶜAbd al-Qādir: *al-Madkhal ilā madhhab al-imām Aḥmad b. Ḥanbal* (The Entryway into the School of the Leader Aḥmad b. Ḥanbal"), Cairo n.d., p. 221 = ed. by ᶜAbd Allāh b. ᶜAbd al-Muḥsin al-Turkī, Beirut 1401/1981), pp. 434–435. Khiraqī's *Mukhtaṣar* was the first epitome of Ḥanbalī positions, whose publication provided the nascent Ḥanbalī school with a basis comparable to that provided to the Māliki school by the epitomes of Ibn ᶜAbd al-Ḥakam (d. Old Cairo, 214/829) and Abū Muṣᶜab al-Zuhrī (d. Medina, 242/857) and to the Shāfiᶜī by the epitomes of al-Buwayṭī (d. Baghdad, 231/846?) and al-Muzanī (d. Old Cairo, 264/877?). On their significance, see further Melchert, Christopher: The Formation of the Sunnī Schools of Law, in: Wael B. Hallaq (ed.): *The Formation of Islamic Law*, Aldershot 2004, pp. 351–366, at pp. 352–354. For biographical information concerning al-Khiraqī, see Laoust, Califat, p. 84. There is some disagreement over al-Futūḥī's name. Ibn Badrān gives the form *Taqī al-Dīn Aḥmad b. al-Najjār*, whereas Brockelmann indicates rather *Muḥammad b. Aḥmad b. al-Najjār*: Brockelmann, Carl: *Geschichte der arabischen Litteratur*, Supplementband, Leiden 1937–1942, vol. 2, p. 447, which see for biographical information. Brockelmann's form is confirmed by Çelebī, Kātib: *Keşf al-zunun*, ed. by Şerefettin Yaltkaya and Rifat Bilge, Istanbul 1941, 1943, p. 1853. Brockelmann also (more doubtfully) proposes the spelling

ing [153] purposes. If we are to write a proper history of the Ḥanbalī school, we must consider citations and teaching texts as well as entries in biographical dictionaries.

As for the special purposes of this study, the chief results of my counting citations in Mardāwī, *al-Inṣāf*, are immediately clear: Ibn Taymiyya appears as a relatively minor figure, less often cited than many other Ḥanbalī jurisprudents, while Ibn al-Qayyim does not even appear among the top twenty (in fact, appears just twice in the sample). It also becomes clear, incidentally, that there has been a considerable break in the tradition between Mardāwī's time and ours, for a majority of the books associated with these twenty-one most-cited jurisprudents have never been printed, so far as I have been able to determine, notwithstanding their importance in the fifteenth century. Ibn Taymiyya and Ibn al-Qayyim are the most famous fourteenth-century Ḥanābila today, but other fourteenth-century Ḥanābila did more to shape the characteristic doctrines of the school.

The reason for Ibn Taymiyya's being seldom cited is not that Mardāwī looks down on him. Mardāwī usually names his authorities in series. Here is a typical passage, for example, concerning whom the leader should permit to join the army on *jihād*:

> He also forbids boys, according to the sound opinion of the school. A number have mentioned this. (The author of) *al-Furūʿ* puts it first. (The authors of) *al-Mughnī*, *al-Kāfī*, *al-Bulgha*, *al-Sharḥ*, *al-Riʿāya al-kubrā*, and others say that he forbids young children (*al-ṭifl*). The Author (*al-muṣannif*) and the Commentator (*al-shāriḥ*) [Ibn Abī ʿUmar] add that it is permissible for him to give permission to whatever boys are strong.[6]

Al-Mardāwī occasionally names Ibn Taymiyya in a series of names like this, but more often quotes him making a special point; for example, [154] not long after the passage just quoted, concerning the employment of non-Muslim subjects in positions of authority:

> (Ibn Mufliḥ al-Qāqūnī) says in *al-Furūʿ*, "There are two versions (of what Aḥmad said) concerning this problem. The first is that it is forbidden, which was the choice of our shaykh (meaning al-Shaykh Taqī al-Dīn) and others as well, for it entails corruption or leads to it. It is more pressing than the question of *jihād*." The shaykh Taqī al-Dīn said, "Whoever of them (the polytheists) operates a ministry (*dīwān*) for the Muslims has violated the terms of his pact, for it goes

---

Khujāwī: Brockelmann, *Geschichte der arabischen Litteratur*, suppl., vol. 2, p. 447, which also see for biographical information.

6. Al-Mardāwī, *al-Inṣāf fī maʿrifat al-rājiḥ*, vol. 4, p. 104 (*K. al-Jihād, bāb mā yalzamu al-imām wa-al-jaysh*, after *qawluhu fa-man lā yaṣluḥu lil-ḥarb*). *Al-Bulgha* (The Sufficiency) was a one-volume abridgement of al-Majd, *al-Kāfī*, by Aḥmad b. Ibrāhīm al-Ḥazzamī (d. Damascus, 711/1311), for biographical information on whom see Ibn Rajab, *al-Dhayl*, vol. 2, pp. 358–360. As remarked above, 'the Author' indicates Ibn Qudāma, author of *al-Muqniʿ*, 'the Commentator' Ibn Abī ʿUmar.

> against humiliation (*al-ṣaghār*)." [Ibn Ḥamdān] says in *al-Riʿāya* that it is discouraged except when necessary.[7]

Ibn Taymiyya is not the only shaykh quoted as explaining a rule, as here; however, al-Mardāwī seems to quote none other so regularly to explain his preference, nor anyone else so regularly to bring up a ramification not discussed elsewhere. Al-Mardāwī plainly respected Ibn Taymiyya as a significant original thinker. In a short work, al-Mardāwī even names Ibn Taymiyya as a recent example of *al-mujtahid al-muṭlaq*, someone capable of inferring rules directly from the revealed sources, not bound to adhere to a pre-existing school.[8] This is to place him at a level with Aḥmad b. Ḥanbal, above the rest of the Ḥanbalī school. However, Al-Matroudi is justified in concluding that al-Mardāwī, although well acquainted with Ibn Taymiyya's views, remained in the end more a reporter of them than an advocate.[9]

As for the apparent insignificance of Ibn Qayyim al-Jawziyya, it might be objected that, although he is little cited in the whole of *al-Inṣāf fī maʿrifat al-rājiḥ*, he may yet appear a leading authority in some specialized parts of the law. The obvious example is the law of non-Muslim subjects, for Ibn al-Qayyim wrote a long (and useful) book on precisely this topic, *Aḥkām ahl al-dhimma* (The Ordinances Concerning the Protected Peoples).[10] I have therefore also [155] counted citations in the section of *al-Inṣāf fī maʿrifat al-rājiḥ* that deals with the law of non-Muslim subjects.[11] Here is a list of those authorities whom Mardāwī there cites ten times or more:

(1) Ibn Ḥamdān, 59 citations.
(2) Abū Yaʿlā, 56 citations.
(3) Ibn Qudāma, 53 citations.
(4) ʿAbd al-Raḥmān, 40 citations.
(5) Al-Majd, 34 citations.

7. Ibid., vol. 4, p. 105 (*K. al-Jihād, bāb mā yalzamu al-imām wa-al-jaysh*, after *qawluhu wa-lā yastaʿīnu bi-mushrik*).

8. Al-Mardāwī, ʿAlāʾ al-Dīn ʿAlī b. Sulaymān: *Qāʿida nāfiʿa jāmiʿa li-ṣifat al-riwāyāt al-manqūla ʿan al-imām Aḥmad* (A Beneficial, Comprehensive Principle Concerning the Character of Transmitted Versions of [the Position of] the Leader Aḥmad), appended to idem, *al-Inṣāf fī maʿrifat al-rājiḥ*, vol. 12, pp. 177–218, at p. 191.

9. Al-Matroudi, *The Ḥanbalī School*, pp. 145–150.

10. Ibn Qayyim al-Jawziyya, Shams al-Dīn: *Aḥkām ahl al-dhimma*, ed. by Ṣubḥī al-Ṣāliḥ, n.p. n.p. 1381/1961, reprint Beirut 1401/1981. I have looked at two other editions. That of Ṭāhā ʿAbd al-Raʾūf Saʿd, Beirut 1415/1995, is a mere retyping of Ṣubḥī al-Ṣāliḥ's, to be avoided. That of Abū Barāʾ Yūsuf b. Aḥmad al-Bakrī and Abū Aḥmad Shākir b. Tawfīq al-ʿĀrūrī, Dammam and Beirut 1418/1997, offers many more notes and occasionally a more careful reading of, apparently, the same manuscript source.

11. Al-Mardāwī, *al-Inṣāf fī maʿrifat al-rājiḥ*, vol. 4, pp. 156–186 (*K. al-Jihād, bāb ʿaqd al-dhimma*).

(6) Aḥmad b. Ḥanbal, 33 citations (with multiple, contradictory versions at 11). Ibn al-Jawzī, ʿAbd al-Raḥmān b. ʿAlī (d. Baghdad, 597/1201), 33 citations.[12] Ibn Abī ʿUmar, 33 citations.
(9) Ibn Munajjā, 28 citations.
(10) ʿIzz al-Dīn al-Maqdisī, 26 citations.
(11) Ibn al-Sarī al-Dujaylī, 22 citations.
(12) Abū al-Khaṭṭāb al-Kalwadhānī, 17 citations.
(13) Ibn Taymiyya, 15 citations.
(14) Al-Sāmarrī, 11 citations.
(15) Al-Zarkashī, 10 citations. Al-Ādamī, 10 citations. ʿAlāʾ al-Dīn b. al-Laḥḥām, ʿAlī b. Muḥammad (d. Cairo, 803/1401), 10 citations.[13]

The list is fairly similar to the list of those most cited in *al-Inṣāf* as a whole. In this section of the *Inṣāf*, there is just one citation of Ibn al-Qayyim, as author of *Badāʾiʿ al-fawāʾid* (The Astonishing Benefits) and *Aḥkām ahl al-dhimma*. Al-Mardāwī certainly knew of Ibn al-Qayyim's work and singles him out as Ibn Taymiyya's [156] disciple (*ṣāḥib*), just two others in the larger sample being referred to thus as someone's disciple, Ghulām al-Khallāl (d. 363/974) and Abū al-Khaṭṭāb, disciple to the kadi Abū Yaʿlā. Despite al-Mardāwī's respect for Ibn al-Qayyim, he evidently did not think him much help at identifying and elaborating the peculiar rules of the Ḥanbalī school. At the level of identifying rules, even on a section of the law about which he had written a long, specialized book, Ibn al-Qayyim was a fairly minor Ḥanbalī.

My second project is to characterize Ibn al-Qayyim's jurisprudence, especially what the Ḥanbalī school meant to him. As a first essay at identifying its place within the Ḥanbalī tradition, I have randomly chosen and analysed in various ways a sample of seventy items in Ibn al-Qayyim, *Aḥkām ahl al-dhimma*. Among these were 17 examples of Aḥmad's opinion (24 percent), of only one of which was a variant version mentioned. Eleven items were primarily theological (16 percent), one was historical without obvious legal application, leaving 58 questions of *aḥkām*; that is, the classification of actions (83 percent). Eleven items in the sample were supported by hadith from the Prophet (16 percent), eight by sayings of Companions (eleven percent), four by sayings of Followers (six percent). There was only one example of Hadith criticism. The Shāfiʿī position was cited eight times (eleven percent), the Ḥanafī four (six percent), the Mālikī three (four per-

12. Of *al-Mudhhab al-aḥmad* (The Most Praiseworthy Gilt [Book]") and *Masbūk al-dhahab* (The Smeltery of Gold). For biographical information, see Laoust, Califat, pp. 112–116, also Swartz, Merlin: *Ibn al-Jawzī's* Kitāb al-Quṣṣāṣ wal-mudhakkirīn, Beirut 1971, pp. 15–38.

13. Of *Tajrīd al-ʿināya* (The Stripped Attention) and *al-Qawāʿid al-uṣūliyya* (The Originating Principles). For biographical information, see al-ʿUlaymī, *al-Manhaj al-aḥmad*, vol. 5, pp. 190–191.

cent), the Ẓāhiri just once (one percent). Abū ʿUbayd (d. Mecca, 224/838–839?) is quoted six times (nine percent), usually quoting someone else in turn.

Ibn al-Qayyim appears from this to have been something of a Ḥanbalī-fundamentalist. He is a fundamentalist in the sense that he wants to go back to basics, avoiding the complexity of accumulated tradition by reaching behind it; he is a Ḥanbalī-fundamentalist inasmuch as what he goes back to is the opinion of Aḥmad b. Ḥanbal himself.[14] In avoiding the complexity of the tradition, he is similar to today's Salafi primitivists. However, whereas they seek to identify directly prophetic law, before the rise of schools, Ibn al-Qayyim stresses Aḥmad's [157] doctrine, before the rise of the Ḥanbalī school but well after the age of the Prophet.

Knowing Aḥmad's doctrine was a complex issue for the tradition, as indicated by the frequency with which it reported multiple versions of what Aḥmad had said. Several collections of Aḥmad's opinions from immediate disciples of his are extant.[15] Contradictions are found among them, the consequence of Aḥmad's changing his mind, being misunderstood, or having things put in his mouth that he did not actually say but that the quoter thought he must have said, had someone asked him. However, such contradictions in the earliest record come nowhere near concerning every third question, as in quotations of Aḥmad reported by al-Mardāwī.[16] Most of the multiple versions in al-Mardāwī were evidently the consequence of *takhrīj*, attributing to the eponym of the school an opinion not that he was remembered as expressing but that seemed, to the writer, to follow from his principles.[17] Mardāwī himself defines *takhrīj* as the transfer of an assessment from

14. "Fundamentalist" has a particular meaning with regard to 20th-century Protestantism, having been invented by a Protestant faction to designate themselves: Shepard, William: "Fundamentalism" Christian and Islamic, in: *Religion*, vol. 17 (1987), pp. 355–378. However, it seems to have some scholarly usefulness when defined not by particular fundamentals but an interest in going past the tradition back to original sources and a tendency to simplify, for which see Marty, Martin E. and Appleby, R. Scott: *Fundamentalisms Observed, Fundamentalism Project 1*, Chicago 1991, introduction.

15. On the *masāʾil* collections, see Melchert, *Ahmad*, chap. 3, pp. 59–81, esp. pp. 68–70. To those cited now add *Masāʾil al-imām Aḥmad b. Ḥanbal wa-Isḥāq b. Rāhawayh*, recension of al-Kawsaj, ed. by Abū al-Ḥusayn Khālid b. Maḥmūd al-Rabāṭ, Wiʾām al-Hāwishī, and Jumʿa Fatḥī, 2 vols., Riyadh 1425/2004, and *Masāʾil al-imām Aḥmad b. Muḥammad b. Ḥanbal wa-Isḥāq b. Rāhawayh*, recension of Ḥarb b. Ismāʿīl al-Kirmānī, ed. by Nāṣir b. Saʿūd b. ʿAbd Allāh al-Salāma, Riyadh 1425.

16. For a sample of contradictions among the *masāʾil* collections, see Ibn al-Farrāʾ: *al-Masāʾil al-ʿaqdiyya min K. al-Riwāyatayn wal-wajhayn* (The Creedal Questions from *The Book of the Two Versions and the Two Aspects*), ed. by Saʿūd b. ʿAbd al-ʿAzīz al-Khalaf, Riyadh (Aḍwāʾ al-Salaf) 1419/1999.

17. Al-Mardāwī names three possible bases of a version (*riwāya*): Aḥmad's express declaration (*naṣṣ*), an indirect indication by him of his opinion (*īmāʾ*), and *takhrīj* on the part of adherents of the school: *Qāʿida nāfiʿa*, vol. 12, p. 196. I have not remarked any estimate from him of how many versions were based on each of these, but he certainly seems less naive than the many writers of the present who assume that contradictory quotations are invariably the product of someone's changing his mind, not back projection of opinions from later generations. On *takhrīj* in Islamic legal literature generally, see Hallaq, Wael B.: *Authority, Continuity and Change in Islamic Law*, Cambridge 2001, chapter 2. For examples

one question to another, similar one, considering them equivalent (*naql ḥukm masʾala ilā mā yushbihuhā wa-al-taswiya baynahumā fīh*).[18] Ibn Taymiyya describes it as a famous [158] question among his fellow adherents of the Ḥanbalī school. He considers the authority of an opinion arrived at by *takhrīj* to lie somewhere between that of what Aḥmad said expressly (*al-madhhab al-manṣūṣ*) and something his known position does not manifestly entail.[19] Many reports of alternative versions are quite late; for example (in chronological order), from Abū Yaʿlā, Abū al-Khaṭṭāb, Ibn al-Jawzī, Ibn Munajjā, Sāmarrī, Ibn Abī ʿUmar, ʿAbd al-Raḥmān, Ibn Ḥamdān, and Ibn Taymiyya in the section of al-Mardāwī's *al-Inṣāf fī maʿrifat al-rājiḥ* on *ʿaqd al-dhimma*. These can hardly go back to contradictory quotations in collections of Aḥmad's opinions by his immediate disciples. It is often unclear how Ibn al-Qayyim himself knows what Aḥmad's position was. Even if he relies on a source as early as the *Mukhtaṣar* of al-Khiraqī (d. Damascus, 334/945–946), he risks confusing the tradition with what the imam verifiably said; that is, although trying to get behind the tradition to Aḥmad himself, he still has little more than the tradition to tell him what Aḥmad said, and the tradition includes a good deal of back projection.[20]

To get a sense of how typical Ibn al-Qayyim was of Ḥanbalī jurisprudents, I thought to examine a sample of similar size from Ibn Qudāma, *al-Mughnī*. I found there rather more citations of prophetic hadith (21 percent of all items), less than half as many citations of Aḥmad b. Ḥanbal's own opinion (11 percent as opposed to 24), relatively more citations of the Ḥanbalī school's position or the opinions of individual Ḥanābila (14 percent). What we see in al-Mardāwī, Ibn Qudāma, and also al-Mardāwī's favorite source, the *Furūʿ* of Ibn Mufliḥ al-Qāqūnī, is a striking feature of the classical schools of law, mainly insistence on legitimate disagreement (*ikhtilāf*)—something we see much less of in Ibn al-Qayyim, especially disagreement within the Ḥanbalī school. Ibn al-Qayyim does not completely ignore [159] disagreement within the school or the complication of multiple versions of Aḥmad's position, but he does bring them up notably less often than mainstream Ḥanbalī writers.[21] His fundamentalism thus manifests itself not only in avoiding the complexity

in the early record of Shāfiʿī's opinions, see Melchert, Christopher: The Meaning of *qāla al-Shāfiʿī* in Ninth-Century Sources, in: Montgomery, James E. (ed.): *Abbasid Studies*, Leuven 2004, pp. 277–301 [*HPL 14].

18. Al-Mardāwī, *al-Inṣāf fī maʿrifat al-rājiḥ*, vol. 1, p. 17; idem, *Qāʿida nāfiʿa*, vol. 12, p. 190.

19. Ibn Taymiyya, Taqī al-Dīn: *al-Qawāʿid al-nūrāniyya al-fiqhiyya*, ed. by Muḥammad Ḥāmid al-Fiqī, Cairo 1370/1951, p. 258.

20. Al-Khiraqī: *al-Mukhtaṣar*, ed. by Muḥammad Zuhayr al-Shāwīsh, Damascus 1378; also published as idem: *al-Matn*, ed. by Abū Ḥudhayfa Ibrāhīm b. Muḥammad, Tanta 1413/1993. Comparison with the extant *masāʾil* collections of Aḥmad's opinions shows that Khiraqī usually offers a faithful summary of his known position. However, he also often articulates a definite rule where Aḥmad was vague or infers a rule from Aḥmad's known position on other matters. See provisionally Khalid, Anas: *The Mukhtasar of Al-Khiraqi*, PhD thesis, New York University 1992, and Hurvitz, Nimrod: The Mukhtaṣar of al-Khiraqī, in: Shaham, Ron (ed.): *Law, Custom, and Statute in the Muslim World*, Leiden 2007, pp. 1–16.

21. E.g., Ibn Qayyim al-Jawziyya, *Aḥkām ahl al-dhimma*, pp. 452–453, where he names five disciples

of accumulated tradition by reaching behind it to the opinion of Aḥmad b. Ḥanbal but also in downplaying the difficulty of knowing what Aḥmad actually said.

Why, then, should Ibn Taymiyya have been, if not a major figure in the Ḥanbalī legal tradition, at least a much more prominent one than his disciple Ibn al-Qayyim? As an example of Ibn Taymiyya's legal writing, I have examined two short works, *al-Qawāʿid al-nūrāniyya*, just quoted concerning *takhrīj*, and *al-Masāʾil al-māradīniyya*.[22] It transpires first that Ibn Taymiyya's approach is somewhat closer to Ibn Qudāma's than Ibn al-Qayyim's: the Prophet is cited twice as often as Aḥmad b. Ḥanbal, and Ibn Taymiyya regularly acknowledges alternative versions of Aḥmad's own position. Qualitatively, Ibn Taymiyya much more often describes legitimate disagreement, usually among different schools but also sometimes within the Ḥanbalī school; for example, to observe that the tenth- and eleventh-century ʿUkbaris such as Abū Ḥafṣ and Abū ʿAlī b. Shihāb on the one hand and the Baghdadis such as Abū ʿAbd Allāh b. Ḥāmid and the kadi Abū Yaʿlā on the other disagreed over a certain property transfer.[23] Ibn Taymiyya did not write as a typical Ḥanbalī, and that evidently limited his effect on the elaboration of Ḥanbalī rules. Sometimes he proposes rules completely at odds with the Ḥanbalī tradition, as that Muslims should be allowed to inherit from non-Muslims, lest anyone refrain from converting to Islam for fear of missing an inheritance—an opinion that not even Ibn al-Qayyim [160] embraced.[24] Tellingly, though, he sometimes proposes novel opinions but plays down their novelty by referring to unspecified precedents. He wrote at least more traditionally than his disciple Ibn al-Qayyim, with more deference to the discursive tradition, which must partly account for the relatively greater attention that later Ḥanābila paid to Ibn Taymiyya's expositions of the rules.

Conclusion

To sum up, then, it appears that Ibn Taymiyya's disciples (with exceptions, Ibn Mufliḥ al-Qāqūnī prominent among them) were impatient with the indeterminacy of the tradi-

who related three different versions of Aḥmad's position on the question of whether someone may inherit from a Muslim who has converted to Islam some time between the Muslim's death and the division of his property. By contrast, Ibn Qudāma names only two versions of Aḥmad's position on this point: Ibn Qudāma, *al-Mughnī*, ed. by ʿAbd Allāh ʿAbd al-Muḥsin al-Turkī and ʿAbd al-Fattāḥ Muḥammad al-Ḥulw, Cairo 1406–11/1986–90), vol. 9, p. 160.

22. Ibn Taymiyya, Taqī al-Dīn: *al-Masāʾil al-māradīniyya*, ed. by Muḥammad Ḥāmid al-Fiqī, Cairo 1980.

23. Ibn Taymiyya, Taqī al-Dīn: *al-Qawāʿid al-nūrāniyya al-fiqhiyya*, ed. by Muḥammad Ḥāmid al-Fiqī, Cairo 1370/1951, p. 106. On Abū Ḥafṣ al-ʿUkbarī (d. 387/997), see Laoust, Califat, p. 88; on Ibn Shihāb al-ʿUkbārī (d. 428/1037), ibid., p. 98; on Ibn Ḥāmid (d. 403/1012–13), ibid., pp. 93–94.

24. Mardāwī, *al-Inṣāf fī maʿrifat al-rājiḥ*, vol. 7, p. 259. Many further examples in Al-Matroudi, *Ḥanbalī School*, chapter 4.

tion. Books like Ibn Qudāma, *al-Mughnī*,[25] Ibn Mufliḥ al-Qāqūnī, *al-Furūʿ*,[26] and al-Mardāwī, *al-Inṣāf*,[27] report a cloud of disagreement on one question after another, not only between the Ḥanbalī school and others but also within the Ḥanbalī school. All of them mention the opinions of other Ḥanābila more often than they do the opinions of Aḥmad b. Ḥanbal himself, along with much disagreement over what Aḥmad said. The God-given rule for each case apparently became impossible to discern with certainty. Somewhat in the fashion of modern Salafi fundamentalists, Ibn Taymiyya's disciples sought a certainty the tradition denied them by going behind it back to original sources: above all to Aḥmad b. Ḥanbal's opinions in the case of Ibn al-Qayyim, to prophetic Hadith in the parallel case of Ibn Kathīr (d. Damascus, 774/1373).[28] A difficulty they faced was for Ibn al-Qayyim to know Aḥmad b. Ḥanbal's opinions, Ibn Kathīr to know what the Prophet had said and done, without depending on the very scholarly tradition they wanted to go behind. (Ibn Kathīr probably faced his problem more frankly, since [161] he worked extensively in the field of Hadith and continually discusses the reliability of particular Hadith reports in his Koran commentary; however, his solution was largely to assume that the great ninth-century Hadith collectors had effectively culled the correct versions of what the Prophet had said from the mass of incorrect. The comparable problem for modern Salafiyya is similarly to know what the Prophet said and to interpret the Koran without depending on the very medieval scholarly tradition that they try to go behind when it comes to the schools of law. Like Ibn Kathīr but probably less excusably, they tend to assume that the great ninth-century hadith collectors, above all Bukhārī (d. 256/870), were not men of their time with accordingly limited horizons, similarly to Aḥmad b. Ḥanbal and al-Shāfiʿī (d. 204/820) and their followers, but somehow transcended it, offering us directly what the Prophet said, not just what various later Muslims thought the Prophet must have said.)

As Ibn al-Qayyim largely skipped over the Ḥanbalī tradition between himself and Aḥmad, so the ongoing Ḥanbalī tradition largely, with some justice, ignored him. Ḥanābila of the following centuries paid much more attention to Ibn Taymiyya than to Ibn al-Qayyim in the field of positive law (*furūʿ*). The reason is probably that he seemed more engaged with the tradition, which is to say he seemed to think the same way they did. He did cite previous Ḥanbalī jurisprudents; he propounded original opinions so as to keep them within the spectrum of Ḥanbalī opinion, not so as to make it his evident

25. Ibn Qudāma, *al-Mughnī* (cited in n. 21).

26. Ibn Mufliḥ al-Qāqūnī: *K. al-Furūʿ*, ed. by ʿAbd al-Laṭīf Muḥammad al-Subkī and ʿAbd al-Sattār Aḥmad Farrāj, Cairo 1379–88/1960–67, reprinted Beirut 1402.

27. Al-Mardāwī, *al-Inṣāf fī maʿrifat al-rājiḥ*.

28. For Ibn Kathīr as a fundamentalist bent on simplistically going back to original sources, see Calder, Norman: Tafsīr from Ṭabarī to Ibn Kathīr: Problems in the Description of a Genre, Illustrated with Reference to the Story of Abraham, in: G.R. Hawting and Abdul-Kader A. Shareef (eds.): *Approaches to the Qurʾān*, London 1993, pp. 101–140.

intention to supersede all earlier Ḥanbalī opinion. However, Ḥanābila of the following centuries paid yet more attention to numerous other Ḥanbalī jurisprudents: men such as Ibn Ḥamdān and Ibn Abī ʿUmar before Ibn Taymiyya, ʿIzz al-Dīn al-Maqdisī and Ibn Qāḍī al-Jabal after him. Insofar as the Ḥanbalī school constituted a peculiar set of answers to juridical problems, Ibn Taymiyya had a significant but limited effect on it. It was when the plundering of *waqf* foundations, the rise of technical education in engineering, medicine, and other fields, mass literacy, and other developments had debilitated the system of schools that Ibn Taymiyya and Ibn al-Qayyim came to the forefront in the 20th century.

Index of Premodern Persons and Groups

Note: The transliteration symbols used for hamza (ʾ) and ʿayn (ʿ) as well as the definite article (al-) are disregarded for purposes of alphabetization.

RESOURCES IN ARABIC AND ISLAMIC STUDIES

Number 3
Hadith, Piety, and Law: Selected Studies
by Christopher Melchert
(2015)

Number 2
The Economy of Certainty: An Introduction to the Typology of Islamic Legal Theory
by Aron Zysow
(2013)

Number 1
A Reader of Classical Arabic Literature
by Seeger Bonebakker and Michael Fishbein
(2012)